Slovenia

D0462003

Eastern Slovenia
p184

Lake Bled & the
Julian Alps
p71

Western Slovenia
& the Soča Valley
p109

★ Ljubljana
p34

Southeast Slovenia
& the Krka Valley
p157

The Karst &
the Coast
p127

THIS EDITION WRITTEN AND RESEARCHED BY
Carolyn Bain, Steve Fallon

Contents

SOČA RIVER P111

PREŠERNOV TRG P37

BORUT TROJNA/GETTY IMAGES ©

TOMASI706/GETTY IMAGES ©

KASTO80/GETTY IMAGES ©

Contents

LAKE BLED AND BLED ISLAND P84

Welcome to Slovenia

A paradise of snow-capped peaks, turquoise rivers and Venetian-style coastline, Slovenia enriches its natural treasures with harmonious architecture, rustic culture and sophisticated cuisine.

Jaw-Dropping Beauty

From the soaring peaks of the Julian Alps and the subterranean magic of Postojna and Škocjan Caves, to sparkling emerald-green lakes and rivers and the short but sweet Adriatic coast, Slovenia has it all. An incredible mixture of climates brings warm Mediterranean breezes up to the foothills of the Alps, where it can snow even in summer. And with more than half of its total territory covered in forest, Slovenia really is one of the greenest countries in the world.

Architectural & Cultural Treasures

You might be forgiven for thinking that anything of beauty in this greenest of green lands is, well, all natural. But it ain't necessarily so. Where humans intrude it's often to good effect, such as at Lake Bled, where a tiny baroque chapel on a picturesque island with a dramatic castle looming above complete a harmonious whole. The architecture is wonderfully varied – from the Venetian harbour towns of the coast and the rustic Hungarian-style farmhouses of Prekmurje to the Gothic church of Gorenjska and art nouveau splendours of Ljubljana – the museums are rich and the culture vibrant.

Outdoor Pursuits

Slovenia is a top outdoor destination. Locals favour active holidays, and you'll be invited – even expected – to join in. The list of activities on offer is endless, with the most popular pursuits skiing, walking and hiking in the mountains and, increasingly, cycling. Fast rivers like the Soča cry out to be rafted and there are ample chances to try out more niche activities like horseback riding, ballooning, caving and canyoning. If all this sounds a bit much, you can always decamp to the coast and sunbathe on the Adriatic.

A Matter of Taste

Slovenian cooking borrows a little something from each of its neighbours – Italy, Austria, Hungary and the Balkans – synthesising and reinventing dishes so they emerge both familiar and unique. Slovenians have an obsession with using only fresh and locally sourced ingredients. This is a terrific foodie destination, where you'll sample dishes in unusual combinations such as scrumptious pasta dumplings of potato, chives and bacon, salads drizzled with nutty pumpkin seed oil, and multi-layered *gibanica,* a wildly decadent dessert. Slovenian wine is an unheralded strength, and regional whites and reds pair well with local specialities.

Why I Love Slovenia

By Steve Fallon, Writer

Even serial visitors to Slovenia like myself often stop and stare, mesmerised by the sheer beauty of this land. The wondrous bucolic valley of Logarska Dolina brings heaven to earth, and at the dramatic Vršič pass through the Alps I feel on top of the world in every sense. I can never tire of the wonderful and varied architecture, excellent wines and traditional dishes, and vibrant folk culture. But for me the country's greatest attribute is the Slovenes themselves: quietly conservative, deeply self-confident, remarkably broadminded, especially tolerant and very, very hospitable.

For more about our writers, see page 288

Above: Logarska Dolina (p185)

Slovenia

Kranjska Gora
Glamping in the serene Sava Dolinka Valley (p101)

Vršič Pass
Breathtaking, zigzagging Alpine pass (p107)

Soča River
Raft it from adventure capital, Bovec (p111)

Mt Triglav
Slovenia's highest, most legendary mountain (p101)

Lake Bled
A lake, an island, a fairy-tale castle (p84)

Vipava Valley
Source of Slovenia's finest wine (p120)

Piran
Slovenia's best preserved medieval Venetian port (p147)

Škocjan Caves
Gargantuan, dramatic underground canyons (p136)

Postojna Caves
A vast labyrinth of subterranean marvels (p129)

Predjama Castle
A fortress perched in a cavern's mouth (p132)

AUSTRIA

ITALY

CROATIA

Wolfsberg
Feldkirchen
Villach
Klagenfurt
Tarvisio
Ratece
Kranjska Gora
Mangart (2679m)
Gozd Martuljek
Rombon (2208m)
Vršič Pass (1611m)
Mojstrana
Prevalje
Jalovec (2645m)
Razor (2601m)
Kanin (2587m)
Triglav (2864m)
Jesenice
Mežica
Bovec
Triglav National Park
Stol (2236m)
Zgornje Jezersko
Črna na Koroškem
Kobarid
Krn (2244m)
Lake Bled
Bled
Lesce
Tržič
Storžič (2132m)
Solčava
Raduha (2062m)
Vogel (1922m)
Stara Fužina
Radovljica
Kamnik - Savinja Alps
Logarska Dolina
Grintovec (2558m)
Luče
Mozirje
Lake Bohinj
Bohinjska Bistrica
Jelovica Hills
Koprivna
Joze Pučnik Airport
Krvavec
Radmirje
Gorpji Grad
Nazarje
ITALY
Tolmin
Porezen (1630m)
Železniki
Cerklje na Gorenjskem
Kamnik
Cividale
Most na Soči
Škofja Loka Hills
Kranj
Brnik
Kozjak
Kanal
Cerkno
Blegoš (1562m)
Lubnik (1025m)
Škofja Loka
Menges
Radomlje
Domžale
Idrija Hills
Spodnja Idrija
Žiri
Medvode
Šmarna Gora (676m)
Slivna (880m)
Žagorje
Gorizia
Nova Gorica
Idrija
Rovte
Dragomer
LJUBLJANA
Litija
Smartno pri Litiji
Ronchi
Montfalcone
Vipavski Križ
Branik
Ajdovščina
Vrhnika
Logatec
Ljubljanica
Ig
Škofljica
Borovnica
Grosuplje
Ivančna Gorica
Mirna
Trebnje
Santa Croce
Komen
Vipava
Predjama Castle
Postojna Caves
Rakek
Cerknica
Postojna
Višnja Gora
Muljava
Krka
Fužina
Opicina
Villa
Karst
Sežana
Prestranek
Dolenje Jezero
Stene Sv Ana (963m)
Sodražica
Dvor
Soteska
Trieste
Lipica
Divača
Škocjan Caves
Reka
Pivka
Lož Valley
Markovec
Nova Štifta
Ribnica
Dolenjske Toplice
Ankaran
Muggia
Ilirska Bistrica
Velika Gora
Veliki Rog (1099m)
Piran Koper
Izola
Bertoki
Slavnik (1028m)
Kočevje
Kočevski Rog
Portorož
Hrastovlje
Mirna Gora (1047m)
Sečovlje
Opatija
Rijeka
Delnice
Pazin
Vrbovsko

N
0 — 50 km
0 — 25 miles

Fürstenfeld

Kalsdorf

Feldbach   Heiligenkreuz

AUSTRIA

Leibnitz

Arnfels

Goričko Hills   Šalovci   Oriszentpeter

Mačkovci

HUNGARY

Dravograd   Muta   Kobansko Hills   Selnica   Mura   Bad Radkersburg   Moravske Toplice

Radlje ob Dravi   ob Muri

Ravne   Vuzenica   Vuhred   Drava   Slovenske Gorice   Gornja Radgona   Murska Sobota   Bogojina

na Koroškem   Lovrenc na   Selnica ob   Dobrovnik

Pohorju   Dravi   Lenart   Beltinci

Slovenj   Velika Kopa   Ruše   Maribor   Banovci   Redics

Gradec   (1543m)   Pohorje Massif   Spodnje   Bučkovci

Mislinja   Žigartov   Hoče   Ljutomer   Lendava

Šoštanj   Rogla   (1347m)   Mursko

(1517m)   Slovenska   Središče

Velenje   Zreče   Bistrica   Središče

Šempeter   Slovenske   Pragersko Kidričevo   Ptuj   Dornava   Ormož   ob Dravi

Žalec   Konjice   Ptujska   Goričak

Celje   Poljčane   Gora   Cirkulane

Šentjur   Donačka   Sotla   Varaždin

Rogaška   Gora   Haloze Hills

Silavec   Slatina   (884m)   Maceljsko

Rogatec

Laško   Đurmanec

Zidani   Podčetrtek   Krapina   Ptuj

Most   Radeče   Kozjansko   Medieval town of red roofs

Sevnica   Regional   and narrow streets (p200)

Boštanj   Senovo   Park   Bistrica

Brestanica   Orlica   ob Sotli

Mokronog   Krško   Podsreda Castle

Šmarjeta   Posavje   Rogaška Slatina

Brežice   Historic hot springs with

Šentjernej   Terme Čatež   Mokrice   indulgent cures (p197)

Novo   Pleterje   Castle   CROATIA

Mesto   Monastery   Kostanjevica   Obrežje   Križevci

na Krki

Trdinov Vrh   Gorjanci Hills

(1178m)   ZAGREB   Dugo

Selo

Metlika   Ljubljana   ELEVATION

Božakovo   Vibrant capital with a

Podzemelj   hilltop castle (p34)

Črnomelj   2000m

Kupa   1500m

Adlešiči   1000m

750m

Žuniči   500m

Vinica   Karlovac   300m

Črnomelj   200m

Home to Slovenia's oldest   100m

international folklore festival (p180)   0

Petrinja

Slovenia's
Top 12

1

Climbing Mt Triglav

1 They say you're not really a Slovene until you climb Mt Triglav (p101) and get 'spanked' at the summit. And it's all but stamped in locals' passports once they've made the trek up the country's tallest mountain. The good news for the rest of us is that Triglav is a challenging but accessible peak that just about anyone in decent shape can 'conquer' with an experienced guide. There are several popular approaches, but whichever path you choose, the reward is the same: sheer exhilaration.
Triglav National Park (p100)

Ljubljana

2 Slovenia's capital city (p34) strikes that perfect yet elusive balance between size and quality of life. It's big enough to offer discoveries yet small enough to walk – or better yet, cycle – around at a leisurely pace. And no place in Slovenia waltzes through architecture so adroitly as the capital named 'beloved', from its ancient hilltop castle and splendid art nouveau banks to local boy Jože Plečnik's wondrously decorative pillars, obelisks and orbs found everywhere.

Piran

3 Venice in Slovenia? That busy merchant empire left its mark up and down the Adriatic coast, and Slovenia was lucky to end up with one of the best-preserved medieval Venetian ports anywhere. It's true that Piran (p147) attracts tourist numbers on a massive scale in season, but the beautiful setting means it's never less than a constant delight. Enjoy fresh fish on the harbour, then wander the narrow streets and end up for drinks and people-watching in a glorious central square.

River Adventures

4 Rarely does a river beckon to be rafted as convincingly as Slovenia's Soča (p111). Maybe it's that piercing sky-blue-bordering-on-green – or is it turquoise? – colour of the water, or the river's refreshing froth and foam as it tumbles down the mountains. Even if you're not the rafting type, you'll soon find yourself strapping on a wetsuit for that exhilarating ride of the summer. Outfitters in Bovec, Bled and Kobarid specialise in guided rafting trips. For gentler floats, try the Krka River. Soča Valley (p111)

Lake Bled

5 With its sky-blue lake, picture-postcard church on a tiny island, a medieval castle clinging to a rocky cliff and some of the country's highest peaks as backdrops, Bled (p84) seems to have been designed by the very god of tourism. But Slovenia's biggest draw is more than just a pretty face. There's a raucous adventure scene too, with diving, cycling, rafting and canyoning, among other active pursuits, as well as excellent camping grounds, hostels and hotels.

Ptuj

6 Its name might sound like a cartoon character spitting, but Ptuj (p200) is no joke. Rather, it's one of Slovenia's richest historical towns. Everyone since the Romans has left their mark, and the centre is still a maze of red roofs and medieval streets, dotted with churches, towers and museums, as well as street cafes to enjoy the passing scenes. Ptuj is within easy reach of some of the country's best (mostly white) wine-producing regions. Drava Tower (p201)

Postojna Cave

7 The cave system at Postojna (p129) is Slovenia's biggest subterranean attraction. The entrance might not look like much, but when you get whisked 4km underground on a train and only then start exploring, you start to get a sense of the scale. The caverns are a seemingly endless parade of crystal fancies – from frilly chandeliers and dripping spaghetti-like stalactites, to paper-thin sheets and stupendous stalagmites, all laid down over the centuries by the simple dripping of mineral-rich water.

JOCHEN SCHLENKER/ROBERTHARDING/GETTY IMAGES ©

Predjama Castle

8 Slovenia is over-endowed with castles and caves, but one inside the other? Now that's something special. Few fortresses have a setting as grand as this, wedged halfway up a cliff face at the foot of valley (p132). The location has a story behind it that's equally dramatic: Slovenia's 'Robin Hood', Erazem Lueger, apparently taunted besieging troops here by hurling fresh cherries at them that he collected via a secret passage. He came to a swift and rather embarrassing end, however.

Traditional Spas

9 A spa in central Europe can often mean a fusty 19th-century royal relic with lots of great architecture but not much in the way of modern treatments. Slovenia's natural and thermal spas have the architecture, but more importantly they offer a wealth of high-quality wellness and beauty treatments including massage, mud baths, saunas, warm sea-water baths and more. Most of the spas are situated in the eastern half of the country and usually offer in-house (or nearby) accommodation as well; Rogaška Slatina (p197) is a fine spot to take the waters.

Škocjan Caves

10 Where Postojna is baroque, the caves at Škocjan (p136) are positively Gothic. It's all about melodrama here – think Jules Verne, Tolkien and Wagner all in one. Forget crawling in tiny underground spaces; the Murmuring Cave has walls reaching a hundred metres high, while the Cerkevnik Bridge crosses a gloomy chasm with a 45m plunge to where the Reka River carves its way through the rock. Visiting the caves is a truly awesome experience.

Crossing the Vršič Pass

11 Making your way – whether by car or (yikes!) bike – across this breathtakingly scenic Alpine pass (p107) that zigs and zags through peaks and promontories, it's hard not to think of the poor Russian WWI POWs who built the road – now called *Ruska cesta* (Russian road) in their honour. This summer-only roadway links Kranjska Gora with Bovec, 50km to the southwest, and includes a number of photo-op rest stops and several mountain huts along the way.

Vipava Valley Wines

12 Slovenia is blessed with the means to produce some of the region's best wines and the Vipava Valley (p120) particularly stands out. It enjoys a warm Mediterranean climate freshened by cold winter winds, making it the ideal destination for those wanting to treat their palates. Wineries with some of the best merlots in the world? Check. The best air-dried *pršut* ham? Yep. Pick up some local fruits and olives and you've got a Slovenian picnic to remember.

Need to Know

For more information, see Survival Guide (p255)

Currency
Euro (€)

Language
Slovene (slovenščina)

Visas
Generally not required for stays up to 90 days though some nationalities will need a valid EU Schengen visa.

Money
ATMs widely available. Credit and debit cards accepted by most businesses throughout the country.

Mobile Phones
Local SIM cards can be used in European, Australian and some American phones. Mobile phones with SIM available from the airport for under €50.

Time
Central European Time (GMT/UTC plus one hour).

When to Go

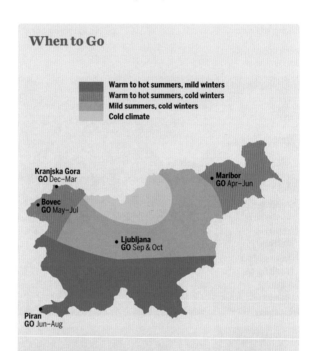

Warm to hot summers, mild winters
Warm to hot summers, cold winters
Mild summers, cold winters
Cold climate

Kranjska Gora
GO Dec–Mar

Maribor
GO Apr–Jun

Bovec
GO May–Jul

Ljubljana
GO Sep & Oct

Piran
GO Jun–Aug

High Season
(Jun–Aug)

➡ Mostly sunny skies with occasional rain.

➡ Crowds in Ljubljana and the coast; advance accommodation booking essential.

➡ Museums and other attractions open for business.

➡ Party atmosphere everywhere.

Shoulder (Apr & May, Sep & Oct)

➡ Sunny, dry September is a great time for climbing Mt Triglav.

➡ Lower tariffs are in effect at many hotels.

➡ Rafting is great by late May; swimming is over by October.

➡ Best overall time for hiking.

Low Season
(Nov–Mar)

➡ Ski season runs from mid-December to March or even April.

➡ Christmas through New Year can be crowded.

➡ Attractions in smaller towns may close or have limited hours.

Useful Websites

Slovenian Tourist Board (www.slovenia.info) Info on every conceivable sight and activity.

Slovenia Times (www.sloveniatimes.com) Website of the independent quarterly magazine.

E-uprava (http://e-uprava.gov.si/e-uprava/en/portal.euprava) Official info-packed government portal.

Lonely Planet (www.lonelyplanet.com/slovenia) Info, bookings and forum.

Important Numbers

All landline phone numbers have an area code (🖉 01 in Ljubljana) followed by a seven-digit number. Mobile phone numbers have a three-digit prefix (eg 🖉 030 or 🖉 040) and then a six-digit number.

Slovenia country code	🖉 386
Ambulance (Reševalci)	🖉 112
Fire brigade (Gasilci)	🖉 112
Police (Policija)	🖉 113 (emergencies)
Road emergency or towing (AMZS)	🖉 1987

Exchange Rates

Prices are quoted in euros (€) unless otherwise stated. €1 = 100 cents.

Australia	A$1	€0.64
Canada	C$1	€0.68
Japan	¥100	€0.74
New Zealand	NZ$1	€0.60
UK	UK£1	€1.36
US	US$1	€0.88

For current exchange rates see www.xe.com.

Daily Costs

Budget: Less than €50

➡ Hostel dorm bed or low-cost guesthouse: €15–€20

➡ Street food and self-catering: €10

➡ Train/bus tickets: €10

➡ Bicycle rental: €15

➡ Pint of beer: €3

Midrange: €80–100

➡ Room in a midrange hotel or pension: €40–€60

➡ Dinner in a good restaurant: €30

➡ Train/bus tickets: €10

➡ Lipica Stud Farm entry €12

Top End: More than €100

➡ Room in the best place in town: €80–€100

➡ Dinner in good restaurant: €40

➡ Train/bus/taxi: €20

➡ Postojna Cave entry: €23

Opening Hours

Opening hours can vary throughout the year. We've provided high-season opening hours here.

Banks 8.30am–12.30pm and 2–5pm Monday to Friday

Bars 11am–midnight Sunday to Thursday, to 1am or 2am Friday and Saturday

Restaurants 11am–10pm daily

Shops 8am–7pm Monday to Friday, to 1pm Saturday

Arriving in Slovenia

Jože Pučnik Airport (**Ljubljana**; p265) Buses run to Ljubljana's train station hourly on weekdays (every two hours on weekends). Shuttle (€9) and taxi (around €40) services will transfer you to the centre in around half an hour.

Ljubljana train station (p69) and **Ljubljana bus station** (p68) are opposite one another north of the city centre, about a 500-metre walk from the Old Town. It's an easy walk, but should you need to take a taxi, nothing should cost more than €8.

Getting Around

Bus Generally efficient and good value but very crowded on Friday afternoons and severely restricted on Sundays and holidays.

Car A great way to explore the countryside, with rental firms everywhere and the airport.

Train Cheaper but usually slower than buses (with the exception of intercity high-speed services). Getting from A to B often requires returning to Ljubljana.

For much more on **getting around**, see p268

If You Like...

Dramatic Scenery

For such a small country, Slovenia packs an amazing amount of diversity and stunning natural beauty. Snow-capped Alps; long, green valleys; and lakes and rivers so blue they almost hurt your eyes.

Vršič Pass This curving WWI-era highway crosses the Alps at an elevation of 1611m as it runs from near Kranjska Gora to Bovec. (p107)

Velika Planina High-altitude Alpine pasture land that offers some of the best mountain photo ops we've ever seen. (p74)

Soča River Valley Hair-raisingly steep verdant valleys and deep gorges cut through by impossibly blue water. (p109)

Lake Bohinj Bled's lesser-known (but larger) sister lake is no wallflower. It's an emerald-green mountain paradise with a quieter, more rustic feel and a glimpse of Mt Triglav. (p93)

Logarska Dolina The 'pearl of the Alpine region' offers caves, springs, rock towers and waterfalls – as well as rare fauna such as mountain eagles. (p185)

Historic Towns

Slovenia's most attractive cities and towns are the kind of places where you feel you can walk through the past (be it Roman times, the Middle Ages or the Communist era).

Ljubljana Roman Emona flanks a medieval core ringed with art nouveau creations and a Communist hinterland of pre-fabs. (p34)

Ptuj One of the oldest towns in Slovenia, this former metropolis from the Middle Ages boasts a symphony of red-tiled roofs. (p200)

Škofja Loka The 'Bishop's Meadow' is a perfectly preserved medieval town with an intact square and a spooky hilltop castle. (p74)

Kropa This one-horse, former iron-working town is a perfectly preserved living museum of the country's once-mighty industrial tradition. (p83)

Piran It's hard to imagine a more romantic spot anywhere than this little Venetian port jutting out into the Adriatic. (p147)

Radovljica A colourful main square of 16th-century townhouses and the delightful Beekeeping Museum. (p79)

Castles & Churches

Slovenia had so many hilltop fortress in the Middle Ages, it was known as the 'country of castles'. It is also blessed with some of the most beautiful houses of worship in Central Europe.

Predjama Castle Could easily be called 'pre-drama' for its dramatic perch tucked high inside a cliffside cave. (p132)

Ljubljana Castle For history, look no further than the capital's hilltop fortress that's been around since at least the 12th century. (p36)

Celje Castle There's not much inside this 13th-century fortress but it evokes the past like few others and the views are commanding. (p189)

Church of St John the Baptist Gazing out at Bohinj, this tiny church is awash in delightful 15th- and 16th-century frescoes. (p93)

Church of the Holy Trinity You'll never forget the macabre 15th-century Dance of Death fresco at this church by the coast. (p143)

Basilica of the Patroness Mary Only recently made a basilica, this hilltop church contains a stunningly carved altar. (p206)

Top: Predjama Castle (p132)

Bottom: *Prekmurska gibanica*, a rich local pastry

Walks & Hikes

Slovenia is crossed by thousands of kilometres of hiking trails, many passing through points of considerable natural beauty or paired to teach the lessons of the country's moving history.

Climbing Mt Triglav The ultimate Slovenian hike involves a trek to the top of Mt 'Three Heads'; at 2864m, it's a point of considerable national pride, especially for those who reach the top! (p100)

Trail of Remembrance This trail wends its way 34km around the capital along the boundary where German barbed wire once enclosed the city during WWII. (p51)

Walk of Peace This 5km-long trail starting from Kobarid is the prettiest open-air museum of wartime atrocities that you're ever likely to see. (p116)

Jeruzalem-Ljutomer wine road Walk or cycle this lovely trail that begins at Ormož and continues for 18km north to Ljutomer, passing many wine cellars and restaurants en route. (p206)

Lake Bled If you're looking for something easy and relaxing, a two-hour circuit around lovely Lake Bled is just the ticket. (p84)

Food

Slovenia is in the midst of a slow-food, organic-food, local-food revolution that prizes original recipes and fresh, quality ingredients. The country's excellent wine has been sorely underrated.

Odprta Kuhna This weekly food festival in Ljubljana's main market square allows you to taste your way round Slovenia. (p59)

Izola The port of Piran likes to think it has the country's best seafood, but for our money, the freshest fish is a few kilometres east in Izola. (p144)

Groats If Slovenian cooking has a signature side, it would have to be these stick-to-your-ribs barley or buckwheat groats. (p250)

Žlikrofi Pasta stuffed with potatoes, chives and a local version of bacon is worth the trip alone to Idrija. (p122)

Pumpkin seed oil Slovenia's most unique condiment, it can be green or red nut, roasted or cold-pressed but always nutty.

Prekmurska gibanica Slovenia's tongue-twister dessert is a rich concoction of pastry filled with poppy seeds, walnuts, apples, raisins and cheese and topped with cream.

Wine, Brandy & Beer

Teran This ruby-red, peppery wine with high acidity is made from Slovenian Refošk grapes and pairs beautifully with *pršut* (air-dried ham) and black olives.

Vipava Valley The best reds in Slovenia are produced here, especially merlots. (p120)

Zlata Radgonska Penina This classic sparkling wine is based on Chardonnay and Beli Pinot.

Žganje Classic brandy distilled from a variety of fruits – from plums and pears to cherries and blueberries.

Beer Leave Union and Laško in the dust in favour of a craft beer such as Human Fish, Bevog or Pelicon.

Outdoor Activities

Slovenia is an active holiday destination. And while hiking and biking are still the most popular ways to relax, there are lots of chances to swim, boat, raft or jump out of a plane.

Rafting the Soča The signature Slovenian outdoor adventure involves a breath-taking float down one of Europe's fastest and most beautiful rivers. (p111)

Adrenaline A growing number of operators – particularly at Bovec, Bled and Bohinj – offer the chance to try ballooning, canyoning and paragliding, among other instant rushes. (p85)

Caving Slovenia has dozens of caves, and some are extraordinary: Škocjan (p136) has walls that run 100m high, while Postojna's caverns (p129) are vast and bejewelled.

Skiing The Julian Alps offers myriad chances to hit the slopes. Kranjska Gora is the centre of the country's ski universe, but is just one of several popular resorts. (p25)

Mt Triglav Slovenia's only national park covers a huge swath of Slovenian turf in the northwest. It's a world of rivers, streams, waterfalls and hiking trails. (p100)

Spas

Slovenia counts upwards of 15 thermal spa resorts, most of them in Štajerska, Dolenjska and Prekmurje. They are excellent places not just for 'taking the cure' but for relaxing and meeting people.

Rogaška Slatina Slovenia's oldest and largest spa town, a veritable 'cure factory' with a fin-de-siècle feel to it. (p197)

Dolenjske Toplice Cosy and very wooded resort town with all the mod cons dating back to the 17th century. (p164)

Radenci Slightly down-at-the-heel but atmospheric spa town that also boasts Slovenia's premier mineral water. (p223)

Terme Olimia Enormous spa complex on the Croatian border with a great fortress looming above it. (p195)

Atlantis Not a spa but a Ljubljana water park, this place has everything, including more than a dozen types of sauna. (p50)

Unique Sleeps

Why stay in a hotel when a bunk in a former prison beckons or you can sleep in a pod hanging from a tree limb?

Garden Village Bled Forget air mattresses and sleeping bags and embrace glamping ('glam camping'). Hire a pier tent over a stream, a safari tent or a treehouse. (p91)

Celica Hostel In Ljubljana, this stylishly revamped former prison has 20 'cells' designed by different artists. (p55)

Kaki Plac Escape the package-tour feel of Portorož by sleeping in a tent under a wooden shelter in a hidden field. (p154)

MCC Hostel Another creative take on the hostel model is situated in a converted brew house in Celje, with each room bearing a unique theme and decor. (p191)

Nebesa Watch paragliders fly by from your chalet's view-enriched terrace near Kobarid high above the Soča. (p115)

DomKulture MuziKafe Magical place in Ptuj with idiosyncratically decorated rooms and great cafe with events. (p204)

Month by Month

January

This is for the most part a quiet month after the holidays, though skiing is generally very good and it's the time of one of the most important sporting events in the year.

☆ Women's World Cup Slalom & Giant Slalom Competition

One of the world's major international ski events held only for women – the coveted Zlata Lisica (Golden Fox) trophy – takes place on the main piste of the Maribor Pohorje ski grounds for four days in late January/early February (p212).

February

A normally cold and snowy month keeps things busy on the ski slopes near Kranjska Gora. Watch for crowds around mid-month, when school kids have their annual winter break.

✷ Kurentovanje

Ptuj's 'rite of spring' is celebrated for 10 days up to Shrove Tuesday (February or early March) and is the most popular Mardi Gras celebration in Slovenia (p203).

✷ Laufarija

Another folkloric pre-Lenten carnival, this is Cerkno's big annual free-for-all held over two days before Ash Wednesday (p125).

March

Still plenty of good skiing in the higher elevations; elsewhere the country is relatively quiet.

☆ Men's Slalom & Giant Slalom Vitranc Cup Competition

The number one downhill ski event of the year in early March – the Vitranc Cup – takes place at Kranjska Gora in early March (p103).

April

Flowers bloom and trees blossom in lower elevations. Depending on the winter, there's skiing at higher elevations. The Vršič Pass opens to cars by mid-month.

✷ Spring Horticultural Fair

Slovenia's largest flower and gardening show takes place at an arboretum in Volčji Potok, near Kamnik, in late April (p73).

May

Hit the Alpine valleys for a breakout of mountain wildflowers. Expect sunshine and warm daytime temperatures. It's too cold yet to swim in the Adriatic, but days are ideal for a portside promenade.

✷ Druga Godba

Held over three days in late May, this is a festival of alternative and world music in Ljubljana's Križanke (p52).

June

June can be gloriously sunny or depressingly rainy. It's the best month for white-water rafting, as rivers swell after the spring thaw and temps warm up enough to make the idea palatable.

☆ International Rowing Regatta

One of the country's most exciting (and fastest) sporting events, now in its seventh decade, is held over three days in mid-June on Lake Bled (p89).

⚜ Idrija Lace-Making Festival

This red-letter annual event held in mid June has a contest at the end of up to 100 competitors.

⚜ Lent Festival

A two-week extravaganza of folklore and culture in Maribor's Old Town (p209).

July

Mostly warm and sunny, this month is big for festivals. Nearly every village and town has something going on. Trekkers, watch out for freak storms at higher elevations.

⚜ Ljubljana Festival

The nation's premier festival of classical entertainment (music, theatre and dance) held in July and August (p52).

August

The traditional summer holiday month for Europeans finds resorts like Piran and Portorož filled to brimming. Camping grounds are packed, and the waters of lakes Bohinj and Bled warm up enough to swim.

⚜ Trnfest

Probably the most popular annual festival in the capital, this month-long party at the KUD France Prešeren cultural centre showcases music, dance and theatre from around the world (p52).

⚜ Radovljica Festival of Classical Music

One of the most important festivals of ancient classical music in Europe is staged over 10 days in August (p81).

September

An autumn chill comes to the mountains. Swimming winds down on the Adriatic coast and resorts such as Bled and Bohinj hold their last big shindigs of the season. Mushroom-hunting shifts into high gear.

⚜ Cows' Ball

Zany weekend of folk dance, music, eating and drinking in Bohinj to mark the return of the cows from their high pastures to the valleys in mid-September (p97).

⚜ Dormouse Night, Cerknica

A celebration and feast during the short dormouse-hunting season of late September in the forests around Snežnik Castle.

⚜ Slovenian Film Festival

A pivotal event in Slovenia's cinema world, this three-day festival in Portorož in late September sees screenings and awards.

October

Coastal areas quieten down for the year and the action shifts to big cities like Ljubljana, where the cultural season of classical concerts, ballet and theatre is in full swing.

⚜ City of Women

Ljubljana's 10-day international festival focusing on contemporary arts and culture by women (p52).

🏃 Ljubljana Marathon

First run in 1996, this marathon draws an increasingly international field (p52).

November

The solemn holiday of All Saints Day (1 November) sets the tone for the rest of this mostly dark, chilly month. On this day, Slovenians bring candles and red lanterns to the cemetery to remember the departed.

⚜ St Martin's Day

Nationwide celebration to mark the day (11 November) when *mošt* (must; fermenting grape juice) officially becomes new wine.

December

Christmas (25 December) is the high point of this dark and cold month. Ski season gets under way in the mountains.

☆ Christmas Concerts

Held throughout Slovenia, but the most famous are in Postojna Cave, where you can also attend the Live Christmas Crib, a re-enactment of the Nativity. Held early to mid-December. (p129)

Itineraries

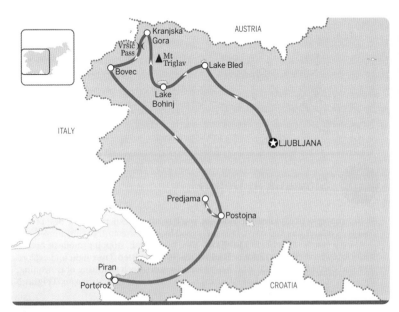

 ### Essential Slovenia

This route is ideal for first-time visitors wanting to experience the highlights of the country's alpine, karst and coastal regions.

Begin in the country's capital, **Ljubljana**, allowing at least two nights to take in the sights, restaurants and beautiful riverside setting. Next, head north to **Lake Bled**, overnighting to allow time for lakeside ambles and taking a *pletna* (gondola) to Bled Island. Lovely **Lake Bohinj**, 26km southwest of Lake Bled, makes for a more rustic, less touristy base and has direct views to **Mt Triglav**.

From here, travel northward to **Kranjska Gora**, the country's skiing capital and another good base for hiking. It's the northern terminus of the spectacular **Vršič Pass**, a high-altitude roadway (open May to October) that zigzags for some 50km down to the white-water rafting capital of **Bovec**. Overnight here and the next day continue along routes 102 and 103 to the amazing cave at **Postojna**. An easy side-trip from here is **Predjama**, where an impregnable castle set in a cliffside cave defies description.

It's just a skip to the coastal resorts of Piran and Portorož. If you're seeking romance, choose **Piran**; if it's sun and fun, **Portorož** is the centre of the action.

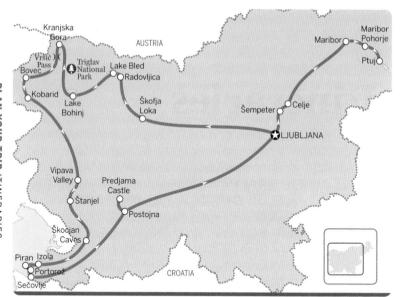

2 WEEKS Slovenia in Depth

With two weeks to explore little Slovenia, you'll be able to experience the best of the country's mountains and coast, plus get a good look at the country's untrampled east.

Allow a couple of nights in **Ljubljana**, then head north, stopping at one or both of the historic towns of **Škofja Loka** or **Radovljica**, to **Lake Bled**. Overnight and explore the lake and Bled Island, or stay a bit longer for adventure, such as rafting or canyoning. To the southwest, picturesque **Lake Bohinj** is an excellent base for exploring **Triglav National Park** or even climbing Mt Triglav itself.

Next head north to ski-capital **Kranjska Gora** to start your climb up and then down to the Soča Valley via the **Vršič Pass**. After 50km of hairpin turns you'll arrive at the country's white-water rafting capital of **Bovec**. Overnight here – especially if you plan to do any adventure sports – or in nearby **Kobarid**, a pretty town with a Mediterranean feel, an amazing WWI history and some of Slovenia's best restaurants.

Continue southward through Nova Gorica to the **Vipava Valley** and on to the Karst region. Little towns here, like **Štanjel** to the west, are rich in olives, ruby-red Teran wine, *pršut* (air-dried ham) and red-tiled roofs.

Further south, following the main Hwy E70 to the coast near Divača, is the awe-inspiring **Škocjan Caves**, part of an immense system of limestone caves. From here, go coastal. **Piran** is the most romantic spot on the Adriatic, but **Izola** has better restaurants and **Portorož** is more fun. Nearby is **Sečovlje** and its famous saltpans.

The return journey to Ljubljana passes through **Postojna**, another amazing cave, with a side trip to **Predjama Castle**. Avoid the capital altogether and continue driving along Hwy E57 to Celje, stopping to visit the awesome Roman necropolis at **Šempeter**. **Celje** is worth an afternoon for its wonderful castle and rich museums but **Maribor**, Slovenia's second-largest city and regional centre, awaits. The surrounding highlands, the **Maribor Pohorje**, rate a look but by now you might just want to spend some downtime along the Drava in atmospheric Lent.

Finish your journey in **Ptuj**, a charming town with a delightful castle and some excellent accommodation.

 Mountain Majesty

 Wine & Spas

What Slovenia has in spades is mountains. Active travellers can head for the hills near Kamnik, climb the dizzying heights of the Julian Alps and then descend into the adventure land of the Soča Valley.

Begin in **Ljubljana**, where you can stock up on hiking gear and regional maps, then make your way to **Kamnik** and the picturesque, high-altitude pastureland of **Velika Planina**. Heading back toward Kranj, continue north to impossibly cute **Radovljica**. Overnight here or a few kilometres north at **Lake Bled**.

Use Bled or nearby **Lake Bohinj** for forays into **Triglav National Park**. Both are popular approaches for scaling **Mt Triglav**. Proceed northward to ski centre **Kranjska Gora** and the heart-stopping **Vršič Pass** (closed winter). The road down deposits you in the **Soča Valley**. Following the Soča River will bring you to the activities centre of **Bovec** and the WWI battlegrounds around **Kobarid**. From here, head down through Tolmin to the sleepy town of **Cerkno**, famous for its pre-Lenten carnival. Route 210 is a sinuous mountain road through the Škofja Loka Hills, a region of steep slopes, deep valleys and ravines, to the charming town of **Škofja Loka** and back to Ljubljana.

Eastern and southern Slovenia are known for both their wines and spas. This tour includes the best of each.

From **Ljubljana** drive southeast to the delightful spa town of **Dolenjske Toplice**. **Otočec ob Krki** and its stunning castle isn't far away. Further east, **Brežice** draws visitors to its Terme Čatež spa complex and the wonderful **Bizeljsko-Sremič wine district**, known for medium-dry whites and reds and for *repnice* (caves for storing wine).

Head north on route 219 to **Podčetrtek** and another inviting spa, Terme Olimia. From here it's a short distance through the Haloze Hills to atmospheric **Rogaška Slatina**, Slovenia's oldest and largest spa, a veritable 'cure factory' with a dozen hotels and far more treatments offered.

Head north to the charming town of **Ptuj** and its nearby Terme Ptuj spa then go east to Ormož, for the start of the important **Jeruzalem-Ljutomer district**, home to the some of the country's best whites. Walk or hike the wine trail here.

The region's biggest city and cultural hub, **Maribor**, is not very far away. Who could possibly resist seeing the world's oldest (and still productive) grapevine dating back more than three centuries?

Plan Your Trip

Outdoor Slovenia

Slovenes are naturally outdoorsy and the country is blessed with a magnificent natural environment of mountains, lakes and rivers that lend a breathtaking backdrop to any activity. Popular pursuits include hiking, skiing and mountain biking, but there's also a world of more intrepid activities – from white-water rafting and caving to horseback riding and canyoning.

The Best...

Hiking
Julian Alps, Triglav National Park, Kamnik-Savinja Alps, Pohorje Massif

Skiing
Maribor Pohorje, Kranjska Gora, Vogel, Rogla

Cycling
Lake Bohinj, Krka Valley, Logarska Dolina

Rafting
Soča Valley, Krka River, Kolpa River

Caves
Škocjan, Postojna

Summer Activities
Hiking, walking, cycling, swimming

Spring Activities
White-water rafting, birdwatching

Autumn Activities
Climbing, especially Mt Triglav

Winter Activities
Skiing (mid-December to early April), bathing at hot springs

Hiking & Walking

Hiking is a national pastime. The country has an excellent system of well-marked trails that run to a total length of more than 9000km. Most trails are marked by a red circle with a white centre, with periodic updater signs along the way indicating distances and walking times. In addition, most regional tourist offices and bookshops stock a comprehensive selection of hiking maps.

The most popular areas for hikes include the Julian Alps and the Kamnik-Savinja Alps in in the northwest, as well as the Pohorje Massif in the northeast, but there are wonderful trails in all of the country's regions. Some of the best of these are linked with less obviously salubrious activities such as wine tasting.

Many trails can also be cycled, with the notable exception being the trails in the Triglav National Park. Maps usually indicate which trails are suitable for cycling with a bicycle sign.

Great Slovenian Hikes

➡ The **Slovenian Mountain Trail** runs for 500km from Maribor to Ankaran on the coast via the Pohorje Massif, the Kamnik-Savinja Alps, the Julian Alps and the Cerkno and Idrija hills. It was opened back in 1953 and was the first such national trail in Europe.

→ The 470km-long **Sub-Alpine Trail** covers Slovenia's hill country – from Cerkno and Idrija to Posavje via Notranjska – and is for less-ambitious, but equally keen, walkers and hikers.

→ A great *vinska cesta* (wine road) is the **Jeruzalem-Ljutomer wine road** in eastern Slovenia, which begins at Ormož and continues for 18km north to Ljutomer, via the beautiful hilltop village of Jeruzalem. There are many wine cellars along the way, and this road can also be biked.

→ The **Haloze Mountain Path** is a lovely wine-oriented 31km-long footpath that takes in the gentle landscape of the Haloze Hills wine region. It is accessible from near Štatenberg.

Major European Trails

→ The 350km **E6 European Hiking Trail** runs from the Baltic to the Adriatic seas and enters Slovenia at Radlje ob Dravi in northeastern Slovenia. It continues on to a point south of Snežnik in southern Slovenia.

→ The 600km **E7 European Hiking Trail** connects the Atlantic with the Black Sea. It

crosses into western Slovenia at Robič and runs along the Soča Valley. From here, it continues through the southern part of the country eastward to Bistrica ob Sotli, before exiting into Croatia.

→ Slovenia has joined Austria, Germany, Liechtenstein, Switzerland, Italy, France and Monaco to develop the **Via Alpina** (www.via-alpina.com), a system of five long trails that follow the entire arc of the Alps from Trieste to Monaco. Two of the trails pass through northern Slovenia: the 14-stage Red Trail (220km) and the 10-stage Purple Trail (120km).

→ The 590km Alpe Adria Trail (www.alpe-adria-trail.com) through Austria, Italy and Slovenia, enters Slovenia at the Jepca mountain pass on the Austrian border and continues for 145km, exiting at Milje above Trieste.

Skiing

Skiing rivals hiking as the most popular recreational pursuit in Slovenia, and many Slovenians even believe the sport was invented here. Today an estimated 300,000 people – some 15% of the population – ski regularly. Just about everyone takes to the slopes or trails in season, and you can too on the more than three-dozen ski grounds and resorts of varying sizes listed in the Slovenian Tourist Board's useful *Ski Resorts in Slovenia*.

Most of Slovenia's ski areas are small and relatively unchallenging compared to the Alpine resorts of France, Switzerland and Italy, but they do have the attraction of lower prices and easy access. For more details, as well as the latest weather and snow reports, check out the Ski Resort Info website (www.skiresort.info) or **Snow Telephone** (Snežni Telefon; ☏041 182 500, 031 182 500; www.snezni-telefon.si).

Julian Alps

→ **Kranjska Gora** (p103) (800m to 1215m), has 20km of pistes, but the skiing here is fairly straightforward and suited mostly to beginners and intermediates. Nevertheless, for foreign visitors, it is probably Slovenia's best-known and most popular ski resort, being easily accessible from Austria and Italy.

→ **Vogel** (p96) (570m to 1800m), above shimmering Lake Bohinj, offers dazzling views of Mt Triglav and reliable snow cover on 22km of slopes.

HIKING HELP

→ The Ljubljana-based Alpine Association of Slovenia (p257) is the fount of all information on hikes and treks. The organisation is a good first stop for basic info and arranging mountain guides. It also publishes hiking maps and maintains an up-to-date list of mountain huts, refuges and bivouacs throughout Slovenia on its website.

→ The Slovenian Tourist Board (www.slovenia.info) publishes the excellent *Hiking in Slovenia* brochure with more than 30 suggested itineraries.

→ *The Julian Alps of Slovenia* (Cicerone) by Justi Carey and Roy Clark, features 58 walking routes and short treks. The same pair's *Trekking in Slovenia: The Slovene High Level Route* (Cicerone) includes 500km of mountain and upland trail walking. *Thematic Paths in Slovenia*, published by the Slovenian Tourist Board and the Alpine Association of Slovenia, features two-dozen walks and hikes.

➡ **Krvavec** (p<OT>) (1450m to 1971m), in the hills northeast of Kranj, is one of the best-equipped ski areas in the country, with 30km of pistes and 40km of trails. In addition you'll find a number of ski (alpine and telemark) and snowboard schools, equipment rental, a ski shop and some good restaurants and bars. As it's only an hour's drive from Ljubljana, it's best avoided at the weekends.

Eastern Slovenia

➡ The biggest downhill skiing area is Maribor Pohorje (p212) (325m to 1327m) in the hills south of Maribor, with 42km of linked pistes and 27km of cross-country trails suitable for skiers of all levels. It offers a ski and snowboard school, equipment rental and floodlit night skiing, as well as being a good starting point for ski touring through the forested hills of the Pohorje.

Cycling & Mountain Biking

Cycling is a popular pastime in Slovenia and the country is an excellent cycling destination. Ljubljana is a bike-friendly big city, with marked cycling paths, an active bike-riding population, and several rental outfits, including an innovative rent-as-you-go cycling scheme, called Bicike(lj) (p69).

The Slovenian Tourist Board (www.slovenia.info) publishes a large-format brochure called *Cycling in Slovenia,* with information for on- and off-road biking and accommodation, as well as a 1: 260,000-scale map with the same name. On its website, the STB identifies 14 areas that it considers to be true 'cycling destinations', based on the existence of marked bike trails, good signage, and rental and repair shops.

Mountain bikers will want to focus on the Julian Alps and Soča Valley areas, particularly around Bovec, Lake Bohinj and Kranjska Gora. The last offers free-riding possibilities, where cyclists are whisked up the hill on a ski lift and then hurtle downward at breakneck speed. Around Lake Bohinj, ask for the *Bohinj Cycling Routes* map, available at the tourist information centre, which marks out a half-dozen trails, from family-friendly to downright crazy. Another popular adrenaline destination is Logarska Dolina and the surrounding Upper Savinja Valley in eastern Slovenia. Buy a copy of the *Upper Savinja Valley Cycling Map* (€3).

Slower, more scenic rides can be found around Lake Bled, and in the Krka Valley in Dolenjska, which has become something of a cycling centre.

Rafting, Kayaking, Canoeing & Canyoning

The centre for rafting and canoeing is the Soča River at Bovec. The Soča is famed as one of the best white-water rafting and kayaking rivers in Europe, and it is one of only half-a-dozen rivers in the European Alps whose upper waters are still unspoiled.

Other rafting centres include the Krka River and the Kolpa in southern Slovenia, the Sava River at Bohinj, the Savinja River at Logarska Dolina and the Drava River near Dravograd in northeastern Slovenia.

Canyoning, a sport that has grown by leaps and bounds in recent years, will have you descending through gorges, jumping over and sliding down waterfalls, swimming in rock pools and abseiling/rappelling. It's been described as being in one

---

'TAKING THE CURE' SLOVENIAN-STYLE

Slovenia has a score of thermal-spa resorts – two on the coast at Portorož and Strunjan and the rest in the eastern half of the country. They are excellent places not only for 'taking the cure' but also for relaxing and meeting people. Many resorts use the Italian *terme* for 'spa' instead of the Slovene words *toplice* (thermal spring) or *zdraviliščp*.

Only two – Dolenjske Toplice in the south and Rogaška Slatina in the east – are really spa towns as such, with that distinctive 19th-century feel about them. Others, like Terme Ptuj in Štajerska, are loud, brash places dedicated to all the hedonistic pursuits you care to imagine, complete with swimming pools, waterslides, tennis courts, saunas, massage services and wellness centres.

BEDDING DOWN ON HIGH

The Alpine Association of Slovenia (www.pzs.si) maintains some 178 mountain huts throughout the land and these are ranked according to category.

➡ A bivouac is the most basic hut in Slovenia's mountains, providing shelter only.

➡ A refuge has refreshments, and sometimes accommodation, but usually no running water.

➡ A *koča* (hut) or *dom* (house) can be a simple cottage or a grand establishment.

➡ A bed for the night runs from €16 to €22 in a Category I hut, the most remote hut, depending on the number of beds in the room, and from €10 to €18 in a Category II, defined as being within an hour's walk of motor transport. Category III huts are allowed to set their own prices but usually cost less than Category I huts.

➡ There are 50 mountain huts in the Julian Alps, most of them open at least between June and September; some huts at lower altitudes are open all year.

➡ Huts are never more than five hours' walk apart. You'll never be turned away if the weather looks bad, but some huts on Triglav can be unbearably crowded at weekends – especially in August and September.

huge, natural water park. Operators at Lake Bled can set you up for the day.

Caving

It is hardly surprising that the country that gave the world the word 'karst' is riddled with caves – around 7500 have been recorded and described. The main potholing regions in Slovenia are in the Karst around Postojna and the Julian Alps, and there are about 20 caves that are open to visitors.

Some caves, such as Škocjan (p136) and Postojna (p129), can be visited easily on a guided tour, others are demanding undertakings requiring more pre-planning. The **Speleological Association of Slovenia** (Jamarska Zveza Slovenije; ☎01-429 34 44; www.jamarska-zveza.si; Lepi pot 6) in Ljubljana can provide information on the requirements for visiting caves and put you in touch with guides and caving clubs.

Diving

Diving is popular in Lake Bled, in the Kolpa River in southern Slovenia and at Ankaran, Portorož and especially Piran on the coast, where you can take lessons. For more information, contact the **Slovenian Diving Federation** (Slovenska Potapljaška Zveza; ☎01-433 93 08; www.spz.si; 25 Celovška cesta) in Ljubljana.

Cave diving is a popular sport in Slovenia but is permitted only under the supervision of a professional guide. It can be done at Postojna, Škocjan and in the tunnel at Wild Lake (Divje Jezero) near Idrija.

Bird-Watching

Slovenia has some of the best bird-watching in Central Europe. Some 376 species have been sighted here, 219 of which are breeders.

The Ljubljana Marsh, south of Ljubljana, Lake Cerknica in southern Slovenia and the Sečovlje salt pans near Portorož on the coast are especially good for sighting waterbirds and waders, as is the Drava River and its reservoirs in northeast Slovenia.

An especially wonderful sight is the arrival of the white storks in Prekmurje in March/April. Other important habitats are the Julian and Savinja Alps, the Karst area and the Krakovski Forest north of Kostanjevica na Krki in southern Slovenia.

For more information, contact the Ljubljana-based **Bird Watching & Study Association of Slovenia** (Društvo za Opazovanje in Proučevanje Ptic Slovenije (DOPPS); ☎01-426 58 75; www.ptice.si; Tržaška cesta 2, Ljubljana), a member of Bird Life International.

Fishing

Slovenia's mountain streams are teeming with brown and rainbow trout and grayling, and its lakes and more-sluggish rivers are home to pike, perch, carp, chub and other fish. The best rivers for angling

SLOVENIA'S LONE NATIONAL PARK: MT TRIGLAV

Slovenia has several regional parks and a few dozen small 'landscape' parks, but Triglav National Park (p100) in the far northwestern corner, is the country's only true national park. Covering about 840 sq km (4% of the country's total land area), it's one of the European continent's largest protected natural landscapes.

The park's main attraction is Mt Triglav, which at 2864m is both the country's tallest mountain and the highest peak in the Julian Alps range. In addition to this and several other peaks that top 2500m, the park boasts scenic waterfalls, gorges, ravines, rivers, streams and the source lands of two major river systems: the Sava and Soča.

The main Triglav National Park Information Centre (p108) is located in the village of Trenta, about 24km south of Kranjska Gora along the Vršič Pass highway. In addition to providing general information on the park, there's a small museum, a gift shop and a small restaurant. Perhaps more convenient are the centres in Bled (p92) and the new one at Stara Fužina (p100) near Lake Bohinj.

Recommended hiking and trekking maps include the PZS 1:50,000-scale *Triglavski Narodni Park* (*Triglav National Park*; €9.10). Both Kartografija and Sidarta do a 1:25,000-scale map of *Mt Triglav* (€9). The *Triglav Hiking Guide* (Sidarta, €13) by Tine Mihelič and Peter Pehani is a classic.

are the Soča, the Krka, the Kolpa, the Sava Bohinjka near Bohinj, and the Unica in southern Slovenia.

Fishing is not cheap in Slovenia – a permit at the more popular rivers will cost from €55 to €150 for two or three days. Catch-and-release permits are cheaper. You can usually buy short-term fishing permits at local tourist information offices.

For information on licences and seasons, contact the **Slovenian Fishing Institute** (Zavod za Ribištvo Slovenije; ☎01-244 34 00; www.zzrs.si; Župančičeva ulica 9) in Ljubljana.

Horseback Riding

Slovenia is a nation of horse riders. The world's most famous horse – the Lipizzaner of the Spanish Riding School fame in Vienna – was first bred in Lipica at the Lipica Stud Farm (p138) is still the best place for serious riders to improve their skills.

For a simple day out on the horses, the Mrcina Ranč (p96) in Studor near Lake Bohinj, offers a range of guided tours on horseback, many of which are suitable for children.

Mountaineering & Rock Climbing

The principal rock- and ice-climbing areas in Slovenia include Mt Triglav's magnificent north face – where routes range from the classic 'Slovene Route' (Slovenski Pot; Grade II/III; 750m) to the modern 'Sphinx Face' (Obraz Sfinge; Grade IX+/X-; 140m), with a crux 6m roof – as well as the impressive northern buttresses of Prisank overlooking the Vršič Pass.

The best mountaineering guidebook readily available is *Mountaineering in Slovenia* (Sidarta) by Tine Mihelič, which describes more than 80 tours in the Julian Alps as well as the Kamnik-Savinja Alps and the Karavanke.

Športno plezanje (sport climbing) is very popular here too. The revised *Slovenija Športnoplezalni Vodnik* (*Sport Climbing Guide to Slovenia*; Sidarta) by climber Janez Skok et al covers 92 crags, with good topos and descriptions in English.

Paragliding, Ballooning & Flying

Paragliding has taken off in Slovenia, especially around Lake Bohinj and at Bovec. The TIC (p264) in Ljubljana can organise hot-air balloon flights.

Every town in Slovenia seems to have an airstrip or aerodrome, complete with an *aeroklub* whose enthusiastic members can take you 'flight-seeing'. The Ljubljana-based **Aeronautical Association of Slovenia** (Letalska Zveza Slovenije; ☎01-422 33 33; www.lzs-zveza.si; Tržaška cesta 2) has a list.

Plan Your Trip
Travel with Children

Slovenia is prime family-holiday territory, especially in July and August when Europeans hit the road and celebrate the summer break. Waterparks, caves, swimmable lakes and walking trails designed for little legs are just part of the story – many businesses go out of their way to make families welcome.

Slovenia for Kids

Slovenia gets a big tick for its friendly locals, accessible nature, unique attractions and short travel distances. Get your kids involved in your travel plans; if they've helped to work out where you're going and they've heard plans of dancing white horses, train rides through caves, or dragons on bridges, they'll have plenty to look forward to.

Sights & Activities

Parents should enquire at local tourist information centres – there are many attractions where kids are king, so get some recommendations on sights, activities and how to spend a rainy day.

Newer museums are interactive (some have dedicated kids sections), and there are parks, playgrounds, swimming pools and year-round waterparks. Many attractions allow free admission for kids up to about age seven and half-price (or substantially discounted) entry for those up to about 15. Family tickets are usually available.

Outdoors, there are loads of family-friendly activities. Kids (and adults) will enjoy paddling on a lake at Bled or Bohinj, swimming in the Adriatic, taking a cable car up a mountain at Vogel or Velika Planina, or riding a train through a cave at mighty Postojna. Winter activities include ski schools – close to Ljubljana there's Krvavec

Best Regions for Kids

Ljubljana

Capital attractions include a bridge guarded by dragons, a castle reached by funicular, a zoo, the House of Experiments and a mega-waterpark.

Lake Bled & the Julian Alps

Cable cars to mountaintops, lakes to swim in, boat rides, gorges, waterfalls and glamping.

Western Slovenia & the Soča Valley

More waterfalls and gorges, great campgrounds, and a river perfect for family adventures.

The Karst Region & Coast

Enormous caves fuel the imagination, plus castles, dancing horses, and seaside activities.

Eastern Slovenia

More castles, forest trails, waterparks, and uncrowded ski areas.

ski centre; in the west, Kranjska Gora is well set up; and the east has Maribor Pohorje.

Popular warm-weather activities such as rafting on the Soča River can be done from around age five; other adventures (kayaking, canyoning) are possible from around age 10.

Sleeping & Eating

In peak season (July and August) campgrounds are hives of activity, and many organise activity programs for junior guests; some are attached to waterparks. Campgrounds often have bungalows for rent, while glamping brings some creature comforts to the great outdoors; with options such as log cabins, treehouses and safari tents, it's a fun way to amuse the kids.

Some hostels are geared more to young backpackers, while others are set up for, and welcoming to, families. Rooms may sleep up to six (in bunks); there will invariably be kitchen and lounge facilities. Check out the apartments at Jazz Hostel in Bled, or family rooms at Hostel Pod Voglom on Lake Bohinj. Farmstays offer a rural idyll and/or the chance to get your hands dirty and are perfect for families. Many guesthouses and hotels offer family-sized rooms, and self-catering villas and apartments are plentiful.

On the whole, restaurants welcome children. Many have highchairs and kids menus, or serve the kind of food kids will eat (eg pizza and pasta). Self-catering is a breeze if you stay somewhere with kitchen facilities. Larger supermarkets stock all you'll need (including baby items), but may be open shorter hours than you might expect. There are oodles of prime picnic spots.

Transport

Having your own vehicle will make life a lot easier, but getting around using public transport isn't impossible. A cycling holiday may be doable with older kids, as distances between towns are not vast. Larger bike-rental outfits supply kids' bikes.

Planning

The best time for families to visit Slovenia is the best time for most travellers – between May and September. Local school holidays run from late June to early September. On the plus side, good weather is likely, attractions are in full swing, and your kids are likely to meet other kids. On the downside, beaches and attractions are busy, and accommodation is in demand (and charges peak prices).

All car-rental firms have children's safety seats for hire; make sure you book one in advance. Likewise, book cots (cribs).

Children's Highlights
Castles

Ljubljana (p36) Ride the funicular to the castle.

Bled (p84) A cool mountain-top fortress with views. Halloween celebrations here are awesome.

Predjama (p132) A castle in a cave with history that involves a toilet – it's every kid's dream.

Waterparks

Atlantis (p50) Sixteen (16!) pools in the capital.

Terme Čatež (p174) Near Brežice, with watery activities and a campground bursting with family fun.

Terme Ptuj (p204) Out east, with indoor and outdoor pools and lots of waterslides.

Dolenjske Toplice (p164) Ahoy! The Laguna at Balnea Wellness Centre has a pool with pirate ship.

Terme Olimia (p195) At Podčetrtek, with abundant slides, pools, activities, plus a child-care club.

Natural Wonders

Vintgar Gorge (p90) Near Bled, this is an easy path (1.6km each way) on a wooden walkway through fabulous nature.

Postojna Cave (p129) Stalagmites, stalactites, a train ride through a cave, and eyeless human fish.

Križna Cave (p134) Don boots and a lamp, and take a short boat ride across a lake inside a cave.

Kozjak Waterfall (p114) From Kobarid, a forested walk to a beautiful chute.

Fresh-Air Fun

Bled (p83) For lake swimming, rowboats, bike rides and *kremšnita* cream cake.

Bohinj (p93) More lake swimming, boat rides, horse-riding, and a cable-car ride up Vogel.

Bovec (p111) Family river-rafting is perfect, the older/braver can try canyoning and kayaking.

Portorož (p153) The most active city on the coast has lots of seaside activities.

Logarska Dolina (p185) The Fairytale Forest perfectly pairs walking trails with storytelling.

Regions at a Glance

Ljubljana

Entertainment
Architecture
Food

Thriving Culture

Ljubljana has a thriving cultural scene year-round. Come summer, nearly every weekend brings a festival or event, and buzzing riverside cafes lend the feeling of a perpetual street party.

Elegant Edifices

Ljubljana may be Europe's greenest city but it's also home to some of its finest architecture. You can't miss the work of architect and designer extraordinaire Jože Plečnik, whose bridges and baubles, pylons and pyramids are both playful and elegant.

Gastronomic Delights

Food has become almost an obsession in the capital in recent years, with locally sourced ingredients topping most shopping lists. Take a gastronomic tour of Slovenia without leaving town by grazing through the city's weekly Open Kitchen food festival.

p34

Lake Bled & the Julian Alps

Scenery
Hiking
Activities

Mountain Vistas

The Vršič Pass, lakes Bled and Bohinj, Alpine peaks: if you're seeking awe-inspiring natural beauty and Instagram-worthy vistas, you've come to the right place.

Hiking Heaven

Go easy with lakeside trails, or amp it up with hikes through gorges, over Alpine pastures or to spectacular waterfalls. If you're feeling ambitious, the mother of all Slovenian hikes is a Mt Triglav ascent.

Natural Waterpark

In summer, lakes Bled and Bohinj are a scenic soup of swimmers and boaters. National-park rivers and gorges beckon wetsuit-clad rafters and canyoners keen for rapids, natural pools and rocky water slides.

p71

Western Slovenia & the Soča Valley

Activities
Food & Wine
History

River Antics

The Soča Valley is one of Slovenia's best (and most beautiful) outdoor playgrounds. The Soča River's aquamarine waters are made for rafting, kayaking and canyoning, and its trails for hiking and biking.

Fruits & Wine

Tour the vineyards of Goriška Brda and the Vipava Valley, tasting olive oils, stone fruits and excellent indigenous wine varieties. Stop in at Idrija for some *žlikrofi* (potato-filled dumplings).

Military & Mining History

Idrija boasts Unesco-recognised mercury-mining heritage. Museums and monuments honour the tragic tales of WWI's Isonzo Front battles, particularly in Kobarid.

p109

32

LAN YOUR TRIP REGIONS AT A GLANCE

The Karst & the Coast

Caves
Coast
Animals

Underground Splendour

Tours of monumental Postojna and Škocjan caves reveal the surprising Slovenia hidden below the surface – vast, ancient and extraordinary.

Coastal Gems

Slovenia's 47km-long coast is rich in history, Venetian architecture, seafood, resorts and popular swimming spots. The jewel in the crown is perfectly poised Piran.

Animal Encounters

With dancing white Lipizzaner horses, strange cave-dwelling salamanders, and brown bears roaming the forests, this is the place to encounter rare and unusual creatures.

p127

Southeast Slovenia & the Krka Valley

Castles
Scenery
Activities

Treasure-Laden Castles

Castles dazzle with five-star accommodation at Otočec ob Krki, a glorious riverside perch at Žužemberk, breathtaking frescoes at Brežice, and tales of a local hero at Bogenšperk.

Slow Travel, Scenic Vistas

Rolling green hills, meandering rivers, church spires, forested slopes and fields filled with grapevines and fruit trees. It's as idyllic and tranquil as it sounds.

Aquatic Fun

Dolenjske Toplice and Čatež ob Savi offer thermal-water spas and waterparks. The winding Krka and Kolpa Rivers serve up rafting, kayaking, delightful riverside camping, hiking and biking.

p157

Eastern Slovenia

Spas
Food
Activities

Healing Waters

This region is dedicated to the art of taking mineral-rich spring waters for health and pleasure, as well as a decent amount of pampering. Top on the list is Rogaška Slatina, largest and oldest of Slovenia's spa towns.

Borderland Cuisine

Prekmurje's cuisine, celebrated throughout Slovenia, has a strong Hungarian influence; help yourself to paprika-rich *golaž* (goulash) and for dessert try *gibanica*, a calorific layered pastry of walnuts, apples and cottage cheese.

Hiking & Skiing

Hike or mountain bike through the lush green valley of Logarska Dolina or up in the Maribor Pohorje highlands, where, in winter, you can explore the same slopes on skis or snowboard.

p184

On the Road

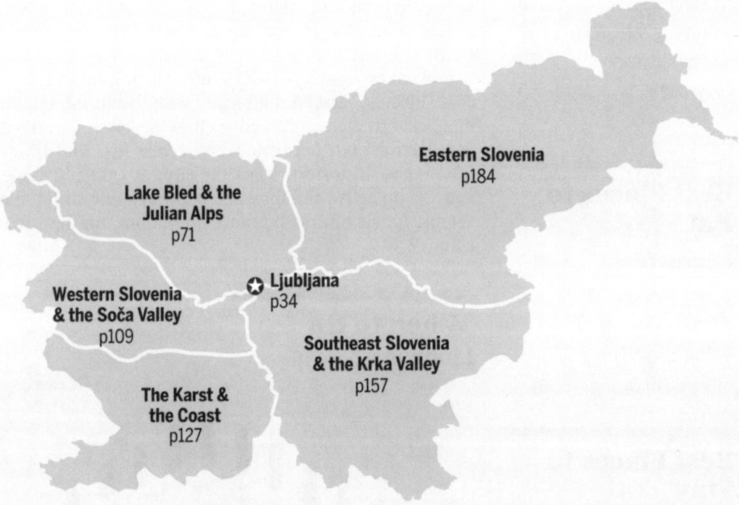

Eastern Slovenia
p184

Lake Bled & the
Julian Alps
p71

Western Slovenia
& the Soča Valley
p109

Ljubljana
p34

Southeast Slovenia
& the Krka Valley
p157

The Karst &
the Coast
p127

Ljubljana

🔗 01 / POP 278,800 / ELEV 297M

Best Places to Eat

➡ Strelec (p56)

➡ Taverna Tatjana (p57)

➡ Druga Violina (p56)

➡ Špajza (p57)

➡ Prince of Orange (p58)

Best Places to Stay

➡ Antiq Palace Hotel & Spa (p55)

➡ Cubo (p55)

➡ Celica Hostel (p55)

➡ Hostel Tresor (p54)

➡ Adora Hotel (p52)

➡ Vander Urbani Resort (p53)

Why Go?

Slovenia's capital and largest city also happens to be one of Europe's greenest and most liveable capitals. Indeed, the European Commission awarded Ljubljana with the coveted Green Capital of Europe title for 2016. Car traffic is restricted in the centre, leaving the leafy banks of the emerald-green Ljubljanica River, which flows through the city's heart, free for pedestrians and cyclists. In summer, cafes set up terrace seating along the river; it almost feels like a nightly street party.

Slovenia's master of early-modern, minimalist design, Jože Plečnik, graced Ljubljana with beautiful buildings and accoutrements; attractive cities are often described as 'jewel boxes', but here the name really fits. And bringing life to these historical riches, the city's 50,000-odd students support an active clubbing and cultural scene, and the museums, hotels and restaurants are among the best in the country.

When to Go
Ljubljana

Apr & May Sunny days, blossoms, and cafe terraces on the banks of the Ljubljanica.

Jul & Aug Street theatre, happenings every week, and the lively Ljubljana Festival.

Sep & Oct Warm temperatures during the day, and an autumn cultural program.

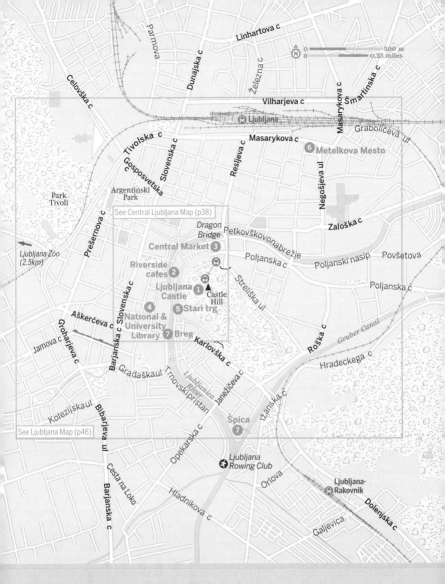

Ljubljana Highlights

1 Enjoy a ride on the funicular to **Ljubljana Castle** (p36) for an overview of the city's past and present.

2 Spend an evening at an outside table at **Slovenska Hiša** (p60) or any other riverside cafe.

3 Indulge in fresh fruits, vegetables and some delicious fish at Ljubljana's **central market** (p59).

4 Consider the genius of Slovenian architect and designer Jože Plečnik at his masterpiece, the **National & University Library** (p43).

5 Stroll through lovely **Stari trg** (p41) and marvel that this pretty place is actually the capital of a European country.

6 Crawl through the Old Town's waterfront pubs and end up at the alternative clubs at **Metelkova Mesto** (p64).

7 Enjoy the redesigned embankment from **Breg** (p43) south to **Špica** (p61).

History

Ljubljana began life in the 1st century AD as a smallish Roman city of 5000 inhabitants called Emona. The city thrived as a strategic crossroad on the routes linking Upper Pannonia in the south, with the Roman colonies at Noricum and Aquileia to the north and west. Remnants of the old Roman walls, dwellings and early churches can still be seen throughout Ljubljana and new discoveries are constantly being made.

Emona was sacked and destroyed by the Huns, Ostrogoths and Langobards (Lombards) from the mid-5th century; by the end of the next century tribes of early Slavs began to settle here.

First mentioned in writing as 'Laibach' in 1144, Ljubljana changed hands frequently in the Middle Ages. The last and most momentous change came in 1335, when the Habsburgs became the town's new rulers, a position they would retain almost without interruption until the end of WWI in 1918.

The town and its hilltop castle were able to repel the Turks in the late 15th century, but a devastating earthquake in 1511 reduced much of medieval Ljubljana to a pile of rubble. This led to a period of frantic construction in the 17th and 18th centuries that provided the city with many of its pale-coloured baroque churches and mansions – and the nickname *Bela Ljubljana* (White Ljubljana).

When Napoleon established his Illyrian Provinces in 1809 in a bid to cut Habsburg Austria's access to the Adriatic, he made Ljubljana the capital (though Austrian rule was restored just four years later). In 1821 Ljubljana walked onto the world stage when the four members of the Holy Alliance (Austria, Prussia, Russia and Naples) met at the Congress of Laibach to discuss measures to suppress the democratic revolutionary and national movements in Italy.

Railways linked Ljubljana with Vienna and Trieste in 1849 and 1857, stimulating economic development of the town. But in 1895 another, more powerful earthquake struck, forcing the city to rebuild once again. To Ljubljana's great benefit, the Secessionist and art nouveau styles were all the rage in Central Europe at the time, and many of the wonderful buildings erected then still stand.

During WWII Ljubljana was occupied by the Italians and then the Germans, who encircled the city with a barbed-wire fence creating, in effect, an urban concentration camp. Ljubljana became the capital of the Socialist Republic of Slovenia within Yugoslavia in 1945, and remained the capital after Slovenia's independence in 1991.

◉ Sights

The easiest way to see Ljubljana is on foot. The oldest part of town, with the most important historical buildings and sights (including Ljubljana Castle) lies on the right (east) bank of the Ljubljanica River. Center, which has the lion's share of the city's museums and galleries, is on the left (west) side of the river.

◉ Castle Hill

Begin an exploration of the city by making the trek up to **Castle Hill** (Grajska Planota) to poke around grand Ljubljana Castle. The castle area offers a couple of worthwhile exhibitions, and the castle watchtower affords amazing views over the city.

★**Ljubljana Castle**   CASTLE
(Ljubljanski Grad; Map p38; ☑ 01-306 42 93; www.ljubljanskigrad.si; Grajska Planota 1; adult/child incl funicular & castle attractions €8/5, castle attractions only €6/3; ⊙ castle 9am-11pm Jun-Sep, 9am-9pm Apr, May & Oct, 10am-8pm Jan-Mar & Nov, 10am-10pm Dec, castle attractions 9am-9pm Jun-Sep, to 8pm Jan-May & Oct-Nov, 10am-6pm Dec) Crowning a 375-metre-high hill east of the Old Town, the castle is an architectural mishmash, but most of it dates to the early 16th century when it was largely rebuilt after a devastating earthquake. It's free to ramble around the castle grounds, but you'll have to pay to enter the Watchtower and the Chapel of St George, see the worthwhile Exhibition on Slovenian History, visit the new Puppet Theatre and take the Time Machine tour.

There are several ways to access the castle, with the easiest (and for kids, the most fun) being a 70m-long funicular that leaves from Old Town not far from the market on Vodnikov trg. There's also an hourly tourist train that departs from south of the Ljubljana Tourist Information Centre. There are three main walking routes: Študentovska ulica, which runs south from Ciril Metodov trg; steep Reber ulica from Stari trg; and Ulica na Grad from Gornji trg.

You can explore the castle's various attractions at your own pace, or join one of the highly recommended 90-minute **Time Machine tours** (Časovni Stroj; Map p38; www.ljubljanskigrad.si; Ljubljana Castle; castle admission incl Time Machine tour €10/7; ⊘ tours 11am, 1pm, 3pm & 5pm daily Jul-Sep, 11am & 3pm daily May-Jun, 11am & 3pm Sat & Sun Oct-Apr), led by costumed guides who walk you through six of the city's most noteworthy periods, starting with Roman Emona.

The castle's 19th-century watchtower is located on the southwestern side of the castle courtyard. The climb to the top, via a double wrought-iron staircase (95 steps from the museum level) and a walk along the ramparts, is worth the effort for the views down into the Old Town and across the river to Center. Within the watchtower, there is a 12-minute video tour of Ljubljana and its history in several languages.

Situated below the watchtower down a small flight of stairs, the remarkable Chapel of St George (Kapela Sv Jurija) is one of the oldest surviving remnants of the castle, dating from 1489. It is covered in frescoes and the coats of arms of the Dukes of Carniola.

The Slovenian History Exhibition (Razstava Slovenska Zgodovina) is an interesting and well-presented interactive exhibition on Slovenian history through the ages, running from the very earliest Roman times, through the Middle Ages, the 19th century, WWI and WWII, and ending with socialist Yugoslavia and independence.

Also worth a look, the castle's latest attraction, the Museum of Puppetry (Lutkovni Muzej), explores the world of puppetry, from the manufacture of marionettes and glove puppets to the staging of the shows themselves. It's very interactive and lots of fun.

The Ljubljana Castle Information Centre (Map p38; ☑ 306 42 93; www.ljubljanskigrad. si; Grajska Planota 1; ⊘ 9am-9pm Apr-Sep, 9am-6pm Oct-Mar) can advise on tours and events that might be on during your visit.

◎ Prešernov Trg & Around

Prešernov Trg   SQUARE
(Map p38) The centrepiece of Ljubljana's wonderful architectural aesthetic is this marvellous square, a public space of understated elegance that not only serves as the link between the Center district and the Old Town but as the city's favourite meeting point. Taking pride of place is the Prešeren monument (Map p38), 1905, designed by Maks Fabiani and Ivan Zajc, and erected in honour of Slovenia's greatest poet, France Prešeren (1800–49). On the plinth are motifs from his poems.

Immediately south of the statue is the city's architectural poster-child, the small but much acclaimed Triple Bridge (p37). To the east of the monument at No 5 is the Italianate Central Pharmacy, an erstwhile cafe frequented by intellectuals in the 19th century. To the north sits the Franciscan Church of the Annunciation (p37), and on the corner of Trubarjeva cesta and Miklošičeva cesta, the delightful Secessionist Palača Urbanc (Palača Urbanc; Map p38; Prešernov trg) building from 1903, which now houses a fancy department store. Diagonally across the square at No 1 is another Secessionist gem: the Hauptman House (Map p38; Prešernov trg). Two doors down at Wolfova ulica 4 you'll see a terracotta figure peeking out from a window. It's Julija Primič gazing at her lifelong admirer Prešeren.

Franciscan Church of the
Annunciation   CHURCH
(Map p38; ☑ 01-242 93 00; www.marijinooznanjenje.si; Prešernov trg 4; ⊘ 10am-6pm) The 17th-century salmon-pink Franciscan Church of the Annunciation stands on the northern side of Prešernov trg. The interior has six side altars and an enormous choir stall. The main altar was designed by the Italian sculptor Francesco Robba (1698–1757). To the left of the main altar is a glass-fronted coffin with the spooky remains of St Deodatus.

Triple Bridge   BRIDGE
(Tromostovje; Map p38) Running south from the square to the Old Town is the much celebrated Triple Bridge. Originally called Špital (Hospital) Bridge when it built as a single span in 1842, it was nothing spectacular, but between 1929 and 1932 superstar architect Jože Plečnik added the two pedestrian side bridges, furnished all three with stone balustrades and lamps and forced a name change. Stairways on each of the side bridges lead down to the poplar-lined terraces along the Ljubljanica River.

Miklošičeva Cesta   ARCHITECTURE
(Map p38) This 650m-long thoroughfare links Prešernov trg with Trg OF and the train and bus stations; the southern end boasts a splendid array of Secessionist buildings and a fine park.

The cream-coloured former People's Loan Bank (Map p38; Miklošičeva cesta 4), 1908, at No 4 is topped with blue tiles and the figures of two women holding symbols of industry (a beehive) and wealth

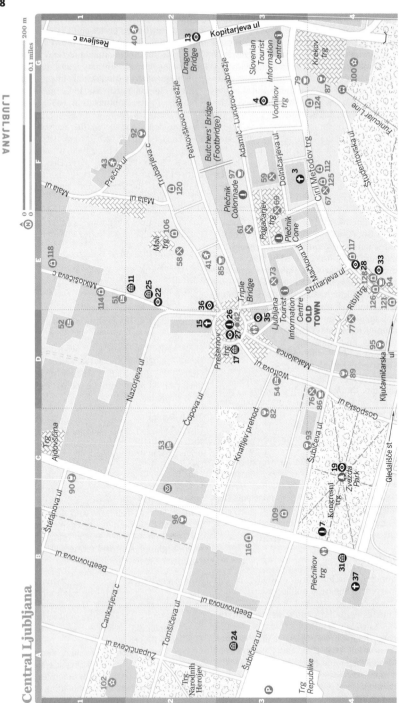

200 m
0.1 miles

Kopitarjeva ul

Dragon
Bridge

Slovenian
Tourist
Information
Centre

Krekov
trg

Vodnikov
trg

Petkovškovo nabrežje

Butchers' Bridge
(Footbridge)

Dolničarjeva ul

Ciril Metodov trg

Funicular Line

Študentovska ul

Trubarjeva c

Plečnik
Colonnade

Pogačarjev
trg

Plečnik
Cone

Mala ul

Prečna ul

Mali
trg

Mačkova ul

Stritarjeva ul

Ribji trg

Triple
Bridge

Ljubljana
Tourist
Information
Centre

OLD
TOWN

Miklošičeva c

Prešernov
trg

Makalonca

Wolfova ul

Ključavničarska
ul

Nazorjeva ul

Čopova ul

Knafljev prehod

Gosposka ul

Subičeva ul

Gledališče st

Trg
Ajdovščina

Zvezda
Park

Kongresni
trg

Štefanova ul

Plečnikov
trg

Beethovnova ul

Cankarjeva c

Tomšičeva ul

Beethovnova ul

Subičeva ul

Zupančičeva ul

Trg
Narodnih
Herojev

Trg
Republike

Resljeva c

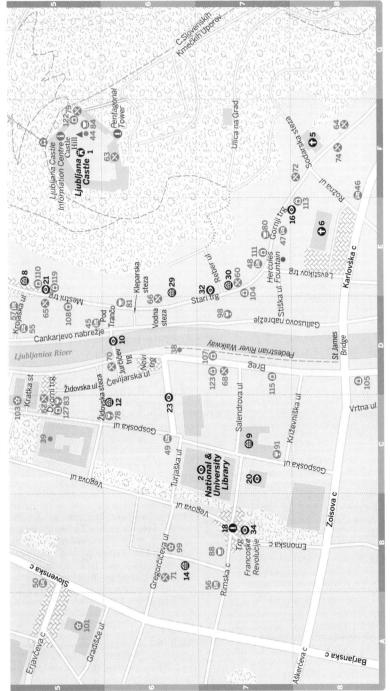

C Slovenskih Kmečkih Uporov

122·75

Pentagonal Tower

Ljubljana Castle
Information Centre
Castle
Castle
Hill
44 84

Ljubljana Castle
Castle 1

63

Ulica na Grad

5

64

72

74

Sodarska steza

Rožna ul

46

80
Gornji trg
47 16
113

Hercules
Fountain

6

Levstikov trg

Karlovška c

48 111
30
60

Reber ul

Kleparska steza

29

32
Stari trg
104

Stiška ul

8
110
119

21
Mestni trg

65
108

Kroja čka ul

55
45
81
Pod
Trančo

66

Vodna
steza

98

Galusovo nabrežje

Cankarjevo nabrežje

Ljubljanica River

Pedestrian River Walkway

10
Jurčičev
trg

70
Novi
trg

38

St James
Bridge

Kratka st

Židovska ul

Čevljarska ul

107

123 68

115

105

Vrtna ul

62
Dvorni trg

103

127 83

Židovska steza

78
12

23

Salendrova ul

Breg

Križevniška ul

39

Gosposka ul

49

Turjaška ul

9

91

Gosposka ul

Zoisova c

2
National &
University
Library

20

Vegova ul

Vegova ul

18
34
Trg
Francoske
Revolucije

Emonska c

Gregorčičeva ul

71
99

88

14

Rimska c

56

Slovenska c

50

101

Erjavčeva c

Gradišče ul

Barjanska c

Aškerčeva c

Central Ljubljana

(a purse). The one-time **Cooperative Bank** (Map p38; Miklošičeva cesta 8) at No 8 was designed by Ivan Vurnik, and the red, yellow and blue geometric patterns were painted by his wife Helena in 1922. Just opposite is the Grand Hotel Union (p52), the grande dame of Ljubljana hotels built in 1905. About 150m to the north is **Miklošičev Park**, laid out by Fabiani in 1902. Many of the buildings facing it are art nouveau masterpieces.

◎ **Old Town**

Ljubljana's Old Town (Staro Mesto) occupies a narrow swathe of land along the right (eastern) bank of the Ljubljanica River. This is the city's oldest and most important historical quarter. It's comprised of three contiguous long squares that include Mestni trg (Town Square), Stari trg (Old Square) and Gornji trg (Upper Square) as you move south

and east. It's an architectural goldmine, with a large portion of the buildings baroque and some townhouses along Stari trg and Gornji trg retaining their medieval layout.

Mestni Trg   SQUARE
(Town Sq; Map p38) The first of the Old Town's three squares is dominated by the town hall. In front of it stands the bright-white **Robba Fountain** (Map p38; Mestni trg) (1751); the three titans with their gushing urns represent the three rivers of Carniola – the Sava, Krka and Ljubljanica – but are modern copies. The original, worn down by time and eaten away by urban pollution, is now housed in the National Gallery.

Town Hall   TOWN HALL
(Mestna Hiša; Map p38; ☑ 01-306 30 00; Mestni trg 1; ⊙ 8am-5pm Mon-Fri) The seat of the city government and sometimes referred to as

the Magistrat or Rotovž, the town hall was erected in the late 15th century and rebuilt in 1718. The Gothic courtyard inside, arcaded on three levels, is where theatrical performances once took place and contains some lovely graffiti. If you look above the south portal leading to a second courtyard you'll see a relief map of Ljubljana as it appeared in the second half of the 17th century.

Stari Trg SQUARE
(Old Square; Map p38) Lined with 19th-century wooden shop fronts, quiet courtyards and cobblestone passageways, this is the heart of the Old Town. From behind the medieval houses on the eastern side, paths once led to Castle Hill, which was a source of water. The buildings fronting the river had large passageways built to allow drainage in case of flooding.

Cobblers' Bridge BRIDGE
(Čevljarski Most; Map p38) In the midst of Old Town, a small street running west from Stari trg called Pod Trančo (Below Tranča) leads to this evocatively named footbridge. During the Middle Ages this was a place of trade, and a tolled gateway led to the town. Craftsmen worked and lived on bridges (in this case 16 shoemakers) to catch the traffic and avoid paying town taxes – a medieval version of duty-free.

Schweiger House HISTORIC BUILDING
(Map p38) Between Stari trg Nos 11 and 15 – the house that should bear the number 13 but now says 11a – there's a lovely rococo building with a large Atlas supporting the upper balcony. The figure has his finger raised to his lips, asking passers-by to be quiet (the owner's name means 'Silent One' in German). In this part of the world,

bordellos were traditionally located at house No 13 of a street, and he probably got quite a few unsolicited calls.

Gornji Trg   SQUARE

(Upper Sq; Map p38) The five medieval houses at Nos 7 to 15 of this square have narrow side passages (some with doors) where rubbish was once deposited so that it could be washed down into the river. Look for the **Church of St Florian** (Cerkev Sv Florijana; Map p38), built in 1672 and dedicated to the patron saint of fires after a serious blaze destroyed much of the Old Town. Plečnik renovated it in 1934. From here, Ulica na Grad is an easy way to reach the castle.

Church of St James   CHURCH

(Cerkev Sv Jakoba; Map p38; ☏ 01-252 17 27; Gornji trg 18; ⊙ 7am-8pm) The Church of St James, built in 1615, houses Robba's main altar (1732), though far more interesting is the one in the church's Chapel of St Francis Xavier to the left, with statues of a 'White Queen' and a 'Black King'.

Botanical Garden   GARDENS

(Botanični Vrt; Map p46; ☏ 01-427 12 80; www. botanicni-vrt.si; Ižanska cesta 15; tropical glasshouse adult/child €2.80/1.30; ⊙ 7am-8pm Jul & Aug, to 7pm Apr-Jun, Sep & Oct, to 5pm Nov-Mar) **FREE** About 800m southeast of the Old Town along Karlovška cesta and over the Ljubljanica River, this 2.5-hectare botanical garden was founded in 1810 as a sanctuary of native flora. It contains 4500 species of plants and trees, about a third of which are indigenous.

◉ Central Market & East

The market area extends east of the Triple Bridge along the eastern edge of the Ljubljanica River, following Adamič-Lundrovo nabrežje. There are not many traditional sights here, but it's a great place to stroll and naturally pay a visit to the Central Market (p59), where you can stock up on fresh local produce, fish and deli items.

Cathedral of St Nicholas   CHURCH

(Stolna Cerkev Sv Nikolaja; Map p38; ☏ 01-234 26 90; http://lj-stolnica.rkc.si; Dolničarjeva ulica 1; ⊙ 10am-noon & 3-6pm) A church has stood here since the 13th century, but the existing twin-towered building dates from the start of the 18th century. Inside it's a vision of pink marble, white stucco and gilt and contains a panoply of baroque frescoes. Have a look at the magnificent carved choir stalls, the organ and the angels on the main altar.

Two stunning bronze doors were added in 1996 to commemorate a visit by the late Pope John Paul II. The (main) west door facing the Bishop's Palace recounts the history of 1250 years of Christianity in Slovenia. The six bishops on the south door fronting Ciril Metodov trg depict the history of the Ljubljana diocese.

◉ Center

This large district on the left bank of the Ljubljanica is the nerve centre of modern Ljubljana. It is filled with shops, commercial offices, government departments and

LJUBLJANA IN...

One Day

Take the funicular up to **Ljubljana Castle** to get an idea of the lay of the land. Come down and explore the **Central Market**. After a seafood lunch at **Ribca** and cake at **Torta Ljubljana**, explore the **Old Town**, walking through the three contiguous squares – Mestni trg, Stari trg and Gornji trg – before crossing over St James Bridge. Walk north along Vegova ulica to **Kongresni Trg** and **Prešernov Trg**. Plan your evening over a fortifying libation at one of the many cafes along the Ljubljanica such as **Tozd** or **Slovenska Hiša**, from where you might head to atmospheric **Taverna Tatjana** for some fine seafood, before hitting **Metelkova Mesto** for some alternative culture.

Two Days

On your second day check out some of the city's excellent museums and galleries – the rich **National Museum of Slovenia** for history and icons, the **Museum of Modern Art** for the best in contemporary art – and then stroll or cycle on a **Ljubljana Bike** or **Bicike(lj)** through **Park Tivoli**, stopping for an oh-so-local horse burger at **Hot Horse** along the way. In the evening, take in a performance at the **Križanke** or **Cankarjev Dom**. Otherwise dine at **Gujžina** and then head for the club at **Nebotičnik**.

embassies. Center is divided into several distinct neighbourhoods centred on squares.

Novi Trg
SQUARE

(New Sq; Map p38) South of Cobblers' Bridge, this was a walled settlement of fisherfolk outside the town administration in the Middle Ages. Remnants include the very narrow street to the north called Židovska ulica and its offshoot Židovska steza (Jewish Lane), once the site of a synagogue in the Middle Ages.

Breg, the city's port when the Ljubljanica River was still commercially navigable this far inland, runs south from the square and is entirely pedestrianised.

★National & University Library
ARCHITECTURE

(Narodna in Univerzitetna Knjižnica (NUK); Map p38; ☑01-200 11 10; www.nuk.uni-lj.si; Turjaška ulica 1; ◷8am-8pm Mon-Fri, 9am-2pm Sat) This library is Jože Plečnik's masterpiece, completed in 1941. To appreciate this great man's philosophy, enter through the main door (note the horse-head doorknobs) on Turjaška ulica – you'll find yourself in near darkness, entombed in black marble. As you ascend the steps, you'll emerge into a colonnade suffused with light – the light of knowledge, according to the architect's plans.

The Main Reading Room (Velika Čitalnica), open to nonstudents only by group tour (adult/child €4/2.50) in July and August, has huge glass walls and some stunning lamps, also designed by Plečnik.

Kongresni Trg
SQUARE

(Map p38) This lovely square, with leafy Zvezda Park (Star Park) at its centre and a new underground car park beneath, was named in honour of the Congress of the Holy Alliance, convened by Austria, Prussia, Russia and Naples in 1821 and hosted by Ljubljana. Today, the square is a popular venue for open-air concerts and national celebrations. To the south at No 12 is the central building of Ljubljana University, erected as a ducal palace in 1902.

The small gilded statue on top of a column at the western end of the square is a copy (the original is in the National Museum) of the Roman-era Citizen of Emona (Map p38), dating from the 4th century and unearthed not far from here in 1836. Just south is a newly excavated section of the city's northern gate.

Ursuline Church of the Holy Trinity
CHURCH

(Uršulinska Cerkev Sv Trojice; Map p38; ☑01-252 48 64; Slovenska cesta 21; ◷6-7.30am, 9-11am & 5-7pm) This church, which faces Kongresni trg from across Slovenska cesta and dates from 1726, is the most beautiful baroque building in the city. It contains a multi-coloured altar by Robba made of African marble.

Slovenian School Museum
MUSEUM

(Slovenski Šolski Muzej; Map p38; ☑01-251 30 24; www.ssolski-muzej.si; Plečnikov trg 1; adult/child €2/1; ◷8am-4pm Mon-Fri, 10am-2pm 1st Sat of the month) This rather esoteric museum explores how Slovenian kids learned the three Rs in past centuries. The mock-ups of the old classrooms are excellent and there is some explanatory material in English.

Trg Francoske Revolucije
SQUARE

(French Revolution Sq; Map p38) For centuries this was the headquarters of the Teutonic Knights of the Cross (Križniki). They built a commandery here in the early 13th century, which was transformed into the Križanke (Map p38; ☑01-241 60 00; Trg Francoske Revolucije 1-2) monastery complex in the early 18th century, which today serves as a concert hall and performance space. The Ilirija Column (Map p38) in the centre of the square recalls Napoleon's Illyrian Provinces (1809–13), when Slovene was taught in schools for the first time.

City Museum of Ljubljana
MUSEUM

(Mestni Muzej Ljubljana; Map p38; ☑01-241 25 00; www.mgml.si; Gosposka ulica 15; adult/child €4/2.50, special exhibits €6/4; ◷10am-6pm Tue, Wed & Fri-Sun, to 9pm Thu) The excellent city museum established in 1935 focuses on Ljubljana's history, culture and politics via imaginative multimedia and interactive displays. The reconstructed street that once linked the eastern gates of the Roman colony of Emona (today's Ljubljana) to the Ljubljanica River, and the collection of well-preserved classical artefacts in the basement treasury are worth a visit in themselves. So too are the models of buildings that the celebrated architect Jože Plečnik never got around to erecting.

Trg Republike
SQUARE

(Republic Sq; Map p46) Center's main plaza is dominated by a pair of glowering, grey tower blocks – TR3, housing offices and embassies, and the headquarters of Nova

Ljubljanska Banka – and a couple of garish revolutionary monuments. But the car park that once created such an eyesore is gone and the square has been cobbled in lovely blue Slovenian granite.

Parliament Building
HISTORIC BUILDING

(Parlament; Map p38; ☎01-478 97 88; www. dz-rs.si; Šubičeva ulica 4; ⊘tours by prior arrangement) FREE The parliament building at the northeast corner of Trg Republike, built between 1954 and 1959 by Vinko Glanz, is no beauty-pageant winner on the outside, but the mammoth portal festooned with bronze sculptures is noteworthy. If you can time it right, it's worth booking a guided tour to see the inside, especially the period-piece mural by Slavko Pengov.

Early Christian Centre Archaeological Park
HISTORIC SITE

(Zgodnjekrščansko Arheološki Park; Map p46; ☎01-241 25 00; www.mgml.si; Erjavčeva cesta 18; adult/child €2/1; ⊘10am-6pm Apr-Oct) Behind Cankarjev Dom, the city's premier cultural and conference centre, is this important site, with the remains of an early Christian church portico with mosaics from the 4th century, a total-immersion baptistery and

hypocaust system. Opposite and to the west of the Cankarjev Dom are the remains of a Roman wall (Map p46; Erjavčeva cesta) dating from 14–15 AD. The city's northern gate is closer to Kongresni trg.

◉ Museum Area

Four of Ljubljana's most important museums are located in this area, which is only a short distance to the northwest of Trg Republike.

National Museum of Slovenia
MUSEUM

(Narodni Muzej Slovenije; Map p46; ☎01-241 44 00; www.nms.si; Prešernova cesta 20; adult/ student €6/4, with National Museum of Slovenia Metelkova or Slovenian Museum of Natural History €8.50/6, 1st Sun of month free; ⊘10am-6pm Fri-Wed, to 8pm Thu) Housed in a building dating from 1888, highlights at this museum include a highly embossed Vače situla, a Celtic pail from the late 6th century BC unearthed in a town east of Ljubljana, and a Stone Age bone flute discovered near Cerkno in western Slovenia in 1995. There are also examples of Roman glass and jewellery found in 6th-century Slavic graves, as well as a huge

---

JOŽE PLEČNIK: ARCHITECT EXTRAORDINAIRE

Few architects anywhere in the world have had as great an impact on the city of their birth as Jože Plečnik. His work is eclectic, inspired, unique – and found everywhere in the capital.

Born in Ljubljana in 1872, Plečnik was educated at the College of Arts in Graz and studied under the architect Otto Wagner in Vienna. From 1911 he spent a decade in Prague teaching and later helping to renovate Prague Castle.

Plečnik's work in his hometown began in 1921. Almost singlehandedly, he transformed the city, adding elements of classical Greek and Roman architecture with Byzantine, Islamic, ancient Egyptian and folkloric motifs to its baroque and Secessionist faces. The list of his creations and renovations is endless – from the National & University Library (p43) and the colonnaded Central Market (p59) to the magnificent cemetery at Žale (p50).

Plečnik was also a city planner and designer. Not only did he redesign the banks of the Ljubljanica River (including Triple Bridge and the monumental lock downstream (Map p46)), and entire streets such as Zoisova cesta and Park Tivoli, but he also set his sights elsewhere: on monumental stairways (Kranj) and public buildings (Kamnik). An intensely religious man, Plečnik designed many furnishings and liturgical objects – chalices, candlesticks, lanterns – for churches throughout the land (such as Škofja Loka's Church of St James (p75)). One of Plečnik's designs that was never realised was an extravagant parliament, complete with an enormous cone-shaped structure, to be built on Castle Hill after WWII.

Plečnik's eclecticism and individuality alienated him from the mainstream of modern architecture during his lifetime, and he was relatively unknown (much less appreciated) outside eastern and central Europe when he died in 1957. Today he is hailed as a forerunner of post-modernism.

glass-enclosed Roman lapidarium outside to the north.

Check out the ceiling fresco in the foyer of the main building, which features an allegorical Carniola surrounded by important Slovenes from the past and the statues of the Muses and Fates relaxing on the stairway banisters.

Slovenian Museum of Natural History
MUSEUM
(Prirodoslovni Muzej Slovenije; Map p46; ☑01-241 09 40; www.pms-lj.si/en; Prešernova cesta 20; adult/student €3/2.50, with National Museum of Slovenia €8.50/6, 1st Sun of month free; ⊙10am-6pm Fri-Wed, to 8pm Thu; ℗) Housed in the same impressive building as the National Museum, the Natural History Museum contains the usual reassembled mammoth and whale skeletons, stuffed birds, reptiles and mammals. However, the mineral collections amassed by the philanthropic Baron Žiga Zois in the early 19th century and the display on Slovenia's unique salamander *Proteus anguinus* are worth the visit.

National Gallery of Slovenija
MUSEUM
(Map p46; ☑01-241 54 15; www.ng-slo.si; Prešernova cesta 24; adult/child €5/3, 1st Sun of month free; ⊙10am-6pm Tue, Wed & Fri-Sun, to 9pm Thu) Slovenia's foremost assembly of fine art is housed over two floors both in an old building (1896) and a modern wing. It exhibits copies of medieval frescoes and wonderful Gothic statuary as well as Slovenian landscapes from the 17th to 19th centuries (check out works by Romantic painters Pavel Künl and Marko Pernhart). Other noteworthies: impressionists Jurij Šubic *(Before the Hunt)* and Rihard Jakopič *(Birches in Autumn)*, the pointillist Ivan Grohar *(Larch)* and Slovenia's most celebrated female painter, Ivana Kobilca *(Summer)*.

The bronzes by Franc Berneker and Alojz Gangl are exceptional. In the entrance vestibule stands the original Robba Fountain, which was moved here from Mestni trg in the Old Town in 2008.

Museum of Modern Art
MUSEUM
(Moderna Galerija; Map p46; ☑01-241 68 00; www.mg-lj.si; Cankarjeva cesta 15; adult/student €5/2.50, with Museum of Modern Art €7.50; ⊙10am-6pm Tue-Sun, to 8pm Thu Jul & Aug) This gallery houses the very best in modern Slovenian art. Keep an eye out for works by painters Tone Kralj *(Family)*, the expressionist France Mihelič *(The Quintet)* and the surrealist Stane Kregar *(Hunter at*

LJUBLJANA'S DRAGONS

Ljubljana's **town hall** (p40) is topped with a golden dragon, a symbol of Ljubljana, but not an ancient one, as many people assume. Just before the turn of the 20th century a wily mayor named Ivan Hribar apparently persuaded the authorities in Vienna that Ljubljana needed a new crossing over the Ljubljanica, and he submitted plans for a 'Jubilee Bridge' to mark 50 years of the reign of Franz Joseph. The result was the much-loved **Dragon Bridge** (Zmajski Most; Map p38), which stands northeast of the Old Town, just beyond Vodnikov trg. City folk joke that the winged bronze dragons supposedly wag their tails whenever a virgin crosses the bridge, which is usually followed up with a smile and observation that they've never seen it happen.

Daybreak) as well as sculptors like Jakob Savinšek *(Protest)*. The museum also owns works by the influential 1980s and 1990s multimedia group Neue Slowenische Kunst (NSK; *Suitcase for Spiritual Use: Baptism under Triglav)* and the artists' cooperative Irwin *(Capital)*.

Serbian Orthodox Church
CHURCH
(Srbska Pravoslavna Cerkev; Map p46; http://spc-ljubljana.si; Prešernova cesta; ⊙9am-noon & 2-6pm Tue-Sun) The interior of the Serbian Orthodox Church, built in 1936 and dedicated to Sts Cyril and Methodius, is covered from floor to ceiling with colourful modern frescoes. There is a richly carved iconostasis separating the nave from the sanctuary.

⊙ Trubarjeva Cesta, Tabor & Metelkova Mesto

North of Castle Hill across the Ljubljanica River, this bustling street lined with waterholes and eateries gives way to leafy, residential Tabor, home to three world-class museums and Metelkova Mesto, Ljubljana's centre of alternative culture.

Slovenian Ethnographic Museum
MUSEUM
(Slovenski Etnografski Muzej; Map p46; ☑01-300 87 45; www.etno-muzej.si; Metelkova ulica 2; adult/child €4.50/2.50, 1st Sun of month free; ⊙10am-6pm Tue-Sun) Housed in the 1886

Ljubljana

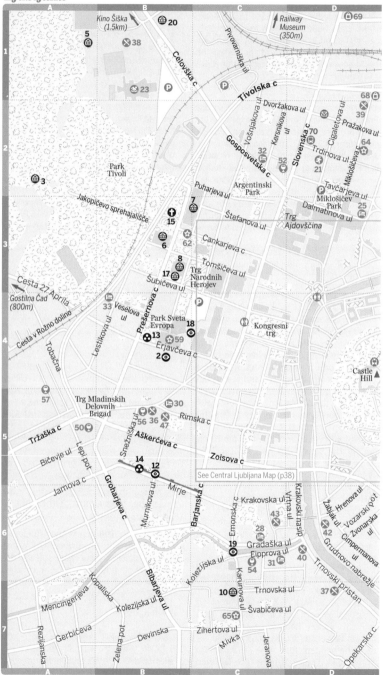

Kino Šiška
(1.5km)

20

5

38

Railway
Museum
(350m)

69

Celovška c

Pivovarniška ul

23

P

P

Tivolska c

Dvoržakova ul

Vošnjakova ul

Kersnikova ul

Gosposvetska c

Pražakova ul

Cigaletova ul

68

39

Slovenska c

70

Trdinova ul

64

Miklošičeva c

32

52

21

Park
Tivoli

3

Puharjeva ul

Argentinski
Park

Tavčarjeva ul

Miklošičev
Park

25

Jakopičevo sprehajališče

7

Štefanova ul

Trg
Ajdovščina

Dalmatinova ul

15

6

62

Cankarjeva c

Cesta 27 Aprila

8

Tomšičeva ul

17

Trg
Narodnih
Herojev

Šubičeva ul

Gostilna Čad
(800m)

Cesta v Rožno dolino

33

Veselova
ul

Prešernova c

Lestnikova ul

Park Sveta
Evropa

P

18

Kongresni
trg

Tobačna

13

59

2

Erjavčeva c

Castle
Hill

57

Trg Mladinskih
Delovnih
Brigad

30

56 **36**

47

Rimska c

Tržaška c

50

Bičevje ul

Lepi pot

Snežniška ul

Aškerčeva c

Zoiska c

See Central Ljubljana Map (p38)

14

12

Groharjeva c

Murnikova ul

Mirje

Barjanska c

Jamova c

Ernonska c

Krakovska ul

Vrtna ul

Žabjak ul

Hrenova ul

Vozarski pot

43

Zvonarska ul

28

42

Vilharjeva c

Cimpermanova
ul

19

Gradaška ul

Eiprova ul

31

40

Krakovski nasip

Grudnovo nabrežje

Koleziska ul

54

Trnovski pristan

Bibarjeva ul

Karunova ul

10

Trnovska ul

37

Mencingerjeva

Kopališka

Kolezijska ul

65

Švabičeva ul

Rezljanska

Gerbičeva

Devinska

Zihertova ul

Mivka

Jeranova

Opekarska c

Zelena pot

Kopališka

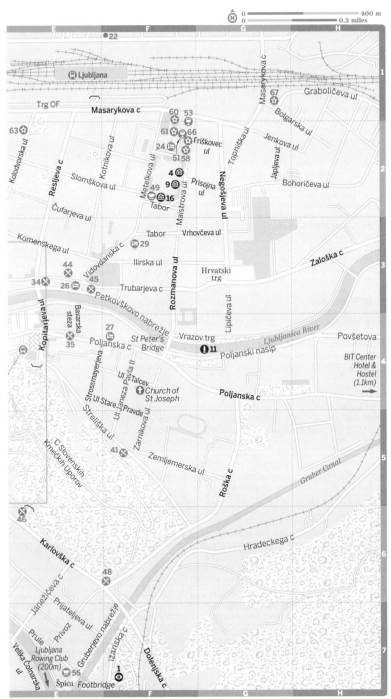

0 — 400 m
0 — 0.2 miles

Ljubljana

Graboličeva ul

Masarykova c

Bolgarska ul

Trg OF

Masarykova c

60 53
61 66
24 Friškovec ul
51 58

Jenkova ul

Japljeva ul

63

Kolodvorska ul

Resljeva c

Kotnikova ul

Slomškova ul

Metelkova c

4
9
49
16
Tabor

Maistrova ul

Prisojna ul

Negošjeva ul

Bohoričeva ul

Čufarjeva ul

Komenskega ul

Tabor

Vrhovčeva ul

Vidovdanska c

29

Ilirska ul

Hrvatski trg

Zaloška c

44
45

34
26

Trubarjeva c

Rozmanova ul

Lipičeva ul

Petkovškovo nabrežje

Bavarska steza

27
35

Poljanska c

St Peter's Bridge

Vrazov trg

11

Ljublanica River

Povšetova

Poljanski nasip

BIT Center Hotel & Hostel (1.1km)

Kopitarjeva ul

Strossmayerjeva

Ul Janeza Pavla II

Talcev

Church of St Joseph

Poljanska c

Ul Stare Pravde

Streliška ul

Zarnikova ul

41

Zemljemerska ul

Roška c

Gruber Canal

C Slovenskih Kmečkih Uporov

46

Karlovška c

48

Janežičeva c

Prijateljeva ul

Hradeckega c

Prule

Privoz

Gruberjevo nabrežje

Ižanska c

Dolenjska c

Ljubljana Rowing Club (200m)

Velika Čolnarska ul

55

Špica

Footbridge

1

Ljubljana

Belgian Barracks on the southern edge of Metelkova, this museum has a permanent collection on the 2nd and 3rd floors. There's traditional Slovenian trades and handicrafts – everything from beekeeping and blacksmithing to glass-painting and pottery making – and some excellent exhibits directed at children.

National Museum of Slovenia

Metelkova   MUSEUM

(Narodni Muzej Slovenije Metelkova; Map p46; ☑01-230 70 30; www.nms.si; Maistrova ulica 1; adult/student €6/4, with National Museum of Slovenia €8.50/6, 1st Sun of month free; ☺10am-6pm Tue-Sun) This modern building in what is now becoming known as the Museum Quarter contains a bizarre assortment of mostly applied art and *objets d'art* (furniture, icons, paintings, sporting goods etc) that are tenuously linked through themes (Seating & Lighting). It's a rich collection spread over two very large floors.

Museum of Contemporary Art GALLERY
(Muzej Sodobne Umetnosti; Map p46; ☑01-241 68 00; www.mg-lj.si; Maistrova ulica 3; adult/student €5/2.50, with Museum of Modern Art €7.50; ☺10am-6pm Tue-Sun, to 8pm Thu Jul & Aug) This new gallery in a sleekly redesigned faceless block picks up the thread from its sister institution, the Museum of Modern Art, with Eastern European (mostly ex-Yugoslav) works from the 1960s to today. Plenty of obscure material here, but just as much of it is challenging and thought-provoking.

⊚ Park Tivoli & Around

Laid out in 1813, this 510-hectare park is Ljubljana's leafy playground and the perfect spot for a walk or bike ride. One of the highlights is the Jakopičevo sprehajališče, the monumental 'Jakopič Promenade', designed by Plečnik in the 1920s and '30s.

International Centre of Graphic Arts MUSEUM
(Mednarodni Grafični Likovni Center; Map p46; www.mglc-lj.si; Pod Turnom 3; adult/senior & student €3.40/1.70, at biennial €6/3; ☺10am-6pm Tue-Sun) This museum and gallery dedicated to the graphic arts regularly hosts rotating exhibitions and is home to the International Biennial of Graphic Arts every odd-numbered year (2017, 2019 etc). The centre is located in the 17th-century Tivoli Mansion (Grad Tivoli) and has a delightful terrace cafe with views over the park.

Museum of Contemporary History of Slovenia MUSEUM
(Muzej Novejše Zgodovine Slovenije; Map p46; ☑01-300 96 10; www.muzej-nz.si; Celovška cesta 23; adult/student €3.50/2.50, 1st Sun of month free; ☺10am-6pm Tue-Sat) This museum, housed in the 18th-century Cekin Mansion (Grad Cekinov), traces the history of Slovenia in the 20th century through multimedia and artefacts. Note the contrast between the sober earnestness of the communist-era rooms and the exuberant, logo-mad commercialism of the industrial exhibits. The sections focusing on Ljubljana under occupation during WWII are very effective. The gloriously baroque Ceremonial Hall (Viteška Dvorana) on the

1st floor is how the whole mansion once looked. Cutting-edge special exhibits too.

Ljubljana Zoo ZOO
(Živalski Vrt Ljubljana; ☑01-244 21 82; www.zoo-ljubljana.si; Večna pot 70; adult/child €8/5.50; ☺9am-7pm Apr-Aug, to 6pm Sep, to 5pm Mar & Oct, to 4pm Nov-Feb; ☐18 to Večna pot) The 20-hectare zoo, on the southern slope of Rožnik Hill (394m), contains some 500 animals representing almost 120 species and is an upbeat and well-landscaped menagerie. There's a petting zoo and lots of other activities for children; consult the website for feeding schedules.

Union Experience MUSEUM
(Union doživetje; Map p46; ☑041 303 050; www.union-experience.si; Union Brewery, Celovška cesta 22; adult €5-7, child €2.5-3; ☺tours noon, 3pm & 5pm Mon-Fri; ☐1, 3 or 5 to Tivoli) FREE This museum at the Union brewery offers various displays of brewing, a film and a tasting. The more expensive tour at noon only includes a visit to the production facilities. Walk here from Center.

Railway Museum MUSEUM
(Železniški Muzej; Map p46; ☑01-291 26 41; www.slo-zeleznice.si; Parmova ulica 35; adult/child €3.50/2.50; ☺10am-6pm Tue-Sun; ☐14 to Parmova) A trainspotter's dreamland, there's a boiler room here with 10 locomotives (one going back to 1861 and one you can climb all over) and carriages. In the old ticket office opposite you'll find maps, uniforms, lanterns and signalling equipment. It's just north of Center.

⊚ Krakovo & Trnovo

These two attractive districts south of Center are Ljubljana's oldest suburbs, and they have a number of interesting buildings and historic sites. The neighbourhood around Krakovska ulica, with all its two-storey cottages, was once called the Montmartre of Ljubljana because of all the artists living there.

The Roman wall (Map p46) running along Mirje from Barjanska cesta dates from about AD 15; the archway topped with a pyramid (Map p46) is a Plečnik addition. Spanning the picturesque canal called Gradaščica to the south is little Trnovo Bridge (Map p46), designed in 1932 by Plečnik, who added five of his trademark pyramids.

Plečnik House MUSEUM
(Hiša Plečnik; Map p46; ☑01-280 16 00; www.
mgml.si; Karunova ulica 4-6; adult/child €6/4;
☺10am-6pm Tue-Sun) Recently reopened after
two years' conservation work, this is the little house in Trnovo where Jože Plečnik lived
and worked for almost 40 years. There's an
excellent introduction by hourly guided tour
to this almost ascetically religious man's life,
inspiration and work.

☉ Žale & Beyond

Žale Cemetery CEMETERY
(Pokopališče Žale; ☑01-420 17 00; www.zale.si;
Med Hmeljniki 2; ☺7am-9pm Apr-Sep, to 7pm Oct-
Mar; ☐2, 7 or 22 to Žale) This cemetery, some
2km northeast of Tabor, is Ljubljana's answer to Père Lachaise in Paris or London's
Highgate. It is 'home' to a number of Slovenian actors, writers, painters and a certain
distinguished architect – *Gospod* Plečnik
himself – but is best known for the ornamental gates, chapels and colonnades designed by the architectural master in 1940.
There are also the graves of Austrian, Italian
and German soldiers from both world wars
and a small Jewish section.

**Museum of Architecture
& Design** MUSEUM
(Muzej za Arhitekturo in Oblikovanje; ☑01-548
42 80; www.mao.si; Fužine Castle, Pot na Fužine
2; adult/child €3/1.50, 1st Sun of month free;
☺10am-6pm Tue-Sun; ☐20 or 22 to Fužine) This
museum, housed in a stunningly preserved
16th-century Fužine castle (worth the visit
alone) about 5.5km east of the centre, pre-

serves some 150,000 items from architects,
designers and photographers and hosts temporary themed exhibitions.

☂ Activities

Ballooning

The Ljubljana TIC organises **hot-air balloon rides** (☑306 12 15; www.visitljubljana.com;
adult/child €130/65; ☺btwn 6 & 7.30am Wed, Fri &
Sun Apr-Oct) (one to 1½ hours actually in the
air) with stunning views of the city, Ljubljana Marsh and the Julian Alps. Departure is
from the Slovenian Tourist Information Centre (p68); times vary.

Boating & Rafting

Ljubljana Rowing Club BOATING
(Veslaški Klub Ljubljana; ☑01-283 87 12; www.
vesl-klub-ljubljanica.si; Velika Čolnarska ulica 20; per
hour €5-7; ☺11am-10pm mid-May–Sep) This club
in Trnovo has dinghies and larger rowing
boats for hire on the Ljubljanica River.

Skok Sport BOATING
(☑01-512 44 02; www.skok-sport.si; Marinovše-
va cesta 8; ☺8am-1pm & 3-8pm May-Oct; ☐8 to
Brod) In Šentvid, 9km northwest of Center,
this place organises combination cycling
and rafting trips on the nearby Sava, lasting
2½ to three hours and costing €32. It can
also arrange kayak and canoe excursions on
the Ljubljanica and runs a kayaking school.
Rental kayaks for half/full day start at €7/10.

Swimming & Sauna

Atlantis SWIMMING
(☑01-585 21 00; www.atlantis-vodnomesto.si; BTC
City, Šmartinska cesta 152; day pass adult/child

A GALLERY OF GALLERIES

Ljubljana is awash with galleries, both public and commercial, so head straight to a few of
the best to get a taste of contemporary Slovenian art culture.

City Art Gallery (Mestna Galerija; Map p38; ☑01-241 17 70; www.mestna-galerija.si; Mestni
trg 5; ☺11am-7pm Tue, Wed, Fri & Sat, 11am-9pm Thu, to 3pm Sun) Old Town gallery with
rotating displays of modern and contemporary painting, sculpture, graphic art and
photography.

DESSA Architectural Gallery (Map p38; ☑01-251 60 10; www.dessa.si; Židovska steza 4;
☺noon-6pm Tue-Fri, 11am-1pm Sat) Small gallery spotlighting contemporary Slovenian and
international architecture and architects.

Equrna Gallery (Galerija Equrna; Map p38; ☑01-252 71 23; www.equrna.si; Gregorčičeva ulica
3; ☺11am-7pm Mon-Fri) Still the most innovative modern gallery in town thanks to the
discerning owner/curator.

Škuc Gallery (Galerija Škuc; Map p38; ☑01-251 65 40; www.galerija.skuc-drustvo.si; Stari trg
21; ☺noon-8pm Mon-Fri) Cutting-edge contemporary art gallery with a studenty vibe in
the heart of the Old Town.

Mon-Fri €15.30/12.90, Sat & Sun €17.60/15.20; ⊗9am-9pm Sun-Thu, to 10pm Fri & Sat; ▣27 to BTC Emporium) The largest of Ljubljana's water parks, with separate theme areas: Adventure World, with a half-dozen pools and water slides; Thermal Temple, with indoor and outdoor thermal pools; and Land of Saunas, with a dozen different types of saunas. The complex is about 3km northwest of the centre.

Tivoli Recreation Centre SWIMMING
(Map p46; ☑01-431 51 55; www.sport-ljubljana. si; Celovška cesta 25) In Park Tivoli, this centre run by Sport Ljubljana has an indoor swimming pool (open mid-September to June), a fitness centre, clay tennis courts and a roller-skating rink, which becomes an ice rink in winter. It also has a popular sauna.

Walking & Hiking
Popular with walkers and joggers, the marked **Trail of Remembrance** (Pot Spominov) runs for 34km around Ljubljana where German barbed wire once completely enclosed the city during WWII. The easiest places to reach the trail are from the **AMZS headquarters** (Slovenian Automobile Association; www.amzs.si; Dunajska cesta 128) – take bus 6, 8 or 11 to the AMZS stop – or from Trg Komandanta Staneta just northwest of LPP (p70) central office (take bus 1 to the Remiza stop). You can also join it from the northwestern side of Žale Cemetery (p50; take bus 19 to the Nove Žale stop), or south of Trnovo (take bus 9 to the Veliki Štradon stop).

☞ Tours

The Ljubljana Tourist Information Centre (p68) organises a number of guided tours of the city and even has a **digital tour guide** (€10), which takes in 17 sights and lasts about two hours.

Ljubljana Free Tours WALKING TOUR
(Map p38; ☑040 604 476; www.ljubljana freetour.com; Prešernov trg; donation expected; ⊗11am & 3pm) All right, yes, 'free tours' is a bit of a misnomer, because these yellow-clad guides that gather up groups twice a day in Prešernov trg do expect a tip. We suggest you pay as much as you would for a regular tour. Walking tours last almost 2½ hours and your guide will take you past – and recount the stories behind – every sight worth seeing in this fair city.

SLOVENIAN HERITAGE

If you are searching for your Slovenian roots, check first with the *mestna občina* (municipal government office) or *občina* (county office); it usually has birth and death certificates going back a century. Vital records beyond the 100-year limit are kept at the **Archives of the Republic of Slovenia** (Arhiv Republike Slovenije; ☑01-241 42 00; www. arhiv.gov.si; Gruber Palace, Zvezdarska ulica 1; ⊗8am-2pm Mon-Fri, to 3pm in winter). Ethnic Slovenes living abroad might be interested in contacting the **Slovenian Emigrants Centre** (Slovenska Izseljenska Matica; ☑01-241 02 80; www. zdruzenje-sim.si; 2nd fl, Cankarjeva cesta 1; ⊗by appointment).

Barka Ljubljanica BOAT TOUR
(Ljubljanica Boat; Map p38; ☑041 386 945; www. barka-ljubljanica.si; Breg 2; adult/child €8/free; ⊗sailings hourly 10am-8pm May-Oct, 11am-8pm Nov-Jan) There are more and more boat tours up and down the river in Ljubljana but only the creatively named Barka Ljubljanica (Ljubljanica Boat) sails a wooden vessel. It's 10m long and carries up to 48 people plus crew on a 45-minute tour. Board it on the west bank of the river, just down from Novi trg.

Ljubljananjam TOUR
(☑041 878 959; www.ljubljananjam.si; 3-4hr tour €30-55) Our cup runneth over with food tours in Ljubljana these days, but we'll always make room for Ljubljananjam (roughly 'Ljubljana Yum'). Epicure Iva Gruden, whose enthusiasm is both fetching and catching, will have you eating out of bakers' hands, nibbling goat cheese in the market, scoffing Carniola sausage in the Old Town and slurping fair-trade espresso below the castle. *Dober tek* (bon appetit)!

CurioCity TOUR
(☑051 640 750; www.curiocity.si; per person €30-45) This unusual outfit organises a number of personal tours – from best selfie locations to expeditions in search of dragons – but the most innovative is their From Ljubljana with Love, which introduces you to the people and the stories behind six socially responsible businesses: from secondhand shops and fair-trade cafes to restaurants supporting those with learning disabilities.

✻ Festivals & Events

Druga Godba   WORLD MUSIC
(Another Story; http://festival.drugagodba.si; ☺ May)
This festival of alternative and world music
takes place in the Križanke in late May.

Ljubljanska Vinska Pot   WINE
(Ljubljana Wine Route; www.ljubljanskavinskapot.
si; ☺ Jun) Held on a Saturday in June, this
event brings winemakers from around the
country to central Ljubljana, where visitors
spend the day wandering around and tasting the offerings.

**Ana Desetnica International
Street Theatre Festival**   THEATRE
(www.anamonro.org; ☺ Jun-Jul) Organised by
the Ana Monro Theatre in late June/early
July, this festival is not to be missed.

Ljubljana Festival   MUSIC
(www.ljubljanafestival.si; ☺ Jul-Aug) The number
one event on Ljubljana's social calendar is
the Ljubljana Festival, a celebration from
early July to late August of music, opera,
theatre and dance held at venues throughout the city, but principally in the open-air
theatre at the Križanke.

Trnfest   MUSIC
(www.kud.si; ☺ Jul-Aug) An international festival of alternative arts and culture and many
Ljubljančans' favourite annual event, Trnfest takes place at the KUD France Prešeren
(p65) in Trnovo and at other venues from
late July to late August.

City of Women   CULTURAL
(www.cityofwomen.org; ☺ Oct) Held in the first
half of October in venues throughout Ljubljana, it showcases all forms of artistic ex-
pression by women.

**International Ljubljana
Marathon**   MARATHON
(www.ljubljanskimaraton.si; ☺ Oct) Sponsored by
Volkswagen, this major sporting event takes
place on the last Sunday in October.

🛏 Sleeping

Accommodation prices in Ljubljana are the
highest in the country, so expect to shell out
a bit more here than elsewhere. For tight-
er budgets, there is a growing number of
high-quality modern hostels, some with
private singles and doubles. The TIC website (www.visitljubljana.com) maintains a
comprehensive list of hotels and sleeping
options, including private rooms (single/

double/triple from €30/50/75). A few of
these are in the centre but most require a
bus trip north to Bežigrad or beyond.

🏠 Prešernov Trg & Around

Hotel Emonec   HOTEL €€
(Map p38; ☏ 01-200 15 20; www.hotel-emonec.
com; Wolfova ulica 12; s/d/tr from €64/77/96;
🅿 ❄ @ 🛜) After a complete revamping, the
decor remains simple and functionally modern at this 54-room hotel. Everything is spotless and you can't beat the central location.
Air-con costs extra but fans are free. There's
a small in-house spa with fitness and sauna.

Grand Hotel Union   HOTEL €€€
(Map p38; ☏ 01-308 12 70; www.gh-union.
si; Miklošičeva cesta 1; s €90-194, d €109-224, ste
€150-455; 🅿 ❄ @ 🛜) The 194-room Grand
Hotel Union, the art-nouveau southern wing
of a two-part hostelry, was built in 1905 and
remains one of the most desirable address-
es in town. It has glorious public areas and
guests can use the indoor pool and fitness
centre of the adjacent 133-room **Grand Hotel Union Business** (Map p38; ☏ 308 11 70;
www.gh-union.si; Miklošičeva cesta 3; s €85-130,
d €99-160, ste €210-250; 🅿 ❄ @ 🛜 🖥), in the
renovated modern wing.

🏠 Old Town

Ad Hoc Hostel   HOSTEL €
(Map p38; ☏ 051 268 288; www.adhoc-hostel.
com; Cankarjevo nabrežje 27; dm €17.50-21, d €40-
54; ❄ @ 🛜) This very well-situated, efficiently run 106-bed hostel on the Ljubljanica has
brightly painted, airy dorms with four to
eight metal bunks and eight doubles. Room
Nos 104 and 106 overlook the river. There
are also four apartments. Great kitchen, too.

★ Adora Hotel   HOTEL €€
(Map p38; ☏ 08 205 72 40; www.adorahotel.si/
en; Rožna ulica 7; s €68-109, d €78-119, apt €110-
150; 🅿 ❄ @ 🛜) This small hotel below Gornji
trg is a welcome addition to accommodation
in the Old Town. The 10 rooms are small but
fully equipped, with lovely hardwood floors
and tasteful furnishings. The lovely breakfast room looks out onto a small garden,
bikes are free for guests' use and the staff
are overwhelmingly friendly and helpful.

Consider splashing out on one of the two
gorgeous apartments that are partially located in the archway that spans Karlovška
cesta.

Allegro Hotel BOUTIQUE HOTEL €€

(Map p38; ☑ 059 119 620, 0401 557 908; www.
allegrohotel.si; Gornji trg 6; s €95-100, d €85-120,
tr €170-200; P ⊛ @ 🕏) This 17-room historic
boutique hotel in Old Town is a symphony
of designer chic with rooms that give on to
Gornji trg and a charming back courtyard.
Room Nos 2 and 3 have a balcony, No 15 a
small terrace and No 12 at the top sleeps four.

The front lounge – a parlour, really – is
on two levels and we love the old piano and
original wooden staircase.

Maček Rooms PRIVATE ROOMS €€

(Sobe Maček; Map p38; ☑ 01-425 37 91; www.
sobe-macek.si; Krojaška ulica 5; s/d €61/96, apt
€126-156; ⊛ @ 🕏) In an ancient building
hard by the Ljubljanica, these five gorgeous
rooms and two apartments (all but one of
which overlook the river) are owned by the
city's most popular riverfront cafe-bar and
are among the most sought-after in town (so
book well in advance).

★ **Vander Urbani Resort** BOUTIQUE HOTEL €€€

(Map p38; ☑ 01-200 90 00; www.vanderhotel.
com; Krojaška ulica 6; r €109-190; ⊛ @ 🕏 🕏)
This stunning new boutique hotel in the
heart of Ljubljana's Old Town was formed
from four 17th-century buildings. But history stops there, for this hostelry – with 16
rooms over three floors – is as modern as
tomorrow. Designed by the trendsetting Sa-
dar Vuga architectural firm, the rooms are

not huge but each is unique and makes use
of natural materials.

One of the best rooms in the hotel is
No 36, with views of the Ljubljanica and a
large bathroom with a shower and tub. The
rooftop terrace boasts an infinity pool and
heart-stopping views of Ljubljana Castle and
the Old Town.

Antiq Hotel BOUTIQUE HOTEL €€€

(Map p38; ☑ 01-421 35 60; www.antiqhotel.si;
Gornji trg 3; s €75-120, d €95-125; ⊛ @ 🕏) This
attractive boutique hotel has been cobbled
together from several townhouses in the Old
Town. There are 16 spacious rooms and a
multitiered back garden. The decor is kitsch
with a smirk and there are fabulous touches
everywhere. Among our favourite rooms are
enormous No 8, with views of the Hercules
Fountain, and No 13, with glimpses of Ljubljana Castle.

Central Market & East

Hostel 24 HOSTEL €

(Map p46; ☑ 040 780 036; www.hostel-spa24.
com; Poljanska cesta 15; dm €10-19, d €34-60,
q €60-84; ⊛ @ 🕏) One of four hostels in
a chain, this one is just east of the market
and Dragon Bridge on a street that seems
to be gaining momentum (and a few bars
and restaurants). It's got 14 rooms including
doubles, quads and dorms with up to 12
beds, all with bathroom. There's a great

LJUBLJANA FOR CHILDREN

The website of the Ljubljana Tourist Information Centre (p68) is a good source of
quick info for events suitable for children.

Park Tivoli, with a couple of children's playgrounds, swimming pools (p51) and a
zoo (p49), is an excellent place to take children, as are the two water parks, Laguna
(☑ 01-589 01 41; www.laguna.si; Dunajska cesta 270; day pass adult/child Mon-Fri €14/10, Sat &
Sun €16/12; ☉ 9am-8pm May-Sep; 🚍 6, 8 or 11 to Ježica) and Atlantis (p50).

In the warmer months the Mini Summer for Children International Festival
(☑ 01-434 36 20; www.mini-teater.si; Grajska planota 1; ☉ 11am & 6.30pm Sun late-Jun–Aug)
stages puppet shows from around the world for kids at Ljubljana Castle. Also, check out
the program at the Ljubljana Puppet Theatre (p65).

A super place for kids is the House of Experiments (Hiša Eksperimentov; Map p38;
☑ 01-300 68 88; www.h-e.si; Trubarjeva cesta 39; admission €6; ☉ 11am-7pm Sat & Sun), a
hands-on science centre with almost four-dozen inventive and challenging exhibits that
successfully mix learning with humour. There's a science adventure show daily at 5pm.

The best museums for children, with handouts, hands-on exhibits and trails to follow,
are the Natural History Museum (p45), the City Museum (p43) and the Ethnographic Museum (p45).

Fun for everyone is Mala Ulica (Little Street; Map p38; ☑ 01-306 27 00; www.malaulica.
si; Prečna ulica 7; family/child €4/2; ☉ 9am-7pm Mon-Fri, 10am-6pm Sat & Sun), a 'public living-
room' for parents and preschool children, with workshops, crafts, puppet shows and so on.

kitchen and lounge area plus an in-house bakery.

BIT Center Hotel
HOTEL €€

(☏01-548 00 55; www.bit-center.net; Litijska cesta 57; dm/s/d €16/45/65; P@☎) The BIT Center, with clean and light modern decor, offers one of the best-value deals in Ljubljana (although, at 3km east of the centre, it's a bit far from the action). In addition to the 39 single and double rooms in the main hotel, there's hostel accommodation with 35 beds in rooms of four to 10 beds.

Guests receive a 50% discount at the sports centre next door. To reach here, catch bus 5, 9 or 13 to the Emona stop.

Center

★ Hostel Tresor
HOSTEL €€

(Map p38; ☏01-200 90 60; www.hostel-tresor.si; Čopova ulica 38; dm €15-24, s/d €40/70; ❄@☎) This new 28-room hostel in the heart of Center is housed in a Secessionist-style former bank, and the money theme continues right into rooms named after currencies and financial aphorisms on the walls. Dorms have between four and 12 beds but are spacious. The communal areas (we love the atrium) are stunning; breakfast is in the vaults.

Slamič B&B
PENSION €€

(Map p46; ☏01-433 82 33; www.slamic.si; Kersnikova ulica 1; s €65-75, d €95-110, ste from €135; ❄☎) It's slightly away from the action but Slamič, a B&B above a famous cafe and teahouse, offers 17 bright, refurbished rooms all with en-suite facilities and large comfortable beds. Choice rooms include the ones looking on to a back garden and the one just off an enormous terrace used by the KavaČaj (CofeeTea), a gem of a cafe on the ground floor.

Penzion Pod Lipo
PENSION €€

(Map p46; ☏031 809 893; www.penzionpodlipo.com; Borštnikov trg 3 & Rimska cesta 17; d/tr/q €58/75/100, ste from €125; ❄@☎) Overlooking a leafy square with a 400-year-old linden in the centre, this guesthouse has 10 rooms that are simply furnished but large, very airy and spotless, with original hardwood floors. Try to get one of the rooms facing east; they have balconies with deck chairs and are quieter than those over the courtyard, with its ever-popular restaurant.

Pri Mraku
HOTEL €€

(Map p38; ☏01-421 96 00; www.daj-dam.si; Rimska cesta 4; s €58-68, d €88-96; P❄@☎) 'At Twilight' is a smallish, very central hotel with 35 refurbished (if dark) rooms in an old building. Rooms on the ground and 4th floors have air-con. Almost opposite the Križanke on Trg Francoske Revolucije, it's ideally located for culture vultures. The back courtyard with grape arbour is a bonus.

A RACE AGAINST THE CLOCK: LJUBLJANA'S ESCAPE GAMES

In the last few years, Ljubljana has picked up on the quirky emerging trend of live escape games, in which teams of between two and 12 people willingly lock themselves in a set of rooms in order to spend an hour or so working through numerous riddles that will eventually unlock the door back to freedom.

Each game has a distinct theme and story and involves not only the solving of puzzles but, crucially, the ability to identify the puzzles in the first place. Some tips for first-timers: try all of your ideas; search everywhere; and request extra clues from your captors!

Escape Room Enigmarium (Map p46; ☏031 334 488; www.escape-room.si; Trdinova ulica 8; 2-5 players €60; ☉9.30am-10pm) Ljubljana's first – and some would say best – escape game has three different themes to choose from: the Agatha Christie-inspired Salvation Room, the Classroom of Doom and – our favourite – the Escape Igloo, based on a really icy one set up in Kranjsla Gora in winter. Teams of two to five players can test their puzzling skills on scenarios that will have them tapping out messages in Morse Code and ice-fishing for clues to riddle their way free in 60 minutes.

Key Escape Room (Map p38; ☏030 232 323; www.thekey.si; Obrežna steza 2; 2-3/4-5/10-12 players €50/60/100; ☉11am-9pm) The central Key has two escape rooms – one named after Da Vinci and the other after Sherlock Holmes. You're really stretching your detective, scientific and artistic skills to the limit here and in this case you must get out of both locked rooms in just 70 minutes. Riddle-dee-dee.

★Antiq Palace Hotel & Spa

BOUTIQUE HOTEL €€€

(Map p38; ☑040 638 163, 083 896 700; www.antiqpalace.com; Gosposka ulica 10; s/d €180/210; ❋@☎) The city's most luxurious sleeping option, the Antiq Palace occupies a 16th-century townhouse, about a block from the river. Accommodation is in 21 individually designed rooms and suites, some stretching to 250 sq m in size and with jacuzzi. Many retain their original features (hardwood floors, floor-to-ceiling windows) and are furnished in an eclectic manner with quirky rococo touches.

Amenities include a very attractive spa with three types of sauna and a fitness centre. If for no other reason, stay here for the lavish breakfast, served in the enormous back lounge or, in fine weather, the small but perfectly formed courtyard garden.

Cubo

BOUTIQUE HOTEL €€€

(Map p38; ☑01-425 60 00; www.hotelcubo.com; Slovenska cesta 15; s/d €120/140; ❋@☎) The stylish 26-room Cubo has raised the bar of Ljubljana accommodation. The overall design is minimalist, with an emphasis on neutral tones of grey, beige and charcoal. Unusual are some of the high-quality materials used in the furnishings: check out the silver thread in the guestroom drapes that cost a king's ransom and the bedside lamps made with silkworm cocoons.

The modern art – especially the calligraphy – adorning the guestroom walls and public areas is well chosen. The in-house restaurant has gained quite a following in Ljubljana.

City Hotel Ljubljana

HOTEL €€€

(Map p46; ☑01-239 00 00; www.cityhotel.si; Dalmatinova ulica 15; s €65-105, d €96-135; P❋@☎) An attractive high-rise hotel offering 202 clean, basic rooms and a central location. Rooms vary from 'economy' to 'comfort', with the latter larger and air-conditioned. It's an odd place – primary colours splashed hither and yon, a kind of circus makeup feel, trees and books in the lobby, but it all works and, frankly, we love it here.

Ask to see the top floor in-the-round suite with dazzling views of the castle.

Museum Area

Vila Veselova

PENSION €€

(Map p46; ☑051 655 254, 059 926 721; www.v-v.si; Veselova ulica 14; dm/d/q €21/68/100; P❋@☎) In the centre of the museum district, this attractive 42-bed yellow villa has its own garden and offers mostly hostel accommodation in five colourful rooms with four to eight beds. A double and two apartments with attached facilities and access to a kitchen make it an attractive midrange option too. Some rooms face Park Tivoli across busy Tivolska cesta.

Trubarjeva Cesta, Tabor & Metelkova Mesto

H2Ostel

HOSTEL €

(Map p46; ☑041 662 266; www.h2ohostel.com; Petkovškovo nabrežje 47; dm €17-22, d €36-57, q €68-88; @☎) One of our favourite hostels in Ljubljana, this seven-room place wraps around a tiny courtyard bordering the Ljubljanica River and one room has views of the castle. Private doubles are available and guests have access to a common kitchen.

Celica Hostel

HOSTEL €€

(Map p46; ☑01-230 97 00; www.hostelcelica.com; Metelkova ulica 8; dm €18-26, s/d cell €58/62; @☎) This stylishly revamped former prison (1882) in Metelkova has 20 'cells', designed by different artists and architects and complete with original bars. There are nine rooms and apartments with three to seven beds and a packed, popular 12-bed dorm. The ground floor is home to a cafe and restaurant (set lunch €5 to €7). Bikes cost €3/6 for a half/full day.

The hostel even boasts its own gallery where everyone can show their work.

Hotel Park

HOTEL €€

(Map p46; ☑01-300 25 00; www.hotelpark.si; Tabor 9; s €60-110, d €70-130; P❋@☎) This renovated tower-block hotel is a very good-value midrange choice in central Ljubljana. The 198 pleasant 'standard' and 'comfort' (air-conditioned) rooms are bright and unpretentiously well equipped. Cheaper 'hostel' rooms are available on the 7th and 12th floors; some have shared facilities and others en suite showers (dorm €19 to €23).

Krakovo & Trnovo

★Hostel Vrba

HOSTEL €

(Map p46; ☑064 133 555; www.hostelvrba.si; Gradaška ulica 10; dm €15-18, d €40; @☎) Probably our favourite new budget accommodation in Ljubljana, this nine-room hostel on the Gradiščica Canal is just opposite the bars and restaurants of delightful Trnovo. There are three doubles, dorms with four to eight beds, hardwood floors and always a warm welcome. Free bikes, too, in summer.

Sax Hostel HOSTEL €
(Map p46; ☑040 168 804; www.saxhostelljub ljana.com; Eiprrova ulica 7; dm €12-20, d €48-54; ✳@⊛) This hostel with five rooms named after jazz greats like Ray Charles and Charlie Parker is attached to the Sax Pub in Trnovo, so it's the place to choose if you want to party. There are a couple of doubles and three dorms with four to nine beds. There's a pretty back garden but the 1st-floor rooms with sloped ceilings feel cramped.

🛏 Žale & Beyond

Ljubljana Resort CAMPGROUND €
(☑01-568 01 41; www.ljubljanaresort.si; Dunajska cesta 270; adult €9.50-13.50, child €6.50-9.50, hotel s €57-64, d €74-84; P✳@⊛; ☐6, 8 or 11 to Ježica) It's got a grandiose name, but wait till you see the facilities at this attractive 6-hectare camping ground-cum-resort 4km north of the centre. Along with a 60-room hotel and 12 stationary mobile homes (€99 to €137), there's the Laguna water park next door, which is half-price for guests.

🍴 Eating

Ljubljana has Slovenia's best selection of restaurants. Although prices tend to be higher here than elsewhere, it is still possible to eat well at moderate cost; even the more expensive restaurants usually offer an excellent-value three-course *dnevno kosilo* (set lunch) for under €10.

🍴 Castle Hill

Gostilna na Gradu SLOVENIAN €€
(Inn at the Castle; Map p38; ☑031 301 777; www. nagradu.si; Grajska planota 1; mains €10-16.50; ☺10am-midnight Mon-Sat, noon-6pm Sun) Within the Ljubljana Castle complex, Na Gradu is much too stylish to be just a *gostilna* (inn-like restaurant). The award-winning chefs use only Slovenian-sourced breads, cheeses and meats, and age-old recipes to prepare a meal to remember. If you really want to taste your way across the country, try the four-/five-course gourmet tasting menus for €30/42.

★Strelec SLOVENIAN €€€
(Archer; Map p38; ☑031 687 648; www.kaval group.si/strelec.asp; Grajska Planota 1; mains €17-38; ☺noon-10pm Mon-Sat) This is *haute cuisine* from on high – Ljubljana Castle's Archer's Tower, no less – with a menu that traces the city's history chosen by ethnologist Janez Bogataj and prepared by Igor Jagodic, recognised as one of the top chefs in Slovenia. Tasting menus are priced from €28 to €59 for between three and six courses.

Make sure to try Jagodic's 'poor man's bread', a potato stuffed with egg yolk, potato foam and truffles in red wine; the scrumptious local *sulec* freshwater trout (or Danube salmon) with Jerusalem artichokes prepared in several ways; and his signature apple strudel. The wine list is impressive – the sommelier even more so.

🍴 Prešernov Trg & Around

Sushimama JAPANESE €€€
(Map p38; ☑040 702 070; www.sushimama.si; Wolfova ulica 12; mains €17-35; ☺11.30am-10.30pm Mon-Sat; ⊛) Ljubljana's first and still arguably best Japanese restaurant has simple, restful decor and the full range of Japanese dishes – from rice and soup noodles – but with fish this fresh, it would be a shame not to indulge in the mixed sushi or sashimi (€11 to €20).

🍴 Old Town

★Druga Violina SLOVENIAN €
(Map p38; ☑082 052 506; Stari trg 21; mains €5-9, set lunch from €6; ☺8am-midnight) Just opposite the Academy of Music, the 'Second Fiddle' is an extremely pleasant and affordable place for a meal in the Old Town. There are lots of very Slovenian dishes like *ajdova kaša z jurčki* (buckwheat groats with ceps) and *obara* (a thick stew of chicken and vegetables) on the menu. It's a social enterprise designed to help those with disabilities.

Güjžina SLOVENIAN €
(Map p38; ☑083 806 446; www.prekmurska-gostilna.si; Mestni trg 19; mains €7-16; ☺8am-midnight) This charming vaulted restaurant in the Old Town serves dishes from Prekmurje, Slovenian's flat-as-a-pancake province in the far northeast. Try the *dödoli* (dumplings; €11) with crackling, the *bujta repa* (pork hotpot with sour turnips; €6), the Hungarian-inspired *bograč* (€10), a thick meaty stew served in a large copper kettle, and for dessert, the multi-layered cake *gibanica* (€5).

Repete SLOVENIAN €
(Map p38; Gornji trg 23; mains €7-11; ☺8am-1am Mon-Fri, 10am-1am Sat, to 5pm Sun; ☑) Subtitled 'Jazz & Okrepčila' (Jazz & Snacks), this is where you come to get both. Locally sourced vegetarian fare only midweek, with carnivorous offerings emerging at the weekend (some serious burgers here). It's a tiny place, with sleek and minimalist decor, but warm and cosy. Jazz concerts at 8pm on Thursday.

Klobasarna SLOVENIAN €
(Map p38; ☑051 605 017; www.klobasarna.si; Ciril Metodov trg 15; dishes €3.50-6; ☺10am-9pm Mon-Sat, 10am-3pm Sun) This hole-in-the-wall eatery in the Old Town specialises in that most Slovenian of dishes, *Kranjska klobasa*, an EU-protected fatty sausage. Buy 'em by the half/whole with a bit of cabbage, bread and mustard on the side. If you're really hungry, add *jota,* a hearty soup of beans and pickled turnip, or *ričet,* a thick barley stew.

Ribca SEAFOOD €
(Map p38; ☑01-425 15 44; www.ribca.si; Adamič-Lundrovo nabrežje 1; dishes €4-12; ☺8.30am-3pm Mon, to 9pm Tue-Sat, 11am-6pm Sun) This basement seafood bar near the fish market below the Plečnik Colonnade in Pogačarjev trg is one of the best for tasty fried squid, sardines and herrings. The setting is informal, though the cuisine is top notch. Set lunch on weekdays is €9.50.

Yildiz Han TURKISH €
(Map p46; ☑01-426 57 17; www.yildiz-han.com; Karlovška cesta 19; mains €8.50-12; ☺noon-midnight Mon-Sat) If Turkish is your thing, head for authentic 'Star House'. For starters try the *yaprak dolma* (stuffed vine leaves) or *sigara burek* (cheese-filled pastry rolls) and move on to any of the kebabs or the *karniyarik* (aubergine filled with ground lamb and baked). There's a small terrace for outside dining on warm evenings. And belly dancing on Friday and Saturday nights.

★**Taverna Tatjana** SEAFOOD €€
(Map p46; ☑01-421 00 87; www.taverna-tatjana.si; Gornji trg 38; mains €9-25; ☺5pm-midnight Mon-Sat) This charming little tavern bordering Old Town specialises in fish and seafood (though there's beef and foal on the menu too). Housed in several vaulted rooms of an atmospheric old townhouse with wooden ceiling beams, the fish is fresher than a spring shower. Go for something you wouldn't normally find elsewhere like *bro-*

det (Croatian fish stew with polenta) or cuttlefish black risotto.

In warmer weather, try to bag a table in the lovely walled back courtyard.

Špajza SLOVENIAN €€
(Map p38; ☑01-425 30 94; www.spajza-restaurant.si; Gornji trg 28; mains €18-24; ☺noon-11pm Mon-Sat, to 10pm Sun) The 'Pantry' attracts as much with its homey decor as with its Slovenian cuisine, executed with a modern touch. Several rooms in an ancient townhouse filled with rough-hewn tables and chairs, wooden floors and nostalgic bric-a-brac lead to a small garden. Expect less common meats on the menu: rabbit, lamb and *žrebičkov z jurčki* (colt with ceps, €24).

Gostilnica 5-6 KG SLOVENIAN €€
(Map p38; ☑01-320 08 04; Gornji trg 33; mains €9-32) This attractive bistro in the upper reaches of the Old Town is where to head when you could really eat a, well, pig. It specialises in all things porcine (the name suggests the perfect size of a suckling pig) and it's all *od glave do repa* (from nose to tail) here. Some excellent pasta and fish dishes, too.

TaBar TAPAS €€
(Map p38; ☑031 764 063; www.tabar.si; Ribji trg 6; tapas €3-10, 3-/5-course menu €17/26; ☺noon-midnight Mon-Thu, to 1am Fri & Sat) Seriously inventive (and borderless) tapas, with an excellent wine list, amid sleek, postmodern surrounds. Unmissable.

Julija INTERNATIONAL €€
(Map p38; ☑01-425 64 63; http://julijarestaurant.com; Stari trg 9; mains €9-19; ☺noon-10pm) This is arguably the best of a trio of restaurants standing side by side on touristy Stari trg. We love the baroque decor and the three-course set lunches (€9) served on the sidewalk terrace. The cuisine here revolves around risottos and pastas, though the duck confit with polenta and sour cherries was one of the best meals this visit.

✖ Central Market & East

Gostilna Dela INTERNATIONAL €
(Map p46; ☑059 925 446; Poljanska cesta 7; mains €6-7, set lunch €6.80-9.20; ☺8am-4pm) This delightful little bistro just east of the Slovenia TIC serves tasty home-style cuisine, only much better. From the soups and the meat and vegetarian main courses to the shop-made *štruklji* (dumplings), it's all

memorable. What's more, Dela (Work) is helping to create job opportunities for local youth otherwise excluded from the working world. Lunch only.

Nyama
VEGAN €

(Map p46; ☑059 047 280; www.nyama.si; Streliška ulica 22; mains €10.50-12.50; ☺10am-11pm Mon-Sat) 'Gourmet vegan' doesn't have to be an oxymoron and this place delivers superbly prepared dishes, regardless of your dietary restrictions. For starters, try the trio of pumpkin spreads, then move on to the truffle *žlikrofi* (like ravioli) on beetroot noodles or the buckwheat cheese *štruklji* (dumplings).

⚜ Center

★ Gelateria Romantika
ICE CREAM €

(Map p38; ☑040 978 566; www.gelateriaromantika.si; Dvorni trg 1; 2 scoops €2.20; ☺10am-11pm Sun-Thu, to midnight Fri & Sat) Quite simply the best ice cream and sorbet – us, exaggerate? – in the world, with flavours so unexpected, so fruit and vegetable-y (pumpkin seed oil, cucumber, bilberry), you'll be back for more once you've reached the bottom of Dvorni trg. Wonder if they ship...

Paninoteka
SANDWICHES €

(Map p38; ☑040 349 329; www.paninoteka.si; Jurčičev trg 3; soups & toasted sandwiches €4-15; ☺8am-12.30am; ☎) Paninoteka now has a large sit-down restaurant attached but we still come to the cafe side by the river for healthy sandwich creations, salads and breakfast (€4 to €7).

Thai Inn Pub
THAI €

(Map p46; ☑040 429 537; http://thaipub.si; Rimska cesta 17; mains €7.50; ☺11am-10pm Mon-Fri, noon-8pm Sat; ☎) This Thai place is popular with students, who come for the well-above-average and authentic fare (the cooks are Thai) as well as the general party atmosphere. There's a lovely garden beside a park, which makes for a perfect lunchtime setting. Great beer selection.

Pizzeria Foculus
ITALIAN €

(Map p38; ☑01-421 92 95; www.picerija.net/foculus.htm; Gregorčičeva ulica 3; pizza €6-9; ☺11am-midnight) This cavernous pizzeria, with a wood-fired oven, boasts comfy outdoor seating and a vaulted indoor ceiling painted with spring and autumn leaves for when the weather turns nasty. The pizzas are excellent, with thin crusts and quality toppings.

Gostilna Rimska XXI
SLOVENIAN €€

(Map p46; ☑01-256 56 54; www.r-g.si/xxi; Rimska cesta 21; mains €8.50-16; ☺11am-11pm Mon-Fri, noon-5pm Sat) This popular inn specialises in traditional Slovenian cooking, using locally sourced ingredients and lots of homemade extras, including their own beer. There's no English menu, so ask the server what looks good in the kitchen. If they're on the menu, try the Istrian *fuži* (a type of homemade noodle) with truffles (€12.50).

Namaste
INDIAN €€

(Map p38; ☑01-425 01 59; www.restavracija-namaste.si; Breg 8; mains €10-20; ☺11am-midnight Mon-Sat, to 10pm Sun; ☑) Should you fancy a bit of Indian, head for this place on the left bank of the Ljubljanica. You won't get high-street-London curry but the thalis and tandoori dishes are very good. The choice of vegetarian dishes is better than average and weekday set lunch is €6.50 to €8.50.

JB Restavracija
FUSION €€€

(Map p46; ☑01-430 70 70; www.jb-slo.com; Miklošičeva cesta 17; mains €25-30; ☺noon-10pm Mon-Fri, 6-11pm Sat) Old-world charm, a hybrid international menu, a top-notch wine list and very stylish decor have made this restaurant one of the most popular in town for a fancy meal. Feast your way through one of chef Janez Bratovž's tasting menus of three/five/eight courses for €50/70/80.

⚜ Trubarjeva Cesta & Tabor

★ Prince of Orange
ITALIAN €

(Map p46; ☑083 802 447; Komenskega ulica 30; dishes €4.50-9, set lunch from €7; ☺7.30am-9.30pm Mon-Thu, 9.30am-midnight Fri, 10am-2pm Sat) This true find – a bright and airy cafe just above Trubarjeva cesta – serves outstanding shop-made soups and bruschetta. Ask for some of the farmer's goat cheese and the link between the cafe and King William III of England (the pub sign on the wall is a clue).

Skuhna
INTERNATIONAL €

(Map p46; ☑041 339 978; www.skuhna.si; Trubarjeva cesta 15; set menu €6-11; ☺11.30am-5pm Mon-Wed, to 10pm Thu & Fri, noon-8pm Sat) This unique eatery is the work of two Slovenian non-profit organisations that are helping the city's migrant community to integrate. A half-dozen chefs from countries as diverse as Sri Lanka, Tunisia and and Colombia take turns cooking everyday, and the result is a cornucopia of authentic world cuisine. Choicest tables are in the kitchen.

Falafel
MIDDLE EASTERN €

(Map p46; ☑041 640 166; www.falafel.si; Trubarjeva cesta 40; sandwiches €4-7; ⊙10am-midnight Mon-Sat, 1-10pm Sun) Authentic Middle Eastern food, like falafel and hummus, served up to go or eat in at a few tables and chairs scattered about. Perfect choice for a quick meal on the run or the late-night munchies.

Ajdovo Zrno
VEGAN €

(Map p38; ☑041 832 446; www.ajdovo-zrno. si; Trubarjeva cesta 7; mains €4-6, set lunch €7.50; ⊙10am-7pm Mon-Fri; ☑) 'Buckwheat Grain' serves soups, lots of different salads and baked vegetarian dishes. It also has terrific, freshly squeezed juices. Enter from Mali trg.

Park Tivoli & Around

Hot Horse
BURGERS €

(Map p46; ☑031 709 716; www.hot-horse.si; Park Tivoli, Celovška cesta 25; small/large burger €2.50/5, set menu €7; ⊙9am-6am) This little place in the city's biggest park supplies *Ljubljančani* (local people) with their favourite treat: horseflesh. It's a little place – a kiosk, really – just down the hill from the Museum of Contemporary History, but it's open almost round the clock, so an all-time favourite of merrymakers and party-goers. Still not tempted? Veggie burgers are €3.

Gostilna Čad
BALKAN €€

(Pod Rožnikom; ☑01-251 34 46; www.gostilna-cad. si; Cesta na Rožnik 18; mains €6-18; ⊙11am-11pm) This place under Rožnik Hill, just downwind from the zoo in Park Tivoli, serves southern Slav-style grills, like *pljeskavica* (spicy meat patties) with *ajvar* (roasted red peppers, tomatoes and eggplant cooked into a purée) and starters such as *prebranac* (onions and beans cooked in an earthenware pot). At 120-plus years of age, it's the oldest show in town and phenomenally popular.

Krakovo & Trnovo

Pizzeria Trta
PIZZA €

(Map p46; ☑01-426 50 66; www.trta.si; Grudnovo nabrežje 21; pizza €6-9.50; ⊙noon-10pm Mon-Sat; ☎) This award-winning pizzeria, with large pies cooked in a wood-fired oven, is just south of the Old Town centre, across the river from Krakovo.

Harambaša
BALKAN €

(Map p46; ☑041 843 106; www.harambasa.si; Trnovski pristan 4a; dishes €4.50-7.50; ⊙10am-10pm Mon-Fri, noon-10pm Sat, noon-6pm Sun) At this small place in Trnovo you'll find authentic Bosnian – Sarajevan to be precise – dishes like *čevapčiči* (spicy meatballs of beef or pork) and *pljeskavica*. Great terrace overlooking the Ljubljanica.

Pri Škofu
SLOVENIAN €€

(Map p46; ☑01-426 45 08; Rečna ulica 8; mains €9-22; ⊙10am-11pm Tue-Fri, noon-11pm Sat & Sun; ☎) Run by women, this wonderful little place south of the centre in tranquil Krakovo serves some of the best prepared local dishes and salads in Ljubljana, with an ever-changing menu. Start with ginger soup (€3) and for dessert try the traditional cherry-and-cheese dumpling. Weekday/weekend (€8/10) set lunches are good value.

TO MARKET, TO MARKET

Central Market (Centralna Tržnica; Map p38; Vodnikov trg; ⊙open-air market 6am-6pm Mon-Fri, 6am-4pm Sat summer, 6am-4pm Mon-Sat winter) Central Market is Ljubljana's larder and worth a trip both to stock up on provisions or just have a good snoop (and sniff) around. Go first to the vast open-air market (Tržnica na Prostem) just across the Triple Bridge to the southeast of Prešernov trg on Vodnikov trg. Here you'll find a daily farmers market (except Sunday). In the next neighbouring square – Pogačarjev trg – there are always stalls selling everything from foraged wild mushrooms and forest berries to honey and homemade cheeses.

Pogačarjev trg also hosts an **organic market** on Wednesday and Sunday, and on Friday in summer it's the venue for **Odprta Kuhna** (Open Kitchen; www.odprtakuhna.si; Pogačarjev trg; ⊙8am-8pm Fri mid-Mar–Oct, up to 10pm in summer), a weekly food fair with local and international specialities cooked on site from restaurants around the city and beyond.

The **covered market** (Pokrita Tržnica; Map p38; Dolničarjeva ulica; ⊙7am-4pm Mon-Fri, 7am-2pm Sat) nearby also sells meats and cheeses, and there's also a **fish market** (Ribarnica; Map p38; Adamič-Lundrovo nabrežje 1; ⊙7am-4pm Mon-Fri, 7am-2pm Sat) below the Plečnik Colonnade. You'll also find open-air fish stands selling fried calamari for as low as €6.50.

Manna SLOVENIAN €€€

(Map p46; ☑059 922 308; www.restaurant-manna.com; Eipprova ulica 1a; mains €18-49; ⏱11am-midnight Mon-Sat, to 9pm Sun) Splashed across the front of this canalside restaurant in Trnovo is the slogan '*Manna: Božanske Jedi na Zemlji*' (Manna: Heavenly Dishes on Earth). Indeed, its divine contemporary Slovenian cuisine includes delicacies such as cold smoked trout, trout terrine and *žlikrofi* of bear meat from Kočevje. For mains there's plenty of fish from the Adriatic and a scrumptious roast lamb dish.

Manna has very stylish decor and a wonderful covered inner terrace for dining almost al fresco.

 Drinking & Nightlife

Ljubljana offers a dizzying array of drinking options, whether your tipple is beer, wine and spirits or tea and coffee. In summer, the banks of the Ljubljanica River transform themselves into one long terrace and serve as the perfect spot for supping, sipping and people-watching. In practice there's often little distinction between 'pubs and bars' and 'cafes and teahouses' here. Most cafes also serve beer and wine, and many pubs and bars start the day out as cafes before morphing into nightspots after sundown.

 Castle Hill

Grajska Kavarna CAFE

(Map p38; ☑01-439 41 40; www.grajskakavarna.si; Grajska planota 1; ⏱9am-11pm, to midnight in summer) This welcoming cafe at Ljubljana Castle offers respite on a hot day and is a great place to kick back with a coffee, beer or light meal after a long slog up the hill.

 Prešernov Trg & Around

Kavarna Cacao CAFE

(Map p38; ☑01-430 17 72; www.cacao.si; Petkovškovo nabrežje 3; ⏱8am-10pm, to midnight in summer) Just steps from central Prešernov trg, Cacao is one of the most stylish cafes on the river. The chocolate-brown interior is a great place to chill out with a slice of cake or freshly prepared fruit smoothie, but most come for the ice cream; it regularly gets voted the best in town.

Kavarna Zvezda CAFE

(Map p38; ☑01-421 90 90; www.zvezdaljubljana.si; Wolfova ulica 14; ⏱7am-11pm Mon-Sat, 10am-

8pm Sun; 🛜) Perhaps the best 'olde worlde' cafe in Ljubljana is the 'Star', with entrances off both Kongresni trg and Wolfova ulica. It has all the usual varieties of tea and coffee (just about the strongest in town), but is celebrated for its housemade cakes, particularly its *skutina pečena* (€3.90), a baked eggy cheesecake.

Makalonca COCKTAIL BAR

(Map p38; ☑01-620 94 36, 030 362 450; Hribarjevo nabrežje 19; ⏱8am-3am) Why sit on the embankment when you can sit *below* it? This striking cafe and cocktail bar with a 100m-long terrace within the columns of the Ljubljanica embankment is the perfect place to nurse a drink and watch the river roll by. It even has tables floating *in* the river. Good breakfasts (€4 to €7.50) and burgers (€7.50 to €10).

Cutty Sark Pub PUB

(Map p38; ☑051 686 209; www.cuttysarkpub.si; Knafljev prehod 1; ⏱8am-1am Mon-Wed, to 3am Thu-Sat, 9am-1am Sun; 🛜) A pleasant and well-stocked pub with colourful bright-yellow windows and a long history. Set in the courtyard behind Wolfova ulica 6, the ivy-covered Cutty Sark is a congenial place for a *pivo* (beer) or glass of *vino* (wine). Happy hour is from 4pm to 6pm.

 Old Town

★**Slovenska Hiša** COCKTAIL BAR

(Slovenian House; Map p38; ☑083 899 88 11; www.slovenskahisa.com; Cankarjevo nabrežje 13; ⏱8am-1am Sun-Thu, to 3am Fri & Sat) Our favourite new boozer along the river is so cute it's almost twee. Sourcing only Slovenian products makes the cocktails that much more inventive (gin – yes, tonic – no), meat and cheese plates (€4 to €7) are worthy blotter, and should you want cigarettes, you must buy from a Kompas 'Duty-Free Shop', as they're not made in Slovenia.

★**Pritličje** CAFE

(Ground Floor; Map p38; ☑040 204 693; www.pritlicje.si; Mestni trg 2; ⏱9am-1am Sun-Wed, to 3am Thu-Sat) One of the very few LGBT-friendly places in town, the 'Ground Floor' offers something for everyone: cafe, bar, live music, cultural centre and comic-book shop. Events are scheduled almost nightly and the location next to the Town Hall, with good cruising views across Mestni trg, couldn't be more perfect.

Tozd
BAR

(Map p38; ☑ 040 727 362; Gallusovo nabrežje 27; ⊙ 8.30am-1pm) A watering hole on a section of the river still largely overlooked by tourists, Tozd is a retro (the name refers to an old socialist association) cafe–pub–wine bar with brick walls, red leather benches, and original photography from contemporary Slovenian artists. We love the waterfront terrace under the trees and the speciality Ruster, a cold-brew coffee unlike anything we've ever tasted.

Cafe Kolaž
CAFE

(Map p38; ☑ 059 142 824; www.facebook.com/kafe.kolaz; Gornji trg 15; ⊙ 10am-1am Mon-Sat, to midnight Sun; ☎) One of the most chilled places to drink (and eat) in the Old Town, the gay-friendly 'Collage' picks up where the much missed Open Cafe just round the corner left off. Exhibitions, literary nights and DJ evenings, with sandwiches and snacks (€2.80 to €4.50) as welcome blotter.

Čajna Hiša
TEAHOUSE

(Tea House; Map p38; ☑ 01-252 70 10; www.cha.si; Stari trg 3; ⊙ 8am-10pm Mon-Fri, to 3pm Sat, 10am-2pm Sun; ☎) This elegant and centrally located teahouse takes its teas very seriously. They also serve light meals (lunch €10) and there's a tea shop next door.

Maček
CAFE

(Map p38; ☑ 01-425 37 91; http://sobe-macek.si; Krojaška ulica 5; ⊙ 9am-12.30am Mon-Sat, to 11pm Sun; ☎) The place to be seen on a sunny summer afternoon, the 'Cat' is one of a number of spots on the right bank of the Ljubljanica to relax over a coffee or alcoholic beverage. It starts to really hop after sundown, when it morphs pretty seamlessly into a cocktail bar. Happy hour is 4pm to 7pm.

Špica
CAFE

(Map p46; ☑ 051 368 658, 070 803 532; http://www.kaval-group.si/spica_caffe.asp; Gruberjevo nabrežje; ⊙ 8am-midnight Mon-Thu, to 1am Fri & Sat) This new cafe/bar at the Špica, the point of land south of the Old Town where the Ljubljanica river splits before entering the city, is tailor-made for a relaxing sundowner after jumping ship from any of the boats that moor at the new pier here. It's opposite the Botanical Gardens.

🌑 Central Market & East

⭐ Klub Daktari
BAR

(Map p38; ☑ 059 055 538; www.daktari.si; Krekov trg 7; ⊙ 8am-1am Mon-Sat, 9am-midnight Sun) This rabbit-warren of a watering hole at the foot of the funicular to Ljubljana Castle is so chilled there's practically frost on the windows. The decor is retro-distressed, with shelves full of old books and a player piano in the corner. More of a cultural centre than club, Daktari hosts live music sets and an eclectic mix of other cultural events.

Cafe Čokl
CAFE

(Map p38; ☑ 041 837 556; http://cafecokl.si/; Krekov trg 8; ⊙ 7am-11pm Mon-Fri, 9am-11pm Sat, 9am-8pm Sun) This fair-trade place at the foot of the lower funicular station takes its java very seriously indeed – roasting it themselves and featuring daily special recommendations on a chalkboard outside. Serves a mean cup of coffee.

Torta Ljubljana
CAFE

(Ljubljana Cake; Map p38; ☑ 01-242 06 65, 030 300 618; www.tortaljubljana.com; Adamič-Lundrovo nabrežje; slice €3.60, small cake €8; ⊙ 8am-4pm) This little cafe in the Plečnik Arcade facing the market is the birthplace of 'Ljubljana Cake', a newly created sweet (but one with a creation myth that adds on a few more years) using only locally sourced ingredients, with great success: gluten-free buckwheat flour, pumpkin seeds, sweet chestnuts and honey.

🌑 Center

⭐ Nebotičnik
CLUB

(Map p38; ☑ 040 233 078, 040 601 787; www.neboticnik.si; 11th fl, Štefanova ulica 1; ⊙ 10pm-3am Thu-Sat) An elegant old cafe with its breathtaking terrace atop Ljubljana's famed art deco Skyscraper (1933) and spectacular 360-degree views attract punters throughout the day but Ljubljana's beau monde returns at night to party in the flashy club and lounge on the floor below — No 11.

Žmavc
PUB

(Map p46; ☑ 01-251 03 24; Rimska cesta 21; ⊙ 7.30am-1am Mon-Fri, from 10am Sat, from 6pm Sun; ☎) Žmavc is the best place to slum it in Ljubljana, with a smallish bar inside packed day and night. The decor is great — check out the manga comic-strip scenes and figures scurrying up the walls. There's a pretty garden terrace for summer evening drinking, but try to arrive early to snag a table.

Dvorni Bar
WINE BAR

(Map p38; ☑ 01-251 12 57; www.dvornibar.net; Dvorni trg 2; ⊙ 8am-1am Mon-Sat, 9am-1am Sun)

This large, L-shaped venue just up from the Ljubljanica on the river's west bank is a bit of a Dr Jekyll and Mr Hyde – a delightful cafe and lunch venue by day and one of the best wine bars in town in the evening. It stocks more than 100 varieties and has wine tastings every month (usually the second Wednesday).

BiKoFe
BAR

(Map p38; ☑ 040 168 804; Židovska steza 2; ☺ 9am-1am Mon-Fri, 10am-1pm Sat & Sun; ☕) A favourite alternative place for a younger crowd, this cupboard of a bar under new management has studenty art on the walls and DJ nights on Wednesday and Friday. The fun spills out on to the shady outdoor patio.

Le Petit Café
CAFE

(Map p38; ☑ 01-251 25 75; www.lepetit.si; Trg Francoske Revolucije 4; ☺ 7.30am-midnight; ☕) Just opposite the Križanke, this pleasant, boho place offers great coffee and a wide range of breakfast goodies, lunches and light meals, plus an excellent restaurant on the 1st floor with a provincial-style decor and menu.

Top Six Club
CLUB

(Map p38; ☑ 040 667 722, 040 668 844; www.topsixclub.si; Tomšičeva ulica 2; ☺ 11pm-5am Wed-Sat) Not quite the magnet it was a few years ago when it starred on television, this retro cocktail bar and lounge on the 6th floor of the Nama department store becomes a popular dance venue towards the end of the week and attracts a chi-chi crowd. Take the glass-bubble lift from along Slovenska cesta or the lift in the passageway linking Cankarjeva cesta and Tomšičeva ulica.

Pod Skalco
PUB

(Under the Rock; Map p38; ☑ 01-426 58 20; Gosposka ulica 19; ☺ 7.30am-3am Mon-Fri, 5pm-3am Sat & Sun) This old dive south of the City Museum has been given a complete makeover and it really swings (there are bar-stool swings) most nights but especially on DJ Fridays.

Klub K4
CLUB

(Map p46; ☑ 040 212 292; www.klubk4.org; Kersnikova ulica 4; ☺ 8pm-4am Sun & Tue-Thu, 8pm-6am Fri & Sat) This evergreen venue in the basement of the Student Organisation of Ljubljana University (ŠOU) headquarters features rave-electronic music Friday and Saturday, with other styles of music on weeknights, and a popular gay and lesbian night on Sunday.

Pr' Skelet Disco Bar
CLUB

(Map p38; ☑ 040 852 366; www.prskelet.com; Kongresni trg 3; ☺ 9pm-5am Wed-Sat; ☕) The skeleton-themed basement bar in the Old Town has crossed the Ljubljanica and occupied an even larger dungeon as a club on Kongresni trg. Cocktails still two for one.

Trubarjeva Cesta, Tabor & Metelkova Mesto

★ **Postaja Centralna**
COCKTAIL BAR

(Central Station; Map p38; ☑ 059 190 400; www.centralnapostaja.com; Trubarjeva cesta 23; ☺ 8am-1am Mon-Wed, to 3am Thu & Fri, 9am-3am Sat) This classy place tries — and largely succeeds – at being just about everything to everyone. It's a slightly louche cocktail bar, with street-art tags on the walls and lots of dazzling neon, a

---

GAY & LESBIAN VENUES

Ljubljana may not be the most gay-friendly city in Central Europe, but there are a few decent options. For general information and advice, contact the Q Cultural Centre (Kulturni Center Q; Map p46; ☑ 01-430 35 35; www.kulturnicenterq.org; Metelkova Mesto, Masarykova cesta 24). Two LGBT-friendly venues in the Old Town are Cafe Kolaž (p61) and Pritličje (p60).

Roza Klub (Map p46; www.klubk4.org; Kersnikova ulica 4; ☺ 10pm-6am Sun Sep-Jun) A popular spot for both gays and lesbians alike is this Sunday (and occasionally Saturday) night disco at Klub K4. The music takes no risks, but the crowd is lively. See the website for dates and details.

Klub Tiffany (Map p46; www.kulturnicenterq.org/tiffany/klub; Metelkovo Mesto, Masarykova cesta 24; ☺ vary) On again, off again club for gay men located in the Metelkova Mesto complex.

Klub Monokel (Map p46; www.klubmonokel.com; Metelkovo Mesto, Masarykova cesta 24; ☺ vary) Club for lesbians situated in the Metelkova Mesto complex.

club with DJs at the weekend, a cafe with its own homemade fruit teas and a restaurant with burgers.

Anything else? Oh, yes, it's also a gallery where anyone can exhibit and an information centre with a surfeit of brochures and two computers for plotting your next move in Slovenia. You might never go home.

Kavarna SEM CAFE
(Map p46; ☑01-300 87 00; www.etno-muzej.si; Metelkova ulica 2; ◎7am-1am Sun-Tue, to 2am Wed & Thu, to 3am Fri & Sat; ☏) This delightful cafe attached to the Slovenian Ethnographic Museum is all glass and modern art, with views of the attached pottery workshop and live swing music on Tuesday and salsa on Friday.

Park Tivoli & Around

Klub Cirkus CLUB
(Map p46; ☑051 631 631; www.cirkusklub.si; Trg Mladinskih Delovnih Brigad 7; admission €5; ◎10pm-5am Wed, Fri & Sat, special events Tue & Thu) Located in the former Kinoklub Vič arthouse cinema, this is one of the most popular clubs in town and within easy walking distance of the centre. Lots of themed nights and DJs; opens on Tuesday and Thursday for special events and parties.

Zoo CLUB
(Map p46; ☑070 656 066; www.zoo-club.si; Tržaška cesta 2; ◎pub 8am-midnight, club 10pm-5am Fri & Sat) Located in the deep recesses of a former tobacco factory complex, this venue run by the Maribor Student Club stays comatose till the weekend when it turns into a raucous place with music and dancers all over the shop.

Krakovo & Trnovo

Šank Pub PUB
(Map p46; ☑041 748 491; Eipprova ulica 19; ◎7am-1am Mon-Fri, 8am-1am Sat & Sun; ☏) Down in studenty Trnovo, the Šank is one of a number of inviting bars and cafes along this stretch of Eipprova ulica. This raggedy little place, with a brick ceiling and wooden floor, is a relaxed option and has a great choice of craft beers, including Bervog's Ond smoked porter and its Baja oatmeal stout.

☆ Entertainment

Ljubljana in Your Pocket (www.inyourpocket.com/ljubljana), which comes out every two months, is an excellent English-language source for what's on in the capital. Buy tickets for shows and events at the venue's box office, online through **Eventim** (☑430 24 05; http://www.eventim.si/en/), or at Ljubljana Tourist Information Centre (p68). Expect to pay €10 to €20 for tickets to live acts.

Live Music

★Sax Pub JAZZ
(Map p46; ☑040 168 804; www.saxhostelljubljana.com/sax-pub.html; Eipprova ulica 7; ◎8am-1am) More than a quarter-century in Trnovo and decorated with colourful murals and graffiti outside, the tiny and convivial Sax has live jazz as well as blues, folk and hip-hop at 8pm on Thursday year-round. Canned stuff rules at other times.

Orto Bar LIVE MUSIC
(Map p46; ☑01-232 16 74; www.orto-bar.com; Graboličeva ulica 1; ◎9pm-2am Tue & Wed, to 4am Thu & Sat, to 5am Fri) A popular bar and live-music venue for late-night drinking and dancing amid a crowd of leather-clad partygoers. It's just a 300m stroll northeast from Metelkova. Note the program takes a two-month hiatus during July and August.

Gala Hala LIVE MUSIC
(Map p46; www.galahala.com; Metelkova Mesto, Masarykova cesta 24) Metelkova's biggest and best venue to catch live alternative, indie and rock music several nights a week. There's an open-air performance space from May to September.

Kino Šiška LIVE MUSIC
(☑030 310 110, box office 01-500 30 00; www.kinosiska.si; Trg Prekomorskih brigad 3; ◎pub 8am-midnight, events 8pm-2am) This renovated old movie theatre now houses an urban cultural centre, hosting mainly indie, rock and alternative bands from around Slovenia and the rest of Europe. Box office is open 3pm to 8pm Monday to Friday.

Jazz Club Gajo JAZZ
(Map p46; www.jazzclubgajo.com; Cankarjeva cesta; ◎9am-midnight Mon-Sat, to 10pm Sun mid-Apr–mid-Oct) Peripatetic Gajo, now occupying an open space opposite the National Gallery, remains the city's premier venue for live jazz and attracts both local and international talent. Music kicks off from 9.30pm, jam sessions are on Monday and there's a jazz brunch on Sunday.

☆ Classical Music & Opera

Cankarjev Dom CLASSICAL MUSIC
(Map p46; ☎01-241 71 00, box office 01-241 72 99; www.cd-cc.si; Prešernova cesta 10; ⊙box office 11am-1pm & 3-8pm Mon-Fri, 11am-1pm Sat, 1hr before performance) Ljubljana's premier cultural and conference centre has two large auditoriums (the Gallus Hall is said to have perfect acoustics) and a dozen smaller performance spaces offering a remarkable smorgasbord of performance arts.

Opera Ballet Ljubljana OPERA
(Map p38; ☎01-241 59 00, box office 01-241 59 59; www.opera.si; Župančičeva ulica 1; ⊙box office 10am-1pm & 2-6pm Mon-Fri, 10am-1pm Sat, 1hr before performance) Home to the Slovenian National Opera and Ballet companies, this historic neo-Renaissance theatre has been restored to its former glory in recent years. Enter from Cankarjeva cesta.

Slovenia Philharmonic Hall CLASSICAL MUSIC
(Slovenska Filharmonija; Map p38; ☎01-241 08 00; www.filharmonija.si; Kongresni trg 10; ⊙box office 11am-1pm & 3-6pm Mon-Fri) Home to the Slovenian Philharmonic founded in 1701, this small but very atmospheric venue in the southeast corner of Kongresni trg also stages concerts and hosts performances of the Slovenian Chamber Choir (Slovenski Komorni Zbor) founded in 1991. Haydn, Beethoven and Brahms were honorary Philharmonic members, and Gustav Mahler was resident conductor for a season (1881–82).

Križanke PERFORMING ARTS, CLASSICAL MUSIC
(Map p38; ☎01-241 60 00, box office 01-241 60 26; www.ljubljanafestival.si; Trg Francoske Revolucije 1-2; ⊙box office 10am-8pm Mon-Fri, 10am-1pm Sat Apr-Sep, noon-5pm Mon-Fri Oct-Mar, 1hr before performance) The open-air theatre seating more than 1200 spectators at this sprawling 18th-century monastery, remodelled by Plečnik in the 1950s, hosts the events of the summer Ljubljana Festival. The smaller Knights Hall (Viteška Dvorana) is the venue for chamber concerts.

Theatre

Ljubljana has half-a-dozen theatres, so there should be something on stage for everyone. Slovenian theatre is usually quite visual with a lot of mixed media, so you don't always have to speak the language to enjoy the production. In addition to concerts and other musical events, Cankarjev Dom (p64) regularly stages theatrical productions.

National Drama Theatre THEATRE
(Narodno Gledališče Drama; Map p38; ☎01-252 14 62, box office 01-252 15 11; www.en.drama.si; ⊙box office 11am-8pm Mon-Fri, 6-8pm Sat, 1hr before performance) Built as a German-language theatre in 1911, this wonderful art nouveau building is home to the national theatre company. Performances are in Slovenian.

SOMETHING COMPLETELY DIFFERENT: METELKOVA MESTO

For a scruffy alternative to trendy clubs, head for **Metelkova Mesto** (Metelkova Town; Map p46; www.metelkovamesto.org; Masarykova cesta 24), an ex-army garrison taken over by squatters in the 1990s and converted into a free-living commune. In this two-courtyard block, a dozen idiosyncratic venues hide behind brightly tagged doorways, coming to life generally after midnight daily in summer and on Friday and Saturday the rest of the year. While it's certainly not for the genteel and the quality of the acts and performances varies with the night, there's usually a little of something for everyone.

Entering the main 'city gate' from Masarykova cesta, the building to the right houses **Gala Hala** (p63), which features live bands and club nights, and **Channel Zero** (Map p46; www.ch0.org; ⊙hours variable), with punk and hardcore. Above it on the 1st floor is **Mizzart** (Map p46; ⊙hours variable) with a great exhibition space (the name is no comment on the quality of the creations). Easy to miss in the first building to the left is **Q Cultural Centre** (p62) including **Klub Tiffany** (p62) for gay men and **Klub Monokel** (p62) for lesbian women. Due south is the ever-popular **Jalla Jalla** (Map p46; ⊙hours variable), a congenial pub with concerts. Beyond the first courtyard to the southwest, **Klub Gromka** (Map p46; www.klubgromka.org; ⊙hours variable) has folk concerts, theatre and lectures. Next door are **Menza pri Koritu** (Map p46; ☎01-434 03 45; www.menzaprikoritu.org), under the creepy ET-like figures, and new-kid-on-the-block **Bizarnica pri Mariči** (Map p46), hosting performance and concerts. If you're staying at the **Hostel Celica** (p55), all of this is just around the corner!

Glej Theatre

THEATRE

(Gledališče Glej; Map p38; ☑01-251 66 79, 01-421 92 40; www.glej.si; Gregorčičeva ulica 3) The 'Look' has been Ljubljana's foremost experimental theatre since the 1970s, working with companies that include Betontanc (dance) and Grejpfrut (drama). It stages about five productions – theatre, mime, puppetry, multimedia – each year.

KUD France Prešeren

THEATRE

(Map p46; ☑01-283 22 88, 051 657 852; www.kud-fp.si; Karunova ulica 14; ⊙10am-10pm Mon-Sat, 1-10pm Sun) This 'noninstitutional culture and arts society' in Trnovo stages concerts as well as performances, literary events, exhibitions, workshops etc on most nights. Trnfest (p52) takes place here in August.

Ljubljana Puppet Theatre

THEATRE

(Lutkovno Gledališče Ljubljana; Map p38; ☑box office 01-300 09 82; www.lgl.si; Krekov trg 2; ⊙box office 9am-7pm Mon-Fri, to 1pm Sat & 1hr before performance) The Ljubljana Puppet Theatre stages its own shows throughout the year and hosts Lutke, the International Puppet Festival (Mednarodni Lutkovni Festival), every even-numbered year in September.

Cinema

Foreign films are never dubbed into Slovene but are shown in their original language with subtitles.

Kinoteka

CINEMA

(Map p46; ☑01-434 25 10; www.kinoteka.si; Miklošičeva cesta 28) The Kinoteka shows archival art and classic films in their original language usually with Slovenian subtitles.

Kinodvor

CINEMA

(Map p46; ☑01-239 22 17, 040 632 570; www.kolodvor.org; Kolodvorska ulica 13) The 'Court Cinema' screens both contemporary art films as well as films on general release.

🛍 Shopping

Ljubljana has plenty on offer in the way of folk art, antiques, music, wine, food and, increasingly, fashion. If you want everything under one roof, head for **BTC City** (☑01-585 22 22; www.btc-city.com; Šmartinska cesta 152; ⊙9am-8pm Mon-Sat; 🚌27 to BTC Emporium) or **City Park** (☑01-587 30 50; www.citypark.si; Šmartinska cesta 152g; ⊙9am-9pm Mon-Sat, to 3pm Sun), sprawling malls side by side with hundreds of shops in Moste, northeast of Center. They can be reached on bus 27.

🏰 Castle Hill

Rustika

FOLK ART

(Map p38; ☑031 704 038; Ljubljanski grad; ⊙10am-7pm, to 9pm in summer) This attractive gallery and shop, with wooden floors and a really 'rustic' feel, is good for folk art and conveniently located in Ljubljana Castle.

🏰 Prešernov Trg & Around

Ljubljanček

GIFTS

(Map p38; ☑059 025 727; www.ljubljana-souvenirs.com; Miklošičeva cesta 1; ⊙8am-2pm & 3.30-5pm Mon-Fri, to 1pm Sat, to noon Sun) This small souvenir shop in the Grand Hotel Union specialises in products and souvenirs with a Ljubljana brand, so expect lots of dragon motifs and idylls along the Ljubljanica.

Peko

SHOES

(Map p38; ☑059 089 068; www.peko.si; Miklošičeva cesta 14; ⊙8am-8pm Mon-Fri, to 1pm Sat) Once the provenance of good solid socialist shoes manufactured in the good solid socialist town of Tržič, northwest of Ljubljana, Peko has gone all trendy and its shoes vie in quality only with its new line of handbags.

🏰 Old Town

⭐Kraševka

FOOD & DRINK

(Map p38; ☑01-232 14 45; www.krasevka.si; Ciril Metodov trg 10; ⊙9am-7pm Mon-Fri, 8am-3pm Sat) 🍴 This fantastic delicatessen with more than 300 products from farms (mostly) in the Karst stocks *pršut* (dry, cured ham) in all its variations and cheeses, as well as wines and spirits, oils and vinegars, and honeys and marmalades.

⭐Lina

FASHION

(Map p38; ☑01-421 08 92, 041 245 276; www.svila-lina.net; Gornji trg 14; ⊙10am-1pm & 3-7pm Mon-Fri, to 1pm Sat) Dušanka Herman's scrumptious painted silk accessories include unevenly cut ties and scarves for men and daringly coloured dresses for women. Just try to leave without buying something.

Vinoteka Movia

DRINK

(Map p38; ☑01-452 54 48, 051 304 590; www.movia.si; Mestni trg 2; ⊙noon-midnight Mon-Sat) As much a wineshop as a wine bar, this is always our first port of call when buying a bottle. Although Movia is its own label, the knowledgeable staff here will advise you on and sell you wine from other vintners.

Soven Natura Ljubljana   CLOTHING
(Map p38; ☑040 190 293; www.soven.si; Ciril Metodov trg 5; ☺9am-7pm Mon-Fri, to 3pm Sat) Purveyors of the finest organic Styrian knitting wool and wool products available in Slovenia: ponchos, capes, hats, gloves, scarves and slippers.

Trgovina Ika   GIFTS
(Map p38; ☑01-232 17 43; www.trgovina-ika.si; Ciril Metodov trg 13; ☺10am-7.30pm Mon-Fri, 9am-6pm Sat, 10am-2pm Sun) This gift shop-cum-art gallery-cum-fashion designer opposite the cathedral and market sells handmade items that put a modern spin on traditional forms and motifs. More than 100 designers have clothing, jewellery, porcelain etc on sale here.

Katarina Silk   FASHION
(Map p38; ☑040 846 448; www.facebook.com/Katarina.Silk; Gornji trg 5; ☺10am-7pm Mon-Fri, to 4pm Sat May-Sep, 10am-1pm & 3-7pm Mon-Fri, 4pm Sat Oct-Apr) Silk scarves so fine they'll pass through a ring, as well unique ceramic and glass jewellery, all designed and hand-crafted by Aleksandra Vrhovec.

3 Muhe   HANDICRAFTS
(3 Flies; Map p38; ☑01-421 07 15; www.3muhe.si; Stari trg 30; ☺10am-8pm Mon-Fri, to 2pm Sat) Only fair-trade products make it to the shelves of this new social enterprise, be it coffee from Uganda, spices from Sri Lanka, baskets from Ghana or stemware from Guatemala. You'll feel noble just walking in.

Galerija Idrijske Čipke   GIFTS
(Idrija Lace Gallery; Map p38; ☑01-425 00 51; www.idrija-lace.com; Mestni trg 17; ☺10am-1pm & 3-7pm Mon-Fri, to 3pm Sat, later hours in summer) If Idrija in Primorska is not on your itinerary but you hanker for some of the fine lace for which that town is renowned, visit this shop. It has a large collection of curtains, tablecloths and bed linen on sale, as well as smaller items like handkerchiefs, doilies and even a Christmas tree ornament in the shape of a dragon.

Oliviers & Co   FOOD & DRINK
(Map p38; ☑01-232 22 92; www.oliviers-co.si; Ciril Metodov trg 20; ☺9.30am-8pm Mon-Sat, 10am-1pm Sun) Part of a French chain, this shop has gone totally local and sells the finest oils from, including olive oil from Slovenian Istria, the unusual spruce oil (*smrekovo olje*) and the finest of both cold-pressed and roasted pumpkin seed oil (*bučno olje*) from Kocbek.

Rogaška Crystal   GLASS
(Map p38; ☑01-241 27 01; www.steklarna-rogaska.si; Mestni trg 22; ☺9am-8pm) The town of Rogaška Slatina in eastern Slovenia is as renowned for its high-quality crystal as it is for its mineral water. If you aren't heading for Štajerska, choose from a wide range of leaded crystal glasses and other household items from this outlet run by the factory.

Honey House   FOOD
(Map p38; ☑040 477 473; Mestni trg 7; ☺9am-7pm, to 8pm in summer) Slovenia is one of the largest producers of honey and honey-related products in Europe, and this place stocks enough varieties of the sweet sticky stuff to satisfy any taste. Medica (honey liqueur) and propolis available too (though royal jelly requires refrigeration).

Piranske Soline   BEAUTY
(Piran Saltpans; Map p38; ☑01-425 01 90; www.soline.si; Mestni trg 8; ☺9am-8pm Mon-Fri, to 3pm Sat, 10am-3pm Sun) This place in the Old Town sells bath sea salts and other products from Sečovlje along the Adriatic coast. Half the products are intended for the bathroom – bath salts of various scents, sea-mud soap and peeling salts – while the rest belongs in the kitchen, including the delightful *fleur de sel* (salt flower), a distinctive-tasting salt from the saltpans.

Trubarjev Antikvariat   BOOKS
(Map p38; ☑01-244 26 83; Mestni trg 25; ☺10am-8pm Mon-Fri, 9.30am-1.30pm Sat, closes at 6pm weekdays in winter) Come here for antiquarian and secondhand books. There's a good selection of antique maps upstairs.

Center

★Geonavtik   BOOKS
(Map p38; ☑01-252 70 27; www.geonavtik.com; Kongresni trg 1; ☺9am-8pm Mon-Fri, to 2pm Sat) This superb shop stocks travel and nautical guides, maps and books about Slovenia in English. There's a popular cafe/bar attached.

Art & Flea Markets   MARKET
(Cankarjevo nabrežje; Map p38; ☺8am-2pm Sat & Sun) It's worth checking out the weekly art market (Saturday) and flea market (Sunday) held year-round along riverside Breg south of Cobblers' Bridge.

Vinoteka Dvor WINE
(Map p38; ☑ 01-251 36 44; www.kozelj.si; Dvorni trg 2; ☺ 10am-8pm Mon-Fri, to 2pm Sat) Just up from the Dvorni Bar, this small but perfectly formed and independently run wineshop has a large selection of wine as well as fruit brandies.

Skrina HANDICRAFTS
(Map p38; ☑ 01-425 51 61, 040 460 460; www.skrina.si; Breg 8; ☺ 10am-6pm Mon-Fri, to 1pm Sat & Sun) This is a good shop for distinctly Slovenian (and affordable) folk craft such as Prekmurje black pottery, Idrija lace, beehive panels with folk motifs, decorated heart-shaped honey cakes, painted Easter eggs, colourful bridal chests and stepped stools.

Lotos FOOD
(Map p38; ☑ 040 832 108; www.sm-lotos.com; Breg 16; ☺ 10am-9pm Mon-Sat, to 5pm Sun) Come here for the jams and marmalades, with more than two-dozen varieties available. From strawberry and mandarin to pomegranate and kiwi, they are loaded with fruit. Lotos is a family-run business and they do things in the old-fashioned way – no artificial colouring and no artificial preservatives – so it's probably best to buy small jars if bought as gifts.

Mladinska Knjiga BOOKS
(Map p38; ☑ 01-241 46 84; www.mladinska.com; 1st fl, Slovenska cesta 29; ☺ 8am-8pm Mon-Fri, 9am-2pm Sat) 'MK' is the city's biggest and best-stocked bookshop, with lots of guidebooks, maps, pictorials, fiction, and newspapers and periodicals in English. There's a branch (Map p46; ☑ 01-234 27 81; Miklošičeva cesta 40; ☺ 7am-7pm Mon-Fri, 9am-1pm Sat) on Miklošičeva cesta.

Trubarjeva Cesta & Tabor

Počen Lonec HOMEWARES
(Map p38; ☑ 031 285 968, 041 718 598; www.pocenlonec.si; Trubarjeva cesta 18; ☺ 11am-7pm Mon-Fri, to 5pm Sat, 1-5pm Sun) This little outlet with the funny name of 'Cracked Pot' sells colourful and very nostalgia-driven enamelled metal teapots, mugs, plates and bowls. If you're under 35, you probably don't remember them first hand, which is just as well – they never looked as good as these do.

Antika Carniola 1989 ANTIQUES
(Map p38; ☑ 01-231 63 97; Trubarjeva cesta 9; ☺ 4-7pm Mon, 10am-1pm & 4-7pm Tue-Fri, 10am-1pm Sat) With a large selection of items from

the 1950s and '60s, this long-established shop is among the best and most helpful antique galleries in town.

Krakovo & Trnovo

Annapurna OUTDOOR EQUIPMENT
(Map p38; ☑ 031 740 838; www.annapurna.si; Krakovski nasip 4; ☺ 9am-7pm Mon-Fri, to 1pm Sat) If you've forgotten your sleeping bag, ski poles, hiking boots, climbing gear or rucksack, this shop in Krakovo can supply you with all of it – and more. Very helpful and knowledgeable staff.

Žale & Beyond

Paviljon Wineshop WINE
(Map p46; ☑ 051 261 118; www.kaval-group.si/paviljon.asp; Jurček Pavilion, Dunajska cesta 18; ☺ 8am-10pm Mon-Sat) If you're serious about wine, this enormous pub and wine cellar in the Ljubljana Fairgrounds north of Center is for you. It has a selection of hundreds of wines, most of which are Slovenian.

Lovec OUTDOOR EQUIPMENT
(☑ 01-585 17 99; www.koptex.com; BTC City, Hall A, Šmartinska cesta 152; ☺ 9am-7pm Mon-Sat) For those into ridin', fishin' and shootin', 'Hunter' has all the kit and equipment you'll need under one roof out at the BTC City shopping mall.

ⓘ Information

DISCOUNT CARDS

The **Urbana-Ljubljana Tourist Card** (www.visitljubljana.com/en/ljubljana-card; per 24/48/72 hours adult €23/30/35, child aged 6-14 €14/18/21), available from the tourist office for 24/48/72 hours, offers free admission to 15 attractions, walking and boat tours, unlimited travel on city buses and internet access.

INTERNET ACCESS

Many cafes and restaurants offer free wi-fi for customers and **WiFreeLjubljana** (www.wifree ljubljana.si/en) offers visitors one hour of free internet access a day. Most hostels and some hotels have a public computer for guests to surf the internet. The Slovenian Tourist Information Centre has computers on-hand to check email (€1 per 30 minutes).

LEFT LUGGAGE

Left Luggage in Bus Station (Trg OF 4; per day €2; ☺ 5am-10.30pm Mon-Sat, 5.30am-10.30pm Sun) Window No 3.

Left Luggage in Train Station (Trg OF 6; per day €2-3; ☺ 24hr) Coin lockers on platform 1.

MEDICAL SERVICES

University Medical Centre Ljubljana (Univerzitetni Klinični Center Ljubljana; ☑ 01-522 50 50, 01-522 23 61; www.kclj.si; Zaloška cesta 2; ⊙ 24hr) University medical clinic with 24-hour accident and emergency service.

Community Health Centre Ljubljana (Zdravstveni Dom Ljubljana; ☑ 01-472 37 00; www. zd-lj.si/en; Metelkova ulica 9; ⊙ 7.30am-7pm Mon-Fri, 8am-4pm Sat) For non-emergencies.

Barsos Medical Centre (☑ 01-242 07 00; www.barsos.net; Gregorčičeva ulica 11; ⊙ 8am-8pm Mon-Fri) Private clinic, with prices starting at around €40 per consultation.

Central Pharmacy (Centralna Lekarna; ☑ 01-230 61 00; Prešernov trg 5; ⊙ 7.30am-7.30pm Mon-Fri, 8am-3pm Sat) Central option for pharmaceutical goods; in an Italianate building that was once a cafe frequented by intellectuals in the 19th century.

MONEY

There are ATMs at every turn, including several outside the main Ljubljana Tourist Information Centre office. At the train station you'll find a **bureau de change** (☑ 01-432 10 14; ⊙ 7am-8pm) changing cash for no commission but not travellers cheques.

Abanka (☑ 01-300 15 00; www.abanka.si; Slovenska cesta 50; ⊙ 8.30am-5pm Mon-Fri)

Nova Ljubljanska Banka (NLB; ☑ 01-477 20 00; www.nlb.si; Trg Republike 2; ⊙ 8am-6pm Mon-Fri)

POST

Main Post Office (Map p38; Slovenska cesta 32; ⊙ 8am-7pm Mon-Fri, to noon Sat) Holds poste restante for 30 days and changes money.

Post Office Branch (Map p46; Pražakova ulica 3; ⊙ 8am-6pm Mon-Fri, to noon Sat) Just southwest of the bus and train stations.

TOURIST INFORMATION

Ljubljana Tourist Information Centre (TIC; Map p38; ☑ 01-306 12 15; www.visitljubljana. com; Adamič-Lundrovo nabrežje 2; ⊙ 8am-9pm Jun-Sep, to 7pm Oct-May) Knowledgeable and enthusiastic staff dispense information, maps and useful literature and help with accommodation. Maintains an excellent website.

Slovenian Tourist Information Centre (STIC; Map p38; ☑ 01-306 45 76; www.slovenia.info; Krekov trg 10; ⊙ 8am-9pm Jun-Sep, 8am-7pm Mon-Fri, 9am-5pm Sat & Sun Oct-May) Good source of information for the rest of Slovenia, with internet and bicycle rental also available.

TRAVEL AGENCIES

STA Travel (☑ 01-439 16 90, 041 612 711; www. sta-lj.com; 1st fl, Trg Ajdovščina 1; ⊙ 8am-5pm Mon-Fri) Discount airfares for students.

USEFUL WEBSITES

Alongside the websites of the Slovenian Tourist Information Centre (www.slovenia.info) and Ljubljana Tourist Information Centre (www. visitljubljana.si), some additional sites provide helpful information on upcoming events.

City of Ljubljana (www.ljubljana.si/en) Comprehensive city hall information portal on every aspect of life and tourism.

In Your Pocket (www.inyourpocket.com/ ljubljana) Insider info on the capital updated bimonthly.

Slovenia Times (www.sloveniatimes.com) News in English.

❶ Getting There & Away

BUS

Buses to destinations both within Slovenia and abroad leave from the **bus station** (Avtobusna Postaja Ljubljana; Map p46; ☑ 01-234 46 00; www.ap-ljubljana.si; Trg Osvobodilne Fronte 4; ⊙ 5am-10.30pm Mon-Sat, 5.30am-10.30pm Sun) just next to train station. Next to the ticket windows are multilingual information phones and a touch-screen computer. There's another touch-screen computer outside too.

You do not usually have to buy your ticket in advance; just pay as you board the bus. But for long-distance trips on Friday, just before the

BUSES FROM LJUBLJANA

Some sample one-way fares (return fares are usually double) from the capital:

DESTINATION	PRICE	DURATION	DISTANCE	FREQUENCY
Bled	€6.30	1½hr	57km	hourly
Bohinj	€8.70	2hr	91km	hourly
Koper	€12	2½hr	122km	5 daily with more in season
Maribor	€12	3hr	141km	2-4 daily
Novo Mesto	€8	1hr	72km	up to 7 daily
Piran	€12	3hr	140km	up to 7 daily
Postojna	€6	1hr	53km	up to 24 daily

TRAINS FROM LJUBLJANA

The following are some one-way, 2nd-class domestic fares, travel times, distances and frequencies from Ljubljana (return fares are double the price, and there's a surcharge of €1.80 on domestic InterCity (IC) and EuroCity (EC) train tickets).

DESTINATION	PRICE	DURATION	DISTANCE	FREQUENCY
Bled	€6.60	55min	51km	up to 21 daily
Koper	€9.60	2½hr	153km	up to 4 daily, with more in summer
Maribor	€9.60	1¾hr	156km	up to 25 daily
Murska Sobota	€13	3¼hr	216km	up to 5 daily
Novo Mesto	€6.60	1½hr	75km	up to 14 daily

school break and public holidays, you run the risk of not getting a seat – book one the day before and reserve a seat (€1.50/2.20 domestic/international).

You can reach virtually anywhere in the country by bus – as close as Kamnik (€3.10, 50 minutes, 25km, every half-hour) or as far away as Murska Sobota (€16, three hours, 199km, one or two a day).

CAR & MOTORCYCLE

Most of the big international car-hire firms have offices in Ljubljana and at the airport. You can rent locally on the spot or often snag a better deal renting in advance over the company website.

Avis (☑ 01-421 73 40; www.avis.si; Miklošičeva cesta 3; ⊗ 8am-4pm Mon-Fri, to noon Sat & Sun) At airport, too.

Atet Rent a Car (☑ 01-513 70 17, 01-320 82 30; www.atet.si; Devova ulica 6a; ⊗ 8am-6pm Mon-Fri, to 1pm Sat & Sun) Office also at airport.

Central Rent (☑ 040 216 084, 059 014 550; www.centralrent.si; Slovenska cesta 36; ⊗ 9am-4pm Mon-Fri, 8am-1pm Sat) Offers some of the best car-rental deals in town.

Europcar (☑ 059 070 512, 031 382 052; www.europcar.si; City Hotel Ljubljana, Dalmatinova ulica 15; ⊗ 8am-6pm Mon-Fri, to noon Sat & Sun) At airport, too.

Hertz (☑ 01-434 01 47; www.hertz.si; Trdinova ulica 9; ⊗ 8am-4pm Mon-Fri, to 1pm Sat, to noon Sun) Office at airport, too.

TRAIN

Domestic and international trains arrive at and depart from central Ljubljana's **train station** (Železniška Postaja; ☑ 01-291 33 32; www.slo-zeleznice.si; Trg Osvobodilne Fronte 6; ⊗ 5am-10pm), where you'll find a separate information centre on the way to the platforms. Buy domestic tickets from windows No 1 to 8 and international ones from either window No 9 or the information centre.

ⓘ Getting Around

TO & FROM THE AIRPORT

The cheapest way to Ljubljana's **Jože Pučnik Airport** (p265) is by **public bus** (€4.10, 45 minutes, 27km) from stop No 28 at the bus station. These run at 5.20am and hourly from 6.10am to 8.10pm Monday to Friday; at the weekend there's a bus at 6.10am and then one every two hours from 9.10am to 7.10pm. Buy tickets from the driver.

Two airport-shuttle services that get consistently good reviews are **GoOpti** (☑ 01-320 45 30; www.goopti.com) and **Markun Shuttle** (☑ 041 792 865, 051 321 414; www.prevozi-markun.com), which will transfer you from Brnik to central Ljubljana for €9 in half an hour. Book by phone or online.

A taxi from the airport to Ljubljana will cost from €35 to €45.

BICYCLE

Ljubljana is a pleasure for cyclists, and there are bike lanes and special traffic lights everywhere.

Ljubljana Bike (☑ 01-306 45 76; www.visitljubljana.si; Krekov trg 10; per 2hr/4hr/day €2/4/8; ⊗ 8am-7pm Apr, May & Oct, to 9pm Jun-Sep) rents two-wheelers in two-hour or full-day increments from April through October from the **Slovenia Tourist Information Centre** (p68).

For short rides, you can hire bicycles as needed from 32 **Bicike(lj)** (☑ 080 23 34; www.bicikelj.si; subscription weekly/yearly €1/€3 plus hourly rate ; ⊗ 24hr) stations with 300 bikes located around the city. To rent a bike requires pre-registration and subscription over the company website plus a valid credit or debit card. This costs just €1/3 per week/year. After registering simply submit your card or an **Urbana** (p70) card plus a PIN number. The first hour of the rental is free, the second hour costs €1, the third hour €2, and each additional hour €4. Bikes must be returned within 24 hours.

CAR & MOTORCYCLE

The centre is walkable and many streets are off limits to motor vehicle traffic, so you're best advised to stow your car on arrival and walk or take public transport as needed to get around. Parking in Ljubljana is tight, especially on work days. Most parking in the centre is metered parking (per hour €0.70 to €1.20, from 8am to 7pm Monday to Friday, and 8am to 1pm Saturday). There are enclosed car parks throughout the city, and their locations are indicated on most maps. Parking rates normally start at 60 cents to €2.40 per hour; expect to pay a day rate from around €25.

PUBLIC TRANSPORT

Ljubljana's city buses, many of them running on methane, operate every five to 15 minutes from 5am (6am on Sunday) to around 10.30pm. There are also a half-dozen night buses. A flat fare of €1.20 (good for 90 minutes of unlimited travel, including transfers) is paid with a stored-value magnetic **Urbana** (☏ 01-474 08 00; www.jhl.si/en/single-city-card-urbana) card, which can be purchased at newsstands, tourist offices and the

LPP Information Centre (Map p46; ☏ 01-430 51 74; www.lpp.si/en; Slovenska cesta 56; ⏱7am-7pm Mon-Fri) for €2; credit can then be added (from €1 to €50).

Kavalir (☏ 031 666 332, 031 666 331; ⏱8am-8pm) is an LPP-run transport service that will pick you up and drop you off anywhere in the pedestrianised Old Town free of charge. All you have to do is call (and wait – there are only three golf cart-like vehicles available April to October and just one the rest of the year).

TAXI

Metered taxis can be hailed on the street or hired from ranks (eg near the train station, at the Ljubljana TIC on Stritarjeva ulica, in front of the Grand Hotel Union). Flagfall is €0.80 to €1.50 and the per-kilometre charge ranges from €0.70 to €1.70, depending on the company and whether you call ahead (cheaper) or hail a taxi on the street.

Laguna Taxi (☏ 031 492 299, 080 12 33; www.taxi-laguna.com) Reliable radio taxi with English-speaking operators.

Lake Bled & the Julian Alps

Best Places to Stay

➡ Garden Village Bled (p91)
➡ Rustic House 13 (p98)
➡ Pr' Gavedarjo (p104)
➡ Natura Eco Camp (p104)
➡ Kekčeva Domačija (p108)
➡ Pristava Lepena (p108)

Best Places to Eat

➡ Finefood – Penzion Berc (p92)
➡ Štrud'l (p98)
➡ Skipass Hotel Restaurant (p106)
➡ Gostilna Repnik (p74)
➡ Vila Podvin (p82)

Why Go?

This is the Slovenia of the tourist posters: mountain peaks, Alpine meadows, postcard-perfect lakes. Prepare to be charmed by Lake Bled (an island *and* a castle!), and surprised by Lake Bohinj (how does Bled score all that attention when down the road is Bohinj?). Mt Triglav's lofty peak may dazzle you enough to prompt an ascent.

This region, known as Gorenjska (Upper Carniola in English), is home to the country's one and only national park – and it's a beauty. Hiking and biking are high on many travel itineraries, but a leisurely outing on the lakes also delivers fresh air and inspiring panoramas. Winter brings its own rewards, with snowy peaks and plentiful ski slopes.

Mother Nature has blessed the region with ample treasure, but human effort deserves praise too: historic towns like Kamnik, Škofja Loka and Radovljica are architectural treasures, while the road over the spectacular Vršič Pass represents a remarkable wartime legacy.

When to Go
Bled

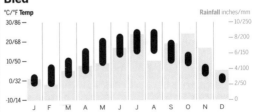

May & Jun River rafting, waterfalls and wildflowers at their peak.

Jul & Aug Swimming season is short and sweet (and draws the crowds) at lakes Bled and Bohinj.

Dec–Apr Decent skiing conditions can last through to spring.

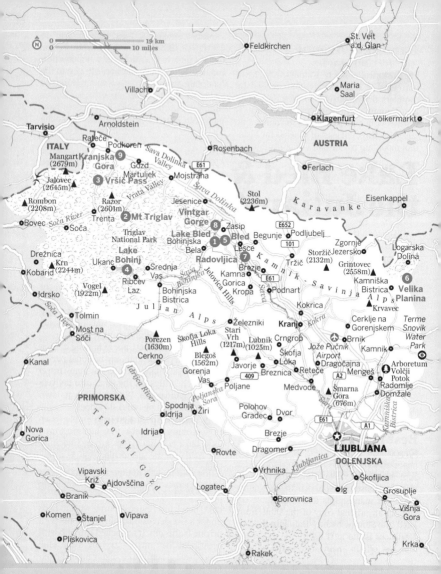

Lake Bled & the Julian Alps Highlights

1 Enjoy **Lake Bled** (p84) with a shoreline cycle or walk, a swim, a *pletna* (gondola) ride or from the castle terrace.

2 Climb to the top of **Mt Triglav** (p101), Slovenia's tallest peak.

3 Drive or bike over the hair-raising (and spine-tingling) **Vršič Pass** (p107).

4 Paddle a kayak or an SUP surrounded by the immense natural beauty of **Lake Bohinj** (p93).

5 Spend an unforgettable day canyoning, rafting or ballooning, starting from **Bled** (p83).

6 Ride the cable car to the photogenic Alpine pastureland of **Velika Planina** (p74).

7 Investigate bees, beers, *lectar* (gingerbread) and fine food in **Radovljica** (p79).

8 Walk the easy, super-scenic trail through **Vintgar Gorge** (p90).

9 Test out glamping, from tree-pod tents at **Natura Eco Camp** (p104) in Kranjska Gora to treehouses in Bled.

Kamnik & Around

🗲 01 / POP 13,803 / ELEV 375M

The historical town of Kamnik, just 23km northeast of Ljubljana, is often missed by travellers drawn directly to Bled or Bohinj. But Kamnik's attractive medieval core is worth a visit, and the town is surrounded by great side trips, not least of which is the beautiful mountain pastures of Velika Planina.

◉ Sights & Activities

Šutna   STREET

A walk along the main street is a trip back in time: pretty, pastel-coloured houses arrayed in a row, many sporting guild and craft signs. In the centre of Šutna stands the Church of the Immaculate Conception (built in the mid-18th century), with a detached Gothic spire.

Mali Grad   HILL

From near central Glavni trg (main square), climb the steps up history-filled Mali Grad hill to enjoy great panoramas from the 'balcony of Kamnik', taking in red rooftops against the backdrop of the Kamnik-Savinja Alps. In summer you can visit the unique, three-level Romanesque Chapel (Mali Grad; adult/child €2.50/1.50; ⊙ 9am-7pm mid-Jun–mid-Sep) here (two storeys plus a crypt), with its 15th-century frescoes and Gothic stone reliefs.

Franciscan Monastery   MONASTERY

(Frančiškanski Samostan; 🗲01-831 80 37; http://franciskani-kamnik.rkc.si; Frančiškanski trg 2; ⊙by appointment) Just west of Glavni trg, the Franciscan monastery has a rich 10,000-volume library of manuscripts and incunabula (including an original copy of the Bible translated into Slovene by Jurij Dalmatin in 1584). Next door is the 1695 Church of St James and just off the main altar is the tent-like Chapel of the Holy Sepulchre, which was designed by Jože Plečnik in 1952 and is full of symbols relating to Christ and Christianity. The church and chapel are usually open daily.

Kamniška Bistrica   NATURE RESERVE

This pretty little settlement in a valley near the source of the Kamniška Bistrica River is 12km north of Kamnik, and well worth a drive for its delightful setting: crystal-clear springs, chapel, Alpine backdrop, a lodge with beds and food. Kamniška Bistrica is the springboard for popular hikes in the Kamnik-Savinja Alps.

More ambitious treks include one to Grintovec (2558m; nine hours return), the highest peak in the range and a popular destination. Shorter hikes head northwest to the mountain pass at Kokra Saddle (Kokrsko Sedlo; 1793m), and north to Kamnik Saddle (Kamniško Sedlo; 1876m). Both passes have mountain huts open in summer. Ask at the TIC, or see more at www.hiking-trail.net.

Arboretum Volčji Potok   GARDENS

(🗲01-831 23 45; www.arboretum-vp.si; Volčji Potok 3; adult/child €7.50/6; ⊙ 8am-8pm Apr-Aug, shorter hrs Sep-Mar) About 6km south of Kamnik is Volčji Potok, Slovenia's largest and most beautiful garden. The 80-hectare arboretum has more than 2500 varieties of trees, shrubs and flowers from all over the world; spring is, needless to say, abloom with colour (April's tulips are especially magnificent).

Terme Snovik   WATER PARK

(🗲01-834 41 00; www.terme-snovik.si; Snovik 7, Laze v Tuhinju; 4hr adult/child €13/10; ⊙indoor pools 9am-8pm daily, outside pools Jun–Sep) Terme Snovik is a year-round thermal water park with indoor and open-air pools in the emerald-green Tuhinj Valley, 10km east of Kamnik. Water temperatures range from 26°C (79°F) outdoors up to 36°C (97°F) inside. There's a range of wellness services and accommodation here – see the website.

🍽 Sleeping & Eating

Hostel Pod Skalo   HOSTEL $

(🗲01-839 12 33; www.hostel-kamnik.si; Maistrova ulica 32; dm/s/d/tr €14/30/48/66; ⓅⓈ) This is a first-rate budget option about 500m east of the centre, opposite a public swimming pool and small campground (note: no kitchen). There's just one cosy dorm, with 10 beds under a wooden ceiling, plus 10 rooms with private bathroom. It's attached to a pub with occasional live music – try the local 'Mali Grad' beer. There's free bike rental; breakfast is €4.

Kamp Alpe   CAMPGROUND $

(🗲041 816 477; www.kamp-alpe.com; Kamniška Bistrica 2; campsite adult/child/tent/motorhome €8/4/2/5; ⊙May-Sep; ⓅⓈ) This shady campground sits in the area surrounding the cable car to Velika Planina (9.5km from Kamnik), with more facilities across the road at Kraljev Hrib (including hostel beds for €17). There are cute wooden huts at Kampe Alpe (per person €25) and a restaurant-bar at Kraljev Hrib.

LAKE BLED & THE JULIAN ALPS KAMNIK & AROUND

Picerija Napoli   PIZZA $

(☑ 01-839 27 44; www.picerijanapoli.com; Sadnikar-jeva ulica 5; pizzas €7-9; ⊙ 11am-10pm) South of Mali Grad, this homey pizzeria is one of the few places for a meal in central Kamnik. It has a shady terrace and does takeaway as well.

★**Gostilna Repnik**   SLOVENIAN $$

(☑ 01-839 12 93; www.gostilna-repnik.si; Vrhpolje 186; s/d from €55/90, mains €12-18; ⊙ restaurant 10am-10pm Tue-Fri, noon-10pm Sat, noon-3pm Sun; P ✳ ⊜) Long a locals' favourite for top-notch Slovenian cuisine, Gostilna Repnik (about 1.5km east of the centre) now boasts fabulous boutique accommodation to give you more reason to linger. Great service and fresh, local produce are the hallmarks. There's usually no menu, but a well-priced offering of, say, trout, veal shank and delicious dessert – all showcasing tradition with a twist.

The nine rooms feature stylishly rustic design elements; guests have free use of bikes and excellent insider travel trips from host Peter.

ℹ Information

Tourist Information Centre (TIC; ☑ 01-831 82 50; www.kamnik-tourism.si; Glavni trg 2; ⊙ 9am-9pm Jul & Aug, 10am-6pm Mon-Sat, 10am-2pm Sun Sep-Jun) Helpful office; hiking maps available, bikes for rent. Can assist in working out transport details to Velika Planina.

ℹ Getting There & Away

Buses from Ljubljana (€3.10, 50 minutes, 25km) run two to four times an hour (less frequent on weekends). Only two or three buses a day continue north to Kamniška Bistrica.

Kamnik is also on a direct rail line to/from Ljubljana (€2.58, 40 minutes, 23km, up to 15 a day).

Škofja Loka

☑ 04 / POP 11,739 / ELEV 348M

Škofja Loka (Bishop's Meadow), just 26km from Ljubljana, is among the most beautiful and oldest settlements in Slovenia. Its evocative Old Town has been protected as a historical monument since 1987. It can be explored as a day trip from the capital or as an overnight stay (though book accommodation in advance since there's just a handful of lodging options). When the castle and other old buildings are illuminated on weekend nights, Škofja Loka takes on the appearance of a fairy tale. It's also an excellent springboard for walking in the Škofja Loka Hills to the west.

⊙ Sights

Ask the TIC for the pamphlet *Walk around the Town and Surroundings*.

★**Loka Castle & Museum**   CASTLE, MUSEUM

(Loški Grad & Muzej; ☑ 04-517 04 00; www.loski-muzej.si; Grajska pot 13; adult/child €5/3; ⊙ 10am-6pm Tue-Sun) The town's premier sight is this

---

> **WORTH A TRIP**
>
> ### VELIKA PLANINA
>
> Velika Planina, loosely translated as 'Great Highlands', wonderfully combines heritage and scenery. It's accessible by cable car from the lower station 9.5km north of Kamnik. Lots of info is online at www.velikaplanina.si, including up-to-date transport timetables.
>
> The journey to the top unfolds in two stages: first a dramatic **cable-car ride** (☑ 031 680 862; www.velikaplanina.si; adult/child return incl chairlift €17/12, cable car only €11/8; ⊙ hourly 8.30am-5.30pm) and then a 15-minute **chairlift**. Once on top, there's little to do except walk the pristine fields, drink in the views, and admire a herding and dairy economy little changed for hundreds of years.
>
> Velika Planina is where traditional dairy farmers graze their cattle between June and September, and the pastures are scattered with around 60 **traditional shepherds' huts** (and the tiny **Church of Our Lady of the Snows**) unique to the area. Regrettably, all but one of these – the tiny two-room **Preskar Hut** (Preskarjeva Bajta; admission €2; ⊙ 10am-4pm) that's now a small museum – are replicas. The originals, dating from the early-20th century, were burned to the ground by Germans in WWII.
>
> While on the top, have a meal at **Zeleni Rob** (⊙ 8am-6pm Jun-Sep, to 4pm Oct-May), a small restaurant a short walk from the first (lower) stop on the chairlift. It's said by some to serve Slovenia's best *štruklji* (sweet dumplings stuffed with curd cheese). In summer, the area's friendly shepherds in their big black hats will sell you curd and white cheese.

commanding castle, overlooking the settlement from a grassy hill west of Mestni trg. It dates from the 13th century and was extensively renovated after an earthquake in 1511. Today the castle houses the **Loka Museum**, which boasts an excellent ethnographic collection spread over two-dozen galleries on two floors.

Exhibits run the gamut from taxidermied animals to church frescoes by way of local painters, lace-making traditions and WWII partisans; English labelling can be patchy for some exhibits. In the garden, you'll find a typical **peasant house** from nearby Pušta dating from the 16th century. Don't miss the four spectacular golden altars in the castle **chapel**. These date from the 17th century and were taken from a church destroyed during WWII in Dražgoše, northwest of Škofja Loka.

Two paths lead up to the castle from the Old Town; one starts just opposite Kavarna Homan, the other next to Martin House. A longer walking trail, the **Three Castles Path**, begins at the castle and travels a circular, forested path for about 5km (two hours), past the ruins of the Krancelj Tower and the Old Castle. The TIC has a brochure with map.

★**Mestni Trg**　　　　　　　　SQUARE
The group of pastel-hued 16th-century **burghers' houses** on this square have earned the town the nickname 'Colourful Loka'. Almost every one is of historical and architectural importance, but arguably the most impressive is **Homan House** (Homanova Hiša; Mestni trg 2), dating from 1511 with graffiti and bits of frescoes of St Christopher and of a soldier.

Another building to look out for is the former **Town Hall** (Stari Rotovž; Mestni trg 35), remarkable for its three-storey Gothic courtyard and the 17th-century frescoes on its facade. Further south, 17th-century **Martin House** (Martinova Hiša; Mestni trg 26) leans on part of the old town wall. It has a wooden 1st floor, a late-Gothic portal and a vaulted entrance hall. The **Plague Pillar** (Mestni trg), in the centre of Mestni trg, was erected in 1751.

Parish Church of St James　　CHURCH
(Župnijska Cerkev Sv Jakoba; Cankarjev trg; ⊙7am-6pm) The town's most important church dates back to the 13th century, with key features like the nave, the presbytery with star vaulting (1524), and the tall bell tower (1532) added over the next three centuries.

The dozen or so distinctive ceiling lamps and the baptismal font were designed by Jože Plečnik.

Inside the church, look up to the vaulted ceiling to see bosses with portraits of the Freising bishops (the town's founders), saints, workers with shears and a blacksmith; the two crescent moons in the presbytery are reminders of the Turkish presence. Outside the church, on the south side, is the church's rectory, part of a fortified aristocratic manor house built in the late 16th century.

Spodnji Trg　　　　　　　　SQUARE
The main square to the east of Mestni trg was where the poorer folk lived in the Middle Ages; today it is used as a busy thoroughfare with admittedly not much to see – this may change, as town authorities plan a bypass that will take most car traffic off the road. The 16th-century **granary** (kašča; Spodnji trg 1) at the square's northern end is where the town's grain stores, collected as taxes, were once kept. Over two floors in the granary house you'll find **France Mihelič Gallery** (Galerija Franceta Miheliča; ☑04-517 04 00; www.loski-muzej.si; Spodnji trg 1; admission €1.50; ⊙by appointment), which displays the works of the eponymous artist born in nearby Virmaše in 1907. You can arrange a visit through the Loka Museum.

★**Capuchin Bridge**　　　　HISTORIC SITE
(Kapucinski Most) The Capuchin Bridge (sometimes called the Stone Bridge) leading from the Capuchin monastery originally dates from the 14th century and is an excellent vantage point for the Old Town and castle as well as the river.

To capture the bridge in its full photogenic glory, cross the footbridge over the river just to the east.

Capuchin Monastery　　　MONASTERY
(Kapucinski Samostan; ☑04-506 30 05; Kapucinski trg 2; ⊙by appointment) The 18th-century Capuchin monastery, west of the bus station, has a priceless **library** of medieval manuscripts, as well as the *Škofja Loka Passion*, a processional with dramatic elements, from around 1720. Arrange a visit with the TIC or the monastery itself.

Church of the Annunciation　　CHURCH
(Cerkev Marijinega Oznanenja; Crngrob; ⊙interior by appointment) This small church in the village of Crngrob, 4km north of Škofja Loka, has one of the most treasured frescoes in Slovenia. Look for it on the outside wall

Škofja Loka

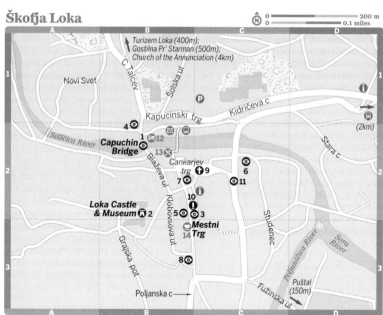

Škofja Loka

under a 19th-century portico near the church entrance. Called Holy Sunday (*Sveta Nedelja*) and produced in 1460, the fresco explains in pictures what good Christians do on Sunday (pray, go to Mass, help the sick) and what they don't do (gamble, drink or fight).

Note that even when the church is locked the Holy Sunday fresco is still viewable – although some of its detail is hard to discern. (There's a helpful replica inside the Loka Museum.)

It's a nice walk or cycle to reach Crngrob – the *Path to Crngrob* brochure from the TIC outlines the way.

🏃 Activities

Hiking

The **Škofja Loka Hills** to the west, a region of steep slopes, deep valleys and ravines, is an excellent area for walks or hikes, and there are several huts with accommodation in the area. If you're serious about exploring, buy a copy of the map and guide for cyclists, hikers and drivers entitled *Škofjeloško, Idrijsko in Cerkljansko Hribovje* (*Škofja Loka, Idrija and Cerkno Hills*; €12 from the TIC).

One of the easiest trips is to **Lubnik**, a 1025m peak northwest of the Old Town, which can be reached on foot in two hours via Vincarje (a difficult route), or via the castle ruins near Gabrovo. A shorter option (40 minutes) is from the village of Breznica. A mountain hut near the summit, **Dom na Lubniku** (☑ 04-512 05 01, 031 655 556; www.pd-skofjaloka.com; Lubnik; per person €20; ⊗ Tue-Sun), has four rooms (12 beds) plus a restaurant and a terrace with great views.

A hike to 1562m **Blegoš**, further west, would be more demanding, but it takes only about three hours from Javorje, a village accessible by bus from Škofja Loka. With your own wheels, drive to the village of Črni Kal and you can reach it within an hour. There is an excellent mountain hut in the area: **Koča na Blegošu** (☑ 051 614 587; www.pd-skofjaloka.com; Blegoš; per person €16-20; ⊗ Tue-Sun May-Oct, Sat & Sun Nov-Apr), at 1391m, with 61 beds (in rooms and dorms), restaurants and good family facilities.

Swimming

In the summer heat, join the locals at the town's fabulous riverside swimming area. It's in Puštal, about a 10-minute walk southeast of the Old Town (signposted from Fužinska ulica). There's a summertime cafe-bar here, as well as the wooden 'Devil's Footbridge'.

Skiing

Stari Vrh Ski Centre   SKIING
(☑ 041 650 849; www.starivrh.si; Stari Vrh; day pass adult/child €27/16) The Stari Vrh ski centre, 12km west of Škofja Loka, is situated at altitudes of 580m to 1217m and features 12km of pistes suitable for all levels.

⭐ Festivals & Events

Škofja Loka Passion Play   RELIGOUS
(www.pasijon.si; ⊗ late Mar/Apr) The staging of the Škofja Loka Passion Play is the biggest outdoor theatre production in Slovenia – it involves as many as 800 actors and 80 horses (and hundreds of volunteers). It's staged every six years (the next is scheduled for 2021), and is held throughout the Old Town in the three weeks prior to Easter.

Historial   CULTURAL
(www.historial-skofjaloka.si; ⊗ Jun) A medieval-inspired festival held on the third Saturday in June.

Pisana Loka   MUSIC
(http://pisanaloka.si; ⊗ Jul-Aug) This arts festival (the name means 'Colourful Loka') stages music and theatre performances, film screenings and children's events over 10 days in late-July/August. Event locations

include the various town squares and the castle.

🛏 Sleeping

Camp Smlednik   CAMPGROUND $
(☑ 01-362 70 02; www.dm-campsmlednik.si; Dragočajna 14a; per adult/child €8/4, 2-/4-person bungalow €40/60; ⊗ May–mid-Oct; P 🅿 🛜) This campground for 400 guests in Dragočajna, 11km to the east, is the closest camping to Škofja Loka (it's also handy for Kranj). It's in a green setting on the east bank of the Sava River and beside Lake Zbilje. There is a beach and separate facilities set aside for naturists, plus good extras including restaurant, playground and sports facilities.

Kavarna Vahtnca   PENSION $
(☑ 04-512 14 79; www.vahtnca.si; Mestni trg 31; s/d €30/48; 🛜) This modern cafe in the heart of Škofja Loka's Old Town has two compact, good-value rooms upstairs that put you in the centre of the action.

Turizem Loka   PENSION $$
(☑ 04-515 09 86; www.loka.si; Stara Loka 8a, Stara Loka; s/d/apt from €40/60/85; P ✳ @ 🛜) A 10-minute walk from the bus station in the small village of Stara Loka, where you'll find this very comfortable pension (and a nearby neighbour, Gostilna Pr' Starman). On offer are bright, spotless rooms and family-sized apartments, plus a good breakfast spread and a sunny hostess, Saša. With advance notice, they offer pick-up from the train station.

Hotel Garni Paleta   HOTEL $$
(☑ 041 874 427; www.hotel-skofjaloka.si; Kapucinski trg 17; d/q €62/112; P ✳ 🛜) Welcoming Igor and Irene run this upbeat place next door to an art-supplies shop (thus the name), just by Capuchin Bridge. There are six no-frills rooms – three rooms have a set of bunks, suitable for families. Rooms 1, 3, 5 and 6 have views of the river and the castle; there are discounts for stays longer than one night. Igor can also guide driving tours of the region.

🍴 Eating

Gostilna Pr' Starman   SLOVENIAN $
(☑ 04-512 64 90; www.gostilnastarman.si; Stara Loka 22, Stara Loka; mains €7-17; ⊗ 7am-10pm Mon-Thu, to midnight Fri & Sat) This popular *gostilna* (inn-like restaurant) is about 1km from the bus station (a 15-minute walk) in the charming village of Stara Loka. It serves authentic traditional Slovenian cooking in an informal tavern setting; prepare for

KRVAVEC – SKIING & HIGH-ALTITUDE DINING

Krvavec Ski Centre (☑04-25 25 911; www.rtc-krvavec.si; day pass adult/child €27/14.50) Krvavec ski centre, only 25km north of Ljubljana and 8km from the international airport, is one of the most popular (and crowded) skiing areas in Slovenia. Thirty kilometres of ski runs are maintained at 1450m to 1971m, and there are all the required ski rental, ski school and après-ski activities. Access is via a cable car near the village of Cerklje na Gorenjskem.

In summer, the cable car grants access to lots of **hiking and biking trails**, and if you feel like dining at altitude – with splendid views, of course – once or twice a month a **sunset dinner** (per person €50) is held. Diners are served three courses over three hours, while riding their private cabin up and down the mountain (each cabin holds two to four guests). Check out the details at www.jezersek.si/en/events, and book ahead.

stomach-expanding portions of pork cutlets, homemade sausage and stuffed calamari. There's an al fresco terrace, too.

Jesharna   ITALIAN $
(☑04-512 25 61; Blaževa ulica 10; pizza & pasta €6-10; ⊙10am-11pm Mon-Thu, to 11.30pm Fri & Sat, 11.30am-10pm Sun; ☑) This friendly pizzeria and spaghetti house serves the town's best pizza, good salads and pasta dishes that are so big they could easily be shared. It's directly across the bridge from the bus station, with steps down to its riverside terrace. Note: kitchen closes at 10pm.

Kašča   SLOVENIAN $$
(☑04-512 43 00; Spodnji trg 1; mains €8-18; ⊙noon-midnight Mon-Sat) This attractive (and huge) pub and wine bar in the cellar of the town's 16th-century granary is Škofja Loka's most upscale dining option, and the perfect venue for a big meal out. The menu is heavy on traditional Slovenian food but there's also an appealing range of pizzas.

Gostilna Pri Danilu   SLOVENIAN $$$
(☑04-515 34 44; www.pridanilu.com; Reteče 48; degustation €45; ⊙noon-10pm Wed-Sat, to 4pm Sun) Winning praise from influential French restaurant guide Gault Millau, this traditional, family-run *gostilna* serves up some of the region's best food. It adheres to Slow Food principles and has a knockout wine list; eight courses for €45 is the deal – and it's wonderful value. It's found in the village of Reteče, about 6km east of Škofja Loka; book ahead.

🍷 Drinking & Nightlife

Kavarna Vahtnca   CAFE
(☑04-512 14 79; www.vahtnca.si; Mestni trg 31; ⊙8am-10pm Sun-Thu, to midnight Fri & Sat) With a tiered back terrace peeking up at the cas-

tle, and tables on the main square, this attractive modern cafe in the heart of the Old Town is an appealing place to refuel. The cafe rents out rooms on the upper floor.

Kavarna Homan   CAFE
(☑04-512 30 47; Mestni trg 2; ⊙8am-11pm Mon-Thu, to midnight Fri & Sat, to 10pm Sun) This ground-floor cafe in historical Homan House is always busy, especially in the warm weather when tables are set out on Mestni trg under the giant linden tree. Homemade ice cream and cakes, too.

❶ Information

Most practical facilities for visitors are located a short walk from the bus station on Kapucinski trg. These include banks and the post office. There's a supermarket and ATM on Mestni trg.

Tourist Information Centre – Old Town (TIC; ☑04-512 02 68; www.skofja-loka.com; Mestni trg 7; ⊙8.30am-7.30pm Mon-Fri, 9am-5pm Sat & Sun Jun-Sep, 8.30am-7pm Mon-Fri, 8.30am-12.30pm Sat Oct-May) Excellent source of general information. Has books and maps on the area; sells decent souvenirs.

Tourist Information Centre (TIC; ☑04-517 06 00; www.skofja-loka.com; Kidričeva cesta 1a; ⊙8am-6pm May, Jun, Sep, to 8pm Jul & Aug, to 4pm Mon-Sat Oct-Apr) A roadside office, as you enter the town centre.

❶ Getting There & Away

BUS
Škofja Loka is well served by regional buses at the **bus station** (Kapucinski trg). Count on at least hourly buses weekdays to/from Ljubljana (€3.10, 36 minutes, 25km). There are fewer departures at the weekend.

To travel on to lakes Bled or Bohinj or to Kranjska Gora, take one of the frequent buses to Kranj (€2.30, 24 minutes) and change there.

Škofja Loka can be reached by up to 17 trains a day from Ljubljana (€1.85, 25 minutes, 20km).

Some 15 services go north to Jesenice via Kranj, Radovljica and Lesce-Bled. Up to seven of these cross the border for Villach, 87km to the north in Austria.

The train station is 2.5km northeast of the Old Town; buses run the route frequently (€0.50).

Radovljica

📍 04 / POP 5997 / ELEV 490M

The town of Radovljica (sometimes shortened to Radol'ca) is filled with charming, historic buildings and blessed with scenic views of the Alps, including Triglav. It was settled by the early Slavs, and by the 14th century had grown into an important market town centred on a large rectangular square, today's Linhartov trg, and fortified with high stone walls. Much of the original architecture, amazingly, is still standing and looks remarkably unchanged from those early days.

Radovljica has just a couple of places to stay, so it's advisable to book in advance or turn to the TIC to snag a private room. It's an easy day-trip from Bled, just 7km away.

🔘 Sights

★ **Linhartov Trg**   SQUARE

Radovljica's colourful main square is the town's leading attraction, lined with houses from the 16th century. Look especially for **Thurn Manor** (Linhartov trg 1), a baroque palace that is home to museums and school of music, and **Koman House** (Komanova Hiša; Linhartov trg 23), identified by a baroque painting of St Florian on its facade. **Mali House** (Malijeva Hiša; Linhartov trg 24) has a barely visible picture of St George slaying the dragon. **Vidič House** (Vidičeva Hiša; Linhartov trg 3) has a corner projection and is painted in red, yellow, green and blue.

At the southern end of the square, take the small street beside house number 28 to find a lovely **viewpoint** over the Lipnica valley, with information boards detailing walking tracks in the area.

★ **Beekeeping Museum**   MUSEUM

(Čebelarski Muzej; 📞 04-532 05 20; www.muzeji-radovljica.si; Linhartov trg 1; adult/child €3/2; ⊙10am-6pm Tue-Sun May-Oct, 8am-3pm Tue, Thu & Fri, 10am-noon & 3-5pm Wed, Sat & Sun Mar, Apr, Nov & Dec, 8am-3pm Tue-Fri Jan & Feb) More in-teresting than it sounds, this apiculture museum takes a closer look at the long tradition of beekeeping in Slovenia. The museum's collection of illustrated beehive panels from the 18th and 19th centuries, a folk art unique to Slovenia, is the largest in the country, and there are some rather astounding beehives in improbable shapes: (life-sized) people, a miniature mansion, even a lion. You can also observe a live beehive in action, filled with a family of indigenous Carniolan bees.

Bees are still kept in Slovenia for their honey and wax but much more lucrative are such by-products as pollen, propolis and royal jelly.

The somewhat esoteric **municipal museum** shares the building with the beekeeping museum (open the same hours; combined ticket €5/3). It tells the history of the town, especially as it relates to the life of Anton Tomaž Linhart (1756–95). Linhart was Slovenia's first dramatist and historian, and was born in Radovljica.

Šivec House   MUSEUM

(Šivčeva Hiša; 📞 04-532 05 23; www.muzeji-radovljica.si; Linhartov trg 22; adult/child €3/2; ⊙10am-1pm & 5-8pm Tue-Sun May-Oct, shorter hrs Nov-Apr) Possibly the most important house on Linhartov trg is 16th-century Šivec House, which is an interesting hybrid: Renaissance on the outside and Gothic within. On the ground floor is a vaulted hall, which now serves as a **gallery** (changing exhibitions). On the 1st floor are three restored rooms, including a **'black kitchen'** and a wood-

---

SUMMER IN RADOL'CA

Doing it's best to woo visitors away from Lake Bled, Radovljica creates a summertime program of weekly concerts and performances in Linhartov trg, plus flea markets and street festivals. Events run from late June to the start of September.

There are weekly free guided walking tours (held on Tuesday mornings in 2015, June to September), plus the introduction of a hop-on, hop-off bus circuit twice a week in July and August that take in Bled, Radovljica and small neighbouring villages. An all-day ticket on these circuits is €5.

Stop by the TIC for further info and schedules, or check online: www.radolca.si.

Radovljica

panelled, late-Gothic **drawing room** with a beamed ceiling used as a wedding hall. Our favourite feature is the 2nd-floor collection of children's book illustrations by celebrated Slovenian artists.

Curiously, there is only a charge to visit the 1st floor – if you say you're visiting the 2nd floor, it's free to enter, and you will pass the restored rooms on your way up the stairs.

Gingerbread Museum MUSEUM
(Lectarski Muzej; ☑ 04-537 48 00; www.lectar.com; Linhartov trg 2; admission €1.50; ⊙noon-10pm, closed Tue Sep-Jun) In the cellar of Gostilna Lectar is this small, super-sweet showroom, which demonstrates in living colour the particularly Slovenian art of *lectarstvo*, the making, shaping and decorating of honey dough into hearts, figures and so on. It's cute as a button, with plenty to buy.

Parish Church of St Peter CHURCH
(Župnijska Cerkev Sv Petra; Linhartov trg; ⊙7am-8pm) At the end of Linhartov trg is the Gothic Parish Church of St Peter, a hall church modelled after the one in Kranj. The three portals are flamboyant Gothic, and the sculptures inside were done by Angelo Pozzo in 1713. The building with the arcaded courtyard south of the church is the **rectory** *(župnišče)*, where exhibitions are sometimes held.

☞ Tours

18sedem3 TOUR
(☑ 031 641 481; www.facebook.com/18sedem3; Gorenjska cesta 1) From its central farmers-market foodstore, this company (the name means 1873) seeks to provide back-to-nature experiences visiting farmers and food producers in unspoilt countryside. There's a range of possibilities: visit a beekeeper, strawberry farm or herbalist. Take a guided cycle or walk with a picnic, or arrange a cooking course. Prices vary depending on tour and size of group, but begin around €40 per person.

Per-person prices are reduced if the group is larger. Even if you're not taking a tour, stop by the shop to check out the tasty produce, from apple juice to honey to cheese.

★ Festivals & Events

Chocolate Festival FOOD
(www.festival-cokolade.si; ⊙mid-Apr) Who can resist a chocolate festival? Radol'ca takes it's 'honestly sweet' slogan seriously over this

weekend in mid-April, with cooking demonstrations, tastings and kids' workshops.

Festival Radovljica
MUSIC

(www.festival-radovljica.si; ☉ Aug) The biggest event of the year is the two-week Festival Radovljica, one of the most important festivals of early classical music in Europe. Culture and music blend nicely in the town's historic setting.

🛏 Sleeping

Camping Šobec
CAMPGROUND $

(☑ 04-535 37 00; www.sobec.si; Šobčeva cesta 25, Lesce; camping per adult/child €14.50/10.70, bungalows for 2/6 €130/160; ☉ mid-Apr–Sep; P 🛜) The largest and quite possibly the best-equipped campground in Slovenia is in Lesce, about 2.5km northwest of Radovljica. Situated on a small lake near a bend of the Sava Dolinka River, the camping resort offers no end of summer activities and recreation facilities: beach, playgrounds, bike hire, swimming, fishing, guided walks. The bungalows (really timber chalets) are top quality. Note that prices listed are for the July–August peak; it's cheaper outside this period. Cyclists and backpackers get a discounted rate.

Vidic House
HOSTEL $

(Vidičeva Hiša; ☑ 031 810 767; www.vidichouse. com; Linhartov trg 3; per person €17-25; 🛜) This 400-year-old historic townhouse on the main square offers accommodation in four large, homely apartments, with postcard views over Linhartov trg. There's a kitchen in each apartment, and access to a laundry, plus a cool cafe downstairs.

★ Gostilna Lectar
PENSION $$

(☑ 04-537 48 00; www.lectar.com; Linhartov trg 2; s/d €65/99; ✿🛜) The nicest place in town, this delightful B&B on the main square has nine individually decorated rooms done up in folk motif – painted headboards and room signs made of *lect* (gingerbread) – that could have ended up kitsch but instead feel like those in a village farmhouse from the 19th century, but with modern creature comforts. Note: prices are reduced outside August.

Sport Hotel Manca
HOTEL $$

(☑ 04-531 40 51; www.manca-sp.si; Gradnikova cesta 2; s/d/q €50/68/100; P 🛜✿) This good-value small hotel is on the northern outskirts of town, about 1.5km from Linhartov trg. It offers 16 spic-and-span modern rooms and all sorts of sports facilities – from swimming pool and sauna to tennis court and bicycles for hire. Some rooms have views of the Karavanke range, others of Mt Triglav.

Vila Podvin
GUESTHOUSE $$$

(☑ 083-843 470; www.vilapodvin.si; Mošnje 1; s/d/ste €89/139/169; P ✿🛜) Not content with wowing diners with fabulous food, Vila

LAKE BLED & THE JULIAN ALPS RADOVLJICA

THE BOARDS & THE BEES

Radovljica is known throughout Slovenia as a centre for beekeeping, an integral part of Slovenian agriculture since the 16th century. Slovenians were at the forefront in developing early ways to improve beekeeping techniques, including the invention of what became known as the *kranjič* hive, with removable boxes that resembled a chest of drawers. This created multiple hives and solved an early problem of damaging an entire hive when the honeycomb was removed. It also led to the development of one of Slovenia's most important forms of folk art.

The *kranjič* hives are constructed with front boards above the entrance, and enterprising beekeepers soon began the practice of painting and decorating these panels with religious and other motifs. Radovljica's **Beekeeping Museum** (p79) has an extensive collection on display, and some of the artwork is nothing short of phenomenal.

The first panels, dating back to the mid-18th century, were painted in a 'folk baroque' style and the subjects were taken from the Old and New Testaments (Adam and Eve, the Virgin Mary, and especially patient Job, the patron of beekeepers), and history (the Turkish invasions, Napoleon, and the Counter-Reformation, with Martin Luther being driven to hell by a devil).

The painting of beehive panels in Slovenia enjoyed its golden age between about 1820 and 1880; after that the artform went into decline. The introduction of a new and much larger hive by Anton Žnidaršič at the end of the 19th century obviated the need for small illustrations, and the art degenerated into kitsch.

Podvin also has a handful of modern rooms and suites on offer, in the former stables of the Grad Podvin estate (3km east of Linhartov trg). Room are on the pricier side, but the setting is lovely and the hospitality warm.

✗ Eating

Gostilna Lectar
SLOVENIAN $$

(☑04-537 48 00; www.lectar.com; Linhartov trg 2; mains €9-16; ⊙noon-10pm, closed Tue Sep-Jun) Take your time to peruse the huge, multilingual menu of local specialities here. Some items may not immediately appeal (eg, pickled beef tongue, sausage in hog's grease), while others boast of a long family pedigree and almost demand to be sampled: the homemade *štruklji* (cheese dumplings) and *žlikrofi* (ravioli of cheese, bacon and chives), for example, and the Lectar strudel.

This main-square inn has been going strong since 1822. Book ahead on weekends or to snag a table on the back terrace with mountain views. The rustic interior is lovely in cool weather.

Gostilna Avguštin
SLOVENIAN $$

(☑04-531 41 63; Linhartov trg 15; mains €8-17; ⊙11am-11pm) The huge portions match the big welcome at this delightful central restaurant (the name is often anglicised to Augustin). It serves excellent Slovenian dishes to order and bans pizzas. Don't miss the cellar dining room, which was once part of a prison (and may have seen an execution or two), and the wonderful back terrace with views of Triglav.

★ Vila Podvin
MODERN SLOVENIAN $$$

(☑083-843 470; www.vilapodvin.si; Mošnje 1; mains €24-28; ⊙noon-10pm Tue-Sat, to 5pm Sun) Winning plaudits from diners local and foreign, this elegant establishment is 3km east of Linhartov trg, on the 14th-century Grad Podvin Estate. Kitchen creativity combines with quality local produce and some time-honoured techniques to produce meals that match the beauty of the setting. Lunch is great value (three courses for €15), as is the chef's tasting menu (four/six courses €39/59).

Gostilna Kunstelj
SLOVENIAN $$$

(☑04-531 51 78; www.kunstelj.si; Gorenjska cesta 9; mains €9-22; ⊙10am-10pm, closed Mon & Thu) There's a fresh, appealing menu at this old-time *gostilna* (from 1873), and a great summer terrace with relaxing verdant views.

Begin with an inventive salad (say, with local trout and honey), then move on to venison medallions or fried chicken. Or: how about the all-day breakfast (€12), full of local ingredients (honey, homemade bread and butter, farm-fresh eggs etc).

🍷 Drinking & Nightlife

Vidic House
CAFE

(Vidičeva Hiša; www.vidichouse.com; Linhartov trg 3; coffee €1-2; ⊙9am-10pm) The most charming of several cafes located along historic Linhartov trg, Vidic House specialises in coffee, cakes and ice cream. The cute vaulted interior is jammed with found items.

Beer Shop
BAR

(☑040 233 917; Gorenjska cesta 19a; ⊙8am-11pm) A short walk from the centre, this bar and store is a mecca for beer-lovers: it stocks almost all Slovenian craft brews, from Kamnik's Mali Grad label to the Vipava Valley's Pelicon by way of Tolmin's Reservoir Dogs – with plenty more besides.

Vinoteka Sodček
WINE BAR

(☑04-531 50 71; www.vinoteka-sodcek.si; Linhartov trg 8; ⊙9am-9pm Mon-Sat) We applaud the deal at this wine bar: for €12, you can enjoy five tastes of Slovenian wines, served with *pršut* (air-dried ham from the Karst), plus local cheese and olive oil.

❶ Information

Most conveniences for tourists, including banks and the post office, are centrally located on and around Gorenjska trg (north of Linhartov trg).

Tourist Information Centre (TIC; ☑04-531 51 12; www.radolca.si; Linhartov trg 9; ⊙9am-7pm Jun-Sep, to 4pm Oct-May) Centrally located, helps book rooms, sells good local hiking and cycling maps, rents bikes, and has a computer on hand for gratis surfing. The office also sells local souvenirs.

❶ Getting There & Away

BUS

The **bus station** (Kranjska cesta) is 400m northwest of Linhartov trg. The best place for bus schedule info is at www.alpetour.si.

Roughly half-hourly services depart for Bled (€1.80, 14 minutes, 7km) from around 5am to 11pm (hourly on weekends). Services to Ljubljana are also frequent, running half-hourly or hourly from 5am to 9pm (€5.60, one hour, 50km). There are also regular buses to Lake Bohinj (€4.70, 50 minutes, 36km) and Kranjska Gora (€5.20, 53 minutes, 41km).

THE FORMER FORGING VILLAGE OF KROPA

In the early years of the Industrial Revolution, the towns and villages around Radovljica grew wealthy through forging and metal working. While much of that activity was stilled decades ago, the custom still lives on in the pretty hillside village of Kropa (population 764), 13km southeast of Radovljica.

Kropa has been a 'workhorse' for centuries, mining iron ore and hammering out the nails and decorative wrought iron that can still be seen in many parts of Slovenia. Today, the village has turned its attention to screws – the German-owned Novi Plamen factory is based here – but artisans continue their work, clanging away in the workshop on the village's single street. The work of their forebears is evident in weather vanes, shutters and ornamental street lamps shaped like birds and dragons.

Kropa's sleepy charm lies in the town's remote feel and the lovely, centuries-old former workers' housing that lines a fast-flowing mountain stream, the Kroparica, that runs right through the centre of town.

The main sight is the Iron Forging Museum (Kovaški Muzej; ☑04-533 72 00; www. muzeji-radovljica.si; Kropa 10; adult/child €3/2; ☉10am-6pm Tue-Sun May-Oct, reduced hrs Nov-Apr), which traces the history of iron mining and forging in Kropa and nearby Kamna Gorica from the 14th to the early 20th centuries. Nail and spike manufacturing was the town's main industry for most of that period; from giant ones that held the pylons below Venice together to little studs for snow boots, Kropa produced more than 100 varieties in huge quantities.

The museum also has working models of forges, a couple of rooms showing how workers and their families lived in very cramped quarters (up to 45 people in one house) and a special exhibit devoted to the work of Jože Bertoncelj (1901–76), who turned out exquisite wrought-iron gratings, candlesticks, chandeliers and even masks.

Just across the street from the museum, pop in to the UKO Kropa forgers' workshop (☑04-533 73 00; www.uko.si; Kropa 7a; ☉8am-3pm Mon-Fri), which exhibits and sells all manner of articles made of wrought iron – from lamps and doorknobs to garden gates.

Kropa is not exactly awash with dining and lodging options, though don't miss a chance to try the traditional Slovenian cooking at Gostilna Pr' Kovač (At the Smith's; ☑04-533 63 20; Kropa 30; mains €9-16; ☉10am-11pm Tue-Sun). There's a no-pizza rule, and the menu sings with home-grown produce and local favourites like red-bean soup and pork filet. The buckwheat omelette with cheese comes recommended. Sit outside in warm weather or dine in an evocative period setting inside the 400-year-old house.

If you don't have your own car, the best way to get here is by bus from Radovljica. Up to 15 buses a day run between the towns (€2.30, 20 minutes, 13km), but not on weekends. Buses stop in front of the Mercator supermarket at the bottom of the village. The summertime (July and August) hop-on, hop-off bus visits Kropa on Tuesday, from Bled and Radovljica. Nail-forging demonstrations and free guided tours of the village coincide with the bus visits.

With your own wheels, the winding 25km drive to Kropa from Škofja Loka via Železniki is a delight. Be sure to stop at the superbly sited Jamnik Church, a five-minute walk from the road.

TRAIN

The train station is 100m below the Old Town on Cesta Svobode. International trains use the nearby station at Lesce-Bled.

Radovljica is on a main rail line linking Ljubljana (€4.28, one hour, 48km) with Jesenice (€1.85, 17 minutes, 16km) via Škofja Loka, Kranj and Lesce-Bled. Around 12 trains a day pass through the town in each direction.

Bled

☑04 / POP 5120 / ELEV 481M

Yes, it's every bit as lovely in real life. With its emerald-green lake, picture-postcard church on an islet, a medieval castle clinging to a rocky cliff and some of the highest peaks of the Julian Alps and the Karavanke as backdrops, Bled is Slovenia's most popular resort, drawing everyone from honeymooners lured by the over-the-top romantic setting to backpackers, who come for the hiking, biking, watersports and canyoning possibilities.

Not surprisingly, Bled can be overpriced and swarming with tourists in midsummer. But as is the case with many popular destinations around the world, people come in droves – and will continue to do so – because the place is so special.

History

Bled was the site of a Hallstatt settlement in the early Iron Age, but as it was far from the main trade routes, the Romans gave it short shrift. From the 7th century the early Slavs came in waves, establishing themselves at Pristava below the castle, on the tiny island and at a dozen other sites around the lake.

Around the turn of the first millennium, the German Emperor Henry II presented Bled Castle and its lands to the Bishops of Brixen in South Tyrol, who retained secular control of the area until the early 19th century when the Habsburgs took it over.

Bled's beauty and its warm waters were well known to medieval pilgrims who came to pray at the island church; the place made it into print in 1689 when Janez Vajkard Valvasor described the lake's thermal springs in *The Glory of the Duchy of Carniola*. But Bled's wealth was not fully appreciated at that time, and in the late 18th century the keeper of the castle seriously considered draining Lake Bled and using the clay to make bricks.

Fortunately, along came a Swiss doctor named Arnold Rikli, who saw the lake's full potential. In 1855 he opened baths where the casino now stands, taking advantage of the springs, the clean air and the mountain light. With the opening of the railway from Ljubljana to Tarvisio (Trbiž) in 1870, more and more guests came to Bled and the resort was a favourite of wealthy Europeans from the turn of the century right up to WWII. In fact, under the Kingdom of Serbs, Croats and Slovenes, Bled was the summer residence of the Yugoslav royal family (and later of Tito).

◎ Sights

★ Lake Bled   LAKE

(Blejsko jezero) Bled's greatest attraction is its exquisite blue-green lake, measuring just 2km by 1.4km. The lake is lovely to behold from almost any vantage point, and makes a beautiful backdrop for the 6km walk along the shore. Mild thermal springs warm the water to a swimmable 26°C (79°F) from June through August. The lake is naturally the focus of the entire town: you can rent boats, go diving or simply snap countless photos.

★ Bled Castle   CASTLE, MUSEUM

(Blejski Grad; Map p86; ☑ 04-572 97 82; www.blejski-grad.si; Grajska cesta 25; adult/child €9/4.50; ☺ 8am-9pm mid-Jun–mid-Sep, to 8pm Apr–mid-Jun & mid-Sep–Oct, to 6pm Nov-Mar) Perched atop a steep cliff more than 100m above the lake, Bled Castle is how most people imagine a medieval fortress to be, with towers, ramparts, moats and a terrace offering magnificent views. The castle houses a museum collection that traces the lake's history from earliest times to the development of Bled as a resort in the 19th century.

The castle, built on two levels, dates back to the early 11th century, although most of what stands here now is from the 16th century. For 800 years it was the seat of the Bishops of Brixen. Among the museum holdings, there's a large collection of armour and weapons, and jewellery found at the early Slav burial pits at Pristava. The smallish 16th-century Gothic chapel contains paintings of castle donor Henry II and his wife Kunigunda on either side of the main altar.

The entry price is steep. Our best tip: book a table at the excellent Castle Restaurant (p92) and admission to the castle is free.

You can reach the castle on foot via one of three trails sign-posted 'Grad'. The first trail starts from the car park behind the Bledec Hostel; the second is a tortuous path up from the Castle Baths; and the third starts just north of the Parish Church of St Martin.

★ Bled Island   ISLAND

(Blejski Otok; Map p88; www.blejskiotok.si) Tiny, tear-shaped Bled Island beckons from the shore. There's the Church of the Assumption and a small museum, but the real thrill is the ride out by *pletna* (gondola). The *pletna* will set you down on the south side at the monumental South Staircase (Južno Stopnišče), built in 1655. The staircase comprises 99 steps – a local tradition is for the husband to carry his new bride up them.

There is no charge to visit the island, except for what you pay to travel there (eg the *pletna* ride or hire of a rowboat); you are free to wander and visit the cafe and souvenir store. However, there is an admission charge to enter the church.

Church of the Assumption CHURCH
(Cerkev Marijinega Vnebovzetja; Map p88; ☑ 04-576 79 79; www.blejskiotok.si; Bled Island; adult/child €6/1; ☺ 9am-7pm May-Sep, to 6pm Apr & Oct, to 4pm Nov-Mar) The baroque Church of the Assumption dates from the 17th century, though there's been a church here since the 9th century. Go inside to see some fresco fragments from the 15th century, a large gold altar and part of the apse of a pre-Romanesque chapel. The 15th-century **belfry** contains a 'wishing bell' you can ring to ask a special favour.

The admission charge includes entry to the newly restored **Bell Tower** with pendulum clock, and to the exhibition space on the 1st floor of the **Provost's House** (Map p88; www.blejskiotok.si; Bled Island).

🏃 Activities

Adventure Sports

Several local outfits organise a wide range of outdoor activities in and around Bled, including trekking, mountaineering, rock climbing, ski touring, cross-country skiing, mountain biking, rafting, kayaking, canyoning, horse riding, paragliding and ballooning.

There's a cluster of agencies around the bus stop, while accommodation providers (especially hostels) can often book you onto their own (or affiliated) tours and activities.

★3glav Adventures ADVENTURE SPORTS
(Map p86; ☑ 041 683 184; www.3glav-adventures.com; Ljubljanska cesta 1; ☺ 9am-noon & 4-7pm mid-Apr–Sep) The number-one adventure-sport specialists in Bled for warm-weather activities. 3glav Adventures' most popular trip is the Emerald River Adventure (€75), an 11-hour hiking and swimming foray into Triglav National Park and along the Soča River that covers a huge sightseeing loop of the region (from Bled over the Vršič Pass and down the Soča Valley, with optional rafting trip).

There are loads more options. A two-day guided ascent of Mt Triglav costs €199. If you don't fancy scaling mountains, a half-day of scenic hiking/mountain biking in the national park is €65/60.

On the water, a 2½-hour rafting trip down the mild Sava Bohinjka River costs €32; on the Soča is €38 (but the latter trip starts from near Bovec). Popular canyoning trips cost €60.

The menu extends to paragliding, ballooning, diving, kayaking and horseback riding – see the website for details. They also rent bikes (per day €15).

Life Adventures ADVENTURE SPORTS
(Map p86; ☑ 040 508 853; www.lifeadventures.si; Grajska cesta 10) Offers a wide range of adventure activities, including a two-day ascent of Mt Triglav from €170. Can help put together self-guided tour itineraries for Slovenia and Croatia (walking, cycling, driving, activity-based), and has a comprehensive menu of winter-time options: backcountry skiing, snowshoeing, ice climbing, sledding etc in the Julian Alps, and even a winter Triglav ascent.

Note that you can start some of their summer day-trips from Bled or Ljubljana.

Mamut ADVENTURE SPORTS
(Map p86; ☑ 040 121 900; www.slovenija.eu.com; Cesta Svobode 4) Offers a full menu of outdoor activities (rafting, canyoning, hiking etc), plus rental of bikes and SUP boards. If Bled is your only stop in Slovenia, Mamut gives you the opportunity to explore further afield via excellent day trips: eg to Logarska Dolina; Postojna Cave and Predjama Castle; Lipica and the Škocjan Caves. Day trips start at €59 per person.

Ballooning

Balonarski Center Barje BALLOONING
(☑ 041 664 545; www.bcb.si; flight €150) Hot-air ballooning offers an incredible vantage point for taking in Bled's breathtaking early-morning peace and beauty (weather permitting, of course). Grega, the owner and balloon pilot, has flown all over the world and is trained as a meteorologist. Book direct, or easily via 3glav Adventures (p85).

Boating & Watersports

Lake Bled is open to rowboats (motorboats are banned); there are also plenty of summertime kayakers and stand-up paddleboarders (SUP) on the water. Rental agencies are in various locations, including at **Mlino waterfront** (Map p88); the **Castle Lido** (Map p86); the beach in front of **Camping Bled** (Map p88); and the lido by **Grand Hotel Toplice** (Map p86). Kayaks generally cost €7 per hour, SUPs €10, and rowboats €12 to €20.

Bled

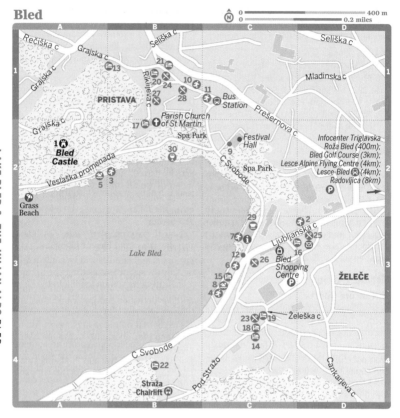

LAKE BLED & THE JULIAN ALPS BLED

Gondola Ride
BOATING

(☑ 041 427 155; www.pletnabled.com; per person return €12) Riding a piloted gondola (known as a *pletna*) out to Bled Island is the archetypal tourist experience. There is a convenient jetty just below the TIC (Map p86) and another in Mlino (Map p88) on the south shore. You get about half an hour to explore the island. In all, the trip to the island and back takes about 1¼ hours.

Diving

Diving Bled
DIVING

(Map p88; ☑ 040 422 407; www.divingbled.com; Kidričeva cesta 10c; ☺ guided shore dive from €40) If it's not enough to simply swim or boat on the lake, consider a guided dive. From their base at the beach on the western shore of Lake Bled, this company offers guided dives and diving courses from beginner to advanced (introduction to scuba diving is €60).

Fishing

Fishing is allowed on Lake Bled, provided you have a permit. The surrounding lakes and streams are rich with all manner of river fish.

Fauna
FISHING

(Map p86; ☑ 041 633 147; www.faunabled.com; Cesta Svobode 12; ☺ 8am-noon & 3-7pm Mon-Fri, 8am-noon Sat, 8-10am Sun) One-stop shopping for all your fishing needs, including guiding (on request), advice, map and gear rental. Sells fishing permits valid for a day on the lake (€25), and licences required for fishing the various local rivers.

Flying

Lesce Alpine Flying Centre
SCENIC FLIGHTS

(Alpski Letalski Center Lesce; ☑ 04-532 01 00; www.alc-lesce.si; Begunjska cesta 10) The flying centre, 4km southeast, has panoramic flights in light aircraft over Bled (€90 for three people), Bohinj (€150) and Mt Triglav (€210), or anywhere you want for €270 an hour. All prices are valid for three passengers.

Golf

Bled Golf Course
GOLF

(☑ 01-200 99 01; www.golfbled.com; Vrba 37a, Lesce; 9/18 holes €35/70) The 18-hole, par-72 Bled Golf Course, 3km east of the lake near Lesce, is Slovenia's best course and, with its dramatic mountain backdrop, one of the most beautiful in Europe. You can rent clubs and carts; bookings advised.

Hiking

There are many short and easy, signposted hikes around Bled (numbered signs correspond to numbered routes on local hiking maps; good maps are available in town for around €6).

One of the best trails is No 6 from the southwest corner of the lake. There, a steep forested path takes about 45 minutes to reach Mala Osojnica (685m), and another 20-minute walk leads to the top of Velika Osojnica (756m). The view from the top – over the lake, island and castle, with the peaks of the Karavanke in the background – is stunning, especially toward sunset. This peak is a photographer's favourite.

Skiing

Straža Bled Ski Centre
SKIING

(Map p88; ☑ 04-578 05 30; www.straza-bled.si; day pass adult/child €17/9; ☺ mid-Dec–mid-Mar) Beginners and families will be content with the tiny (6-hectare) ski centre close to town. A chairlift takes you up the hill to the 634m summit in three minutes; you'll be down the short slope in no time. Equipment is available for hire on-site.

Outside of winter, Straža is transformed into a family-friendly adventure area: there's a 520m toboggan run down the slope, and Pustolovski Park (http://pustolovski-park-bled.si), an 'adrenaline park' of ropes courses, at the summit. Both activities are pricey, though, with the chairlift and one toboggan ride costing €9/6 per adult/child; two hours at Pustolovski Park costs €20/10 per adult/child.

Swimming

Bled's warm (23°C/73°F at source) and crystal-clear water – it rates a Blue Flag (a voluntary and independent eco-label awarded to beaches around the world for their cleanliness and water quality) – makes it suitable for swimming all summer, and there are decent beaches around the lake, including a popular one near the campground (rich in activity options) and a lovely grass one on the northern side.

The public lido is excellent, and there are a couple of private lidos too, including a refined one at the Grand Hotel Toplice (Map p86; Cesta Svobode; admission €15, hotel guests free).

Castle Lido
SWIMMING

(Grajsko Kopališče; Map p86; ☑ 04-578 05 28; www.kopalisce-bled.si; Veslaška promenada 11; day

Lake Bled

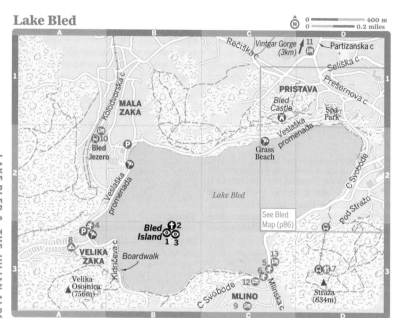

pass adult/child €7/4.50; ⊙9am-7pm Jun–mid-Sep) The popular public lido below the castle offers lake swimming behind protected enclosures as well as waterslides and other family-friendly amusements. You can rent lockers, deckchairs and umbrellas. It closes at 8pm for most of July; it's also closed on rainy days. There are slightly cheaper tickets if you arrive after noon, or after 5pm. At the lido's entrance, you can rent kayaks, SUP boards and rowboats.

☞ Tours

Tourist Train   TOUR
(Map p86; adult/child €4/2.50; ⊙9am-9pm Jun-Sep, 10am-5pm Sat & Sun May & Oct) This easy, family-friendly 45-minute twirl around the lake departs from just south of the TIC up to 20 times a day in season, making stops at a number of convenient places (Mlino, the campground, the Castle Lido).

Horse-Drawn Carriages   TOUR
(Map p86; www.fijaker-bled.si) A romantic way to experience Bled is to take a horse-drawn carriage (fijaker) from the stand near the Festival Hall, in the Spa Park. A spin around the lake costs €40, and it's the same price to the castle (an extra 30 minutes inside costs €50 total). You can even get a carriage for four to Vintgar Gorge; the two-hour return trip costs €90.

✯✯ Festivals & Events

A number of special events take place during the summer in Bled, including summertime concerts at the Festival Hall and the Parish Church of St Martin, or theatrical performances at Bled Castle. There are frequent live-music performances at lakeside venues like the Park Cafe terrace. You may like to track down the pop-up open-air yoga classes. See more details on www.bled.si/en/events.

International Rowing Regatta   SPORTS
(www.veslaska-zveza.si; ☉ mid-Jun) The biggest of a number of rowing events held on the lake.

Bled Film Festival   FILM
(http://bledff.com; ☉ mid-Jun) A new five-day festival (first held in 2014), with feature films and documentaries screened and judged.

Festival Bled   MUSIC
(www.festivalbled.com; ☉ Jul) A fortnight of concerts in beautiful venues (primarily classical music, but also jazz and other genres). Includes masterclasses with accomplished musicians, and an international viola and violin competition.

Bled Days   ARTS
(www.bled.si; ☉ Jul) Over a weekend in mid-July, plenty of concerts and an arts-and-crafts fair bring the crowds. The highlight is Bled Night on the Saturday: fireworks and spectacular illuminations of the lake.

Okarina Etno Festival   MUSIC
(www.festival-okarina.si; ☉ late Jul-Aug) A festival chock-full of great international folk and world music artists, with free concerts by the lake (and ticketed gigs in the castle).

Biathlon World Cup   SPORTS
(www.biathlon-pokljuka.com; ☉ Dec) The Pokljuka Plateau, west of Bled, is the venue for this championship of cross-country skiing and rifle shooting.

🛌 Sleeping

Bled has a wide range of accommodation – from Slovenia's original hostel to a five-star hotel in a villa that was once Tito's summer retreat. It's not advisable to arrive in July or August without a booking.

Private rooms and apartments are offered by dozens of homes in the area. Both Kompas and the TIC have lists, with prices for singles ranging from €16 to €33 and doubles €24 to €50. Apartments for two cost from €35 to €63 and for four €62 to €110.

Note that prices listed here are for peak season (July and August); there may be discounts in the quieter periods – hotel websites will list all prices. If you're driving, it's worth asking about parking options at or near your accommodation.

**★ Jazz Hostel
& Apartments**   HOSTEL, GUESTHOUSE $
(Map p88; ☏ 040 634 555; www.jazzbled.com; Prešernova cesta 68; dm €20, d without/with bathroom €50/60, apt d/q €60/85; P @ 🛜) If you don't mind being a little way (a short walk) from the action, this is a first-class budget choice. Guests rave about Jazz, mainly thanks to Jani, the superbly friendly owner who runs a sparkling, well-kitted-out complex. There are dorms (bunk-free, and with underbed storage) and colourful en-suite rooms, plus family-sized apartments with full kitchen.

Camping Bled   CAMPGROUND $
(Map p88; ☏ 04-575 20 00; www.camping-bled. com; Kidričeva cesta 10c; site per adult/child €13.40/9.38, glamping huts from €61; P @ 🛜) Bled's hugely popular, amenity-laden campground is in a rural valley at the western end of the lake, about 4km from the bus station. There's a rich array of family-friendly activities possible, and on-site are a restaurant and store.

The campground is also home to glamping possibilities: four family-sized 'mobile homes' (far nicer than they sound, with kitchen and bathroom), and a dozen cute wooden A-frame huts, some equipped with hot tubs.

Traveller's Haven   HOSTEL $
(Map p86; ☏ 041 396 545; www.travellers-haven.si; Riklijeva cesta 1; dm/d from €21/48; P 🛜) This is arguably the nicest of several hostels clustered on a hillside on the eastern shore of the lake, about 500m north of the centre. The setting is a renovated villa, with six rooms (including one double), a great kitchen and low-cost laundry and bike hire. Plus a couple of parking spots, and a supermarket across the road.

Vila Viktorija   HOSTEL $
(Map p86; ☏ 082-052 740; www.vila-viktorija.si; Cesta Svobode 27; dm €18-25, tr/q €56/84; P 🛜) In a sweet lakeside location (better placed than other hostels in town), Vila Viktorija offers old-world Bled glamour at budget prices. An 1871 villa now houses various dorm rooms (sleeping four to 12), plus a couple of

private rooms sleeping three or four. It's a well-run and sociable place with the requisite cheap breakfasts and good travel info.

Bledec Hostel   HOSTEL $

(Map p86; ☑04-574 52 50; www.bledec.si; Grajska cesta 17; dm €25-27, s/d €40/60; ℗@🛜) This well-organised HI-affiliated hostel in the shadow of the castle has 12 rooms of three to eight beds with attached bathrooms. It also has a bar, and an inexpensive restaurant (breakfast €5, dinner €10). Extra points for laundry room, and cheap bike hire.

★Old Parish House   GUESTHOUSE $$

(Map p86; ☑070 865 738; www.blejskiotok.si/hotel; Slovenski trg 3; s/d from €50/68; ℗🛜) In a privileged position, the Old Parish House (Stari Farovž) belonging to the Parish Church of St Martin has been newly transformed into a simple, welcoming guesthouse, with timber beams, hardwood floors and neutral, minimalist style. Pros include car parking, lake views, and waking to church bells.

Penzion Berc   PENSION $$

(Map p86; ☑04-574 18 38; www.penzion-berc.si; Želeška cesta 15; s €35-55, d €65-90; ℗🛜) Rooms at this snug pension are in demand, and it's not hard to see why: a quiet position a few minutes walk from town, a delightful 19th-century farmhouse aesthetic, and a garden that's home to a great restaurant.

There's also the chance to arrange small-group sightseeing trips.

Garni Hotel Berc   HOTEL $$

(Map p86; ☑04-576 56 58; www.berc-sp.si; Pod Stražo 13; s/d €55/80; ⊙Apr-Oct; ℗🛜) Not to be confused with Penzion Berc across the road, this charming 15-room place is reminiscent of a Swiss chalet, with a cosy traditional feel and lots of pine wood in its simple, appealling rooms. It's one of a great pocket of guesthouses in a quiet location above the lake. Free bikes a bonus.

Penzion Mayer   PENSION $$

(Map p86; ☑04-576 57 40; www.mayer-sp.si; Želeška cesta 7; s/d €57/82, apt from €120; ℗🛜) This flower-bedecked, 12-room inn in a renovated 19th-century house sits in a lovely garden in a quiet location above the lake. The larger apartment is in a delightful wooden cabin and the in-house restaurant (primarily for guests) is excellent.

Pletna B&B   PENSION $$

(Map p88; ☑04-574 37 02; www.pletna.com; Cesta Svobode 37, Mlino; s €45-50, d €70-75, tr €85; ℗🛜) This friendly, well-run pension with attached souvenir shop has five compact, pretty rooms facing the lake – each with balcony. It's in the hamlet of Mlino on the southern shoreline about 2km from Bled's town centre.

DON'T MISS

VINTGAR GORGE

One of the easiest and most satisfying half-day trips from Bled is to Vintgar Gorge (Soteska Vintgar; ☑031 344 053; www.vintgar.si; adult/child €4/2; ⊙8am-7pm late Apr–Oct), some 4km to the northwest of Bled village.

The highlight is a 1600m wooden walkway through the gorge, built in 1893 and continually rebuilt since. It crisscrosses the swirling Radovna River four times over rapids, waterfalls and pools before reaching 16m-high Šum Waterfall.

The entire walk is spectacular, although it can get pretty wet and slippery. There are little snack bars at the beginning and the end of the walkway; the path to view Šum Waterfall is behind the kiosk at the walkway's end.

It's an easy walk to the gorge from Bled. Head northwest on Prešernova cesta then north on Partizanska cesta to Cesta Vintgar. This will take you to Podhom, where signs show the way to the gorge entrance. To return, you can either retrace your steps or, from Šum Waterfall, walk eastward over Hom (834m) to the ancient pilgrimage Church of St Catherine (signed 'Katarina Bled'), which retains some 15th-century fortifications. From there it's due south through Zasip to Bled. Count on about three hours all in.

From June to September, a tourist bus (☑04-532 0440; www.alpetour.si; one-way €1.80-2.30) leaves Bled bus station daily at 10am and heads for Vintgar, stopping at Panorama Restaurant by Grand Hotel Toplice, Mlino, the far end of the lake (Zaka) and Bled Castle, arriving at 10.26am. It returns from Vintgar at 12.30pm. There is an additional 9am bus travelling to the gorge in July and August.

Penzion Mlino
PENSION **$$**

(Map p88; ☑04-574 14 04; www.mlino.si; Cesta Svobode 45, Mlino; s/d €55/80; ⓟ🛜) This 13-room pension, as well known for its restaurant as its accommodation, is just about as close as you'll get to the lake at this price. Decor is a little tired but the service is warm. Free bike use for guests.

★Garden Village Bled
RESORT **$$**

(Map p88; ☑083-899 220; www.gardenvillage bled.com; Cesta Gorenjskega odreda 16; pier tent €110, treehouse €290, glamping tent €340; ⊙Apr-Oct; ⓟ@🛜⛱) Garden Village embraces and executes the eco-resort concept with aplomb, taking glamping to a whole new level and delivering lashings of wow factor. Accommodation ranges from small two-person tents on piers over a trout-filled stream (shared bathroom), to family-sized treehouses and large safari-style tents. Plus there are beautiful grounds, a natural swimming pool and an organic restaurant. Superb.

Hotel Triglav Bled
BOUTIQUE HOTEL **$$$**

(Map p88; ☑04-575 26 10; www.hoteltriglav bled.si; Kolodvorska cesta 33; s/d/ste from €139/159/299; ⓟ✳@🛜⛱) This elegant 22-room hotel resides in a painstakingly restored inn dating from 1906 and enjoys delightful panoramas from its out-of-the-way location on a hill above the northern lakeshore. Its dining room (Restaurant 1906) has an esteemed reputation to match the views, while rooms feature hardwood floors, oriental carpets and antiques. There's also a wine cellar, wellness area, and polished service.

Vila Mila
APARTMENT **$$$**

(Map p86; ☑04-576 50 00; www.vila-mila.si; Grajska cesta 20; apt €90-140; ⓟ✳🛜) Six new, elegant and very spacious apartments are on offer at Vila Mila, each with living space and kitchen. There's a lovely common outdoor area with grill, and undercover parking. A fine choice.

Hotel Lovec
HOTEL **$$$**

(Map p86; ☑04-620 41 00; www.lovechotel. com; Ljubljanska cesta 6; d without/with view €140/160, ste €188; ⓟ✳@🛜⛱) This Best Western member boasts 60 of some of the most attractive hotel rooms in Bled. We love the suites (such as 402, 403 and 404) with blondwood walls, red carpet, and bath with Jacuzzi in front of a massive window facing the lake. Service is polished; the indoor pool and wellness centre is a bonus.

Grand Hotel Toplice
HOTEL **$$$**

(Map p86; ☑04-579 10 00; www.hotel-toplice. com; Cesta Svobode 12; d without/with view €200/250, ste €350; ⓟ✳@🛜⛱) With a history that goes back to the 19th century, the 87-room Toplice is Bled's 'olde worlde' five-star hotel, with attractive public areas and superb views of the lake. It's one of only two Slovenian members of Small Luxury Hotels of the World. Features include a lovely wellness area and indoor thermal pool, and a private lakeside lido (p87).

There are five more Bled hotels that are part of the Sava Hotel group, covering a range of prices and facilities – full details are online (www.sava-hotels-resorts.com/en/bled).

🍴 Eating

Slaščičarna Šmon
CAFE **$**

(Map p86; ☑04-574 16 16; www.smon.si; Grajska cesta 3; kremna rezina €2.70; ⊙7.30am-10pm) Bled's culinary speciality is the delicious *kremna rezina*, also known as the *kremšnita*: it's a layer of vanilla custard topped with whipped cream and sandwiched between two layers of flaky pastry. While Šmon patisserie may not be its place of birth, it remains the best place in which to try it – retro decor and all.

Park Restaurant & Cafe
CAFE

(Map p86; ☑04-579 18 18; Cesta Svobode 10; kremna rezina €3.50; ⊙9am-10pm) The Park Cafe has a huge terrace and a commanding position over the lake's eastern end – it's a good spot for coffee and *kremna rezina*. The cafe is said to be the place where the cake was first created – as well as the original recipe, you can now try variants with fruit or chocolate.

Pizzeria Rustika
PIZZA **$**

(Map p86; ☑04-576 89 00; www.pizzeria-rustika.com; Riklijeva cesta 13; pizza €7-11; ⊙noon-11pm) The best pizza in town is conveniently located on the same hill as many of Bled's hostels. A cool terrace, ample topping options, and home delivery offered too.

Ostarija Peglez'n
SEAFOOD **$$**

(Map p86; ☑04-574 42 18; Cesta Svobode 19a; mains €9-23; ⊙noon-10.30pm) Fish is the main game at the lovely, central 'Iron Inn'. Enjoy the cute retro decor with lots of antiques and curios, and choose from a tempting menu of trout from local rivers, John Dory from the Adriatic coast, and a host of calamari, seafood pasta and fish soup options. Meaty mains and veggie options also offered.

Grajska Plaža
SLOVENIAN $$

(Map p86; ☑031 813 886; www.grajska-plaza. com; Veslaška promenada 11; mains €8-20; ☺9am-11pm May–mid-Oct) Even the locals say that dining at this place feels like a summer holiday. It's built on a terrace over the Castle Lido and has a relaxed vibe, helpful service and an easy all-day menu that stretches from morning coffee to end-of-day cocktails. Meal options like grilled trout or octopus salad are generous and tasty.

Gostilna Murka
SLOVENIAN $$

(Map p86; ☑04-574 33 40; www.gostilna-murka. com; Riklijeva cesta 9; mains €9-19; ☺10am-10pm Mon-Fri, noon-11pm Sat & Sun) This traditional eatery set within a large, leafy garden may at first appear a bit theme-park-ish – but the food is super-authentic (lots of old-school national dishes) and the welcome warm. Offers good-value lunch specials for around €5.

Penzion Mlino
SLOVENIAN $$

(Map p88; ☑04-574 14 04; www.mlino.si; Cesta Svobode 45; mains €9-24; ☺noon-11pm) A good choice along the quieter southern strip of the lake. The restaurant is known for trout and game dishes (including venison, wild boar and duck), and the fish or meat platters for two are enormous. Never fear – there are a few veg-friendly options too.

★ Finefood – Penzion Berc
SLOVENIAN $$$

(Map p86; ☑04-574 18 38; www.penzion-berc.si; Želeška cesta 15; mains €16-30; ☺5-11pm late Apr-late Oct) In a magical garden setting, Penzion Berc sets up a summertime restaurant, with local produce served fresh from its open kitchen. Try sea bass with asparagus soufflé, homemade pasta with fresh black truffle, deer entrecote or Black Angus steak. Finefood's reputation for high-class flavour and atmosphere is growing: book ahead.

★ Castle Restaurant
MODERN SLOVENIAN $$$

(Map p86; ☑04-620 34 44; www.jezersek.si/ en/bled-castle-restaurant; Grajska cesta 61; mains €15-25; ☺11am-10pm) It's hard to fault the superb location of the castle's restaurant, with a terrace and views straight from a postcard. What a relief the food is as good as it is: black risotto with octopus, lake trout fillet, veal fillet with tarragon dumplings. Book in advance to score a table with a view – note: with a reservation, you don't pay to enter the castle.

Okarina
INTERNATIONAL $$$

(Map p86; ☑04-574 14 58; www.okarina.com; Ljubljanska cesta 8; mains €10-22; ☺noon-3pm & 6-11pm Mon-Fri, noon-midnight Sat & Sun; ☑) Expect a mixed bag of international flavours from this colourful, upmarket restaurant. The menu wanders from local classics (trout amandine, grilled calamari) to pastas and Balkan grilled meats. The most interesting section of the menu features a cuisine not often seen in Slovenia: Indian (including favourites like chicken masala and rogan josh). There's a top choice of vegetarian dishes too.

🍷 Drinking & Nightlife

Pub Bled
PUB

(Map p86; Cesta Svobode 19a; ☺9am-1am Sun-Thu, to 3am Fri & Sat) The pick of the town's pubs, this friendly place sits above the Oštarija Peglez'n restaurant and has great cocktails and, on some nights, a DJ.

Vila Prešeren
CAFE, BAR

(Map p86; ☑04-575 25 10; www.vilapreseren. si; Veslaška promenada 14; ☺8am-midnight) A consummate all-rounder, this glamorous cafe-bar-restaurant-guesthouse sits in pole position on the lakeside promenade, with a huge terrace that's designed for people (and lake) watching. It morphs from coffees to cocktails and has a crowd-pleasing menu that helpfully flags dishes that bring you a taste of Bled, Slovenia or 'Ex Yu' (Yugoslavian).

ℹ Orientation

'Bled' refers both to the lake and to the settlements around it, particularly the built-up area to the northeast where most of the hotels are located.

Bled's main road, Ljubljanska cesta, runs eastward from here. Footpaths and a busy road called Cesta Svobode (when south of the lake), Kidričeva cesta (to the southwest) and Veslaška promenade (to the northwest and north) circle the lake.

ℹ Information

Online, good sources of info include Lake Bled News (www.lakebled.com) and In Your Pocket (www.inyourpocket.com/bled).

Gorenjska Banka (Cesta Svobode 15) Just north of the Park Hotel.

Infocenter Triglavska Roža Bled (☑04-578 02 05; www.tnp.si; Ljubljanska cesta 27; ☺8am-6pm mid-Apr–mid-Oct, to 4pm mid-Oct–mid-Apr) An excellent info centre for Bled and the entire region, with maps, guides and displays on Triglav National Park. Free exhibitions, plus an on-site cafe and gift shop. Worth a stop.

Kompas (☑ 04-572 75 01; www.kompas-bled. si; Bled Shopping Centre, Ljubljanska cesta 4; ⊗ 8am-7pm Mon-Sat, 9am-2pm Sun) Helpful, full-service travel agency offering sightseeing tours to Bohinj, Radovljica and Ljubljana (among other destinations), plus airport transfers and transport, guiding, and bike and ski rental. Also arranges good-value accommodation in private homes and apartments throughout the region.

SKB Banka (Ljubljanska cesta 4) In the Bled Shopping Centre.

Tourist Information Centre (Map p86; ☑ 04-574 11 22; www.bled.si; ⊗ 8am-9pm Mon-Sat, 9am-5pm Sun Jul & Aug, reduced hrs Sep-Jun) Occupies a small office behind the Casino at Cesta Svobode 10; sells maps and souvenirs, rents bikes and has internet access. It's open year-round: until at least 6pm Monday to Friday, to 3pm Sunday.

❶ Getting There & Away

BUS

Bled is well connected by bus; the **bus station** (Map p86; Cesta svobode 4) is a hub of activity at the lake's northeast. **Alpetour** (☑ 04-532 04 45; www.alpetour.si) runs most of the bus connections around Gorenjska, so check its website for schedules.

Popular services:

Kranjska Gora (€4.70, 50 minutes, 40km, up to 12 daily) Note: these buses depart from Lesce-Bled train station, not from Bled.

Lake Bohinj (€3.60, 37 minutes, 29km, up to 12 daily)

Lesce-Bled train station (€1.30, nine minutes, 5km, up to five an hour)

Ljubljana (€6.30, 80–90 minutes, 57km, up to 15 daily)

Radovljica (€1.80, 14 minutes, 7km, at least half-hourly)

Check out the hop-on, hop-off bus circuit that runs in the area in July and August – twice a week (Tuesdays and Thursdays in 2015) the circuit takes in Bled, Radovljica and small neighbouring villages. On Saturday and Sunday it runs from Bled to Bohinj and includes a number of villages and national-park destinations on its route. Stop by any of the TICs in the region for further info and schedules.

TRAIN

Bled has two train stations, though neither one is close to the centre.

Lesce-Bled station, 4km east of Bled township on the road to Radovljica. It's on the rail line linking Ljubljana with Jesenice and Austria.

Trains to/from Ljubljana (€5.08 to €6.88, 40 minutes to one hour, 51km, up to 20 daily) travel via Škofja Loka, Kranj and Radovljica. Buses connect the station with Bled.

Bled Jezero station, on Kolodvorska cesta northwest of the lake. Trains to Bohinjska Bistrica (€1.85, 20 minutes, 18km, seven daily), from where you can catch a bus to Lake Bohinj, use this smaller station. You can travel on this line further south to Most na Soči and Nova Gorica.

❶ Getting Around

You can order a local taxi on ☑ 041 710 747 or ☑ 031 205 611. Bikes can be rented from various accommodation providers and tour agencies for around €12 to €15 per day.

Car parking in Bled is in short supply, and is expensive (€2 an hour in some locations, charged from 8am to 8pm, with a maximum stay of two hours). It's a good idea to leave your car at your accommodation (if it has free parking) and walk, cycle or take the wee tourist train to get around.

There's free parking at the castle, and usually spaces available in the large parking lot behind Hotel Krim, off Ljubljanska cesta (€2 an hour, maximum four hours). Further out, there is unrestricted parking in a lot behind the Infocenter Triglavska Roža Bled (€5 for 24 hours).

Bohinj

☑ 04 / POP 5146 / ELEV 542M

Many visitors to Slovenia say they've never seen a more beautiful lake than Bled…that is, until they've seen Lake Bohinj, just 26km to the southwest. We'll refrain from weighing in on the Bled versus Bohinj debate other than to say we see their point.

Admittedly, Bohinj lacks Bled's glamour, but it's less crowded and in many ways more authentic. It's an ideal summer holiday destination. People come primarily to chill out or to swim in the crystal-clear, blue-green water, with leisurely cycling and walking trails to occupy them. There are lots of outdoor pursuits like kayaking, hiking and horseback riding if you've got the energy, and the charming villages to the lake's northeast, remarkably, have remained faithful to traditional occupations like dairy herding and farming.

◉ Sights

★**Church of St John the Baptist**   CHURCH
(Cerkev Sv Janeza Krstnika; Ribčev Laz; ⊗ 10am-6pm mid-Jun–mid-Sep) This postcard-worthy church, at the head of the lake and right

by the stone bridge, is what every medieval church should be: small, surrounded by natural beauty, and full of exquisite frescoes. The nave is Romanesque, but the Gothic presbytery dates from about 1440. Many walls and ceilings are covered with 15th- and 16th-century frescoes.

As you face the arch from the nave, look for the frescoes on either side gorily depicting the beheading of the church's patron saint. On the opposite side of the arch, to the left, is Abel making his offering to God and, to the right, Cain with his inferior one. Upon the shoulder of history's first murderer sits a white devil – a rare symbol. Behind you on the lower walls of the presbytery are rows of angels, some with vampire-like teeth; look for the three men above them singing. They have goitres, once a common affliction in mountainous regions due to the lack of iodine in the diet. The carved wooden head of St John the Baptist on the side altar to the right dates from 1380.

Hours are limited outside of summer and bigger holidays like Easter and New Year – enquire at the TIC.

★ **Savica Waterfall** WATERFALL
(Slap Savica; Ukanc; adult/child €2.50/1.30; ⊙ 8am-8pm Jul & Aug, 9am-7pm Apr-Jun, 9am-5pm Sep-Nov) The magnificent Savica Waterfall, which cuts deep into a gorge 78m below, is 4km from Ukanc and can be reached by a walking path from there in 1½ to two hours. By car, you can continue past Ukanc via a sealed road to a carpark beside the Savica restaurant, from where it's a 20-minute walk up more than 500 steps and over rapids and streams to the falls. Wear decent shoes for the slippery path.

Opening hours may vary depending on weather conditions; the falls may be open in winter if weather permits – ask at the TIC.

Vogel MOUNTAIN
(📞 04-572 97 12; www.vogel.si; cable-car return adult/child €13.50/9; ⊙ cable car 7.30am-7pm) The glorious setting and spectacular panoramas make it worth a trip up Vogel – during winter, when it's a popular ski resort (p96), but also in its 'green season', when walks and photo ops abound. The cable car operates from Ukanc – the base station is at 569m, the top station at 1535m.

Alpine Dairy Farming Museum MUSEUM
(Planšarski Muzej; 📞 04-577 01 56 04-577 01 56; www.bohinj.si; Stara Fužina 181; adult/child €2.60/2.10; ⊙ 11am-7pm Tue-Sun Jul & Aug, 10am-noon & 4-6pm Tue-Sun Sep, Oct & Jan-Jun, closed Nov & Dec) This museum in Stara Fužina, 1.5km north of Ribčev Laz, has a small collection related to Alpine dairy farming – look for it behind Gostilna Mihovc. The four rooms of the museum – once a cheese dairy itself – contain a mock-up of a mid-19th-century herder's cottage, old photographs, cheese presses, wooden butter moulds, copper vats, enormous snowshoes and sledges, and wonderful hand-carved shepherds' crooks.

Until the late 1950s, large quantities of cheese were still being made on 28 highland pastures, but a modern dairy in nearby Srednja Vas does it all now.

Oplen House MUSEUM
(Oplenova Hiša; 📞 04-572 35 22; www.bohinj.si; Studor 16; adult/child €2.60/2.10; ⊙ 11am-7pm Tue-Sun Jul & Aug, 10am-noon & 4-6pm Tue-Sun Sep, Oct & Jan-Jun, closed Nov & Dec) The hamlet of Studor, about 3.5km from Ribčev Laz, is home to Oplen House – a typical old peasant's cottage with a chimney-less 'black kitchen' that has been turned into a museum focusing on the domestic life of peasants in the Bohinj area.

Studor's real claims to fame are its many toplarji, the photogenic, double-linked hayracks with barns or storage areas at the top. Look for the ones at the entrance to the village; they date from the 18th and 19th centuries.

🏃 Activities

Adventure Sports

There are exhilarating pursuits available, including canyoning, caving, and paragliding from the top of Vogel, among others. Two Bohinj companies, Alpinsport and PAC Sports, specialise in these activities and offer broadly similar programs and prices, plus lots of activity-gear rental. Both companies offer guides for hiking and mountaineering, and a menu of winter activities (skiing, snowshoeing, ice climbing).

Expect to pay the following: canyoning (from €49 to €79, depending on the length and difficulty), tandem paraglider flight (€90 to €130), and caving (€85). Check the websites for details.

Alpinsport ADVENTURE SPORTS
(📞 041 596 079, 04-572 34 86; www.alpinsport.si; Ribčev Laz 53; ⊙ 9am-8pm) Rents equipment: canoes, kayaks, SUPs and bikes in summer,

Lake Bohinj

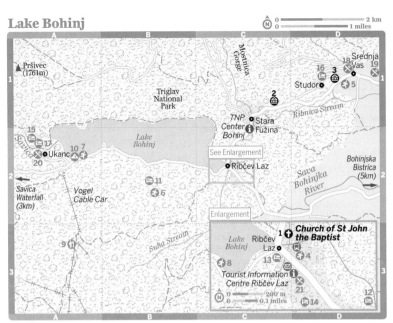

skis and snowboards in winter. It also operates guided rafting and canyoning trips. Its base is opposite Hotel Jezero in Ribčev Laz.

PAC Sports   ADVENTURE SPORTS
(☑04-572 34 61; www.pac-sports.com; Hostel Pod Voglom, Ribčev Laz 60; ⊙8am-10pm Jun-Sep, to 8pm Oct-May) Popular sports and adventure company, based in Hostel Pod Voglom, 2km west of Ribčev Laz; also has a summertime lakeside kiosk at Camp Zlatorog (p98). Rents bikes, canoes, SUPs and kayaks, and operates guided canyoning, rafting and caving trips. In winter, they rent sleds and offer ice climbing and snowshoeing.

Boating

Summertime boating is popular on the lake. Both Alpinsport and PAC Sports rent kayaks, canoes and SUP boards (you're looking at from €5 to €9 per hour, with hourly prices decreasing the longer you rent; Alpinsport is cheaper).

Both companies also offer guided rafting and canoeing trips on Lake Bohinj and along the Sava Bohinjka River – PAC Sports has the most options in this category. Prices start at around €29 per person, including equipment, guide and transfers. Expect relatively mild rapids in June and a slower pace by August.

🛈 GET YOUR BEARINGS IN BOHINJ

Lake Bohinj, 4.5km long, 1200m wide and up to 45m deep, lies in a valley basin on the southern edge of Triglav National Park.

There is no town called Bohinj; the name refers to the entire valley, its settlements and the lake (in Slovenian, Bohinjsko Jezero). The largest town is Bohinjska Bistrica (population 1750), 6km east of the lake.

At the lake, Ribčev Laz is the main hub, where you can find everything of a practical nature. Ukanc is a smaller hamlet on the lake's southwest shore. To the northeast is a string of idyllic villages, many with rooms for rent: Stara Fužina, Studor and Srednja Vas. There are no settlements on the lake's northern side.

Tourist Boat BOATING

(Turistična Ladja; ☎ 04-574 75 90; www.tourist-boat.eu; one-way adult/child/family €9/6.50/19, return €10.50/7.50/24; ◷ Apr-Oct) An easy family-friendly sail from Ribčev Laz to Camp Zlatorog in Ukanc (and back). It's worth checking the timetable online – from June to August, boats depart Ribčev Laz at 80-minute intervals from 9.30am to 5.30pm.

Cycling

Lake Bohinj is perfect for cyclists of all skill sets – in fine weather, cycling is the best way to get around. There's a well-marked 11km asphalt cycling route running along the river from Bohinjska Bistrica to Stara Fužina, which then continues to Studor and Srednja Vas. The route from Ribčev Laz west to Savica is also relatively flat and easy.

For anyone looking for more adventure, there is a summertime mountain-bike park at Vogel (www.vogel.si/summer). PAC Sports (p95) has mountain-biking tours from €20.

From the TICs, pick up the free *Cycling Routes* map, which illustrates routes and their difficulty level. You can rent bikes from both Alpinsport (p94) and PAC Sports (half day/whole day around €11/14).

Fishing

Lake Bohinj is home to lake trout and char, and the jade-coloured Sava Bohinjka river, which starts at the stone bridge in front of the church in Ribčev Laz, is rich in brown trout and grayling. You can buy fishing licences (lake €25, river as far as Bitnje for catch/catch and release €60/42) valid for a day from the TICs and some hotels. The season runs from March to late October.

Hiking

Lake Bohinj is an ideal destination for hiking and walking. A good easy walk around the lake (12km) from Ribčev Laz should take between three and four hours. Otherwise you could just do parts of it by following the hunters' trail in the forest above the south shore of the lake to Ukanc and taking the bus back, or walking along the more tranquil northern shore under the cliffs of Pršivec (1761m).

Another excellent hike is the two-hour walk north from Stara Fužina through the Mostnica Gorge to the **Mostnica Waterfalls** (Mostniški Slapovi), which rival Savica Waterfall after heavy rain.

For recreational hikers, a recommended map is the *Bohinj Hiking Trails* map, outlining 22 marked trails and a handful of cycling routes (€5.50 from the TICs).

There are several day hikes and longer treks that set out from Vogel. Experienced hikers might try the ascent up to Vogel (1922m) from the cable car's upper station. Take a map and compass. The whole trip should take about four hours.

Horse Riding

Mrcina Ranč HORSE RIDING

(☎ 041 790 297; www.ranc-mrcina.com; Studor; 1/4hr €22/55) Pretty Mrcina Ranč in Studor offers a range of guided tours on horseback through unspoiled countryside. Tours can last from one to seven hours; in spring and autumn overnight trips are possible. Tours are on sturdy Icelandic horses, and kids can be catered to. Bookings are required.

Skiing

Vogel Ski Centre SKIING

(☎ 04-572 97 12; www.vogel.si; day pass adult/child €29/16; ◷ mid-Dec–Apr) Vogel Ski Centre lies 1540m above the lake's southwestern corner and is accessible by cable car form Ukanc. With skiing up to 1800m, the season can be long, sometimes from late November to the start of May. Vogel has 22km of ski runs.

Swimming

Lake Bohinj's chilly waters warm to a swimmable 22°C (72°F) in July and August. Swimming is not restricted and you can enter the water from any point on shore, though there are decent, small beaches on both the northern and southern shores. Some beaches on the northern shore are reserved for naturists.

Aquapark Bohinj WATER PARK
(Vodni Park Bohinj; ☎082-004 080; www.vodni-park-bohinj.si; Triglavska cesta 17, Bohinjska Bistrica; pools adult/child 3hr €12.70/8; ⏰9am-9pm) This water park is open year-round and overflows with indoor and outdoor pools, slides and play areas, as well as saunas, steam rooms, and fitness and wellness centres. If you're travelling with kids, it can be a lifesaver in winter or a rainy-day treat in summer. It's located in Bohinjska Bistrica, next to the Bohinj Park Hotel.

Festivals & Events

International Wildflower Festival BOTANICAL
(www.bohinj.si/alpskocvetje; ⏰late-May–early Jun) Held over two weeks, this festival celebrates Bohinj's botanical riches and includes guided walks and tours, birdwatching, traditional craft markets and concerts.

Cows' Ball FOLK TRADITIONS
(Kravji Bal; www.bohinj-info.com/en; ⏰mid-Sep) The Cows' Ball is a wacky weekend of folk dance, music, eating and drinking to mark the return of the cows from their high pastures to the valleys. It shares the weekend celebrations with a cheese and wine festival.

Hiking Festival HIKING
(www.bohinj.si/pohodnistvo; ⏰Sep-Oct) A month-long program that celebrates the great outdoors, with guided walks and hikes as well as more adventurous activities like dry canyoning and nighttime hiking and canoeing.

Sleeping & Eating

The TICs can arrange accommodation in the region: private rooms (€14 to €20 per person), plus apartments and holiday houses. Apartments for two/six in summer start at €48/116. Prices vary with season, quality and location. The website www.bohinj.si has more details.

Many of the better restaurants are out of Ribčev Laz, and require a modest hike, or a car or a bike to reach them. There's a **Mercator** (Ribčev Laz 49; ⏰7am-8pm Mon-Sat, to 5pm Sun) supermarket next to the TIC in Ribčev Laz.

Ribčev Laz

Hostel Pod Voglom HOSTEL $
(☎04-572 34 61; www.hostel-podvoglom.com; Ribčev Laz 60; dm €16-18, r per person €19-27; P@🛜) Bohinj's lively, well-run hostel, 1.5km west of Ribčev Laz on the road to Ukanc, is a hive of activity – and a hub for activities. There are big grounds, and 130 beds in two buildings: the 'hostel' building has rooms and dorms (maximum four beds), all with shared facilities; rooms in the annex have private bathrooms.

Note: there's no kitchen, but cheap dinners (€9) are available. Guests get discounts with PAC Sports (p95), which is based here. The hotel is popular with sports groups and school groups.

★**Hotel Kristal** HOTEL $$
(☎04-577 82 00; www.hotel-kristal-slovenia.com; Ribčev Laz 4a; half-board per person €48-70; P🛜) There's a great energy at Kristal, thanks in large part to the super-friendly management, walls filled with original artwork, and an Ayurvedic wellness centre and yoga room (plus appealing massage pavilion in the garden). Add some simple, classy guestrooms and a quality restaurant and you can't go wrong. It's about 800m from the lakeshore.

Hotel Gasperin HOTEL $$
(☎041 540 805; www.gasperin-bohinj.com; Ribčev Laz 36a; d €70-104; P❄@🛜) This spotless chalet-style hotel is 350m southeast of the Ribčev Laz TIC and run by a friendly British-Slovenian couple who offer loads of local info and insight (including bike hire). Most of the 24 rooms and apartments have balconies; apartments have cooking facilities. The (cheaper) upper-storey rooms can get hot in summer, but each has air-con.

Hotel Jezero HOTEL $$$
(☎04-572 91 00; www.hotel-jezero.si; Ribčev Laz 51; s/d €78/136; P@🛜🏊) The largest lakeside hotel, the 76-room Jezero offers decent if characterless rooms, plus an indoor swimming pool and fitness centre. Staff are friendly and there are two on-site restaurants, but more interesting options lie elsewhere.

Hotel Kristal Restaurant SLOVENIAN $$
(☎04-577 8200; www.hotel-kristal-slovenia.com; Ribčev Laz 4a; mains €10-22) A number of Bohinj hotels offer half-board, and eating options aren't especially memorable. Happily, this polished hotel restaurant bucks

the trend, with a menu of interesting local flavours: brook trout with asparagus, grilled calamari with saffron risotto, wild game (stag fillet, smoked goose breast). Bookings advised.

Ukanc

★Camp Zlatorog — CAMPGROUND $
(☑059-923 648; www.camp-bohinj.si; Ukanc 5; per person €10-15; ☺May-Sep; ℗🐾) This tree-filled campground can accommodate up to 750 guests and sits photogenically on the lake's southwestern corner, 5km from Ribčev Laz. Prices vary according to site location, with the most expensive (and desirable) sites right on the lake. Facilities are very good – including restaurant, laundry and watersport rentals, and the tourist boat docks here. Tents can be hired.

Pension Stare — PENSION $$
(☑040 558 669; www.bohinj-hotel.com; Ukanc 128; s/d €48/76; ℗🐾) This sweet 10-room pension is on the Savica River in Ukanc, surrounded by a large, peaceful garden. If you really want to get away from it all without having to climb mountains, this is your place. Rooms are no-frills; there's a half-board option, too. The owner has an adjacent three-bedroom villa that sleeps eight in comfort – weekly bookings are preferred in high season (see www.rent-villa-slovenia.com).

★Vila Park — BOUTIQUE HOTEL $$$
(☑04-572 3300; www.vila-park.si; Ukanc 129; d €100-120; ℗🐾) Vila Park creates a great first impression, with sunloungers set in expansive riverside grounds, and balconies overflowing with flowers. The interior is equally impressive, with eight elegant rooms plus a handsome lounge and dining area. Note: it's a kid-free zone.

Gostišče Erlah — SLOVENIAN $$
(☑04-572 33 09; www.erlah.com; Ukanc 67; mains €8-18; ☺11am-10pm) Local trout is king at this relaxed eatery, and it comes perfectly prepared: smoked, grilled or *en brochette* (skewered). There's a rustic, timber-lined terrace, and families will be happy with the kids playground right next door. Rooms are also available.

Northeast Villages

★Rustic House 13 — PENSION $$
(Hiša 13; ☑031 466 707; www.studor13.si; Studor 13; d/q €70/110; ℗🐾) Cosy and rustic down

to the last detail (from the wooden balcony to the garden area), Rustic House gives you a delightful taste of village life. It's owned by an Australian-Slovenian couple and houses two super suites that each sleep up to four. There's a shared kitchen and lounge – admire Andy's photos of the surrounds (he also offers photography tours).

Note: there's a three-night minimum in summer.

Gostilna Rupa — SLOVENIAN $$
(☑04-572 34 01; www.gostilna-rupa.si; Srednja Vas 87; mains €8-21; ☺11am-10pm, kitchen closes 9pm) If you're under your own steam, head for this country-style restaurant at the eastern edge of Srednja Vas. Among the excellent home-cooked dishes are *ajdova krapi*, crescent-shaped dumplings made from buckwheat and cheese, various types of local *klobasa* (sausage) and Bohinj trout.

Gostilna Pri Hrvatu — SLOVENIAN $$
(☑04-572 36 70; Srednja Vas 76; mains €6-15; ☺8am-midnight) Get an eyeful of mountain views from the sweet creek-side terrace of this relaxed inn in Srednja Vas. Flavourful homemade dishes include buckwheat dumplings, polenta with porcini, local chamois in piquant sauce, and grilled trout.

Bohinjska Bistrica

Bohinj Park Hotel — HOTEL $$$
(☑082-004 000; www.bohinj-park-hotel.si; Triglavska cesta 17, Bohinjska Bistrica; per person from €88; ℗❄@🐾🏊) We might not have chosen this modern, high-rise 102-room hotel at first glance – located in Bohinjska Bistrica it's a full 6km from Lake Bohinj. But it's a green, eco-minded hotel, it has an excellent in-house restaurant (named 2864, after Triglav's height), there's bowling and a small cinema, and Aquapark Bohinj (p97) is at the back door and included in the price.

★Štrud'l — SLOVENIAN $
(☑041 541 877; www.strudl.si; Triglavska cesta 23; mains €6-12; ☺7am-10pm) This modern take on traditional farmhouse cooking is a must for foodies keen to sample local specialities. Overlook the incongruous location in the centre of Bohinjska Bistrica, and enjoy dishes like *ričet s klobaso* (barley porridge with sausage and beans).

The *hišni krožnik* (house plate) is a hearty sampling of native flavours, including ham, sausage, mashed beans and sauerkraut, potato mash, and cooked buckwheat.

ZLATOROG & HIS GOLDEN HORNS

The oft-told tale of Zlatorog, the mythical chamois (*gams* in Slovene) with the golden horns who lived on Mt Triglav and guarded its treasure, almost always involves some superhuman (or, in this case, super-antelopine) feat that drastically changed the face of the mountain. But don't let Slovenes convince you that their ancient ancestors passed on the tale.

The Zlatorog story first appeared in the *Laibacher Zeitung* (*Ljubljana Gazette*) in 1868 during a period of Romanticism and national awakening. It tells of how the chamois created the Triglav Lakes Valley, a wilderness of tumbled rock almost in the centre of Triglav National Park.

Zlatorog roamed the valley (at that time a beautiful garden) with the White Ladies, good fairies who kept the mountain pastures green and helped humans whenever they found them in need.

Meanwhile, down in the Soča Valley near Trenta, a plot was being hatched. It seemed that an innkeeper's daughter had been given jewels by a wealthy merchant from Venice. The girl's mother demanded that her daughter's suitor, a poor but skilled hunter, match the treasure with Zlatorog's gold hidden under Mt Bogatin and guarded by a multi-headed serpent. If not, he was at least to bring back a bunch of Triglav roses to prove his fidelity. This being mid-winter, it was an impossible task.

The young hunter, seething with jealousy, climbed the mountain in search of the chamois, figuring that if he were to get even a piece of the golden horns, the treasure of Bogatin – and his beloved – would be his. At last the young man spotted Zlatorog, took aim and fired. It was a direct hit.

The blood gushing from Zlatorog's wound melted the snow, and up sprang a magical Triglav rose. The dying chamois nibbled on a few petals and – presto! – was instantly back on his feet. As the chamois leapt away, roses sprang up from under his hooves, luring the hunter onto higher and higher ground. But as they climbed, the sun caught Zlatorog's golden horns. The glint blinded the hunter, he lost his footing and plunged into a gorge.

The once kind and trusting Zlatorog was enraged that a mere mortal would treat him in such a manner. In his fury he gored his way through the Triglav Lakes Valley, leaving it much as it looks today. He left the area with the White Ladies, never to return.

And the fate of the others? The innkeeper's daughter waited in vain for her lover to return home. As spring approached, the snow began to melt, swelling the Soča River. One day it brought her a sad gift: the body of her young swain, his lifeless hand still clutching a Triglav rose. As for the innkeeper's rapacious wife, we know nothing.

Observant (and thirsty) travellers will see the face of Zlatorog everywhere they go in Slovenia. It's on the label of the country's most popular beer.

ℹ Information

MONEY

There's an ATM in Ribčev Laz, next to the tourist office. **Gorenjska Banka** (Trg Svobode 2b, Bohinjska Bistrica) is next to the post office.

POST

Post Office Ribčev Laz (Ribčev Laz 47)
Post Office Bohinjska Bistrica (Trg Svobode 2, Bohinjska Bistrica)

TOURIST INFORMATION

There are two main tourist information centres in the Bohinj area. The office in **Ribčev Laz** is closer to the lake and handier for most visitors than the office in **Bohinjska Bistrica**. Both have a wealth of free material, sell souvenirs and local food products, book rooms in private homes, and offer free internet.

Both offices sell the **Bohinj Guest Card** (www.bohinj.si; adult/family €15/20), which entitles the holder to free parking in the lake area and free bus rides, along with discounts at local businesses.

The newest additon is the **national park centre**, which is well worth a stop.

Tourist Information Centre Bohinjska Bistrica (TIC; ☑ 04-574 75 90; www.bohinj.si; Triglavska cesta 30, Bohinjska Bistrica; ⊙7am-5pm Mon-Fri, 9am-5pm Sat & Sun Jul & Aug, 7am-3pm Mon-Fri, 9am-1pm Sat, 9am-noon Sun Sep-Jun)

Tourist Information Centre Ribčev Laz (TIC; ☑ 04-574 60 10; www.bohinj-info.com; Ribčev Laz 48; ⊙8am-8pm Mon-Sat, 8am-6pm Sun

ⓘ MOTORAIL

Driving around Slovenia and short on time? If your itinerary takes in Bled or Bohinj, and you then want to head west but can't spare the time to drive up and over the Vršič Pass – consider taking the *autovlak* (motorail, ie a train that carries cars too).

The *autovlak* runs south of Bohinjska Bistrica via a rail tunnel under the mountains, and is the only direct option to the Soča Valley.

From Bohinjska Bistrica, four trains run daily to Podbrdo (€9.10 for car and driver, 10 minutes, 7km) and two or three to Most na Soči (€14, 35 minutes, 28km). Bikes and motorbikes can also be transported. Find more info on the Slovenian Railways website (www.slo-zeleznice.si – search 'motorail' on the site).

Jul & Aug, 8am-6pm Mon-Sat, 9am-3pm Sun Sep-Jun)

TNP Center Bohinj (☑ 04-578 0245; www.tnp.si; Stara Fužina 37-38; ⊘ 8am-5pm Jul-Aug, 10am-3pm Mon-Fri, to 5pm Sat & Sun Sep-Jun) A brand-new national park info centre about 1km north of the Church of St John the Baptist, full of exhibits, maps and books, and a lovely Room With A View. There's a summer program of free events that includes talks, walks and stargazing. You can also arrange a trekking guide here, or a guide for an ascent of Mt Triglav.

ⓘ Getting There & Away

BUS

The easiest way to get to Lake Bohinj is by bus – services run frequently from Ljubljana, via Bled and Bohinjska Bistrica. **Alpetour** (☑ 04-532 04 45; www.alpetour.si) is the major bus operator for the region.

Services from Lake Bohinj (departing from Ribčev Laz, near the TIC):

Bled (€3.60, 40 minutes, 29km, up to 12 daily)
Bohinjska Bistrica (€1.80, eight minutes, 7km, up to 20 daily)
Ljubljana (€8.30, two hours, 86km, up to nine daily)

TRAIN

Bohinjska Bistrica station is the closest you can get to the lake by train.

Several trains daily make the run to Bohinjska Bistrica from Ljubljana (€7.17, two hours, six daily), though this route requires a change in

Jesenice. There are also trains between Bled's small Bled Jezero station and Bohinjska Bistrica (€1.85, 20 minutes, 18km, seven daily).

From Bohinjska Bistrica, passenger trains to Nova Gorica (€5.80, 1¼ hours, 61km, up to eight a day) make use of a century-old, 6.3km tunnel under the mountains that provides the only direct option for reaching the Soča Valley.

ⓘ Getting Around

In July and August there is a bus loop linking Bohinjska Bistrica with the lake via the villages of Stara Fužina, Studor and Srednja Vas, and another loop from Ribčev Laz west to Ukanc, the Vogel cable car and Savica waterfall (sample fare: Ribčev Laz to Savica €1.80). A timetable is posted at the bus stops, or ask at the TICs.

It's generally necessary to pay for car parking in popular spots around the lake (€1.50 per hour). Buy a Bohinj Guest Card (which includes parking and local buses) if you plan to stay a few days. Or better – leave your car at your accommodation and walk or cycle.

Triglav National Park

☑ 04, 05 / ELEV UP TO 2864M

Triglav National Park (Triglavski Narodni Park; commonly abbreviated as TNP), with an area of 840 sq km (over 4% of Slovenian territory), is one of the largest national reserves in Europe. It is a pristine, visually spectacular world of rocky mountains – the centrepiece of which is Mt Triglav (2864m), the country's highest peak – as well as river gorges, ravines, lakes, canyons, caves, rivers, waterfalls, forests and Alpine meadows.

History

Although Slovenia counts three large regional parks and 44 smaller country (or 'landscape') parks, TNP is the country's only gazetted national park, and it includes almost all of the Alps lying within Slovenia. The idea of a park was first mooted in 1908 and realised in 1924, when 1600 hectares of the Triglav Lakes Valley were put under temporary protection. The area was renamed Triglav National Park in 1961 and expanded 20 years later to include most of the eastern Julian Alps.

Today the park stretches from Kranjska Gora in the north to Tolmin in the south and from the Italian border in the west almost to Bled in the east. The bulk of the park lies in Gorenjska administrative region, but once you've crossed the awesome Vršič Pass – at 1611m, Slovenia's highest – and begun the descent into the Soča Valley, you've entered Primorska.

◉ Sights

Mt Triglav   MOUNTAIN

The 2864m limestone peak called Triglav (Three Heads) has been a source of inspiration and an object of devotion for Slovenes for more than a millennium – it even appears on the country's flag. The early Slavs believed the mountain to be the home of a three-headed deity who ruled the sky, the earth and the underworld.

No one managed to reach the summit until 1778, when an Austrian mountaineer and his three Slovenian guides climbed it from Bohinj. For Slovenes under the Habsburgs in the 19th century, the 'pilgrimage' to Triglav became, in effect, a confirmation of one's ethnic identity, and this tradition continues to this day: a Slovene is expected to climb Triglav at least once in his or her life.

Pokljuka Plateau   NATURE RESERVE

Close to Bled, the forests and meadows of the Pokljuka Plateau offer plenty of walking trails and winter-sports facilities. While Vintgar Gorge (p90) gets all the limelight, the 2km-long Pokljuka Gorge (Pokljuška Soteska) is also impressive, and sees far fewer visitors. Access is possible by bus from Bled to Krnica. Note that Pokljuka is the favoured departure point for ascents of Triglav.

ⓘ Orientation

It's easy to enjoy TNP from one of countless hubs – the biggest include Bled, Bohinj, Kranjska Gora and Trenta (in Gorenjska region), and Bovec, Kobarid and Tolmin (in the Soča Valley). One of the most spectacular – and easy – trips to get you to the heart of TNP is to follow the paved road over the Vršič Pass.

These hubs offer natural features you can visit (waterfalls, gorges etc), and activities that grant you access to the park's natural beauty: hiking, mountain biking, skiing, fishing, rafting, swimming. Marked trails in the park lead to countless peaks and summits besides Mt Triglav, but it's not only about climbing mountains. There are easy hikes through beautiful valleys, forests and meadows, too.

ⓘ Information

Information centres Regular tourist information centres have loads of information, brochures and maps, and there are dedicated TNP info centres at **Bled** (p92), **Stara Fužina** (p100) in Bohinj, and **Trenta** (p108) on the Vršič Pass. These info centres have great displays on park flora and fauna and are well worth a stop. They have a good program of activities in summer (including guided walks), and can put you in touch with mountain guides.

Websites and apps Good starting points are www.tnp.com and www.slovenian-alps.com. There is a free app named 'Julius Guide' with coverage of TNP.

Maps Several good hiking maps are available from tourist information centres. Two good options: the laminated 1:50,000-scale *Triglavski Narodni Park* (€9; buy online from http://shop.pzs.si) from the Alpine Association of Slovenia (PZS), and Kartografija's widely available 1:50,000-scale *Triglavski Narodni Park* (€8; www.kartografija.si).

Books *The Julian Alps of Slovenia* (Cicerone; www.cicerone.co.uk) by Justi Carey and Roy Clark outlines 58 mountain walks and short treks. Includes high-mountain routes.

Kranjska Gora

🎵 04 / POP 1556 / ELEV 806M

Nestling in the Sava Dolinka Valley some 40km northwest of Bled, Kranjska Gora (Carniolan Mountain) is among Slovenia's largest and best-equipped ski resorts. It's at its most perfect under a blanket of snow, but its surroundings – nudging both the Austrian and Italian borders – are wonderful to explore at other times too. There are endless possibilities for hiking, cycling and mountaineering in Triglav National Park, which is right on the town's doorstep to the south, and few travellers will be unimpressed by a trip over Vršič Pass, the gateway to the Soča Valley.

◉ Sights

Liznjek House   MUSEUM

(Liznjekova Domačija; www.gmj.si; Borovška cesta 63; adult/child €2.50/1.70; ◷10am-6pm Tue-Sat, to 5pm Sun) The endearing late-18th-century Liznjek House contains a good collection of traditional household objects and furnishings peculiar to this area. Among the various exhibits are some excellent examples of trousseau chests covered in folk paintings, some 19th-century icons painted on glass and a collection of linen tablecloths (the valley was famed for its flax and its weaving).

Antique carriages and a sled are kept in the massive barn out the back, which once housed food stores as well as pigs and sheep. The stable reserved for cows below the main building now contains a memorial room dedicated to the life and work of Josip

Julian Alps & Triglav National Park

Vandot (1884–1944). Vandot was a writer born in Kranjska Gora who penned the saga of Kekec, the do-gooder shepherd boy who, together with his little playmate Mojca and his trusty dog Volkec, battles the evil poacher and kidnapper Bedanec. It's still a favourite story among Slovenian kids and has been made into several popular films.

★ **Zelenci**　　　　　　　　NATURE RESERVE
About 5km west of Kranjska Gora, signed just off the main road, is this idyllic nature reserve. It's the perfect leg-stretcher, with a short path to a turquoise-coloured lake that

is the source of the Sava Dolinka River. You can easily walk here in about two hours on a path from Kranjska Gora via Podkoren and on to Rateče. These Alpine villages are notable for their medieval churches, rustic wooden houses and traditional hayracks.

Slovenian Alpine Museum　　MUSEUM
(Slovenski Planinski Muzej; ☑ 083-806 730; www. planinskimuzej.si; Triglavska cesta 49, Mojstrana; adult/child €6/3.60; ☉ 9am-7pm Jun–mid-Sep, to 5pm mid-Sep–May) The town of Mojstrana, the starting point for the northern approaches to Triglav, lies about 15km south of

AUSTRIA

0 — 10 km
0 — 5 miles

Mojstrana
Slovenian Alpine Museum

Jesenice

Pokljuka Plateau

See Lake Bled Map (p88)

Lake Bled · Bled

Bohinjska Bela

Bohinjska Bistrica · Sava Bohinjka

Avtovlak (Rail Tunnel)

Podbrdo

Kranjska Gora. Here you'll find this pricey but nicely designed museum, celebrating the history, importance and beloved pastime of mountain exploration in Slovenia.

🏃 Activities

Skiing

Skiing is Kranjska Gora's bread and butter and the resort can get very crowded in January and February. The season usually lasts from mid-December to early March.

There are a number of ski schools and ski-rental outlets – a good source of information is the website www.kranjska-gora.si.

Kranjska Gora Ski Centre   SKIING

(RTC Žičnice; ☑ 04-580 94 00; www.kr-gora.si; Borovška cesta 103a; day pass adult/child €31.50/20; ☉ Dec-Mar) Kranjska Gora's main ski area is just five minutes' walk from the centre of town. The slopes of Vitranc mountain run for several kilometres west to Podkoren and Planica, making effectively one big piste. All up, there are 18 slopes of varying technical difficulty, at altitudes of 800m to 1215m. There's also 40km of cross-country trails, and a fun park for snowboarders.

Planica Ski-Jump Centre   SKI JUMPING

(☑ 04-588 70 60; www.planica.si; Planica) The gorgeous Planica Valley, 6km west of Kranjska Gora, is renowned for ski jumping and its newly enlarged facilities host frequent competitions (open to spectators) – including the annual Ski Jumping World Cup held in mid-March. Check the website for ticketing info.

Hiking

The area around Kranjska Gora and into Triglav National Park is excellent for hikes and walks, ranging from the very easy to the difficult. Before heading out, buy the 1:30,000-scale *Kranjska Gora* hiking map published by LTO Kranjska Gora and available at the TIC for €6.50 – it details 20 walking routes and 15 cycling tracks.

There's a well-marked trail from Planica to the Category II, 50-bed mountain hut, **Planinski dom Tamar** (Dom v Tamarju; ☑ 04-587 60 55; www.pzs.si; per person €8-20) at 1108m in the Tamar Valley – reserve ahead. The one-hour walk here from the Planica Ski-Jump Centre is spectacular, and lies in the shadow of Mojstrovka (2332m) to the east and Jalovec (2645m) to the south. From the hut, the Vršič Pass is about three hours away on foot.

Cycling

In recent years, Kranjska Gora has evolved into one of the country's leading centres for mountain biking and alpine downhilling, the kind of extreme riding where you take your bike up on a chairlift and race downhill.

There are plenty of easier, family-friendly rides as well. The 1:30,000-scale *Kranjska Gora* map (€6.50) marks out 15 cycling routes of varying difficulty. Most of the ski-rental outfits hire out bikes in summer; expect to pay €10 to €15 for a full-day rental.

Bike Park Kranjska Gora   MOUNTAIN BIKING

(☑ 041 706 786; www.bike-park.si; Borovška cesta 107; day pass €22; ☉ 9am-5pm daily Jun-Aug,

ℹ CLIMBING MT TRIGLAV

Patriotic locals – and curious tourists – are naturally drawn to Triglav's 2864m-high peak. And despite the fact that on a fine summer's day hundreds of people will reach the summit, Triglav is not for the unfit or faint-hearted. In fact, its popularity is one of the main sources of danger. On the final approach to the top, there are often scores of people clambering along a rocky, knife-edge ridge in both directions, trying to pass each other.

If you are relatively fit and confident, have a good head for heights, and have the right equipment, then by all means go for it. However, we *strongly* recommend hiring a guide, even if you have some mountain-climbing experience. A local guide will know the trails and conditions, and can prove invaluable in helping to arrange sleeping space in mountain huts and trailhead transport. Guides can be hired through **activity operators in Bled or Bohinj** (p85), or via the TNP info centres or the Alpine Association of Slovenia (Planinska Zveza Slovenije or PZS; http://en.pzs.si).

The prime time to climb is from early July (or when the snow melts) to mid-October (or before the snow comes); the best months are August and September. Most people allow two days for the trip, one day up and one down.

It bears stressing: never underestimate the extremes of mountain weather. The list of items to take reflects common sense: quality boots, warm clothes, hat, gloves, rain gear, sun protection, map, compass, whistle, head torch, first-aid kit, and emergency food and drink.

Huts are operated by different Alpine clubs, but a comprehensive list is published on the website of the Alpine Association of Slovenia, with contact details and access information. Expect to pay around €20 for a bed.

There are many ways to reach the peak, with the most popular approaches coming from the south, either starting from Pokljuka, near Bled, or from near Lake Bohinj. You can also climb Mt Triglav from the north and the east (Mojstrana and the Vrata Valley). All of the approaches offer varying degrees of difficulty (differing in altitude and length of ascent) and have their pros and cons.

Fri-Sun May, Sep & Oct) On the central slopes of Vitranc, this park is a mecca for mountain bikers – a chairlift takes you up the hill and you descend on trails of varying difficulty. The park offers rental of bikes and protective gear, plus guided and shuttle tours into the surrounding mountains.

🛏 Sleeping

Accommodation demand (and prices) peak from December to March and in midsummer. There are a number of large chain hotels but these are generally pricey and uninspiring; there are some real gems to uncover in the smaller, family-run places.

The Kranjska Gora TIC books private rooms (per person €15 to €23) and apartments (for two €39 to €50, for four €67 to €95), with prices depending on size, quality and time of year.

⭐ **Natura Eco Camp**   CAMPGROUND **$**
(📞 064 121 966; www.naturaecocamp.si; camping adult/child €13/7, safari tent €95, tree tent €65; ☉ Jun-Sep; 🅿) 🪷 This back-to-nature site

some 600m north of the highway (signposted) sits in a green glade and is as close to paradise as we've been for a while. Pitch a tent or stay in one of the safari tents or the unique tree tents (great teardrop pods suspended from branches, with mattresses on a platform inside).

⭐ **Pr' Gavedarjo**   B&B **$$**
(📞 031 479 087; http://prgavedarjo.si; Podkoren 72; s €45-75, d €80-140; 🅿 🛜) There's a lot to love about the new incarnation of this century-old homestead, especially the clever design and fun decor that celebrates Slovenian heritage and melds old with new in each of its five guestrooms. Added bonus: its location on a pretty village square in Podkoren, about 3km west of Kranjska Gora.

Youth Hostel Barovc   HOSTEL **$$**
(📞 04-582 04 00; http://hostel-barovc.com; Naselje Ivana Krivca 22; s/d/tr €32/56/78; 🅿 🛜) Head south out of town (on the Vršič Pass) and you'll see a sign for this lovely new option, with fresh, simple rooms (all with bathroom), great service, a budget-friendly

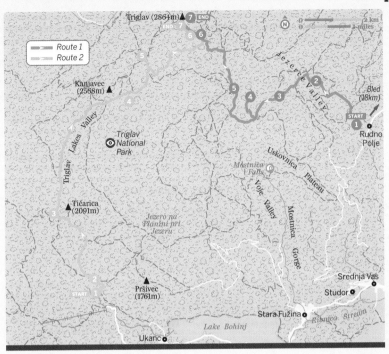

🏃 Walking Tour
Mt Triglav: Reaching the Summit

START LAKE BLED (ROUTE 1)
LENGTH TWO DAYS

The shortest (and considered to be the easiest) ascent of Mt Triglav starts from ① **Rudno Polje** (1347m) on the Pokljuka Plateau, 18km southwest of Bled. An experienced climber could do this in under 12 hours out and back, but most mortals choose to stay overnight.

The route follows a well-marked trail under ② **Viševnik** (2050m) and over the ③ **Studor Saddle** (1892m), before contouring around the slopes of ④ **Tosc** (2275m). Three hours of hiking brings you to the ⑤ **Vodnikov Dom na Velem Polju** mountain hut, at 1817m. You can sleep here, or continue another two hours to the ⑥ **Dom Planika pod Triglavom** at 2401m (book ahead to stay as it gets full). From here, it's an hour and a half of steep climbing and scrambling along the summit ridge, grabbing hold of metal spikes and grips, to the ⑦ **summit of Triglav.**

START LAKE BOHINJ (ROUTE 2)
LENGTH THREE DAYS

Approaching from Bohinj is longer and involves more ascent than from the north, but it's more gently graded. It's often used for descent. Start near ① **Savica Waterfall**, at the western end of Lake Bohinj. It's a lovely route, with vistas of the Triglav Lakes Valley. The path zigzags up steep and tricky ② **Komarča Crag** (1340m). A helmet is recommended due to the risk of falling stones. Four hours north of Savica is ③ **Koča pri Triglavskih Jezerih** (1685m), at the southern end of the Triglav Lakes Valley, where you spend the first night. For views over the valley, climb to Tičarica (2091m) to the northeast (about an hour).

Day two, hike north along the valley, then northeast to the ④ **Hribarice Plateau** (2358m). Descend to the Dolič Saddle (2164m) and the ⑤ **Koča na Doliču hut** at 2151m. Stay here or carry on to ⑥ **Dom Planika pod Triglavom**, about two hours northeast. From here it's another hour and a half of steep climbing to the ⑦ **top of Triglav.**

restaurant and a terrace with views over the pretty Jasna Lake area. It's a 15-minute walk from the town centre.

Hotel Kotnik   HOTEL $$

(☑041 671 980; www.hotel-kotnik.si; Borovška cesta 75; s €55-70, d €70-90; P🛜) This charming, bright-yellow, flower-adorned hotel sits plumb in the heart of town. It has 15 cosy rooms, a great restaurant and pizzeria downstairs, and bikes for hire.

Hotel Miklič   HOTEL $$

(☑04-588 16 35; www.hotelmiklic.com; Vitranška ulica 13; s €58-66, d €86-1116; 🛜) There's warm, personalised service at this pristine 17-room hotel south of the centre. Most of the rooms are large, with living space, and families are well accommodated (there's a kids' playroom). Half-board is possible at the high-quality on-site restaurant.

Penzion Lipa   PENSION $$

(☑04-582 00 00; www.penzion-lipa.si; Koroška cesta 14; s €45-72, d €60-96; P🛜) Decor and facilities at this 10-room pension are hotel-standard, especially in the classy superior rooms. Downstairs is a popular restaurant-pizzeria and light-filled conservatory dining room. It's right by where the buses stop.

Skipass Hotel   BOUTIQUE HOTEL $$$

(☑04-582 10 00; www.skipasshotel.si; Koroška ulica 14c; r €120-170; P🛜) This is a stylish new addition to the town's offerings: a 10-room boutique hotel with Scandi-chic, timber-lined rooms. It's run by Skipass Travel Agency and has an excellent restaurant on-site.

✗ Eating

Gostilna Pri Martinu   SLOVENIAN $

(☑04-582 03 00; Borovška cesta 61; mains €5-16; ⊗10am-11pm; 🛜) Ask a local where to eat and they'll invariably suggest here: it's an atmospheric tavern-restaurant with a country farmhouse vibe, and you will certainly not leave hungry. Dishes are old-school (house specialities include roast pork, beef goulash and sausage with sauerkraut) and portions are huge.

★ Skipass Hotel Restaurant   INTERNATIONAL $$

(☑04-582 10 00; www.skipasshotel.si; Borovška cesta 14c; mains €15-21; ⊗5-10pm Mon-Fri, 1-10pm Sat & Sun) At the most upmarket dining option in town, the geometric timber feature above the bar creates a fresh first impression, and the menu follows its lead. It's an appealling combination of influences from across the nearby Italian and Austrian borders, the food given a local twist and sharp presentation. The three/five-course chef's menu is €28/45. It's generally open for lunch in ski season, too.

Hotel Kotnik   SLOVENIAN $$

(☑041 204 408; www.hotel-kotnik.si; Borovška cesta 75; mains €9-20) Behind it's cute sunshine facade, central Kotnik does double duty at mealtimes: there's a smart, linen-napkin restaurant doing a nice line in steak and fish dishes, and an adjoining pizzeria (pizzas €5.50-8) with a wood-burning stove, for the best pies in town.

Penzion Lipa   SLOVENIAN $$

(☑04-582 00 00; www.penzion-lipa.si; Koroška cesta 14; mains €8-20; ⊗11am-11pm) Hedging its bets with a range of cheaper pastas and pizzas plus some upmarket main dishes (oven-baked octopus, beefsteak with black truffles), this attractive restaurant has something on the menu to please most diners and budgets.

🍷 Drinking & Nightlife

Sport Point Café   CAFE

(☑04-588 4892; www.sport-point.si; Borovška cesta 93a; ⊗7.30am-5pm Mon-Thu, to 8pm Fri-Sun) This convenient spot on the main drag is a good place to relax over coffee and pastry and plan the day's events.

Vopa Pub   PUB

(☑041 502 908; Borovška cesta 92; ⊗7am-1am Sun-Thu, to 5am Sat & Sun) This bar near the post office is practically the only place in town with a pulse after 10pm. The ground-floor pub operates year round, while a club of the same name downstairs is the place to go during the ski season. Count on DJs and a pretty lively aprés-ski scene on weekends.

ℹ Information

Most facilities for visitors, including banks, post office and supermarket, are in a cluster around central Borovška cesta, west of the TIC.

Skipass Travel (☑04-582 1000; www.skipasstravel.si; Borovška cesta 14c; ⊗7.30am-5pm Mon-Fri, to noon Sat & Sun) A full-service travel agency that offers ski instruction and equipment rental as well as airport transfers and special skiing excursions to nearby Italy and Austria. Based at **Skipass Hotel** (p106).

Tourist Information Centre (TIC; ☑04-580 94 40; www.kranjska-gora.si; Kolodvorska ulica 1c; ⊗8am-8pm Jun-Sep, to 6pm Oct-May)

ℹ️ Getting There & Away

The closest train station is in Jesenice, 23km southeast of Kranjska Gora. Buses are your best option; these are run by **Alpetour** (☑04-201 32 15; www.alpetour.si); the main bus stop is on Koroška ulica.

Popular bus routes:

Bled (€5.20, 64 minutes, 43km) Only two direct services daily – however, there are hourly buses to Lesce-Bled train station (€4.70, 50 minutes, 40km).

Jesenice (€3.10, 28 minutes, 23km, hourly).

Ljubljana (€8.70, two hours, 91km, up to nine daily).

Vršič Pass Alpetour runs buses to Bovec (€6.70, one hour 40 minutes, 46km) via Trenta (€4.70, 70 minutes, 25km) from late June through August. Check the website for timetables; there are five or six departures daily.

In July and August (and weekends in September), a big red **tourist bus** runs a loop through the villages of the Upper Sava Valley, from Mojstrana to Podkoren and Rateče, with brief stops for photos at Planica and Zelenci; the aim is a hop-on, hop-off bus but it doesn't quite run often enough. Still, if you are without your own wheels, it's worth investigating (day ticket €9). Ask at the TIC for the schedule and map.

Vršič Pass

Just a couple of kilometres from Kranjska Gora is one of the road-engineering marvels of the 20th century: a breakneck, Alpine road that connects Kranjska Gora with Bovec, 50km to the southwest. The trip involves no fewer than 50 pulse-quickening hairpin turns and dramatic vistas as you cross the Vršič Pass at 1611m.

The road was commissioned during WWI by Germany and Austria-Hungary in their epic struggle with Italy. Much of the hard labour was done by Russian prisoners of war, and for that reason, the road from Kranjska Gora to the top of the pass is now called the Ruska cesta (Russian Road).

The road over the pass is usually open from May to October and is easiest to navigate by car, motorbike or bus (in summer, buses between Kranjska Gora and Bovec use this road). It is also possible – and increasingly popular – to cycle it.

When the mountain pass is closed, you can travel between Kranjska Gora and Bovec via Tarvisio in Italy and the Predel mountain pass (also spectacular). The road from Bovec to Trenta is usually open year-round.

🔘 Sights

Jasna Lake LAKE

(Jezero Jasna) Jasna Lake lies just south of Kranjska Gora and if you're heading over the Vršič Pass it's the first spot of interest. It's a small, blue glacial lake with white sand around its rim and the little Pivnica River flowing alongside. Standing guard is a bronze statue of **Zlatorog** (p99). The lake is a popular recreation area; there's a pocket of accommodation on the hill above.

Vršič Pass MOUNTAIN PASS

(Prelaz Vršič) Sitting at a view-enhanced elevation of 1611m, this mountain pass is about 13km southwest of Kranjska Gora, via a storied road that zigzags madly and passes numerous sites of interest as it climbs. From the pass itself, the peak-tastic views take in **Mojstrovka** (2332m) to the west and **Prisojnik/Prisank** (2547m) to the east; to the south the valley of the **Soča River** points the way to western Slovenia.

From Kranjska Gora, as the road reaches just over 1100m you come to the beautiful wooden **Russian Chapel** (Ruska kapelica), erected on the site where more than 300 Russian POWs were buried in an avalanche in March 1916. From here the climb begins in earnest as the road meanders past a couple of huts and corkscrews up the next few kilometres to the pass itself.

From here, a hair-raising descent of about 10km ends just short of a **monument to Dr Julius Kugy** (1858–1944), a pioneer climber and writer whose books eulogise the beauty of the Julian Alps.

The road continues to the settlements of Trenta and Soča, 8km downstream. The activity hub of Bovec is 12km west of Soča. En route, the narrow **Lepena Valley** is well worth a detour, for accommodation, splendid vistas and a range of walks.

Alpinum Juliana GARDENS

(☑01-241 09 40; www.pms-lj.si/juliana/en; Trenta; adult/child €3/2; ⊗8.30am-6.30pm May-Sep) About 600 different plant species prosper in this botanical garden, established in 1926. Most of them are Alpine species, but because of the relatively low altitude, quite a few Karst species can also be found.

Trenta VILLAGE

The elongated mountain village of Trenta (elevation 620m) is the main settlement along the road over the Vršič Pass. The lower section, Spodnja Trenta (Lower Trenta), is home to the Triglav National Park Information Centre (p108). In the same building you'll find the **Trenta Museum** (☑05-388 93 30; www.tnp.si; adult/child €5/3.50; ☉9am-7pm Jul-Aug, 10am-6pm May, Jun, Sep & Oct, 10am-2pm Mon-Fri Jan-Apr, closed Nov-Dec), which focuses on the park's geology and natural history.

🏃 Activities

Source of the Soča
WALKING
(Izvir Soče) From close to the monument to Dr Julius Kugy on the road over the Vršič Pass, a side road takes you about 1.3km to a simple mountain lodge (named Koča pri Izviru Soče, with beds and food), and from here you can take a 15-minute walk along the first part of the Soča Trail to the source of the Soča River.

Fed by an underground lake, the infant river bursts from a dark cave before dropping 15m to the rocky bed from where it begins its long journey to the Adriatic.

Soča Trail
WALKING
(Soška Pot; www.soca-trenta.si) The Soča Trail extends 20km along the turquoise Soča River, from its source west as far as the edge of Triglav National Park at Kršovec. From here, a trail known as the **Bovec Walking Trail** continues to Bovec. All up, it's a marked, five-hour, easy walking trail, with scenic highlights including the footbridges that cross the river at several points.

😴 Sleeping

Campgrounds abound, especially west of Trenta. There are also several mountain huts on or near the Vršič road, all of which offer beds and basic meals. Expect to pay €15 to €20 per person for a bunk. Most are open from May through September.

Camp Korita
CAMPGROUND $
(☑051 645 677; www.camp-korita.com; Soča 38; campsite per adult/child €10/6, glamping per person €16-25; ☉May-Sep; 🅿) A great riverside spot in Soča, Korita has a smorgasbord of camping options: regular pitches, plus fab glamping options like wooden A-frame huts, or tents under wooden shelters. You can even choose a sleeping hammock strung between trees. There are more standard mattresses on the floor of the 'hostel', and a couple of old bungalows.

Tičarjev Dom na Vršiču
MOUNTAIN HUT $
(☑04-586 60 70, 051 634 571; www.pdjesenice-drustvo.si; elev 1620m, Trenta 85; per person €18-26; ☉mid-May-mid-Sep; 🅿) This category-II cyclists' and hikers' haven has 60 beds and sits right on the pass itself. It also has a popular restaurant serving basic meals

★ Kekčeva Domačija
GUESTHOUSE $$$
(Kekec Homestead; ☑041 413 087; www.kekceva-domacija.si; Trenta 76; per person €65; 🅿 ♨) The enchanting Kekčeva Domačija, off the main road and 700m past the source of the Soča, has rooms named after characters in the Kekec children's tales (the eponymous movie was filmed nearby in 1951). It's a delightful spot, with fabulous food (€80 delivers half-board). There are lovely walks, views, and even a small rockpool for cooling off.

★ Pristava Lepena
RESORT $$$
(☑05-388 99 00, 041 671 981; www.pristava-lepena.com; Lepena 2; per person €61-69; ☉mid-May-mid-Oct; 🅿 🛜 ♨) This positively idyllic 'hotel village' is set in an Alpine meadow above the Lepena Valley. It's a small collection of rustic houses and rooms, run by a charming Slovenian-Uruguayan couple. In a beautiful setting, there's a pool, high-quality restaurant (open to all), sauna and tennis court, and fishing and horse-riding opportunities.

ℹ️ Information

Triglav National Park Information Centre (Dom Trenta; ☑05-388 93 30; Trenta; ☉9am-7pm Jul-Aug, 10am-6pm May, Jun, Sep & Oct, 10am-2pm Mon-Fri Jan-Apr, closed Nov-Dec) Displays, maps and information on the park, and the region. On-site is the **Trenta Museum** (p108). There's accommodation upstairs (apartments from €54), a simple restaurant next door, and a grocery store across the road.

ℹ️ Getting There & Away

From late June through August, **Alpetour** (☑04 201 31 30; www.alpetour.si) runs buses in both directions over the pass, connecting Kranskja Gora and Bovec (€6.70, one hour 40 minutes, 46km) via Trenta. Check the website for timetables; there are five or six departures daily. Buses stop at most of the major landmarks and accommodation on the route.

Western Slovenia & the Soča Valley

Best Places to Stay

➡ Dobra Vila (p113)

➡ Adrenaline Check Eco Place (p112)

➡ Majerija (p120)

➡ Nebesa (p115)

➡ Hotel Kendov Dvorec (p124)

Best Places to Eat

➡ Hiša Franko (p116)

➡ Topli Val (p116)

➡ Majerija (p120)

➡ Faladur (p121)

➡ Gostilna Pri Lojzetu (p121)

Why Go?

Rivers don't come much more scenic than the Soča (pronounced so-cha). This aquamarine-coloured watercourse threads through the Soča Valley (Dolina Soče) from its source in the Julian Alps and gives rise to a smorgasbord of sights like gorges and waterfalls. Loads of activities get travellers up close to the natural splendour from busy centres like Bovec and Kobarid, where tour operators help adrenaline-seekers ride river rapids or paraglide from hillsides. But it doesn't have to be all high action: cycling and walking trails get you out among stunning panoramas.

As ever in this pocket-sized country, there's more to explore behind the scenes. There's rich history to delve into – particularly relating to WWI, when millions of troops fought on the mountainous battlefront here. Tucked away east of the Soča is a Unesco-recognised mercury-mining town, and small regions like Goriška Brda and the Vipava Valley enchant with idyllic landscapes and long wine-making traditions.

When to Go

Bovec

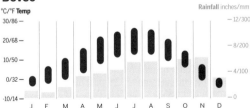

Feb–Mar See Cerkno's fascinating Laufarija Mardi Gras in the run-up to Lent.

May–Jun Meltwater swells the Soča River for the most dramatic white-water rafting.

Sep–Oct The grape harvest – ideal for wine and food touring in Goriška Brda and the Vipava Valley.

Western Slovenia & the Soča Valley Highlights

1 Marvel over the exquisite green waters of the **Soča River** (p111) while rafting or kayaking on them.

2 Take one of the area's loveliest short walks to **Kozjak Waterfall** (p114) in Kobarid.

3 Tour the idyllic, under-the-radar villages and vineyards of **Goriška Brda** (p119).

4 Dine superbly and get a lesson in indigenous wine varieties in the **Vipava Valley**. (p120).

5 Push your limits with activities like canyoning or hydrospeeding from **Bovec** (p111).

6 Check out World Heritage–listed history in **Idrija** (p122),

followed by a plate of *žlikrofi* (ravioli-like pasta pockets).

7 Wonder over the human spirit at Cerkno's **Franja Partisan Hospital** (p125).

8 Stretch your legs and admire the views at **Most na Soči** (p117).

SOČA VALLEY

Bovec

📍 05 / POP 1593 / ELEV 456M

Soča Valley's de-facto capital, Bovec offers plenty for adventure-sports enthusiasts. With the Julian Alps above, the Soča River below and Triglav National Park (p100) all around, you could spend a week here rafting, hiking, kayaking, mountain biking and, in winter, skiing, without ever doing the same thing twice.

History

The area around Bovec is first mentioned in documents dating back to the 11th century, but in the modern era it has seen a lot of destruction. On two occasions Napoleon's army attacked Austria from here, and much of the town was destroyed in the fighting around the Soča Valley during WWI. It was rebuilt in the 1920s, but then suffered again as a result of severe earthquakes in 1976 and 1998.

◉ Sights

Boka Waterfall   WATERFALL
(Slap Boka) With a sheer vertical drop of 106m (and a second drop of 30m), Boka is the highest waterfall in Slovenia – and it's especially stunning in the spring, when snowmelt gives it extra oomph. It's 5.5km southwest of Bovec – you can drive or cycle to the area and park by the bridge, then walk about 15 minutes to the viewpoint.

Alternatively, take a walk from town: follow the relatively easy B2 marked path via the village of Plužna and the Virje waterfall, or the more difficult S1 on the *Bovec z Okolico* (Bovec and Surrounds) map.

Kluže Fortress   CASTLE
(Trdnjava Kluže; 📞 05-388 6758; www.kluze.net; adult/child/student €3/1; ⏱ 9am-8pm Jul & Aug, 10am-5pm Jun & Sep, 10am-5pm Sat & Sun May & Oct) Built by the Austrians in 1882 on the site of a 17th-century fortress above a 70m ravine on the Koritnica River, Kluže Fortress is 4km northeast of Bovec. It was the site of an Austro-Hungarian garrison during WWI, right behind the front line of the Isonzo battlefield. Exhibitions outline its turbulent history.

Even more dramatic is the upper fortress, **Fort Hermann**, built halfway up Mt Rombon to the west in 1900. You can walk to these ruins from Kluže in about half an hour.

🏃 Activities

Cycling

Ask the TIC for the *Biking Trails* pamphlet, which lists 16 trips of various degrees of difficulty. Most sports agencies (p112) rent mountain bikes from €15/20 for a half-/full day, and offer guided trips (from €30).

Hiking & Walking

The 1:25,000-scale *Bovec z Okolico* (*Bovec with Surroundings*; €7) map lists a number of walks, from two-hour strolls to the ascent of Mt Rombon (2208m), a good five hours one way.

Great areas to explore: Lepena, en route to Trenta; the spectacular Mangart Saddle (at 2072m, reached by Slovenia's highest road); the alpine valley of Loška Koritnica. Ask for more info at the TIC.

Skiing

Bovec Kanin Ski Centre   SKIING
Bovec Kanin Ski Centre offers skiing up to 2300m – the highest in Slovenia, often with good spring skiing into early May. It's a cross-border ski resort, too, connected to Sella Nevea on the Italian side of the mountain.

In 2013, however, the ski centre and cable car ceased operating – in 2015, a large government grant was announced to reopen the resort. All going to plan, the ski centre will be functioning again by the time you read this.

Once the cable car is functioning again, summer activities on Kanin should again take off (mountain biking and hiking, paragliding from the mountain). Enquire at the TIC.

Rafting & Kayaking

Rafting and kayaking on the beautiful Soča River (10% to 40% gradient; Grades I to IV) is a major draw. The season lasts from April to October, with the highest water levels in the spring. Almost every agency (p112) sells trips, and generally travels the same stretch of river (from Boka to Trnovo ob Soči). Companies operate three rafting trips a day in high season. Children are welcome – generally from five years for rafting, eight for other activities, but this may depend on water levels and weather conditions.

Rafting trips on the Soča over a distance of around 8km (1½ hours) cost €35 to €40; longer trips may be possible when water levels are high. Prices include guiding, transport to/from the river, a neoprene suit, boots, life jacket, helmet and paddle. Wear a swimsuit; bring a towel.

WESTERN SLOVENIA & THE SOČA VALLEY BOVEC

Minirafting uses a smaller boat than a raft, carrying two or three people. The key difference: there is no guide in the boat (the guide accompanies you in a kayak). You navigate the waters on your own (with advice), making it good for more-experienced paddlers. Trips cost around €45.

Kayaking courses for beginners are on offer (from €60); guided kayak trips (around 8km) are also available (€50). Kayaks and canoes can be hired.

If you're experienced and prefer to DIY, a number of companies will rent you equipment and help with transport.

Canyoning & Hydrospeeding

Canyoning along the Soča, in which you descend through gorges, swim through pools, slide down rocks and jump over falls attached to a rope, costs around €45 for a two-hour trip through Bovec agencies (p112). Longer, more-demanding canyons can be tackled for around €90.

Hydrospeeding (also known as riverboarding) is growing in popularity – this involves surfing the rapids with flippers on your feet, holding on to a flotation device. Expect to pay €40 to €50.

🛏 Sleeping

The TIC has dozens of private rooms and apartments (from €20) on its lists.

Don't discount the many scenic options along the road to Trenta towards the Vršič Pass (p108), especially if you have a campervan for camping.

★ Adrenaline Check

Eco Place   CAMPGROUND **$**

(✆041 383 662; www.adrenaline-check.com; Podklopca 4; campsite per person €12; ⊙May-Sep; P🐾) About 3km southwest of town, this fun, fabulous campground makes camping easy: hire a tent under a lean-to shelter that comes with mattresses and linen (per person €20), or a big, furnished safari-style tent (€100). Cars are left in a carpark, and you walk through to a large, picturesque clearing (so it's not for campervans).

Owners Matic and Katja are fonts of local knowledge, and loads of activities can be organised here. Pick-up from the bus station can be arranged.

★ Hostel Soča Rocks   HOSTEL **$**

(✆041 317 777; http://hostelsocarocks.com; Mala Vas 120; dm €13-15, d €34-40; P@🐾) This welcome new arrival sleeps 68 and is a new breed of hostel: colourful, spotlessly clean and social, with a bar that never seems to quit. Dorms sleep maximum six; there are also a few doubles (all bathrooms shared). Cheap meals are served (including summertime barbecue dinners), and a full activity

---

BOVEC ADVENTURE SPORTS AGENCIES

There are dozens of adrenaline-raising companies in Bovec; some specialise in one activity (often rafting), while others offer multiday packages so you can try various activities (rafting, canyoning, kayaking, paragliding, climbing, caving, ziplining). Some agencies offer winter sports, too, like dog-sledding and snowshoeing.

Accommodation providers can often book you onto their own (or affiliated) tours and activities. Alternatively, if you choose a package from a sports company, they can usually arrange accommodation as part of the deal.

Central booking offices are generally open long hours in summer (9am to 7pm).

Aktivni Planet (✆040 639 433; www.aktivniplanet.si; Trg Golobarskih Žrtev 19) Offers multiday packages so you can try all its various activities (rafting, canyoning, kayaking, caving, zipline, biking, hiking). Affiliated with Soča Rocks hostel.

Bovec Rafting Team (✆041 338 308; www.bovec-rafting-team.com; Mala Vas 106) On-the-water specialists (rafting, minirafting, kayaking, hydrospeed, canyoning). Also offers caving, paragliding and winter activities like snowshoeing and dog-sledding.

Soča Rafting (✆041 724 472, 05-389 62 00; www.socarafting.si; Trg Golobarskih Žrtev 14) Offers rafting, canyoning, kayaking, ziplines and mountain-biking (and simple bike rental). Winter activities, too.

Sport Mix (✆031 871 991, 05-389 61 60; www.sportmix.si; Trg Golobarskih Žrtev 18) Good FAQs on its website, and a full range of water activities (rafting, kayaking, canyoning etc), plus mountain-biking, rock climbing and caving.

menu is offered: the hostel is affiliated with Aktivni Planet (p112).

Hotel Mangart
HOTEL $$

(☑05-388 42 50; www.hotel-mangart.com; Mala Vas 107; B&B per person €40-55; ⓟ❋🛜🏊) A good option on the outskirts of Bovec is this modern Alpine hotel. Rooms are handsome, service is good, and there's a lovely outdoor terrace. There are a handful of 'hostel' rooms with bunks – these are good value at €25 per person. The best feature: a small artificial rock pool for cooling off in.

Martinov Hram
GUESTHOUSE $$

(☑05-388 62 14; www.martinov-hram.si; Trg Golobarskih Žrtev 27; per person from €30; 🛜) This central guesthouse has 11 comfy, well-equipped rooms and a good restaurant with an emphasis on specialities from the Bovec region.

★ Dobra Vila
BOUTIQUE HOTEL $$$

(☑05-389 64 00; www.dobra-vila-bovec.si; Mala Vas 112; d €120-165; ⓟ❋@🛜) This stunning 10-room boutique hotel is housed in an erstwhile telephone-exchange building dating from 1932. Peppered with art deco flourishes, interesting artefacts and objets d'art, it has its own library and wine cellar, and a fabulous restaurant with a winter garden and outdoor terrace.

Hotel Sanje ob Soči
HOTEL $$$

(☑05-389 6000; www.sanjeobsoci.com; Mala Vas 105a; r €89-109, apt €125-180; ⓟ🛜) 'Dream on the Soča' is an architecturally striking, newly built hotel on the edge of town. Interiors are minimalist, room sizes range from 'economy' on the ground floor to studios and family-sized apartments (named after the mountain you can see from the room's windows). There's friendly service, a sauna area, and a great breakfast spread (€10).

✖ Eating & Drinking

Gostilna Sovdat
SLOVENIAN $

(☑05-388 60 27; www.gostilna-sovdat.si; Trg Golobarskih Žrtev 24; mains €7-20; ⊙10am-10pm) Sovdat isn't strong on aesthetics and its outdoor terrace isn't as pretty as others in town, but the crowd of locals attests to its popularity and value. Lots on the menu falls under €10, including plentiful pastas and bumper burgers. You can go upmarket, too, with the likes of gnocchi with truffle or roast beef with gorgonzola.

Martinov Hram
SLOVENIAN $$

(☑05-38 86 214; www.martinov-hram.si; mains €8-18; ⊙10am-10pm Tue-Fri, to midnight Sat & Sun) This traditional restaurant gets mixed reviews, but on a good day you'll enjoy well-prepared local specialities including venison, Soča trout and mushroom dishes. The best place to enjoy them is from the street-front terrace, under the grapevines.

Dobra Vila Restaurant
MODERN SLOVENIAN $$$

(☑05-389 64 00; www.dobra-vila-bovec.si; Mala Vas 112; 3/4/5 courses €28/36/45) Easily the best place to eat in town is the polished restaurant at Dobra Vila – preferably in the pretty garden in summer. A carefully constructed menu of local, seasonal ingredients is served to an appreciative crowd. Setting, service and food are first-class; bookings are essential.

★ Črno Ovca
PUB

(Trg Golobarskih Žrtev 18; ⊙4pm-midnight Mon-Thu, 10am-3am Fri &Sat, 10am-11pm Sun) You may have to search for this tucked-away bar, but the Black Sheep is worth the hunt (hint: it's close to Hotel Kanin). Enjoy the friendly, chilled atmosphere, occasional live music, and opportunity for activities (kids playground, petanque, tennis courts for hire) – or just sit and drink in the mountain views.

ⓘ Orientation

The centre is Trg Golobarskih Žrtev, one of the few named streets in town. Actually, it's a long square that forms the main east–west drag. Services like banks are found along here; buses stop down the side street next to Mercator supermarket.

ⓘ Information

Post Office (Trg Golobarskih Žrtev 8) Just northwest of the TIC.

Tourist Information Centre (TIC; ☑05-384 19 19; www.bovec.si; Trg Golobarskih Žrtev 22; ⊙8am-8pm Jul & Aug, 9am-7pm Jun & Sep, 9am-6pm May, shorter hrs Oct-Apr) The TIC is open year-round. Winter hours will depend on the reopening of the local **ski centre** (p111) – expect long hours when the ski season is in full swing.

ⓘ Getting There & Away

Popular bus routes:

Kobarid (€3.10, 30 minutes, 22km, five daily).

Ljubljana (€13.60, 3¾ hours, 151km, three daily).

Vršič Pass Busline **Alpetour** (🖉 04-532 04 45; www.alpetour.si) runs buses to Kranjska Gora (€6.70, one hour 40 minutes, 46km) via Trenta (€2.70, 30 minutes, 20km) from late June through August. Check the website for time-tables; there are five or six departures daily.

Kobarid

🖉 05 / POP 1115 / ELEV 231M

The charming town of Kobarid is quainter than nearby Bovec, and despite being sur-rounded by mountain peaks it feels more Mediterranean than Alpine, with an Ital-ianate look (the border at Robič is only 9km to the west).

On the surface not a whole lot has changed since Ernest Hemingway described Kobarid (then Caporetto) in *A Farewell to Arms* (1929) as 'a little white town with a campanile in a valley', with 'a fine fountain in the square'. The bell in the tower still rings on the hour, but the fountain has sadly dis-appeared.

Kobarid was a military settlement during Roman times. It was hotly contested in the Middle Ages and was hit by a devastating earthquake in 1976, but the world will al-ways remember Kobarid as the site of the decisive battle of 1917 in which the com-bined forces of the Central Powers defeated the Italian army.

◉ Sights

★Kobarid Museum   MUSEUM
(Kobariški Muzej; 🖉 05-389 00 00; www.kobariski-muzej.si; Gregorčičeva ul 10; adult/child €6/2.50; ⊘9am-6pm Apr-Sep, 10am-5pm Oct-Mar) This museum is devoted almost entirely to the Soča Front and the 'war to end all wars'. Themed rooms powerfully describe the 29 months of fighting, and there's a 20-minute video (available in 10 languages) that gives context. There are many photos document-ing the horrors of the front, military charts, diaries and maps, and two large relief dis-plays showing the front lines and offensives through the Krn Mountains and the posi-tions in the Upper Soča Valley.

The **Krn Range Room** looks at the initial assaults along the Soča River after Italy's entry into the war in May 1915. The **White Room** describes the harsh conditions of war in the snowbound mountains. The **Room of the Rear** describes life behind the battle lines (hospitals, soldiers on leave from the trenches) – a sharp contrast to the **Black Room**'s photographs of the dead and dying. Finally, the **Battle of Kobarid Room** details the final offensive launched by the Austrian and German forces that defeated the Italian army.

★Kozjak Waterfall   WATERFALL
(Slap Kozjak) One of the region's loveliest short walking trails (approximately 30 minutes) leads to the photogenic, 15m-high Kozjak Waterfall, which gushes over a rocky ledge in a cavern-like amphitheatre, into a green pool below. Access the trail from var-ious spots: from a footbridge from Kamp Lazar campground, or from a car park op-posite Kamp Koren. Alternatively, it's part of the Kobarid Historical Trail (p116).

☂ Activities

Kobarid gives Bovec a run for its money in adventure sports, and you'll find several out-fits on the town's main square that organise rafting (from €30), canyoning (from €45), kayaking (from €45), mountain-biking tours (from €30), and tandem paragliding (from €125). Kayaks and mountain bikes can also be hired. (Note that operators in Bovec and Kobarid all raft the same river stretch.)

X Point   ADVENTURE SPORTS
(🖉 05-388 53 08; www.xpoint.si; Trg Svobode 6) Operates from its base at X-Point Hostel.

Positive Sport   ADVENTURE SPORTS
(🖉 040 654 475; www.positive-sport.com; Trg Svo-bode 15) Has its office on the main square.

🛏 Sleeping

Kamp Koren   CAMPGROUND $
(🖉 05-389 13 11; www.kamp-koren.si; Drežniške Ravne 33; campsite per adult/child €12.50/6.25, chalet €55-190; ℙ 🐾) The oldest campground in the valley, this lovely green site is about 500m northeast of Kobarid, by the Soča Riv-er and the road to Drežnica. There are loads of activities and facilities, and some quite luxurious log-cabin chalets that sleep six in comfort.

X Point Hostel   HOSTEL $
(🖉 05-388 53 08; www.xpoint.si; Trg Svobode 6; per person €16-20; 🐾) Above its town-centre activity base, X Point offers six small, neat hostel rooms, with shared bathrooms plus kitchen and laundry facilities.

Hemingway House   APARTMENT $$
(🖉 040 774 106; www.hemingwayhouseslovenia. com; Volaričeva ulica 10; d €40-67; 🐾) A good-

LONG-DISTANCE HIKING TRAILS

Two popular long-distance hiking trails range through the Soča Valley, from the Alps to the Adriatic, and it's easy for visitors to walk a stage or two: the Alpe-Adria-Trail and the Walk of Peace.

Alpe-Adria-Trail

The transnational Alpe-Adria-Trail (www.alpe-adria-trail.com), which is growing in stature, links existing paths in three countries, from the foot of the Grossglockner mountain (Austria's highest peak), through varying regions filled with mountains, lakes, rivers and vineyards, then on to Trieste and the Adriatic coast of Italy. The trail is about 700km in length, broken into stages that are roughly 20km long (each stage takes about six hours to walk). The route can be walked in either direction.

The walk is designed for recreational walkers: as far as possible there are only slight differences in altitude. Six stages pass through Slovenia:

Stage 23 Kranjska Gora to Trenta

Stage 24 Trenta to Bovec

Stage 25 Bovec to Drežnica (6km northeast of Kobarid)

Stage 26 Kobarid to Tolmin

From Tolmin the route enters Italy, but dips back into Slovenia around Goriška Brda. Full details are on the website, including route details, accommodation and trip packages.

Walk of Peace

The 100km-long Walk of Peace (Pot Miru; www.potmiru.si) connects the outdoor museums and the most important remains and memorials of the Isonzo Front of the Upper Soča Region. It ranges in five sections from Log pod Mangartom in the north to near Tolmin in the south; there's an excellent visitor centre (p116) in Kobarid where you can get information. Guiding is possible too, especially at outdoor museums.

Note, too, that the Walk of Peace can be extended south, encompassing wartime sites down to the Adriatic coast.

value option in the centre of town, honouring Papa Hemingway and owned by Marie, a Canadian. The house has five apartments (each with bathroom and kitchen) over three floors – they sleep between two and five people, and share a lovely garden where breakfast (€5) can be served. Off-season and weekly rates, too.

★**Hiša Franko**   GUESTHOUSE **$$$**
(📞05-389 41 20; www.hisafranko.com; Staro Selo 1; r €120-148; 🅿🛜) This foodie favourite is in an old farmhouse 3km west of Kobarid in Staro Selo, halfway to the Italian border. Here 10 rooms ooze character, with rich colours and fabrics and interesting artworks. A handful of rooms have huge bathtubs; others have terraces. All offer a sumptuous breakfast. And best of all: the acclaimed restaurant downstairs.

★**Nebesa**   CHALET **$$$**
(📞05-384 46 20; www.nebesa.si/en; Livek 39; d €186-270; 🅿🛜) The name translates as 'Heaven', and it's fitting. These four heavenly mountain retreats sit at the top of a 7km winding road from the village of Idrsko (2km south of Kobarid) and enjoy stupendous views. Each sleeps two and is large and self-contained, with kitchenette and terrace; there is also a communal house that includes a kitchen and a wine cellar, plus saunas.

There's also a help-yourself breakfast, and complimentary wine and cheese.

Hotel Hvala   HOTEL **$$$**
(📞05-389 93 00; www.hotelhvala.si; Trg Svobode 1; s/d from €72/104; 🅿🛜) At the super-central Hotel Thanks (actually it's the family's name), the snazzy elevator shaft is decorated with artworks that take you on a vertical tour of Kobarid (illustrations include Soča trout, and Papa Hemingway at work). The standard rooms are tired but the suites are smart; the hotel's best feature is its fabulous on-site restaurant.

KOBARID HISTORICAL TRAIL

The TIC offers a free brochure describing the 5km-long Kobarid Historical Trail.

From the Kobarid Museum (p114) walk to the north side of Trg Svobode and take the winding road lined with the Stations of the Cross to the Italian Charnel House (Italijanska Kostnica), which contains the bones of more than 7000 Italian soldiers killed on the Soča Front. It's topped by the 17th-century Church of St Anthony.

From here, a path leads north (bearing left) for just over 1km to the ancient fortified hill of Tonocov Grad, then descends through the remains of the Italian Defence Line (Italijanska Obrambna Črta), past cleared trenches, gun emplacements and observation posts, before crossing the Soča over a 52m footbridge. A path leads up a side valley that takes you to the foot of the beautiful Kozjak Waterfall (p114). The return path leads over Napoleon Bridge (Napoleonov Most), a replica of a bridge built by the French in the early 19th century and destroyed in 1915, and finishes at a small Cheese Museum that explores the local cheese-making tradition, just a short walk from the trail's starting point.

✗ Eating

Topli Val
SEAFOOD $$

(📞05-389 9300; www.hotelhvala.si; Trg Svobode 1; mains €10-20; ⊘noon-3pm & 6-10pm) Diners are spoiled for choice in Kobarid. Seafood is the focus here, and it's excellent, from the carpaccio of sea bass to the Soča trout and signature lobster with pasta. It's not exclusively aquatic – the 'mountains meet the sea' here: venison is also a speciality, and vegetarians will fare well. For dessert, try the *kobariški štruklji* (stuffed with walnuts and raisins).

Restaurant Lazar
SLOVENIAN $$

(📞05-388 53 33; http://lazar.si; Trnovo ob Soči 1b; mains €7-22; ⊘8am-10pm Apr-Oct, shorter hrs Nov-Mar) Where do top locals chefs recommend for a casual meal? This fun, rustic outdoor restaurant-bar at the riverside Lazar holiday centre (camping and quality rooms also available). The menu here ranges from cheap, filling pancakes to Black Angus steaks, and fire-roasted lamb and pork ribs. It's well placed for the walk to/from Kozjak Waterfall.

★ Hiša Franko
MODERN SLOVENIAN $$$

(📞05-389 41 20; www.hisafranko.com; Staro Selo 1; 5/9 courses €60/80; ⊘lunch Sat & Sun, dinner Tue-Sun) Provenance is everything at this restaurant in Staro Selo, just west of town. Impeccable tasting menus change monthly and showcase produce from Chef Ana's garden, plus berries, trout, mushrooms, cheese, meat and fish delivered by local farmers and foragers. The resulting dishes are innovative and delicious, and ably paired with top-notch wines (predominantly Slovenian). Service is first-class.

ℹ Orientation

The centre of town is Trg Svobode, dominated by the Gothic Church of the Assumption and that famous bell tower. Practical services (banks, post office, supermarket) are found here, and just west on Markova ulica. Buses stop in front of the Cinca Marinca bar-cafe at Trg Svobode 10.

ℹ Information

Tourist Information Centre (TIC; 📞05-380 04 90; www.dolina-soce.com; Trg Svobode 16; ⊘9am-8pm Jul & Aug, to 7pm May, Jun & Sep, 9am-4pm Mon-Fri, 10am-4pm Sat Oct-Apr) Good local maps and brochures, plus information on **Triglav National Park** (p100).

Walk of Peace Visitor Centre (📞05-389 01 67; www.potmiru.si; Gregorčičeva ulica 8; ⊘9am-6pm Mon-Fri, from 10am Sat & Sun) Based opposite the Kobarid Museum, this foundation provides information about the **Walk of Peace** (p115) long-distance trail and the various heritage sites of the Isonzo Front. There are maps and books, plus guiding services can be organised.

ℹ Getting There & Around

The closest train station is at Most na Soči (22km south, and good for trains to/from Bohinjska Bistrica and Bled Jezero). Popular bus services from Kobarid:

Bovec (€3.10, 30 minutes, 22km, five daily) In July and August, two of these services connect with buses over the Vršič Pass to Kranjska Gora.

Ljubljana (€11.60, 3¼ hours, 131km, four daily).

Most na Soči (€3.10, 50 minutes, 22km, five daily).

Tolmin (€2.70, 20-30 minutes, 18km, eight daily).

NOVA GORICA

♫ 05 / POP 12,985 / ELEV 99M

Nova Gorica is a modern university city adjoining the Italian border. It's the largest city in the area and has interesting recent history, but it lacks natural beauty or historic charm. Its tourist 'appeal' lies in the casinos that draw Italians from across the border who can't gamble at home.

There's no reason to linger long – it's better to end up in one of the attractive neighbouring regions: the Soča Valley to the north, or the postcard-pretty wine-growing areas of Goriška Brda and the Vipava Valley.

History

When the town of Gorica was awarded to the Italians under the Treaty of Paris in 1947 and became Gorizia, the Yugoslav government set about building a model town on the eastern side of the border 'following the principles of Le Corbusier'. Appropriately enough they called it 'New Gorica' and erected a chain-link barrier between the two towns.

This 'mini-Berlin Wall' was finally pulled down to great fanfare in 2004 after Slovenia joined the EU, leaving Trg Evrope (or Piazza della Transalpina, as the Italians call it) straddling the now nonexistent border right behind Nova Gorica train station.

◎ Sights

Kostanjevica Monastery MONASTERY

(Samostan Kostanjevica; **♫** 05-330 77 50; www.samostan-kostanjevica.si; Škrabčeva ulica 1; tombs/library €2/1; ☉ 8am-noon & 3-5pm Mon-Sat, 3-5pm Sun) On a 143m hill south of the train station (signed 'Grobnica Bourboni'), this monastery was founded by the Capuchin Franciscans in the early 17th century and has a library with 10,000 volumes and 30 incunabula. In the crypt of the Church of the Annunciation is the **Tomb of the Bourbons**, which contains the mortal remains of the last members of the French house of Bourbon. This includes Charles X (1757–1836), who died of cholera while on holiday in Gorizia and was buried here.

Goriško Museum MUSEUM

(Goriški Muzej; **♫** 05-333 11 40; www.goriskimuzej.si; Grajska cesta 1, Kromberk; adult/child €2/1; ☉ 9am-7pm Mon-Fri, 1-7pm Sun May-Oct, to 5pm Nov-Apr) Three kilometres east of the town, the Goriško Museum resides in the impressive, 17th-century **Kromberk Castle**. The collection spans rich period furnishings to modern artworks, incorporating religious carvings and details of the Vipava Valley in the Roman era. There's a lovely restaurant in the castle too, and summertime music events held here.

☞ Tours

★ Slocally TOUR

(**♫** 041 432 488; www.slocally.com; guiding per hr €25-35) Based about 10km north of Nova Gorica in a village called Plave, Vesna runs this company with a goal of encouraging slow travel and giving curious travellers a range of unique and affordable local

---

TOLMIN

Tolmin (population 3461), a town in the Soča Valley 16km southeast of Kobarid, is enjoying a growing reputation as a paragliding hot spot and a summertime music-festival hub – annual metal, punk rock and reggae festivals are staged in July and August. The week-long MetalDays (www.metaldays.net) is especially well attended. We like Tolmin best for some of the natural attractions on its doorstep.

Tolmin Gorges (Tolminska Korita; **♫** 05-380 04 80; www.dolina-soce.com; adult/child €4/2; ☉ 8.30am-7.30pm Jun-Aug, shorter hrs Apr, May, Sep & Oct) A scenic river confluence is found here, at the southernmost entry point of Triglav National Park (p100). The ticket kiosk is a 2km walk northeast of Tolmin town (by road, follow the signs to Zatolmin), and the circular walk through the gorges formed by the Tolminka and Zadlaščica Rivers takes about an hour. A short detour off the main path leads to the much-photographed Medvedova glava, a wedged rock in the shape of a bear's head.

Most na Soči The name of this settlement 5km south of Tolmin literally means 'Bridge on the Soča River'. The village (population 422) sits, in fact, on a beautiful green lake – surprisingly, it's an artificial lake at the confluence of the Soča and Idrijca Rivers, created by a nearby hydroplant. It's a super-scenic place to pause for a lakeside walk or some boating; rowboats and kayaks can be hired.

experiences (herb picking, wine or cheese tours, woodcraft, culinary workshops etc). You can also 'rent-a-local' for guiding.

The options range all over western Slovenia and further afield – check the website. Vesna also offers homestays with her family.

🛏 Sleeping

Perla Casino & Hotel HOTEL $$$
(✍ 05-336 30 00; www.hit.si; Kidričeva ulica 7; d €95-160; P ❀ ❄ ❁ ❀) To observe what makes Nova Gorica tick, head here. It's a huge, flashy place – a favourite with Italians, who can't get enough of the casino. It's in a big glass-and-steel modern structure, and is home to 250 rooms and suites, restaurants, bars and a wellness centre.

🍴 Eating & Drinking

Delpinova ulica and Bevkov trg are lined with fast-food eateries and cafe-bars.

Rusjan SLOVENIAN $
(✍ 05-330 22 56; Delpinova ulica 18b; lunch €4-10; ☺ restaurant 10am-3pm Mon-Thu, to 11pm Fri, noon-11pm Sat) Rusjan is in a handy spot – next to the TIC and across from the bus station. Downstairs is a cafe with long opening hours, ideal for coffee and sweets; upstairs is a modern dining room where the changing daily lunch menu costs little more than small change.

Vinoteka Solum WINE BAR
(✍ 05-998 20 87; Bevkov trg 6; ☺ 9am-10pm Tue-Thu, to 1am Fri & Sat) This handsome new wine bar takes great pride in offering loads of local wines and foodstuffs (from just across the border, too). There are more than 150 wines from 50 producers, plus cheeses, meats and nibbles.

❶ Orientation

Nova Gorica is a long town, running about 5km from the crossing with Italy at Rožna Dolina (Casa Rossa) in the south to Solkan in the north.

THE SOČA (ISONZO) FRONT

The breakthrough in the Soča Front (more commonly known to historians as the Isonzo Front) by the combined Austro-Hungarian and German forces near Caporetto (Kobarid) in October 1917 was one of the greatest and bloodiest military campaigns fought on mountainous terrain in history. By the time the fighting had stopped 17 days later, hundreds of thousands of soldiers lay dead or wounded, gassed or mutilated beyond recognition.

In May 1915, Italy declared war on the Central Powers and their allies and sent its army to the strategically important Soča Valley; from there, they hoped to move on the heart of Austria-Hungary. However, the Austrians had fortified the lines with trenches and bunkers for 80km from the Adriatic to the mountain peaks overlooking the Upper Soča Valley. While the Italians' First Offensive was initially successful – including the occupation of Kobarid – the attack stalled after the first month.

The Italians launched 11 offensives over the next two and a half years, but the difficult terrain meant a war of attrition between the two entrenched armies. The fighting in the mountains and the limestone plateau to the south was horrific, but the territorial gains were minimal. With the stalemate, much of the fighting shifted to Gorica (Gorizia).

On 24 October 1917 the stalemate was broken when the Austro-Hungarians and Germans moved hundreds of thousands of troops, arms and materiel (including seven German divisions) into the area between Bovec and Tolmin, with Kobarid as the first target. The surprise 12th Offensive – the Austrians' first – began with heavy bombardment.

The 'miracle of Kobarid' routed the Italian army and pushed the fighting back deep into Italian territory. The sketches of one Lieutenant Erwin Rommel (later the 'Desert Fox' commander of Germany's North African offensive in WWII) are invaluable for understanding the battle, but no account is more vivid than the description of the Italian retreat in Hemingway's *A Farewell to Arms*. The novelist himself was wounded on the Gorica battlefield in the spring of 1917 while driving an Italian ambulance.

The 12th Offensive was the greatest breakthrough in WWI, and it employed some elements of what would later be called 'lightning war' (*blitzkrieg*). The Italians alone lost 500,000 soldiers, and another 300,000 were taken prisoner. Casualties on the Soča Front for the entire 1915–17 period, including soldiers and civilians behind the lines, number almost a million.

The main square is Bevkov trg, with major services (banks, supermakets) in the vicinity. The bus station is nearby at Kidričeva ulica 22. The train station is at Kolodvorska ulica 6, about 1.5km to the west.

ℹ Information

Tourist Information Centre (☑ 05-330 46 00; www.novagorica-turizem.com; Delpinova ulica 18b; ⊙ 8am-5pm Mon-Fri, 9am-1pm Sat & Sun) Central, helpful and offers cheap bike rental (€3 per day). Open until 8pm weekdays in summer.

ℹ Getting There & Away

BUS

Being a large university town, transport connections are good:

Bovec (€7.50, two hours, 79km, five daily) via Kobarid. In July and August, two of these services connect with buses over the Vršič Pass to Kranjska Gora.

Idrija (€6.30, 2¼ hours, 96km, three daily).

Ljubljana (€10.70, two to 2½ hours, 117km, 11 daily).

Nova Gorica is an easy way to get to/from Italy; hourly buses run between the Nova Gorica train station and its counterpart in Gorizia (€1), just a couple of kilometres away.

TRAIN

About a half-dozen trains head northeast each day for Jesenice (€6.99, two hours, 89km) via Most na Soči and Bled Jezero (€6.59, 1¾ hours, 79km) – arguably Slovenia's most beautiful train journey. You can change at Jesenice for Ljubljana – or, alternatively, travel southeast from Nova Gorica and change at Sežana. The travel times are similar (around three hours). To reach Trieste in Italy, change trains in Sežana.

GORIŠKA BRDA

☑ 05 / ELEV UP TO 800M

Picture-perfect Goriška Brda ('Gorica Hills') is a tiny wine-producing region that stretches from Solkan west to the Italian border. It's a charmer, reminiscent of Tuscany, full of rolling hills topped with small settlements and churches, its hillsides lined with grapevines and orchards.

In addition to its grapes and wine, Goriška Brda is celebrated for its fruit and olive oil, in particular its cherries (usually available from early June).

Your own wheels (two or four) are recommended for explorations. A good place to start is **Dobrovo** (population 328), 18km northwest of central Nova Gorica, where there's a castle, *vinoteka* and information centre.

◉ Sights & Activities

Dozens of small, family-run wineries offer tastings in Goriška Brda, though you should call ahead – or ask at the TIC for recommendations.

★ Šmartno   VILLAGE

The Goriška Brda area has been under the influence of northern and central Italy since time immemorial, and you'll think you've crossed the border as you go through little towns with narrow streets and the remains of feudal castles. One perfect example is Šmartno (San Martino; population 210), a photogenic fortified village with stone walls and a 16th-century tower. It's 4km east of Dobrovo.

Dobrovo Castle   CASTLE

(Grad Dobrovo; ☑ 05-395 95 86; Grajska cesta 10; adult/child €2/1; ⊙ 8am-4pm Tue-Fri, 1-6pm Sat & Sun) The Renaissance-style Dobrovo Castle, dating from 1606, has a handful of rooms filled with artworks and period furnishings (limited labelling). There's a decent restaurant here, and in the cellar is **Vinoteka Brda** (☑ 05-395 92 10; www.vinotekabrda; Grajska cesta 10; tastings from €7; ⊙ 11.30am-9pm), where you can sample local vintages (white rebula and chardonnay or the pinot and merlot reds), which go nicely with the cheese and nibbles on offer.

Vinska Klet Goriška Brda   WINE TASTING

(☑ 05-331 01 44; www.klet-brda.si; Zadružna cesta 9, Dobrovo) Usually open to groups only is the wine cooperative Vinska Klet Goriška Brda, with the largest wine cellar in Slovenia. It's just downhill from Dobrovo Castle and has a shop open Monday to Saturday selling plenty of local drops; in July and August there is a tour and tasting open to the public at 2pm for €10 (it's advisable to call to confirm time, or enquire at the TIC).

🛏 Sleeping & Eating

A number of wineries engage in *agriturismo*, with rooms and meals available.

Hotel San Martin   HOTEL $$

(☑ 05-330 56 60; www.sanmartin.si; Šmartno 11; s/d/q €50/75/120; ☏) To stay in the area, atmospheric Šmartno is a top choice. This new hotel is close to the entrance to the fortified village and has polished service, bright, good-value rooms (including family-sized) and a highly regarded restaurant showcasing regional produce and enjoying a view-enriched terrace. Note: restaurant closed Wednesday.

Hiša Marica　　　　　GUESTHOUSE **$$**
(☑ 05-304 1039; www.marica.si; Šmartno 33; s/d €50/80; ✱ ⓢ) This charming old inn lies within the fortified walls of Šmartno and offers four excellent, spacious rooms. Also here is a wine bar serving up local flavours, including home-cured hams and salamis, and Soča Valley cheeses. Note: wine bar closed Tuesday.

VIPAVA VALLEY

☑ 05 / ELEV 180M

The fertile, wine-rich Vipava Valley (Vipavska Dolina in Slovenian) stretches southeast from Nova Gorica into the Karst region. It's an excellent place to tour by car or bike, with outstanding gourmet treats and idyllic rural scenery. The valley's mild climate encourages the cultivation of stone fruits such as peaches and apricots – the trees are pretty with blossoms in spring, while autumn foliage is deeply colourful and photogenic.

The area has a rich history: under the Roman Empire, this was the first important station on the road from Aquileia to Emona (Ljubljana). The landmark **Mt Nanos** looms above the valley – a mountain plateau from which the Vipava River springs, and a popular recreation area for hiking, mountain biking, climbing and paragliding.

There are two main towns in the valley that make for handy hubs: **Ajdovščina** (population 6596) and **Vipava** (population 1946), only about 7km apart. There are also loads of villages and hamlets, home to family-owned wine producers.

South of the village of Branik lies the unofficial border between the Vipava Valley and Karst wine region (p137). In both areas, beware the local *burja* or bora, a notoriously strong and disruptive wind from the northeast, occurring primarily in winter. Note the stones that have been placed on roofs to prevent tiles blowing off. The wind is that strong – gusts of up to 180km/h have been recorded.

🛏 Sleeping

★ **Youth Hostel Ajdovščina**　　HOSTEL **$**
(Hiša Mladih; ☑ 05-368 93 83; www.hostel-ajdovscina.si; Cesta IV Prekomorske 61a; per person €18-21; ℗ @ ⓢ) This is a high-quality hostel, with bright, fresh features and cool design. Rooms sleep four to eight (with a 24-bed room for groups). All bathrooms are shared; there's also a kitchen (breakfast €3) and laundry. It's on the northern edge of Ajdovščina in a great park-like setting, alongside a youth centre, bar and summertime concert venue.

Camp Lijak　　　　　CAMPGROUND **$**
(☑ 05-308 85 57; www.parklijak.com; Ozeljan 6a, Šempas; camp site per adult/child/van €10.70/8.20/5.10; ℗ ⓢ ⛴) About 6km east of Nova Gorica, this year-round campground has a focus on activities: summertime hiking, cycling and mountain-biking tours can be arranged, and year-round paragliding. Family-sized bungalows are available (sleeping two/four €66/88); 'hobbit holes' are timber cubicles that sleep one or two (per person €16.30).

Apartmaji Koren　　　　GUESTHOUSE **$$**
(☑ 040 217 213; www.apartmaji-koren.com; Glavni trg 2, Vipava; r/apt for 2 €60/75; ⓢ) A friendly option right next door to the TIC in the heart of Vipava, so a good choice for travellers using the bus. Homely rooms and apartments are available, plus a breakfast room full of atmosphere and a small *vinoteka* for wine tasting.

★ **Majerija**　　　　　GUESTHOUSE **$$**
(☑ 05-368 50 11; www.majerija.si; Slap 18; s/d €69/96; ℗ ⓢ) Four kilometres from Vipava in the hamlet of Slap, Majerija has a fun, unique offering: 10 rooms built underground – under the herb garden, in fact. These simple, stylish rooms feature custom-made timber furniture, skylights above the bed, and a herb theme (they're named for the lavender, basil and assorted plants growing above).

🍴 Eating & Drinking

Make a beeline for Faladur (p121) for excellent local options and knowledgeable service.

★ **Majerija**　　　　MODERN SLOVENIAN **$$**
(www.majerija.si; Slap 18; mains €15; ⊘ lunch & dinner Thu-Sat, lunch Sun) Local produce shines in skilled, contemporary dishes at this farmhouse idyll – how about Vipava ham

WINE TASTING IN THE VIPAVA VALLEY

The constant winds, plus the proximity of the sea, and the sun on steep slopes contribute to ideal conditions for wine production. Reds and whites are produced, including fresh whites from the indigenous zelen and pinela grapes.

Recommended labels to try (and estates to track down) include Guerila (www.guerila.si); Tilia Estate (www.tiliapremiumwines.com), the 'house of pinots'; Burja (www.burja estate.com); and Batič (www.batic-wines.com).

It may help to get a big-picture view of wines, producers and flavours before you take to the backroads. Faladur and Vinoteka Vipava are ideal for this, and Winestronaut offers tours.

Faladur (☑ 040 232 987; www.faladur.si; Lokarjev Drevored 8b, Ajdovščina; ⊙10am-6pm Mon-Fri, to 2pm Sat) Faladur is a wine shop and tasting room where you're in very capable hands: host Matej can recommend wines to try, put together a platter of valley-produced cheeses, hams and olives to accompany, and tell you about homegrown varietals and labels. Faladur also provides tastings of the craft beer produced in Ajdovščina, **Pelicon** (www.pelicon.beer).

By arrangement, Faladur can organise more complex tastings and food events.

Vinoteka Vipava (☑ 05-368 70 41; Glavni trg 1, Vipava; ⊙9am-7pm Jul-Sep, to 6pm Mon-Fri, to 2pm Sat Oct-Jun) Attached to Vipava's tourist information centre, this friendly, well-informed *vinoteka* stocks some 180 bottles from 45 local winemakers. For €5 you can sample 10 wines (refunded if you buy a bottle).

Winestronaut (☑ 040 166 042; www.winestronaut.com; per person from €49) Winestronaut is a new operator with a goal of exploring local wine culture (eg harvest events), tasting wine and food, and getting tourists into selected cellars and to meet the winemakers. Tours are flexible (minimum two guests); pick-up is offered in the Vipava Valley but can be arranged elsewhere.

with lavender honey and salted peaches as a starter? The multicourse menus are great value (three/five courses for €26/34). Service is exemplary, the setting is rustic and charming.

Gostilna Pri Lojzetu   MODERN SLOVENIAN **$$$**
(☑ 05-368 70 07; www.zemono.si; Dvorec Zemono; mains €18-27; ⊙5-11pm Wed & Thu, from noon Fri-Sun) For gourmands, this is a must. Make an advance booking, and make the trip 2km north of Vipava to Dvorec Zemono, a frescoed mansion built in 1680. Here, you'll find innovative, locavore Gostilna Pri Lojzetu, ranked by many as among Slovenia's finest restaurants: 'Michelin-star-worthy' is common praise.

❶ Information

Tourist Information Centre Ajdovščina (TIC; ☑ 05-365 91 40; www.tic-ajdovscina.si; Cesta IV Prekomorske 61a, Ajdovščina; ⊙10am-6pm Mon-Fri, 8am-noon Sat May-Sep, 8am-4pm Mon-Fri, 8am-noon Sat Oct-Apr) At the youth hostel complex.

Tourist Information Centre Vipava (TIC; ☑ 05-368 70 41; www.izvirna-vipavska.si; Glavni trg 1, Vipava; ⊙9am-7pm Jul-Sep, to 6pm Mon-Fri, to 2pm Sat Sep-Jun) In the centre of town.

❶ Getting There & Around

About a dozen buses daily connect Ljubljana and Nova Gorica, travelling via Postojna, Vipava and Ajdovščina (Ljubljana–Vipava €7.90, 1¾ hours, 83km).

In the Vipava Valley, the TICs and numerous accommodation providers have bicycles for rent.

CENTRAL PRIMORSKA

If you're heading to the Soča Valley from Ljubljana (rather than through the Julian Alps), you'll pass through central Primorska, a land of steep slopes, deep valleys and innumerable ravines with plenty of good hiking. The region is dominated by the Cerkno and Idrija Hills, foothills of the Julian Alps.

The towns here don't feature too high on traveller radars, but that, combined with some quirky attractions, may be a large part of their appeal.

Idrija

☑ 05 / POP 5903 / ELEV 325M

Idrija means three things: *žlikrofi*, lace and mercury. The women of Idrija have been taking care of the first two for centuries, while the men went underground to extract the latter, making Idrija one of the richest towns in Europe during the Middle Ages.

Idrijski žlikrofi are pasta pockets not unlike small ravioli; they're made with a potato filling (with pork fat, onion and herbs); in 2010 they were awarded a protected geographical status (the first Slovenian dish to get such recognition). Bigger things were to come for the town: in 2012 Unesco granted World Heritage status to Idrija's mercury mine (together with a similar mine in Almadén, Spain).

History

The first mine opened at Idrija in 1500; within three centuries Idrija produced 13% of the world's quality mercury. Its uses ranged widely, from the extraction of gold and silver in the mines of the New World to treatments for syphilis. Miners faced many health hazards, but the relatively high wages attracted workers from all over the Habsburg Empire and because of the toxic effects of mercury, doctors and lawyers flocked as well.

The mines are no longer in operation, but their legacy remains: Idrija sits on 700km of shafts that descend 15 levels, and expensive measures continue to be taken to ensure the town doesn't sink.

⊙ Sights

★ **Municipal Museum**   MUSEUM
(Mestni Muzej; ☑ 05-372 66 00; www.muzej-idrija-cerkno.si; Prelovčeva ulica 9; adult/child €5/3; ⊙ 9am-6pm) This award-winning museum is housed in the hilltop **Gewerkenegg Castle** (Prelovčeva ulica 9). The excellent collections, which deal with mercury, lace and local history (but, sadly, not *žlikrofi*) are exhibited in three wings centred on a beautiful courtyard, and an accompanying booklet guides visitors through the rooms.

Exhibits span rocks and fossils (and a bowl of mercury in room 3) to lifestyles of the miners and the growth of the town. Head down the steps of the Mercury Tower (room 7) to see the mining tools used, and also the lovely modern sculpture of mercury drops suspended in perspex.

Another highlight is the wing given over entirely to the bobbin lace *(klekljana čipka)* woven here. Check out the tablecloth that measures 3m by 1.8m. It was designed for Madame Tito and took 5000 hours to make.

The castle itself was built in the 1520s to serve as the administrative headquarters of the Idrija mine.

★ **Anthony Mine Shaft**   MINE
(Antonijev Rov; ☑ 05-377 11 42; www.antonijevrov.si; Kosovelova ulica 3; adult/child €9/5; ⊙ tour 10am & 3pm daily Apr-Nov, Sat & Sun Dec-Mar) The mine is a 'living museum', allowing you to get a feel for the working conditions of mercury miners in Idrija. The entrance is the Anthony Shaft, built in 1500, which led to the first mine: 1.5km long, 600m wide and 400m deep. The tour covers about 1200m and lasts 1½ hours; it begins in the 'call room' of an 18th-century building where miners were selected each morning and assigned their duties.

You'll be supplied overcoats and helmets; the temperature in the mine is around 13°C (55°F). There are additional tour times in summer – see the website.

Idrija Lace School   NOTABLE BUILDING
(Čipkarska Šola Idrija; ☑ 05-373 45 70; http://cipkarskasola.si; Prelovčeva ulica 2; adult/child €2.50/free; ⊙ 9am-3pm Mon-Sat Jul-Aug, 10am-1pm Mon-Fri Sep-Jun) The Idrija Lace School was founded in 1876 (it's the biggest and oldest lace school in the world), and continues to offer lace-making skills to younger generations. The showroom exhibits remarkable pieces made by students aged six to 15. There are also items for purchase, made locally.

Miner's House   NOTABLE BUILDINGS
(Rudarska Hiša; ☑ 05-372 66 00; www.muzej-idrija-cerkno.si; Bazoviška 4; adult/child €3/2; ⊙ 9am-4pm by appointment) Laid out across the slopes encircling the valley are Idrija's distinctive miners' houses. Large wooden A-frames with cladding and dozens of windows, they usually had four storeys with living quarters for three or four families. You can visit a traditional miner's house above the centre of town, accompanied by a guide from the museum.

Wild Lake   NATURE RESERVE
(Divje Jezero) A 3km trail called **Pot ob Rakah** follows the Idrijca River Canal from the **Kamšt** (an 18th-century waterwheel used by the mines) to Wild Lake, a tiny, impossibly green lake fed by a deep karst spring. After heavy rains, water gushes up from the

Idrija

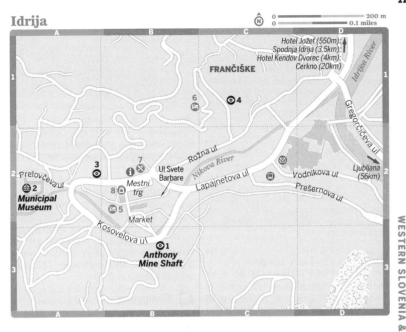

Idrija

⊙ Top Sights
1 Anthony Mine Shaft B3
2 Municipal Museum A2

⊙ Sights
Gewerkenegg Castle .... (see 2)
3 Idrija Lace School A2
4 Miner's House C1

⊜ Sleeping
5 Gostilna Pri Škafarju B2
6 Hostel Idrija B1

⊗ Eating
Gostilna Pri Škafarju .... (see 5)
7 Žlikrof Plac... B2

⊛ Shopping
8 Studio Koder B2

tunnel like a geyser and the lake appears to be boiling. With your own wheels, take the road out of town towards Ljubljana and turn at the sign to Idrijska Bela – it's 600m to the lake.

West of the lake, there's a footbridge and a river-swimming area, which is used in summer when the water averages about 20°C (68°F).

🛌 Sleeping

Hostel Idrija   HOSTEL $
(📞 05-373 40 70; www.youth-hostel.si; Ulica IX Korpusa 17; dm from €9, d €26; P 🖥) Basic budget beds with shared bathroom, about 600m northeast of Mestni trg.

Gostilna Pri Škafarju   GUESTHOUSE $
(📞 05-377 32 40; www.skafar.si; Ulica Svete Barbare 9; s/d €35/50; 🖥) In addition to food, this popular *gostilna* (inn) offers accommodation in four smallish but well-appointed mansard rooms. If you want a central location, you've got it.

Hotel Jožef   HOTEL $$$
(📞 082-004 250; www.hotel-jozef.si; Vojkova 9a; d €110-130; P 🖥) Jožef is a small (12 rooms), newly built hotel about 800m north of the town centre. It features modern design and facilities catering to a business crowd, plus it offers good service and there's an excellent on-site restaurant.

STONE AGE MUSIC

Despite our preconceptions, our prehistoric forebears were a sophisticated bunch. In 1995, palaeontologists looking for Stone Age tools were directed to Divje Babe, a cave some 200m above the main road linking Cerkno with the Tolmin–Idrija highway. After careful digging they found a piece of cave bear femur measuring 10cm long and perforated with four aligned holes (two intact, two incomplete) at either end. It looked exactly like, well, a flute.

The flute was dated using electron spin resonance techniques and is believed to be around 43,000 years old. Although dubbed the 'Neanderthal flute' in Slovenia, some debate persists about whether or not it was made by that species or by Cro-Magnons – modern humans. (There is also conjecture that the punctures may simply have been made by a carnivore bite, but studies cast doubt on this theory.)

If it *is* a flute, Slovenia can claim the oldest known musical instrument on earth. And – in case you were wondering – it could play a tune (search for 'Neanderthal Bone Flute Music' on YouTube, in which a replica is played). It's on display at the National Museum of Slovenia (p44) in Ljubljana.

Hotel Kendov Dvorec   HOTEL $$$
(②05-372 51 00; www.kendov-dvorec.com; Na Griču 2, Spodnja Idrija; s/d from €130/180; ℗⊚) The most characterful, romantic option in the area is this 'castle hotel' 4km north of Idrija. There are 11 rooms in a converted manor, the oldest part of which dates from the 14th century. Antique furniture, pretty gardens and dreamy views along the Idrijca Valley add to the allure.

✗ Eating

There are no standout dining venues, but you're able to get your fill of *žlikrofi* everywhere. Traditionally they are eaten with *bakalca*, a meat sauce made with mutton, but they are also popular with gorgonzola, mushrooms or pork. They can be served as a main dish, or a side.

Žlikrof Plac   SLOVENIAN $
(②041 666 646; Mestni trg 4; mains €4-8; ⊙7am-3pm Mon, to 9pm Tue-Fri, 8am-9pm Sat, 11am-5pm Sun) A central and bright cafe serving up all manner of easy eats (pasta, salads, pizza, including cheap daily lunch specials). But you're here for the *žlikrofi*, and this place serves them traditional-style but also with inventive fillings – including vegetarian, or even sweet dessert ones.

Gostilna Pri Škafarju   SLOVENIAN $
(②05-377 32 40; www.skafar.si; Ulica Svete Barbare 9; mains €5-13; ⊙10am-4pm Mon-Thu, to 9pm Fri & Sat, 11am-8pm Sun) Pizza baked in a wood-burning tile stove is why many people come to this friendly *gostilna*, but there are plenty of other things on the menu, such as a tasting plate of *žlikrofi* with various sauces (for two people; €20) and tasty *štruklji* (pastries) of spinach and cheese.

🔒 Shopping

Studio Koder   ARTS & CRAFTS
(②05-377 13 59; www.idrija-lace.si; Mestni trg 16; ⊙10am-noon & 4-7pm Mon-Fri, 10am-noon Sat) Idrija lace is among the finest in the world, and a small piece makes a great gift or souvenir. There are several shops; we like the superior Studio Koder, a stylish shop across from the town hall.

ℹ Information

Tourist Information Centre (TIC; ②05-374 39 16; www.visit-idrija.si; Mestni trg 2; ⊙9am-7pm Mon-Fri, to 6pm Sat & Sun May-Sep, 9am-4pm Mon-Fri, 10am-3pm Sat & Sun Oct-Apr) Centrally placed; can help with info and accommodation.

ℹ Getting There & Away

From the **bus station** (Lapaijnetova ulica), bus services include the following:

Bovec (€9.20, 2½ hours, 99km, two daily) via Tolmin and Kobarid.

Cerkno (€3.10, 28 minutes, 21km, hourly).

Ljubljana (€6.30, 1¼ hours, 56km, roughly hourly).

Cerkno

②05 / POP 1550 / ELEV 323M

A sleepy village in the Cerknica River Valley, Cerkno is an important destination for ethnologists and party-goers alike when the

Laufarija, the ancient Shrovetide celebration, takes place. Nearby are the intriguing remains of a secret Partisan hospital from WWII.

◉ Sights

Cerkno Museum   MUSEUM
(Cerkljanski Muzej; ☑ 05-372 31 80; www.muzej-idrija-cerkno.si; Bevkova ulica 12; adult/child €3.50/2.50; ⊙ 9am-3pm Tue-Fri, 10am-1pm & 2-6pm Sat & Sun) The town's museum is not far southwest of Glavni trg. Its main displays trace the development of the region from earliest times to the modern period, but its biggest draw is the collection of Laufarija masks contained in the exhibit 'Pust Is to Blame'.

★ Franja Partisan Hospital   MEMORIAL
(Partizanska Bolnica Franja; ☑ 05-372 31 80; www.muzej-idrija-cerkno.si; adult/child €5/3; ⊙ 9am-6pm Apr-Sep, to 4pm Oct) This clandestine hospital, hidden in a canyon near Dolenji Novaki, about 5km northeast of Cerkno, treated wounded Partisan soldiers from Yugoslavia and other countries from late 1943 until the end of WWII. A memorial to humanity and self-sacrifice, it had more than a dozen wooden cabins, including treatment huts, operating theatres, X-ray rooms and huts for convalescence. Nearly 600 wounded were treated here, and the mortality rate was only about 10%.

The complex, hidden in a ravine by a stream, had an abundance of fresh water, which was also used to power a hydroelectric generator. Local farmers and Partisan groups provided food, which was lowered down the steep cliffs by rope; medical supplies were diverted from hospitals in occupied areas or later air-dropped by the Allies. The hospital came under attack by the Germans twice but it was never taken.

There's another remarkable thing about the hospital: it was almost entirely destroyed by flood in 2007, and has been completely reconstructed. It's extremely well done; access is via a lovely 500m stream-side walking path.

☆ Activities

The brochure *Cerkno Map of Local Walks,* available from the TIC and Hotel Cerkno, lists eight walks in the Cerkno Hills (Cerkljansko Hribovje), most of them pretty easy and lasting between 1½ and four hours return. Walk number 7 leads to the Franja Partisan Hospital (3½ hours) and back. The *Cerkno Cycling Tracks* brochure outlines five mountain-biking routes in the hills; bikes can be hired from Hotel Cerkno.

✷ Festivals & Events

Laufarija   CULTURAL
(www.laufarija-cerkno.si; ⊙ Feb/Mar) The biggest annual event in these parts unfolds on Glavni trg in the days before Lent begins (the Sunday and Tuesday before Ash Wednesday). This ancient carnival sees masked participants chasing and executing the Pust, a character representing winter and the old year.

THE LAUFARIJA TRADITION

Ethnologists believe that the Laufarija tradition and its distinctive masks came from Austria's South Tyrol. *Lauferei* means 'running about' in German, and that's just what the crazily masked participants do as they nab their victims.

Special (and mostly male) Laufarji societies organise the annual event. Those aged 15 and over are allowed to enter, after proving themselves as apprentices by sewing costumes. Outfits are made fresh every year, with leaves, pine branches, straw or moss stitched onto a hessian backing. They take quite a beating during the festivities.

The action takes place on the Sunday before Ash Wednesday and again on Shrove Tuesday. The main character is the Pust, with a horned mask and heavy costume of moss. He's the symbol of winter and the old year – and he *must* die.

The Pust is charged with many grievances – a bad harvest, inclement weather, lousy roads – and always found guilty. Other Laufarji characters represent crafts and trades – Baker, Thatcher, Woodsman – with the rest including the Drunk and his Wife, the Bad Boy, Sneezy and the accordion-playing Sick Man. The Old Man, wearing Slovenian-style lederhosen and a wide-brimmed hat, executes the Pust with a wooden mallet, and the body is rolled away on a caisson.

🛏 Sleeping & Eating

Gačnk v Logu   GUESTHOUSE **$**

(☑ 05-372 40 05; www.cerkno.com; Dolenji Novaki 1; r per person €21-29; ☎) This friendly, century-old inn is close to the turn-off for the Franja Partisan Hospital (about 3.5km north of Cerkno centre). It has nine homely rooms (including family-sized ones), a kids' play area, and a **restaurant** (mains €6 to €12) serving up locally grown ingredients – specialities include mushroom soup, fresh trout, *žlikrofi* and venison.

Hotel Cerkno   HOTEL **$$**

(☑ 05-374 34 00; www.hotel-cerkno.si; Sedejev trg 8; budget s/d €32/50, standard €60/90; @ ☎ ✖) The decor at this large hotel is tired but facilities are decent and service is excellent. Standard rooms are quite pricey for what you get – better value are the budget 'hostel' rooms (which still have private bathroom, TV and wi-fi). There's an indoor pool and free bike use for guests, plus a restaurant and cafe.

ℹ Information

Glavni trg, where the buses stop, is the main square and the centre of Cerkno.

Tourist Information Centre (TIC; ☑ 05-373 46 45; www.turizem-cerkno.si; Močnikova ulica 2; ⊗ 9am-4pm Tue-Fri, 8am-3pm Sat & Sun) Just off Glavni trg. It's best not to visit Cerkno on a Monday, when both the museum and the TIC are closed.

ℹ Getting There & Away

On weekdays, there are hourly bus departures to Idrija (€3.10, 28 minutes, 21km), and up to eight buses daily to Ljubljana (€7.50, 1¾ hours, 77km). Services drop by about 50% on weekends.

The Karst & the Coast

Best Places to Stay

➡ Kaki Plac (p154)

➡ Old Schoolhouse Korte (p146)

➡ PachaMama (p151)

➡ Lipizzaner Lodge (p130)

➡ Kempinski Palace Portorož (p155)

Best Places to Eat

➡ Capra (p142)

➡ Hiša Torkla (p146)

➡ Etna (p137)

➡ Restaurant Proteus (p131)

➡ Cantina Klet (p152)

Why Go?

Slovenia's astonishing diversity comes to the fore in this region. Separated by short distances, you can traipse through remarkable Unesco-recognised caves that yawn open to reveal karstic treasures, go bear-watching in dense green forests, or admire the Venetian history and architectural legacy of photogenic seaside towns.

Continue the winning mix of history-meets-scenery: view dancing white Lipizzaner horses at the estate that first bred them in the late 16th century, then inspect the marvellous detail of the 15th-century *Dance of Death* fresco at remote Hrastovlje. Visit the historic salt pans of Sečovlje then enjoy a salt scrub at the stylish open-air day spa in their midst.

Flavours are equally diverse and delectable. Lunch on *pršut* (air-dried ham) accompanied by ruby-red teran wine for the definitive taste of the Karst; dine on seafood washed down with local *malvazija* wine on the coast – best savoured with a sunset view of the Adriatic.

When to Go
Piran

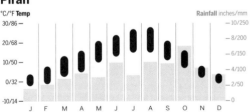

Jun–Aug The summer peak: prime weather, crowds, beaches and activities in full swing.

Sep The perfect time for swimming in the Adriatic, when the tourist numbers have died down.

Dec See the living nativity scene inside Postojna Cave.

The Karst & the Coast Highlights

1 Descend into the netherworld with a tour of the **Škocjan Caves** (p136).

2 Enjoy the catch of the day amid the glorious Venetian architecture of **Piran** (p147).

3 Marvel at a train *inside* a cave and look for human fish at **Postojna Cave** (p129).

4 Unwind at the peaceful **Lepa Vida Thalasso Spa** (p156) in the salty Sečovlje Salina Nature Park.

5 Be dazzled by the detail of the frescoes lining the interior of the **Church of the Holy Trinity** (p143) in Hrastovlje.

6 Admire the stories told at **Predjama Castle** (p132), an impregnable castle perched in a cliffside cave.

7 Get off the beaten track (and potentially spot a bear) in the forests of the **Lož Valley** (p134).

KARST REGION

The Karst region (Kras in Slovenian; www.visitkras.info) is a limestone plateau stretching from the Gulf of Trieste to the Vipava Valley. Rivers, ponds and lakes can disappear and then resurface in the Karst's porous limestone through sinkholes and funnels, often resulting in underground caverns like the caves at Škocjan and Postojna.

Along with caves, the Karst is rich in olives, fruits, vineyards producing ruby-red teran wine, *pršut* (air-dried ham, not unlike prosciutto), old stone churches and red-tiled roofs.

Postojna

🎵 05 / POP 9366 / ELEV 546M

The karst cave at Postojna, one of the largest in the world, is among Slovenia's most popular attractions, and its stalagmite and stalactite formations are unequalled anywhere. It's a busy destination – the amazing thing is how the large crowds at the entrance seem to get swallowed whole by the size of the cave, and the tourist activity doesn't detract from the wonder.

The cave has been known – and visited – by residents of the area for centuries (you need only look at Passage of New Signatures inside the Vivarium Proteus). But people in the Middle Ages knew only the entrances; the inner parts were not explored until April 1818, just days before Habsburg Emperor Franz I (r 1792–1835) came to visit. The following year the Cave Commission accepted its first organised tour group, including Archduke Ferdinand, and Postojna's future as a tourist destination was sealed.

Since then, more than 36 million people have visited it (with some 6000 a day in August; rainy summer days bring the biggest crowds). It's a big, slick complex – and it doesn't come cheap (beginning with a €4 charge for parking).

👁 Sights & Activities

⭐ Postojna Cave   CAVE

(Postojnska Jama; 🎵 05-700 01 00; www.postojnska-jama.eu; Jamska cesta 30; adult/child €22.90/13.70, with Predjama Castle €31.90/19.10; ⊙ tours hourly 9am-5pm or 6pm May-Sep, 3-4 daily 10am-3pm or 4pm Oct-Apr) The jaw-dropping Postojna Cave system, a series of caverns, halls and passages some 24km long and two million years old, was hollowed out by the Pivka River, which enters a subterranean tunnel near the cave's entrance.

Visitors get to see 5km of the cave on 1½-hour tours; 3.2km of this is covered by a cool electric train. Postojna Cave has a constant temperature of 8°C to 10°C with a humidity of 95%, so a warm jacket and decent shoes are advised.

The train takes you to the Great Mountain cavern, on a trip that's like entering the secret lair of a James Bond villain. From here a guide escorts you on foot through tunnels, halls, galleries and caverns in one of six languages (audioguides are available in many more tongues).

These are dry galleries, decorated with a vast array of stalactites shaped like needles, enormous icicles and even fragile spaghetti. The stalagmites take familiar shapes but there are also bizarre columns, pillars and translucent curtains that look like rashers of bacon.

From the Velika Gora cavern you continue across the Russian Bridge, built by prisoners of war in 1916, through the 500m-long Beautiful Caves that are filled with wonderful ribbon-shaped stalactites and stalagmites that are two million years old (it takes 30 years to produce 1mm of stalactite). The halls of the Beautiful Caves are the farthest point you'll reach; from here a tunnel stretches to the Black Cave (Črna Jama) and Pivka Cave (these can also be visited on additional tours).

The tour continues south through the Winter Hall, past the 5m, snow-white Brilliant stalagmite (also sometimes called the Diamond) and the neighbouring baroque pillar, which have become symbols of the cave. You then enter the Concert Hall, which is the largest in the cave system and can accommodate 10,000 people for musical performances. In the week between Christmas and New Year, the Live Christmas Crib (Jaslice) – the Nativity performed by miming actors – also takes place in the cave. Visitors reboard the train by the Concert Hall and return to the entrance. The river continues its deep passage underground, carving out several series of caves, and emerges again as the Unica River.

Green felt capes can be hired at the entrance for €3.50. There are few steps to climb. Check the website for package deals, including various combination tickets that include Vivarium Proteus (p130), the new Expo (p130) and the don't-miss Predjama

Castle (p132). Postojna is a less-strenuous option than Škocjan Caves (p136).

Vivarium Proteus MUSEUM

(☑ 05-700 01 00; www.postojnska-jama.eu; adult/child €8/4.80, with Postojna Cave €28.90/17.30; ☺ 8.30am-6.30pm Jul & Aug, to 5.30pm May, Jun & Sep, 9.30am-4.30pm Apr & Oct, 9.30am-3.30pm Nov-Mar) Just near the entrance to the Postojna Cave is the Vivarium, the cradle of a special branch of biology: speleobiology. Postojna provides shelter to dozens of cave-dwelling animal species – visitors can get to know some of the most interesting ones in more detail here, including the 'human fish' (p131).

Expo Postojna Cave Karst MUSEUM

(☑ 05-700 01 00; www.postojnska-jama.eu; adult/child with Postojna Cave €28.90/17.30; ☺ 8.30am-6.30pm Jul & Aug, to 5.30pm May, Jun & Sep, 9.30am-4.30pm Apr & Oct, 9.30am-3.30pm Nov-Mar) The newest addition to the Postojna Cave complex is this well-designed, kid-friendly space. It displays details of karst phenomena in an engaging manner, and tracks cave exploration. Most interesting is all the memorabilia and vintage posters detailing the 200-year history of tourism to Postojna Cave (eg, the cave got electric lighting in 1883, a decade before Ljubljana).

Planina Cave CAVE

(Planinska Jama; ☑ 041 338 696; www.planina.si; adult/child €7/4; ☺ 3pm Sat, 3pm & 5pm Sun Apr-Sep) Planina Cave, 12km to the northeast of Postojna Cave, is the largest water cave in Slovenia and a treasure-trove of fauna (including *Proteus anguinus*). The cave's entrance is at the foot of a 100m rock wall. It's 6.5km long, and you are able to visit about 900m of it in an hour. There are no lights so take a torch.

With prior warning, tours can be arranged most days in July and August – including a longer, five-hour tour with boat (€30).

★Underground Adventures ADVENTURE TOUR

(☑ 05-700 01 00; www.postojnska-jama.eu; tours per person €30-80) Want to escape the crowds and get a taste of spelunking? Guided tours have been designed to visit Pivka Cave and Black Cave, parts of the Postojna cave system that are not open on regular tours. These tours can be relatively tame, or involve hardhats, overalls, water obstacles and a little abseiling, depending on your wishes.

Tours last from 1½ to six hours, with expert guiding and equipment provided. They are available year-round; bookings must be made at least three days in advance.

🛏 Sleeping

★Youth Hostel Proteus Postojna HOSTEL $

(☑ 05-726 52 91; www.proteus.sgls.si; Tržaška cesta 36; dm/s/d €15/23/34; P @ 🛜) Don't be fooled by the institutional exterior – inside, this place is a riot of colour. It's surrounded by parkland and is a fun, chilled-out space, with three-bed rooms (shared bathrooms), kitchen and laundry access, and bike rental. The year-round hostel shares the building with student accommodation, so facilities are good. It's about 500m southwest of Titov trg.

Camping Pivka Jama CAMPGROUND $

(☑ 05-720 39 93; http://camping-postojna.com; Veliki Otok 50; campsite adult/child €11.90/8.90, 4-bed bungalow €84-99; ☺ Apr-Oct; P 🛜 ☀) This large, attractive forested site is about 4km past the Postojna Cave complex, near the entrance to Pivka Cave. Some of the cosy, family-sized, stone-and-wood bungalows have kitchens, and there's a swimming pool, restaurant and activity options. Note: campervanners might wish to simply overnight at the parking stop by the cave complex (24 hours €18).

★Lipizzaner Lodge GUESTHOUSE $$

(☑ 040 378 037; www.lipizzanerlodge.com; Landol 17; s/d/q from €45/70/90; P 🛜) In a relaxing rural setting 9km northwest of Postojna Cave, a Welsh-Finnish couple have established this very hospitable, affordable guesthouse. They offer seven well-equipped rooms (including family-sized, and a self-catering apartment); great-value evening meals on request (€14); and brilliant local knowledge (check out their comprehensive website for an idea). Forest walks (including to Predjama in 40 minutes) plus bike rental.

Rooms & Apartments Proteus GUESTHOUSE $$

(☑ 081-610 300; www.postojnska-jama.eu; Titov trg 1a; d €82-114, q €140-176; P ❄ 🛜) Above and behind the excellent Proteus Restaurant on Postojna's main square, this newly-built complex of 15 sparkling rooms and apartments offers fresh decor and good facilities (including air-con and free parking). Apartments have a kitchen and can sleep up to six. Breakfast is additional (€7).

THE HUMAN FISH

Postojna is home to the blind eel-like *Proteus anguinus*, or olm. A kind of salamander with a colour not unlike pink human flesh, it lives hidden in the pitch black for up to a century and can go a decade without food.

The chronicler Janez Vajkard Valvasor wrote about the fear and astonishment of local people when an immature 'dragon' was found in a karst spring in the late 17th century. Several other reports about this four-legged 'human fish' (*človeška ribica* as it's called in Slovene) were made before a Viennese doctor described it for science in 1786, naming it for the protector of Poseidon's sea creatures in Greek mythology and the Latin word for 'snake'.

Proteus reaches 30cm long, with a swimming tail and stubby legs. Although blind, with atrophied eyes, *Proteus* has an excellent sense of smell and is sensitive to weak electric fields in the water, which it uses to move around in the dark, locate prey and communicate. It breathes through frilly, bright-red gills. The skin entirely lacks pigmentation but looks pink in the light due to its blood circulation.

Cool pitch-black caves slow down life cycles – the gills are a strange evolutionary throwback to the animals' tadpole stage, which it never fully outgrows, instead reaching sexual maturity at 14 years. No wonder it's always been a creature of local fascination.

You can see *Proteus* in an aquarium inside the Postojna Cave (p129), or at the Vivarium Proteus (p130).

Hotel Kras
HOTEL $$$

(☑ 05-700 23 00; www.hotel-kras.si; Tržaška cesta 1; s/d/ste €87/109/141; P ✳ ⓢ) Smart modern option in the heart of the town, on the main square. There's a nice ground-floor cafe with a large summer terrace.

Hotel Jama
HOTEL $$$

(☑ 05-700 01 00; www.postojnska-jama.eu; Jamska cesta 30) This huge, concrete, socialist-era hotel is part of the Postojna Cave complex and was under major renovation at the time of research. It is expected to re-open by mid-2016, no doubt refreshed and offering all mod-cons (with prices to match). See the Postojna Cave website (p129) for updates.

✖ Eating & Drinking

Štorja Pod Stopnicami
SLOVENIAN $

(☑ 05-992 78 98; www.storja.si; Ulica 1 Maja 1; mains €7-15; ⊗ 7am-11pm) Just southeast of Titov trg, this cute and crowd-pleasing cafe-restaurant has a menu covering all bases: coffee and cake, cracking burgers, pasta and gnocchi, and fancier fare. It has great lunch-time specials (€5.50).

Čuk
PIZZA $

(☑ 05-720 13 00; www.pizza-cuk.si; Pot k Pivki 4; pizza & pasta €6-10; ⊗ 11am-10pm Wed-Mon; 🚗) A large, no-frills, family-style restaurant south-west of Titov trg, off Tržaška cesta, Čuk takes its pizza seriously but offers a wide range of Slovenian mains too. There's a large playground for kids.

★ Restaurant Proteus
MODERN SLOVENIAN $$

(☑ 081-610 300; Titov trg 1; mains €12-20; ⊗ 8am-10pm) The fanciest place in town: inside is modern and white, with booths fringed by curtains, while the terrace overlooking the main square is a fine vantage point. Accomplished cooking showcases fine regional produce – house specialities include venison goulash and steak with teran (red wine) sauce. It's hard to go past the four-course Chef's Slovenian Menu (€35) for value and local flavour.

Modrijan Homestead
SLOVENIAN $$

(☑ 05-700 01 00; www.postojnska-jama.eu; Postojna Cave complex; mains €12-20; ⊗ 10am-6pm Apr-Sep) As you'd imagine, eating at the touristy complex surrounding Postojna Cave is not cheap, but here you'll get some very tasty grilled meats to fuel exploration. The menu is listed in an impressive seven languages and includes grilled trout, salmon and veggies. The meats – roast suckling pig, *klobasa* (sausage) and *čevapčiči* (spicy meatballs) – are excellent.

Guštarna
WINE BAR

(☑ 031 339 211; www.gustarna.com; Tržaška cesta 35; ⊗ 9am-noon & 3-7pm Mon-Fri, 9am-noon Sat) Stop by this attractive wine store for advice on local drops, tastings, and the chance

PREDJAMA CASTLE

Predjama Castle (☎ 05-700 01 00; www.postojnska-jama.eu; Predjama 1; adult/child €11.90/7.10, with Postojna Cave €31.90/19.10; ☺ 9am-7pm Jul & Aug, to 6pm May, Jun & Sep, 10am-5pm Apr & Oct, 10am-4pm Nov-Mar) Predjama Castle is 9km from Postojna and is one of the world's most dramatic castles. It teaches a clear lesson: if you want to build an impregnable fortification, put it in the gaping mouth of a cavern halfway up a 123m cliff. Its four storeys were built piecemeal over the years from 1202, but most of what you see today is from the 16th century. It looks simply unconquerable.

An audioguide (available in 15 languages) details the site's highlights and history. The castle holds great features for kids of any age – holes in the ceiling of the entrance tower for pouring boiling oil on intruders, a very dank dungeon, a 16th-century chest full of treasure (unearthed in the cellar in 1991), and an eyrie-like hiding place at the top called Erazem's Nook, named for Erazem (Erasmus) Lueger.

Lueger was a 15th-century robber-baron who, like Robin Hood, stole from the rich to give to the poor. During the wars between the Hungarians and the Austrians, Erazem supported the former. He holed up in Predjama Castle and continued his daring deeds with the help of a secret passage that led out from behind the rock wall. In 1484 the Austrian army besieged the castle, but it proved impregnable. Erazem mocked his attackers, even showering them with fresh cherries to prove his comfortable situation. But the Austrians had the last laugh – finally hitting him with a cannonball as he sat on the toilet. An ignoble fate for a dashing character.

The cave below the castle is part of the 14km Predjama cave system. It's open to visitors from May to September (closed in winter so as not to disturb its colony of bats during their hibernation). Another adventure option is to visit the narrow Erazem's Passage, through which the besieged knight was connected with the outside world (some climbing skills are required for this). Tours need to be booked at least three days in advance; caving tours range in price from €24 to €80.

Gostilna Požar (☎ 05-751 52 52; www.gostilna-pozar.com; Predjama 2; mains €7-15; ☺ 10am-10pm Jul-Aug, closed Wed Apr-Jun & Sep-Dec, open weekends Jan-Mar) is a simple, traditional restaurant conveniently located next to the ticket kiosk and in perfect view of the castle. Basic rooms are available (double €54).

Joint tickets can be bought for the castle and Postojna Cave (p129). In July and August, a handy shuttle-bus service runs between the cave and the castle; it's free for guests who buy a combined ticket for both attractions.

to sample and buy local delicacies (hams, cheeses, oils etc).

❶ Orientation

The Postojna Cave tourist complex is about 1.5km northwest of Titov trg, the main square in the town centre. Follow Jamska cesta to reach it.

Postojna's bus station is at Titova cesta 2, about 200m southwest of Titov trg. Note that some intercity buses will stop at the cave complex too (on timetables this is *Postojnska jama*). The train station is on Kolodvorska cesta about 800m east of the square.

❶ Information

Kompas Postojna (☎ 05-721 14 80; www. kompas-postojna.si; Titov trg 2a) In town, this travel agency is a good source of information. It also arranges private rooms.

Tourist Information Centre Postojna (TIC; ☎ 064 179 972; tic.postojna.info@gmail. com; Tržaška cesta; ☺ 9am-9pm Jul & Aug, to 6pm Jun & Sep, shorter hrs Oct, Nov, Apr & May, closed Jan-Mar) A smart new pavilion has been built in the town's west, on the road into town (by the supermarket Mercator). It's ideal for motorists, not so good for those on public transport. There is also a small info area inside the library at Trg Padlih Borcev 5, not far southwest of Titov trg.

❶ Getting There & Away

BUS

Bus destinations from Postojna include:
Cerknica (€2.70, 27 minutes, 17km, seven daily)
Divača (for Škocjan; €3.60, 30 minutes, 28km, seven daily)

Koper (€6.90, 1¼ hours, 68km, up to eight daily)

Ljubljana (€6, one hour, 54km, hourly)

Piran (€8.30, 1¾ hours, 86km, four daily)

Trieste (€6.50, 1¼ hours, 52km, two to three daily)

Vipava (€3.60, 34 minutes, 29km, 12 daily)

TRAIN

Postojna is on the main train line linking Ljubljana (€5.80, one hour, 67km) with Sežana and Trieste via Divača, and is an easy day trip from the capital. As many as 20 trains a day make the run from Ljubljana to Postojna and back.

You can also reach Koper (€8.79, 1½ hours, 86km) on the coast. There are up to six trains a day; these may involve a change at Divača.

🛈 Getting Around

In July and August there is a free shuttle bus from the train station to Postojna Cave. Enquire at your accommodation for the closest bike rental, or head to **Youth Hostel Proteus Postojna** (p130). For a taxi, call ☑ 031 777 974 or ☑ 031 413 254.

Green Karst

The undulating, heavily forested Notranjska ('Inner Carniola') region – which encompasses Postojna and Predjama – is full of woodlands, castles, caves, and sinkholes created by 'disappearing' rivers and lakes. Its isolated setting has spawned some of Slovenia's most cherished myths and legends, notably that of the Turk-slayer Martin Krpan, made famous in Fran Levstik's book of the same name.

The region has recently been repackaged and promoted as the 'Green Karst' (Zeleni Kras; www.zelenikras.si) – it's an apt name, as this is a peaceful rural pocket that flies under the radar of most travellers' attention. This may change, when word spreads about its natural beauty, friendly tourist farms – and bear-spotting potential.

Access is easy from Postojna, the hub of the region; exploration is best with your own transport.

Cerknica & Around

☑ 01 / POP 3981 / ELEV 572M

Cerknica is the largest town on a lake that isn't always a lake – one of Slovenia's most unusual natural phenomena. It's a good springboard for the gorge at Rakov Škocjan and Notranjska Regional Park as a whole.

◉ Sights

Lake Cerknica LAKE

Since ancient times, periodic Lake Cerknica (Cerniško Jezero) has baffled and perplexed people, appearing and disappearing with the seasons. Cerknica is a *polje*, a field above a collapsed karst cavern riddled with holes like a Swiss cheese. During rainy periods, usually in the autumn and spring, water comes rushing into the *polje*. As the water percolates between the rocks, the sinkholes and siphons can't handle the outflow underground, and the *polje* becomes Lake Cerknica – sometimes in less than a day.

The *polje* is fed by a disappearing river, the Stržen, and also collects water underground from the Bloke Plateau and the Javornik Mountains. The surface area of Lake Cerknica can reach 38 sq km (under ordinary conditions it usually reaches around 28 sq km), but it is never more than a few metres deep. When full it is an important wetland, attracting some 250 species of birds each year. During dry periods (usually July to September or later), farmers drive cattle down to the *polje* to graze among the sinkholes.

The lake really begins at the village of Dolenje Jezero, 2.5km south of Cerknica.

Lake House Museum MUSEUM

(Muzej Jezerski Hram; ☑ 01-709 40 53, 051 338 057; www.jezerski-hram.si; Dolenje Jezero 1e; adult/child €7/5) In the village of Dolenje Jezero you will find the Lake House Museum, with a 5m by 3m, 1:2500-scale working model of Lake Cerknica. It shows how the underground hydrological system actually works in a 1¼-hour demonstration and video about the lake in the four seasons. There's also ethnological exhibits about local fishing and boat building.

The demonstration is open to the public once daily; it occurs Monday to Saturday July to August (start time varies), and up to a few times a week in other months. It's best to check the website or call/email for times. Note that you can also arrange a private demonstration.

Notranjska Regional Park NATURE RESERVE

(Notranjska Regijski Park; www.notranjski-park.si) This 222-sq-km park holds within its borders a good deal of the region's karst phenomena, including the intermittent Lake Cerknica, forests, meadows, wetlands, caves (including Križna Cave) and Rakov Škocjan gorge. There is also a wealth of cultural heritage in the form of orchards, preserved buildings and old hayracks. Great hiking, cycling and birdwatching lie within its borders. The area's TICs (p134) can provide info.

Rakov Škocjan
GORGE

Rakov Škocjan is a beautiful, 2.5km-long gorge lying some 6km west of Cerknica. The Rak River, en route to join the Pivka River at Planina Cave, has sculpted 2.5km of hollows, caves, springs and rocky arches – including the Veliki and Mali Naravni Most, the Big and Little Natural Bridges. There are lots of hiking and biking trails through and around the gorge and it is surrounded by Notranjska Regional Park.

Heritage House
CULTURAL CENTRE

(Hiša Izročila; ☑ 01-709 63 10; www.hisaizrocila. si; Dolenja Vas 70c) This new project aims to preserve the cultural and natural heritage of the Notranjska Regional Park, and to that end it stages public events and organises unique activities and workshops. This could be a guided walk, birdwatching, boat-building demonstration, or an evening of folk music and storytelling. Advance booking required; contact the organisation for details, prices etc.

🏃 Activities

Ask at the TICs for activities in the area – these range from cave tours to animal-spotting (including bears) and horse riding to sport fishing. There are good hiking trails, including the 91km, three-day Great Krpan Trail (Velika Krpanova Pot), which connects the entire Green Karst region, beginning in the town of Pivka and ending in Postojna. Shorter legs can be walked; it's also suitable for cyclists.

🎉 Festivals & Events

Pust v Cerknici
RELIGIOUS

(http://pust.si; ☺ Feb-Mar) Cerknica is famous for its pre-Lenten carnival, Pust, which takes place for four days over the weekend before Ash Wednesday. Mask-wearing merrymakers and witches parade up and down while being provoked by *butalci* (hillbillies) with pitchforks.

🛏 Sleeping & Eating

Prenočišča Miškar
GUESTHOUSE $

(☑ 081 602 284; www.miskar.si; Žerovnica 66; s/d/ tr €35/46/60; 🅿🛜) It's nicer to stay out on the rural properties around Cerknica, and this four-room guesthouse is a very good

choice, on forested grounds about 7km southeast of town (and only about 5km from Križna Cave). The owners are friendly, the balcony views superb.

Valvasorjev Hram
SLOVENIAN $

(☑ 01-709 37 88; Partizanska cesta 1; mains €6-14; ☺ 8am-11pm Mon-Sat, 3-10pm Sun) This simple eatery serves hearty dishes like *jota* (bean soup) and *klobasa* (sausage) as well as pizza. It has its own wine cellar and outside seating in summer.

ℹ️ Information

Tourist Information Centre (TIC; ☑ 01-709 36 36; ticerknica@cerknica.si; Tabor 42; ☺ 10am-5pm) For local information, including for Notranjska Regional Park. Bike rental available.

ℹ️ Getting There & Around

Bus connections from Cerknica:

Ljubljana (€6, 1¼ hours, 47km, up to 17 daily).

Postojna (€2.70, 27 minutes, 17km, six daily).

Ratek (€1.30, nine minutes, 9km, nine daily) The closest train station.

Lož Valley
☑ 01 / ELEV 586M

The secluded Lož Valley (Loška Dolina) southeast of Cerknica is a green and tranquil taste of rural Slovenia. In summer look out for its trademark *ostrnice* (tall slender haystacks) in mowed meadows. Plus: it's bear-spotting country!

👁 Sights & Activities

⭐ Križna Cave
CAVE

(Križna Jama; ☑ 041 632 153; www.krizna-jama. si; adult/child €8/5.50; ☺ tours 11am, 1pm, 3pm & 5pm daily Jul & Aug, 11am, 1pm & 3pm Sep, 3pm Sat & Sun Apr-Jun) You can explore plenty of Slovenia's caves on foot, but Križna (Cross) Cave is one of the few caves where you can take a subterranean boat ride. This is also the country's only tourist cave without electric lighting – visitors are given lamps (and boots) for their visit, which lasts one to 1½ hours and tours the dry part of the cave, including a short boat ride at the first lake. No prebooking is required for this tour.

Križna is one of the most magnificent water caves in the world. It's 8.8km long and counts 22 underground lakes filled with green and blue water. It's well known for the amount of fossilised cave-bear bones found inside.

BEAR-WATCHING TOURS

Slovenia is one of the rare countries in Europe with a stable brown bear population – in fact, thanks to good management and protection in the last half-century or so, bear numbers have increased significantly (from an estimated 40 in 1900 to up to 700 today).

There is a good-sized bear population in the forests of Notranjska, and there are experienced guides that can help you observe them in their natural habitat from April to September (with luck, there may also be viewings of lynx and/or wolves, which also reside in local forests).

Gostišče Mlakar (☑ 041 582 081; www.slovenianbears.com; Markovec 15a) From his family's **guesthouse** (p135) in the hamlet of Markovec, Miha runs customised nature programs, from multiday wildlife photography workshops to seasonal bear-watching tours. He offers a network of 10 observation hides and professional photography hides in pristine forest – prices are €80 to €120 per day.

Tourist Information Centre Tours (TIC; ☑ 081 602 853; www.loskadolina.info; Cesta 19 Oktobra 49, Lož; 1/2/3 people: €90/120/150) The TIC in Lož can arrange an evening with a local guide at a wildlife observation lookout. The tour begins at the TIC, takes around three hours (including a short forest walk to the lookout), and there is a maximum of three on the tour. Advance booking required.

With advance booking, you go as far as the Kalvarija chamber by rubber raft via 13 lakes (€45 to €65 according to group size). It's a physical, four-hour tour, and the price includes all equipment. Visitor numbers are restricted to about 1000 annually, so it's a good idea to book ahead. In winter (October to March), there is a seven-hour tour, too (€200; restricted to about 100 per year).

The cave is signposted off the main road about halfway between Cerknica (11km northwest) and Snežnik Castle (10km south).

Snežnik Castle
CASTLE
(Grad Snežnik; ☑ 01-705 78 14; www.nms.si; Kozarišče 67; adult/child €5/3; ☺ tours hourly 10am-6pm Apr-Sep, to 4pm Tue-Sun Oct-Mar) Surrounded by parkland, the restored 16th-century Renaissance Snežnik Castle is one of the loveliest and best-situated fortresses in Slovenia.

Entrance is via a 45-minute guided tour. The four floors are richly decorated with period furniture and portraits – the household inventory of the Schönburg-Waldenburg family, who bought the castle in 1853 and used it as a summer residence and hunting lodge until WWII.

The castle's isolation means you really need your own wheels to visit. There is an inn offering accommodation and food in the grounds.

🛏 Sleeping & Eating

★ Gostišče Mlakar
GUESTHOUSE **$$**
(☑ 041 582 081, 01-705 86 86; mlakar.markovec@gmail.com; Markovec 15a; per person €30; P ☎) In the hamlet of Markovec, Miha and his family run a comfy five-room guesthouse and a restaurant beloved of locals, serving homemade regional specialities. The cherry on top: Miha runs customised nature programs (see the boxed text, above).

Pristava Snežnik
APARTMENT **$$**
(☑ 081 614 200; www.pristave-sneznik.si; Kozarišče 69; apt €60-150; P ☎) In the grounds of the lovely Snežnik Castle, an outbuilding has been very nicely converted into five modern apartments, with a restaurant on the ground floor. Apartments are of varying size, most with kitchen and living space; the largest two-bedroom unit can sleep six. It's a gorgeous place to unwind, with a castle outside your window.

The **restaurant** serves traditional cuisine – lots of potatoes, cabbage, stews and game, but also lighter dishes such as local trout.

ℹ Information

Tourist Information Centre (TIC; ☑ 081 602 853; www.loskadolina.info; Cesta 19 Oktobra 49, Lož; ☺ 10am-6pm May-Sep, to 4pm Mon-Fri Oct-Apr) Friendly, helpful office in the wee hamlet of Lož.

Škocjan Caves

🎿 05 / ELEV 402M

The immense system of karst caves at Škocjan, a Unesco World Heritage site, easily rival those at Postojna, and for many travellers a visit here will be a highlight of their Slovenia trip – a page right out of Jules Verne's *A Journey to the Centre of the Earth*.

◉ Sights & Activities

★ **Škocjan Caves**   CAVE

(Škocjanske Jame; 🎿 05-708 21 10; www.park-skocjanske-jame.si; Škocjan 2; cave tour adult/child €16/7.50; ⊙ tours hourly 10am-5pm Jun-Sep, 2-3 daily Oct-Apr) Touring the huge, spectacular subterranean chambers of the 6km-long Škocjan Caves is a must. This remarkable cave system was carved out by the Reka River, which enters a gorge below the village of Škocjan and eventually flows into the Dead Lake, a sump at the end of the cave where it disappears. It surfaces again as the Timavo River at Duino in Italy, 34km northwest, before emptying into the Gulf of Trieste. Dress warmly and wear good walking shoes.

There are two options for touring the caves. The first is a two-hour guided tour through the caves (the most popular option for visitors, called **Through the Underground Canyon**). Visitors walk in groups from the ticket office for about 600m down a gravel path to the main entrance in the Globočak Valley. Through a 116m-long tunnel built in 1933, you soon reach the head of the so-called **Silent Cave**, a dry branch of the underground canyon that stretches for 500m. The first section, called **Paradise**, is filled with beautiful stalactites, stalagmites and flowstones that look like snowdrifts; the second part (called **Calvary**) was once the riverbed. The Silent Cave ends at the **Great Hall**, 120m wide and 30m high. It is a jungle of exotic dripstones and deposits; keep an eye out for the mighty stalagmites called the Giants and the Pipe Organ.

The sound of the Reka River heralds your entry into the **Murmuring Cave**, with walls 100m high. To get over the Reka and into Müller Hall, you must cross **Cerkevnik Bridge**, suspended nearly 50m above the riverbed and surely the highlight of the trip.

Schmidl Hall, the final section, emerges into the Velika Dolina (Big Valley). From here you walk past **Tominč Cave**, where finds from a prehistoric settlement have been unearthed, and over a walkway near the **Natural Bridge**. The tour ends at a funicular lift that takes you back to the entrance (or you can opt to walk, which takes about 30 minutes).

The Škocjan Caves are home to a surprising amount of flora and fauna; your guide will point out mounds of bat guano. The temperature is constant at 12°C so bring along a jacket or sweater. Also note the paths are sometimes slippery. In total, visitors walk 3km on this tour. There's a 'no photos' rule.

From April to October, visitors can choose a second tour option, called **Following the Reka River Underground**. This is a guided (or self-guided) 2km walk following the path of the Reka River, entering the first part of the cave through the natural entrance carved by the river below the village of Škocjan. Tickets for this option cost adult/child €11/5.50; a combined ticket with Through the Underground Canyon costs €21/11.

Škocjan Education Trail   WALKING TOUR

If you have time before or after your cave tour, follow the circular, 2km Škocjan Education Trail around the dolines of the cave system and into nearby hamlets. If time is short, take the path leading north and down some steps from the caves' ticket office – after 250m you'll reach a **viewpoint** that enjoys a superb vista of the Velika Dolina and the gorge where the Reka starts its subterranean journey.

🛏 Sleeping & Eating

If you have your own wheels, consider staying at the lovely Hostel Kras (p137), 25km away.

Pr' Vncki Tamara   GUESTHOUSE $$

(🎿 05-763 30 73, 040 697 827; pr.vncki.tamara@gmail.com; Matavun 10; d €70; 🅿) This welcoming, relaxed spot in Matavun is just steps south of the entrance to the caves. It has four traditionally styled rooms with a total of 10 beds in a charming old farmhouse; we love the rustic old kitchen with the open fire. Bikes can be rented; meals can be arranged (and are highly praised).

Hotel Malovec   HOTEL $$

(🎿 05-763 33 33; www.hotel-malovec.si; Kraška cesta 30a, Divača; s/d hotel €54/80, pension €40/56; 🅿 ❄ 🛜) This new build in the centre of Divača, some 4km northwest of the caves, has 20 compact, modern rooms. There's a similar number of simpler rooms in Malovec's original pension right next door, at a cheaper price. Part of the complex is a popular **restaurant** (open noon to 11pm), which serves hearty, meat-heavy Slovenian favourites to an appreciative crowd.

Etna
ITALIAN

(📞 031 727 568; www.etna.si; Kolodvorska ulica 3a, Divača; mains €8-18; ⊙ 11am-11pm Tue-Sun) Etna takes the classic pizza-pasta-meat-dishes menu and gives it a creative twist, with surprisingly tasty (and beautifully presented) results. All the essentials are homemade (pasta, pizza dough from wholemeal flour); pizza choices are divided between classic or seasonal. The desserts are pretty as a picture.

❶ Getting There & Around

The Škocjan Caves are about 4.5km by road southeast of Divača. A bus connection runs from Divača's neighbouring train and bus stations to the caves a couple of times a day – the caves office recommends you call for times, as these change seasonally. Alternatively, there's a one-hour signed walking trail to the caves.

Buses between Ljubljana and the coast stop at Divača. Destinations:

Koper (€4.70, 45 minutes, 40km, up to 11 daily)

Ljubljana (€7.90, 1½ hours, 82km, seven daily)

Postojna (€3.60, 30 minutes, 28km, seven daily)

Train destinations from Divača:

Koper (€4.28, 50 minutes, five daily)

Ljubljana (€7.70, 1½ hours, up to 14 daily)

Postojna (€3.44, 35 minutes, up to 14 daily)

Lipica

🗐 05 / ELEV 396M

The impact of Lipica, some 9km southwest of Divača and 2km from the Italian border, has been far greater than its size would suggest. This tiny village lives for and on its white Lipizzaner horses, which were first bred here for the Spanish Riding School in Vienna in the late 16th century.

History

In 1580 Austrian Archduke Charles founded a stud farm here for the imperial court in Vienna. Andalusian horses from Spain were coupled with the local Karst breed that the Romans had once used to pull chariots – and the Lipizzaner was born. But they weren't quite the white horses we know today. Those didn't come about for another 200 years when white Arabian horses got into the act.

The breed has subsequently become scattered – moved to Hungary and Austria after WWI, to the Sudetenland in Bohemia after the Germans during WWII, and then shipped off to Italy (along with the studbooks) by the American army in 1945. Only 11 horses returned when operations resumed at Lipica in 1947.

Today more than 300 Lipizzaners remain at the original stud farm while others are bred in various locations around the world, including Piber in Austria, which breeds the horses for the Spanish Riding School. Everyone claims theirs is the genuine article –

THE KARST WINE REGION

If you have your own wheels and a taste for wine and scenery, you might like to explore a picturesque wine region or two. Along the Italian border, the *terra rossa* (iron-rich red soil) of the Karst wine region produces full-bodied, ruby-red teran, a genuine Slovenian wine with designated origin, made from Refošk grapes and perfect to pair with another local speciality: *pršut* (air-dried ham). North of Branik, the **Vipava Valley** (p120) wine region extends northwest to Nova Gorica.

The **Karst Wine Road** (www.vinskacestakras.si) connects dozens of small family-owned producers; pick up maps and brochures from local tourist information centres. There are charming villages and back roads to explore – a favourite destination is the ancient fortified village of **Štanjel** (population 370; www.stanjel.eu), with its own castle and some lovely gardens just outside its walls.

About 10km southwest of Štanjel – and 25km from Škocjan Caves – is the fabulous **Hostel Kras** (📞 05-764 02 50, 041 947 327; www.hostelkras.com; Pliskovica 11; dm/d €16/40; 🛜). It's in a 400-year-old house in the idyllic hamlet of Pliskovica, surrounded by lavender bushes and grapevines. The rooms are simple (all bathrooms shared); there's a kitchen, laundry and bike rental, plus you can pitch a tent in the garden.

patriotic Slovenia even has a pair of Lipizzaners on the reverse side of its €0.20 coin.

◉ Sights

Lipica Stud Farm FARM
(☑ 05-739 15 80; www.lipica.org; Lipica 5; tour adult/child €12/6, incl performance €19/9.50; ⊙ tours hourly 10am-5pm Apr-Oct, 4 daily 10am-3pm Nov-Mar) The stud farm can be visited on very popular, 50-minute guided tours. The interesting, informative tours are available in a number of languages; a tour covers the farm's unique heritage and the breeding of the animals, and visits the pastures and stables. It ends at the very good, hands-on museum called Lipikum (entrance included in tour). A highlight is the performance of these elegant horses (p138) as they go through their complicated paces pirouetting and dancing to Viennese waltzes with riders *en costume*.

Performances take place at 3pm on Tuesday, Friday and Sunday, May to September. On Wednesday, Thursday and Saturday, you can watch training sessions at 10am and 11am (adult/child €14/7 including guided tour). It pays to check the website or call to confirm these schedules, rather than arrive and be disappointed.

Horse-drawn carriage jaunts around the estate might appeal (15/30/60 minutes €14/20/40, not available Mondays).

In April and October there is a reduced number of performances and training sessions; from November to March there are none. You can still take a tour in winter, but there are fewer horses around. Hint: if you can, avoid visiting on Mondays, when there are no performances, training sessions or carriage rides.

🏃 Activities

Lipica Stud Farm HORSE RIDING
(☑ 05-739 15 80; www.lipica.org; Lipica 5; 45/90min trail ride €40/60) Experienced riders only can sign up for a trail ride of 45 or 90 minutes' duration – these must be arranged at least three days in advance, and proper riding gear must be worn. There is also an eight-day riding program involving lessons and grooming (€682, including meals and accommodation). Again, experience (and pre-booking) is a must.

Golf is also available here, and bikes can be hired. See the website for full details.

🛏 Sleeping & Eating

Hotel Maestoso HOTEL $$
(☑ 05-739 15 80; www.lipica.org; Lipica 5; d €60-96; 🅿 @ 🛜) You get to enjoy the stud's farms bucolic setting without the crowds if you stay at this 59-room hotel on the estate. Rooms are clean and comfy but decor is looking a little timeworn in parts. Facilities are decent – including restaurant, golf course and bike hire.

Restaurant Maestoso SLOVENIAN $
(☑ 05-739 17 31; www.lipica.org; Lipica 5; mains €6-16; ⊙ 10am-10pm) At Hotel Maestoso, this restaurant seems to cope well with summertime lunch crowds, and caters to the hotel's overnight guests at dinner. Pizzas are surprisingly good, and there are plenty of options with local *pršut* and olives. Also on the estate is an open-air summer cafe with a terrace serving drinks and ice cream.

❶ Getting There & Around

Most people visit Lipica as a day trip from Sežana, 6km to the north, or Divača, 10km to the northeast, both of which are on a rail line and

---

DANCING HORSES OF LIPICA

Lipizzaners are the finest riding horses in the world. Intelligent, sociable, robust and graceful, they are much sought-after for *haute école* dressage.

Breeding is paramount. Today six stallions are recognised as the foundation bloodstock of the breed, all from the late-18th and early-19th centuries. When you walk around the stables at Lipica you'll see charts on each horse stall with complicated names and dates tracing their lineage.

Lipizzaners foal between January and May, and the foals remain in the herd for about three years. They are then separated for four years of training.

Lipizzaners are born grey, bay or even chestnut. The celebrated 'imperial white' comes about when their hair loses its pigment between five and 10 years old. They are not true 'white horses', as their skin remains grey. When they are ridden hard enough to sweat, they appear mottled.

PRIMORSKA PRIMER

It may come as a surprise to many that Primorska, the name of the long slender province that extends from Austria and Triglav National Park to Istria and the Adriatic Sea, means 'Littoral' in Slovene. With Slovenia's coastline measuring only 47km long, why such an extravagant name? It all has to do with weather. Almost all of Primorska gets the warm winds from the coast that influence the valleys as far as Kobarid and Bovec and inland. As a result, the climate and the flora are distinctly Mediterranean right up to the foothills of the Alps. Yet the province has four distinct regions: the Soča Valley; central Primorska with its rolling Cerkno and Idrija hills; the unique Karst; and the coast itself (sometimes called Slovenian Istria). We cover the first two regions of Primorska in the Western Slovenia & the Soča Valley chapter, and the latter two in the Karst & the Coast chapter.

---

accessible from Ljubljana or Koper. An infrequent bus runs from Sežana to Lipica (€1.80), otherwise a taxi will cost around €10.

At Lipica, bikes can be hired at the golf course reception (two hours/day €5/10).

THE COAST

Slovenia has just 47km of coastline on the Adriatic Sea. Three seaside towns – Koper, Izola and glorious Piran – are full of important Venetian Gothic architecture, and have clean beaches, boats for rent and rollicking bars. It's overbuilt, and jammed from May to September, so if you want solitude head for the hinterland to the south or east where 'Slovenian Istria' still goes about its daily life. You could also sample a portion of the **Parenzana Trail**, a 120km walking and cycling trail (numbered D8) that runs along the old narrow-gauge Parenzana railway, which once connected Trieste in Italy with Poreč in Croatia. About 30km runs through Slovenian Istria. See www.parenzana.info for more details.

You'll find Italian as an official second language here in many of the municipalities, with bilingual signs. Campgrounds, and some of the hotels and restaurants here close or curtail their opening times during the November to March/April off-season. General info is online at www.slovenska-istra.si.

Koper

☑ 05 / POP 25,459

Coastal Slovenia's largest town, Koper (Capodistria in Italian) at first glance appears to be a workaday port city that scarcely gives tourism a second thought. Your first impression may be underwhelming as you see all the industry and shopping malls on the outskirts, but Koper's central core is delightfully medieval and far less overrun than its ritzy cousin Piran.

Koper's recreational area, the seaside resort of Ankaran, is to the north across Koper Bay.

History

Koper has been known by many names during its long history– as Aegida to ancient Greeks, Capris to the Romans and Justinopolis to the Byzantines. In the 13th century it became Caput Histriae – Capital of Istria – from which its Italian name Capodistria is derived. Its golden age was during the 15th and 16th centuries under the Venetian Republic, when the town monopolised the salt trade. But when Trieste, 20km to the northeast, was proclaimed a free port in the early 18th century, Koper lost much of its importance.

Between the World Wars Koper was controlled by the Italians. After WWII the disputed Adriatic coast area – the so-called Free Territory of Trieste – was divided into two zones, with Koper going to Yugoslavia and Trieste to Italy. Today Koper is the centre of the Italian ethnic community of Slovenia.

⊙ Sights & Activities

Although the city has no standout attractions, it's a great place to wander and enjoy some architectural riches. The easiest way to see Koper's Old Town is to walk from the marina on Ukmarjev trg east along Kidričeva ulica to Titov trg and then south down Čevljarska ulica, taking various detours along the way.

Carpacciov Trg   SQUARE
One of the most colourful streets in Koper, Kidričeva ulica, starts at Carpacciov trg, where the **Column of St Justina**

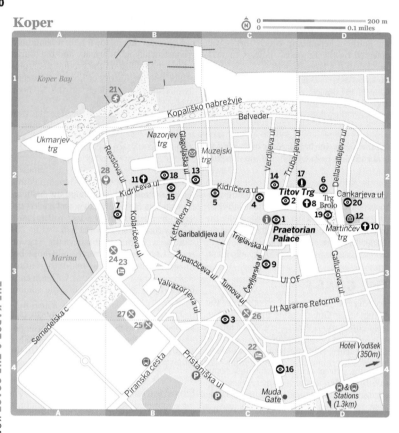

Koper

Koper

◎ Top Sights
1 Praetorian Palace	C2
2 Titov Trg	C2

◎ Sights
3 Almerigogna Palace	C3
4 Armoury	C2
5 Belgramoni-Tacco Palace	C2
6 Brutti Palace	D2
7 Carpacciov Trg	B2
8 Cathedral of the Assumption	D2
9 Čevljarska Ulica	C3
10 Church of St James	D3
11 Church of St Nicholas	B2
City Tower	(see 8)
Column of St Justina	(see 7)
12 Fontico	D2
13 Kidričeva Ulica	B2
Koper Regional Museum	(see 5)
14 Loggia	C2
15 Medieval Town Houses	B2
16 Prešernov Trg	C4

17 Rotunda of John the Baptist	D2
Taverna	(see 7)
18 Totto Palace	B2
19 Trg Brolo	D2
20 Vissich-Nardi Palace	D2

◎ Activities, Courses & Tours
21 Beach	B1

◎ Sleeping
22 Hostel Histria	C4
23 Hotel Koper	B3

◎ Eating
24 Capra	B3
25 Fritolin	B4
26 Istrska Klet Slavček	C3
27 Market	B3

◎ Drinking & Nightlife
28 Kavarna Kapitanija	A2

(Steber Sv Justine; Kidričeva ulica) commemorates Koper's contribution – a galley – to the Battle of Lepanto, in which Turkey was defeated by the European powers in 1571. Just north is a large Roman covered basin that now serves as a fountain. The western edge of the square is marked by the large arched Taverna (Carpacciov trg), a one-time salt warehouse dating from the 15th century.

Kidričeva Ulica   STREET

On the north side of Kidričeva ulica are several churches from the 16th century, including the Church of St Nicholas (Cerkev Sv Nikolaja; Kidričeva ulica 30), plus some restored Venetian houses and the 18th-century baroque Totto Palace (Palača Totto; Kidričeva ulica 22a), with winged lion relief. Opposite the palace are wonderful medieval town houses (Kidričeva ulica 33), with protruding upper storeys painted in a checked red, yellow and green pattern.

Koper Regional Museum   MUSEUM

(Pokrajinski Muzej Koper; ☑ 05-663 35 70; www. pokrajinskimuzejkoper.si; Kidričeva ulica 19; adult/ child €5/2.50; ☉ 9am-5pm Tue-Fri, 11am-5pm Sat, 11am-3pm Sun) The 17th-century Belgramoni-Tacco Palace (Palača Belgramoni-Tacco; Kidričeva ulica 19) houses the Koper Regional Museum, whose history collection spans prehistory to more recent times. In beautiful surrounds is art dating from the 15th century, and displays of armoury and musical heritage.

★ Titov Trg   SQUARE

In the centre of old Koper, Titov trg is a Venetian-influenced stunner; mercifully, like much of the Old Town's core, it is closed to traffic. On the north side is the arcaded Venetian Gothic Loggia (Loža; Titov trg 1) built in 1463 (a perfectly placed cafe lives here); attached is the Loggia Gallery, with changing art exhibits.

To the south is the Praetorian Palace, once the symbol of Venetian power in the region. On the square's western side, the Armoury (Armeria; Titov trg 4) was a munitions dump four centuries ago and is now university offices. Opposite is the Cathedral of the Assumption and its belfry.

★ Praetorian Palace   NOTABLE BUILDING

(Pretorska Palača; ☑ 05-664 64 03; Titov trg 3; adult/child €3/2; ☉ tours 10am, noon, 2pm, 4pm & 6pm Jul-Sep, 11am, 1pm & 3pm Oct-Jun) On the southern side of Titov trg is the white Praetorian Palace, a mixture of Venetian Gothic and Renaissance styles dating from the 15th century and the very symbol of Koper. Now serving as town hall, it contains a reconstructed old pharmacy and the tourist information office on the ground floor, plus exhibits on the history of Koper and a ceremonial hall for weddings on the 1st floor. Access is via guided tour.

The facade of the palace, once the residence of Koper's mayor who was appointed by the doge in Venice, is festooned with medallions, reliefs and coats of arms.

Cathedral of the Assumption   CATHEDRAL

(Stolnica Marijinega Vnebovzetja; Titov trg) Plumb on Titov trg is the Cathedral of the Assumption and its 36m-tall belfry, now called the City Tower (adult/child €3/2; ☉ 9am-1pm & 4-8pm Jul-Sep, 9am-5pm Oct-Jun), with 204 climbable stairs for primo views. The cathedral, partly Romanesque and Gothic but mostly dating from the mid-18th century, has a white classical interior with a feeling of space and light that belies the sombre exterior.

Behind the cathedral to the north is the circular Romanesque Rotunda of John the Baptist (Rotunda Janeza Krstnika; Titov trg), a baptistery dating from the second half of the 12th century with a ceiling fresco.

Trg Brolo   SQUARE

Linked to Titov trg to the east, Trg Brolo is a wide and leafy square of fine old buildings, including the late-18th-century baroque Brutti Palace (Palača Brutti; Trg Brolo 1), now the central library, to the north. On the eastern side is the 17th-century Vissich-Nardi Palace (Palača Vissich-Nardi; Trg Brolo 3) containing government offices and the Fontico (Fontiko; Trg Brolo 4), a granary where the town's wheat was once stored, with wonderful medallions and reliefs. Close by is the disused Church of St James (Cerkev Sv Jakoba; Martinčev trg) dating to the 14th century.

Čevljarska Ulica   STREET

Atmospheric Čevljarska ulica (Cobbler St), a narrow commercial street for pedestrians, runs south from Titov trg. As you walk under the arch of the Praetorian Palace, look to the right. The little hole in the wall with the Italian inscription 'Denontie' was where anonymous denunciations of officials could be made.

Almerigogna Palace   NOTABLE BUILDING

(Palača Almerigogna; Gortanov trg 13) At the end of Čevljarska ulica and down the stone steps is the Almerigogna Palace, a painted Venetian Gothic palace (now with a very basic pub on ground level). It's one of Koper's most beautiful buildings, despite the severely faded paintwork. Look high to see the colour remaining under the eaves.

Prešernov Trg
SQUARE

The 17th-century Italian family who erected the fountain in Prešernov trg was named Da Ponte; thus it is shaped like a bridge (*ponte* in Italian). At the square's southern end is the **Muda Gate** (Vrata Muda; Prešernov trg). Erected in 1516, it's the last of a dozen such entrances to remain standing. On the south side of the archway you'll see the city symbol: the face of a youth in a sunburst.

Beach
BEACH

(Mestno Kopališče; Kopališko nabrežje; ⊙ 8am-7pm May-Sep) **FREE** Buzzing in summer, Koper's tiny beach lies on the northwest edge of the Old Town. It has a small bathhouse with toilets and showers, grassy areas for lying in the sun, and a bar and cafe. On hot summer nights, people pay little heed to the 'closing' hour and swim until late.

Sleeping

Hotel offerings are generally lacklustre.

Hostel Histria
HOSTEL $

(☑ 083 824 038; www.hostel-histria.si; Ulica pri Velikih Vratih 17; dm €15-17; ❄ @ 🛜) Supremely placed in the core of the Old Town, this cosy place is in a 200-year-old house, with decent facilities (including air-con and laundry). Dorms have six or eight beds; bathrooms are shared.

Camping Adria Ankaran
CAMPGROUND $

(☑ 05-663 73 50; www.adria-ankaran.si; Jadranska cesta 25; campsite adult €11-13.50, child €5-6.75; ⊙ mid-Apr–mid-Oct; 🅿 @ 🛜 ⛱) This enormous, well-run campground is on the seashore in Ankaran, 10km to the north and the closest site to Koper (with regular bus connections). Choose from 430 pitches, plus cabins, apartments and hotel rooms and loads of facilities (bowling, minigolf, wellness centre, watersports). The camping charge includes use of the seawater swimming pools (nonguests pay €5/7 weekdays/weekends).

Hotel Vodišek
HOTEL $$

(☑ 05-639 24 68; www.hotel-vodisek.com; Kolodvorska cesta 2; s/d/tr/q €59/88/107/126; 🅿 ❄ @ 🛜) Don't be disheartened by its appearance or location – this small hotel is in a shopping centre halfway between the Old Town and the train and bus stations. Rooms are decent and well-priced; the waterfront is a 10-minute walk away (and there are free bikes for guest use).

Hotel Koper
HOTEL $$$

(☑ 05-610 05 00; Pristaniška ulica 3; per person €73-81; ❄) This 65-room property on the edge of the historic Old Town is Koper's only central hotel. Its location was the best thing going for it – it was in need of renovation when we last visited. However, in late 2015 it comes under new ownership, so hopefully renovations are in its future.

Eating & Drinking

Fritolin
FISH & CHIPS $

(Pristaniška ulica 2; dishes €2-7) There's an outdoor fresh-food market not far from the shore, and it's surrounded by cheap eating spots and cafe-bars popular with locals. We love tiny Fritolin for its fish and chips: calamari fried or grilled, sardines, portions of seabass or bream, or *fritto misto* (mixed fried seafood). There are benches out front, or a park nearby.

Istrska Klet Slavček
SLOVENIAN $

(☑ 05-627 67 29; Župančičeva ulica 39; dishes €3-10; ⊙ 8am-10pm Mon-Fri) The Istrian Cellar, situated below the 18th-century Carli Palace, is one of the most colourful places for a meal in Koper's Old Town. Come for authentic home cooking (hearty soups and stews, roast pork), wine from the barrel, and truly vintage decor that hasn't changed in 30-odd years.

★ Capra
MEDITERRANEAN $$

(☑ 041 602 030; www.capra.si; Pristaniška ulica 3; mains €8-21; ⊙ 8am-11pm) Capra is a sexy new indoor-outdoor venue with a touch of Scandi style. Its appeal extends all day, from coffee to lounge-y cocktails, and the creative, ambitious menu covers many bases with great seafood, salad and pasta options (how's homemade pasta with scampi and truffle?). Presentation is first-class, as are the desserts.

Kavarna Kapitanija
CAFE-BAR

(☑ 040 799 500; www.kavarna-kapitanija.si; Ukmarjev trg 8; ⊙ 7am-midnight) A number of all-day cafe-bars face the water along Pristaniška ulica. This chilled-out, tropical-ish space, with its open terrace and wicker lounges, would be even more inviting if the souvenir kiosks didn't mar the harbour view. Coffee, juices, cocktails and ice cream help to compensate.

ℹ️ Information

Tourist Information Centre (TIC; ☎ 05-664 64 03; www.koper.si; Titov trg 3; ⊙ 9am-8pm Jul-Sep, to 5pm Oct-Jun) On the ground floor of the Praetorian Palace.

ℹ️ Getting There & Away

The joint bus and train station is 1.5km south-east of the Old Town on Kolodvorska cesta.

There's a handy central bus stop for local services (including to other coastal cities) on Piranška ulica (just south of the market).

BUS

Arriva (☎ 090 74 11; www.arriva.si) is the bus operator on the coast; see its website for schedules. Buses go to Izola (€1.80, 15 minutes, 9km), Portorož (€2.70, 40 minutes, 19km) and Piran (€2.70, 45 minutes, 22km) up to three times an hour on weekdays (hourly on weekends). Five daily buses make the run to Ljubljana (€11.10, 1¾ hours, 122km).

Arriva and Croatian-based Črnja Tours (www.crnja-tours.hr) run regular buses to Italian and Croatian destinations. Buses to Trieste (€3.30, 45 minutes) run up to nine times daily Monday to Saturday. Črnja Tours has a daily service to Venice (€18, three hours). Destinations in Croatia include Rovinj (€11, three hours) via Umag, Novi Grad and Poreč.

TRAIN

Five trains a day link Koper to Ljubljana (€11.36, 2½ hours, 153km) via Postojna and Divača.

To get to Buzet and Pula in Croatia from Koper, you must change at Hrpelje-Kozina for any of the two to three trains a day.

ℹ️ Getting Around

BUS

Red local buses link the bus and train stations to the rest of the town; line L2 and 2A will get you to the Tržnica stop on Piranška ulica, by

---

> **WORTH A TRIP**
>
> ### HRASTOVLJE'S DANCE OF DEATH
>
> The Romanesque church in the tiny Karst village of Hrastovlje (population 139) is small, surrounded by medieval walls with corner towers, and covered inside with extraordinary 15th-century frescoes, including the famous *Dance of Death*. This is the reason to make the trip here – as difficult as it can be.
>
> Hrastovlje is 30km southwest of Divača off the main highway to the coast; Koper is 18km to the northwest. Without a car or bicycle it is hard to reach. There is a weekday afternoon train from Koper (€1.85, 16 minutes), however there is no return train. The church is about 1km northwest of Hrastovlje's train station.
>
> **Church of the Holy Trinity** (Cerkev Sv Trojice; ☎ 031 432 231; adult/child €3/1.50; ⊙ 9am-noon & 1-5pm) What attracts most people to this little church is the famous **Dance of Death** or Danse Macabre, a fresco that shows 11 skeletons leading the same number of people forward to a freshly dug grave. A 12th holds open a coffin. The doomed line-up includes peasants, kings, cardinals, and even a moneylender (who attempts to bribe his skeletal escort with a purse): all are equal in the eyes of God.
>
> The church was built between the 12th and 14th centuries in the southern Romanesque style, with fortifications added in 1581 in advance of the Ottomans. Its sombre exterior is disarming in the extreme.
>
> The *Dance of Death* is not the only fresco, the interior is completely festooned with paintings by John of Kastav from around 1490. They helped the illiterate understand the Old Testament stories, the Passion of Christ and the lives of the saints. Spare the 12 minutes it takes to listen to the taped commentary (in four languages, including English) that will guide you around the little church.
>
> Facing you as you enter the church is the 17th-century altar, the central apse with scenes from the **Crucifixion** on the ceiling and portraits of the **Trinity and the Apostles**. On the arch, **Mary** is crowned queen of heaven. To the right are episodes from the seven days of **Creation**, with **Adam and Eve**, and **Cain and Abel** on the right.
>
> On the ceilings of the north and south aisles are scenes from daily life as well as the liturgical year and its seasonal duties. Christ's **Passion** is depicted at the top of the southernmost wall, including his **Descent into Hell**, where devils attack him with blazing cannons. Below the scenes of the Passion is the *Dance of Death*.

the market. Line 7 does a circle around the Old Town. Local buses are €1.50 if you pay the driver, €0.80 if you prepurchase your ticket (from vending machines or kiosks).

PARKING

Parking in much of the Old Town is severely restricted – or banned altogether – between 6am and 3pm. Ask your accommodation provider for advice, or leave your vehicle in the pay carparks along Pristaniška ulica.

TAXI

To order a taxi in Koper, call ☑ 031 386 000 or ☑ 031 230 320.

Izola

☑ 05 / POP 11,188

Izola, a fishing port 7km southwest of Koper, is the poor relation among the historical towns on the Slovenian coast. As a result, it is often bypassed by foreign visitors – but Izola does have a certain Venetian charm, together with a large marina, some narrow old winding streets and excellent restaurants and bars where you might linger. If Piran is solidly booked (or its prices too high), Izola makes a good fall-back.

History

The Romans built a port called Haliaetum at Simon's Bay (Simonov Zaliv) southwest of the Old Town, and you can still see parts of the original landing when the tide is very low. While under the control of Venice in the Middle Ages, Izola – at that time an island (*isola* is Italian for 'island') – flourished, particularly in the trading of such commodities as olives, fish and wine. But a devastating plague in the 16th century and the ascendancy of Trieste as the premier port in the northern Adriatic destroyed the town's economic base. During the period of the Illyrian Provinces in the early 19th century, the French pulled down the town walls and used them to fill the channel separating the island from the mainland. Today, Izola is the country's foremost fishing port.

◉ Sights

Izola isn't overly endowed with important historical sights; Napoleon and his lot took care of that.

Parish Church of St Maurus   CHURCH
(Župnijska Cerkev Sv Mavra; Garibaldijeva ulica) This renovated, salmon-coloured, 16th-century church and its detached bell tower sit on the hill above the town.

Besenghi degli Ughi Palace   NOTABLE BUILDING
(Besenghijeva Palača; Gregorčičeva ulica 76) Izola's most beautiful building – but looking a little worse for wear – is this late-baroque palazzo below the Parish Church of St Maurus. Built between 1775 and 1781, the mansion has windows and balconies adorned with stuccos and wonderful wrought-iron grilles painted light blue. It is now a music school.

Municipal Palace   NOTABLE BUILDING
(Mestna Palača; Veliki trg) On Veliki trg is the Municipal Palace, which now houses offices of the local council. It was built in Gothic style in 1325, but the present baroque facade is from the 17th century.

Church of St Mary of Haliaetum   CHURCH
(Cerkev Sv Marije Alietske; Veliki trg) This central church dates from around the latter 11th century and has been lovingly restored.

Manzioli House   NOTABLE BUILDING
(Manziolijev trg 5) The Venetian Gothic Manzioli House was built in 1470 and was the residence of an Istrian chronicler in the 16th century. Today it houses the bureau looking after the interests of the *communità italiana* (Italian community) in Izola – and a wine bar.

Strunjan Landscape Park   NATURE RESERVE
(Krajinski Park Strunjan; www.parkstrunjan.si) For centuries the people who lived at Strunjan, a peninsula halfway between Izola and Piran, were engaged in salt-making. Today the old salt-pan area is protected, along with other natural and cultural heritage sites, inside Strunjan Landscape Park.

Although there has been much development (resorts and public beach areas) around Strunjan Bay to the southwest, much of the peninsula's northern coast is remarkably unspoiled.

The north is bounded by a 4km-long flysch cliff, up to 80m high. There are pathways along the clifftop and some good viewpoints; it is also possible to walk along the rocky shoreline below.

Buses linking the coastal towns stop at Strunjan Bay; you can also access the park's walks from the Belvedere resort west of Izola.

Activities

There are popular pebble beaches to the north and southeast of the Old Town, but the best one is at Simon's Bay about 1.5km to the southwest. It has a grassy area for sunbathing.

Ask at the tourist office about sailing excursions – a number of boats offer tours from the main port of Izola, just off Veliki trg. Destinations include Venice (once a week), and more frequent sailings to Piran, Portorož and Sečovlje Salina Nature Park.

Along the waterfront there are a few operators renting boats for the day, but they don't come cheap (from around €130).

Sleeping

Hostel Alieti HOSTEL $
(☑ 051 670 680; www.hostel-alieti.si; Dvorišćna ulica 24; dm €18-22; ❋ ☜) This might just be the coast's best hostel. Tucked away off a winding alley, it's small and modern with fresh decor – beds are in dorms sleeping four to six (shared bathrooms; kitchen facilities). Plus there's air-con, and a simple breakfast included in the price. Owner Uroš is friendly and welcoming.

Laguna Izola ACCOMMODATION SERVICES $
(☑ 05-640 0278; www.lagunaizola.com; Istrska Vrata 7; d €28-50, apt for 2 from €43) This central agency can help with accommodation in and around Izola – rooms, apartments, hotels. Details including locations, photos and prices are on its website.

Belvedere CAMPGROUND, RESORT $
(☑ 05-660 51 00; www.belvedere.si; Dobrava ulica 1a; campsites adult €10-13, child €5-6.50; ☺ Apr-early Oct; ℗ ☜ ☲) This large campground sits on a pine-shaded bluff 3km west of Izola and has views of the town and the Adriatic, and sites for 500 campers. No bookings are taken. It's part of a larger resort complex that includes rooms and apartments, a restaurant and swimming pool. There's a path down to a beach, also serviced by the resort's shuttle bus. Peak-season rooms start at €95 for two people.

Hotel Marina HOTEL $$$
(☑ 05-660 41 00; www.hotelmarina.si; Veliki trg 11; s €62-133, d €82-192; ℗ ❋ @ ☜) Behind its somewhat incongruous chocolate-brown exterior, this super-central, 52-room hotel offers friendly service, a popular seafood restaurant and appealing extras (such as bike hire, boat trips and a wellness centre).

Rates vary with the season and room type: superior rooms have sea view and terrace, standard rooms have neither, but all are comfy and well equipped.

Eating

Izola is the best place on the coast to enjoy a seafood meal. Tip: ask the exact price of the

Izola

Izola

Sights
1 Besenghi degli Ughi Palace A2
2 Church of St Mary of Haliaetum A2
3 Manzioli House.....................................A2
4 Municipal Palace..................................A2
5 Parish Church of St Maurus A1

Sleeping
6 Hostel Alieti A2
7 Hotel Marina A2
8 Laguna Izola A2

Eating
9 Gostilna Bujol A2
10 Gušt B3
Marina Restaurant.......................(see 7)
11 Mercator B3
12 Mercator A2

Drinking & Nightlife
13 Bariera..A2

THE KARST & THE COAST IZOLA

fish. As seafood is sold by decagram (usually abbreviated as *dag* on menus) or kilogram, you might end up eating (and paying) a lot more than you expected. And be sure to have a glass of *malvazija*, the local white wine that is light and dry.

Mercator SUPERMARKET $
(Trg Republike 4; ☉7am-9pm Mon-Sat, 8am-9pm Sun) There's a supermarket opposite the bus stops and a more central **Mercator** (Veliki trg; ☉7am-9pm Mon-Sat, 8am-9pm Sun) near the inner port.

Gušt MEDITERRANEAN $$
(☑031 606 040; http://gostilnica-gust.si; Drevored 1 Maja 5; mains €8-21; ☉11am-10am Mon-Thu, to 11pm Fri-Sun) Away from the seafront, Gušt is stylishly appealing indoors and out. Choose from a menu full of flavour: pizzas, home-made pasta, creative salads and tasty mains like seabass fillet on seasonal salad with avocado and truffle, or risotto of octopus and red Refošk wine.

Marina Restaurant SEAFOOD $$
(☑05-660 41 00; www.hotelmarina.si; Veliki trg 11; mains €9-20; ☉noon-10pm) At the Marina Hotel, this much-loved restaurant serves a stellar range of seafood (with accessible prices): fish soup, salt-crusted seabass, lobster with pasta. Meat dishes are no slouch (pork fillet with olive polenta and fresh truffle). There are a range of good-value set menus available, including the daily three-course menu for a bargain €18.

Gostilna Bujol SEAFOOD $$
(☑041 799 490; Verdijeva ulica 10; mains €8-16; ☉11am-10pm Wed-Sun) A place recommended by locals (especially for its cod-fish pate, or *bakalar na belo*), rustic Bujol has a selection of fresh fish offered fried or grilled (the menu is only in Slovenian but staff are helpful). Mussels, calamari and pasta with seafood are all good choices.

 Drinking & Nightlife

Bariera CAFE-BAR
(☑031 392 572; Sončno nabrežje 26; ☉7am-1am) Waterside seating and a friendly atmosphere make this a popular spot for a drink throughout the day and night.

Ambasada Gavioli CLUB
(☑040 663 366; www.ambasadagavioli.si; Industrijska cesta 10; cover €10-15; ☉11pm-6am Fri & Sat) Big capacity (2300 people), mad decor (inside and out) and a procession of big-name international and local DJs have led to a cult following for this club, found in the industrial area southeast of the port. It holds the crown as queen of Slovenia's electronic clubs. See the website for events.

ⓘ Orientation

Almost everything of a practical nature is located around central Trg Republike. Buses stop in at Cankarjev drevored; to reach the Old Town and its main square, Veliki trg, walk north along the waterfront promenade.

WORTH A TRIP

KORTE

If the coast is a bit too crowded for your liking, retreat is possible: head inland. Korte (population 802) is a sweet hilltop village about 9km from Izola, with a few good reasons to visit. Buses connect it with Izola only a handful of times a day (€2.30).

Old Schoolhouse Korte (Stara Šola Korte; ☑05-642 11 14, 031 375 889; www.hostel-starasola.si; Korte 74; r per person €19-25, apt €80-100; ℗❀☎) This renovated old school is home to 17 bright, modern rooms with two to four beds (with shared or private bathrooms), plus a couple of two-bedroom apartments. It's beautifully done, with idyllic views and pretty common areas. Apartments have a kitchen but there are no cooking facilities for room guests. Breakfast is available (€5) and Korte has two excellent restaurants.

Hiša Torkla (☑05-620 96 57; www.hisa-torkla.si; Korte 44b; mains €17-28; ☉noon-10pm Wed-Sun) One of our most memorable meals was enjoyed here, where Andreja and Sebastijan provide warm service in a stylish setting, with fine local flavours accentuated by accomplished, not-too-fussy cooking (Black Angus steak cooked to perfection on an indoor flame-grill). The chef's menu is outstanding value (three/four/five plates for €28/40/50). Be guided by staff on local wine choices. Bookings advised.

ℹ️ Information

Tourist Information Centre (📞 05-640 10 50; www.izola.eu; Ljubljanska ulica 17; ⊙ 9am-8pm summer, to 4pm winter, to 6pm autumn & spring) Signposted from the waterfront promenade.

ℹ️ Getting There & Away

Arriva (📞 090 74 11; www.arriva.si) is the busline serving the coast; see its website for schedules and prices.

Buses run east to Koper (€1.80, 15 minutes, 9km) and west to Portorož (€1.80, 24 minutes, 9km) and Piran (€2.30, 30 minutes, 13km) up to three times an hour on weekdays (hourly on weekends).

Three daily buses make the run to Ljubljana (€11.40, 2½ hours, 130km), via Koper.

International routes include two buses a day to Trieste (€4.40, one hour, 32km) in Italy; and two in summer to Umag (€5, 40 minutes, 26km), Pula (€7, 1½ hours, 57km) and Rovinj (€10, 2½ hours, 81km) in Croatia.

ℹ️ Getting Around

You can rent bicycles from **Koloset** (📞 059 977 886; www.koloset.si; Gorkijeva ulica 8; from €15; ⊙ 9am-1pm & 4-7pm Mon-Fri, 9am-1pm Sat) or from **Hotel Marina** (p145) for €5/8 for three hours/all day.

From June to August a tourist train does an hourly loop around town from Trg Republike, stopping at beaches and Belvedere resort (adult/child €4/2.50).

Order a taxi on 📞 040 602 602 or 📞 041 706 777.

Piran

📞 05 / POP 3975

Picturesque Piran (Pirano in Italian), sitting pretty at the tip of a narrow peninsula, is everyone's favourite town on the Slovenian coast. Its Old Town – one of the best-preserved historical towns anywhere on the Adriatic – is a gem of Venetian Gothic architecture, but it can be a mob scene at the height of summer. In quieter times, it's hard not to fall instantly in love with the atmospheric winding alleyways, the sunsets and the seafood restaurants.

History

It's thought that Piran's name comes from the Greek word for the fires *(pyr)* lit at the very tip of the peninsula, to guide ships to the port at Aegida (now Koper). The Romans estab-

lished a settlement here called Piranum, and were followed by the early Slavs, Byzantines, Franks and the Patriarchs of Aquileia.

Five centuries of Venetian rule began in the late 13th century, and Piran was a major salt supplier for its rulers. The Venetian period was the town's most fruitful, and many of its beautiful buildings and fortifications were erected then.

⦿ Sights

⭐ **Tartinijev Trg** SQUARE
The much-photographed, pastel-toned Tartinijev trg is a marble-paved square (oval-shaped, really) that was the inner harbour until it was filled in 1894. The **statue** (Tartinijev trg) of the nattily dressed gentleman in the centre is of native son, composer and violinist Giuseppe Tartini (1692–1770).

To the east is the 1818 **Church of St Peter** (Cerkev Sv Petra; Tartinijev trg). Across from the church is **Tartini House**, the composer's birthplace.

The **Court House** (Sodniška Palača; Tartinijev trg 1) and the porticoed 19th-century **Municipal Hall** (Občinska Palača; Tartinijev trg 2), the latter home to the tourist information centre, dominate the western edge of the square.

The 15th-century stone pillars of the two **flagpoles** at the entrance to the square bear Latin inscriptions praising Piran, the town's coat of arms, a relief of St George (the patron) to the left and one of St Mark (with the lion symbol) on the right.

⭐ **Venetian House** HISTORIC BUILDING
(Benečanka; Tartinijev trg 4) One of Piran's most eye-catching structures is the red mid-15th-century Gothic Venetian House, with its tracery windows and balcony, in the northeast of Tartinijev trg.

There is a story attached to the stone relief between the two windows – a lion with a banner in its mouth and the Latin inscription *Lasa pur dir* above it. A wealthy merchant from Venice fell in love with a beautiful local girl, but she soon became the butt of local gossips. To shut them up (and keep his lover happy), the merchant built her this little palace complete with a reminder for his loose-lipped neighbours: 'Let them talk'.

Tartini House NOTABLE BUILDING
(Tartinijeva Hiša; 📞 05-671 00 40; www.pomorskimuzej.si; Kajuhova ulica 12; adult/child €1.50/1; ⊙ 9am-noon & 6-9pm Jul & Aug, shorter hrs Sep-Jun) Tartini House was the birthplace

Piran

Piran

Bathing Area

Preševo nabrežje

Punta

12

6

Pebble
Beach

Pusterla

Bonifacijeva ul

Vegova ul **23**

Gregorčičeva ul

Preševo nabrežje

25 **15**

Trg 1
Maja

Kosovelova ul

Židovski
trg

Trubarjeva ul

Verdijeva ul

Levstikova ul

27

28

Obzidna ul

Zelenjavni
trg

Vidaljeva ul

Piran
Bay

Bathing
Area

Tomažičev
trg

Tomažičeva ul

18

Stjenkova ul

24

30

Kidričeva nabrežje

Marina

A D R I A T I C
S E A

Piran
Harbour

Customs
Wharf

Dantejeva ul

Pri Mari (65m);
Apartments Mia Chanel (180m);
Rizibizi (1.2km);
Hotel Marko (2.25km);
Portorož (5km)

of composer and violinist Giuseppe Tartini. Today it's the base of Piran's Italian community and is used for cultural events and exhibitions. On the 1st floor is the **Tartini Memorial Room**, containing his violins and music scores.

⭐ **Cathedral of St George**   CATHEDRAL
(Župnijska Cerkev Sv Jurija; www.zupnija-piran.si; Adamičeva ulica 2) A cobbled street leads from behind the Venetian House to Piran's hilltop cathedral, baptistery and bell tower. The cathedral was built in baroque style in the early 17th century, on the site of an earlier church from 1344.

The cathedral's doors are usually open and a metal grille allows you to see some of the richly ornate and newly restored interior, but full access is via the **Parish Museum of St George** (☑ 05-673 34 40; Adamičeva ulica 2; adult/child €1.50/0.75; ⊙ 10am-4pm Wed-Mon), which includes the church's treasury and catacombs.

Items of interest include a silver-plated St George slaying a dragon, and a wooden model of the church dating from 1595.

The highlight of the cathedral interior (not visible from the grille) is the remarkable, early-14th-century wooden sculpture, **The Crucified from Piran**, depicting Christ on the cross.

⭐ **Bell Tower**   TOWER
(Zvonik; Adamičeva ulica; admission €1; ⊙ 10am-8pm summer) The Cathedral of St George's freestanding, 46.5m bell tower, built in 1609, was clearly modelled on the campanile of San Marco in Venice and provides a fabulous backdrop to many a town photo. Its 147 rickety stairs can be climbed for superb views of the town and harbour. Next to it, the octagonal 17th-century **baptistery** (*krstilnica*) contains altars and paintings. It is now sometimes used as an exhibition space. To the east is a 200m-long stretch of the 15th-century **town wall**.

Minorite Monastery   MONASTERY
(Bolniška ulica 20) The Minorite Monastery has a lovely cloister, and the attached **Church of St Francis Assisi** was built originally in the early 14th century but enlarged and renovated over the centuries. Inside are ceiling frescoes and the Tartini family's burial plot.

⭐ **Sergej Mašera Maritime Museum**   MUSEUM
(☑ 05-671 00 40; www.pomorskimuzej.si; Cankarjevo nabrežje 3; adult/child €3.50/2.10; ⊙ 9am-

Piran

noon & 5-9pm Tue-Sun Jul & Aug, 9am-5pm Tue-Sun Sep-Jun) Located in the 19th-century **Gabrielli Palace** on the waterfront, this museum's focus is the sea, with plenty of salty-dog stories relating to Slovenian seafaring. In the archaeological section, the 2000-year-old Roman amphorae beneath the glass floor are impressive. The antique model ships upstairs are very fine; other rooms are filled with old figureheads and weapons, including some lethal-looking blunderbusses. The folk paintings are offerings placed by sailors on the altar of the pilgrimage church at Strunjan for protection against shipwreck.

Museum of Underwater Activities   MUSEUM
(Muzej Podvodnih Dejavnosti; ☑041 685 379; Župančičeva ulica 24; adult/child €4.50/3; ☺10.30am-8pm Jun-Sep, 11am-6pm Fri-Sun Oct-May) One for diving enthusiasts, this museum makes much of Piran's close association with the sea and diving. Particularly noteworthy are all the old diving suits and helmets.

Trg 1 Maja   SQUARE
Trg 1 Maja (1st May Square) may sound like a socialist parade ground, but it was the centre of Piran until the Middle Ages, when it was called Stari trg (Old Square). The surrounding streets are a maze of pastel-coloured overhanging houses, vaulted passages and arcaded courtyards.

The square is surrounded by interesting baroque buildings, including the **former town pharmacy** on the north side (now the Fontana restaurant). In the centre of the square is a large baroque **cistern** (*vodnjak*) that was built in the late 18th century to store fresh water; rainwater from the surrounding roofs flowed into it through the fish borne by the stone putti cherubs in two corners.

Punta Lighthouse   LIGHTHOUSE
Punta, the historical 'point' of Piran, still has a lighthouse, but today's is small and relatively modern. Attached to it, however, is the round, serrated tower of the **Church of St Clement** (Prešernovo nabrežje), which evokes the ancient beacon from which Piran got its name. The church was originally built in the 13th century but altered 500 years later; it has a lovely (though decrepit) stuccoed ceiling.

🏃 Activities

Cruises & Excursions
Several agencies in Piran and Portorož can book you on boat cruises and bus excursions – from a loop that takes in the towns along the coast to day-long excursions to Slovenian highlights (Bled or Postojna, for example), or to Venice and Trieste in Italy.

Subaquatic
BOAT TOUR

(☑041 602 783; www.subaquatic.si; adult/child €15/9; ☺cruises 10am, 2pm, 4.15pm & 6.30pm Apr-Sep) Subaquatic offers 1½-hour coastline cruises from Piran to Fiesa and Strunjan (and return). Panoramas are enjoyed above and under the water, with windows under the deck. Check tour schedules online – in cooler months, there may be only two a day.

Diving

Sub-Net
DIVING

(☑041 746 153; www.sub-net.si; Prešernovo nabrežje 24; shore/boat dive €33/45) Organises shore and boat-guided dives, runs PADI open-water courses and hires equipment. A 'discover scuba diving' course is €60.

Swimming

Piran has several 'beaches' – rocky areas along Prešernovo nabrežje – where you might get your feet wet. They are a little better on the north side near Punta (and you can hire umbrellas and sunlounges), but as long as you've come this far keep walking eastward on the paved path for just under 1km to Fiesa (p151), which has a small beach.

✹ Festivals & Events

Piran Summer Festival
CULTURAL

(www.piranfestival.si; ☺Aug) For a little over two weeks in early August, performers (dance and music of varying genres) take to a stage set up in Tartinijev trg at 9pm for free performances.

Tartini Festival
MUSIC

(www.tartinifestival.org; ☺late-Aug–Sep) The two-week Tartini Festival of classical music takes place in venues throughout Piran, including the vaulted cloister of the Minorite Monastery. A handful of events are staged in Koper.

🛏 Sleeping

Prices are higher in Piran than elsewhere on the coast, and it's not a good idea to arrive without a booking in summer. If you need to find a private room, start at the Maona Tourist Agency or Turist Biro (p153).

If you are getting around by car, ask your hotel for their advice on parking.

Val Hostel
HOSTEL $

(☑05-673 25 55; www.hostel-val.com; Gregorčiče-va ulica 38a; per person €22-25; @ 🛜) Location is the winner here – this central hostel has 22 rooms (including a few singles) with shared bathrooms, and access to kitchenette and laundry.

Kamp Fiesa
CAMPGROUND $

(☑05-674 62 30; kamp.fiesa@gmail.com; Fiesa 57b; adult/child €12/free; ☺May-Sep; P) The closest campground to Piran is at Fiesa, 4km by road but about 1km if you follow the coastal path east. It's tiny and becomes crowded in summer but it's in a valley by two small, protected ponds and right by the beach.

★PachaMama
GUESTHOUSE, APARTMENT $$

(☑059 183 495; www.pachamama.si; Trubarjeva 8; per person €30-35; ✳🛜) Built by travellers for travellers, this excellent new guesthouse ('PachaMama Pleasant Stay') sits just off Tartinijev trg and offers 12 simple, fresh rooms, decorated with timber and lots of travel photography. Cool private bathrooms and a 'secret garden' add appeal. There are also a handful of studios and family-sized apartments under the PachaMama umbrella, dotted around town and of an equally high standard.

★Max Piran
B&B $$

(☑041 692 928, 05-673 34 36; www.maxpiran.com; Ul IX Korpusa 26; d €65-70; ✳🛜) Piran's most romantic accommodation has just six handsome, compact rooms, each bearing a woman's name rather than a number, in a delightful, coral-coloured, 18th-century townhouse. It's just down from the Cathedral of St George, and excellent value.

Miracolo di Mare
B&B $$

(☑051 445 511, 05-921 76 60; www.miracolodimare.si; Tomšičeva ulica 23; d €65-75; 🛜) A lovely and decent-value B&B, the Wonder of the Sea has a dozen charming (though smallish) rooms, some of which (like No 3 and the breakfast room) give on to a pretty garden. Floors and stairs are wooden and original.

Hotel Piran
HOTEL $$$

(☑05-666 71 00; www.hotel-piran.si; Stjenkova ulica 1; high-season d €140-180; ✳🛜) The town's flagship hotel has a commanding waterside position, great service and a century of history. There are 74 modern rooms and 15 suites – sea view is the way to go, if you can. Downstairs is a wellness centre, cafe and restaurant with large terrace; on the rooftop is a fab summertime champagne bar for hotel guests only.

Vila Piranesi APARTMENTS $$$
(☑ 05-600 99 77; www.piranesi.si; Kidričevo na-brežje 4; apt for 2 €75-180; ❋ ☎) Decor is in-offensively bland but location and facilities at this apartment complex are first-rate. Each of the 18 modern, one-bedroom apart-ments has kitchen and living room; larger apartments have sofabeds suitable for kids. Low-season rates are particularly good.

Hotel Tartini HOTEL $$$
(☑ 05-671 10 00; www.hotel-tartini-piran.com; Tartinijev trg 15; d €102-128; ❋ ☎) This attrac-tive, 45-room property faces Tartinijev trg and manages to catch a few sea views from the upper floors (for an additional €10 you can score a sea-view balcony). The staff are especially friendly and helpful. If you've got the dosh, splash out on suite No 40A; we're suckers for eyrie-like round rooms with million-euro views.

The summertime rooftop terrace is a winner.

Apartments Mia Chanel APARTMENT $$$
(☑ 041 711 888; apartma.piran@gmail.com; Dante-jeva ulica 31; d/q from €100/120; P ❋ ☎) At the entrance to town, Mia Chanel has six studios and apartments set behind a pret-ty garden, directly across the road from the sea. As a bonus, it's the only central accom-modation offering free on-site parking. It's a short walk to good restaurants and the centre of town.

✖ Eating

One of Piran's attractions is its plethora of fish restaurants, especially along Prešernovo nabrežje. Most cater to the tourist trade and are rather overpriced.

The seafood pairs well with the local *mal-vazija* white wine.

★ Cantina Klet SEAFOOD $
(Trg 1 Maja 10; mains €5-9; ⊙ 10am-11pm) This small wine bar sits pretty under a grapevine canopy on Trg 1 Maja. You order drinks from the bar (cheap local wine from the barrel or well-priced beers), but we especially love the self-service window (labelled 'Fritolin pri Cantini') where you order from a small blackboard menu of fishy dishes, like fish fillet with polenta, fried calamari, or fish tortilla.

Market MARKET $
(Zelenjavni trg; ⊙ 7am-1pm Mon-Sat) There's an outdoor market in the small square behind the Municipal Hall – and a **Mercator** (Levs-tikova ulica 5; ⊙ 7am-9pm Mon-Sat, 8am-8pm Sun) supermarket here, too.

Pirat SEAFOOD $$
(☑ 05-673 14 81; Župančičeva ulica 26; mains €8-18; ⊙ noon-10pm) It's not the fanciest place in town but the atmosphere is top-notch and Rok and his crew do their best to ensure you have a good time. Seafood is king, from the fresh-fish carpaccio to pasta with lob-ster and grilled seabass filleted at the table. All nicely accompanied by local *malvazija* white wine.

Pri Mari MEDITERRANEAN $$
(☑ 05-673 47 35, 041 616 488; www.primari-piran.com; Dantejeva ulica 17; mains €8-22; ⊙ noon-10pm Tue-Sat, to 6pm Sun) This stylishly rustic and welcoming restaurant run by an Ital-ian-Slovenian couple serves the most inven-tive Mediterranean and Slovenian dishes in town – lots of fish, a good selection of local wines. Space is restricted, so it pays to book ahead.

La Bottega dei Sapori MEDITERRANEAN $$$
(☑ 05-992 04 74; Kajuhova ulica 12; mains €12-33; ⊙ 10am-10pm Tue-Sun) An elegant, upmarket feel combines with a prime main-square lo-cation at this polished (but pricey) charmer, which cherry-picks from local, Italian and French cuisines. The menu sings with prime local produce, especially fresh white and black truffles. Have them alongside scampi with pasta or risotto, or with beefsteak.

♟ Drinking & Nightlife

Mestna Kavarna CAFE-BAR
(☑ 082 056 393; Tartinijev trg 3; ⊙ 7am-midnight) A morning coffee or smoothie goes well with a strong dose of people-watching, and this cafe-bar on the main square delivers. By night, the orders turn to cocktails.

Žižola Kantina CAFE-BAR
(☑ 041 516 822; Tartinijev trg 10; ⊙ 9am-2am) This nautically themed cafe-bar – named after the jujube (Chinese date) that grows prolifically along the Adriatic – has tables right on the main square.

★ Café Teater CAFE-BAR
(☑ 041 638 933; Stjenkova ulica 1; ⊙ 9am-mid-night) With a grand waterfront terrace and faux antique furnishings, this is where any-one who's anyone in Piran can be found. Per-fect for sundowners.

🛍 Shopping

Piranske Soline GIFTS
(☑05-673 31 10; www.soline.si; Tartinijev trg 4; ⊙9am-9pm) In the Venetian House, this place sells nicely packaged cooking salts and bath sea salts, along with other products all made from the salt of Sečovlje.

Čokoladnica Olimje FOOD
(http://cokoladnica-olimje.si; Tartinijev trg 5; ⊙9am-8pm) Slovenia's best-known chocolate is produced by this chocolaterie, based in the hamlet of Olimje in the east of the country. This boutique outlet is a Willy Wonka world of deliciousness.

ℹ Information

Banka Koper (Tartinijev trg 12)
Maona Tourist Agency (☑05-673 45 20; www.maona.si; Cankarjevo nabrežje 7; ⊙9am-8pm Mon-Sat, 10am-1pm & 5-7pm Sun) Travel agency organising everything from private rooms to activities and cruises.
Post Office (Cankarjevo nabrežje 5)
Tourist Information Centre (TIC; ☑05-673 44 40; www.portoroz.si; Tartinijev trg 2; ⊙9am-10pm Jul & Aug, to 5pm Sep-Jun) In the impressive Municipal Hall.
Turist Biro (☑05-673 25 09; www.turist-biro-ag.si; Tomažičeva ulica 3; ⊙9am-1pm & 4-7pm Mon-Sat, 9am-1pm Sun) Travel agency opposite Hotel Piran. Can book rooms and apartments all over the coast. Double rooms/apartments in summer start at €31/46.

ℹ Getting There & Away

BUS

Arriva (☑090 74 11; www.arriva.si) is the busline serving the coast; see its website for schedules and prices.

From the **bus station** (Dantejeva ulica) south of the centre, buses run frequently to Portorož (€1.30, six minutes, 4km) and up to four times an hour to Izola (€2.30, 30 minutes, 12km) and Koper (€3.10, 45 minutes, 22km).

Three buses daily make the journey to Ljubljana (€12, three hours, 140km), via Divača and Postojna.

For international destinations, one bus daily goes to Trieste (€5.90, 1½ hours, 43km) in Italy, and one bus daily in summer heads south for Croatian Istria, stopping at Umag, Poreč and Rovinj (€9, 2¾ hours). There are more frequent services from Izola and Koper.

FERRY

From late June through August, **Trieste Lines** (☑040 200 620; www.triestelines.it) operates

---

ℹ **PARKING IN PIRAN**
....

Traffic is heavily restricted in town for non-residents – ask your accommodation provider for advice. You may be able to enter the town for 15 minutes to drop off luggage.

The best option is to park at the huge Fornače carpark about 1km south of the centre and walk or take a free shuttle bus into the centre. It's €17 to park at Fornače for 24 hours (some hotels offer a discounted rate). Arze is a cheaper carpark east of town (€12 per day) but it doesn't have a shuttle service.

a daily (except Wednesday) catamaran from Piran's harbour to Trieste in Italy (€8.80, 30 minutes), and in the other direction to Rovinj in Croatia (€21.60, 70 minutes). Buy tickets through the TIC.

ℹ Getting Around

From the southwest corner of Tartinijev trg, free, frequent minibuses shuttle to Piran's bus station and the Fornače carpark. Timetables are posted – in high summer, the shuttles operate roughly every 15 minutes from 5.25am to 1.46am.

Rent bikes from the TIC (€10 for 48 hours), or from **Luma Šport** (☑041 781 414; www.lumasport.com; Dantejeva 3; per hour/day €3/15), opposite the bus station.

Portorož

☑05 / POP 2961
Every country with a coast has got to have a honky-tonk beach resort and Portorož (Portorose in Italian) is Slovenia's.

Portorož's beaches are relatively clean (if wall-to-wall people in summer), and there are spas and wellness centres where you can take the waters or cover yourself in curative mud. The vast array of accommodation options makes Portorož a useful fall-back if everything's full in Piran, only 4km up the road.

◉ Sights

Forma Viva PARK
FREE Perched atop the Seča Peninsula south of town (beyond the marina), Forma Viva is an outdoor sculpture garden with some 130 works carved in stone. The real reason for coming is the peace and quiet, and the fantastic view of Portorož and Piran Bays. The

saltpans at Sečovlje are a short walk to the south.

🏃 Activities

Cruises & Excursions

In summer, a couple of boats make runs from the main pier in Portorož to explore the immediate coastline, visiting various combinations of Piran, Izola and Koper, possibly including Strunjan or the saltpans at Sečovlje.

Full-day trips are offered in high season to Venice (by boat or bus) for around €70, and there are bus excursions to Slovenia's big-ticket attractions (Ljubljana, Bled, Postojna).

Stroll along the pier to see the offerings, or visit travel agencies like Go Portorož.

Spas

All the major hotels have wellness centres. If this is your cup of tea, don't miss the Lepa Vida Thalasso Spa (p156) at Sečovlje Salina Nature Park.

Terme & Wellness LifeClass   SPA

(☑ 05-692 80 60; www.lifeclass.net; Obala 43) The 'LifeClass' hotel group includes six hotels in town (chief among them the four-star Grand Hotel Portorož). Part of the offering is this comprehensive spa, offering 'medical wellness', relaxation, spa and recreation facilities – everything from palatial indoor swimming pools to a 'sauna park', gym, Thai massage, thalasso centre and Ayurveda clinic. All activities, opening hours and prices are online.

Swimming

Portorož Central Beach   BEACH

(Centralna Plaza Portorož) FREE Portorož Central Beach accommodates 3300 fried and bronzed bodies. There are loads of waterslides and kiddie playgrounds; beach chairs (€5) and umbrellas (€5) are available for rent. Beaches are patrolled by lifeguards during the day, and are off-limits between 11pm and 6am. Sleeping overnight on the beach is strictly forbidden.

Water Sports

Lunos Sport Centre   WATER SPORTS

(☑ 041 617 205; www.sportaction.si; 1hr kayak/SUP rental €10/12) Right in the main beach area, you can hire kayaks, small sailboats, windsurfing and SUP boards and various other sea-going paraphernalia, or sign up for lessons.

🛏 Sleeping

Portorož counts dozens of hotels; few of them fit into the budget category. Rates can be very high during summer; many close for the winter in October or November and re-open in April.

Travel agencies can help with private rooms and apartments, prices vary widely and depend on season and category. Some of the cheapest rooms are up on the hillside, quite a walk from the beach. Getting a room for fewer than three nights (for which you must pay a supplement) or a single any time can be difficult.

★ Kaki Plac   CAMPGROUND $

(☑ 041 359 801; www.adrenaline-check.com/sea; Liminjan 8, Lucija; tent site per person €13, with hired tent €15, lean-to €20; ☺ May-Nov; 🅿 🛜) A small, chilled-out and eco-friendly retreat tucked into the woods outside Lucija, on the outskirts of Portorož. Tents with air mattresses can be hired – some sit snugly under thatched Istrian lean-tos, and include linen. There's a sociable communal eating area, free bike hire, and welcoming owners can arrange activities and give great local recommendations.

To reach it, head for the police station in Lucija (signposted), and look for signs from there. Free pick-up can be arranged, from Lucija or Portorož.

Europa Hostel   HOSTEL $

(☑ 059 032 574; www.ehp.si; Senčna pot 2; per person €22-27; 🅿 ❄ 🛜) This is a good, central budget choice, close to the bus station and with the Auditorium as its neighbour. It's geared to travellers, with bunk-filled rooms named after European destinations. Private rooms are possible, with and without bathroom. Bonus: parking, air-con, garden terrace. Note: no kitchen.

Camp Lucija   CAMPGROUND $

(☑ 05-690 60 00; www.camp-lucija.si; Seča 204; campsite adult €8-17, child €5-6; ☺ Apr-Oct; 🅿 🛜) This large, well-run campground is on the Seča Peninsula, just south of the huge marina complex and about 2km from the bus station. It offers all sorts of sporting facilities including a beachfront area, and can (and often does) accommodate 1000 guests.

Hotel Marko   HOTEL $$

(☑ 05-617 40 00; www.hotel-marko.com; Obala 28; d €80-130; 🅿 ❄ 🛜) Truly midrange hotels are thin on the ground in Portorož, and peak summer rates at the Marko are high (we recommend the midrange options in Piran). But this place gets good reviews for its location close to the beach, plus its service and surrounding garden; decor is a little faded.

★ **Kempinski Palace Portorož**   HOTEL $$$
(☑ 05-692 70 00; www.kempinski.com/portoroz; Obala 45; s/d from €135/170; P ✱ @ 🛜 🛋) This 19th-century grande dame is a 181-room, five-star masterpiece in the Kempinski stable, with a new and an old wing masterfully combining traditional and contemporary design, with all the required bells and whistles.

The Palace has been renovated within an inch of her life – you'll look high and low for any original features (stone staircase, chandeliers in the Crystal Hall). Keep your eyes instead on things like the rose-themed rooms, the faux-baroque furniture, the front balconies with sea views and the interconnecting indoor and outdoor pools.

✖ Eating

There's no shortage of big, basic restaurants catering to the tourist crowd with so-so food, but it's worth the hunt to find a few gems.

Oštarija   SLOVENIAN $$
(☑ 05-674 40 04; www.ostarija.eu; Obala 16; mains €7-18; ⊙ 10am-midnight) Big, bustling and beachfront, but maintaining quality and reasonable prices – there's a lot to like here. The menu rolls through classic Istrian specialities; good choices include *pršut* with truffles, fish soup, calamari in various guises, and fresh fish sold by the gram.

Rizibizi   SLOVENIAN $$$
(☑ 059 935 320; www.rizibizi.si; Vilfanova 10; mains €20-30; ⊙ noon-11pm) In a tucked-away, elevated position (signed off the road between Portorož and Piran), Rizibizi earns accolades as one of the coast's finest dining options. Savour sea views and a locavore ethos – best value are the various tasting menus (€33 to €49). Truffle-lovers, your dreams have come true: six courses, every one with a truffle flavour, for €55. Bookings advised.

★ **Montagu**   INTERNATIONAL $$$
(☑ 05-990 04 77; www.montagu.si; Obala 14b; mains €9-35; ⊙ noon-midnight) Super-chic, this new restaurant and cocktail bar shines like a beacon on the main strip. The short menu hones in on some serious steak (eg, Argentinian Black Angus) with price tags to match, but salads and burgers come in at considerably cheaper rates. You can opt to

simply sup wine or cocktails on the handsome, sprawling beachfront terrace.

🍷 Drinking & Entertainment

★ **Kavarna Cacao**   CAFE-BAR
(☑ 05-674 10 35; http://cacao.si; Obala 14; ⊙ 8am-1am Sun-Thu, to 3am Fri & Sat) This place wins the award as the most stylish cafe-bar on the coast and boasts a fabulous waterfront terrace thronged by beachgoers. The menu is rich with coffee, juices and smoothies, cocktails, ice creams and cakes, served into the wee hours.

Kanela Bar   BAR
(☑ 068 139 765; Obala 14a; ⊙ 10am-3am) Secreted between the beach and the Cacao, the 'Cinnamon' is a workhorse of a rock-'n'-roll bar up late (and early) with frequent live concerts.

Portorož Auditorium   THEATRE
(Portorož Avditorij; ☑ 05-676 67 00; www.avditorij. si; Senčna pot 10) The main cultural venue in Portorož has two indoor theatres and an open-air amphitheatre, and is 200m behind where the buses stop. Keep an eye out for events like upcoming concerts, or check the calendar online.

ⓘ Orientation

Portorož's main development looks onto the bay from Obala, but there are satellite resorts and hotel complexes to the northwest at Bernardin and south near the Portorož Marina at Lucija. Buses stop opposite the main beach on Postajališka pot.

ⓘ Information

Go Portorož (☑ 040 461 000; www.goportoroz.si; Obala 14) Travel agency on the waterfront, in a hard-to-miss golfball-shaped kiosk. Plans excursions and activities, can help with accommodation and transport too. Also has boats, bikes, scooters and cars for rent.

Tourist Information Centre (☑ 05-674 22 20; www.portoroz.si; Obala 16; ⊙ 9am-10pm Jul & Aug, to 5pm Sep-Jun) Helpful office opposite the Kempinski; bike rental available.

ⓘ Getting There & Away

Arriva (☑ 090 74 11; www.arriva.si) is the bus line serving the coast; see its website for schedules and prices.

Buses run frequently to Piran (€1.30, eight minutes, 4km), and up to four times an hour to Izola (€1.80, 30 minutes, 8km) and Koper

(€2.70, 40 minutes, 18km). These buses all stop at Lucija, Bernadin and Strunjan.

Three buses daily make the journey to Ljubljana (€12, 2¾ hours, 137km), via Divača and Postojna.

For international destinations like Trieste and Croatian Istrian towns, services are the same as from **Piran** (p153); there are more-frequent services from Izola and Koper.

Sečovlje

Salt-making is a centuries-old business along the Slovenian coast. The best place to get a briny taste is at the old saltpans of the Sečovlje Salina Nature Park.

◎ Sights & Activities

Sečovlje Salina Nature Park NATURE RESERVE
(Krajinski Park Sečoveljske Soline; ☑ 05-672 13 30; www.kpss.si; adult/child €7/5; ◎ 8am-9pm Jun-Sep, to 5pm Oct-May) This 750-hectare saltpan-studded area, criss-crossed with dikes and channels, has a wealth of birdlife – 290 species have been recorded here.

It's important to note that there are two sections of the park: the main (north) part is at Lera, just south of Seča and off the main road from Portorož. The south part is at Fontanigge, right on the border with Croatia; to reach it you must pass through Slovenian immigration and customs first, so don't forget your passport.

The Lera and Fontanigge sections are not connected – they are separated by the Drnica Channel, and different entrances must be used for each. You can get around each section on bike or foot. The area was once a hive of salt-making activity and was one of the biggest money-spinners on the coast in the Middle Ages.

Lera, where salt is still harvested using traditional methods, is home to a **multimedia visitor centre** (free) and neighbouring cafe. It also has a shop selling Piranske Soline salt products (cooking salt and beauty products; www.soline.si). Lera is also home to the Lepa Vida spa, away to the north in an oasis of calm.

Fontanigge is home to the excellent Saltworks Museum. It's a couple of kilometres from the park's entrance to the museum – free bikes are available to cover the ground.

Saltworks Museum MUSEUM
(Muzej Solinarstva; www.kpss.si; Fontanigge; ◎ 10am-1pm Wed & Fri) In the centre of the Fontanigge section of the nature park is the wonderful Saltworks Museum. The exhibits relate to all aspects of salt-making and the lives of salt-workers and their families. At the time of research, the opening hours were restricted, with some doubt over the museum's future path.

It's best to enquire about hours at local TICs or direct with the park.

★ Lepa Vida Thalasso Spa SPA
(☑ 05-672 13 60; www.thalasso-lepavida.si; Lepa; 2/4hr incl park admission €18/30; ◎ 9am-9pm mid-May–Sep) This gorgeous open-air spa sits at the breezy northern end of the saltpans. There's a great set-up: saltwater swimming pool, brine pools for soaking, and a massage pavilion and cafe (drinks only). It's peaceful and quiet, with a maximum 50 guests (no kids under 12). Bookings are essential, and a golf cart will shuttle you from the park entrance to the spa.

You can opt for pool time only, or book a variety or soaks, scrubs and massages. Note: opening hours are weather dependent.

ⓘ Getting There & Away

If driving, follow the signs to the park to reach the park at Lera. The nicest way to arrive is by bike, along the coastal bike trail from Lucija. A few tour companies offer cruises that stop at Lera.

Southeast Slovenia & the Krka Valley

Best Places to Eat

➡ Grad (p170)

➡ Oštarija Debeluh (p175)

➡ Oštarija (p165)

➡ Gostilna Vovko (p170)

Best Places to Stay

➡ Hotel Balnea (p165)

➡ Šeruga Farmhouse (p170)

➡ Otočec Castle Hotel (p170)

➡ Glamping Malerič (p182)

➡ Domačija Novak (p164)

➡ Vila Castanea (p173)

Why Go?

Slovenia's southeast doesn't announce itself as loudly as other parts of the country, preferring subtle charms over big-ticket attractions. Dolenjska (Lower Carniola) and Bela Krajina are regions where life slows down considerably – all the better to enjoy the meandering rivers and rolling hills covered with forest, orchards and grapevines. Villages cluster around church spires and distinctive *toplarji* hayracks shelter neat woodpiles.

Low-key tourist attractions come in the shape of grand monasteries and restored castles, thermal water resorts, and surprisingly good regional museums and galleries. Local farms and vineyards welcome travellers with rustic accommodation, farm-to-plate food and unique wine. The area encourages outdoor exploration, too: walking and cycling trails take in the bucolic splendour; kayaking and rafting get you onto those green rivers. With some time up your sleeve and a desire to see beyond Slovenia's headline acts, you could craft an itinerary where slow travel brings its own rewards.

When to Go

Novo Mesto

Mar–May Put on your hiking boots as spring blooms and temperatures warm up.

Jun–Sep Mix summer sun with kayaking on the waters of the Kolpa or Krka Rivers.

Sep–Oct Take to the cycling trails during cooler autumn days, and enjoy the autumn grape harvest.

Southeast Slovenia & the Krka Valley Highlights

1 Cycle the back roads of the picturesque **Krka River valley** (p163).

2 Kayak the rapid-water run on the **Kolpa River** (p183) from Stari Trg to Vinica.

3 Walk the island of **Kostanjevica na Krki** (p171), and explore the art that fills its ancient monastery outside town.

4 Castle-hop from Renaissance Bogenšperk to fresco-rich Brežice, stopping for a sumptuous night in regal surrounds at **Otočec** (p170).

5 Take in a music performance at the stunning Knights' Hall during the annual **Seviqc Brežice** (p175) festival.

6 Embrace the local wine culture by staying in a vineyard cottage, sampling new wine varieties, and touring fascinating wine caves in **Bizeljsko-Sremič wine country** (p177).

7 Soak in thermal waters at **Dolenjske Toplice** (p164) or **Terme Čatež** (p174).

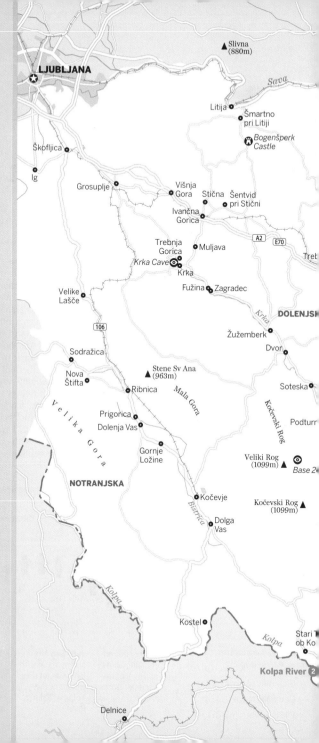

DOLENJSKA

Dolenjska was settled early on and is well known for its Hallstatt (early Iron Age) ruins, especially near Stična, Šmarjeta and Novo Mesto. The Romans made the area part of the province of Upper Pannonia (Pannonia Superior) and crossed it with roads.

In the Middle Ages, the population clustered around the many castles along the river, such as those at Žužemberk and Otočec, while monasteries sprung up at Stična, Kostanjevica na Krki and Šentjernej.

Dolenjska declined after the Middle Ages and progress only came in the late 19th century when a railway line linked Novo Mesto with Ljubljana.

Ribnica & Around

✔ 01 / POP 9530 / ELEV 493M

Ribnica is the oldest and most important settlement of western Dolenjska. It sits in the area known locally as Kočevsko – all woods, underground rivers and brown bears. It is a good springboard for the unspoiled forests of the Kočevski Rog, and worth a stop for anyone interested in local handicraft traditions.

Ribnica's main street, Škrabčev trg, lies on the east bank of the tiny Bistrica River and runs parallel to it.

Note, too, that if you're searching online for Ribnica, there are a few Slovenian towns by the same name, and Ribnica na Pohorju in northeast Slovenia has a stronger online presence! This town is Ribnica na Dolenjskem in online bus schedules etc.

◉ Sights

Ribnica Handicraft Centre CULTURAL CENTRE
(Rokodelski center Ribnica; ✔ 01-836 11 04; www.rodelskicenter-ribnica.si; Cesta na Ugar 6; ⊙ 9am-5pm Mon-Fri, to 1pm Sat) This is a great addition to the town – a centre tasked with preserving and promoting the area's longstanding handicraft traditions. The *suha roba* made in the region can be translated as 'dry goods', but that doesn't quite do justice to the finely crafted wooden and wicker implements (pottery is another local product). Stop by to see the shop here, and learn about production methods. There are occasionally workshops where you can see local artisans in action.

The centre also acts as the town's tourist information office.

Ribnica Castle & Museum CASTLE
(Muzej Ribnica; ✔ 01-835 03 76; www.muzej-ribnica.si; Gallusovo nabrežje; 10am-1pm & 4-7pm May-Oct) Ribnica Castle was originally built in the 11th century and expanded over the centuries. Only a small section – a Renaissance wall and two towers – survived bombings during WWII. Today the castle is set in lovely parkland and houses a small museum detailing the traditional crafts of the area, plus an interesting exhibition on local witch trials from the 15th century.

Parish Church of St Stephen CHURCH
(Župnijska Cerkev Sv Štefana; Škrabčev trg) Built in 1868 on the site of earlier churches, this parish church would not be of much interest were it not for the two striking towers added by Jože Plečnik in the form of his signature steeples in 1960, to replace the ones toppled during WWII.

Mikel House Gallery GALLERY
(Galerija Miklova Hiša; ✔ 01-835 03 78; www.galerija-miklovahisa.si; Škrabčev trg 21; ⊙ 10am-noon & 4-6pm) FREE Mikel House is a lovely cream-and-white building dating from 1858; it houses exhibitions of contemporary art and does double duty as the town's library.

Church of the Assumption of Mary CHURCH
(Cerkev Marijinega Vnebovzetja; ✔ 01-836 99 43; Nova Štifta 3; ⊙ 10am-noon & 2-6pm) The church at Nova Štifta, in the foothills of the Velika Gora 7km west of Ribnica, is one of the most important pilgrimage sites in Slovenia. Completed in 1671, the baroque church is unusual for its octagonal shape. The interior of the church, with its golden altars and pulpit, is blindingly ornate.

In the courtyard opposite the Franciscan monastery (where the church key is kept) stands a wonderful old *toplar* and a linden tree, planted in the mid-17th century, complete with a treehouse that has been there for over a century.

🏃 Activities

Ribnica is the base for many excellent walks. Ask at the TIC (p161) for information.

A well-marked trail leads northeast of the town for about 4.5km to **Stene Sv Ana** (the Walls of St Anne; 963m), with fantastic views over the Ribnica Valley.

The Sv Ana hilltop is one of the points along the **Ribnica Hiking Trail**, which comprises 17 points scattered around the Ribnica valley and surrounding mountains. The highest peak of the trail is Turn (1254m), southwest of town.

✯ Festivals & Events

Ribnica Fair CULTURAL
(Ribniški Semenj; www.ribnica.si; ☉ late-Aug–Sep) A town fair with events over two weeks, combined with a celebration of Ribnica's handicrafts heritage.

⊨ Sleeping & Eating

There are slim pickings in Ribnica.

★**Harlekin Gostilna** GUESTHOUSE
(☑ 01-836 15 32; www.harlekin.si; Gorenjska cesta 21; s/d incl breakfast €50/80) The nicest place in town to bed down, with half-a-dozen large, modern, timber-floored rooms above an excellent restaurant.

Gostišče-Penzion Makšar GUESTHOUSE €€
(☑ 01-837 31 60; http://penzion-maksar.si/; Breze 18A; s/d incl breakfast €50/80) Simple, agreeable rooms in a guesthouse in a hamlet 5km northwest of Ribnica. There's also a well-priced traditional restaurant here, and the chance to try the Makšar beer made in the small on-site brewery.

Harlekin Pizzerija SLOVENIAN €€
(☑ 01-836 15 32; www.harlekin.si; Gorenjska cesta 21; mains €7-15; ☉ 10am-10pm) Not just pizzas – Harlekin has a big menu of crowd-pleasers. Stick with wood-fired pizzas, or taste local flavours like forest mushroom soup, wild boar goulash, tagliatelle with truffles or squid stuffed with shrimp and mozzarella.

ⓘ Information

Tourist Information Centre (TIC; ☑ 01-836 11 04; Cesta na Ugar 6; ☉ 9am-5pm Mon-Fri, to 1pm Sat) The Ribnica Handicraft Centre acts as the town's tourist office, with brochures, maps and local advice.

ⓘ Getting There & Around

Buses run at least hourly north to Ljubljana (€5.60, 65 minutes, 47km), and south to Kočevje (€2.70, 25 minutes, 17km). Buses stop on Škrabčev trg in front of the church.

Stična

☑ 01 / POP 850 / ELEV 363M
The abbey at Stična is the oldest monastery in Slovenia and one of the country's most important religious monuments. Only 35km from Ljubljana, it's an easy day trip from the capital.

◉ Sights

Stična Cistercian Abbey ABBEY
(Cistercijanska Opatija Stična; ☑ 01-787 78 63; www.mks-sticna.si; Stična 17; adult/child €7/2; ☉ tours 8.30am, 10am, 2pm & 4pm Tue-Sat, 2pm & 4pm Sun) Established in 1136 by the Cistercians (famous for their vows of silence), this abbey was for centuries the most important religious, economic, educational and cultural centre in Dolenjska. The walled monastery, an incredible combination of Romanesque, Gothic, Renaissance and baroque architecture, currently has 14 monks in residence.

Entry is on the east side of the monastery, across a small stream. On the north side of the central courtyard is the Old Prelature, a 17th-century Renaissance building, which contains the **Slovene Museum of Christianity** (Muzej Krščanstva na Slovenskem), a hotchpotch mix of antique clocks, furniture, icons and old documents (though note, the medieval documents are facsimiles).

On the west side of the courtyard is the **Abbey Church** (1156), a buttressed, three-nave Romanesque cathedral, rebuilt in the baroque style in the 17th and 18th centuries. Look inside for the Renaissance red-marble tombstone of Abbot Jakob Reinprecht in the north transept and the blue organ cupboard with eight angels (1747) in the choir loft. The greatest treasures here are the Stations of the Cross painted in 1766 by Fortunat Bergant.

South of the church is Stična's vaulted **cloister**, mixing Romanesque and early Gothic styles. The arches and vaults are adorned with frescoes of the prophets and Old Testament stories and allegorical subjects. The carved stone faces on the west side were meant to show human emotions and vices.

On the south side of the cloister is a typically baroque monastic **refectory**, with an 18th-century pink ceiling with white stucco decoration. **Neff's Abbey**, built in the mid-16th century by Abbot Volbenk Neff, runs to the west. The arches in the vestibule on the ground floor are painted with a dense network of leaves, blossoms, berries and birds.

The Cistercians sell their own products (honey, wine, herbal teas, liqueurs) in a small shop inside the complex.

ℹ️ Getting There & Away

Stična is served by up to a dozen buses a day from Ljubljana (€4.10, 50 minutes, 35km) on weekdays, with fewer on weekends.

Another option is the train, which stops at Ivančna Gorica, a larger town 2.5km south of the abbey. Frequent Ljubljana–Novo Mesto trains stop here (€3.44, 50 minutes in either direction).

Bogenšperk Castle

📍 01 / ELEV 413M

The 16th-century Bogenšperk Castle is in many respects the secular equivalent of the Cistercian Abbey at Stična. It celebrates the life and works of the castle's most noteworthy resident, the great natural historian Janez Vajkard Valvasor.

◉ Sights

Bogenšperk Castle CASTLE
(Grad Bogenšperk; 📞 01-898 76 64; www.bogensperk.si; Bogenšperk 5; adult/child €4.50/3.50; ⏲ tours hourly 10am-5pm Tue-Sat, to 6pm Sun Jul & Aug, shorter hours Sep-Jun, closed Dec-Feb) This Renaissance-style castle was the home of the celebrated 17th-century polymath Janez Vajkard Valvasor, who spent the most productive two decades of his life here. The castle, with its rectangular courtyard and three towers (the fourth burned down in the 19th century), now houses a museum devoted to the great man, his work and Slovenian culture.

Valvasor bought the castle in 1672 and installed his printing press, engraving workshop and extensive library here. But due to the enormous debts incurred in getting his magnum opus published, he was forced to sell up 20 years later.

Valvasor's library is now used as a wedding hall, but his study, with its beautiful parquetry, black limestone columns and painted ceiling, is pretty much the way he left it when he performed his last alchemical experiments here. Other rooms contain examples of Valvasor's original cartography and etching, an original four-volume set of his famous work, a working printing press and a collection of hunting trophies, including a 360kg brown bear. The most interesting exhibits, however, are the ones that deal with folk dress, superstition and medicine.

ℹ️ Getting There & Away

Bogenšperk is tough to reach without your own transport. Half-hourly trains link Ljubljana with Litija (€3.44, 30 minutes, 31km), but it's still another 6km south to the castle – much of it uphill.

Krka Valley

The Krka River springs from a karst cave southwest of Stična, near the village of Trebnja Gorica, and runs to the southeast and east until it joins the mightier Sava near Brežice. At 94km, it is Dolenjska's longest waterway.

VALVASOR, SLOVENIA'S RENAISSANCE MAN

Most of our knowledge of Slovenian history, geography, culture and folklore before the 17th century comes from the writings of one man, Janez Vajkard Valvasor – and more specifically his book *The Glory of the Duchy of Carniola*.

Valvasor was born to a noble family from Bergamo in 1641, in Ljubljana's Old Town. After a Jesuit education there and in Germany, he joined Miklós Zrínyi, the Hungarian count and poet, in the wars against the Turks and travelled widely, visiting Germany, Italy, North Africa, France and Switzerland. He collected data on natural phenomena and local customs as well as books, drawings, mineral specimens and coins.

In 1672 Valvasor installed himself, his books and his precious collections at Bogenšperk Castle, where he conducted scientific experiments (including alchemy) and wrote. In 1689 he completed his most important work, *The Glory of the Duchy of Carniola*. It ran to four volumes, comprising 3500 pages with 535 maps and copper engravings, and remains one of the most comprehensive works published in Europe before the Enlightenment – such a wealth of information on the Slovenian patrimony that it's still explored and studied to this day.

Valvasor never enjoyed the success of his labours. Publishing such a large work at his own expense ruined him financially and he was forced to leave Bogenšperk in 1692. He died a year later at Krško, 65km to the east on the Sava River.

KRKA CRUISING

If you have your own transport, you can make a maze-like trip through Dolenjska by following Route No 216 along the Krka River, which cuts a deep and picturesque valley along its upper course. Along the way, you'll chance upon historical churches, mighty castles and even a couple of caves worth visiting. A few buses from Ljubljana to Novo Mesto via Dolenjske Toplice follow this route but they are very infrequent.

The journey begins about 9km south of Ivančna Gorica, in the village of Krka, where you can find a pair of caves, one of which is the source of the Krka River. Carry on for another 13km or so and you'll reach Žužemberk, a town dominated at street level by a multi-turreted castle but watched from on high by the sizeable Parish Church of Sts Mohor and Fortunat (Župnijska Cerkev Sv Mohorja in Fortunata), built over six decades in the 18th century. Nine kilometres to the south of Žužemberk at Soteska are the ivy-covered ruins of Soteska Castle, a fortress admired by Valvasor but more or less razed during WWII. Nearby is the irresistibly sweet Garden Pavilion (in Slovenian known as Hudičev Turn – literally the 'Devil's Tower'), a cylindrical structure from the late 17th century standing photogenically in a field.

At Soteska you can elect to carry on south on Route 216 to the spa town of Dolenjske Toplice or turn east on to Route No 419 and continue following the Krka River. If you choose the latter, within 6km you'll reach Straža, which boasts the massive Church of the Assumption of Mary (Cerkev Marije Vnebovzete), built at the very end of the 18th century and featuring some impressive illusionist paintings. Then it's on to Dolenjska's main city, Novo Mesto.

The river's fast-flowing waters are popular for kayaking and canoeing, but there are considerably fewer commercial opportunities for tours here than in the Soča Valley, for instance. It may be a matter of asking around at tourist centres and accommodation to find equipment and/or a guide.

Rafting is most popular on the upper section of the river, from the village of Lese to Šmihel – this stretch has numerous natural dams. Relaxed canoeing is best on the calmer lower section of the river.

◉ Sights & Activities

Krka Cave   CAVE
(Krška Jama; ☏ 041 276 252; www.tdkrka.si; Gradiček 6; adult/child €3/2; ⊘ 2-4pm Sat & Sun Apr-Oct) Krka Cave lies above the Krka spring on the northern side of the village Gradiček, just northwest of Krka village. It's nowhere close to the league of Postojna or Škocjan Caves, but along the 200m route you get to see some stalactites shaped like ribbons and fragile-looking 'spaghetti', a century-old specimen of *Proteus anguinus* (human fish) and a 30m-deep siphon lake. The cave temperature is 8°C to 9°C.

Carpe Diem   KAYAKING
(☏ 01-780 60 11, 041 739 771; www.kayak.si; Krka 27; per person €20-30) Offers a range of kayaking trips on the Krka River, based out of Krka village.

Žužemberk

☏ 07 / POP 1023 / ELEV 220M
This old market town is a good place to stretch your legs and impress the locals with your Slovenian pronunciation (it's zhoozhem-berk).

◉ Sights

Žužemberk Castle   CASTLE
(td.suha-krajina@siol.net; Grajski trg 1; ⊘ 9am-6pm Mon-Fri, 7am-8pm Sat & Sun Jun-Sep) FREE
The mighty, 13th-century Žužemberk Castle perches photogenically on a terrace overlooking the Krka River. It was refortified in the 16th century, only to be all but flattened during air raids in WWII. Its towers have been partially reconstructed, and the Renaissance walls, the roof, the courtyard and the wine cellar have now been restored. In summer the castle grounds are open daily for a ramble; with prebooking, you can arrange guiding.

The grounds are the setting for a number of summer events; the biggest is the annual Market Town Days, held over a weekend in mid-July.

🛏 Sleeping & Eating

For a great picnic spot, follow the signs south of town to Dolga Vas – there's a great park down here, with a designer treehouse and great castle views.

⭐ Domačija Novak   GUESTHOUSE €€
(📞 041 343 000; www.novakdoma.eu; Sadinja vas pri Dvoru 7; s/d incl breakfast €55/80; 🅿 🛜) Earning raves from smitten guests, this delightful farmhouse is signposted about 3km south of Žužemberk and offers cosy accommodation, top-notch food (much of it homegrown) and local wines, and good activity options – including free bike usage, and the opportunity for fishing, kayaking and even cooking classes. Non-guests can dine here too, but bookings are essential.

Koren   GUESTHOUSE €€
(📞 07-308 72 60; www.turizem-koren.com; Dolga Vas 5; per person incl breakfast €30) At the southern end of Žužemberk, a sign points the way down to a riverside village below town, and here you'll find Koren, with glorious views up to the castle. Rooms here are low on frills but clean and comfy; the restaurant's riverside tables are the real drawcard, as is the good food (mains €6 to €12; try the *štruklji* with mushrooms) and the chance to rent kayaks.

Gostilna Pri Gradu   SLOVENIAN €
(📞 07-308 72 90; www.gostilna-prigradu.si; Grajski trg 4; mains €7-18; ⏰ 6am-11pm) This old-style eatery under a linden in front of Žužemberk Castle has a terrace open in the warmer months. Fare is hearty and local – standard fare, but it's pretty much the only game in the heart of town.

ℹ Getting There & Away

The bus stop is in front of the post office on Grajski trg. Popular destinations:

Dolenjske Toplice (€2.70, 24 minutes, 18km, three daily)

Ljubljana (€6, one hour, 53km, up to five daily)

Novo Mesto (€2.30, 20 minutes, 19km, one daily)

Dolenjske Toplice

🎵 07 / POP 792 / ELEV 176M

Within striking distance of Novo Mesto, this small and sweet thermal resort is one of Slovenia's oldest spa towns. Located in the karst valley of the Sušica (a tributary of the Krka River), and surrounded by the wooded slopes of Kočevski Rog, it's an excellent place in which to hike, cycle or simply relax.

History

The first spa was built here in 1658. The Kopališki Dom (Bathers' House), complete with three pools, was built in the 18th century. Despite getting its own guidebook, tourism didn't really take off until 1899, with the opening of the Zdravilíški Dom (Health Resort House). Strascha Töplitz, as it was then called, was a great favourite of Austrians from around the turn of the 20th century up to WWI.

🏃 Activities

Thermal Spas

Balnea Wellness Centre   SPA
(📞 07-391 97 50; Zdravilíški trg; lagoon day pass adult €10-13, child €8-11; ⏰ lagoon 9am-9pm Sun-Thu, to 11pm Fri & Sat) The large Balnea Wellness Centre is the town's big attraction. It's composed of three parts: the park-like **Lagoon** counts four pools (three outdoor and one inside) with thermal water between 27°C and 32°C. In the **Oasis** section are a host of indoor and outdoor saunas and steam baths. The **Aura** section has treatments and massages. The Lagoon is kid-friendly too (complete with outdoor pirate-ship pool).

Hotel guests get into Lagoon free; access to the Oasis for three hours is €15 to €17 (or €18 to €21 including the Lagoon, for non-hotel guests). There are a number of combination tickets and packages available. There's a cafe-bar on-site.

The centre is as you drive into town, in pretty parkland just north of the hotels – it's connected to the Balnea hotel by walkway.

Hotel Vital   SPA
(📞 07-391 97 50; Zdravilíški trg 11; adult €7-9, child €5-7; ⏰ 7am-8pm) Taking the waters is the *sine qua non* of Dolenjske Toplice: the 36°C mineral water gushing from 1000m below the three indoor thermal pools at the Hotel Vital is used primarily for therapeutic purposes (Balnea is geared to tourists, Vital to therapy).

Hiking & Cycling

A dozen trails are outlined on the free *Dolenjske Toplice Municipal Tourist Trails* handout, but without any explanatory detail. You need to ask at the TIC for more detailed information – it has some two dozen separate sheets with themed hikes, walks and cycle routes.

One is a 2.5km **archaeological walk** west to Cvinger (263m), where Hallstatt tombs and iron foundries have been unearthed. Nature lovers may be interested in the 8km **herbalist trail**, a loop south to Sela and Podturn and back via forest roads, which takes in a herbalist farm and the 15th-century Church of the Holy Trinity at Cerovec. Further afield is the 2km **Dormouse Trail**, which makes a loop from Kočevske Poljane, about 4.5km southwest of Dolenjske Toplice, and could be combined with a hike to Base 20 (p166).

Skiing

Bela Ski Centre　　　　　　　　　SKIING
(Smučarski Center Bela; ☑ 041 182 513; www.sc-bela.si; day pass adult/child €24/19) The Bela Ski Centre is on the edge of the Kočevje forest, 16km south of Dolenjske Toplice en route to Črnomelj. It has 6km of slopes and 7km of cross-country trails on Mt Gače at altitudes between 700m and 965m.

🛏 Sleeping

Kamp Dolenjske Toplice　　CAMPGROUND €
(☑ 040 466 589; www.camping-potocar.si; per adult/child €11/5.50; ⊙ year-round; P 🐾) This small, shady campground sits pretty in a riverside position, its sites defined by trees. It's just off the northern end of Zdraviliški trg, more or less opposite the Balnea spa complex. It's open as a campervan stop in winter too. Bike rental available.

Hotel Pri Mostu　　　　　　GUESTHOUSE €
(☑ 041 755 363; Pionirska cesta 2; s/d/f from €34/49/70; P ❄ 🐾) This brand-new seven-room option (more guesthouse than hotel) is a great choice – central, stylish and competitively priced, and with a choice of rooms, studios and a family-sized apartment. It's above a cafe-bar, where the optional breakfast is served (€5).

Penzion Termal　　　　　　GUESTHOUSE €
(☑ 031 413 588; www.penzion-termal.si; Sokolski trg 2; s/d €30/50; P ❄ 🐾) Simple, spotless rooms in a central location, with a friendly atmosphere – plus the advantage of the town's best restaurant downstairs (making the half-board option at €38 per person a great deal).

★ Hotel Balnea　　　　　　　HOTEL €€€
(☑ 07-391 94 00; www.terme-krka.si; Zdraviliški trg 11; s/d incl breakfast €91/152; P ❄ @ ♨) Few newly built hotels in Slovenia can compare with this 63-room, four-star (plus) palace in terms of design and facilities. It's heavy on timber, natural materials and nature-inspired colours. We love the back-facing rooms with large balconies looking on to the park – and the covered walkway to the Balnea spa centre. Lots of weekend/wellness packages available, and half-board for not much extra.

🍴 Eating & Drinking

Gostišče Račka　　　　　　　SLOVENIAN €
(☑ 07-306 55 10; www.gostisce-racka.si; Ulica Maksa Henigmana 15; pizza & pasta €4-8; ⊙ 8am-10pm Mon-Thu, to 11pm Fri, noon-11pm Sat & Sun) This no-frills pub-style restaurant is a popular local spot for cheap grub (hearty meat dishes, pizza etc). There are basic rooms for rent, too.

★ Oštarija　　　　　　　　　SLOVENIAN €€
(☑ 051 262 990; www.ostarija.si; Sokolski trg 2; mains €7-25; ⊙ noon-11pm Tue-Sat, noon-4pm Sun) There are few eating options in town, so it's a joy to find this place is so good, and so well-priced (tip: make a booking). From the cute courtyard to the old-world interior, the place is pumping, and the kitchen standards are high. Drop in for a three-course lunch for €10 to €12, and marvel at the bargain of a five-course dinner menu for €25.

Pri Mostu　　　　　　　　　CAFE, BAR
(Pionirska cesta 2; ⊙ 7am-11pm) About as central as you'll find, this lively cafe-bar has an outside terrace along the narrow Sušica and offers all-day coffee, booze and snacks.

ℹ Information

Terme Krka Dolenjske Toplice (☑ 08-205 03 00; www.terme-krka.si) Central contact for bookings at the three main hotels (Balnea, plus affiliated Kristal and Vital), beauty and medical treatments etc.

Tourist Information Centre Dolenjske Toplice (TIC; ☑ 07-384 51 88; www.dolenjske-toplice.si; Sokolski trg 4; ⊙ 9am-noon & 2-6pm Mon-Fri, 10am-noon & 2-4pm Sat & Sun)

ℹ Getting There & Around

Useful bus services:

Črnomelj (€4.10, 50 minutes, 33km, one daily)
Ljubljana (€7.20, 1½ hours, 73km, two daily)
Novo Mesto (€2.30, 20 minutes, 13km, hourly)
Žužemberk (€2.70, 25 minutes, 18km, two daily)

Some accommodation providers offer bike rental; otherwise, head to **K2M** (☑ 07-306 68 30; www.k2m.si; Pionirska cesta 3; per day €15).

Kočevski Rog

One of the most pristine areas in Slovenia, Kočevski Rog's virgin forests have been a protected nature area for over a century. As many as 250 brown bears are believed to live here, as well as lynx and wolf.

Base 20 · MONUMENT

(Baza 20; ☑ 041 315 165; www.dolmuzej.com; guiding per person €4; ⊗ grounds 24hr, guiding by arrangement 8am-4pm Apr-Oct) During the early days of WWII the Partisans, under Marshal Tito's command, headquartered in Kočevski Rog's dense forests. Amid the region's limestone caves they operated hospitals, schools and even printing presses. The nerve centre was the so-called Base 20, about 9km southwest of Dolenjske Toplice at 662m, reconstructed and turned into a national monument after the war. The site is always open; exhibitions in two huts are accessible with a guide.

Once a favourite 'pilgrimage' spot for Slovenes and Yugoslavs, it's now a shadow of its former self, its 26 wooden buildings slowly being consumed by the forest. A plaque erected near the site in 1995 diplomatically pays homage to everyone involved in the 'national liberation war', presumably including the thousands of Domobranci (Home Guards) executed here by the Partisans in 1945.

There's no bus service, but Base 20 can be reached by sealed road or on foot or bike from Podturn (it's 2km from Dolenjske Toplice to Podturn, and a further 7km uphill to Base 20). Guiding must be arranged in advance.

Novo Mesto

☑ 07 / POP 23,315 / ELEV 169M

Situated on a sharp, scenic bend of the Krka River, the inappropriately named New Town – it's actually pretty old – is the political, economic and cultural capital of Dolenjska and one of its prettiest towns. It is an important gateway to the historical towns and castles along the lower Krka, the karst forests of the Gorjanci Hills to the southeast, Bela Krajina and Croatia (Zagreb is a mere 75km away).

Today's Novo Mesto shows two faces to the world: the Old Town (with the cobbled square of Glavni trg) on a rocky promontory above the left bank of the Krka; and a new town to the north and south, thriving on business such as the large pharmaceutical company named Krka, and Revoz, which produces Renault cars.

History

Novo Mesto was settled during the late Bronze Age around 1000 BC, and helmets and decorated burial urns unearthed in surrounding areas suggest that Marof Hill, northwest of the Old Town, was the seat of Hallstatt princes during the early Iron Age (8th to 4th century BC). The Illyrians and Celts came later, and the Romans maintained a settlement here until the 4th century AD.

During the early Middle Ages, Novo Mesto flourished as a marketplace at the centre of the estates owned by Stična abbey. But by the 16th century plague, fires, and raids by the Turks on their way to Vienna took their toll on the city.

Prosperity returned in the 18th and 19th centuries: a college was established in 1746, Slovenia's first National Hall (Narodni Dom) opened here in 1875 and a railway line linked the city with Ljubljana in the 1890s. Heavy bombardments during WWII severely damaged the city.

◉ Sights

Cathedral of St Nicholas · CATHEDRAL

(Stolna Cerkev Sv Nikolaja; http://zupnija-stolna-nm.rkc.si/; Kapiteljska ulica) Perched above the Old Town, this Gothic cathedral is Novo Mesto's most important historical monument. It has a 15th-century vaulted (and very floral) presbytery and crypt, wall frescoes, a belfry that had once been a medieval defence tower, and an altar painting of the church's eponymous saint supposedly painted by the Venetian master Jacopo Tintoretto (1518–94).

If the church is locked, you'll find the key at the Provost's House, the yellow building to the northwest of the cathedral built in 1623. Just south of this is a section of the medieval town walls erected in the 14th century.

★ Dolenjska Museum · MUSEUM

(Dolenjski Muzej; ☑ 07-373 11 30; www.dolmuzej.com; Muzejska ulica 7; adult/child €5/3; ⊗ 9am-5pm Tue-Sat Apr-Oct, 8am-4pm Tue-Sat Nov-Mar) The Dolenjska Museum's impressive collection is spread over a campus of buildings. The oldest, which once belonged to the Knights of the Teutonic Order, houses a valuable collection of archaeological finds unearthed in the southern suburb of Kandija in the late 1960s. Don't miss the fine bronze *situlae* (or pails) from the 3rd or 4th century BC embossed with battle and hunting scenes, and the Celtic ceramics and jewellery (particularly the bangles of turquoise and blue glass).

Other collections in the complex include one devoted to recent history, and an excellent ethnographic collection with farm implements, folk art and exhibits covering local practices such as winemaking, bee-keeping and decorative gingerbread.

Jakac House
GALLERY

(Jakčev Dom; ☎ 07-373 11 31; www.dolenjskimuzej.si; Sokolska ulica 1; adult/child €3/2; ☉ 9am-5pm Tue-Sat Apr-Oct, 8am-4pm Tue-Sat Nov-Mar) The Dolenjska Museum administers Jakac House, which exhibits some of its 830-odd works by the prolific painter and local boy Božidar Jakac (1899–1989). The artist visited dozens of countries in the 1920s and 1930s, painting and sketching such diverse subjects as Parisian dance halls, Scandinavian port towns, African villages and American city skylines. But his best works are of Novo Mesto's markets, people, churches and rumble-tumble wooden riverside houses.

Novo Mesto

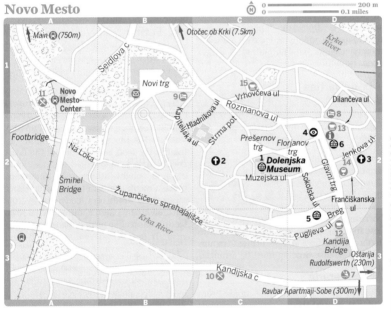

The Dolenjska Museum's permanent collection of paintings from the 17th to 20th centuries is also exhibited here.

Glavni Trg
SQUARE

(Glavni trg 7) On the Old Town's main square, the neo-Renaissance **town hall** (Rotovž), out of step with the square's other arcaded buildings, ostentatiously calls attention to itself at all hours with its bells and unusual facade. The coat of arms on the front is that of Archduke Rudolf IV, the town's 14th-century founder.

Franciscan Church of St Leonard
CHURCH

(Frančiškanska Cerkev Sv Lenarta; Frančiškanska ulica) Southeast of Glavni trg is the yellow Franciscan Church of St Leonard, which was originally built by monks fleeing the Turks in Bosnia in 1472, and the attached Franciscan monastery, whose library contains some 12,000 volumes, including 12th-century incunabula.

Activities

Bar Boter
KAYAKING

(☑040 799 990; Kandijska cesta 9; ⊙7am-midnight) Head to this riverside pub, just south of the Old Town, to rent boats and canoes.

Equestrian School Sport Centre Češča Vas
HORSE RIDING

(KŠSC Češča Vas; ☑07-337 30 40, 041 554 265; www.konji-cescavas.si; per hour €10-20; ⊙by appointment) About 5km west of Novo Mesto, just south of Prečna, this equestrian centre has a riding school and offers cross-country rides by arrangement.

Sleeping

The TIC has a list of private rooms (from €25 per person). The closest campgrounds are at Otočec ob Krki, 10km northeast, and Dolenjske Toplice, 13km southwest.

★ Hostel Situla
HOSTEL €

(☑07-394 20 00; www.situla.si; Dilančeva ulica 1; dm €13.50-19, s/d €25/44; P@🖥) One of Slovenia's nicest hostels, partially built within the walls of an 18th-century town house with rooms over five floors. Iron Age–style art sets off the cosy rooms (we love the attic dormitory under the mansard roof, but perhaps not in midsummer heat). There's no kitchen for guests, but breakfast is included, and the on-site bar-restaurant has a set lunch from €4.

Ravbar Apartmaji-Sobe
APARTMENT €

(☑07-373 06 80, 041 738 309; www.ravbar.net; Smrečnikova ulica 15-17; s/d/tr from €24/35/55, apt for 2/4 from €45/70; P🌦🖥) This family-run guesthouse has rooms and apartments of various size and comfort-category – all are homely, well-equipped and spotlessly clean, and the location is a leafy and quiet suburban area south of the river (a short walk to the centre). The welcome is warm, the prices more than reasonable.

Hotel Krka
HOTEL €€€

(☑07-394 21 00; www.terme-krka.si; Novi trg 1; s/d incl breakfast €72/114; P🌦🖥) This is the town's four-star business hotel. It's nice and central, but the decor is looking well past its use-by date.

Eating

Local restaurants have great-value lunchtime deals (meals around €4) to feed local workers and students (and make travellers very happy).

Oštarija Rudolfswerth
SLOVENIAN €€

(☑07-332 33 35; www.ostarija-rudolfswerth.si; Kandijska cesta 35; mains €5-20; ⊙7am-10pm Mon-Sat) The roadside location is uninspiring but the food is excellent and the decor stylish and detail-oriented – brass buckets used as light fittings, rustic timber and brick, a menu printed on handmade paper. Meals range from beef tenderloin to trout fillet, and there's also local game and Krka River fish – plus creative pizza options.

Don Bobi
SLOVENIAN €€

(☑07-338 24 00; www.don-bobi.com; Kandijska cesta 14; mains €6-20; ⊙10am-11pm Mon-Fri, noon-11pm Sat) Considerably fancier than the name might suggest, this *gostilnica* and pizzeria has great lunch deals, good service and a full menu of fish, steaks, pastas and pizzas (the pizzas win lots of local plaudits).

Gostišče Loka
INTERNATIONAL €€

(☑07-332 11 08; www.gostisce-loka.si; Župančiče-vo sprehajališče 2; mains €7-20; ⊙7am-10pm Mon-Thu, to 11pm Sat, 9am-11pm Sat, 9am-9pm Sun) A cool, all-day riverside spot, just beyond the small footbridge linking the two banks. A huge outdoor terrace and variety of indoor spaces serve a short and relatively simple menu that covers all bases: pasta and risotto, meat and fish. It's equally good for a cuppa-and-cake pitstop, or an evening glass of wine.

🍷 Drinking

⭐ Malamačka   CAFE, BAR
(☑ 031 854 421; http://malamacka.si; Vrhovčeva ulica 14; ☺ 7am-10pm Mon-Thu, to midnight Fri, 9am-midnight Sat) One of those secret local spots you need to hunt down: a chilled-out wine bar and cafe with a garden to relax in, great coffee, lots of wine options (try the local drops, including the region's trademark Cviček red), and snacks.

Čajarna Stari Most   TEAHOUSE
(☑ 07-337 01 60; www.starimost.si; Glavni trg 17; ☺ 7am-10pm Mon-Thu, to midnight Fri, 9am-midnight Sat, to 10pm Sun) This is a cute, colourful and family-friendly space by the bridge into the Old Town. It serves many varieties of tea, as well as drinks, snacks and cakes.

Lokal Patriot   BAR
(☑ 07-337 45 10; www.lokalpatriot.si; Glavni trg 11; ☺ 9am-11pm Mon-Wed, to midnight Thu, to 2am Fri, 5pm-2am Sat) The venue of choice among Novo Mesto's students, this bar-club-cafe has programs throughout the week and DJs (and sometimes live music) at the weekend.

Knjigarna-Kavarna Goga   CAFE
(☑ 07-393 08 01; www.goga.si; Glavni trg 6; ☺ 9am-7pm Mon-Fri, to 1pm Sat) Lovely arcade bookshop stocking the best of Slovene literature, plus a cultural centre staging events, with a small gallery space and a cafe.

ℹ️ Information

Tourist Information Centre (TIC; ☑ 07-393 92 63; www.visitnovomesto.si; Glavni trg 6; ☺ 9am-6pm Mon-Fri, to 2pm Sat) Next door to the town hall. Can arrange guiding, and has bikes for rent (per day €7).

Kompas Novo Mesto (☑ 07-393 15 20; www.kompas-nm.si; Novi trg 10; ☺ 8am-6pm Mon-Thu, to 5pm Fri, 9am-noon Sat) Organises excursions and adventure sports in the Dolenjska and Bela Krajina regions – see its website for suggestions.

ℹ️ Getting There & Away

BUS
The bus station is southwest of the Old Town across the Krka River on Topliška cesta.
Useful bus services:
Brežice (€5.60, 1¼ hours, 50km, two daily)
Črnomelj (€5.60, 1¼ hours, 46km, two daily).
Dolenjske Toplice (€2.30, 20 minutes, 13km, hourly)
Kostanjevica na Krki (€3.60, 45 minutes, 30km, two daily)

Ljubljana (€7.20, 65 minutes, 72km, up to 12 daily)
Otočec ob Krki (to the castle; €1.80, 17 minutes, 8km, up to 17 daily)

TRAIN
Novo Mesto has two train stations: the main one on Kolodvorska ulica, and little Novo Mesto-Center on Ljubljanska cesta at the western edge of the Old Town. Only about 1km separates the two stations.

Up to 14 services a day connect Novo Mesto and Ljubljana (€6.60, 1½ to two hours, 76km). Ten of these continue on to Črnomelj (€3.45, 40 minutes, 31km) and Metlika (€4.30, one hour, 46km), where there are connections to Karlovac in Croatia.

ℹ️ Getting Around

Book taxis by calling ☑ 041 625 108 or ☑ 040 550 785. The TIC rents bicycles.

Otočec ob Krki

☑ 07 / POP 790 / ELEV 167M
The castle at Otočec, on a tiny island in the middle of the Krka River, 7.5km northeast of Novo Mesto, is one of Slovenia's loveliest and most complete fortresses – and the setting is a delight.

The first castle here stood on the right bank of the river, but during the Mongol onslaught in the mid-13th century, a canal was dug on the south side, creating an artificial island. The present castle, which dates from the 16th century, now houses a five-star hotel.

The area around Otočec, the gateway to the lower Krka and the Posavje region, has become something of a recreational centre.

🔴 Sights

Otočec Castle   CASTLE
(Grad Otočec) Perched dramatically in the centre of the Krka River and reached via a wooden bridge, Otočec Castle, 1.5km east of Otočec village, is well worth a visit, even if you're not staying at the hotel here. With late Gothic and Renaissance influences, the castle consists of two wings and an entrance block connected by a pentagonal wall. There are four squat, rounded towers with very thick walls, narrow windows and conical roofs at each end. Admire it all from the courtyard terrace cafe.

Trška Gora   HILL
Postcard-pretty, vineyard-covered Trška Gora (428m) can be reached by road and

trail from Mačkovec, about 5km southwest of Otočec. From there, follow the road north for 1km to Sevno and then continue along the narrow winding track for 2km until you reach the summit and the Church of St Mary.

From the summit there are wonderful panoramas of the Gorjanci Hills, Kočevski Rog and the Krka Valley. Alternatively, from Otočec Castle, a walking trail (1¾ hours) leads to Trška Gora.

🏃 Activities

Kamp Otočec
CANOEING

(☑040 466 589; www.camping-potocar.si; per hour €2) For exploration, rent canoes (€9/20 for three hours/day) and bikes (€5/10 for three hours/day).

Otočec Sports Centre
HEALTH & FITNESS

(☑07-384 86 56; www.terme-krka.si; Grajska cesta 2) The sports centre in the grounds of Hotel Šport has facilities open to the general public: tennis courts, football and basketball courts, gym, bike hire. The hotel includes a new pool and sauna area (admission €11 to €14), while the hotel grounds are home to the Otočec Adventure Park, a forest ropes and climbing course (adult/child €17/13).

Golf Grad Otočec
GOLF

(☑07-307 56 27, 041 304 444; www.golf-otocec.si; 18 holes €50-60; ⊙Mar-Nov) Along the Krka, about 800m from Otočec Castle, the scenic Golf Grad Otočec is Slovenia's newest 18-hole golf course (par 72). Hiring a set of clubs costs €10 and an electric cart is €25. Bookings advised.

🛏 Sleeping

Kamp Otočec
CAMPGROUND €

(☑040 466 589; www.camping-potocar.si; per adult/child €11/5.50; ⊙Apr–mid-Oct; 🖥) This idyllic campground has it all: riverside location, castle views, canoes and bikes for rent. It's on a 2-hectare strip of land running along the south bank of the Krka – to reach it from the castle, cross the second bridge, turn left (east) and walk for 300m.

★Šeruga Farmhouse
GUESTHOUSE €€

(☑07-334 69 00; www.seruga.si; Sela pri Ratežu 15; s/d incl breakfast €38/65; 🖥) If you're seeking rural relaxation, look no further. This postcard-perfect farm (complete with babbling brook) sits in a small valley, in a hamlet about 4km south of Otočec village. The rustic farmhouse rooms are lovely, but the prize booking is the self-contained Granary. You'd

be mad not to take the half-board option: organic farm produce and time-honoured recipes.

Hotel Šport
HOTEL €€

(☑07-384 86 00; www.terme-krka.si; Grajska cesta 2; s/d €61/92; @🖥🖥) This large, recreation-focused hotel has somewhat dated decor but good facilities, including restaurant, a new thermal pool and saunas, gym, tennis courts, bike rental, and an adventure park (a fun ropes course through the forest). It's a short walk from the castle.

★Otočec Castle Hotel
HOTEL €€€

(☑07-384 89 00; www.terme-krka.si; s/d €180/260, ste from €300; 🖥🖥🖥) Suitably regal and refined, the five-star Otočec Castle Hotel is one of the most atmospheric places to stay in Slovenia, and a member of the prestigious Relais & Chateaux group of luxury hotels. The 10 rooms, with polished parquet floors, oriental carpets, marble-topped tables and large baths, are of a uniform size, though you could lose yourself in one of the half-dozen suites.

There's a range of packages involving weekends, romance, golf and/or cuisine.

🍴 Eating

Gostilna Vovko
SLOVENIAN €€

(☑07-308 56 03; www.gostilna-vovko.si; Ratež 48; mains €8-16; ⊙11am-10pm Tue-Fri, noon-10pm Sat, to 4pm Sun) With your own wheels (or on foot), head south from Otočec a couple of kilometres to the village of Ratež, and try this very fine local *gostilna*. The setting is farmhouse chic, the wine options are long and varied, and the food highlights local, seasonal flavours. The speciality is charcoal-grilled meats; dessert of pear stewed in Cviček wine is a winner.

Grad
SLOVENIAN €€

(☑07-384 89 01; www.grad-otocec.com; mains €13-28; ⊙7am-10pm) The restaurant at the Otočec Castle Hotel is as fancy as you would hope: ancient stone walls, stained glass and locally made artisan furniture. It's formal, but not overly so, and service is excellent. The mains aren't as expensive as the setting would lead you to believe – and the degustation menu may be worth the splurge, at €55 for six courses.

The same menu is served all day, with wide-ranging prices (from a cheaper chicken or trout fillet to fancy beefsteak with truffles). We like that anyone can drop in for a coffee in the courtyard. Dinner bookings advised.

ℹ Getting There & Away

Buses link Novo Mesto with Otočec (€1.80, 17 minutes, 8km) up to 17 times daily, and stop at the bridge leading to the castle.

Kostanjevica na Krki

🚗 07 / POP 720 / ELEV 149M

Situated on an islet just 500m long and 200m wide, in a loop of the Krka River, sleepy Kostanjevica is Slovenia's smallest town. And with a charter that dates back to 1252, it is also one of its oldest. It's an important art centre and its location is magical.

◉ Sights

★ **Božidar Jakac Art Museum** MUSEUM
(Galerija Božidar Jakac; 🕿 07-498 81 40; www.galerija-bj.si; Grajska cesta 45; adult/child €4/2;

🕓 9am-6pm Tue-Sun Apr-Oct, to 4pm Tue-Sun Nov-Mar) This is an unexpected treat: superbly varied art in a magnificent setting, in a garden full of sculptures.

About 1.5km southwest of town, this former Cistercian monastery was a very wealthy institution in the Middle Ages, but abandoned in 1786 when monastic orders were dissolved. The beautifully painted main entrance through two squat, candy-striped towers leads to an enormous courtyard enclosed by a cloister with 230 arcades across three floors.

To the west stands the disused **Church of the Virgin Mary** containing elements from the 13th to 18th centuries; it is now used to great effect as exhibition space. Upstairs is an exhibition on the monastery's history and its masterful restoration.

The **galleries** of the museum itself showcase the works of eight Slovenian artists, encompassing paintings, drawings, graphic art

---

WORTH A TRIP

PLETERJE MONASTERY

Pleterje Monastery (Samostan Pleterje; www.kartuzija-pleterje.si; Drča 1; 🕓 church 7.30am-6pm) Located 10km southwest of Kostanjevica na Krki, the enormous Pleterje Monastery belongs to the Carthusians, the strictest of all monastic orders. The Gothic Holy Trinity Church (also called the Old Gothic Church or Stara Gotska Cerkev), 250m up a linden-lined path from the car park, is the only part of the complex open to the general public. But the monastery's location in a narrow valley between slopes of the Gorjanci Hills is so attractive and peaceful that it's worth a visit in any case.

Pleterje was built in 1407 by the Counts of Celje. It was fortified with ramparts, towers and a moat during the Turkish invasions, and all but abandoned during the Protestant Reformation in the 16th century. The Carthusian order, like all monastic communities in the Habsburg Empire, was abolished in 1784. When French Carthusian monks returned in 1899, they rebuilt to the plans of the order's charterhouse at Nancy in France.

You may catch a glimpse of some of the white-hooded monks quietly going about their chores – they take a strict vow of silence – or hear them singing their offices in the Gothic church at various times of the day. But the ubiquitous signs reading *Klavzura – Ni Vstopa* (Enclosure – No Admittance) and *Območje Tišine* (Area of Silence) remind visitors that everything apart from the church is off-limits.

Above the ribbed main portal of the austere church (1420) is a fresco depicting Mary being crowned and the Trinity. Inside, the rib-vaulted ceiling with its heraldic bosses and the carved stone niches by the simple stone altar are worth a look, as is the medieval rood screen, the low wall across the aisle that separated members of the order from lay people.

There's a **monastery shop** (🕓 7.30am-5.30pm Mon-Sat), where the monks sell some of their own products, including beeswax candles, honey, Cviček wine and various fruit brandies, including *hruška* (pear), which comes with a pear grown inside each bottle and then picked when ripe.

To the west of the monastery car park is the sweet **Open-Air Museum Pleterje** (Muzej na Prostem Pleterje; 🕿 07-308 10 50, 041 639 191; www.skansen.si; Drča 1; adult/child €4/3; 🕓 10am-5pm Apr-Oct), with thatched peasant houses, hayracks, a pigsty and even an outhouse. Farmyard animals roam, making for a lovely pastoral scene.

and sculpture. Chief among the artists is the impressionist Božidar Jakac (1899–1989), and brothers France (1895–1960) and Tone Kralj (1900–75), who painted expressionist and surrealist-cum-socialist-realist canvases respectively. France Kralj was particularly prolific, and his sculptures are captivating. There's also a permanent collection of Old Masters from the Carthusian monastery at Pleterje.

The grounds of the Božidar Jakac Art Museum are home to more than 100 large wooden sculptures from **Forma Viva**, sculptural symposiums that were held in several places in Slovenia from 1961 to 1988 and have been revived in recent years. At these symposiums, sculptors work with materials associated with the area. Here it was oak, in Portorož stone, iron at Ravne in Koroška and concrete in Maribor.

Kostanjevica Cave　　　　CAVE
(Kostanjeviška Jama; ☑ 07-498 70 88, 041 297 001; www.kostanjeviska-jama.com; adult/child €8/4; ☉ tours 10am, noon, 2pm, 4pm & 6pm weekends mid-Apr–Oct, daily Jul & Aug) This small cave about 1.5km southeast of town, has 40-minute tours in spring, summer and autumn. The guide will lead you 250m in, past a small lake and several galleries full of stalactites and stalagmites. The temperature is a constant 12°C.

Old Town　　　　NEIGHBOURHOOD

No one's going to get lost or tired touring the Old Town island of Kostanjevica – but you will possibly be charmed. Walk 400m up Oražnova ulica and 400m down Ulica Talcev and you've seen the lot.

On Kambičev trg, across the small bridge from the bus stop (but enter from Oražnova ulica), stands the **Church of St Nicholas** (Cerkev Sv Miklavža), a tiny late-Gothic structure. The presbytery contains brightly coloured frescoes of scenes from the Old and New Testaments painted in 1931.

About 200m northwest along Oražnova ulica is a 15th-century manor house containing the **Lamut Art Salon**, a branch of the Božidar Jakac Art Museum.

Continue along Oražnova ulica, passing a somewhat crumbling fin-de-siècle house (No 24), to the **Parish Church of St James** (Župnijska Cerkev Sv Jakoba), a 13th-century Romanesque building with a mostly baroque interior. Above the carved stone portal on the western side are geometric designs and decorative plants and trees. On the south side is a 15th-century depiction of Jesus rising from the tomb, as well as 1800s grave markers embedded in the wall.

Ulica Talcev, the island's other street, is lined with attractive 'folk baroque' houses.

🏃 Activities

Čolnarna　　　　WATER SPORTS
(☑ 040 883 007; svet.avanture@gmail.com; Oražnova 14) From a house in the village, a local guy rents out canoes, rowboats and SUP boards. If you can't find him, ask at Bar Štraus on the riverfront.

Cviček Wine Cellar　　　　WINE TASTING
(Vinska Klet Cviček; ☑ 07-498 81 40; info@galerija-bj.si; Grajska cesta 45; ☉ by arrangement Tue-Sun) Inside the ancient monastery that now home to the Božidar Jakac Art Museum is the Cviček Wine Cellar. This is a true cellar if there ever was one, with ancient casks and mould a-blooming in the vaulted ceiling. Cviček tastings can be arranged here for groups of 10 people or more – a 40-minute tasting session of three local drops is €8 per person.

Hosta Stud Farm　　　　HORSE RIDING
(Kobilarna Hosta; ☑ 041 690 066, 031 220 059; www.hosta-lipizzans.eu; Sela pri Šentjerneju 6; per hour €15-22) Some 9km southwest of Kostanjevica, this horse stud is one of the largest private Lipizzaner breeders in Slovenia (and

Europe), with 50 horses. It offers rides from two hours to two days in beautiful rolling countryside; it can arrange riding lessons too. Bookings are required. Drop by the stud farm on weekends, when it's open to visitors from 11am to 7pm (free).

🛏 Sleeping

Gostilna Žolnir GUESTHOUSE €
(📞 07-498 71 33; www.zolnir.eu; Krška cesta 4; s/d €30/50; 🅿 🛜) This friendly *gostilna*, about 500m northeast of the island, has 12 double rooms; decor is basic but comfy. The best reason to stay here is the on-site restaurant.

⭐ Vila Castanea GUESTHOUSE €€
(📞 031 662 011; www.vila-castanea.si; Ulica Talcev 9; d €60-80, f €98, incl breakfast; 🅿 ❄ 🛜) A swish renovation has breathed new life into this gracious Old Town villa, and the result is an appealing nine-room guesthouse with elegant decor and muted tones. Superior rooms are lovely and spacious (two have a balcony), while larger rooms can accommodate families.

🍴 Eating & Drinking

Gostilna Žolnir SLOVENIAN €€
(📞 07-498 71 33; www.zolnir.eu; Krška cesta 4; mains €8-18; 🕙 7am-10pm) It's a short walk northeast of the island to this local favourite, which wins praise for its traditional food: lots of *štruklji* (dumpling) options, grilled calamari, gnocchi with game ragù, and a speciality of the house – venison fillet. Its decor is a blend of old and new, with an appealing courtyard space.

Gostilna Kmečki Hram SLOVENIAN €€
(📞 07-498 70 78; www.gkh.si; Oražnova ulica 11; mains €10-20; 🕙 11am-9pm Wed-Thu, to 11pm Fri, 9am-midnight Sat, to 8pm Sun) This old-style inn with retro decor really looks like the Farmers House it calls itself. The central location and summer garden alongside the river are its best features; the food and service receive mixed reviews.

Bar Štraus BAR, CAFE
(📞 07-498 75 30; Ulica Talcev 31; 🕙 5.15am-midnight) Fronting the Krka by the northern bridge, this pleasant little cafe-bar is the ideal spot in which to while away a warm and lazy afternoon in Kostanjevica.

ℹ Information

Although most of Kostanjevica's historical sights are on the island, amenities are on the mainland

to the northwest or southeast, reached by two small bridges.

Tourist Information Centre (TIC; 📞 07-498 81 50; tic-gbj@galerija-bj.si; Grajska cesta 45; 🕙 9am-6pm Tue-Sun Apr-Oct, to 4pm Tue-Sun Nov-Mar) In an old mill at the entrance to the Božidar Jakac Art Museum, and keeping the same hours (ie, closed Mondays).

ℹ Getting There & Away

Useful bus services, from the bus stop south of the island along Ljubljanska cesta:

Brežice (€2.70, 30 minutes, 20km, up to eight daily)

Ljubljana (€9.20, 1¾ hours, 97km, up to four daily)

Novo Mesto (€3.60, 40 minutes, 30km, up to seven daily)

Brežice

📞 07 / POP 6650 / ELEV 163M

From a traveller's perspective, Brežice is the most interesting town in Posavje. One of the best museums in provincial Slovenia is here, and a popular spa and waterpark are just down the road.

History

Situated near where the Krka flows into the Sava, Brežice was an important trading centre in the Middle Ages. Its most dominant feature has always been its castle, mentioned in documents as early as 1249. In the 16th century the original castle was replaced with a Renaissance fortress to strengthen the town's defences against the Turks and later marauding peasants who, during one uprising, beheaded nobles at the castle and impaled their heads on poles. Today the castle houses the Posavje Museum.

⦿ Sights

⭐ Posavje Museum MUSEUM
(Posavski Muzej; 📞 07-466 05 17; www.posavski-muzej.si; Cesta Prvih Borcev 1; adult/child €3/2; 🕙 10am-8pm Tue-Sat, 2-8pm Sun Jul-Aug, to 6pm Apr-Jun & Sep-Oct, to 4pm Nov-Mar) Housed in Posavje Castle, the Posavje Museum is one of provincial Slovenia's richest museums, particularly for its archaeological and ethnographic collections – and for its stunning fresco-filled hall.

From the courtyard you ascend a staircase whose walls and ceiling are illustrated with Greek gods, the four Evangelists and the Attems family coat of arms. Rooms on

Brežice

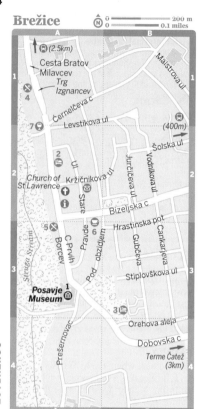

N
200 m
0.1 miles

Brežice

◉ Top Sights
1 Posavje Museum.....................................A3

🛏 Sleeping
2 Hotel Splavar...A2
3 MC Hostel Brežice..................................B3

🍴 Eating
Gostilna Splavar............................(see 2)
4 Oštarija Debeluh..A1
5 Santa Lucija...A3

🍷 Drinking & Nightlife
6 Aquarius Café Bar.....................................A3
7 Jazz Pub...A2

the 2nd floor are archaeological; look out for the 7th-century BC bronze horse bridle and the Celtic and Roman jewellery. In the ethnographic rooms, along with the details of local winemaking, flax weaving and mas-

ter pottery, there is a strange beehive in the shape of a soldier from the early 1800s.

Rooms on the 1st floor cover life in the Posavje region in the 19th century and during the two world wars, with special emphasis on the deportation of Slovenes by the Germans during WWII. There are also galleries of religious artworks and more contemporary pieces.

The museum's real crowd-pleaser is the **Knights' Hall** (Viteška Dvorana), an Italian baroque masterpiece where everything except for the floor is painted with landscapes, and classical gods, heroes, allegories and muses. Concerts and events are sometimes held here.

🏃 Activities

You can rent bikes (per hour/day €3/15) from the tourist information centres. Ask for a free copy of the *Cycling Booklet,* outlining four themed regional rides. Both TICs have plenty of local cycling and hiking advice, as well as info on river watersports in the area including SUP boarding and canoeing.

Terme Čatež   SPA, RESORT
(☎ 07-493 67 00; www.terme-catez.si; Topliška cesta 35) The thermal spring just east of Čatež ob Savi (3km southeast of Brežice) has attracted rheumatics since the late 18th century. Today, the huge Terme Čatež spa and holiday complex is every bit as much a recreational area, popular year-round. There's an outdoor pool playground, year-round indoor complex, saunas, three hotels and an enormous campground, plus wellness centre and various family-friendly activities.

Summer Thermal Riviera   WATERPARK
(Poletna Termalna Riviera; ☎ 07-493 67 00; www.terme-catez.si; Topliška cesta 35; day pass adult/child €15/12.50; ⊙ late-Apr–early Oct) This outdoor area at Terme Čatež is enormous, and full of family fun (with water temperatures between 26°C and 36°C): 10 pools, a 'lazy river' to float down, massive slides, fountains, artificial waves, play areas and so on. Weekday prices slightly cheaper.

Winter Thermal Riviera   WATERPARK
(Zimska Termalna Riviera; ☎ 07-493 67 00; www.terme-catez.si; Topliška cesta 35; day pass adult/child €16/13; ⊙ year-round) Terme Čatež's year-round indoor complex has a water temperature of about 32°C, and lots of pools and kid-friendly spaces. Weekday prices slightly cheaper.

✤ Festivals & Events

Sevíqc Brežice MUSIC
(www.seviqc-brezice.si; ⊘late-Jun–mid-Aug) Culture vultures, this is for you. This is an acclaimed summer-long series of concerts, featuring international early music performances (classical music with authentic instruments), set exclusively at venues of Slovenian cultural heritage – for example, the stunning Knights' Hall at Brežice Castle, and Mokrice Castle. Full program online.

🛏 Sleeping

★ Camping Terme Čatež CAMPGROUND €
(☎07-493 67 00; www.terme-catez.si; Topliška cesta 35; per person €18.50-24.30; ⊘year-round; 🅿🛜🌊) Don't come here looking for peace and quiet at summer's peak – this large campground at the Terme Čatež resort is chockers, with families and facilities. Price includes two day-long passes to the Summer Thermal Riviera. Outside of holidays, expect more breathing space.

The best feature of the ground is its family-sized unique sleeps: an Indian Village of tepees (per night €69 to €89); a covered pioneer wagon (€79 to €105); and the Pirate's Bay featuring a series of bungalows (€97 to €133) built over the water in the middle of the campground's lake. Prices all include linen, so these make for a great family glamping experience.

★ MC Hostel Brežice HOSTEL €
(☎059 083 797; www.mc-hostel.si; Gubčeva ulica 10a; dm €15, d without/with bathroom €36/48; 🅿🛜) Just a short walk through parkland from the town's castle and museum, this great hostel is a breath of fresh air: bright, colourful, with dorm beds and private rooms (including rooms with bathroom). There's a cute outdoor terrace and a kitchen and laundry, and in the same complex is a friendly bar serving beers from around the globe.

Hotel Splavar HOTEL €€
(☎07-499 06 30; www.splavar.si; Cesta Prvih Borcev 40a; s/d/tr incl breakfast €50/75/90; 🅿🛜) The Raftman, with 16 rooms on Brežice's main street, is above the Gostilna Splavar. The plain rooms are in the back and are dark – nothing special, but comfortable and central in town.

Hotel Terme HOTEL €€€
(☎07-493 67 00; www.terme-catez.si; Topliška cesta 35; per person €89-113; 🅿🛜🌊) One of three large, run-of-the-mill hotels at the Terme Čatež complex. This is the nicest (in retro-1980s style) and it benefits from being tucked away a little from the crowds. Still, prices are high (but include waterpark entry and half-board).

🍴 Eating

Santa Lucija PIZZA €
(☎07-499 25 00; www.santalucija-brezice.com; Cesta Prvih Borcev 15; mains €6-15; ⊘11am-11pm) The summer terrace at the back of this restaurant is lovely, and the over-the-top frescoes inside are worthy of admiration. The menu lists dishes featuring game and truffles, but it's best to stick to the basics here, namely pizza and pasta.

★ Oštarija Debeluh SLOVENIAN €€
(☎07-496 10 70; www.debeluh.si; Trg Izgnancev 7; mains €12-25; ⊘noon-10pm Mon-Sat) This cosy, upscale eatery serves the best and most inventive Slovenian and international dishes in the area, from the chef's signature beef tartare with foie gras, to duck with peaches cooked in balsamic. The wine list is admirable, the strudel desserts excellent, and the advice sage. A four-/six-course tasting menu is €38/50. Bookings advised.

Gostilna Splavar SLOVENIAN €€
(☎07-499 06 30; www.splavar.si; Cesta Prvih Borcev 40a; mains €8-22; ⊘7am-10pm) This friendly *gostilna* offers dining inside or on its main-street summer terrace. The menu holds few surprises (pasta, pizza, fish, heavy on grilled meats) and is generally well done. The best is kept for last: Splavar is celebrated for its homemade ice cream.

🍷 Drinking & Nightlife

Jazz Pub PUB
(☎031 412 797; www.jazzpub.si; Trg Izgnancev 2; ⊘7am-midnight) Come for the pub's popular outdoor terrace, good coffee and the beautiful, timber-lined, old-world interior. No live jazz, alas.

Aquarius Café Bar CAFE, BAR
(☎051 252 440; Bizeljska ulica 4; ⊘7am-11pm Sun-Thu, 7am-1am Fri & Sat) Housed on the lower levels of Brežice's unmissable 46m-high pink water tower (1914), this all-day cafe-bar is decorated with old photos of the town and faux antiques. It's a simple pit stop for a daytime coffee or evening beer.

ℹ️ Information

Major services (banks etc) are found on the main street, Cesta Prvih Borcev.

Tourist Information Centre Brežice (TIC; ☑ 064 130 082; www.visitbrezice.com; Cesta Prvih Borcev 22; ⊘10am-6pm Mon-Sat) Part of a complex that offers tourist information, the sale of local products, and a wine shop where it's possible to learn about (and taste) local wines.

Tourist Information Centre Terme Čatež (☑ 07-620 70 35; www.discoverbrezice.com; Topliška cesta 35; ⊘10am-noon & 6-10pm Jun-Aug, 10am-6pm Sep-Nov & Mar-May, to 2pm Dec-Feb) Helpful branch at the Terme Čatež resort.

ℹ️ Getting There & Around

BIKE

You can rent bikes (per hour/day €3/15) from the tourist information centres.

BUS

The bus station is behind the big shopping centre at Cesta Svobode 11, about 1km northeast of the Posavje Castle.

Useful services:

Kostanjevica na Krki (€2.70, 30 minutes, 20km, roughly hourly)

Ljubljana (€10.70, 2¼ hours, 117km, five daily)

Novo Mesto (€5.20, 70 minutes, 45km, roughly hourly)

Terme Čatež (€1.30, five minutes, 3km, at least half-hourly)

TRAIN

As many as 17 trains a day serve Brežice from Ljubljana (€7.70, 1½ to two hours, 107km), but the station is quite inconvenient, about 3km north of the castle at Trg Vstaje 3.

TAXI

Order a taxi on ☑ 041 611 391.

Mokrice Castle

☑ 07 / ELEV 227M

Mokrice Castle, about 10km southeast of Brežice, is the loveliest fortress in the Posavje region and is also a popular hotel. With one of Slovenia's handful of 18-hole golf courses, a 20-hectare 'English park' full of rare plants, a large orchard of pear trees and a small disused Gothic chapel, a trip to the castle makes a lovely excursion from Brežice – especially by bike (take the secondary road from Čatež ob Savi that runs parallel to the highway).

👁️ Sights

Mokrice Castle   CASTLE

(Grad Mokrice) Mokrice castle dates from the 16th century, but there are bits and pieces going back to Roman times built into the structure. It's supposedly haunted by the ghost of the 17th-century countess Barbara, who committed suicide here after her lover failed to return from sea. She's particularly active on her name day (4 December) when she spends the night rolling cannonballs around the joint. The castle is home to a hotel; its lovely grounds are open to all at no charge.

🛏️ Sleeping

Golf Hotel Mokrice Castle   HOTEL €€€

(☑ 07-457 42 40; www.terme-catez.si; Rajec 4; per person incl breakfast €94-126; 🅿️ 📶) Sadly the quality at this four-star castle hotel is nowhere close to that of Otočec to the west. Rooms have beamed ceilings and period furniture, and the huge suites have fireplaces. The setting and lush green surroundings (including golf course) are a delight – it's a pity the dated decor feels so time-warped.

Bizeljsko-Sremič Wine District

☑ 07 / ELEV 175M

Cycling the 17km from Brežice to Bizeljsko is a great way to see the picturesque Bizeljsko-Sremič wine country, stopping off whenever you see a *gostilna, vinska klet* (wine cellar) or *repnica* (flint-stone cave for storing wine) that takes your fancy. A good place to get pre-trip info on wine types and where to visit is the wine shop at the TIC in Brežice.

🏃 Activities

Penine Istenič   WINERY

(☑ 07-495 15 59; www.istenic.si; Stara Vas 7) One of Slovenia's biggest and best sparkling wine producers, Istenič has a *vinska klet* (wine cellar) in the hamlet of Stara Vas, surrounded by an emerald-green lawn. Stop in to sample a few bubbly varieties (the Prestige extra brut is the pick, but Desiree is the big-seller) alongside some charcuterie. A cellar tour can be arranged (it's best to call and book).

There is also well-priced accommodation here, enabling you to enjoy the peaceful surrounds – and more wine. Single/double

SOUTHEAST SLOVENIA & THE KRKA VALLEY MOKRICE CASTLE

VINEYARD COTTAGES

Farmstays have long been popular in Slovenia, but in recent years there's been a growing trend for vineyard stays.

Traditional vineyard cottages are a feature of the Dolenjska, Bela Krajina and Bizeljsko-Sremič wine districts. They stand on the edge of vineyards, on the sunny sides of hills, and offer wonderful views over the surrounding landscape of rolling hills and grapevines, perhaps with church spires and small villages in the panoramic sweep. Vineyard owners have generally built and maintained these cottages (called *zidanice* in Slovenian; singular *zidanica*) for themselves, using them while tending their vines. Many of them have now been renovated in a new tourism trend to rent them to travellers; they are often well-priced and family-friendly (sleeping four and starting around €60 per night), with kitchen facilities. If you're lucky, the owners will include a bottle or two of wine as well.

If you're seeking authentic rural charm and tranquility, you can find some vineyard cottages listed on booking.com and various accommodation websites. Alternatively, check out the local site www.zidanice.si.

rooms from €32/54; stylish rooms in the Istenič Villa from €75.

 Repnice Najger WINERY
(☑07-495 11 15; repnicanajger@siol.net; Brezovica 32; tour & tastings €4; ☺9am-9pm) Follow the sign for 'Repnice/Brezovica' to reach a pocket of small wineries, each with their own *repnica* (flint-stone cave, once used to store *repa,* turnips, over the winter). Family-run Najger will give you a fun tour of their large cave, with tastings of their produce.

🍷 Drinking

Pivoteka Bizeljsko PUB
(☑059 912 329; Stara Vas 58; ☺10am-midnight) A surprise in amongst the vineyards – but a fun one. This is a big barn of a pub, with a wide beer selection and hearty beer snacks to enjoy on the chilled-out terrace. Hungry? Order a metre of chicken wings or a metre of *čevapčiči* (spicy meatballs), enough to feed four.

BELA KRAJINA

Bela Krajina (www.belakrajina.si), the 'White March', is separated from Dolenjska by the scenic Gorjanci Mountains. The 600-sq-km region takes its name from the countless stands of birch trees here, and is a treasure trove of Slovenian folklore.

Flying well under the radar of most travellers, Bela Krajina has the Kolpa River, vineyards, forests and landscape parks offering opportunities for active pursuits and relaxing stops along the heritage trails and wine roads. However, tourism is a different beast in this far southeastern corner of the country – visitor numbers here are noticeably lower, and there is less tourist gloss, a little more grit. The well-oiled tourism machine of the Julian Alps or Soča Valley is nowhere to be found, and that, for some travellers, may be a key part of Bela Krajina's appeal.

Still, there may be frustration when independent travellers try to access some facilities – museums need to be opened by TIC staff, wineries only accept pre-arranged visits by groups, a rural *gostilna* only serves lunch if a group has prebooked, and so on. Our advice is to ask advice from the TICs and from locals, especially from accommodation providers. They are well-placed to know about local offerings and how best to access them.

First up, ask the TIC in Metlika or Črnomelj for the excellent English-language brochure-maps *Hiking Trails through Bela Krajina* and *Cycling Trails through Bela Krajina.*

Metlika
☑07 / POP 3240 / ELEV 156M
Metlika lies in a valley at the foot of the Gorjanci Hills and is a good springboard for hiking and cycling in the area. It is surrounded by Croatia on three sides; the Kolpa River and its 'beaches' lies about 1km to the south.

There was a major Hallstatt settlement here during the early Iron Age, and the Romans established an outpost in Metlika on the road leading to the important river

Metlika

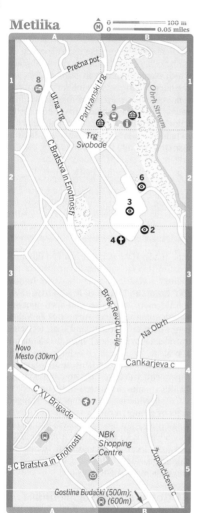

Roman displays, as well as items relating to the area's ethnology and agriculture. A 20-minute film introduces the collection in four different languages.

Slovenian Firefighters' Museum MUSEUM
(Slovenski Gasilski Muzej; ☑ 07-305 86 97; Trg Svobode 5; admission €2; ⊙ 9am-2pm Tue-Sat) Metlika was the first town in Slovenia to have its own fire brigade (1869), commemorated by the Slovenian Firefighters' Museum, which is just outside the castle. There are old fire trucks with enormous wheels, ladders and buckets.

Mestni Trg SQUARE
This colourful, leafy square contains 18th- and 19th-century buildings, including the neo-Gothic **town hall** (Mestni trg 24). At the southern end of the square is the so-called **Commandery** (Komenda; Mestni trg 14), which once belonged to the Knights of the Teutonic Order (note that it has a '2' above the door, but is number 14 on the square). Note the Maltese Cross above the entrance. To the northwest is the **Parish Church of St Nicholas** (Farna Cerkev Sv Nikolaja; Mestni trg). On the ceiling are sobering contemporary frescoes of the Day of Judgment, with devils leading sinners to damnation.

🏃 Activities

The Kolpa River is clean and very warm (up to 28°C to 30°C in summer), so you might want to go **swimming** at the Podzemelj campground.

port of Sisak in Croatia. During the Turkish onslaught of the 15th and 16th centuries, Metlika was attacked 17 times and occupied in 1578.

◉ Sights

Bela Krajina Museum MUSEUM
(Belokranjski Muzej; ☑ 07-306 33 70; www.belokranjski-muzej.si; Trg Svobode 4; adult/child €4/3; ⊙ 9am-5pm Mon-Sat, 10am-2pm Sun) Located in **Metlika Castle** with its splendid courtyard, the Bela Krajina Museum houses a collection of local archaeological finds. There's Hallstatt metalwork from Pusti and

There are a lot of hikes and walks in the surrounding areas, outlined on the map *Hiking Trails through Bela Krajina*. Walk number 19 is an easy 8km trail around Metlika and its old town centre. Number 13 is the circular, 6.3km Urban Walking Trail through vineyards to Grabrovec and back via Veselica, a 233m-high small hill less than 1km north of Metlika, with great views over the town. Number 12 is the 2km Educational Path Zdenc to Vidovec, from the village of Božakovo to the Zdenc and Vidovec karst caves.

Ask the TIC about organised wine tastings at the Vinska Klet (☑07-363 70 52; www.kz-metlika.si; Cesta XV Brigade 2; per person from €5; ☺8am-3pm Mon-Fri, to noon Sat or by appointment), the wine cellar run by the local wine cooperative, which usually requires a minimum group of 10 people.

🎭 Festivals & Events

Vinska Vigred   WINE
(Vineyard Spring; www.metlika-turizem.si; Metlika; ☺May) Metlika's main event is the Vinska Vigred festival held on the first weekend after 15 May. Local wines, foods, folk dancing and music contribute to a merry, much-loved event (enjoyed by more than 20,000 attendees).

🛏 Sleeping

Kamp Podzemelj   CAMPGROUND €
(☑040 753 188; www.kamp-podzemelj.si; Škrilje 11; campsite adult/child €9.80/6.80, d/q from €50/70; ☺mid-Apr–Sep; P🐕🛜🏊) An excellent choice, this large green campground sits on the Kolpa River 7km southwest of Metlika in Podzemelj. It's got lots of family- and activity-focused facilities, including rental of bikes, canoes and rafts. There's a restaurant, fun river-swimming area, fishing permits available, and a great playground and ropes course. For non-campers, you can rent a room or family-sized cabin.

Hotel Bela Krajina   HOTEL €€
(☑07-305 81 23; www.hotel-belakrajina.si; Cesta Bratstva in Enotnosti 28; s/d/tr incl breakfast from €48/76/93; P❄🛜) A former Slovenian socialist holdover pulled into the 21st century with air-con and upgraded furnishings. Look past the orange exterior to find spotless, comfy lodgings, welcoming service and a good on-site restaurant.

🍴 Eating & Drinking

Hotel Bela Krajina   SLOVENIAN €
(☑07-305 81 23; Cesta Bratstva in Enotnosti 28; mains €6-13; ☺7am-10pm) This convivial place, which starts you off with *belokranjska pogača* (local flatbread, not unlike Italian focaccia), is the best place for a meal in Metlika, with house specialities like herb-crusted lamb or venison medallion. Try the *žlikrofi* in mushroom sauce, or the excellent trout in Belokranjec white wine.

Gostilna Budački   SLOVENIAN €
(☑07-363 52 00; Ulica Belokranjskega Odreda 14; mains €7-16; ☺8am-10pm Mon-Sat, noon-5pm Sun) One of the very few 'real' places to eat in the city limits, this bright-yellow *gostilna* 1km south of the town centre (not far from the train station) gets good reviews for its home-style cooking. Fish dishes and pizza are good bets.

Grajska Klet   WINE BAR
(☑031 632 470; Trg Svobode 4; ☺7am-11pm Mon-Thu, to 1am Fri & Sat, 8am-noon Sun) To try some Bela Krajina wine, head for this *vinoteka* in the castle courtyard. This is the cellar for Šturm label wines, and you can sample pinot blanc, chardonnay, rieslings and sweet *rumeni muškat* (yellow muscatel). Do try the Metliška Črnina (the ruby-red 'Metlika Black'), unique to Bela Krajina.

ℹ Information

Tourist Information Centre (TIC; ☑07-363 54 70; www.metlika-turizem.si; Trg Svobode 4; ☺8am-5pm Mon-Fri, 9am-1pm Sat Jun-Aug, 8am-4pm Mon-Fri, 9am-noon Sat Sep-May) In the castle courtyard.

ℹ Getting There & Around

BUS

The bus station is 650m south of the Old Town on Črnomaljska cesta, opposite a shopping centre. Destinations served include:

Črnomelj (€2.30, 30 minutes, 15km, up to seven daily)

Novo Mesto (€3.60, one hour, 30km, two daily)

TRAIN

The train station is on Kolodvorska ulica, about 1km southeast of the town centre.

Metlika has up to nine trains daily to/from Ljubljana (€8.49, 2½ to three hours, 122km). These run via Novo Mesto (€4.28, one hour, 47km) and Črnomelj (€1.85, 18 minutes, 15km). Two trains a day head for Karlovac in Croatia.

Metlika Wine Area

The hills to the north and northeast of Metlika are some of the Bela Krajina wine district's most important areas and produce such distinctive wines as Metliška Črnina (the ruby-red 'Metlika Black') and a late-maturing sweet 'ice wine' called Kolednik Ledeno Vino. They're also superb areas for easy walking.

On the way to Drašiči, an important wine town 6km from Metlika, you'll see (or walk through) *steljniki,* stands of birch trees growing among ferns in clay soil – the very symbol of Bela Krajina.

Drašiči is well known for its folk architecture, and you can sample local wines at several places – get advice from the Metlika TIC.

The much-awarded Prus is the standout cellar to visit in the area around Metlika. Rustically charming Vinska Klet Prus (☑ 07-305 90 98; www.vinaprus.si; Krmačina 6) is in the hamlet of Krmačina, just beyond Drašiči. Be sure to prebook a visit – you can arrange a cellar tour with wine tasting of five wines for €10 per person.

Črnomelj

☑ 07 / POP 5695 / ELEV 145M

The capital of Bela Krajina and its largest town, Črnomelj (pronounced cher-*no*-ml) is on a promontory in a loop where the Lahinja and Dobličica Rivers meet. This relaxed town is the 'folk heart' of Bela Krajina, and its popular Jurjevanje festival attracts hundreds of dancers and singers from the region. There's not a lot to see, but it's a gateway to scenic surrounds.

Črnomelj's Roman presence is evident from the Mithraic shrine at Rožanec, about 4km northwest of the town. During the Turkish invasions in the 15th and 16th centuries, the town was attacked incessantly, but due to its strong fortifications and excellent hilltop lookouts it was never taken. After Italy's surrender in 1943, the town functioned for a time as Slovenia's capital.

Legend has it that Črnomelj (a corruption of the words for 'black miller') got its name when a beggar, dissatisfied with the quality of the flour she'd been given, put a curse on the local miller. The town's symbol today is a smiling baker holding a pretzel.

◎ Sights & Activities

Trg Svobode SQUARE

The main square is surrounded by some of the town's oldest and most important buildings: the castle (Črnomeljski Grad; Trg Svobode 3), parts of which date from the mid-12th century (now home to administrative offices); the Commandery (Komenda; Trg Svobode 1) (the current building dates from 1655; it acts as the regional courthouse); and a grand old bank from the turn of the 20th century.

Parish Church of St Peter CHURCH

(Cerkev Sv Petra; Ulica Staneta Rozmana) The church dates to the 13th century but what you'll see today is a standard-issue baroque structure with a single spire. There are Roman tombstones built into the walls, and on the western exterior above the main entrance is a fresco of St Christopher.

Town Museum Collection MUSEUM

(Mestna Muzejska Zbirka; ☑ 07-620 08 97; www.muzej-crnomelj.si; Ulica Mirana Jarca 3; adult/child €4/2; ☉ noon-4pm Tue, Wed & Fri, to 6pm Thu, 11am-3pm Sat) Houses a bright, interesting take on the history of the town and Bela Krajina.

Primožič House GALLERY

(Primožičeva Hiša; Ulica Mirana Jarca 18; ☉ by arrangement) This cute green house is home to displays of local arts and crafts, including embroidery, woodwork and Bela Krajina's renowned *pisanice,* intricately painted Easter eggs. TIC staff will open it for you.

Mithraeum HISTORIC SITE

About 4km northwest of Črnomelj is Rožanec village; to reach it turn west just after Lokve. From the village centre, a sign points along a trail leading about 400m to the Mithraeum (Mitrej), a temple in a cavern dedicated to the god Mithra, dating from the 2nd century AD. One of the exposed limestone faces is a 1.5m-high carved relief of Mithra sacrificing the sacred bull, watched by the sun and moon with a dog, serpent and scorpion at his feet.

Črnomelj Wine Cellar WINE TASTING

(Črnomaljska Klet; ☑ 07-305 65 30; Ulica Mirana Jarca 2; ☉ by arrangement) The wine cellar, in the basement of the beautifully renovated music school, offers tastings from the Bela Krajina wine-growing district with *belokranjska pogača* (local flatbread) and cheese. Generally it's only for groups of 10 or more, and is arranged through the TIC.

Walking Trails

Some great hikes and walks in the surrounding areas are outlined on the map *Hiking Trails through Bela Krajina*. A number of them connect the smaller villages to Črnomelj's south – eg walk number 1 is a 13km path from Dragatuš to Vinica dedicated to a local poet. Number 2 is a 6km circular path beginning from Obrh (south of Dragatuš) that takes in forest scenery plus vineyards, castle ruins and village churches.

★ Festivals & Events

Jurjevanje CULTURAL

(www.jurjevanje.si; ⊙late Jun) The oldest international folklore festival in Slovenia, Jurjevanje is five days of music, dance and bonfires at the fairground near the train station and other locations around town in late June. It's based on the Zeleni Jurij (Green George), an early Slavic deity of vegetation, fertility and spring.

🛏 Sleeping

There's not a lot of choice for rooms, and the hostel is pretty grim – best to stock up on local maps and groceries and head out of town, where there's some great guesthouse and glamping options (p182).

Nearby riverside campgrounds include those at Podzemelj, 10km northeast of Črnomelj, and Adlešiči, 12km to the southeast.

Gostilna Müller GUESTHOUSE €

(☑07-356 72 00; www.gostilna-muller.si; Ločka cesta 6; s/d incl breakfast €30/50; P❄🐾🛜) This *gostilna* across the river to the south of the Old Town is the best option in town. The four chalet-style rooms are bright and attractive, there's a good restaurant downstairs, and it's an easy walk into central Črnomelj.

✗ Eating & Drinking

Gostilna Müller SLOVENIAN €

(☑07-356 72 00; www.gostilna-muller.si; Ločka cesta 6; mains €5-14; ⊙8am-11pm Tue-Fri, 11am-midnight Sat, to 10pm Sun) A local favourite, this is one of few options in Črnomelj, and it's a sweet place with farmhouse decor, lots of plants, and nice outdoor terrace. The menu is filled with affordable Slovenian culinary standbys: grilled trout, beefsteak, roast pork, calamari, pizza and pasta.

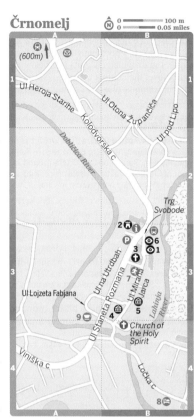

Črnomelj

⊙ Sights

1 Commandery	B3
2 Črnomelj Castle	B3
3 Parish Church of St Peter	B3
4 Primožič House	B3
5 Town Museum Collection	B3
6 Trg Svobode	B3

🎯 Activities, Courses & Tours

7 Črnomelj Wine Cellar	B3

🛏 Sleeping

8 Gostilna Müller	B4

🍽 Eating

Gostilna Müller	(see 8)

🍷 Drinking & Nightlife

9 Črnomaljska Kavarna	A3

Črnomaljska Kavarna　　　CAFE, BAR
(⟟040 741 006; Ulica Lojzeta Fabjana 7; ⊗9am-2pm daily plus 6-11pm Mon-Thu, 6pm-1am Fri & Sat, 5-10pm Sun) An appealingly leafy spot for a drink, the Črnomelj Cafe sits just below the bridge over the Lahinja River and has plenty of drink options, plus a list of burgers for the hungry.

ℹ Information

Tourist Information Centre (TIC; ⟟07-305 65 30; www.belakrajina.si; Trg Svobode 3; ⊗8am-4pm Mon-Fri, 9am-noon Sat) On the ground floor of Črnomelj Castle. Helpful office, with additional Saturday hours (3pm to 7pm) in July and August.

ℹ Getting There & Around

BUS

Buses stop at Trg Svobode. Črnomelj's bus connections are just OK; there are a handful of departures to local villages and Kolpa Valley destinations. See timetables online at www.mpov.si, or ask at the TIC. Services include:

Ljubljana (€9.20, two hours, 100km, two daily)

Metlika (€2.30, 30 minutes, 15km, up to seven daily)

Novo Mesto (€5.20, 70 minutes, 44km, two daily)

TRAIN

The train station is about 1.5km north of the old town, on Železničarska cesta.

Črnomelj has up to nine trains daily to/from Ljubljana (€7.70, two to 2½ hours, 107km). These run via Novo Mesto (€3.45, 40 to 50 minutes, 32km) and continue to Metlika (€1.85, 18 minutes, 15km).

BICYCLE

You can hire bikes from **L Šport** (⟟07-305 24 81; Kolodvorska cesta 13; per day from €10; ⊗8am-7pm Mon-Fri, to noon Sat).

Around Črnomelj

◉ Sights

Lahinja Landscape Park　　　NATURE RESERVE
(Krajinski Park Lahinja) This 200-hectare park, about 9km south of Črnomelj, is a protected karst area rich in birdlife and is the source of the Lahinja River. Trails criss-cross the fields, forest and wetlands. It's possible to access the park via two 'entrances': at the villages of Pusti Gradec and Veliki Nerajec. The latter is the best option – there's a simple information point at Veliki Nerajec 18a, where you can get a map and basic information for walks.

Vera, the owner of the house at Veliki Nerajec 18a, displays and sells local handicrafts – including distinctive 'kingfisher' ceramic whistles she makes, and the *gudalo,* a remarkable local musical instrument.

Walks 1 and 24 outlined on the *Hiking Trails through Bela Krajina* map cover areas of the park.

🛏 Sleeping & Eating

Pri Štefaniču Farmhouse　　　GUESTHOUSE €
(⟟07-305 73 47; www.pri-stefanicu.com; Dragatuš 22; d per person €25; 🅿⟩) This friendly 'farmhouse' sits in the heart of Dragatuš, a village 9km south of Črnomelj. It has good-value, comfy rooms, and its bar is the village hub (food served with prior arrangement). There's a small supermarket next door. It's an excellent starting point for walks in Lahinja Landscape Park.

★**Glamping Malerič**　　　APARTMENT €€€
(⟟07-305 71 20; http://glamping.turizemmaleric.si/en/; Podlog 3C; apt for 4 €130) About 8km south of Črnomelj, in the tiny hamlet of Podlog, is this ace complex: four futuristic hous-

---

MITHRA & THE GREAT SACRIFICE

Mithraism, the worship of the god Mithra, originated in Persia. As Roman rule extended west, the religion became extremely popular with traders, imperial slaves and mercenaries of the Roman army, and spread rapidly throughout the empire in the 1st and 2nd centuries AD. In fact, Mithraism was the principal rival of Christianity until Constantine, a Christian convert, came to the throne in the 4th century.

Mithraism's devotees guarded its secrets well. What little is known of Mithra, the god of justice and social contract, has been deduced from reliefs and icons found in temples, such as the ones at Rožanec near Črnomelj and at Ptuj in Štajerska. Mithra is portrayed in Persian dress sacrificing a white bull in front of Sol, the sun god. From the bull's blood sprout grain and grapes, and from its semen animals grow. Sol's wife Luna, the moon, begins her cycle and time is born.

es arranged by a natural swimming pool, with splendid rural outlooks. The pods are stylishly compact, each with two bedrooms (sleeping four) plus bathroom, kitchenette and living space, plus sundeck.

Down the road (also in Podlog), the owners have a complex of standard apartments too, costing €70/100 for two/four.

Gostilna Balkovec SLOVENIAN €
(☑ 07-305 76 32; Mali Nerajec 3; mains €7-16; ⊗ 8am-11pm) This *gostilna* in Mali Nerajec, southeast of Dragatuš and Veliki Nerajec en route to Vinica, specialises in *pečenka* (roast meat), mostly delicious slow-roasted pork and lamb. The rest of the menu offers few surprises (calamari, schnitzel, pizza), but options in the area are limited and this is a good choice.

Kolpa Valley

☑ 07 / ELEV UP TO 370M

The 118km-long Kolpa River marks the border with Croatia, and is the warmest and one of the cleanest rivers in the country. As a result, it has become a popular recreational area for swimming, fishing and boating, especially around the villages of Vinica, Adlešiči and, to the west, Stari Trg ob Kolpi. Vinica is the largest village, with facilities like a grocery store.

Much of the Slovenian riverbank from Fučkovci (yes, that is a real town name), just north of Adlešiči, as far southwest as Stari Trg ob Kolpi forms the **Kolpa Landscape Park** (Kolpa Krajinski Park; www.kp-kolpa.si), a protected area of natural wonders and cultural monuments.

Activities

This area will appeal to nature and activity fans. There are some good campgrounds and small-time operators that can help you get on the river, and excellent cycling trails along the river valley. Get a copy of the *Cycling Trails through Bela Krajina* map – routes 1 and 5 are especially good for exploring this area.

On the *Hiking Trails through Bela Krajina* map, walks 3, 4, 5 and 18 are good. Walk 18 describes the 'Castle Footpath along the Kolpa River', a flat 26km path through the most attractive part of the park, from the sweet hamlet of Žuniči (full of traditional architecture) to Dragoši.

Grand Kolpa RAFTING
(☑ 041 740 798; www.grandkolpa.si; Stari Trg ob Kolpi 15; rafting tour per person €16-20) From its base in the village of Stari Trg ob Kolpi, this company offers raft and kayak rental, and river-rafting trips ranging from a family-friendly 8km to a longer 25km.

🛏 Sleeping & Eating

★ **Kamp Jankovič** CAMPGROUND €
(☑ 041 622 877; www.kolpas.si; Adlešiči 24a; campsite adult/child €7/5, hut €42; ⊗ mid-Apr–Sep; P) At the southern end of Adlešiči, take the signposted turning and follow the road for about 1km to reach this fabulous, friendly spot. It's a simple riverside camp area with extras including swimming platform, canoe and SUP rental, three small timber glamping huts, and a great barn-like restaurant-bar known as Stari Pod.

★ **Madronič** GUESTHOUSE €
(☑ 031 627 952; www.gostinstvo-madronic.si; Prelesje 10; campsite/room per person €8/23) About 4km downhill from Stari Trg ob Kolpi in the hamlet of Prelesje, this is a handsome riverside complex in a beautiful setting. There's a restaurant to feed you, a choice of beds (from camping to smart, renovated rooms – and also the chance to sleep in a hayloft), and lots of activities, from fishing to rafting to swimming.

ℹ Getting There & Around

This is an area best explored with your own wheels (car or bike). There are infrequent buses – these link Vinica with Črnomelj via Dragatuš, or Adlešiči to Črnomelj – but they are geared to the needs of local workers and students. Bus timetables are at www.mpov.si.

Eastern Slovenia

Best Places to Eat

➡ Restavracija Mak (p210)

➡ Gostilna Rajh (p221)

➡ Gostilna Ribič (p204)

➡ Gostilna Amadeus (p204)

➡ Pri Florjanu (p211)

➡ Gostilna Lovenjak (p222)

Best Places to Stay

➡ DomKulture MuziKafe (p204)

➡ Hotel Mitra (p204)

➡ Grand Hotel Rogaška (p199)

➡ MCC Hostel (p191)

➡ Herbal Glamping Resort Ljubno (p188)

Why Go?

Eastern Slovenia, embracing three provinces, rises from flat agricultural lands to snow-capped peaks. Its mountains, rivers and thermal waters provide a natural playground, while many of its historic towns date back to Roman times.

Sizable Štajerska (Styria) has swathes of farmland, much of it rich with vineyards, obligingly linked by cyclable wine routes. It also claims the Savinja Alps and the Pohorje Massif, an adventure-land of outdoor activities, and historical centres with castles, medieval alleys and ancient churches.

Tiny Koroška (Carinthia) is a region of forests, mountains and highland meadows and is tailor-made for outdoor activities, including skiing, mountain biking and hiking.

In the far northeast, Prekmurje is Slovenia's 'forgotten' corner, mostly a broad, farmed plain 'beyond the Mura River', which has preserved its culture of traditional music, folklore, architecture and food. It's a great place to relax and enjoy taking the waters at its many thermal spas.

When to Go
Maribor

Dec–Mar Skiers head to Maribor Pohorje, Slovenia's biggest downhill skiing centre.

Feb/Mar Crowds flock to Ptuj for the masked Kurentovanje carnival parade; storks arrive in Prekmurje.

Aug–Oct Ideal for walking and climbing in Logarska Dolina; grape harvest begins.

ŠTAJERSKA

Štajerska has long been the crossroads of Slovenia and virtually everyone has 'slept here' – Celts, Romans, early Slavs, Habsburgs and Nazi occupiers. In the 14th century, the German-speaking Counts of Celje were among the richest and most powerful feudal dynasties in Central Europe, and they challenged the Austrian monarchy's rule for a century. Štajerska suffered more than most of the rest of Slovenia during WWII, when many of its inhabitants were murdered, deported or sent to Nazi labour camps.

Upper Savinja Valley

The beautiful Upper Savinja Valley (Zgornja Savinjska Dolina) is bound by forests, ancient churches, traditional farmhouses and high Alpine peaks. There are activities here to suit every taste and inclination – from hiking, mountain biking and rock climbing to fishing, kayaking and swimming in the Savinja.

The valley has been exploited for its timber since the Middle Ages. Rafters transported the timber from Ljubno to Mozirje and Celje and some of the logs travelled as far as Romania. The trade brought wealth to the valley, evident from the many fine buildings still standing here.

The best place to get active is around Logarska Dolina. The free English-language brochures entitled *The Savinjska and Šaleška Valleys* and the *Solčava Panoramic Road* are helpful for exploring the area. Hikers should pick up a copy of the map *Hiking in the Lap of the Alps* (€1) from the TIC or buy the more detailed *Zgornja Savinjska Dolina* GZS map or the *Kamniško Savinjske Alpe* one (both 1:50,000, €8.10) by PZS. Cyclists will want the *Kolesarska Karta Zgornja Savinjska Dolina* (*Upper Savinja Valley Cycling Map*; €3).

Logarska Dolina

☑ 03 / POP 110 / ELEV UP TO 1250M

Most of the glacial 'Forester Valley', which is 7.5km long and no more than 500m wide, has been a country park of just under 24 sq km since 1987. This 'pearl of the Alpine region', with more than 40 natural attractions – caves, springs, peaks, rock towers and waterfalls – as well as endemic flora (golden slipper orchid) and rare fauna (mountain

eagles, peregrine falcons), is a wonderful place to explore for a few days.

◎ Sights & Activities

The tourist office (p188) can organise any number of activities – from guided mountaineering and rock climbing (per hour €25) to paragliding (€75) and canyoning (€110). It also rents mountain bikes (per hour/day €3/12), as does Hotel Plesnik (p188). The valley has the very basic **Logarska Dolina ski grounds** (☑ 03-838 90 04; www.logarska-dolina.si; day pass adult/child €10/7), a 1km-long slope and 13km of cross-country ski trails served by two tows.

Logarska Dolina Country Park PARK
(Krajinski Park Logarska Dolina; Apr-Sep & weekends in Oct admission per car/motorcycle €7/5, pedestrians & cyclists free; ☉year-round) Logarska Dolina Country Park is one of the most beautiful 'hidden' spots of Slovenia and a paradise for those seeking adventure and outdoor activities. A road goes past a chapel and through the woods to the 90m-high **Rinka Waterfall** (Slap Rinka) at 1100m, but there are plenty of trails to explore and up to 20 other waterfalls in the area.

The bottom of the Rinka Waterfall is a 10-minute walk from the end of the valley road. The climb to the top takes about 20 minutes; it's not very difficult, but it can get slippery. From the top to the west you can see three peaks reaching higher than 2250m: Kranjska Rinka, Koroška Rinka and Štajerska Rinka. Until 1918 they formed the triple border of Carniola (Kranjska), Carinthia (Koroška) and Styria (Štajerska). Ask the tourist office for the *Trail through the Logar Valley* brochure, a 14km hike which will take you through the valley in about five hours.

Opposite Dom Planincev is a trail leading to Sušica Waterfall and Klemenča Cave, both at about 1200m.

Matkov Kot VALLEY
Much less explored than neighbouring Logarska Dolina, this magnificent 6km-long valley runs parallel to Logarska Dolina and the border with Austria. Reach here by road by turning west as you leave Logarska Dolina.

🛏 Sleeping & Eating

Dom Planincev CABIN €
(☑ 03-584 70 06, 070 847 639; www.domplanincev.si; Logarska Dolina 15a; per person without/with breakfast €18/23; ☉late-Apr–Oct; 🅿) This

Eastern Slovenia Highlights

1 Wander back through the past via the narrow cobbled streets of medieval **Ptuj** (p200), the jewel of Štajerska.

2 Enjoy the wonderland (and the uncrowded skiing) that is **Rogla** (p214) in winter.

3 Watch the world walk (and maybe even sail) by from a cafe or bar in the waterfront

Lent district of **Maribor** (p206).

4 Stay with locals on a farm holiday in **Logarska Dolina** (p188), the greenest of Štajerska's valleys.

⑤ Take the waters in style at the thermal baths of **Rogaška Slatina** (p197), one of the few true spa towns in Slovenia.

⑥ Satisfy that sweet tooth with a helping of calorific *prekmurska gibanica* (pastry with poppy seeds, walnuts, fruit, cheese and cream)

at **Gostilna Rajh** (p221) in Bakovci.

⑦ Visit Prekmurje's last two remaining **floating mills** (p224) on the Mura River near Veržej and Ižakovci.

wooden mountain hut 2.5km from the Rinka waterfall has a relaxed, rustic feel to it. There are seven rooms with beds for up to 32 people. Party place.

Planšarija Logarski Kot CABIN €
(☎041 210 017; www.logarski-kot.si; Logarska Dolina 15; per person without/with breakfast €20/25; ⏰May-Oct; P) Close to the Rinka falls, this locally run hut has accommodation for two-dozen hikers. It's a bit off the beaten track, quiet and peaceful.

Lenar Farmhouse FARMSTAY €€
(☎03-838 90 06, 041 851 829; www.lenar.si; Logarska Dolina 11; r per person €32-35, apt for 3/6 €70/100; P) This farmhouse has six rooms and a couple of apartments in a farmhouse and a lovely peasant's cottage a couple of kilometres south from the valley entrance. In addition there's dormitory accommodation (per person €12) for up to five people in two rooms with beds made of straw. Free cross-country bikes for guests.

Pension Na Razpotju PENSION €€
(☎03-839 16 50, 031 249 441; www.logarska-narazpotju.si; Logarska Dolina 14; s €40-50, d €80; P @) A very comfortable pension set back from the main road, 'At the Crossroads' has 10 comfortable rooms containing 21 beds. Don't miss the pension's adorable **Fairytale Forest** (Pravljični Gozd; ☎031 249 441; Logarska Dolina 14; adult/child €3.50/2.50, free to pension guests; ⏰9am-6pm) just next door, a series of trails for children weaving through forest and three-dozen recreated staged fairy stories.

Hotel Plesnik HOTEL €€€
(☎03-839 23 00; www.plesnik.si; Logarska Dolina 10; s €89, d €144; P @ 🛜 ≋) A 29-room hotel in the centre of the valley with a pool, sauna, a fine restaurant (open 8am to 10pm) and lovely public area, the Plesnik pretty much *is* Logarska Dolina. Its annexe, the **Vila Palenk** (s/d €50/90), with 11 rooms done up in generic 'Alpine style', takes the overflow.

★ **Herbal Glamping Resort Ljubno** RESORT €€€
(☎059 917 200; www.charmingslovenia.com/sl/herbal-glamping-ljubno/galerija/resort.html; Ter 42, Ljubno ob Savinji; 4-person tent €170-360; P ❄ 🛜 ≋) A rather ordinary camping ground 23km southeast of Logarska Dolina has metamorphosed into one of the most stunning glamping resorts in eastern Slovenia. Surrounding a lovely wooden-decked filtered-water swimming pool are 10 en-suite perma-tents/chalets with two double beds and private outdoor jacuzzi. Great use is made of the extensive herbal garden in the way of beauty treatments. Rates are seasonal.

Orlovo Gnezdo CAFE €
(Eyrie; ☎070 847 639; dishes €4-6; ⏰10am-6pm) In the valley itself, the 'Eagle's Nest' is a simple cafe-pub with snacks, in a tall wooden tower overlooking the falls and reached by a steep set of steps.

Information

The **tourist information centre** (TIC; ☎03-838 90 04, 051 626 380; www.logarska-dolina.si; Logarska Dolina 9; ⏰9am-5pm Mon-Fri, to 6pm Sat & Sun Jul & Aug, 10am-4pm Sep, 10am-4pm Sat & Sun Apr-Jun, 10am-3pm Sat & Sun Oct) is in a small wooden kiosk opposite the Hotel Plesnik car park. The more comprehensive **Center Rinka** (☎03-839 07 10; www.solcavsko.info; Solčava 29; ⏰8am-5pm Jul & Aug, to 3pm Sep-Jun) is in Solčava, 4km before the entrance to the valley.

Getting There & Around

Logarska Dolina isn't well served by public transport. You can reach it from Celje (€7.20, two hours, 75km) on a daily weekday bus in season.

You can rent **bicycles** (per hour/day €4/12) from the tourist office and the **Hotel Plesnik** (p188). The latter also has **electric bikes** (per hour/day €4/16).

Celje

☎03 / POP 37,540 / ELEV 238M

With its time-warp historical centre, fabulous architecture, excellent museums and enormous castle looming over the picturesque Savinja River, Celje might appear to have won the tourism sweepstakes. But as it often gets overlooked in favour of Maribor and Ptuj, making it here feels like something of a discovery.

Celje's compact Old Town sits north of the Savinja River, bordered by the Lower Castle area to the west and the train tracks to the east. The town has two main squares: Glavni trg, at the southern end of pedestrian Stanetova ulica, and Krekov trg, opposite the train station.

History

Celeia was the administrative centre of the Roman province of Noricum between the 1st and 5th centuries. In fact, it flourished to such a degree that it gained the nickname 'Troia secunda', the 'second Troy'.

Celje's second Camelot came in the mid-14th century when the Counts of Celje took control of the area. The counts (later dukes), one of the richest and most powerful feudal dynasties in medieval Central Europe, were the last on Slovenian soil to challenge the absolute rule of the Habsburgs, and they united much of Slovenia for a time. Part of the counts' emblem – three gold stars forming an inverted triangle – has been incorporated into the Slovenian national flag and seal.

Celje was more German than Slovene until the end of WWI, when the town government passed into local hands for the first time.

⊙ Sights

Old Castle Celje   CASTLE
(Stari Grad Celje; ☑ 03-428 79 36, 03-544 36 90; www.grad-celje.com; Cesta na Grad 78; adult/child €4/free; ☉ 9am-9pm Jun-Aug, to 8pm May & Sep, to 7pm Apr, to 6pm Mar & Oct, to 5pm Feb & Nov, 10am-4pm Dec & Jan) The largest fortress in Slovenia, this castle is perched on a 407m-high escarpment about 2km southeast of the Old Town; the walk up via a footpath from Cesta na Grad takes about half an hour. The castle was originally built in the early 13th century and went through several transformations, especially under the Counts of Celje in the 14th and 15th centuries. There's not much inside, though concerts are staged and medieval-themed events take place in the warmer months.

When the castle lost its strategic importance in the 15th century it was left to deteriorate, and subsequent owners used the stone blocks to build other structures, including parts of the Princes' Palace and the Old Counts' Mansion. A surprisingly large portion remains intact, however, and has been restored, including 23m-high Frederick's Tower (Friderikov Stolp).

Celje Regional Museum   MUSEUM
(Pokrajinski Muzej Celje; ☑ 03-428 09 50; www.pokmuz-ce.si/en; adult/child both branches €5/3; ☉ 10am-6pm Tue-Sun Mar-Oct, to 4pm Tue-Fri, 9am-1pm Sat Nov-Feb) A birch-lined park along the Savinja River's northern embankment has an open-air lapidary of Roman remains unearthed in the Celje area, overlooked by the 16th-century Old Counts' Mansion, a lovely Renaissance building housing a branch of the Celje Regional Museum. The collection includes a large lapidarium in the basement with some 200 finds, and a huge collection of folk items and furnishings from the Savinja region on the ground floor.

On the 1st floor a dozen rooms are done up in styles from different periods (eg baroque, neoclassical, Biedemeier, Secessionist), but the main attraction here is the astonishing Celje Ceiling (Celjski Strop) in the central main hall. This is an enormous trompe l'oeil painting of columns, towers, angels frolicking skyward, noblemen and ladies looking down at you looking up. Completed in about 1600 by an Italian artist, the mural was meant to lift the ceiling up to the sky, and it does just that. Other panels represent the four seasons and show scenes from Roman and Greek mythology.

Princes' Palace   HISTORIC BUILDING
(Spodnji grad; www.pokmuz-ce.si/en; Trg Celjskih Knezov 8; adult/child both branches €5/3; ☉ 10am-6pm Tue-Sun Mar-Oct, to 4pm Tue-Fri, 9am-1pm Sat Nov-Feb) Sometimes referred to as the Lower Castle (Spodnij grad), this 4th-century structure houses an important branch of the Celje Regional Museum. In the cellar is the **City under the City**, a complete 3rd-century Roman road brilliantly displayed with excavated statuary and frescoes and parts of the old city walls. On top of these are traces of the medieval buildings up to parts of air-raid shelters built to withstand the bombs of WWII.

On the 1st floor, exhibits trace the history of Celje from the late Stone Age and through Roman Celeia right up to the period of the Counts of Celje. Taking pride of place on the 2nd floor are 18 of the noble skulls on display in back-lit cases.

In the southern wing of the Princes' Palace is the **Gallery of Contemporary Art** (Galarija Sodobnih Umetnosti; ☑ 03-426 51 60; Trg Celjskih Knezov 8; ☉ 11am-6pm Tue-Sat, 2-6pm Sun) FREE, with thematic exhibitions of both local and foreign artists.

Krekov Trg   SQUARE
Opposite the train station is the mammoth neo-Gothic **Celje Hall** (Celjski Dom; Krekov trg 3), built in 1907 and once the centre of social life for German-speaking *Celjani*. It now contains the year-round TIC. To the south and connected to the Hotel Evropa is the 16th-century **Defence Tower** (Obrambni Stolp; Razlagova ulica), and about 150m further on, the **Water Tower** (Vodni Stolp; Razlagova

Celje

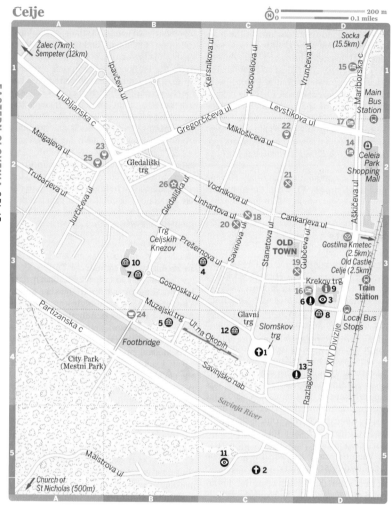

ulica 19), part of the city wall and ramparts, built between 1451 and 1473.

Josip Pelikan Photo Studio MUSEUM

(Fotografski Atelje Josipa Pelikana; ☎03-428 64 28; www.muzej-nz-ce.si; Razlagova ulica 5; adult/child incl main museum entry €3/1.50; ⊙10am-2pm Tue-Fri, 9am-1pm Sat, 2-6pm Sun) Looking like an over-sized greenhouse (to let in the light), the Josip Pelikan Photo Studio is the complete studio of a pioneering early 20th-century Celje photographer and part of the Museum of Recent History. His work is celebrated as he was the first major Slove-

nian photographer to gain national acclaim. Check out the ancient photographic equipment. Enter from the car park at the back.

Celje Museum of Recent History MUSEUM

(Muzej Novejše Zgodovine Celje; ☎03-428 64 10; www.muzej-nz-ce.si; Prešernova ulica 17; adult/child €3/1.50; ⊙10am-6pm Tue-Fri, 9am-1pm Sat, 2-6pm Sun) The permanent exhibition, *Living in Celje: 1900–2000*, records the story of Celje from the late 19th century onwards and includes a re-creation of an early 20th-century street, complete with tailor, hairdresser, clockmaker and goldsmith.

Celje

Abbey Church of St Daniel   CHURCH
(Opatijska Cerkev Sv Danijela; Slomškov trg) A few steps to the northwest of the Water Tower is the Abbey Church of St Daniel, dating from the early 14th century. The church has some magnificent frescoes and tombstones, but its greatest treasure is a 15th-century carved wooden pietà in the **Chapel of the Sorrowful Mother** to the left of the sanctuary. The chapel has carved stone walls and vaults with remnants of frescoes from the early 15th century and carved effigies of the Apostles.

Parts of Celje's medieval walls and ramparts can be seen along Ulica na Okopih, west of the church. Contiguous with Slomškov trg is **Glavni trg**, the heart of the Old Town. It is filled with lovely townhouses dating from the 17th and 18th centuries. In the centre of the square is the requisite **plague pillar** (1776) dedicated to Mary.

**Ugly Duckling Gallery
of Erotic Art**   GALLERY
(Galerija Erotike Grda Račka; ☑ 03-426 51 62, 051 681 995; www.celeia.info; 2nd fl, Gosposka ulica 3; ⊙ 5-8pm Tue-Sat) Located in a former peep show, this gallery exhibits erotica-related art.

Breg   NEIGHBOURHOOD
On the south bank of the Savinja River, a covered stairway with 90 steps at Breg 2 leads to the **Capuchin Church of St Cecilia** (Kapucinska Cerkev Sv Cecilije; Savinja River south bank). The Germans used the nearby monastery (now apartments) as a prison during WWII. Between the church and City Park is the reconstructed Roman **Temple of Hercules** (Heraklejev Tempelj; Maistrova ulica) dating from the 2nd century AD. Further south, you can walk up 396m-high **Nicholas Hill** (Miklavški Hrib), topped by the **Church of St Nicholas** (Cerkev Sv Miklavža), for a wonderful view of the castle, the Old Town and the Savinja.

🏃 Activities

The tourist information centre (p193) has brochures listing a number of **walks** and **hikes** into the surrounding countryside lasting between one and several days. An easy one leads southeast to **Mt Tovst** (834m) and the picturesque village of Svetina via the **Celjska Koča** (☑ 041 718 274, 059 070 400; www.celjska-koca.si; Pečovnik 31), a mountain hut at 650m that has metamorphosed into a delightfully modern three-star hotel with adjacent skiing piste. Ask for the *Dežela Celjska: Vodnik za Pohodnike* (Land of Celje: Guide for Hikers). It also distributes the *Dežela Celjska: Turistična Karta za Kolesarje in Pohodnike* (Land of Celje: Tourist Map for Cyclists and Hikers), with more than 40 routes outlined for Celje and surroundings.

🛏 Sleeping

★ **MCC Hostel**   HOSTEL €
(☑ 03-490 87 42, 040 756 009; www.hostel-celje.com; Mariborksa cesta 2; dm/s/d €15/27/42; @ 🛜) Private rooms and dorms are immaculately presented at this 12-room hostelry, but each is a unique installation, decorated by local

artists to tell a story from Celje's crazy past. Who can resist the room of the Celje ninja (costume included), the giant catfish or the cop who had to arrest himself? Regular music and social events, plus free bike hire.

George's Hostel
HOSTEL €

(☑ 041 329 179; violeta.stojs@sz-atrij.si; Aškerčeva ulica 3; dm €15; ☎) Tiny but very comfortable and central hostel with just one private room with three beds and a dormitory for six people. Go through the courtyard; the door is on the right. There's also a comfortable communal room with TV and kitchen.

Hotel Celeia
HOTEL €€

(☑ 03-426 97 00; www.hotel-celeia.si; Mariborska cesta 3; s €46-56, d €68-88, ste €98-120; P ❄ @ ☎) A change in ownership has taught this old (since 1962!) dog new tricks and it's now a 52-room colourful 'pop-art' hotel with Warhol-like portraits of Elvis, Marilyn and even Obama strewn throughout. The hotel is a favourite with businesspeople, but eschew any of the rooms facing Mariborska cesta – it's a major and very busy highway.

Hotel Evropa
HOTEL €€€

(☑ 03-426 90 00; www.hotel-evropa.si; Krekov trg 4; s €64-83, d €86-126, ste €260; P ❄ ☎) Located near the train station and in the centre of town, this 62-room historic hotel has been lovingly restored and is once again a provincial favourite, almost a century and a half in situ. We love the high-end cafe, the stunning restaurant with the Defence Tower adjacent and the pleasant staff. Rooms on the 3rd and 4th floors are superior. Enter from Razlagova ulica.

✖ Eating

Loving Hut
VEGAN €

(☑ 070 631 501; www.lovinghut.si; Linhartova ulica 7; dishes €2.50-5.50; ⏲ 8am-5pm Mon-Wed, 9am-6pm Thu & Fri, 11am-3pm Sat) Who would have guessed that a meatless restaurant would open so close to Celje's uber-carnivorous market? Vegans (and anyone else!) seeking respite from the meaty offerings of Slovenia's traditional cuisine will find refuge here, where they can happily tuck into scrummy veggie bakes, salads and soups.

Gostilna Jež
SLOVENIAN €

(☑ 03-492 66 03; www.gostilnajez.si; Linhartova ulica 6; dishes €4.20-7.50; ⏲ 9am-4pm Mon-Sat) This very simple eatery is a great place for a cheap and filling lunch – as so many market-goers seem to think. It's now branched out into pizza too, eat-in or takeaway, to attract a younger clientele.

★ Gostilna Kmetec
SLOVENIAN €€

(☑ 03-544 25 55, 041 333 831; www.tlacan.si; Zagrad 140a; mains €8.50-19; ⏲ 10am-10pm Tue-Thu, to midnight Fri & Sat, to 8pm Sun) One of our favourite *gostilne* anywhere, the Kmetec sits high in the hills, looking Celje's old castle square in the face. Offerings are on the meaty side – lamb chops, boar and other game – but don't fail to try the creamy pumpkin soup with a dollop of *bučno olje* (pumpkinseed oil; €3). It's heavenly.

Koper
PIZZA €€

(☑ 059 071 380; www.pizzeria-koper.si; Gubčeva ulica 3; mains €7.50-16; ⏲ 10am-10pm Mon-Thu, 9am-midnight Fri, 11am-midnight Sat, noon-10pm Sun) Despite bearing the name of Slovenia's largest port town, the menu skips the coastal connection, focusing instead on Koper's Italian heritage in its menu of mostly pizza and pasta. The pizzas in particular, baked in a wood-fired stove, are top-notch. Just about the busiest eatery in town – especially the terrace on a warm night.

Restavracija Evropa
INTERNATIONAL €€

(☑ 03-426 90 00; Krekov trg 4; mains €13-22; ⏲ 11am-10pm Mon-Sat, to 9pm Sun) This stunning eatery in the Hotel Evropa (p192) has superb international cuisine and some very inspired decor. We love the Manet-like portraits of film and rock stars (though we don't get the connection either). Have a look at the function room straight ahead; it's the inside the Defence Tower (p189).

Self-Catering

Market
MARKET

(cnr Savinova ulica & Linhartova ulica; ⏲ 6am-3pm Mon-Sat) This outdoor market has fresh fruit, vegetables and other foodstuffs.

Mercator
SUPERMARKET

(Stanetova ulica 14; ⏲ 7am-7pm Mon-Fri, to 1pm Sat, 8am-noon Sun) You'll find a large Mercator supermarket opposite the 1929-Art Deco Kino Metropol (Metropol Cinema).

🍷 Drinking & Entertainment

Miško Knjižko
CAFE

(☑ 03-426 17 52, 031 377 480; www.ce.sik.si; Muzejski trg 1a; cakes €2-3.50; ⏲ 7am-10.30pm Mon-Sat, 8am-9pm Sun) This lovely modern cafe at the Celje Central Library, just at the footbridge over the Savinja, is a lovely place to enjoy the riverfront and a slice of something sweet.

Vrtnica BAR
(☑ 059 071 388; Malgajeva ulica 2a; ⊙ 6am-11pm Mon-Thu, to midnight Fri, 8am-midnight Sat, to 10pm Sun) Probably the most popular cafe-bar in Celje, the colourful 'Rose' (run by the same people who manage the Hotel Evropa) overlooks a leafy garden and attracts a well-heeled clientele.

Kavarna Evropa CAFE
(☑ 03-426 96 07; Krekov trg 4; ⊙ 7am-11pm Mon-Thu, 11am-midnight Fri & Sat, 8am-10pm Sun) This 'olde worlde' cafe in the Hotel Evropa – all dark-wood panelling, gilt mouldings and chandeliers – is a good place for a cup of coffee and a slice of cake.

Maverick Pub PUB
(Ljubljanska cesta 7; ⊙ 6am-midnight Mon-Thu, to 2am Fri & Sat, 10am-10pm Sun) One of several watering holes bunched up opposite Gledališki trg, this is a lively and quite affable place with a large outdoor terrace for people-watching in the warmer months.

Branibor Club LIVE MUSIC
(☑ 03-492 41 44; Stanetova ulica 27; ⊙ 6am-1am Mon-Thu, to 2.30am Fri, 7am-2.30am Sat, 8am-1am Sun) One of the watering holes in central Celje, Branibor has a great big courtyard out the back where frequent live-music concerts get punters up on their feet.

Slovenian People's Theatre THEATRE
(Slovenski Ljudsko Gledališče; ☑ 03-426 42 00, box office 03-426 42 08; www.slg-ce.si; Gledališki trg 5; ⊙ 9am-noon & 3-6pm Mon-Fri, also 1hr before performance) The SLG, which encompasses part of a medieval tower once used as a dungeon on Vodnikova ulica, stages six plays between September and May. Performances are normally – though not always – in Slovene, but the visuals are usually so sophisticated you won't have trouble following the story line.

ℹ Information

Abanka (Aškičeva ulica 10; ⊙ 8am-5pm Mon-Fri, 8-11am Sat)

Banka Celje (Vodnikova ulica 2; ⊙ 8.30-11.30am & 2-5pm Mon-Fri) In a building designed by Jože Plečnik in 1930.

Mladinska Knjiga (☑ 03-428 52 52; Stanetova ulica 3; ⊙ 8am-7pm Mon-Fri, to noon Sat) Sells regional maps and guides.

Post Office (Krekov trg 9; ⊙ 8am-6pm Mon-Fri, to noon Sat) Purpose-built in 1898.

Tourist Information Centre Celje (TIC; ☑ 03-492 50 81, 03-428 79 36; www.celje.si; Celje Hall, Krekov trg 3; ⊙ 9am-5pm Mon-Fri, to 1pm Sat) There's also a TIC branch at the entrance to the **Old Castle Celje** (p189), open when the castle is, which rents bicycles for €3/5/10 per three hours/six hours/day.

ℹ Getting There & Around

BUS
The main bus station is 300m north of the train station, opposite the huge Celeia shopping mall on Aškičeva ulica. Local buses stop south of the train station on Ulica XIV Divizije.

Intercity buses run frequently to Mozirje (€4.10, 50 minutes, 32km), Rogaška Slatina (€4.10, one hour, 34km), Rogatec (€5.20, 70 minutes, 41km) and Zreče (€3.60, 45 minutes, 29km). Count on up to six buses on weekdays and two at the weekend to Ljubljana (€7.50, 1¾ hours, 77km) and Maribor (€6.70, 1¾ hours, 68km). Other destinations accessible by bus from Celje and their frequencies include Logarska Dolina (€7.20, two hours, 75km), and Murska Sobota (€10.70, two hours, 117km).

For local destinations such as Šempeter (€2.60, 20 minutes, 12km), Šentjur, Prebold and Žalec, go to the **bus stops** south of the train station on Ulica XIV Divizije.

TAXI
For a local taxi, ring ☑ 070 801 237.

TRAIN
Celje is a good rail hub. From Ljubljana (€7 to €12.30, 1½ hours, 89km) you can reach Celje up to two dozen times a day by regular train and six times a day by ICS express train.

Celje is also on the line linking Zidani Most (connections to and from Ljubljana and Zagreb) with Maribor (€5.80 to €10.50, one hour, 67km) and the Austrian cities of Graz and Vienna.

WORTH A TRIP

HOPS MUSEUM

Eko Muzej (☑ 03-710 04 34; www.ekomuzej-hmelj.si; Aškerčeva ulica 9a, Žalec; adult/child €2.5/1; ⊙ 9am-5pm Tue-Fri, to noon Sat) Halfway between Šempeter and Celje in Žalec, this museum is dedicated to hops (hmelj) – Štajerska is famous for them – and the noble art of brewing. August to October are the best times to visit, when there are plenty of outdoor activities and demonstrations, from hop picking, the crowning of the hop princess and guided walks. And, yes, they do beer tastings too.

A spur line links Celje with Šempeter (€1.85, 15 minutes, 12km) up to 10 times a day Monday to Saturday in each direction. A third line connects Celje with Zabok in Croatia via Rogaška Slatina (€3.45, 50 minutes, 36km), Rogatec and Dobovec. Up to seven trains arrive and depart on weekdays but only a couple at the weekend.

Šempeter

 03 / POP 2030 / ELEV 271M

◉ Sights

Roman Necropolis　　　　　　　　RUIN
(Rimska Nekropola; ☑ 03-700 20 56, 031 645 937; www.td-sempeter.si; Ob Rimski Nekropoli 2; adult/child €4/3; ⊙ 10am-5pm May-Sep, to 3pm Apr, to 4pm Sat & Sun Oct) Some 12km west of Celje, Šempeter is the site of a reconstructed Roman necropolis of wealthy families living in the area. The burial ground contains four complete tombs and scores of columns, stellae and fragments carved with portraits, mythological creatures and scenes from daily life. They have been divided into about two dozen sections linked by footpaths.

The most beautiful is the Ennius family tomb, with reliefs of animals and, on the front panel, the Phoenician princess Europa riding a bull. The oldest is the Vindonius tomb, while the largest is the 8m-high Spectacius tomb, raised in honour of a Roman official, his wife and son. (Notice the kidnapping scene on the side relief.) If you compare these with the later Secundinus family tomb erected in about 250 AD, it's obvious that Roman power and wealth was on the decline here in the mid-3rd century.

Pekel Jama　　　　　　　　　　CAVE
(Hell Cave; ☑ 03-570 21 38, 035 702 138; Ob Rimski Nekropoli 2; adult/child €8/5; ⊙ 10am-6pm May-Sep, to 5pm Apr, to 5pm Sat & Sun Mar & Oct) A visit to 'Hell Cave' (note the outline of a devil at the entrance), some 4km north of the Roman necropolis, is quite a heavenly experience. A one-hour tour will take you 1200m from the lower wet area to the upper dry section. Among the highlights, you'll pass a 4m-high waterfall, the Silent Hall with perfect acoustics and the Hall of Fantasy, where stalactites and stalagmites become snakes, pigeons, cauliflower and frogs. It's 10°C in there and very slippery; take a wrap and wear sturdy shoes.

Kozjansko Region

Kozjansko is a remote region along the eastern side of the Posavje Mountains and the 90km-long Sotla River, which forms part of the eastern border with Croatia. It is an area of forests, rolling hills, vineyards, scattered farms and the site of one of Slovenia's three regional parks, with much to offer visitors in the way of spas, two impressive castles, hiking, cycling and excellent wine.

Podčetrtek

☑ 03 / POP 535 / ELEV 212M
Most people make their way to this village, on a little bump of land extending into Croatia, to relax at the Terme Olimia thermal spa. Looming overhead are the remains of a castle originally built in the 11th century and an important fortification during the wars with the Hungarians 300 years later.

The town's seemingly unpronounceable name (pronounced pod-*che*-ter-tek) comes from the Slovenian word for 'Thursday' – the day the market took place and the district court sat.

◉ Sights

Podčetrtek Castle　　　　　　　CASTLE
(Grad Podčetrtek) The enormous Renaissance-style Podčetrtek Castle, atop a 355m-high hill to the northwest of town, went up some time in the mid-16th century but was badly damaged by an earthquake in 1974. The castle, which is not open to the public but offers stunning views, can be reached by walking north along Trška cesta and then west on Cesta na Grad for about 1.5km.

Olimje Minorite Monastery　　MONASTERY
(Minoritski Samostan Olimje; ☑ 03-582 91 61; www.olimje.net; Olimje 82; pharmacy adult/child €1/0.50; ⊙ 8am-7pm) The Minorite Olimje Monastery, 3km southwest of Podčetrtek, was built as a Renaissance-style castle in about 1550. Its **Church of the Assumption** contains 17th-century ceiling paintings in the presbytery, one of the largest baroque altars in the country and the ornate **Chapel of St Francis Xavier**. On the ground floor of the corner tower to the left of the main entrance is the monastery's greatest treasure: a 17th-century **pharmacy** painted with religious and medical scenes. The Franciscan monks here grow their own herbs and medicinal plants in the nearby garden.

Čokoladnica Olimje
CHOCOLATE FACTORY

(Olimje Chocolate Boutique; ☑03-810 90 36; http://cokoladnica-olimje.si; Olimje 61; ⊙10am-7pm Jun-Aug, to 5pm Sep-May) Čokoladnica Olimje is just next door to the Olimje Minorite Monastery, and makes and sells the most famous chocolate in Slovenia.

Koča Pri Čarovnici
AMUSEMENT PARK

(Land of Fairytales & Fantasy; ☑031 309 103; www.carovnica.si; Olimje 104; admission €2; ⊙10am-6pm) A little trail in the forest 1.5km above the Olimje Minorite Monastery, laid out by the former local school principal, leads you past dozens of his all-singin', all-dancin' fairytale characters made of recycled materials who act out their roles. There's also a small museum of local life a century ago and a room filled with souvenirs from around the world. Charming.

🏃 Activities

Some of the most rewarding hikes and bike trips in Slovenia can be made in this region. The free *Občina Podčetrtek Sprehajalne Poti* (Podčetrtek Municipality Walking Trails) map outlines several excursions for hikers on marked trails. The 1:50,000-scale *Obsotelje in Kozjansko* cycling map from the TIC outlines 10 paths of varying difficulty for cyclists and mountain bikers.

Terme Olimia
SPA

(☑03-829 70 00; www.terme-olimia.com; Zdraviliška cesta 24) Some 1.2km northeast of Podčetrtek centre, Terme Olimia has thermal water (28°C to 35°C) full of magnesium and calcium for health. These days, though, it places most of the emphasis on recreation and beauty. The centre's **Termalija** (☑03-829 78 05; nonguests adult/child Mon-Fri €13/8.50, Sat & Sun €15/10; ⊙8am-10pm Sun-Thu, to midnight Fri & Sat) pool and spa complex has eight indoor and outdoor pools connected by an underwater passage and covers an area of 2000 sq metres. In addition, the complex has two wellness centres: the **Spa Armonia** at the Hotel Sotelia and the luxurious **Orchidelia**.

🛏 Sleeping

The TIC (p196) has a list of families offering private rooms (per person from €20) in Podčetrtek and the surrounding area.

Pension Podčetrtek
PENSION €

(☑03-582 91 09; www.ciril-youthhostel-bc.si; Zdraviliška cesta 10; r per person €16-20; P@) This pension on the main road just across

Podčetrtek Area

◎ Sights
1 Podčetrtek Castle A3

✚ Activities, Courses & Tours
2 Termalija B3
3 Terme Olimia B3

🛏 Sleeping
4 Hotel Sotelia B3
5 Kamp Natura B2
6 Ortenia Apartments in Nature A3
7 Pension Podčetrtek B2

✕ Eating
8 Mercator A4

from the entrance to the camping ground has 15 basic rooms with two and four beds. Holders of an HI card or equivalent get a 10% discount. It's basic but comfortable enough and convenient to the area's recreational facilities.

Kamp Natura
CAMPGROUND €

(☑03-829 78 33; www.terme-olimia.com; Zdraviliška cesta; campsite per person €12.50-14.50, with pools €16.50-21; ☺mid-Apr–mid-Oct; 🅿🌐) Owned and operated by Terme Olimia (p195), this 1-hectare campground with 200 sites is about 1km north of the Terme Olimia spa complex, on the edge of the Sotla River. It's fairly standard but the location by the Croatian border is stunning. There are also holiday cottages available.

★ Jelenov Greben
FARMSTAY €€

(☑03-582 90 46; www.jelenov-greben.si; Olimje 90; s €54-59, d €98-104, apt for 4 €90-100; 🅿🌐♨) This spectacular property, set on a ridge some 500m south of Olimje at Ježovnik, has 15 cosy rooms and apartments (some with balconies). Along with a popular restaurant, there is a superb wine cellar, a spa and sauna and a shop selling farm products. 'Deer Ridge' is a working farm and 100 head of deer roam freely on six hectares of land.

Hotel Sotelia
HOTEL €€€

(☑03-829 78 36; www.terme-olimia.com; Zdraviliška cesta 24; s/d €99/170 half-board; 🅿✳@🌐♨) ⏀ The Terme Olimia (p195) spa complex offers accommodation in two hotels, an apartment complex and a tourist village. Top of the heap is the four-star, 145-room Hotel Sotelia, a luxurious place that does half- and full-board packages exclusively. It's a very ecofriendly hotel and almost blends into the forest behind it.

Ortenia Apartments in Nature
DESIGN HOTEL €€€

(Ortenia Apartmajo v Naravi; ☑040 373 331; www.ortenia.com; Škofja Gora 36; r €194-224; 🅿✳♨) This award-winning property with a mouthful of a name counts six luxurious apartments with kitchens in three ultra-modern 'pods' – each with enormous glass windows looking up to the castle. The 'nature' part of the name is well-deserved; all materials are natural, with wood and stone in profusion. There's a sauna and small pool and breakfast comes in a basket.

Eating

Restavracija Amon
SLOVENIAN €€

(☑03-818 24 80; www.amon.si; Olimje 24; mains €9-16; ☺11am-10pm Sun-Thu, to 11pm Fri & Sat) This Maison de Qualité establishment up on the hill south of Olimje and opposite the golf course is simply the best place for miles around. It offers high-quality food and or-

ganic wines (including its own organic variety). The set lunch at €10 is excellent value.

Gotišče Jelenov Greben
SLOVENIAN €€

(☑03-582 90 46; Olimje 90; mains €8-16; ☺7am-10pm Mon-Fri, to 11pm Sat & Sun) This rustic-by-design eatery at the lovely 'Deer Ridge' farm is celebrated, not surprisingly, for its venison, as well as its wild mushroom dishes. Desserts emerge from their own in-house bakery. Set lunch is a budget-busting €12 (or €20 if you want venison).

Self-Catering

Mercator
SUPERMARKET

(Cesta Slake 1; ☺7am-7pm Mon-Fri, to 3pm Sat, to noon Sun) In Podčetrtek village.

❶ Information

Banka Celje (Zdraviliška cesta 27c; ☺8.30-11.30am & 2-5pm Mon-Fri) In the shopping mall between the village centre and spa complex.

Post Office (Zdraviliška cesta 27c; ☺8am-9.30am, 10am-5pm Mon-Fri, 8am-noon Sat) Some 200m north of the village centre and next door to Banka Celje.

Tourist Information Centre Podčetrtek (TIC; ☑03-810 90 13; www.turizem-podcetrtek.si; Cesta Škofja Gora 1; ☺8am-3pm Mon-Fri & 8am-noon Sat year-round, plus 9am-noon Sun Apr-Sep) At the central roundabout.

❶ Getting There & Around

The centre of Podčetrtek is at the junction of four roads. All buses stop at the crossroads as well as at the spa and the camping ground. Up to five buses a day pass by Podčetrtek and Terme Olimia on their way from Celje (€4.70, one hour, 39km) to Bistrica ob Sotli (€2.30, 20 minutes, 14km) and vice versa.

Podčetrtek is on the rail line linking Celje (via Stranje) with Imeno. There are three train stations. For the village centre and the castle, get off at Podčetrtek. Atomske Toplice is good for Terme Olimia and the spa hotels. Podčetrtek Toplice is the correct stop for the camping ground. Up to six trains leave the main Podčetrtek station every day for Celje (€3.45, 50 minutes, 35km).

Kozjansko Regional Park

☑03 / ELEV UP TO 685M

⊙ Sights

Kozjansko Park
PARK

(Kozjanski Park; ☑03-800 71 00; www.kozjanski-park.si; Podsreda 45; ☺visitor centre 8am-4pm Mon-Fri) Established in 1999, the 206.5 sq km Kozjansko Park stretches along the Sotla River, from the border with Dolenjska and Bizeljsko in the south to Podčetrtek in the north. Named a Unesco biosphere reserve in 2010, the park's forests and dry meadows harbour a wealth of flora and fauna, notably butterflies, reptiles and birds, including corncrakes, kingfishers and storks. There are a number of trails, including educational ones and the circular 32km-long Podsreda Trail (Pešpot Podsreda), which ends at the wonderfully preserved Podsreda Castle.

Podsreda Castle

CASTLE

(Grad Podsreda; ☑ 03-580 61 18; www.kozjanski-park.si; adult/child €4/2.50; ⊙ 10am-6pm Tue-Sun Apr-Oct) Set amidst the hills of the Kozjansko region, Podsreda Castle is one of the best-preserved Romanesque fortresses in Slovenia, and looks pretty much the way it did when it was built in the mid-12th century, thanks to renovations completed in 2015.

A rough, winding 5km-long road leads to the castle, but you can also reach it via a relatively steep 2km footpath from the village of Podsreda.

A barbican on the south side, with walls 3m thick and a medieval kitchen, leads to a central courtyard with a sgraffito of a knight and angels on the east side and a dungeon hidden beneath a staircase.

The rooms in the castle wings, some with beamed ceilings and ancient chandeliers, now contain a glassworks exhibit (crystal from Rogaška Slatina, vials from the Olimje pharmacy, green and blue Pohorje glass). The fabulous wood-panelled Renaissance Hall hosts classical concerts and, of course, weddings. In the room next to it is a wonderful collection of prints of Štajerska's castles and monasteries taken from Topographii Ducatus Stiria (1681) by Georg Mattäus Vischer (1628–96). There are exhibition spaces of art and photographs in the east and north wings. The tiny Romanesque chapel is above the courtyard to the southeast.

✖ Eating & Drinking

Pekarna-Okrepčevalnica Klavdija   BAKERY

(☑ 040 200 265; Podsreda 53; ⊙ 6am-9pm Mon-Fri, 7am-9pm Sat, 7am-1pm Sun) In Podsreda village, this bakery has a selection of snacks and sandwiches.

Pod Gradom

BAR

(☑ 03-580 61 04; Podsreda 49; ⊙ 6.30am-8pm) This bar is in Podsreda village near Kozjansko Park headquarters.

ℹ Getting There & Away

You can reach Podsreda from Podčetrtek (€3.10, 40 minutes, 33km) on just one weekday bus at 11.13am, though there's another two more during school term at 3pm and 4.13pm.

Rogaška Slatina

☑ 03 / POP 5030 / ELEV 227M

Rogaška Slatina is Slovenia's oldest and largest spa town, a veritable 'cure factory' with a half-dozen posh hotels offering treatments and therapies. It's an attractive place set among scattered forests in the foothills of the Macelj range. Hiking and cycling in the area is particularly good.

The hot spring here was known in Roman times but first made it onto the map in 1572, when the governor of Styria took the waters on the advice of his physician. A century later visitors started arriving in droves and by the early 19th century, Rogaška Slatina was an established spa town.

The heart of Rogaška Slatina is the spa complex, an architecturally important group of neoclassical, Secessionist and Plečnik-style buildings surrounding a long landscaped garden called Zdraviliški trg, or Health Resort Sq.

⊙ Sights

Anin Dvor   MUSEUM

(Ana's Mansion; ☑ 03-620 26 51; www.turizem-rogaska.si; Cvetlična hrib 1a; adult/child €5/3.50; ⊙ 9am-5pm Tue-Sun) This new, very ambitious and surprisingly interesting museum is divided into several distinct sections and includes a close (and mixed-media) look at Rogaška's important glass-making industry as well as a wonderful collection of items from the Yugoslav kingdom and autographs of the great and the good amassed by one man. The water-based art installation is beyond soothing; arborphiles will love the instructive collection of tree bark.

Tempel   HISTORIC BUILDING

(Zdraviliški trg) This lovely art nouveau pavilion at the southern end of Zdraviliški trg was built in 1904.

✦ Activities

Rogaška Slatina's mineral water (called Donat Mg) contains the largest amount of magnesium found in water anywhere in the world and is primarily for drinking, although you might find it tastes a little

Rogaška Slatina

metallic and salty. It's said to aid digestion, alleviate constipation and encourage weight loss. The magnesium alone, it is claimed, regulates 200 bodily functions.

Hot Springs & Spas

Pivnica HOT SPRING

(Zdravilíški trg; admission €2.10, 3-/5-day pass €16/21; ☉7am-1pm & 3-7pm Mon-Sat, 7am-1pm & 4-7pm Sun) You can engage in a 'drinking cure' of your own at the Pivnica, the round glassed-in drinking hall where mineral water is dispensed directly from the springs. Enter via the Rogaška Medical Center. In front is the oval-shaped bandstand where concerts are staged in the warmer months.

Rogaška Medical Center SPA

(☑03-811 70 15; www.rogaska-medical.com; Zdravilíški trg 9; ☉7am-8pm Mon-Fri, 8am-noon & 4-8pm Sat & Sun) The centre of spa action is the 12-storey Rogaška Medical Center (formerly called Terapija), where you'll find everything from pearl baths to lymph-gland drainage. Treatments start from around €25.

Rogaška Riviera SWIMMING

(☑03-818 19 50; Celjska cesta 5; day pass adult/child Mon-Fri €10/6, Sat & Sun €12/8; ☉9am-8pm) This ambitiously named complex at the northern end of Celjska cesta has one indoor and three outdoor swimming pools that are all connected. There's also two whirlpools. Guests at the Grand Hotel Rogaška get free entry to these pools.

Hiking

Walking trails fanning out into the surrounding hills and meadows are listed in the *Rogaška Slatina & the Surrounding Area* free guide available from the TIC. One leads 15km to the hilltop **Church of St Florian**, and to Ložno, from where you can continue on another 4km to **Donačka Gora**, a 1374m-high hill east of Rogatec. To return, walk two hours down to Rogatec to catch a bus or train back.

The walk to **Boč** (979m), northwest of Rogaška Slatina and in the centre of the 886-hectare **Boč Country Park** (Krajinski Park Boč; www.boc.si), will take you about four hours, though you can drive as far as Category III **Dom na Boču** (☑03-582 46 17, 031 671 418; kamensek.b@hotmail.com; Drevenik 7; ☉Tue-Sun year-round), a mountain hut a couple of kilometres south of the peak at 658m with 47 beds in 15 rooms.

✵ Festivals & Events

Ana's Festival

Rogaška Slatina MUSIC FESTIVAL

(www.anin-festival.si; ☉Aug) Ana's Festival is a series of concerts, from chamber music and opera to Slovenian folk music, held in various venues around town including the Tempel pavilion and the Crystal Hall in August.

🛏 Sleeping

The TIC has a list of private rooms for between €16 and €20 per person, and apartments from €80.

Grand Hotel Rogaška   HOTEL €€€
(☑03-811 20 00; www.grandhotel-rogaska.com; Zdraviliški trg 12; s €99-119, d €149-169; P ❊ @ 🛜 ☒) The Grand Hotel Rogaška, along with its two contiguous (and now unnamed) branches, dominates the eastern side of Zdraviliški trg with its 194 rooms. The older wing dates from 1913 and the public areas (especially the sparkling Crystal Hall) are the grandest in town. This is the place if you are looking for atmosphere (with all the mod-cons).

Grand Hotel Sava   HOTEL €€€
(☑03-811 40 00; www.rogaska.si; Zdraviliški trg 6; Grand Hotel Sava s €69-89, d €109-189, Hotel Zagreb s €62-70, d €100-116; P ❊ @ 🛜 ☒) The modern Grand Hotel Sava and the attached older (and cheaper) Hotel Zagreb, each with four stars, are at the northwestern end of Zdraviliški trg and count a total of 284 rooms.

🍴 Eating & Drinking

Gostilna Bohor   SLOVENIAN €
(☑03-581 41 00; Kidričeva ulica; mains €8-18, pizzas €5.60-10.80; ⊙8am-10pm Mon-Thu, to 11pm Fri & Sat, 10am-10pm Sun) For hearty Slovenian fare and better-than-average pizza, try this popular local eatery. The Štajerska pizza (€5.80) has virtually everything from the barnyard on top.

Sonce   MEDITERRANEAN €€
(☑03-819 21 60; Celjska cesta 9; mains €8-19; ⊙9am-10pm Mon-Fri, 11am-9pm Sat & Sun) Quite a sophisticated number at the far end of Celjska cesta, the 'Sun' leans toward the Mediterranean (or perhaps the Adriatic) with a large selection of fish dishes (as well as meat ones) and an excellent wine card. There's a terrace for al fresco dining in the warmer months.

Restavracija Kaiser   INTERNATIONAL €€
(☑03-811 47 10; Zdraviliški trg 6; mains €12-24; ⊙noon-11pm) Rogaška Slatina's fanciest eatery, this international restaurant in the Hotel Zagreb, with some Slovenian favourites thrown in for good measure, faces the main square. Service is sterling and the food sublime; the duck and lamb dishes are espe-

cially good. Tasting menus for four/five/six courses cost €31/35/65.

Central Cafe   CAFE
(☑03-819 08 88; Zdraviliški trg 23; ⊙7am-11pm Mon-Thu, to 3am Fri & Sat, to 10pm Sun) Most visitors to Rogaška Slatina spend their evenings in the hotel bars and cafes; the Central, at the southern end of Zdraviliški trg, is in the thick of things and popular with a local crowd. Ice cream, cakes and cocktails.

🛍 Shopping

Steklarska Rogaška   HOMEWARES
(☑03-818 20 27; Ulica Talcev 1; ⊙8am-7pm Mon-Fri, to 1pm Sat) Rogaška Slatina is as celebrated for its crystal as it is for its mineral water. This outlet, attached to the crystal-making school, which can be visited (adult/child €8/ free), has a wide range of leaded crystal items for sale. It's 2km southeast of the centre.

Afrodita Beauty Shop   BEAUTY
(☑03-812 13 61; Kidričeva ulica 54; ⊙10am-4pm Mon-Sat, 9am-noon Sat) Slovenia's largest cosmetic manufacturer, with more than 600 products, has an outlet about 1.5km south of the train station. After your spa therapy, come here to stock up on locally made lotions, creams and cosmetics.

ℹ️ Information

Post Office (Kidričeva ulica 3; ⊙8am-6pm Mon-Fri, to noon Sat) Just south of the bus station.

SKB Banka (Kidričeva ulica 11; ⊙8am-5pm Mon-Fri) Next to the post office.

Tourist Information Centre Rogaška Slatina (TIC; ☑03-581 44 14; www.rogaska-slatina.si; Zdraviliški trg 1; ⊙8am-7pm Mon-Fri, to noon Sat & Sun Jul & Aug, 8am-4pm Mon-Fri, 8am-noon Sat Sep-Jun) Free internet access.

ℹ️ Getting There & Around

BUS
Rogaška Slatina's bus station is south of Zdraviliški trg on Celjska cesta. Buses to Celje (€4.10, one hour, 34km) and Rogatec (€1.80, 10 minutes, 7km) leave Rogaška Slatina more or less hourly. To reach Maribor (€7.20, 1½ hours, 75km) you must change on Slovenska Bistrica.

TRAIN
The train station is on Kidričeva ulica, 300m south of the bus station. Rogaška Slatina is on the train line linking Celje (€3.45, 50 minutes, 36km) via Rogatec (€1.30, 10 minutes, 6km) and Dobovec with Zabok in Croatia (change here for Zagreb).

Rogatec

📱 03 / POP 1495 / ELEV 296M

This small town, about 7km east of (and accessible by bus and train from) Rogaška Slatina, has two important sights well worth the short trip.

Strmol Manor
CASTLE

(Dvorec Strmol; 📱 03-810 72 22; www.rogatec.si; Pot k Ribniku 6; adult/child/family €3/2.60/6, with Open-Air Museum €5.40/4.10/10.80; ⊘ 10am-6pm Tue-Sun Apr-Oct) This restored 15th-century castle has exhibits in 15 rooms on five floors. Don't miss the original open-hearth 'black kitchen' (*črna kuhinja*); the 17th-century chapel, with its baroque and Renaissance murals; the lovely baroque salon and its pink stucco work; and the exhibit in the loft, which re-creates a mid-19th-century country kitchen, complete with original furnishings and fittings. Work from the local artists' colony is on display on the 2nd floor.

Rogatec Open-Air Museum
MUSEUM

(Muzej na Prostem Rogatec; 📱 03-818 62 00; www.rogatec.si; Ptujska cesta 23; adult/child/family €3/2.30/6; ⊘ 10am-6pm Tue-Sun Apr-Oct) Slovenia's largest and most ambitious *skanzen* (open-air village museum), with more than a dozen mostly original structures, moved here in the early 1980s. The central farmhouse, built by the Šmit family in the early 19th century, barn, a *toplar* (double hayrack), forge, grocery shop and vintner's cottage replicate a typical Styrian hamlet of the 19th and early 20th centuries. There are regular displays (including participation) of activities such as weaving, stone-cutting, bread-making and so on.

Ptuj

📱 02 / POP 17,810 / ELEV 225M

Rising gently above a wide valley, Ptuj (p-too-ee) forms a symphony of red-tile roofs best viewed from across the Drava River. One of the oldest towns in Slovenia, Ptuj equals Ljubljana in terms of historical importance, but the compact medieval core, with its castle, museums, monasteries and churches, can easily be seen in a day. But there are so many interesting side trips and activities in the area that you may want to base yourself here for a while longer.

History

Ptuj began life as a Roman military outpost on the south bank of the Drava River and later grew into a civilian settlement called Poetovio on the opposite side. By the 1st century AD, Poetovio was the largest Roman township in what is now Slovenia, and the centre of the Mithraic cult; several complete temples have been unearthed in the area.

Ptuj received its town rights in 977 and grew rich through river trade. By the 13th century it was competing with the 'upstart' Marburg (Maribor) upriver, in both crafts and commerce. Two monastic orders – the Dominicans and the Franciscan Minorites – settled here and built important monasteries. The Magyars attacked and occupied Ptuj for most of the 15th century.

When the railroad reached eastern Slovenia from Vienna on its way to the coast in the mid-19th century, the age-old rivalry between Maribor and Ptuj turned one-sided: the former was on the line and the latter missed out altogether. The town remained

---

THE HAYRACK: A NATIONAL ICON

Nothing is as Slovenian as the *kozolec*, the hayrack seen almost everywhere in the country. Because the Alpine ground can be damp, wheat and hay are hung from racks, allowing the wind to do the drying faster and more efficiently.

Until the late 19th century, the *kozolec* was just another tool to make a farmer's work easier and the land more productive. But when artist Ivan Grohar made it the centrepiece of many of his Impressionist paintings, the *kozolec* became as much a part of the cultural landscape as the physical one. Today it's virtually a national icon.

There are many different types of Slovenian hayracks: single ones standing alone or 'goat hayracks' with sloped 'lean-to' roofs, parallel and stretched ones and double *toplarji* (hayracks), often with roofs and storage areas on top. Simple hayracks are not unknown in other parts of Alpine Central Europe, but *toplarji*, decorated or plain, are unique to Slovenia.

Hayracks were traditionally made of hardwood (usually oak). Today, however, the hayrack's future is in concrete, and the new stretched ones seem to go on forever.

essentially a provincial centre with a German majority until WWI.

◉ Sights & Activities

Ptuj's Gothic centre, with its Renaissance and baroque additions, can be best viewed on a walking tour.

Minorite Monastery   MONASTERY
(Minoritski Samostan; ☎ 059 073 000; Minoritski trg 1; ☺ by appointment) On the east side of Minoritski trg, with its 17th-century plague pillar, sits the massive Minorite monastery established in the 13th century. Because the Franciscan Minorites dedicated themselves to teaching, the order was not dissolved under the edict issued by Habsburg Emperor Joseph II in the late 18th century, and it has continued to function here for more than seven centuries.

The arcaded baroque structure, which dates from the second half of the 17th century, contains a summer refectory on the 1st floor, with beautiful stucco work and a dozen ceiling paintings of St Peter (north side) and St Paul (south side). It also has a 5000-volume library of important manuscripts.

On the northern side of the inner courtyard, the Church of Sts Peter and Paul (Cerkev Sv Petra in Pavla) is one of the most beautiful examples of early Gothic architecture in Slovenia. Reduced to rubble by Allied bombing in January 1945, it was painstakingly rebuilt over the decades. View fragments of the original church in the side chapel.

Drava Tower   MONUMENT
(Dravski Stolp; Dravska ulica 4) About 150m west of the Minorite Monastery is the circular Drava Tower, a Renaissance water tower built as a defence against the Turks in 1551. It houses the Mihelič Gallery (Miheličeva Galerija; ☎ 02-787 92 50; ☺ 10am-4pm Tue-Fri, to 1pm Sat) `FREE`, which hosts exhibitions of modern art.

Slovenski Trg   SQUARE
Funnel-shaped Slovenski trg is the centre of old Ptuj. In the middle is the 16th-century City Tower (Mestni Stolp). Roman tombstones and sacrificial altars from Poetovio were incorporated into the walls in the 1830s – check the reliefs of Medusa's head, dolphins, a lion and a man on horseback.

In front of the tower stands the 5m-tall Orpheus Monument (Orfejev Spomenik), a

2nd-century Roman tombstone with scenes from the Orpheus myth. Note the holes at the base: it was used as a pillory in the Middle Ages.

On the northern side of the square are several interesting buildings, including the 16th-century Provost's House (Slovenski trg 10), the baroque Old Town Hall (Slovenski trg 6) and Ljutomer House (Slovenski trg 5), now housing the TIC, whose Mediterranean-style loge was built in 1565.

Church of St George   CHURCH
(Cerkev Sv Jurija; Slovenski trg) On the east side of Slovenski trg, this church reveals an array of styles from Romanesque to neo-Gothic. The church contains some lovely late-14th-century choir stalls decorated with animals, a carved relief of the Epiphany dating from 1515 and frescoes in the middle of the south aisle. Here too is the restored Laib Altar, a three-winged altar painting by Konrad Laib completed around 1460. Near the entrance is a carved 14th-century statue of St George slaying the dragon.

Prešernova Ulica   STREET
Pedestrian Prešernova ulica was the town's market in the Middle Ages. The arched spans above some of the narrow side streets support older buildings. The Late Gothic House (Prešernova ulica 1), dating from about 1400, has an unusual projection held up by a Moor's head. Opposite is the sombre Romanesque House (Prešernova ulica 4), the oldest building in Ptuj. The renovated yellow pile called the Little Castle (Mali Grad; Prešernova ulica 33-35) was the home of the Salzburg bishops and various aristocratic families over the centuries.

Ptuj Castle   CASTLE, MUSEUM
(Grad Ptuj; ☎ castle 02-748 03 60, museum 02-787 92 30; http://pmpo.si; Na Gradu 1; adult/child €5/3; ☺ 9am-6pm daily May–mid-Oct, 9am-8pm Sat & Sun Jul & Aug, 9am-5pm daily mid-Oct–Jun) Ptuj castle is an agglomeration of styles from the 14th to the 18th centuries, but is nonetheless a majestic sight, sitting high on the hill overlooking the red-roofed burgher houses of Ptuj and the Drava River. It houses the Ptuj-Ormož Regional Museum but is equally worth the trip for the views of Ptuj and the Drava River. The shortest way to the castle is to follow narrow Grajska ulica, east of the Hotel Mitra, which leads to a covered wooden stairway and the castle's Renaissance Peruzzi Portal (1570).

Ptuj

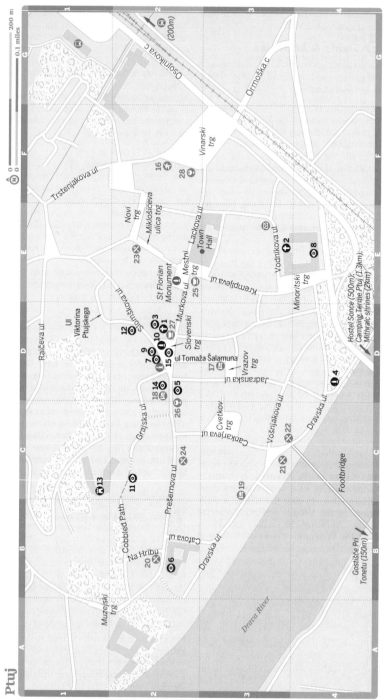

Ptuj

As you enter the castle courtyard, look to the west at the red marble tombstone of Frederick IX, the last lord of Ptuj (who died in 1438). In the former stables just past the ticket office is a large collection of Kurent masks and costumes.

The ground floor of one wing is devoted to an arms collection of some 500 weapons. The suits of armour are particularly fine. Also here is a fascinating musical instruments collection mostly from the 17th to 19th centuries (though there is a Roman double flute from the 2nd or 3rd century AD).

The 1st floor is given over to period rooms – treasure-troves of original tapestries, painted wall canvases, portraits, weapons and furniture mostly left behind by the castle's last owners, the Herbersteins (1873–1945). Notice the coat of arms containing three buckles upon entering the chapel – it belonged to the Leslies, a Scottish-Austrian family who owned the castle from 1656 to 1802. The Chinoiserie Countess's Salon and her rococo bedroom are exquisite.

In Festival Hall you'll find Europe's largest collection of aristocratic Turkerie portraits – some 45 in total – though possibly of more historical rather than artistic interest.

The Castle Gallery on the 2nd floor contains paintings from the 16th to 18th centuries.

Enquire at the museum office if you're interested in visiting Ptuj's unearthed Roman-era Mithraic shrines, dedicated to the sun god Mithras; for a time in the 1st and 2nd centuries AD Mithraism was more widely practised than Christianity. The shrines are located south of the river, a couple of kilometres west of town in suburban Spodnja Hajdina and Zgornji Breg.

Ptujska Klet   WINE TASTING
(Ptuj Wine Cellar; ☑ 02-787 98 10, 041 486 258; www.pullus.si; Vinarski trg 1; tours €7-12; ☉ tours 9am-5pm Mon-Sat) One of the largest and oldest cellars in Slovenia, this is the place to go if you want to learn about local wine, especially Haloze Sauvignon, Chardonnay, Šipon or Laški Rizling, but be sure to book in advance. It also holds Slovenia's oldest vintage: Zlata Trta, the 'Golden Vine' sweet wine dating from 1917. If you can't get on a tour, sample local wines at the attached **Pullus Vinoteka** (☑ 02-787 98 10; Vinarski trg 1; ☉ 9am-5pm Mon-Fri, to 1pm Sat).

✯ Festivals & Events

Kurentovanje   CARNIVAL
(www.kurentovanje.net/en; ☉ Feb) Kurentovanje is a rite of spring celebrated for 10 days in February leading up to Shrove Tuesday; it's the most popular and best-known folklore event in Slovenia.

Days of Poetry & Wine   FESTIVAL
(Dnevi Poezije in Vina; www.versoteque.com; ☉ Aug) This annual festival held in August gathers Slovenian and international poets, writers, storytellers and musicians for readings, concerts and good wine through the summer evenings.

🛏 Sleeping

The TIC (p205) can arrange private rooms (per person €20 to €25) both in the centre and on the south side of the Drava near Terme Ptuj.

Hostel Sonce   HOSTEL €
(☑ 02-788 93 31, 031 361 982; www.hostel-sonce. com; Zagrebška cesta 10; s/d €32/50) This 14-room 'hostel' in a bright-orange building (*sonce* means 'sun') on the south side of the Drava River is really an elegant, budget hotel. The decor is colourful but subdued and the common areas, especially the kitchen and garden terrace, are a delight. The Sonce is just over the footbridge from the centre.

Camping Terme Ptuj   CAMPGROUND €
(☑ 02-749 45 80; www.terme-ptuj.si; Pot v Toplice 9; adult €16-18, child €11-12.50, wine barrels s/d €42/62; ☺ year-round; P @ 🏊) This 1.8-hectare campground next to the thermal spa and water park has 120 sites. Rates include entry to the park and use of pools and other recreational facilities. For something really different, stay in one of the eight oversized (but cosy) wine barrels on the edge of the camping ground.

Gostišče Pri Tonetu   GUESTHOUSE €
(☑ 02-788 56 83, 041 764 407; www.gostisce-svensek.si; Zadružni trg 13; r per person €18; P) This basic guesthouse, with 24 beds in nine rooms and a popular restaurant, is just over the footbridge on the south bank of the Drava. It's clean, comfortable and certainly the right price. Ptuj's thermal baths and the golf course are nearby.

★ DomKulture MuziKafe   HOTEL €€
(☑ 02-787 88 60; www.muzikafe.si; Vrazov trg 1; s €46-62, d €52-85; 🐾) This quirky cracker of a place is tucked away off Jadranska ulica. Everything is bright, with each room idiosyncratically decorated by the hotel's designer owners; we especially love Nos 1 and 7. There's a small kitchen for guests' use, a terrace cafe and courtyard with old cinema chairs, plus a vaulted brick cellar that hosts musical and artistic events.

Šilak B&B   HOTEL €€
(☑ 02-787 74 47, 031 597 361; www.rooms-silak. com; Dravska ulica 13; s €35-48, d €52-64, apt €80-90; P ❄ @ 🐾) This gem of a B&B by the Drava, with 15 rooms and apartments, is in an old tannery that dates back at least to the early 16th century and just oozes character;

some rooms retain their original beams. Breakfast is in the old workshop and apartments have full kitchens.

Hotel Mitra   BOUTIQUE HOTEL €€€
(☑ 02-787 74 55, 051 603 069; www.hotel-mitra.si; Prešernova ulica 6; s €57-92, d €97-112; P ❄ @ 🐾) One of provincial Slovenia's more interesting hotels has 25 generous-sized guest rooms and four humongous suites, each with its own name and story, and specially commissioned paintings on the wall. There are lovely Oriental carpets on the original wooden floors and a wellness centre off an old courtyard cellar. Rooms at the top have mansard ceilings.

🍴 Eating

Pizzerija Slonček   PIZZA €
(☑ 02-776 13 11; Prešernova ulica 19; pizza €5-7; ☺ 9am-10pm Mon-Fri, 10am-11pm Sat, noon-10pm Sun; ☑) The cosy 'Little Elephant', with an interesting marble fountain out front, serves what many think is the best pizza in Ptuj, along with some meatless dishes such as pasta, plus the ubiquitous range of grills. There's a terrace for the warmer months.

Kitajski Vrt   CHINESE €
(☑ 02-776 14 51; Dravska ulica 7; mains €7-11; ☺ 11am-10pm Sun-Thu, to 11pm Fri & Sat) If you need a rice or noodle fix or just a break from traditional Slovenian fare, try the 'Chinese Garden', Ptuj's long-established Chinese restaurant, just opposite the footbridge over the Drava. It has a fair few vegetable dishes on its menu.

★ Gostilna Ribič   SLOVENIAN €€
(☑ 02-749 06 35; Dravska ulica 9; mains €14.50-23; ☺ 10am-11pm Sun-Thu, to midnight Fri & Sat) Arguably the best restaurant in Ptuj, the 'Angler Inn' faces the river, with an enormous terrace, and the speciality here is – not surprisingly – fish, especially trout and pike-perch in their various modes of preparation. The mushroom soup served in a bread-loaf bowl is exceptional. There's live Slovenian music some nights.

Gostilna Amadeus   SLOVENIAN €€
(☑ 02-771 70 51; Prešernova ulica 36; mains €8-18; ☺ noon-10pm Mon & Wed-Sat, to 4pm Sun) This very pleasant *gostilna* (inn-like restaurant) above a pub and near the foot of the road to the castle serves a lot of stick-to-the-ribs Slovenian specialties, such as *štruklji* (dumplings with herbs and cheese, €5) and *ajdova*

KURENT: PARTY TIME IN PTUJ

Ptuj marks Shrovetide with Kurentovanje, a rite of spring and fertility that dates to the time of the early Slavs.

The main character of the rite is Kurent, a Dionysian god of unrestrained pleasure and hedonism. The Kurents (there are many groups of them) are dressed in sheepskins with cowbells dangling from their belts. On their heads they wear huge furry caps decorated with feathers, sticks or horns and coloured streamers. Their leather masks have red eyes, trunk-like noses and enormous tongues hanging down to the chest.

The Kurents process from house to house, scaring off evil spirits with their bells and *ježevke* (wooden clubs) entwined with hedgehog quills. A *hudič* (devil), covered in a net to catch souls, leads each group. Young girls present the Kurents with handkerchiefs, which they then fasten to their belts, and people smash little clay pots at their feet for luck and good health.

Kurentovanje is now an organised carnival and a centrepiece of Ptuj's calendar. Festivities are spread over 11 days, culminating in the Kurent parades on the Saturday and Sunday before Shrove Tuesday, when hundreds of masked and costumed Kurents march through the town. Tens of thousands of spectators visit Ptuj for the parades, so book accommodation well in advance.

kaša z jurčki (buckwheat groats with mushrooms, €7), as well as fish, steak and a preponderance of pork preparations.

Self-Catering

Market `MARKET`
(Novi trg; ☺7am-3pm Mon-Sat) The town's open-air market sells fruit, vegetables and more.

Drinking & Nightlife

Kavarna Kipertz `CAFE`
(☑02-787 74 55; Prešernova ulica 6; ☺8am-11pm Mon-Thu, to midnight Fri-Sun) Named after the very first man in Ptuj to roast coffee beans (in 1786, in fact), this retro-style cafe in the Hotel Mitra attracts Ptuj's boho set with its very own coffee roast and rich desserts.

Kavarna Pod Odrom `CAFE`
(☑02-749 32 50; Murkova ulica 6; ☺7am-11pm Mon-Thu, to 1.30am Fri & Sat, 8am-11.30pm Sun) The 'Under the Stage' cafe is just that – on a sloping street just below the Ptuj City Theatre. It attracts a youngish crowd and is great for a sundowner or a post-theatre drink.

Kavabar Orfej `BAR`
(☑02-772 97 61; Prešernova ulica 5; ☺6.30am-11pm Mon-Thu, to 1am Fri & Sat, 10am-11pm Sun) The Orfej is the anchor tenant of Prešernova ulica and is usually where everyone starts (or ends) the evening. It closes an hour or so later in summer.

Café Evropa `CAFE`
(☑02-771 02 35; Mestni trg 2; ☺7am-10pm Mon-Thu, to midnight Fri, 8am-midnight Sat, 10am-10pm Sun) In the 18th-century Corner House, this is Ptuj's oldest cafe and it still serves the best cakes (€2.50 to €3) in town.

ℹ Information

Nova Ljubljanska Banka (Prešernova ulica 6; ☺8am-5pm Mon-Fri) With an ATM, next door to the Hotel Mitra.

Post Office (Vodnikova ulica 2; ☺8am-6pm Mon-Fri, to noon Sat)

Tourist Information Centre Ptuj (☑02-779 60 11; www.ptuj.info; Slovenski trg 5; ☺9am-8pm May–mid-Oct, to 6pm mid-Oct–Apr) Housed in the 16th-century Ljutomer House.

ℹ Getting There & Around

BUS

Buses to Maribor (€3.60, 45 minutes, 29km) and Ormož (€3.60, 40 minutes, 27km) run frequently, though less so at weekends. One to two buses a day head for Stuttgart (€80, 11½ hours, 720km) via Munich in Germany.

TRAIN

There are plentiful train departures to Ljubljana (€10 to €14.80, two to three hours, 155km) direct or via Zidani Most and Pragersko. Up to a dozen trains go to Maribor (€3.45 to €5.25, 50 minutes, 37km). Up to eight trains a day head for Murska Sobota (€5.80 to €7.60, 1¼ hours, 61km).

TAXI

Book a taxi on ☑031 380 366 or ☑041 514 045.

Around Ptuj

Ptujska Gora

📍 02 / POP 385 / ELEV 337M

👁 Sights

Basilica of the Patroness Mary   BASILICA
(Bazilika Marije Zavetnice; 📞 02-794 42 31; www.
ptujska-gora.si; Ptujska Gora 40; ⊙6am-7pm
year-round) The pilgrimage Basilica of the Patroness Mary, in Ptujska Gora village 14km
southwest of Ptuj, contains one of the most
treasured objects in Slovenia: a 15th-century
carved caped Misericordia of the Virgin
Mary and the Child Jesus. The church itself, built at the start of the 15th century, is
the finest example of a three-nave Gothic
church in Slovenia. It was named a basilica
for its 600th anniversary in 2010.

Among some of the other treasures inside is a small wooden statue of St James
on one of the pillars on the south aisle
and, under the porch and to the right as
you enter, 15th-century frescoes of the life
of Christ and of several saints, including St
Nicholas and St Dorothy with the Child Jesus. Look behind the modern tabernacle in
the chapel to the right of the main altar for
faded frescoes of St Peter and St Michael
the Archangel. The modern stained glass is
exquisite.

MADONNA'S MANTLE

The altar carving above the main altar in
the church at Ptujska Gora, which dates
from 1410, portrays the images of 82
people from all walks of life taking shelter
under Mary's enormous cloak. This is
held aloft by seven angels; another two
are crowning the Virgin. The carving is as
important an historic document as it is a
work of art. Among the lifelike faces looking up to Mary are the Counts of Celje
(Frederick II and the three Hermans).

The protective mantle of the Madon-
na is a not-uncommon motif in Gothic
art. Making use of her large enveloping
cloak, Mary gives shelter to 'outlaws'
and refugees and dispels fear and need
among the faithful of all social classes.
The motif did not evolve into subsequent art styles, and more or less disap-
peared by the 16th century.

The church, perched atop Black Hill
(Črna Gora), is an easy 10-minute walk from
where the bus headed for Majšperk from
Ptuj (up to six a day) will let you off. Drag-
ica is a small bar opposite the church with
snacks and views.

Wine Roads

Ptuj is within easy striking distance of two
important wine-growing areas: the **Haloze**
district and the **Jeruzalem-Ljutomer**
district.

The Haloze Hills extend from Makole,
18km southwest of Ptuj, to Goričak on the
border with Croatia. The footpath taking
in this land of gentle hills, vines, corn and
sunflowers is called the **Haloze Mountain
Path** (Haloška Planinska Pot). It is about
12km and is accessible from near **Štatenberg Manor** (Dvorec Štatenberg; 📞 040 870
835; Štatenberg 89; adult/child €2/1; ⊙visits
by appointment, restaurant noon-7pm Sat & Sun
Jul & Aug, to 6pm Sat & Sun May, Sep & Oct), an
18th-century pile with grand rooms, which
has a bar and restaurant open at weekends
part of the year; the food is just so-so but
the surrounds are spectacular. The manor is
5km outside Makole. The TIC (p205) in Ptuj
will help with maps.

The **Jeruzalem-Ljutomer wine road** begins at Ormož and continues for 18km north
to Ljutomer, the main seat in the area, via the
delightful hilltop village of Jeruzalem. There
are many cellars, small restaurants and pensions along the way where you can sample
the local whites, including at **Taverna Vino
Kupljen** (📞 02-719 41 28; www.vino-kupljen.com;
Svetinje 21; s/d €40/70). For guidance, visit the
Tourist Information Centre Jeruzalem
(📞 02-719 45 45; www.jeruzalem.si; Jeruzalem 8;
⊙9am-7pm Mon-Sat, to 6pm Sun May-Oct, 10am-
5pm Mon-Sat, 11am-4pm Sun Nov-Apr), next door
to the **Dvorec Jeruzalem** (📞 02-741 77 90;
www.dvorec-jeruzalem.com; Jeruzalem 8; s/d/apt
€60/98/140), with a wine cellar, romantic
restaurant and flashy rooms. The TIC rents
bicycles (per hour/day/week €2/10/50) and
distributes the free *Kolesarske in Sprehajalne Poti Ljutomer-Jeruzalem-Ormož* cycling and hiking map.

Maribor

📍 02 / POP 95,880 / ELEV 266M

Despite being the nation's second-largest
city, Maribor has only about a third of the
population of Ljubljana and often feels more

like an overgrown provincial town. It has no unmissable sights but oozes charm thanks to its delightfully patchy Old Town along the Drava River. Pedestrianised central streets buzz with cafes and student life and the riverside Lent district hosts a major summer arts festival. Maribor is the gateway to the Maribor Pohorje, a hilly recreational area to the southwest, and the Mariborske and Slovenske Gorice wine-growing regions to the north and the east.

History

Maribor rose to prominence in the Middle Ages and grew wealthy through the timber and wine trade, financed largely by the town's influential Jewish community. The waterfront landing (Pristan) in the Lent district was one of the busiest river ports in the country. The town was fortified in the 14th century.

Though its fortunes declined in later centuries, the tide turned in 1846 when it became the first town in Slovenia to have train connections with Vienna. Maribor thrived again and began to industrialise.

Air raids during WWII devastated Maribor, and by 1945 two-thirds of the city lay in ruin.

⊙ Sights

Maribor Regional Museum   MUSEUM
(🕿 02-228 35 51; www.pmuzej-mb.si; Grajska ulica 2; adult/child €3/2; ⊙10am-6pm Tue-Sat) Housed inside 15th-century **Maribor Castle**, this museum has one of the richest collections in Slovenia. On the ground floor are archaeological, clothing and ethnographic exhibits, including 19th-century beehive panels with biblical scenes from the Mislinja and Drava Valleys, models of Štajerska-style hayracks, Kurent costumes and wax ex voto offerings from the Ptuj area. Upstairs are rooms devoted to Maribor's history and its guilds and crafts, a fascinating 18th-century pharmacy, and altar paintings and sculptures from the 15th to the 18th centuries.

Taking pride of place are the exquisite statues by Jožef Straub (1712–56) taken from the Church of St Joseph in Studenci. The magnificent rococo staircase near the exit, with its pink walls, stucco work and figures arrayed on the bannisters, is visible from the street when the museum is closed.

Glavni Trg   SQUARE
Maribor's marketplace in the Middle Ages, Glavni trg is just north of the river and the main bridge crossing it. In the centre of the square is Slovenia's most extravagant **plague pillar** (Glavni trg), erected in 1743. Behind it is the **town hall** (Glavni trg 14) built in 1565 by Venetian craftsmen.

Maribor Cathedral   CATHEDRAL
(Stolna Cerkev Maribor; www.stolnicamaribor.si; Slomškov trg) Maribor's cathedral faces the square named after Anton Martin Slomšek (1800–62), the Slovenian bishop and politician beatified in 1999 and the first Slovene to earn such distinction. Parts of the imposing structure date from the 13th century, and it shows elements of virtually every architectural style from Romanesque to modern. Of special interest are the flamboyant Gothic sanctuary and the gilded choir stalls, as well as the lovely modern stained glass and the enormous organ.

Maribor Art Gallery   GALLERY
(Umetnostna Galerija Maribor; 🕿 02-229 58 60; www.ugm.si; Strossmayerjeva ulica 6; adult/child/family €3/2; ⊙10am-6pm Tue-Sun) The Maribor Art Gallery, southwest of Slomškov trg, has a relatively rich collection of modern works by Slovenian artists and excellent changing exhibits.

National Liberation Museum   MUSEUM
(Muzej Narodne Osvoboditve; 🕿 02-235 26 00; www.muzejno-mb.si; Ulica Heroja Tomšiča 5; adult/child €2/1.50; ⊙8am-5pm Mon-Fri, 9am-noon Sat) Housed in a stunning 19th-century mansion, the collections here document Slovenia's struggle for freedom throughout the 20th century, with particular emphasis on the work of the Pohorje Partisans during the Nazi occupation. Riveting.

City Park   PARK
City Park (Mestni Park) is a lovely arboretum with 150 species of trees and three ponds. Here you'll find the small but diverting **Maribor Aquarium-Terrarium** (Akvarij-Terarij Maribor; 🕿 02-234 26 80; http://maribor-pohorje.si/aquarium-terrarium; Ulica Heroja Staneta 19; adult/child €4/3.20; ⊙8am-7pm Mon-Fri, 9am-noon & 2-7pm Sat & Sun), with its diverse collection of fresh- and salt-water critters, reptiles and other exotic creepy crawlies. To the northeast is **Piramida** (386m), where the titans of Marchburg once held sway. Here you'll find an archaeological site and a chapel.

Maribor

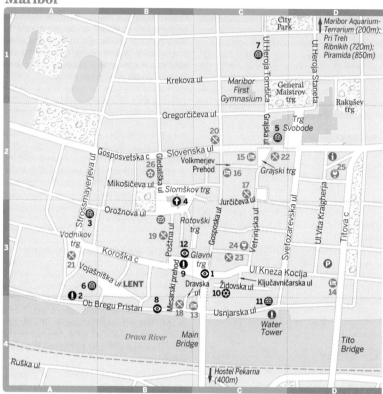

Maribor

Old Vine — LANDMARK

(Stara Trta; Vojašniška ulica 8) About 150m east along the Pristan embankment is Maribor's most celebrated attraction, the so-called Old Vine, which is still producing between 35kg and 55kg of grapes and about 25L of red wine per year after being planted more than four centuries ago. It is tended by a city-appointed viticulturist, and the dark-red Žametna Črnina (Black Velvet) is distributed to visiting dignitaries as 'keys' to Maribor in the form of 0.25L bottles.

Learn more about it and Slovenian viti-culture at the adjacent Old Vine House (Hiša Stare Trta; ☑ 02-251 51 00; http://maribor-pohorje.si; Vojašniška ulica 8; wine tasting €4; ⊙10am-6pm Tue-Sun) **FREE**, where you can taste local wine from its enormous collection. And don't miss the lovely new floor mosaic tracing Maribor's history.

Synagogue — SYNAGOGUE

(☑02-252 78 36; Židovska ulica 4; admission €1; ⊙8am-4pm Mon-Fri) Just north of the pentagonal 16th-century Water Tower on the waterfront, a set of steps leads up to Židovska ulica (Jewish St), the centre of the Jewish district in the Middle Ages, and home to this 15th-century synagogue. It contains Gothic key stones and tomb fragments; the special exhibitions and 15-minute video are enlightening.

Tower Photo Gallery — GALLERY

(Fotogalerija Stolp; ☑02-620 97 13; www.galerijastolp.si; ⊙10am-2pm Tue-Fri, to 1pm Sat) Housed in the Jewish Tower (1465), this gallery has sporadic exhibits of photographs, both Slovenian and foreign.

👁 Lent

The waterfront Lent district contains some of the most important and interesting historical sights in Maribor, including an ancient grape vine.

Minorite Monastery — GALLERY

(Vojašniški ulica 2a) At the western end of the riverfront Pristan is the renovated 13th-century Minorite Monastery, closed by Joseph II in 1784, later used as a military barracks until 1927, and now reborn as the Maribor Puppet Theatre.

Judgement Tower — TOWER

(Ob Bregu Pristan) To the south of the former Minorite monastery along the riverfront, the round Judgement Tower is the first of four defence towers still standing, with curious friezes on the south side.

🎉 Festivals & Events

Maribor hosts a lot of events throughout the year.

Lent Festival — CULTURAL

(www.festival-lent.si; ⊙Jun-Jul) The biggest event on the city's calendar, the Lent Festival is a two-week celebration of folklore, culture and music from late June into July, when stages are set up throughout the Old Town.

Festival Maribor — MUSIC

(www.festivalmaribor.si; ⊙Sep) A 10-day extravaganza of music concerts held in venues across town in September.

Harvesting of the Old Vine — WINE

(http://maribor-pohorje.si; ⊙Oct) Among the most colourful ceremonies in Maribor is the harvesting of the Old Vine for wine in early October.

🛏 Sleeping

The TIC (p212) can organise private rooms (from €25/40 for singles/doubles) and apartments.

Uni Youth Hostel HOSTEL €
(📱 02-250 67 00; www.hotel-orel.si; Volkmerjev prehod 7; HI member/nonmember s €29/33, d €48/54; @) This very central, almost luxurious 53-room 'residence hotel' affiliated with Hostelling International is run by, and attached to, the Orel Hotel (p210), where you'll find reception. Home to students during the academic year, it lets out beds in singles and doubles to visitors during holidays.

★Hostel Pekarna HOSTEL €€
(📱 059 180 880; www.mkc-hostelpekarna.si; Ob Železnici 16; dm/s/d €21/30/54; P 🛜) Part of Maribor's Pekarna alternative cultural centre, this bright and welcoming hostel south of the river is housed in a converted army bakery (*pekarna* is 'bakery' in Slovene). Accommodation is mostly in seven rooms with four beds, but there is also private apartments with kitchens. Facilities, including the great balcony and cosy TV room, are up to the minute.

Hotel Lent HOTEL €€
(📱 02-250 67 69, 059 177 700; www.hotel-lent.si; Dravska ulica 9; s/d €49/69; ❄ 🛜) Chaotically run but enviably located on the river in Lent, this caravansary has 17 well-turned-out and comfortable rooms, though they are a bit cosy. There's a lovely cafe out front.

Orel Hotel HOTEL €€€
(📱 02-250 67 00; www.hotel-orel.si; Volkmerjev prehod 7; s/d/ste €72/105/200; P ❄ @ 🛜) Shiny, pretty and dressed to impress, Maribor's most central hotel has 71 rooms and the price includes entry to the Fontana Terme Maribor. Rooms are sleek and modern but ask for a back room: the front ones face a busy street.

Maribor City Hotel BUSINESS HOTEL €€€
(📱 02-621 25 00; www.cityhotel-mb.si; Ulica Kneza Koclja 22; s €125, d €135-200, ste €250; P ⊕ ❄ 🛜) Maribor's newest hotel, a business destination with 78 rooms and suites done up in chocolates and beiges and oatmeals, wouldn't look out of place in any larger provincial Euro city. But its rooftop terrace restaurant and cafe with fabulous views of the Drava and Pohorje to the south is the wild card in the deck.

Rent electric bicycles from reception for €5/17/25 per hour/four hours/day.

🍴 Eating

Isabella Food & Wine CAFE €
(📱 059 959 450; Poštna ulica 3; dishes €2.80-6.50; ⏰ 8am-midnight Mon-Thu, 9am-2am Fri & Sat, to midnight Sun) This pint-sized eatery on Maribor's liveliest street is a great place for a panini or a salad, though they also do more complex dishes like couscous with chicken. Decent selection of craft beers, including Bevog and Pelicon.

Malca SLOVENIAN €
(📱 059 100 397; www.malcamimogrede.si; Slovenska ulica 4; dishes €4.90-6.60; ⏰ 8am-4.30pm Mon-Fri) This little place with the bankers' hours serves some of the freshest dishes based on seasonal ingredients in town. Dishes are mostly Slovenian, such as *žlikrofi* (ravioli of potato, onion and spiced pork), or savoury dumplings in butter sauce, though they occasionally move toward pastas. Throwing in a salad and a glass of wine won't add more than €2 to the total.

Gril Ranca BALKAN €
(📱 02-252 55 50; www.ranca.si; Dravska ulica 10; dishes €5-7.70; ⏰ 8am-11pm Mon-Sat, noon-11pm Sun) This unpretentious little place in Lent, with its lovely open terrace and full views of the Drava River, serves simple but scrumptious Balkan grills such as *čevapčiči* (spicy meatballs of beef or pork) and *pleskavica* (meat patties). Eat them stuffed into *lepenja,* a flat eastern Mediterranean bread.

Ancora PIZZA €
(📱 02-250 20 33; www.ancora-mb.si; Jurčičeva ulica 7; pizza €6.60-9; ⏰ 7.30am-midnight Sun-Thu, to 1am Fri & Sat) This enormous restaurant and pizzeria just south of Grajski trg pulls in punters with its fast service, low prices and wood-fired stoves.

★Restavracija Mak FUSION €€
(📱 02-620 00 53; www.restavracija-mak.si; Osojnikova ulica 20; mains €17-24, set lunch/dinner from €25/45; ⏰ noon-3pm & 6-9.30pm Tue-Sat) A meal at this unprepossessing restaurant in Obrežje across the Drava River is not just a night out but an event. Forget à la carte and opt for a set dinner, chosen and prepared by owner-chef David Vračko. From amuses-gueule to bite-sized multiple courses to

desserts undreamt of on high, you won't be disappointed.

Pri Florjanu
MEDITERRANEAN €€

(☑ 059 084 850; www.priflorjanu.si; Grajski trg 6; mains €10-22; ☺ 11am-10pm Mon-Thu, to 11pm Fri, noon-11pm Sat; ☑) A great spot in full view of the Column of St Florian, patron of firefighters, this very stylish place has both an open front and an enclosed back terrace and a huge minimalist restaurant in between. It serves rather inspired Mediterranean food, with a good supply of vegetarian options, as well as great coffee and cakes.

Gostilna Pri Treh Ribnikih
SLOVENIAN €€

(☑ 02-234 41 70; www.trijeribniki.si; Ribniška ulica 9; mains €12-20; ☺ 10am-10pm Mon-Sat, to 9pm Sun Apr-Sep) A great place for a meal if you want to get out of the city but don't feel like travelling is 'At the Three Fishponds' in City Park. Along with a handful of fish dishes, you'll find such specialities as cheese *štruklji* (dumplings) and stuffed pork ribs. There's a decent wine list too.

Rožmarin
INTERNATIONAL €€

(☑ 02-234 31 80; www.rozmarin.si; Gosposka ulica 8; mains €13-21; ☺ 7am-midnight Mon-Sat) Anchor tenant in central Maribor for several years now, this stylish place is all things to all men (and women): a restaurant, a cafe, a *vinoteka*, a shop. The steaks are a cut above but the best deals going are the pre- or post-theatre two-/three-course set menus for €18/24. The decor, with its sleek modern design and unusual lighting, has set new standards for 21st-century Maribor. Enjoy.

Self-Catering

Market
MARKET

(Vodnikov trg; ☺ 6.30am-3pm Mon-Sat) There's a market selling produce just north of the Judgement Tower on the Drava.

🍺 Drinking & Nightlife

⭐ Luft Kavica & Zabavica
BAR

(☑ 040 413 514; www.luftbar.si; Ulica Vita Kraigherja 3; ☺ 8am-midnight Mon-Fri, 9am-4am Fri & Sat, 10am-10pm Sun) Always suckers for views and recycling, we love that the old Slavija Hotel is now an office building with its own two-level rooftop cafe-bar. Head for floor 11 and you'll be amazed; go one floor up to the open terrace and you'll be bowled over by the sweeping views of the city and mountains. Service is deft and friendly, cocktails out of this world.

Čajek Cafe
TEAHOUSE

(www.cajek.com; Slovenska ulica 4; ☺ 7.30am-10pm Mon-Fri, 9am-10pm Sat, 3-9pm Sun) Lovely new addition to the Maribor cafe scene, this charming little teahouse attracts students and other readers for its friendly service, great tea selection and housemade cakes.

Cantante Café
BAR

(☑ 040 304 050; Vetrinjska ulica 5; ☺ 8am-midnight Mon-Thu, to 2am Fri, 9am-2am Sat, noon-midnight Sun) This popular place with its Cuban-ish feel does Mexican and Latin American dishes, but we come here for the mojitos and 149 other cocktails on its extensive drinks list.

Gledališka Kavarna
CAFE

(☑ 02-252 37 20; www.gledaliska-kavarna.com; Slovenska ulica 27; ☺ 9am-11pm Mon-Thu, to midnight Fri, 10am-1pm Sat) The very upmarket Theatre Cafe, next to the Slovenian National Theatre (enter from Slomškov trg), attracts a classy crowd both before and after performances. They do great cakes.

⭐ Entertainment

Slovenian National Theatre Maribor
THEATRE

(Slovensko Narodno Gledališče Maribor; ☑ 02-250 61 00, box office 02-250 61 15; www.sng-mb.si; Slovenska ulica 27; ☺ 10am-1pm & 5-7.30pm Mon-Fri, 10am-1pm Sat & 1hr before performance) This branch of the SNG in Ljubljana has one of the best reputations in the country, and its productions have received critical acclaim throughout Europe. The city's ballet and opera companies also perform here. Enter from Slomškov trg.

Jazz Klub Satchmo
JAZZ

(☑ 070 878 387; www.jazz-klub.si; Strossmayerjeva ulica 6; ☺ 7pm-3am Tue-Thu, 7pm-4am Fri, 8pm-4am Sat) Maribor's celebrated jazz club meets in a wonderful cellar in the art gallery building.

ℹ Information

Abanka (Glavni trg 18; ☺ 8am-5pm Mon-Fri, to 11am Sat) In the mall at the eastern end of Glavni trg.

Maribor City Card (www.mariborcitycard.si; 24/48/72hr €7/11/13) Almost unlimited entry to Maribor's attractions and transport.

Mladinska Knjiga (☑ 02-234 31 13; Gosposka ulica 24; ☺ 8am-7pm Mon-Fri, 9am-1pm Sat) Bookshop, selling Lonely Planet guides as well as maps.

Post Office (Slomškov trg 10; ☺8am-6pm Mon-Fri, to noon Sat)

Tourist Information Centre Maribor (☑02-234 66 11; www.maribor-pohorje.si; Partizanska cesta 6a; ☺9am-7pm Mon-Fri, to 5pm Sat & Sun) Helpful TIC in large kiosk opposite Franciscan church.

❶ Getting There & Away

AIR

Adria Airways flies between Maribor and Southend on Sea in Essex in the UK three times a week (June to October, two hours). Maribor's Edvard Rusjan Airport is 10km south of the city.

BUS

You can reach virtually any town in Slovenia (and certain international destinations) from Maribor's huge **bus station** (Partizanska cesta).

Bus services are frequent to Celje (€6.70, 1½ hours, 65km), Murska Sobota (€6.30, 1¼ hours, 59km), Ptuj (€3.60, 45 minutes, 29km) and Ljubljana (€12.40, three hours, 140km). Other destinations include Rogaška Slatina (€7.20, 1½ hours, 75km) via Slovenska Bistrica and Slovenj Gradec (€7.20, two hours, 74km).

There's a daily bus to Sarajevo (€45, nine hours) at 9.35pm (8.35pm on Friday), as well as Munich (€48, six hours) and Vienna (€23, 3½ hours).

TRAIN

From Ljubljana there is the ICS express service (€14.85, two hours, 156km), or more frequent slower trains (€9.50, 2½ hours). Both stop at Celje. Eastbound, services run to Murska Sobota (€9, two hours, 98km).

International connections include Zagreb (€21, three hours, 119km), Vienna (€53.20, 3½ hours, 257km) and Belgrade (€59.40, 8½ hours, 518km).

❶ Getting Around

Maribor and its surrounds are well served by local buses. They depart from the stands south of the train station near Meljska cesta.

Maribor Bike (☑02-234 66 11; per 3hr/1 day €5/10; ☺8am-8pm Apr-Oct) has bicycles available from outside the TIC. Electric bicycles are available from the **Maribor City Hotel** (p210).

For a local taxi, ring ☑02-251 71 51 or ☑031 325 725.

Maribor Pohorje

☑02 / ELEV UP TO 1347M

Maribor's green lung and central playground, the eastern edge of the Pohorje Massif is known in these parts as the Maribor Pohorje (Mariborsko Pohorje). It's in easy reach of the city and has countless activities on offer – from skiing and hiking, to horse riding and mountain biking.

🏃 Activities

Walking

There are heaps of easy walks and more difficult hikes in every direction from the upper ski station atop Žigartov Vrh (1347m). Following a stretch of the marked Slovenian Mountain Trail, which originates in Maribor and goes as far as Ankaran on the coast, first west and then southwest for 5km, will take you to the two Šumik waterfalls and Pragozd, one of the very few virgin forests left in Europe.

Another 6km to the southwest is Black Lake (Črno Jezero), the source of the swift-running Lobnica River, and Osankarica, where the Pohorje battalion of Partisans was wiped out by the Germans in January 1943. PZS produces a 1:50,000-scale Pojorje map (€8.10) while Kartografija's is 1:40,000-scale and costs €12.

Biking

Cycling is an ideal way to explore the back roads and trails of the Maribor Pohorje. The TIC offers the 1:100,000 Pohorje Cycling Map and the simple but useful Kolesarske Poti na Mariborskem Pohorju (Cycle Trails in the Maribor Pohorje). The sport centre rents GT DHI Pro mountain bikes from the lower cable-car station (€40/50 per four hours/day).

Skiing

Maribor Pohorje Ski Grounds　　SKIING

(☑02-603 65 53; www.mariborskopohorje.si; day pass adult/child/student & senior €31/17/26; ☺7am-7pm) Maribor Pohorje ski grounds stretch from the Hotel Habakuk (336m) near the lower cable-car station to Žigartov Vrh (1347m). With 42km of slopes, 27km of cross-country runs and 22 ski lifts, tows and gondola, this is Slovenia's largest ski area. Ski equipment rentals are available from the upper cable-car station, and there's a ski and snowboarding school as well.

🎊 Festivals & Events

Women's World Cup Slalom & Giant Slalom Competition　　SPORTS

(☺Jan/Feb) The annual Women's World Cup Slalom and Giant Slalom Competition – the coveted Zlata Lisica (Golden Fox; www. goldenfox.org) trophy – takes place on the main piste of the Maribor Pohorje ski grounds for four days in late January/early February.

🛏 Sleeping & Eating

There are plenty of places to stay in the Maribor Pohorje, including more than a dozen mountain lodges and holiday homes; ask at the Maribor TIC (p212) for a list and basic map. Places close to main roads are the Category III **Ruška Koča pri Arehu** (🖉 02-603 50 46, 041 666 552; www.ruskakoca. si; ⊙ year-round) with 36 beds at 1246m and the more swish Category III **Poštarski Dom pod Plešivcem** (🖉 02-822 10 55; ⊙ Wed-Mon) with 47 beds at 805m.

Camping Centre Kekec (🖉 040 225 386; www.cck.si; Pohorska ulica 35; adult/child €9.50/6), with three-dozen pitches, is at the foothills of the Maribor Pohorje near the cable car's lower station.

Almost everyone takes their meals in their hotels in the Maribor Pohorje; there are no independent restaurants except for snack bars. Be on the lookout for dishes and drinks that are unique to the region, including *pohorski pisker* (Pohorje pot), a kind of goulash, and *pohorska omleta,* a pancake filled with cranberries and topped with cream.

Hotel Bellevue   HOTEL €€
(🖉 02-607 51 00, 031 691 554; www.hotelbellevue. si; Na Slemenu 35; s/d from €80/90; 🅿 @ 🛜) A Pohorje landmark, this very stylish place with 50 rooms and apartments within tumbling distance of the upper cable-car station is simply the poshest place in the region. Rates include entry to the hotel's fine wellness centre.

Hotel Bolfenk   HOTEL €€
(🖉 02-603 55 00; www.hotel-bolfenk.si; Hočko Pohorje 131; s/d from €80/90; 🅿 @) This well-maintained property next to Hotel Bellevue is an apartment hotel with 20 rooms, some of which are quite grand with living rooms and fireplaces.

Hotel Zarja   HOTEL €€
(🖉 02-603 60 00; www.hotelzarja.si; Frajhajm 34; s €39-44, d €66-80; 🅿 @ 🛜) Just east of the ski fields and upper cable-car station, the chalet-like Zarja has 24 comfortable and airy rooms with wooden floors, a restaurant and a sauna.

ℹ Getting There & Away

To reach the lower station from the train station in Maribor take local bus 6 (€1.10, 20 minutes) and get off at the terminus – the cable-car station is just behind the bus stop.

An easy – and exhilarating – way to get to the Hotel Bellevue and the heart of the Maribor Pohorje is to take the **cable car** (vzpenjača; 🖉 041 959 795; www.mariborskopohorje.si; one-way return €4/6) from the station in Zgornje Radvanje, 6km southwest of Maribor's Old Town. There are clamps on the outside of each of the cable car's cabins for mountain bikes and skis.

On weekdays the cable car runs every hour from 7am to 7pm Monday to Thursday and 7am to 10pm Friday to Sunday. Between 10am and 4pm on Saturday and Sunday the cable car runs continuously. The service is more frequent in winter.

You can drive or, if ambitious, cycle the 20km from the Old Town in Maribor south past the Renaissance-style Betnava Castle, turning west at Spodnje Hoče before reaching a fork in the road at a small waterfall. A right turn and less than 4km brings you to the upper cable-car station. Go left and you'll reach the upper station of the ski lift after about 5km.

Central Pohorje Region

🖉 03 / ELEV 1517M
Travellers can easily sample Pohorje's recreational offerings along its eastern edge from Maribor and its western fringes from Slovenj Gradec and Dravograd in Koroška. But the pear-shaped massif's highest and most beautiful area is in the centre. And although it's true that the Pohorje peaks can't exactly compete with those of the Julian and the Kamnik-Savinja Alps – most barely clear the 1500m mark here – hiking and trekking in the winter here is as good as it is in the summer.

Zreče, some 40km southwest of Maribor, is the springboard for the central Pohorje region; indeed, the region is also known as the Zreče Pohorje (Zreško Pohorje). Although certainly not Slovenia's most attractive town – it's dominated by the tool-manufacturing company Unior – Zreče has a modest spa and is within easy striking distance of the ski and sport centre around **Rogla** (1517m), 16km to the north, where teams – including the Slovenian Olympic one – train.

🏃 Activities

Hiking & Mountain Biking

Kartografija's 1:40,000 *Pohorje* (€12) map outlines various circular hiking trails that are as short as 2km (30 minutes) and as long as 32km (eight hours). It covers the Šumik waterfalls, Black Lake and Osankarica. Another good one is the 12km hike (three hours) that leads northwest to the **Lovrenc Lakes** (Lovrenska Jezera), a turf swamp with 20 small lakes that are considered a natural phenomenon. The free *Rogla-Zreče Karta Pohodnih Poti* hiking map has 14 hikes and walks of between 3km and 33.5km.

Mountain bikers should get hold of a copy of the excellent free 1:100,000 *Pohorje Cycling Map,* with a dozen trails outlined from Maribor in the east to Slovenj Gradec and Dravograd in the west. The spa's map/brochure (1:50,000) called *Rogla Terme Radfahrwege/Cycling Paths* is much more basic with nine trails linking Zreče, Rogla and Areh.

Rogla Cycling & Hiking Centre   HIKING
(Kolesarsko in Pohodriško Center; ☑ 03-757 74 68; www.rogla.eu; Rogla; hard-tail mountain bikes 1hr/half-day/day €8/15/18, full suspension €10/20/24; ⊘ 9am-7pm Thu-Sun Jun & Jul, 9am-7pm daily Aug–mid-Sep) The Rogla Cycling & Hiking Centre organises guided walks in season (per person from €12) and rents mountain bikes and other equipment.

Skiing

Rogla Ski Grounds   SKIING
(☑ 03-757 61 55, 03-757 64 40; www.rogla.eu; day pass adult/child/senior & student €31/17/27; ⊘ 9am-4pm daily & 5-9pm Thu-Sun) The Rogla ski grounds has 13km of ski slopes (mostly easy and intermediate) and 21km of cross-country trails served by two chairlifts and 11 tows. The season is a relatively long one – from the end of November to as late as April.

Rogla Ski School   SKIING
(Smučarska Šola Rogla; ☑ 03-757 74 68; www.rogla. eu; ⊘ 8.30am-4pm daily in season) Based in a little wooden cabin at the base of the ski lift, Rogla Ski School can help you learn to ski and snowboard.

Intersport Rent & Ski Servis   SKIING
(☑ 03-757 74 89; Planja Hotel, Rogla; skis per day adult/child €21/16; ⊘ 8.30am-4.45pm, to 9pm winter) You can rent equipment from the Ski Servis office at the Planja Hotel.

Thermal Spa

Terme Zreče   SPA
(☑ 03-757 61 56; www.terme-zrece.eu; Cesta na Roglo 15; swimming pools adult/child 3hr Mon-Fri €8.50/6.50, Sat & Sun €9.50/8.50, all day Mon-Fri €1/8, Sat & Sun €13/9.50, pools & Sauna Village weekday/weekend €17/19; ⊘ swimming pools 9am-9pm, Sauna Village 11am-9pm Mon-Thu, 10am-9pm Fri-Sun) While Terme Zreče is a serious treatment centre for post-operative therapy and locomotor disorders (especially those involving sports injuries), it is also a place where you can simply have fun. Along with an indoor thermal pool (the water temperature is around 35°C), there are large covered recreational and outdoor swimming pools covering an area of 1600 sq metres.

The attached Sauna Village has the usual array of saunas, jacuzzis and steam rooms.

🛏 Sleeping

The central Pohorje region abounds in farmhouses with rooms and apartments for rent, particularly along Cesta Kmečnega near Resnik, about 7km southwest of Rogla. There are even more farmhouses accepting guests in Skomarje to the southwest. Enquire at the TIC (p215) in Zreče for more information.

Pačnik Farmhouse   FARMSTAY €
(☑ 03-576 22 02; Resnik 21; per person €28; 🅿) One of the best central Pohorje farmstay options, Pačnik farmhouse has four rooms and two apartments. Rooms are comfortable, with lovely views over the mountains. And the food is delicious, prepared with home-grown produce and locally sourced meat and dairy products. It's near Resnik, around 7km southwest of Rogla.

Garni Hotel Zvon   PENSION €€
(☑ 03-757 36 00; www.garnihotelzvon.si; Slomškova ulica 2, Zreče; s €52-60, d €86-100; 🅿 ❋ @) There's no particular reason to stay down in Zreče; all the fun is up in Rogla, especially in winter. But if you're a serious disciple of all things thermal, the pension-like 'Bell' is just opposite the entrance to the spa and has 15 spotless rooms and apartments.

Terme Zreče Villas   VILLA €€
(☑ 03-757 60 00; www.terme-zrece.eu; Cesta na Roglo 15, Zreče; s/d €65/84; 🅿 ❋ 🛜 🏊) Of the spa's several properties in Zreče, accommodation in these villas in a small wooded area 150m from the main spa building is the cheapest. There are 40 apartments and an

equal number of double rooms. The villas are fairly bare-boned but clean and comfortable and set apart on their own.

Atrij Hotel
HOTEL €€€

(☑03-757 60 00; www.terme-zrece.eu; Cesta na Roglo 15, Zreče; s/d €108/188; [P][❄][@][🛜][≋]) Of Terme Zreče's three flashy hotels, the four-star Atrij at the entrance is the flagship, with 45 spacious and well-designed rooms and a comprehensive wellness centre. Several rooms are adapted for guests with disabilities. Make sure you get one of the rooms with a balcony. Includes entry to thermal pools.

Planja Hotel
HOTEL €€€

(☑03-757 71 00; www.terme-zrece.eu; Rogla; Planja s/d from €67/110, Rogla s/d from €55/90; [P][@][🛜][≋]) The poshest place in Rogla is Terme Zreče's 16-room new build called the **Natura** but we still prefer this four-star, 30-room property near the ski lift and whatever might be going on in Rogla. It also has a three-star wing called the **Rogla Hotel**, with 88 rooms that can be brighter and more attractive than those in the main hotel.

🍴 Eating

Koča na Pesku
SLOVENIAN €

(☑03-757 71 67; www.planinske-koce.si/koca_na_pesku; Rogla; dishes €4.50-12.50; ☉7am-9pm Apr-Oct, 8am-5pm Nov-Mar) This mountain lodge (per person half-board €28), 3km north of Rogla on the unsealed road to Koroška, is a popular place for hearty Slovenian fare, especially its celebrated mushroom soup with buckwheat groats (*gobova kremna juha z ajdovimi žganci;* €5) and *pohorski lonec* (Pohorje pot; €5.50), a kind of goulash.

Pizzerija Planja
PIZZA €

(☑03-757 72 50; Rogla; pizza €5.50-7; ☉9am-5pm) Along with pizza, this place – just north of the Planja Hotel in Rogla and near the ski lift – does breakfasts and some Slovenian dishes.

Gostilna Jurček
SLOVENIAN €

(☑041 686 725; Cesta na Roglo 4b, Zreče; mains €6-13; ☉7am-10pm Mon-Fri, to 11pm Sat, 9am-10pm Sun) This *gostilna* in Zreče, on the main road to Rogla and opposite the PTC shopping centre, is a convenient place for a quick meal. Expect hearty, rib-lining Slovenian fare. Comfortable seating in a covered terrace, too.

Stara Koča
SLOVENIAN €€

(☑03-757 74 47; Rogla; set lunch €13; ☉7am-midnight) The Old Hut is the main restaurant – and the original structure – at the Planja Hotel. It retains its rustic mountain-hut vibe and serves hearty Slovenian fare.

❶ Information

Post Office (Cesta na Roglo 11, Zreče; ☉8am-6pm Mon-Fri, to noon Sat) To the southeast of the bank.

Tourist Information Centre Rogla-Zreče (TIC; ☑03-759 04 70; www.destinacija-rogla.si; Cesta na Roglo 11j, Zreče; ☉8am-4pm Mon-Fri, 9am-noon Sat, to 11am Sun) In the PTC shopping centre. They have a complete listing of farmstays in the area.

❶ Getting There & Away

There are regular connections from Zreče to Celje (€3.60, 45 minutes, 26km) via Slovenske Konjice. In winter two buses a day from Celje and a couple from Slovenske Konjice stop at Zreče and then carry on to Rogla. Local buses make the runs from Zreče bus station to Rogla.

In winter there are special ski buses from Zreče (five in each direction), as well as Celje and Slovenske Konjice. At that time **Terme Zreče** (p214) runs buses hourly from 6am to 8.30pm or 9pm up to Rogla for its guests. During the rest of the year there is a bus up at 6am and a return at 10pm only.

KOROŠKA

The truncated province of Koroška is essentially just three valleys bounded by the Pohorje Massif on the east; the last of the Karavanke peaks, Mt Peca, on the west; and the hills of Kobansko to the north. The Drava Valley runs east to west and includes the towns of Dravograd, Muta and Vuzenica. The Mežica and Mislinja valleys fan out from the Drava; the former is an industrial area with such towns as Ravne na Koroškem, Prevalje and Črna na Koroškem, while the latter's main centre is Slovenj Gradec.

There is a reason Koroška is so small. In the plebiscite ordered by the victorious allies after WWI, Slovenes living on the other side of the Karavanke, the 120-km-long rock wall that separates Slovenia from Austria, voted to put their economic future in the hands of Vienna while the mining region of the Mežica Valley went to Slovenia. As a result, the Slovenian nation lost 90,000 of its nationals (7% of the population at the time) as well as the cities of Klagenfurt (Celovec) and Villach (Beljak) to Austria.

Understandably, the results of that vote have never sat very well with the Slovenes on the southern side of the mountains. Still, Koroška holds a special place in the hearts and minds of most Slovenes. The Duchy of Carantania (Karantanija), the first Slavic state dating back to the 7th century, was centred here, and the word 'Carinthia' is derived from that name.

Slovenj Gradec & Around

02 / POP 7475 / ELEV 405M

Slovenj Gradec isn't the 'capital' of Koroška – that distinction goes to the industrial centre of Ravne na Koroškem to the northwest – but it is certainly the province's cultural and recreational heart. A large number of museums, galleries and historical churches line its main square, while the sporting opportunities in the Pohorje Massif to the east are many.

Slovenj Gradec's main street is Glavni trg, a colourful long 'square' lined with old townhouses and shops.

History

The history of Slovenj Gradec is closely tied to Stari Trg, a suburb southwest of the Old Town where there was a Roman settlement called Colatio that existed from the 1st to the 3rd centuries (though there is no trace of it now). At that time an important Roman road from Celeia (Celje) to Virunum (near Klagenfurt in Austria) passed through Colatio. Slovenj Gradec was an important trade centre in the Middle Ages and minted its own coins. Later it became an important cultural and artistic centre with many artisans and craft guilds. Among the prominent Habsburg nobles based in Slovenj Gradec over the centuries were members of the Windisch-Grätz family, a variant of the German name for the town (Windisch Graz).

◉ Sights

Koroška Regional Museum   MUSEUM
(Koroški Pokrajinski Muzej; ☑ 02-884 20 55; www. kpm.si; ground & 2nd fl, Glavni trg 24; adult/child/ family €2.50/1.70; ⊙10am-6pm Tue-Fri, 10am-1pm & 2-5pm Sat & Sun) This museum on two floors of the former town hall has several permanent collections, including a large number of ethnological items relating the history of Slovenj Gradec and the Koroška region,

from painted beehive panels to models of wartime hospital rooms and schools run by Partisans; African folk art brought here by Slovenian doctor Franc Tretjak (1914–2009) in the 1950s and '60s; and items amassed by Jakob Soklič (1893–1972), a priest who began squirreling away bits and bobs in the 1930s.

The Soklič Collection on the 2nd floor is a real hotchpotch, including mediocre watercolours and oils of peasant idylls and the umpteen portraits of composer Hugo Wolf (born at Glavni trg 38 in 1860), green goblets and beakers from nearby Glažuta (an important glass-manufacturing town in the 19th century), local embroidery, religious artefacts and some 18th-century furniture. Tretjak's African photographs are exhibited in five of the old town hall's jail cells on the ground floor.

**Koroška Gallery
of Fine Arts**   GALLERY
(Koroška Galerija Likovnih Umetnosti; ☑ 02-882 21 31; www.glu-sg.si; 1st fl, Glavni trg 24; adult/ child €2.50/1; ⊙10am-6pm Tue-Fri, 10am-1pm & 2-5pm Sat & Sun) The Koroška Gallery of Fine Arts, on the first floor of the former town hall, counts among its permanent collection bronze sculptures by Franc Berneker (1874– 1932) and naive paintings by Jože Tisnikar (1928–98). Tisnikar is among the most interesting and original artists in Slovenia, and his obsession with corpses, distorted figures and oversized insects is at once disturbing and funny. Check out *Birth and Death, Crows under the Cross* and the amusing *Bare Feet.*

Outside the town hall is the **Venetian Horse**, a life-size work by contemporary sculptor/designer Oskar Kogoj, and now something of a symbol for Slovenj Gradec.

Church of St Elizabeth   CHURCH
(Cerkev Sv Elizabete; Trg Svobode) The sombre Church of St Elizabeth, with a 50m-tall belfry, was built in 1251 and is the town's oldest structure. Aside from the Romanesque nave and a couple of windows, almost everything here is baroque, including the massive (and impressive) gold altar and pulpit, and the altar paintings done by local artist Franc Mihael Strauss (1647–1740) and his son Janez Andrej Strauss (1721–83).

Church of the Holy Spirit   CHURCH
(Cerkev Sv Duha; Trg Svobode) The Church of the Holy Spirit (1494), once the chapel of the town hospital, has an interior covered with Gothic frescoes by Andrej of Otting.

The 27 panels on the north wall represent the Passion of Christ; the scenes on the archway are of the Final Judgement. There's a peephole to view them (partially) when the church is locked. Note the 3rd-century recycled Roman tombstone on the exterior north wall.

🏃 Activities

If you are going to do a fair amount of hiking in the western Pohorje, pick up a copy of the 1:40,000-scale *Pohorje* map (€12) from Kartografija. The TIC distributes the free 1:60,000 *Hiking & Biking Koroška* map.

Slovenian Alpine Trail HIKING
The Slovenian Alpine Trail passes through Stari Trg and the centre of Slovenj Gradec before continuing up to Mala Kopa (1524m), where it meets the E6. There is a Category II, 18-bed mountain hut at 1102m to the northwest called **Koča pod Kremžarjevim Vrhom** (☑02-884 48 83, 041 800 947; ⊙ Wed-Mon late-Apr–Sep, Sat & Sun Oct–late-Apr). The E6 heads north through Vuhred and Radlje ob Dravi to Austria, and the Slovenian Alpine Trail carries on eastward to Rogla and Maribor. There is more accommodation on Velika Kopa at 1377m at the 60-bed **Grmovškov Dom pod Veliko Kopo** (☑02-883 98 60, 031 816 754; ⊙year-round).

If you are going to do a fair amount of hiking in the western Pohorje, pick up a copy of the 1:40,000-scale *Pohorje* map (€12) from Kartografija. The TIC distributes the free 1:60,000 *Hiking & Biking Koroška* map.

Kope Ski Grounds SKIING
(☑02-882 27 40; www.pohorje.org; day pass adult/child/student & senior €27/17/24; ⊙9am-6pm) Three ski slopes are within striking distance of Slovenj Gradec, but the closest is Kope, with skiing above the Mislinja Valley on the western edge of the Pohorje Massif. The ski grounds have 8km of runs, 15km of cross-country trails and eight lifts and tows on Mala Kopa and Velika Kopa peaks.

To reach Kope, follow the Velenje road (No 4) for 3km south and then turn east. The ski area is another 13km at the end of the road.

Koroški Splavarij RAFTING
(Koroški Rafters; ☑02-872 33 33; www.splavarjenje.com) The TIC can help organise three-hour rafting trips for about €25 per person on the Drava, though they are usually available to groups only. The trip starts at Vrata, about

Slovenj Gradec

Slovenj Gradec

◉ Sights
1 Church of St Elizabeth A2
2 Church of the Holy Spirit A3
3 Koroška Gallery of Fine Arts A2
　 Koroška Regional Museum .... (see 3)
4 Venetian Horse Statue A2

🛏 Sleeping
5 Hotel Slovenj Gradec A2

🍴 Eating
6 Pizzerija Apachi.....................................B1
7 Restavracija Paradiso A2

🍷 Drinking & Nightlife
8 Mestna Kavarna A2
9 Pisarna Cafe Lounge Bar B2
10 Šlaščičarna Šrimpf A2

🎭 Entertainment
11 Slovenj Gradec Cultural Centre B1

8km east of Dravograd. The price includes food and drink.

Tourist Information
Centre Murska Sobota TOURIST INFORMATION
(TIC; ☑02-534 11 30; tic.sobota@gmail.com; Zvezda ulica 10; ⊙9am-5pm Mon-Fri, to 1pm Sat, shorter hrs in winter)

UNDER THE LINDEN TREES

Slovenia's national tree, the stately linden (or common lime), and its heart-shaped leaf have become something of a symbol of Slovenia and Slovenian hospitality.

The linden *(lipa)* grows slowly for about 60 years and then suddenly spurts upward and outwards, living to a ripe old age. It is said that a linden grows for 300 years, stands still for another 300 and takes 300 years to die.

Linden wood was used by the Romans to make shields and, as it is easy to work with, artisans in the Middle Ages carved religious figures from it, earning linden the title *sacrum lignum,* or 'sacred wood'. Tea made from the linden flower, which contains aromatic oils, has been used as an antidote for fever and the flu at least since the 16th century. More importantly, from earliest times the linden tree was the focal point of any settlement in Slovenia – the centre of meetings, arbitration, recreation and, of course, gossip. The tree, which could never be taller than the church spire, always stood in the middle of the village, and important decisions were made by town elders at a table beneath it.

In fact, so sacred is the linden tree to Slovenes that its destruction is considered a serious offence. In discussing the barbarous acts committed by the Italians during the occupation of Primorska between the wars, one magazine article passionately points out that 'Kobarid had to swallow much bitterness...The fascists even cut down the linden tree...'

Slovenia's oldest linden is the 800-year-old Najevska Lipa under Koroška's Mt Peca, where Slovenian politicians meet in June. We give it another century.

🛏 Sleeping

Gaj Camping Ground
CAMPGROUND €

(🖉 02-885 05 00, 02-620 46 00; www.vabo.si; Mislinjska Dobrava 110; campsite per person €9, 3-person bungalows €45; ⊙ mid-Mar–mid-Oct) This is a small, friendly place with sites for tents and caravans, a half-a-dozen bungalows and a popular pizzeria set among the pine trees of Turiška Vas, just beyond the Gostišče Aerodrom in Mislinjska Dobrava.

Hotel Slovenj Gradec
HOTEL €€

(🖉 02-883 98 50, 051 310 333; www.vabo.si; Glavni trg 43; s €44-52, d €74-84; 🅿 ❄ @ 🤶) The only central hotel option in town is this 68-room property with mostly gloomy rooms and long, dark corridors that seem to go on forever. But we're happy to report that 15 of the rooms have had a complete makeover, with wooden floors, solid (and rather rustic) furnishings and 21st-century plumbing.

Gostišče Aerodrom
INN €€

(🖉 02-883 98 50, 051 310 333; www.vabo.si; Mislinjska Dobrava 110; s/d €52/84; 🅿 ❄ @ 🤶) This pleasant inn by the airfield, about 5km southeast of Slovenj Gradec, has a dozen basic but comfortable and competitively priced rooms. Some of the best cycling tracks in the region are close by.

Hotel Korošica
HOTEL €€

(🖉 02-878 69 12; www.korosica.si; Otiški Vrh 25d; s/d €59/85; 🅿 ❄ @ 🤶) It's a bit of a schlep 10km northwest of town, but this four-star hotel in the village of Otiški Vrh on the Mislinja River en route to Dravograd is about the best in the region. It's not the most attractive from the outside – essentially a big yellow box in a field – but the 30 rooms are comfortable and there's a very popular restaurant, too.

🍴 Eating

Pizzerija Apachi
PIZZA €

(🖉 02-883 17 84; Pohorska cesta 17b; pizza €6-9; ⊙ 9am-11pm Mon-Thu, to 1am Fri, noon-1am Sat, to 10pm Sun) This pizzeria with a wood-burning stove and a 'cowboys and Indians' theme is next to the bus station. Try the all-in-one Pizza Siux (sic).

Restavracija Paradiso
INTERNATIONAL €€

(🖉 02-883 98 50; www.vabo.si; Hotel Slovenj Gradec, Glavni trg 43; mains €8.50-22) The opening of this silver-service restaurant at the (partially) renovated Hotel Slovenj Gradec has raised the standard of dining options here by 100%. The *plošče* (platters) for sharing are especially good value (€20 to €24), as are the daily set menus (€8 to €9). The menu is a mini history lesson on the great and the good of Slovenj Gradec.

Gostilna Murko   SLOVENIAN €€

(☑02-883 81 03; Francetova cesta 24; mains €12-
18; ⊙8am-10pm Mon-Fri, 10am-10pm Sat, to 5pm
Sun) About 400m north of the centre on the
Mislinja River, Gostilna Murko is a four-star
roadside inn popular with Austrian tourists
on the go. It's been here for decades and is still
serving solid and reliable Slovenian dishes.

🍷 Drinking & Entertainment

Šlaščičarna Šrimpf   CAFE

(☑02-884 14 82; Glavni trg 14; ⊙8.30am-7pm Mon-
Sat, 10am-7pm Sun) This long-established cafe
draws the crowds with its fabulous cakes. Try
the *zagrebska* (€2), a rich concoction of custard, cream, chocolate and flaky pastry.

Mestna Kavarna   CAFE

(☑041 324 774; Trg Svobode 7; ⊙7am-10pm Mon-
Thu, to 1am Fri, 8am-11pm Sat, to 10pm Sun) This
retro-style cafe on the corner of Glavni trg is
one of the most comfortable places in town
to tip back a coffee or maybe even something stronger.

Pisarna Cafe Lounge Bar   PUB

(☑041 727 984; Poštna ulica 3; ⊙6am-11pm Mon-
Thu, to 2am Fri, 8am-2am Sat, 9am-8pm Sun) Pub
and bar very popular with students, who like
the upbeat decor, music and free internet
access.

Slovenj Gradec
Cultural Centre   CONCERT VENUE

(Kulturni Dom Slovenj Gradec; ☑02-884 50 05;
www.kulturni-dom-sg.si; Francetova ulica 5) Classical music concerts are sometimes held at
both the Church of St Elizabeth and this
centre, which also has a small cinema showing films between 7pm and 9pm Friday to
Sunday.

ℹ Information

Nova Ljubljanska Banka (Glavni trg 30;
⊙8.30am-12.30pm & 2.30-5pm Mon-Fri)

Post Office (Francetova cesta 1; ⊙8am-6pm
Mon-Fri, to noon Sat) At the northern end of
Glavni trg.

Tourist Information Centre Slovenj Gradec
(TIC; ☑02-881 21 16; www.slovenjgradec.si;
Glavni trg 24; ⊙8am-6pm Mon-Fri, 10am-5pm
Sat & Sun) On the ground floor, near the former
town hall. This office has reams of material on
local activities and places of interest.

ℹ Getting There & Around

Slovenj Gradec is not on a train line. The bus station is at Pohorska cesta 15, about 500m north-

east of the TIC. Destinations served by bus from
Slovenj Gradec include Celje (€7.20, 1½ hours,
55km), Ljubljana (€9.90, two hours, 110km) and
Maribor (€7.20, two hours, 74km).

You can call a taxi in Slovenj Gradec on ☑070
900 300.

PREKMURJE

Prekmurje is Slovenia's 'forgotten' corner –
for the most part a broad, farmed plain 'beyond the Mura River' (as its name describes
it). Relatively isolated until the 1920s, Prekmurje has preserved its traditional music,
folklore, architecture and a distinctive local
dialect.

Until the end of WWI, most of Prekmurje
belonged to the Austro-Hungarian Empire
and it still has a small Magyar minority,
especially around Lendava. In many ways
Prekmurje looks and feels more like Hungary than Slovenia, with its white storks,
large thatched farmhouses, substantial
Roma population, and the occasional Hungarian-style *golaž* (goulash) cooked with
paprika.

Prekmurje, a natural springboard into
Austria or Hungary, is a fine place to relax
and enjoy taking the waters at several thermal spas, and to indulge in *gibanica*, a rich
local pastry.

Murska Sobota & Around

☑02 / POP 11,310 / ELEV 189M

Slovenia's northernmost city, Murska Sobota
sits on a plain flatter than a *palačinka,* the
pancake filled with jam or nuts and topped
with chocolate that is so popular here. The
city itself has little to recommend it except
for its odd architectural mix of neoclassical, Secessionist and 'socialist baroque'
buildings. But the surrounding countryside,
potters' villages and thermal spas make it a
good springboard for the entire region.

History

The town of Murska Sobota was once little
more than a Hungarian market town until
the opening of the railway in 1907, which
linked Murska Sobota with Šalovci in Hungary proper. With the formation of the Kingdom of Serbs, Croats and Slovenes in 1918
and the transfer of territory, Murska Sobota found itself more or less in the centre of
Prekmurje and development really began.

Murska Sobota

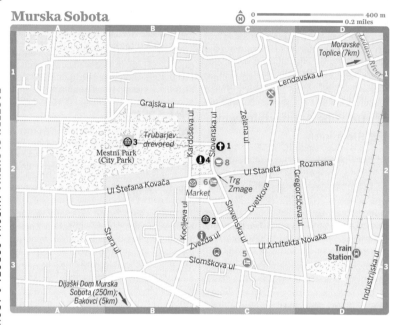

N 0 — 400 m
0 — 0.2 miles

EASTERN SLOVENIA MURSKA SOBOTA & AROUND

◉ Sights

Pomurje Museum Murska Sobota   MUSEUM
(Pomurski Muzej Murska Sobota; ☎02-527 17 06; www.pomurski-muzej.si; Trubarjev drevored 4; adult/child €3/2; ⊙9am-5pm Tue-Fri, to 1pm Sat, 2-6pm Sun Sep-Jun, 10am-4pm Tue-Fri, 9am-noon Sat & Sun Jul & Aug) Housed in 14 rooms of the Renaissance-style Murska Sobota Castle, a sprawling manor house from the mid-16th century, this award-winning museum tells the story of life along the Mura River, from prehistoric times to the end of the 20th century. Highlights include the medieval rubbish pit (room 4), the frescoed Baroque Salon (room 9), the old peasant house interiors in room 11 and the former chapel next to room 14.

Murska Sobota Gallery   GALLERY
(Galerija Murska Sobota; ☎02-522 38 34; www.galerija-ms.si; Kocljeva ulica 7; adult/child €2/1; ⊙9am-noon Mon & Sat, 8am-5pm Tue-Fri Sep-Jun, 9am-noon Sat Jul & Aug) The best gallery in Prekmurje, MSG has a permanent collection of more than 500 works – much of it sculpture – as well as some excellent special exhibitions (admission varies).

Victory Monument   MONUMENT
In Mestni Park, the Victory Monument is an impressive stone grouping Yugoslav Partisans and Soviet soldiers, a rarity in modern Slovenia.

Evangelical Church   CHURCH
(Slovenska ulica) The neo-Gothic Evangelical Church (1910) is the main Lutheran seat in Slovenia. (The majority of Slovenian Protestants live in Prekmurje). The interior, painted with geometric shapes and floral motifs in muted shades of blue, green, brown and gold, is a welcome change from the over-

wrought baroque gold and marble decor found in most Catholic churches here.

Parish Church of St Martin CHURCH

This church in Martjanci, 4km north of Murska Sobota on the road to Moravske Toplice, contains wonderful 14th-century frescoes painted on the sanctuary's vaulted ceiling and walls. Look for the centuries-old graffiti on the walls behind the altar.

🛏 Sleeping

Dijaški Dom Murska Sobota HOSTEL €

(🖉 02-530 03 10; www.d-dom.ms.edus.si; Tomšičeva ulica 15; dm €18.50; ⊙ late-Jul–Aug; 🅿 @) This student dormitory southwest of the centre with 40 rooms accepts travellers in summer only, although there a few rooms that may be available at other times. It has laundry facilities.

Hotel Štrk HOTEL €€

(🖉 02-525 21 58; www.lovenjakov-dvor.si; Polana 40; s/d €41/82; 🅿 ❄ @ 🛜 🛏) The 25-room 'Stork' at the Lovenjakov Dvor (Lovenjak Court) tourist house, 4km northwest of Murska Sobota, boasts many special features – from furnishings from a nearby castle (room 24), views of nesting storks (room 21), and thermal water in its enclosed pool from Moravske Toplice. Rents bikes for €10 a day.

Hotel Zvezda HOTEL €€

(🖉 02-539 15 73; www.hotel-zvezda.si; Trg Zmage 8; s/d €35/60; 🅿 ❄ 🛜) This landmark caravansary (1909) in central Murska Sobota has had a refit and is looking better than ever. It may be just a bit too pink on the outside but enter and you'll find 30 comfortable rooms with all the mod-cons. And the right price.

Great pub-restaurant with a massive terrace attached.

Hotel Diana BUSINESS HOTEL €€

(🖉 02-514 12 00; www.hotel-diana.si; Slovenska ulica 52; s/d €52/84; 🅿 ❄ 🛜 🛏) The 96 rooms at this business hotel are bright and functional. It has a glassed-in swimming pool, sauna and fitness room on the 2nd floor, as well as a decent restaurant.

🍴 Eating

Mini Rajh No 1 INTERNATIONAL €

(🖉 02-523 12 38; Cvetkova ulica 21; pizza & pasta €5.60-8; ⊙ 10am-10pm Tue-Fri, from 11.30am Sat, from 4pm Sun) A self-styled 'mini-restaurant' on the corner of Lendavska ulica, this is an upmarket *špagetarija* and *picerija* with great salads (€6.50 to €8) too.

★Gostilna Rajh SLOVENIAN €€

(🖉 02-543 90 98; www.rajh.si; Soboška ulica 32, Bakovci; mains €9.50-19, tasting menu €35; ⊙ 10.30am-10pm Tue-Fri, 11am-10pm Sat, 11.30am-4pm Sun) Probably the best restaurant in Prekmurje, this lovely *gostilna* in Bakovci, a village 5km southwest of Murska Sobota, serves local specialities with a modern twist. We love the *tünka* (ham preserved in lard), tomato soup with pumpkin seed oil and basil, the boar pâté and *dödoli* (dumplings) with crackling. Oh, and the venison with cranberries.

If there's still room, finish with *gibanica* ice cream – what happens when the rich local pastry gets taken to new dessert heights. There's a large cellar/*vinoteka* of regional wines. Seasonal tasting menu is €35.

WHITE STORKS

The white stork (*Ciconia ciconia*), or *beli štrk* in Slovene, is Prekmurje's most beloved symbol. Country people consider it a symbol of luck and honour for a pair to nest on the rooftop. The storks arrive in spring and spend the warm summer months here. Come mid-August, they migrate south on a 12,000km trek to sub-Saharan Africa for the winter, returning in the spring.

Storks build their nests on church steeples, rooftops or telephone poles. The nest is repaired every year and can weigh as much as 500kg. Storks live on a diet of worms, grasshoppers, frogs and small rodents. If food is scarce, however, it is not unknown for parents to turf their fledglings out of the nest.

Slovenia's stork population (around 350 breeding pairs) has grown over the past two decades. Nevertheless, the white stork remains a vulnerable species, primarily because its hunting and breeding grounds – the meadows – are being destroyed, dried out and regulated.

Gostilna Lovenjak SLOVENIAN €€
(☑ 02-525 21 53; Hotel Štrk, Polana 40; mains €7.50-19; ⊙ 11am-10pm Mon-Thu, to midnight Fri & Sat, 11am-8pm Sun) This atmospheric *gostilna* serves such Prekmurje favourites as *bograč golaž* (Hungarian-style goulash soup), roast suckling pig served with noodles, and indecently rich *prekmurska gibanica*, the local spiced pastry delight. There's a Sunday buffet and live music at weekends. Set lunches are a snip at €10 to €18.

🍷 Drinking & Nightlife

Zvezda Pivnica PUB
(Star Pub; ☑ 02-539 15 73; www.hotel-zvezda.si; Trg Zmage 8; ⊙ 9.30am-10pm Sun-Thu, to 1am Fri & Sat) Anchor tenant in central Murska Sobota, the 'Star' is a large pub with an enormous terrace and decent food. Start or end your evening here.

City CAFE
(Slovenska ulica 27; ⊙ 6.30am-10pm Mon-Thu, to midnight Fri, 7am-midnight Sat, 8am-10pm Sun) Essentially a stylish cafe with drinks, City also serves snacks and is a convenient pit-stop distance from the Pomurje Museum Murska Sobota.

ℹ️ Information

Nova Ljubljanska Banka (Trg Zmage 7; ⊙ 8.30am-5pm Mon-Fri)

Post Office (Trg Zmage 6; ⊙ 8am-6pm Mon-Fri, to noon Sat)

ℹ️ Getting There & Around

BICYCLE

You can rent bikes from **Hotel Štrk** (p221) for €10 a day.

BUS

Buses leave regularly for Radenci (€2.30, 15 minutes, 12km), Maribor (€6, 1¼ hours, 60km) and Moravske Toplice (€1.80, 15 minutes, 9km). Other destinations include Dobrovnik (€2.70, 30 minutes, 20km) and Ljubljana (€16, three hours, 191km) via Maribor and Celje.

TRAIN

Murska Sobota has rail connections to Ljubljana (€13 to €19, 3½ hours, 216km) and Maribor (€7 to €9, 1¾ hours, 98km) and Vienna. From Murska Sobota the train carries on to Budapest.

Moravske Toplice

☑ 02 / POP 760 / ELEV 185M
The thermal spa of Moravske Toplice, 7km northeast of Murska Sobota, boasts the hottest water in Slovenia: 72°C at its source but cooled to body temperature (38°C) for use in its many pools and basins. Though it's one of the newest spas in the country – the spring was discovered in 1960 during exploratory oil drilling – many young Slovenes consider the clientele too old for their liking, preferring the small, partly *au naturel* spa at Banovci to the southwest. But Moravske Toplice is every bit a health resort geared for recreation, with enough upgraded sport facilities to cater to every taste.

POTTERY TOWNS OF PREKMURJE

Explore some of Prekmurje's less-frequented towns and discover thermal spas, pottery workshops and a floating mill.

From Murska Sobota, head north along Route 232, then from Martjanci and its Parish Church of St Martin (p221), head east along Route 442 to the thermal spa (p223) of **Moravske Toplice**. Tešanovci, a couple of kilometres east, is noted for its *lončarstvo* (pottery).

About 2.5km further east is the village of **Bogojina** and its **Parish Church of the Ascension**, which was redesigned by Jože Plečnik around 1926. The interior is an odd mixture of black marble, brass, wood and terracotta; the oak-beamed ceiling is fitted with Prekmurje ceramic plates and jugs, as is the altar.

Filovci, 2km past Bogojina, is famed for its *črna keramika* (black pottery). **Keramika Bojnec** (☑ 041 330 987; www.bojnec.com; Filovci 20; admission €2.50), 200m southwest of the main road, invites visitors to watch them work at the ancient kiln in the *skanzen* (open-air museum displaying village architecture) over the road.

Carry on to Dobrovnik, which has a couple of decent roadside *gostilna* and then southwest through Beltinci to **Ižakovci**, which has one of the last floating mills (p224) on the Mura. From here, Murska Sobota is just 8km to the northwest.

Activities

Terme 3000
SPA

(☑02-512 22 00; www.sava-hotels-resorts.com; Kranjčeva ulica 12; non-guests adult/child €14/10; ⊘8am-9pm May-Sep, 9am-9pm Oct-Apr) This spa complex has a dozen indoor and outdoor pools filled with thermal water, slides and a water tower. The thermal water is recommended for relief of rheumatism and certain minor skin problems. Guests at the resort have free use of the pools and saunas; nonguest admission is reduced before noon and after 3pm. The resort also has a golf course, tennis courts and a fitness room.

Terme Vivat
SPA

(☑02-538 21 00; www.vivat.si; Ulica ob Igrišču 3; full day/after 3pm adult €11.50/8, child €10/6; ⊘8am-8pm Mon-Thu, to 11pm Fri & Sat, to 9pm Sun) Terme Vivat has thermal indoor and outdoor pools connected by a swimming channel, saunas and an ambitious wellness centre.

🛏 Sleeping

The TIC can organise private rooms (from €20 per person); apartments for two cost from €30 to €50, depending on length of stay.

Camping Terme 3000
CAMPGROUND €

(☑02-512 22 00; www.sava-hotels-resorts.com; Kranjčeva ulica 12; per person €16.50-19; P @ ☎) The spa's seven-hectare camping ground, Camping Terme 3000, counts 430 sites and is open year-round. Use of the swimming pool nearby is included in the price.

Terme 3000 Bungalows
BUNGALOWS €€€

(☑02-512 22 00; Kranjčeva ulica 12; half-board s €73-78, d €98-104; P @ ☎) The attractive bungalows at the resort's Prekmurje Village (Prekmurska Vas) are done up to look like traditional peasant cottages, with thatched roofs, cool white-washed walls and a total of 78 double rooms.

Hotel Livada Prestige
HOTEL €€€

(☑02-512 22 00; Kranjčeva ulica 12; half-board s €100-105, d €170-182, ste €115-290; P ❄ @ ☎ ☎) The vast flagship property here has 122 five-star rooms, many with thermal water piped straight into the bathrooms for your own private spa experience.

🍴 Eating

The silver-service restaurant at the Hotel Livada Prestige (p223), serving artful takes on regional specialties created by visiting chefs, gets excellent reviews.

Gostilna Kuhar
SLOVENIAN €€

(☑02-548 12 15; Kranjčeva ulica 13; mains €8-19.50; ⊘9am-11pm Tue-Sun) Opposite the Terme 3000's main entrance, Gostilna Kuhar is a decent and convenient place in which to sample Prekmurje's cuisine.

Gostišče Oaza
SLOVENIAN €€

(☑051 383 141; www.oaza-grill.com; Mljatinci 39; mains from €11; ⊘10am-10pm Tue-Thu, to 11pm Fri & Sat, to 5pm Sun) Enjoy excellent local dishes while overlooking a tiny lake in Mljatinci, just south of the pottery village Tešanovci, about 3km southeast of Moravske Toplice.

ℹ Information

Nova Ljubljanska Banka (Kranjčeva ulica; ⊘8am-5pm Mon-Fri) At the entrance to the Terme 3000 spa.

Post Office (Kranjčeva ulica 5; ⊘8am-6pm Mon-Fri, to noon Sat) On the main road.

Tourist Information Centre Moravske Toplice (TIC; ☑02-538 15 20; www.moravske-toplice.com; Kranjčeva ulica 3; ⊘8am-8pm Mon-Fri, 7am-3pm Sat, 8am-2pm Sun Jul & Aug, shorter hrs Sep-Jun) On the main road northwest of the entrance to the Terme 3000 complex.

ℹ Getting There & Around

Buses leave from Kranjčeva ulica up to six times a day for Murska Sobota (€1.80, 15 minutes, 9km) and Dobrovnik (€2.30, 15 minutes, 11km).

The TIC rents bicycles for €3/12 per hour/day.

Radenci

☑02 / POP 2155 / ELEV 203M

Radenci is best known for its health-spa resort, parts of which still feel like a down-at-the-heel full-of-itself 19th-century spa town. The spa dominates activities for visitors, but when most Slovenes hear the name they think of Radenska Tri Srca – the 'Radenci Three Hearts' mineral water that's bottled here and consumed in every restaurant and cafe in the land.

🏃 Activities

Spas

Terme Radenci
SPA

(☑02-520 27 20; www.sava-hotels-resorts.com; Zdraviliško naselje 12; 3hr/day pools €8.50/11, sauna €15/18.50; ⊘pools 7am-9pm Sun-Thu, 9am-10pm Fri & Sat, sauna 4-9pm Mon-Thu, 10am-10pm Fri & Sat, to 9pm Sun) The Radenci Thermal Spa opened in 1882 and has three claims to fame: water rich in carbon dioxide for

FLOATING MILLS

Floating mills, which date back to Roman times, were very popular on rivers that changed their course abruptly or swelled rapidly after rainfall, as they allowed millers to move to the best possible spots for milling. In Slovenia, floating mills were largely built on the Mura River; there were dozens of them in operation up to WWII. Today, the only ones left are the Babič Mill (Babičev Mlin; ☑ 041 694 087; Prvomajska ulica 24, Veržej; ⏰ 8am-4.30pm Mon-Fri, to 2pm Sat) at Veržej and the Island of Love Mill (Otok Ljubezni Mlin; ☑ 02 541 35 80; Mladinska ulica 2, Beltinci; admission €3; ⏰ 9am-6pm Apr-Jun, Sep & Oct, to 8pm Jul & Aug) at Ižakovci, southwest of Beltinci. The former is the real deal, with grain ground and sold for clients. The latter is more touristy and includes small museum, shop and a raft ride across the Mura.

drinking; mineral-laden thermal water (41°C) for bathing; and sulphurous mud from Lake Negova for therapeutic and beauty treatments. There are 10 pools of varying sizes, including large indoor and outdoor thermal pools with temperatures of 30°C to 33°C, plus various saunas and a large wellness centre.

The spa's thoroughly modern blocks overlook the few remaining older Victorian-style buildings and a wooded park.

Cycling

The spa rents bicycles for €3/6/10 per hour/three hours/day. Cycling excursions can be made into the surrounding wine country; head southwest along the *vinska cesta* (wine road) for about 4km to Janžev Vrh and an old vineyard cottage called Janžev Hram. The region's most celebrated wine is the champagne-like Zlata Radgonska Penina.

🛌 Sleeping

Private rooms are available on Panonska cesta (eg house 21) to the west and south of the spa's main entrance.

Hotel Izvir HOTEL €€€
(☑ 02-520 27 20; www.sava-hotels-resorts.com; Zdraviliško naselje 12; s €90-105, d €120-130; P ※ 🛜 🛒) This is the smaller and quieter of the spa hotels, with a slick modern exterior and 128 well-presented rooms.

Hotel Radin HOTEL €€€
(☑ 02-520 27 22; www.sava-hotels-resorts.com; Zdraviliško naselje 12; s €93-104, d €124-138; P ⊖ 🛜 🛜) Radenci's larger hotel with two wings and a total 291 rooms – comfortable and well-organised, although with the occasional hint of the conference centre about it.

🍴 Eating & Drinking

Gostilna Park SLOVENIAN €
(☑ 02-520 10 00; mains €8.50-14; ⏰ 10am-5pm Tue-Sun) In the heart of the spa's large wooded park and serving local specialties, the aptly named Park is a pleasant place for a meal in summer. Daily specials are just €4.50.

Pub Kavarna Vikend PUB
(☑ 02-566 93 95; Panonska cesta 2; ⏰ 6am-10pm Mon-Thu, to midnight Fri, 8am-midnight Sat, 9am-10pm Sun) This convivial pub-cafe with a large open-air terrace is just opposite the bank and post office, and around the corner from the main entrance to the Terme Radenci. It's got a casino attached, so that's most everyone's needs sorted.

Self-Catering

Mercator SUPERMARKET
(Radgonska cesta 9; ⏰ 7am-6pm Mon-Fri, to noon Sat) Not far from the spa's main entrance.

ℹ Information

Nova Ljubljanska Banka (Panonska cesta 7; ⏰ 8.30am-12.30pm & 2.30-5pm Mon-Fri)
Post Office (Panonska cesta 5; ⏰ 8am-6pm Mon-Fri, to noon Sat)

ℹ Getting There & Away

The bus station is opposite the main entrance to the Terme Radenci spa. There are daily buses to Gornja Radgona (€1.80, 10 minutes, 7km), Ljubljana (€16, three hours, 187km) via Maribor (€5.60, one hour, 49km) and Celje (€9.60, 1¾ hours, 105km), and half-a-dozen buses to Murska Sobota (€2.30, 15 minutes, 12km).

Understand Slovenia

Slovenia Today

Slovenia's 25th birthday was the official reason for celebrating 2016. But what looked like the start of economic recovery after several years of recession and austerity was the real reason some people were breaking out the bubbly. And the European Commission's recognition of Ljubljana as the Green Capital of Europe after all its hard work was the icing on the cake. Is it party time again in Slovenia?

Best in Print

Crumbs (Miha Mazzini, 1987) Slovenian anti-hero with a crazy obsession in the final days of Yugoslavia.

Forbidden Bread (Erica Johnson Debeljak, 2009) A young American follows her poet-lover to his homeland just after independence.

Čefurji Raus! (Goran Vojnovič, 2009) Wry look at ex-Yugoslav immigrants in Slovenia.

Slovenia and the Slovenes: A Small State and the New Europe (James Gow and Cathie Carmichael, 2010) Excellent analysis of Slovenian history, politics, culture and the arts.

Best on Film

Ekspres, Ekspres (*Gone with the Train*, 1997) Surreal comedy on (and off) the rails.

Rezerni Deli (*Spare Parts*, 2003) Dark tale about the trafficking of illegal immigrants.

Petelinji Zajtrk (*Rooster's Breakfast*, 2007) Bittersweet romance with lots of laughs.

Razredni Sovražnik (*Class Enemy*, 2013) Tragedy leads students to revolt against their teacher.

The Economy: Guarded Optimism

As the republic of Slovenia moved closer to marking its quarter-century of independence, the mood was guardedly optimistic. Yes, people were concerned with things like the lack of jobs (especially among young people), what they saw as an absence of strong leadership at the highest levels, and – something new in staunchly egalitarian Slovenia – the perceived rise of an elite class working to its own agenda.

But there was good news, and it had to do with the recovering economy. Just a few short years ago Slovenia was in deep recession, and many feared the possibility of a 'Greek scenario' and EU bailout (though on a more modest scale). In 2015, driven by a very strong export sector, lower oil and commodity prices, and increased government investment, the economy was set to grow 2.6%, a rate twice the EU average. True, the jobless rate stood at a stubborn 9.2% (though down from 11% two years before) and the public deficit stood at 5.5% of GDP, but at this point in time Slovenia seemed to be setting the pace for southeastern Europe just as it had done as the smallest but wealthiest republic in the former Yugoslavia.

Ins & Outs of Government

Slovenia has had four different prime ministers in as many years, and this parliamentary 'revolving door' has begun to seem almost normal to many people here. The days of strong leaders or ones who were able to weather the storm more successfully – the late Janez Drnovšek and Borut Pahor spring to mind – seem a very long time ago indeed.

The current government is a coalition of three parties with very different agendas. These include Prime Minister Miroslav Cerar's centrist Modern Centre Party (SMC), which won 36 of the 90 seats in the snap election of

2014 after Alenka Bratušek, the country's first female prime minister, resigned. The main opposition party, the Slovenian Democratic Party (SDS), led by controversial former Prime Minister Janez Janša, took 21 seats. Though commanding a narrow majority of just under 58%, the coalition has been able to agree on some key reforms, including selling off government-owned enterprises such as banks, which in turn control other formerly state-owned businesses.

Gold for Green

Slovenia is celebrated for its forest cover (58% of its land mass), sparkling alpine air and some of the purest drinking water in the world. Now the European Commission has awarded Ljubljana the coveted Green Capital of Europe title for 2016.

Much of the kudos must go to Zoran Janković, the only mayor to have served two successive terms in the capital since WWII. He closed large chunks of the city centre to traffic, including the main artery Slovenska cesta, spruced up the embankment of the Ljubljanica, added a couple of new footbridges across that little river and either built or renewed a score of drinking fountains, encouraging one and all to forsake bottled water. Most importantly Ljubljana has now become the first EU capital to adopt a zero-waste strategy, under which everything discarded is recycled. It's not hard to see why the city they call the 'Beloved' has been so honoured.

A Sterling Occasion

Slovenia is due to celebrate the 25th anniversary of its establishment as an independent nation on 25 June 2016. Plans for national celebrations include a mix of political speeches meant to lift the country's spirit and (sometimes outlandish) cultural performances, that will likely take place in the capital's picturesque Kongresni trg. (Despite the fact that the country's independence from Yugoslavia was actually declared by then-President Milan Kučan in the much-less-pretty Trg Republike.) Based on previous form, the main celebration is likely to take place the night before, so that everyone can make the most of the national holiday by heading out to the beach or mountains. A toast to the next 25 years!

POPULATION: **2.06 MILLION**

AREA: **20,273 SQ KM**

GDP: **US$49.5 BILLION**

GDP GROWTH: **+2.6%**

INFLATION: **0.2%**

UNEMPLOYMENT: **9.2%**

if Slovenia were 100 people

58 would be Catholic
3 would be Muslim
2 would be Orthodox Christian
1 would be Protestant
36 would be No confirmed faith

ethnic groups

(% of population)

83 Slovenes

17 Others

population per sq km

SLOVENIA   ITALY   UK

🧍 ≈ 100 people

History

Slovenia is as old as the hills and as new as tomorrow. Slovenia the *narod* (nation of people) can trace its origins back at least a millennium and a half. But Slovenia the *nacija*, or nation-state, is a much more recent entity, not until June 1991 did the nation's 'new day' as an independent republic at last arrive. Slovenia's story begins with the mass migration of Celts, but by the late 13th century the Habsburgs moved in and stayed for more than six centuries.

Early Inhabitants

The area of present-day Slovenia has been settled since the Palaeolithic Age. Stone implements that date back to 250,000 BC have been found in a cave at near Orehek, southwest of Postojna.

During the Bronze Age (roughly 2000 to 900 BC), marsh dwellers farmed and raised cattle in the Ljubljansko Barje – the marshland south of present-day Ljubljana – and at Lake Cerknica. They lived in round huts set on stilts and traded with other peoples along the so-called Amber Route linking the Balkans with Italy and northern Europe.

Around 700 BC the Ljubljana Marsh people were overwhelmed by the Illyrian tribes from the south, who brought with them iron tools and weapons. They settled largely in the southeast, built hill-top forts and reached their peak between 650 and 550 BC, during what is called the Hallstatt period. Iron helmets, gold jewellery and *situlae* (embossed pails) with distinctive Hallstatt geometric motifs have been found in tombs near Stična and at Vače near Litija; you'll see some excellent examples of these finds at both the National Museum of Slovenia in Ljubljana and the Dolenjska Museum in Novo Mesto.

Around 400 BC, Celtic tribes from what are now France, Germany and the Czech lands began pushing southward towards the Balkans. They mixed with the local population and established the Noric kingdom, the first 'state' on Slovenian soil.

A primitive bone flute discovered in 1995 in a cave at Divje Babe, near the town of Cerknica, dates back some 35,000 years and is thought to be the world's oldest known musical instrument. It takes pride of place at the National Museum of Slovenia in Ljubljana.

TIMELINE	2000–900 BC	700 BC	400 BC
	Bronze Age settlers build wooden huts on stilts, farm, raise cattle, and produce coarse pottery in the Ljubljansko Barje, a marshy area south of present-day Ljubljana.	Illyrian tribes arrive in the Ljubljana Marsh, bringing with them iron tools, weapons and jewellery featuring geometric Hallstatt patterns.	Continental Celtic tribes led by the Norics establish a kingdom called Noricum on Slovenian soil near the present-day city of Celje in central Štajerska.

The Romans

In 181 BC the Romans established the colony of Aquileia (Oglej in Slovene) on the Gulf of Trieste in order to protect the empire from tribal incursions. Two centuries later they annexed the Celtic Noric kingdom and moved into the rest of Slovenia and Istria.

The Romans divided the area into the provinces of Noricum, Upper and Lower Pannonia and Histria, later called Illyrium, and built roads connecting their new military settlements. From these bases developed the important towns of Emona (Ljubljana), Celeia (Celje) and Poetovio (Ptuj), where reminders of the Roman presence can still be seen.

The Early Slavs

In the middle of the 5th century AD, the Huns, led by Attila, invaded Italy via Slovenia, attacking Poetovio, Celeia and Emona along the way. On their heels came the Germanic Ostrogoths and then the Langobards, who occupied much of Slovenian territory. The last major wave was made up of the early Slavs.

The ancestors of today's Slovenes arrived from the Carpathian Basin in the 6th century and settled in the Sava, Drava and Mura River valleys and the eastern Alps. In their original homelands the early Slavs were a peaceful people, living in forests or along rivers and lakes, breeding cattle and farming by slash-and-burn methods. They were very superstitious, seeing *vile* (both good and bad fairies or sprites) everywhere and worshipping a pantheon of gods and goddesses. As a social group they made no class distinctions, but chose a leader – a *župan* (the modern Slovenian word for 'mayor') or *vojvoda* (duke) – in times of great danger. During the migratory periods, however, they became more warlike and aggressive.

Reminders of the Roman Presence

Citizen of Emona statue in Ljubljana

Roman necropolis at Šempeter near Celje

Mithraic shrines outside Ptuj and Črnomelj

HISTORY THE ROMANS

THE TALE IN THE PAIL

Hallstatt is the name of a village in the Salzkammergut region of Austria where objects characteristic of the early Iron Age (from about 800 to 500 BC) were found in the 19th century. Today the term is used generically for the late Bronze and early Iron Age cultures that developed in Central and Western Europe from about 1200 to 450 BC.

Many regions of Slovenia were settled during this period, particularly the Krka Valley. Burial mounds – more than two dozen in Novo Mesto alone – have yielded swords, helmets, jewellery and especially *situlae* – pails (or buckets) that are often richly decorated with life-like battle and hunting scenes. Hallstatt art is very geometric, and typical motifs include birds and figures arranged in pairs. The *Vače situla* in the National Museum of Slovenia in Ljubljana is a particularly fine example.

1st century AD	5th century	6th century	7th century
The Romans move into Slovenia from Italy and annex Noricum, marking the beginning of the Roman occupation that would last for almost half a millennium.	In about AD 450, the Huns, led by Attila, invade Italy via Slovenia, attacking Roman settlements of Poetovio (Ptuj), Celeia (Celje) and Emona (Ljubljana) along the way.	Early Slavic tribes, divided into two distinct but related groups, the Slaveni and the Antes, settle in the valleys of the Sava, Drava and Mura Rivers and the eastern Alps.	A loose confederation of Slavic tribes establishes the Duchy of Carantania, the world's first Slavic political entity, and establishes its capital somewhere near Celovec (now Klagenfurt in Austria).

From Duchy to Kingdom

The early Magyars were such fierce fighters that a common Christian prayer during the Dark Ages was 'Save us, O Lord, from the arrows of the Hungarians'.

In the early 7th century the alpine Slavs united under their leader, Duke Valuk, and joined forces with the Frankish kingdom. This tribal union became the Duchy of Carantania (Karantanija) – the first Slavic state, with its seat at Krn Castle (now Karnburg) near Klagenfurt (Celovec in Slovene) in Austria.

Within a century, a new class of ennobled commoners called *kosezi* had emerged, and it was they who publicly elected and crowned the new *knez* (grand duke) on the *knežni kamen* ('duke's rock') in the courtyard of Krn Castle. Such a process was unique in the feudal Europe of the early Middle Ages.

In 748 the Frankish empire of the Carolingians incorporated Carantania as a vassal state called Carinthia and began converting the people to Christianity. By the early 9th century, religious authority on Slovenian territory was shared between Salzburg and the Patriarchate (or Bishopric) of Aquileia, now in Italy. The weakening Frankish authorities began replacing Slovenian nobles with German counts, reducing the local peasants to serfs. The German nobility was thus at the top of the feudal hier-

THE PATRIARCHATE OF AQUILEIA

You'd never guess from its present size (population 3370), but the Friulian town of Aquileia north of Grado on the Gulf of Trieste played a pivotal role in Slovenian history, and for many centuries its bishops or 'patriarchs') ruled much of Carniola (Kranjska).

Founded as a Roman colony in the late 2nd century BC, Aquileia fell to a succession of tribes during the Great Migrations and had lost its political and economic importance by the end of the 6th century. But Aquileia had been made the metropolitan see for Venice, Histria and Carniola, and when the church declared some of Aquileia's teachings heretical, it broke from Rome. The schism lasted only a century and when it was resolved Aquileia was recognised as a separate patriarchate.

Aquileia's ecclesiastical importance grew during the mission of Paulinus II to the Avars and Slovenes in the late 8th century, and it acquired feudal estates and extensive political privileges (including the right to mint coins) from the Frankish and later the German kings. It remained a feudal principality until 1420 when the Venetian Republic conquered Friuli, and Venetians were appointed patriarchs for the first time. Aquileia retained some of its holdings in Slovenia and elsewhere for the next 300 years. But the final blow came in 1751 when Pope Benedict XIV created the archbishoprics of Udine and Gorizia. The once powerful Patriarchate of Aquileia had outlasted its usefulness and was dissolved. The rich archaeological area and the cathedral of Aquileia have been on the World Heritage List since 1998.

748	869–74	955	970
The Carolingian empire of the Franks incorporates Carantania as a vassal state called Carinthia; with the establishment of a formal church, the Christianisation of the Slovenes begins.	Carinthian Prince Kocelj rules a short-lived Slovenian 'kingdom' in Lower Pannonia, the area that stretches southeast from Styria (Štajerska) to the Mura, Drava and Danube Rivers.	The marauding Magyars, who had invaded in and settled in Slovenian Pannonia, are stopped in their tracks at a decisive battle at Augsburg by German king Otto I.	Creation of the Freising Manuscripts, the earliest known text written in Slovene (or any Slavic language for that matter), which contain a sermon on sin and penance and instructions for general confession.

archy for the first time in Slovenian lands. This would later become one of the chief obstacles to Slovenian national and cultural development.

With the total collapse of the Frankish state in the second half of the 9th century, a Carinthian prince named Kocelj established a short-lived (869–74) independent Slovenian 'kingdom' in Lower Pannonia, the area stretching southeast from Styria to the Mura, Drava and Danube Rivers. But German King Otto I would soon bring this to an end, after defeating the Magyars in the mid-10th century.

German Ascendancy

The Germans decided to re-establish Carinthia, dividing the area into a half-dozen border regions (*krajina*) or marches. These developed into the Slovenian provinces that would remain basically unchanged until 1918: Carniola (Kranjska), Carinthia (Koroška), Styria (Štajerska), Gorica (Goriška) and the so-called White March (Bela Krajina).

A drive for complete Germanisation of the Slovenian lands began in the 10th century. Land was divided between the nobility and various church dioceses, and German gentry were settled on it. The population remained essentially Slovenian, however, and it was largely due to intensive educational and pastoral work by the clergy that the Slovenian identity was preserved.

Between the 10th and 13th centuries most of Slovenia's castles were built and many important Christian monasteries – such as Stična and Kostanjevica – were established. Towns also began to develop as administrative, trade and social centres from the 11th century.

Early Habsburg Rule

In the early Middle Ages, the Habsburgs were just one of many German aristocratic families struggling for hegemony on Slovenian soil. Others, such as the Andechs, Spanheims and Žoneks (later the Counts of Celje), were equally powerful at various times. But as dynasties intermarried or died out, the Habsburgs consolidated their power. Between the late 13th century and the early 16th century, almost all the lands inhabited by Slovenes passed into Habsburg hands.

By this time Slovenian territory totalled about 24,000 sq km, about 15% larger than its present size. Not only did more towns and boroughs receive charters and rights, but the country began to develop economically with the opening of ironworks at Kropa and mines at Idrija. This economic progress reduced the differences among the repressed peasants, and they united against their feudal lords.

The proto-democratic process that elected the grand duke of Carantania at Krn Castle was noted by the 16th-century French political theorist Jean Bodin, whose work is said to have been a key reference for Thomas Jefferson when he wrote the American Declaration of Independence in 1775–76.

Lake Balaton in Hungary, which the early Slavs reached in their roamings, takes its name from the Slovenian word *blato* (mud).

10th century	Late 13th century	1408	1478–1573
Land is divided between the German nobility and church dioceses in a drive for complete Germanisation of Slovenia, but the population remains mostly Slovenian.	The first feudal holdings on Slovenian territory – the provinces of Carniola, Gorizia, Istria, Carinthia and Styria – fall under Habsburg control and remain in their hands until WWI.	Ottoman Turks start their attacks on southeastern Europe, which will continue for over two centuries and bring them to the gates of Vienna several times.	Peasant-led riots are at their peak; along with the Protestant Reformation in the middle of the 16th century, they are considered a watershed of the Slovenian national awakening.

Raids, Revolts & Reformation

Attacks by the Ottoman Turks on southeastern Europe in the early 15th century helped to radicalise landless peasants and labourers, who were required to raise their own defences *and* continue to pay tribute and work for their feudal lords. More than a hundred peasant uprisings and revolts occurred on Slovenian territory between the 14th and 19th centuries, but they reached their peak between 1478 and 1573. Together with the Protestant Reformation at the end of the 16th century, they are considered a watershed of the Slovenian national awakening

In most of the uprisings, peasant 'unions' demanded a reduction in feudal payments and the democratic election of parish priests. Castles were occupied and pulled down and lords executed, but none of the revolts succeeded as such.

The Protestant Reformation in Slovenia was closely associated with the nobility from 1540 onward and was generally ignored by the rural population except for those who lived or worked on lands owned by the church. But the effects of this great reform movement cannot be underestimated. It gave Slovenia its first books in the vernacular, thereby lifting the status of the language and thus affirming Slovenian culture.

Habsburg Reforms & Napoleon

Ivan Cankar's *Hlapec Jernej in Njegova Pravica* (*The Bailiff Yerney and His Rights*; 1907), a tale of the unequal relationship between servant and master, is read as a metaphor for Slovenia under Habsburg rule.

Reforms introduced by Habsburg Empress Maria Theresa (1740–80) included the establishment of a new state administration with a type of provincial government; the building of new roads; and the introduction of obligatory elementary school in German and state-controlled secondary schools. Her son, Joseph II (1780–90), went several steps further. He abolished serfdom in 1782, paving the way for the formation of a Slovenian bourgeoisie, and allowed complete religious freedom for Calvinists, Lutherans and Jews. He also made primary education in Slovene compulsory. As a result of these reforms, agricultural output improved, manufacturing intensified and there was a flowering of the arts and letters in Slovenia.

But the French Revolution of 1789 convinced the Austrians that reforms should be nipped in the bud, and a period of reaction began that continued until the Revolution of 1848. In the meantime, however, there was a brief interlude that would have a profound effect on Slovenia and its future. After defeating the Austrians at Wagram in 1809, Napoleon decided to cut the entire Habsburg Empire off from the Adriatic. To do this he created six 'Illyrian Provinces' from Slovenian and Croatian regions, and made Ljubljana their capital.

Although the Illyrian Provinces lasted only from 1809 to 1813, France instituted a number of reforms, including equality before the law and

1540–85	16th century	1782	1809
The first printed books appear in Slovene, including a catechism published by Primož Trubar, a complete translation of the Bible by Jurij Dalmatin, and a grammar of Slovene written in Latin.	The Catholic-led Counter-Reformation is in full swing throughout Slovenia; the systematic Germanisation of Slovenia's culture, education and administration begins under the Habsburgs.	Habsburg Emperor Joseph II abolishes serfdom, paving the way for the growth of a Slovenian bourgeoisie, and grants complete religious freedom to Calvinists, Lutherans and Jews.	Ljubljana is named the capital of the French-ruled Illyrian Provinces (1809–13), created by Napoleon from Slovenian and Croatian regions in a bid to cut the Habsburgs off from the Adriatic Sea.

the use of the Slovene language in primary and lower secondary schools and in public offices. Most importantly, the progressive influence of the French Revolution brought the issue of national awakening to the Slovenian political arena for the first time.

Romantic Nationalism & the 1848 Constitution

The period of so-called Romantic Nationalism (1814–48), also known as the Vormärz (pre-March) period in reference to the revolution that broke out across much of central Europe in March 1848, was one of intensive literary and cultural activity and led to the promulgation of the first Slovenian political program. Although many influential writers published at this time, no one so dominated the period as the poet France Prešeren (1800–49). His bittersweet verse, progressive ideas, demands for political freedom and longings for the unity of all Slovenes caught the imagination of the nation then and have never let it go.

In April 1848 Slovenian intellectuals drew up their first national political program under the banner Zedinjena Slovenija (United Slovenia). It called for the unification of all historic Slovenian regions within an autonomous unit under the Austrian monarchy, the use of Slovene in all schools and public offices, and the establishment of a local university. The demands were rejected, as they would have required the reorganisation of the empire along ethnic lines. It must be remembered that Slovenes of the time were not contemplating total independence. Indeed, most looked upon the Habsburg Empire as a protective mantle for small nations against larger ones they considered predators like Italy, Germany and Serbia.

The only tangible results for Slovenes in the 1848 Austrian Constitution were that laws would henceforth be published in Slovene and

SLOVENIA'S NATIONAL ANTHEM

The seventh stanza of France Prešeren's popular poem 'Zdravljica' ('A Toast') forms the lyrics of Slovenia's national anthem:

God's blessing on all nations,
Who long and work for that bright day,
When o'er earth's habitations
No war, no strife shall hold its sway;
Who long to see
That all men free
No more shall foes, but neighbours be.

1821	1848	1867	1918
Members of the Holy Alliance meet at the Congress of Laibach to discuss ways to suppress the democratic revolutionary and national movements in Italy, which lands Slovenia's capital on the world-conference map.	Slovenian intellectuals issue a national political program called United Slovenia, which demands the unification of all historic Slovenian regions within an autonomous unit under the Austrian monarchy.	A number of Slovenes are incorporated into Hungary with the Compromise of 1867, an agreement creating the Dual Monarchy of Austria (the empire) and Hungary (the kingdom).	Austria-Hungary loses WWI and the political system collapses with the armistice of 11 November; the Serbia-dominated Kingdom of Serbs, Croats and Slovenes is established.

that the Carniolan (and thus Slovenian) flag should be three horizontal stripes of white, blue and red. But the United Slovenia program would remain the basis of all Slovenian political demands up to 1918, and political-cultural clubs and reading circles began to appear all over the territory. Parties first appeared toward the end of the 19th century, and a new idea – a union with other Slavs to the south – was propounded from the 1860s onward.

The Kingdom of Serbs, Croats & Slovenes

With the defeat of Austria-Hungary in WWI and the subsequent dissolution of the Habsburg dynasty in 1918, Slovenes, Croats and Serbs banded together and declared the independent Kingdom of Serbs, Croats and Slovenes under Serbian King Peter I. Postwar peace treaties had given large amounts of Slovenian and Croatian territory to Italy, Austria and Hungary, and almost half a million Slovenes now lived outside the borders.

The kingdom was dominated by Serbian control, imperialistic pressure from Italy and the notion of Yugoslav unity. Slovenia was reduced to little more than a province in this centralist kingdom, although it did enjoy cultural and linguistic autonomy. Economic progress was rapid.

In 1929 Peter I's son Alexander seized power, abolished the constitution and proclaimed the Kingdom of Yugoslavia. But he was assassinated five years later during an official visit to France, and his cousin, Prince Paul, was named regent. The political climate changed in Slovenia when the conservative Clerical Party joined the new centralist government in 1935, proving that party's calls for Slovenian autonomy hollow. Splinter groups began to seek closer contacts with the workers' movements; in 1937 the Communist Party of Slovenia (KPS) was formed under the leadership of Josip Broz Tito and the Communist Party of Yugoslavia (KPJ).

WWII & the Partisan Struggle

Josip Broz Tito (1892–1980) was born in Kumrovec, just over the Štajerska border in Croatia, to a Slovenian mother and a Croatian father.

Yugoslavia's involvement in WWII began in April 1941, when the German army invaded and occupied the country. Slovenia was split up among Germany, Italy and Hungary. To counter this, the Slovenian Communists and other left-wing groups formed a Liberation Front (Osvobodilne Fronte, or OF), and the people took up arms for the first time since the peasant uprisings. The OF, dedicated to the principles of a united Slovenia in a Yugoslav republic, joined the all-Yugoslav Partisan army of the KPJ, which received assistance from the Allies and was the most organised – and successful – of any resistance movement during WWII.

After Italy capitulated in 1943, the anti-OF Slovenian Domobranci (Home Guards) were active in western Slovenia and, in a bid to prevent the communists from gaining political control in liberated areas, began

1929	1937	1945	1948
King Alexander seizes absolute power, abolishes the constitution and proclaims the Kingdom of Yugoslavia; he is assassinated five years later by a Macedonian terrorist in France.	The Communist Party of Slovenia (KPS) is formed under the leadership of Josip Broz Tito and the Communist Party of Yugoslavia (KPJ).	Slovenia, occupied by the German army during WWII, is liberated by the Partisans in May and 12,000 Domobranci and anti-communist civilians are executed; Slovenia is included in the Federal People's Republic of Yugoslavia in November.	Yugoslavia distances itself from – and then breaks with – the Soviet Union; exclusion from the markets of the Soviet bloc forces Tito to look to the West.

supporting the Germans. Despite this assistance and the support of the fascist groups in Croatia and Serbia, the Germans were forced to evacuate Belgrade in 1944. Slovenia was not totally liberated until May 1945.

The following month, as many as 12,000 Domobranci and anti-communist civilians were sent back to Slovenia from refugee camps in Austria by the British. Most of them were executed by the communists over the next two months, their bodies thrown into the caves at Kočevski Rog.

Postwar Division & Socialist Yugoslavia

The status of the liberated areas along the Adriatic, especially Trieste, was Slovenia's greatest postwar concern. A peace treaty signed in Paris in 1947 put Trieste and its surrounds under Anglo-American administration (the so-called Zone A) and the areas around Koper and Buje (Istria) under Yugoslav control in Zone B. In 1954 Zone A (with both its Italian and ethnic Slovenian populations) became the Italian province of Trieste. Koper and a 47km-long stretch of coast later went to Slovenia while the bulk of Istria went to Croatia. The Belvedere Treaty (1955) guaranteed Austria its 1938 borders, including most of Koroška.

Tito had been elected head of the assembly, providing for a federal republic in November 1943. He moved quickly after the war to consolidate his power under the communist banner. Serbian domination from Belgrade continued, though, and in some respects was even more centralist than under the Kingdom of Yugoslavia.

Tito distanced himself from the Soviet Union as early as 1948, but isolation from the markets of the Soviet bloc forced him to court the West. Yugoslavia introduced features of a market economy, including workers' self-management. Economic reforms in the mid-1960s as well as relaxed police control and border controls brought greater prosperity and freedom of movement, but the Communist Party saw such democratisation as a threat to its power. What were to become known as the 'leaden years' in Yugoslavia lasted throughout the 1970s until Tito's death in 1980.

Crisis, Renewal & Change

In 1987 the Ljubljana-based magazine *Nova Revija* published an article outlining a new Slovenian national program, which included political pluralism, democracy, a market economy and independence, possibly within a Yugoslav confederation. The new liberal leader of the Slovenian communists, Milan Kučan, did not oppose the demands, and opposition parties began to emerge. But the de-facto head of the central government in Belgrade, Serbian communist leader Slobodan Milošević, resolved to put pressure on Slovenia.

In June 1988 three Slovenian journalists working for the weekly *Mladina (Youth)* – including the former prime minister, Janez Janša – and a

Neil Barnett's relatively slim biography *Tito* (2006), an entertaining and timely read, offers a new assessment of the limits of holding a state like Yugoslavia together by sheer force of personality.

The 2nd edition of *Slovenia and the Slovenes: A Small State and the New Europe* by James Gow and Cathie Carmichael (2010) offers excellent and independent analysis not just of history and politics but of culture and the arts as well.

1956	1980	1987	1988
Tito, in association with India's first prime minister Jawaharlal Nehru and the president of Egypt Gamal Abdul Nasser, founds the Non-Aligned Movement.	Tito, his direct involvement in domestic policy and governing somewhat diminished, dies at age 87, opening the floodgates that lead to the dissolution of the federal republic in the next decade.	*Nova Revija*, a Ljubljana-based magazine, publishes a new Slovenian national program, which Milan Kučan, liberal leader of the Slovenian communists, does not oppose.	The arrest and sentencing of three journalists and a junior army officer for passing on 'military secrets' results in mass demonstrations; independent political parties are established for the first time in more than four decades.

Slovenia 1945: Memories of Death and Survival after World War II (2010), by John Corsellis and Marcus Ferrar, is the harrowing story of the forced return to Slovenia and subsequent execution of thousands of members of the anti-Communist Domobranci after WWII.

junior army officer who had given away 'military secrets' were tried by a military court and sentenced to prison. Mass demonstrations erupted throughout the country.

In the autumn, Serbia unilaterally scrapped the autonomy of Kosovo (where 80% of the population is ethnically Albanian) granted by the 1974 constitution. Slovenes were shocked by the move, fearing the same could happen to them. A rally organised jointly by the Slovenian government and the opposition in Ljubljana early in the new year condemned the move.

In the spring of 1989 the new opposition parties published the May Declaration, demanding a sovereign state for Slovenes based on democracy and respect for human rights. In September the Slovenian parliament amended the constitution to legalise management of its own resources and peacetime command of the armed forces. Serbia announced plans to hold a 'meeting of truth' in Ljubljana on its intentions. When Slovenia banned the meeting, Serbia and all the other republics except Croatia announced an economic boycott of Slovenia, cutting off 25% of its exports. In January 1990, Slovenian delegates walked out on a congress of the Communist Party.

Independence

In April 1990, Slovenia became the first Yugoslav republic to hold free elections. Demos, a coalition of seven opposition parties, won 55% of the vote, and Kučan, head of what was then called the Party of Democratic Renewal, was elected president. The Slovenian parliament adopted a declaration on the sovereignty of the state of Slovenia. Slovenia's own constitution would direct its political, economic and judicial systems; federal laws would apply only if they were not in contradiction to it.

On 23 December 1990, 88.5% of the Slovenian electorate voted for an independent republic, effective within six months. The presidency of the Yugoslav Federation in Belgrade labelled the move 'secessionist' and 'anticonstitutional'. Serbia took control of the Yugoslav monetary system and misappropriated almost the entire monetary issue planned for Yugoslavia in 1991 – US$2 billion. Seeing the writing on the wall, the Slovenian government began stockpiling weapons, and on 25 June 1991 Slovenia pulled out of the Yugoslav Federation for good. 'This evening dreams are allowed', President Kučan told a jubilant crowd in Ljubljana's Kongresni trg the following evening. 'Tomorrow is a new day.'

Indeed it was. On 27 June the Yugoslav army began marching on Slovenia but met resistance from the Territorial Defence Forces, the police and the general population. Within several days, units of the federal army began disintegrating; Belgrade threatened aerial bombardment and Slovenia faced the prospect of total war.

1989	1990	June/July 1991	October 1991
The May Declaration calls for a sovereign state for Slovenes based on democracy and respect for human rights; parliament amends the constitution to legalise peacetime command of armed forces.	The Slovenian electorate overwhelmingly votes for an independent republic within six months; Belgrade brands the action secessionist and anti-constitutional and raids the state coffers of US$2 billion.	Slovenia quits the Yugoslav Federation; fighting erupts when the Yugoslav army marches on Slovenia and meets resistance from the Territorial Defence Forces; the war lasts 10 days and leaves 66 people dead.	Keeping its promise that it would withdraw the federal army from Slovenia within three months, Yugoslavia recalls the last of its soldiers from Slovenian territory.

The military action had not come totally unprovoked. To dramatise their bid for independence and to generate support from the West, which preferred to see Yugoslavia continue to exist in some form or another, Slovenian leaders attempted to take control of the border crossings first. Apparently Belgrade had never expected Slovenia to resist, believing that a show of force would be sufficient for it to back down.

As no territorial claims or minority issues were involved, the Yugoslav government agreed on 7 July to a truce brokered by leaders of what was then called the European Community (EC). Under the so-called Brioni Declaration, Slovenia would put further moves to assert its independence on hold for three months provided it was granted recognition by the EC after that time. The war had lasted just 10 days and took the lives of 66 people.

France Štiglic's 1955 film *Dolina Miru* (*Valley of Peace*) is the bittersweet story of an ethnic German boy and a Slovenian girl trying to find a haven during the tumult of WWII.

WAVING THE FLAG

Slovenia had to come up with a national flag and seal at rather short notice after independence and not everyone was happy with the results. Some citizens said that the flag resembled a football banner while others complained the seal was too similar to that of neighbouring countries such as Croatia.

Though the flag's colours – red, white and blue – were decided in 1848, the national seal was a new design. In order to clear up any confusion, the government information office offered Slovenes and the world an explanation of 'what it all means' on two levels.

'On a national level, the outline of Triglav above a wavy line represents a recognisable sign of the Slovenian regional space, which has been created between the mountain world to the north and west, the Adriatic Sea to the south and the plains of the former Pannonian Sea to the east. The three six-pointed stars of the Counts of Celje symbolise the cultural-statesmanship tradition of the Slovenian lands in relation to their inclusion in the currents of European history.'

And then there's the 'universal' explanation: 'The symbol of a mountain with a water surface along the foothills is a universal archetype symbolising the basic equilibrium of the world. On a human level it also demonstrates the balance between man and woman and, on a planetary level, the balance between civilisation and nature. Such a symbol is understandable to people irrespective of their cultural background since it touches a primal exemplar rooted deep in the subconscious. In addition it is a sign of the future as a postmodern time which once again respects equilibrium on every level. The three gold stars above symbolise spiritual-ethical principles in relation to which the equilibrium is restored. The triangular disposition is a symbol of pluralistic dynamics.' So now we know.

1992	2004	2007	2008
The EC formally recognises independent Slovenia; Slovenia is admitted into the United Nations as the 176th member-state; Serbia's and Montenegro's bid for admission as the Federal Republic of Yugoslavia is rejected.	Slovenia enters the EU as a full member along with nine other countries, and becomes the first transition country to graduate from borrower status to donor partner at the World Bank.	Slovenia becomes the first of the 10 new EU states to adopt the euro, its fourth currency (Yugoslav dinar, tolar scrip, tolar) since independence.	In its most prestigious and high-profile role thus far, Slovenia assumes the presidency of the EU Council in the first half of 2008.

Best Preserved Castles

Ljubljana Castle

Bled Castle

Ptuj Castle

Old Castle Celje

Predjama Castle

The Road to Europe

Belgrade withdrew the federal army from Slovenian soil on 25 October 1991, less than a month after Slovenia introduced its own new currency – the tolar. In late December, Slovenia got a new constitution that provided for a bicameral parliamentary system of government. The head of state, the president, is elected directly for a maximum of two five-year terms. Executive power is vested in the prime minister and his cabinet.

The EC formally recognised Slovenia in January 1992, and the country was admitted to the UN four months later as the 176th member-state. In May 2004, Slovenia entered the EU as a full member and less than three years later adopted the euro, replacing the tolar as its national currency.

2010

The Slovenian parliament ratifies a border arbitration deal with Croatia vital for Zagreb's EU membership bid; Croatia becomes a member three years later.

2012

Janez Janša resumes the premiership in coalition after 3½ years in opposition, and his political opponent and predecessor, former Prime Minister Borut Pahor, unseats President Danilo Türk in a landslide victory.

2013

The coalition collapses over disputes about austerity measures and corruption allegations; Jansa is sentenced to two years in prison for corruption but the conviction is overturned two years later.

2014

The centre-left Miro Cerar Party (SMC), founded by a renowned law professor of that name, wins a snap general election; Cerar forms a coalition government with two other parties.

Slovenian Way of Life

Slovenes are a sophisticated and well-educated people. They have a reputation for being sober-minded, hard-working, dependable and honest – perhaps a result of all those years under the yoke of the Germanic Habsburgs. But they very much retain their Slavic character, even if their spontaneity is sometimes a little more premeditated and their expressions of passion a little more muted than that of their Balkan neighbours. Think quietly conservative, deeply self-confident, broad-minded and tolerant. And mostly happy.

Lifestyle

The population of Slovenia is divided exactly in half between those who live in towns and cities and those who live in the country. But in Slovenia, where most urban dwellers still have some connection with the countryside – be it a village house or a *zidanica*, a cottage in one of the wine-growing regions – the division is not all that great. And with the arrival of large malls on the outskirts of the biggest cities and a Mercator supermarket in virtually every village, the city has now come to the country.

Most Slovenes believe that the essence of their national character lies in nature's bounty. For them a life that is not in some way connected to the countryside is inconceivable. At weekends many seek the great outdoors for some walking in the hills or cross-country skiing. Or at least a spot of gardening, which is a favourite pastime.

Cleveland, Ohio, in the USA is the largest 'Slovenian' city outside Slovenia; other American cities with large concentrations of ethnic Slovenes are Pittsburgh, Pennsylvania, and Chicago, Illinois.

ERICA JOHNSON DEBELJAK: WRITER

Erica Johnson Debeljak is an American writer and translator who moved to Slovenia in 1993. Her memoir *Forbidden Bread* about her own transition to a new culture and language has become required reading for many visitors to Slovenia.

In your writings, you state that the word *priden* 'comes close to defining the essence of the Slovenian soul'. What's it mean? *Priden* is 'diligent' or 'hard-working'. A husband is *priden* when he takes out the garbage. A wife is *pridna* when she waters the geraniums in the window box. Babies are *pridni* if they sleep at night. But Slovenia's nose-to-the-grindstone ideal of itself has been challenged in post-crisis Europe, with corruption, rising unemployment and the flight of young Slovenes abroad. That said, developments in Ljubljana, with its new pedestrian zones and the edginess and sophistication of its festivals and cultural scene, underlie a shift in mentality from the industrial (and being *priden*) to post-industrial, finding a new and more creative way to survive in the new Europe.

You've also hinted at a darker side to the Slovenian character. Explain. That darker side might be embodied in a different Slovenian word: *hrepenenje*. It means something like 'longing' or 'yearning' but it's a more permanent condition – the feeling that life isn't supposed to be perfect, that fulfilment never really comes. This reflects the melancholic side of Slovenes and is the source of its poetry and perhaps its decadence – cigarette smoking, drinking, suicide. But that dark side can also be refreshing after too much Western (especially American) optimism and banality.

It's not hard to reach deep countryside here. Forest, some of it virgin, and woodland covers more than 58% of the land area, the third-most forested country in the EU after Finland and Sweden. And the figure jumps to 66% if you include land reverting to natural vegetation and agricultural plots that have not been used for more than two decades. Land under agricultural use is rapidly diminishing and now accounts for less than a quarter of the total.

With farmstays a popular form of accommodation in Slovenia, it's relatively easy to take a peek inside a local home. What you'll see generally won't differ too much from what you'd see elsewhere in Central and Western Europe, though you may be surprised at the dearth of children. Slovenes don't have many kids – the nation has one of Europe's lowest rates of natural population increase and women usually give birth on the late side (the average age is almost 29). Most families tend to have just one child and if they have a second one it's usually almost a decade further on. And the names of those kids? Overwhelmingly Luka and Jan for boys and Nika and Eva for girls.

Population & Multiculturalism

The French novelist Charles Nodier (1780–1844), who lived and worked in Ljubljana from 1811 to 1813 during the so-called period of the Illyrian Provinces, described Slovenia as 'an Academy of Arts and Sciences' because of the people's flair for speaking foreign languages.

According to the most recent national field census figures, just over 83% of Slovenia's two million people claims to be ethnic Slovene, descendants of the South Slavs who settled in what is now Slovenia from the 6th century AD.

'Others' and 'undeclared', accounting for almost 17% of the population, include (in descending order) ethnic Serbs, Croats, Bosnians, those who identify themselves simply as 'Muslims' and many citizens of former Yugoslav republics who 'lost' their nationality after independence for fear that Slovenia would not grant them citizenship. The status of many as noncitizens in Slovenia – the so-called *izbrisani*, or 'erased' – remains extremely controversial.

The Italians (0.1% of the population) and Hungarians (0.3%) are considered indigenous minorities with rights protected under the constitution, and each group has a special deputy looking after their interests in parliament. Census figures put the number of Roma, mostly living in Prekmurje and Dolenjska, at about 3300, although unofficial estimates are double or even triple that number.

Ethnic Slovenes living outside the national borders number as many as 400,000, with the vast majority in the US and Canada. In addition, 50,000 Slovenes live in the Italian regions of Gorizia (Gorica), Udine (Videm) and Trieste (Trst), another 15,000 or more in Austrian Carinthia (Kärnten in German, Koroška in Slovene) and about 5000 in southwest Hungary.

Slovenes are mostly polyglots, and almost everyone speaks some English, German and/or Italian. The fact that you will rarely have difficulty making yourself understood and will probably never 'need' Slovene shouldn't stop you from learning a few phrases of this rich and wonderful language, which counts as many as three dozen dialects and boasts

SLOVENIA AT THE OLYMPICS

Slovenia punches well above its weight when it comes to winning Olympic medals at the winter and even the summer games. At the 2008 Olympic Games in Beijing, Team Slovenia took gold in the men's hammer throw, two silver medals (women's 200m freestyle swimming and laser sailing) and a bronze each in women's half-heavyweight judo and men's 50m rifle shooting. At the 30th Olympiad in London in 2012, Slovenia won gold in women's half-middleweight judo, silver in men's hammer throw and a bronze each in men's 50m rifle shooting and men's double scull rowing.

not just singular and plural but the 'dual' number in which things are counted in twos (or pairs) in all cases. Any effort on your part to speak the local tongue will be rewarded a hundredfold. *Srečno* (Good luck)!

Sport

Smučanje (skiing) remains the king of sports. The national heroes have been Primož Peterka, ski-jumping World Cup winner in the late 1990s and extreme skier Davo Karničar, who has skied down the highest mountains in each of the seven continents, including the first uninterrupted descent of Mt Everest on skis in 2000. More recent people to follow have been Peter Prevc, who won a silver and a bronze medal at the 2014 Winter Olympics at Sochi and was named Slovenian athlete of the year for the second time, and snowboarder Žan Košir, who took bronze at Sochi. Two women have also helped put Slovenian skiing on the world map. The first is Petra Majdič who, in 2006, was the first Slovenian skier to win a medal in a World Cup cross-country race and went on to collect two dozen more. The second is Tina Maze, the most successful female ski racer in Slovenian history, who won two silvers at the 2010 Winter Olympics in Vancouver and two golds at Sochi. She is the current world champion in giant slalom and holds a world-record number of World Cup points (2414).

Until not so long ago Slovenia was one of the few countries in Europe where *nogomet* (football) was not a national passion. But interest in the sport increased after the national team's plucky performance in the 2000 European Championship and in two of three matches at the 2010 World Cup in South Africa, its second appearance at a World Cup since independence. There are 10 teams in the First Division (Prva Liga), with Maribor, Olimpija Ljubljana and Domžale consistently at the top of the league.

In general *kosarka* (basketball) is the most popular team sport here, and the Union Olimpija team reigns supreme. Other popular spectator sports are *odbojka* (volleyball) and *hokej na ledu* (ice hockey), especially since Anže Kopitar, perhaps the best-known Slovenian athlete in the world, helped the Los Angeles Kings of the US National Hockey League win their first Stanley Cup ever in 2012 and again two years later.

Religion

Although Protestantism gained a very strong foothold in Slovenia in the 16th century, the majority of Slovenes – just under 58% – identified themselves as Roman Catholic in the most recent census. The archbishop of Ljubljana and primate of Slovenia is Stane Zore.

Other religious communities in Slovenia include Muslims (2.4%), Eastern Orthodox Christians (2.2%) and Protestants (less than 1%). Most Protestants belong to the Evangelical (Lutheran) church based in Murska Sobota in eastern Slovenia. Slovenia's first mosque is under construction in the Bežigrad district of northern Ljubljana.

Jews have played a very minor role in Slovenia since they were first banished from the territory in the 15th century. In 2003 the tiny Jewish community of Slovenia received a Torah at a newly equipped synagogue in Ljubljana – basically a room in an office block – the first since before WWII. The chief rabbi of Slovenia is based in Trieste.

Women in Slovenia

Women have equal status with men under Slovenian law but, despite all the work done to eliminate discrimination, bias remains. The share of women in government has improved in recent years: at present more than a third of all MPs are women but only a handful of government departments have a female at the helm. In business about 20% of directorial posts are filled by women.

Every third Slovene regularly takes part in some sort of active leisure pursuit; 3500 sport societies and clubs count a total membership of 400,000 – 20% of the population – across the nation.

For the latest on Union Olimpija and Slovenian basketball see the Eurobasket (www.eurobasket.com/Slovenia/basketball.asp) website.

An excellent guide to the culture and customs of Slovenia is *Culture Smart! Slovenia* by long-term Ljubljana resident Jason Blake.

SLOVENIAN WAY OF LIFE SPORT

The Arts

Slovenia is a highly cultured and educated society, with a literacy rate of virtually 100% among those older than 15 years of age. Indeed, being able to read and write is so ingrained in the culture that the question 'What is your surname?' in Slovene is 'Kako se pišete?' or 'How do you write yourself?' Though few will be able to enjoy Slovenian literature in the original, music, fine art and film are all widespread and accessible.

Literature

Medieval to Modern

The oldest example of written Slovene can be found in the so-called *Freising Manuscripts (Brižinski Spomeniki)* from around AD 970. They contain a sermon on sin and penance and instructions for general confession. Oral poetry, such as the seminal *Lepa Vida (Fair Vida)*, a tale of longing and nostalgia, flourished throughout the Middle Ages, but it was the Reformation that saw the first book in Slovene, a catechism published by Primož Trubar in 1550. A complete translation of the Bible by Jurij Dalmatin followed in 1584. Almost everything else published until the late 18th century was in Latin or German, including an ambitious account of Slovenia, *The Glory of the Duchy of Carniola* (1689), by Janez Vajkard Valvasor (1641–93), from which comes most of our knowledge of Slovenian history, geography, culture and folklore before the 17th century.

The Enlightenment gave Slovenia its first dramatist (Anton Tomaž Linhart), poet (Valentin Vodnik) and modern grammarian (Jernej Kopitar). But it was during the so-called National Romantic Period that Slovenian literature gained its greatest poet of all time: France Prešeren. In the latter half of the 19th century, Fran Levstik (1831–87) brought the writing and interpretation of oral folk tales to new heights with his legends about the larger-than-life hero *Martin Krpan*, but it was Josip Jurčič (1844–81) who published the first novel in Slovene, *Deseti Brat (The 10th Brother)* in 1866.

Slovenia is the third-smallest literature market in Europe (a fiction 'best seller' means 500 to 800 copies sold) and in the EU only the Danes borrow more library books than the Slovenes, the annual average is 10 books per person.

Contemporary Literature

The first half of the 20th century was dominated by two men who single-handedly introduced modernism into Slovenian literature: the poet Oton Župančič (1878–1949) and the novelist and playwright Ivan Cankar (1876–1918). The latter has been called 'the outstanding master of Slovenian prose' and works like his *Hlapec Jernej in Njegova Pravica (The Bailiff Yerney and His Rights*, 1907), influenced a generation of young writers.

Slovenian literature immediately before and after WWII was influenced by socialist realism and the Partisan struggle as exemplified by the novels of Lovro Kuhar-Prežihov Voranc (1893–1950). Since then, however, Slovenia has tended to follow Western European trends: late expressionism, symbolism (poetry by Edvard Kocbek, 1904–81) and existentialism (novels by Vitomil Zupan, 1914–87, and the drama of Gregor Strniša, 1930–87).

The major figures of Slovenian post-modernism since 1980 have been the novelist Drago Jančar (1948–) and the poet Tomaž Šalamun (1941–2014), who has just had a street in Ptuj named after him. Important writers born around 1960 include the poet Aleš Debeljak (1961–) and the writer Miha Mazzini (1961–) whose *Crumbs* (1987) was the best-ever selling novel in Yugoslavia. A personal favourite is Boris Pahor (1913–), a member of the Slovenian minority in Trieste whose books – including *Nekropola (Pilgrim among the Shadows)*, a harrowing memoir of time spent in a concentration camp at the end of WWII – are now being translated into English.

Young talent to watch out for today includes authors dealing with very sensitive issues such as racism and relations with the former Yugloslav republics. The first novel by Andrej E Skubic (1967–), *Fužinski Bluz* (*Fužine Blues*, 2004), takes place on the day of the first football match between independent Slovenia and Yugoslavia. Goran Vojnović (1980–) wrote a satire called *Čefurji Raus!* (2009), which is translated as *Southern Scum Out!* and refers to those from the other former Yugoslav republics living in Slovenia. One of the finest poets to emerge on the Slovenian literary scene in recent years is Katja Perat (1988–) whose *Najboljši So Padli* (*The Best Have Fallen*, 2011) won a best debut award.

Music

As elsewhere in Central and Eastern Europe, music – especially the classical variety – is very important in Slovenia. There is a network of music schools at the secondary level across the nation, and attendance at concerts and recitals is high in cities and towns.

Romantic composers from the 19th century such as Benjamin Ipavec, Fran Gerbič and Anton Foerster incorporated traditional Slovenian elements into their music as a way of expressing their nationalism. But Slovenia's most celebrated composer from that time was Hugo Wolf (1860–1903), born in Slovenj Gradec and best-known for his lieder. Contemporary classical composers whose reputations go well beyond the borders of Slovenia include Primož Ramovš, Marjan Kozina, Lojze Lebič and the ultramodernist Vinko Globokar, who was born in France. Aldo Kumar has received awards for his theatre and film compositions; Milko

The leader of celebrated punk band Laibach, Tomaž Hostnik, died tragically in 1982 when he hanged himself from a *kozolec*, the traditional Slovenian hayrack.

FRANCE PREŠEREN: A POET FOR THE NATION

Slovenia's most beloved poet was born in Vrba near Bled in 1800. Most of his working life was spent as an articled clerk in the office of a Ljubljana lawyer. By the time he had opened his own practice in Kranj in 1846, he was already a sick and dispirited man. He died three years later.

Although Prešeren published only one volume of poetry (*Poezije*, 1848) in his lifetime, he left behind a legacy of work printed in literary magazines. His verse set new standards for Slovenian poetry at a time when German was the literary *lingua franca*, and his lyric poems, such as the masterpiece *Sonetni Venec* (*A Garland of Sonnets*, 1834), are among the most sensitive and original works in Slovene. In later poems, such as his epic *Krst pri Savici* (*Baptism by the Savica Waterfall*, 1836), he expressed a national consciousness that he tried to instil in his compatriots.

Prešeren's life was one of sorrow and disappointment. The sudden death of his close friend and mentor, the literary historian Matija Čop, in 1835 and an unrequited love affair with a young heiress called Julija Primic brought him close to suicide. But this was when he produced his best poems.

Prešeren was the first to demonstrate the full literary potential of the Slovenian language, and his body of verse – lyric poems, epics, satire, narrative verse – has inspired Slovenes at home and abroad for generations.

Lazar is one of the more interesting composer-musicians to emerge in recent years. Opera buffs won't want to miss out on the chance to hear Marjana Lipovšek and Argentina-born Bernarda Fink, the country's foremost mezzo-sopranos.

The bilingual *Slovenian Folk Songs/Slovenske Ljudske Pesmi* (ed Marko Terseglav) is a good introduction to what was (and sometimes still is) sung up in them thar hills.

Popular music runs the gamut from Slovenian *chanson* (as sung by the likes of Vita Mavrič) and folk to jazz and mainstream polka best exemplified by the Avsenik Brothers Ensemble, whose founder Slavko died in 2015. However, it was punk music in the late 1970s and early 1980s that put Slovenia on the world stage. The most celebrated groups were Pankrti, Borghesia and especially Laibach, and they were imitated throughout Eastern Europe. The most popular alternative rock band in Slovenia today remains Siddharta, still going strong after two decades.

Architecture

You'll encounter all styles of architecture – from Romanesque to postmodern – in Slovenia but it is fair to say that for the most part you'll find baroque, with the occasional bits of Gothic and flourishes of art nouveau thrown in to liven things up.

Examples of Romanesque architecture can be found in many parts of Slovenia and include the churches at Stična Abbey in Dolenjska and at Podsreda Castle in Štajerska.

Much of the Gothic architecture in Slovenia is of the late period; the earthquake of 1511 took care of many buildings erected before then (although both the Venetian Gothic Loggia and the Praetorian Palace in

SLAVOJ ŽIŽEK: PHILOSOPHER

Slovenia's best-known son has authored some 60 philosophical works and starred in several films, including the evocatively titled *The Pervert's Guide to Cinema* (2006) and *The Pervert's Guide to Ideology* (2012).

How does it feel to be the most famous Slovene outside the borders? Fame...the irony of it all! But not true in the USA. That would be the ice-hockey star Anže Kopitar or maybe Donald Trump's wife who Germanised her name from Melanija Knavs to Melania Knauss. Maybe she thought it sounded better to be Austrian. You know, *Sound of Music*, Vienna waltzes, the Blue Danube...

And your place in Slovenia? OK, I am Slovene – whatever that means. The official line here is that we are a nation of poets, modest and good. But bad Slovenia is miserly, very Catholic, authoritarian and mean-spirited. An illustration: a fairy appears to a Slovenian farmer and tells him he can have anything he wants but his neighbour will get double. 'OK,' he says, 'take one of my eyes'.

The meaning of life. Discuss. A philosopher knows that asking the right question is more important than providing an answer. My first duty is to disturb the commonplace. And to make you understand what deep shit you are in.

You have quite a following among younger people. How so? Maybe they are tired of postmodern liberal culture and know change is on the way. Look at Occupy Wall St. Or maybe they think I'm a good stand-up philosopher and like my references to popular culture.

Nothing to do with the Lady Gaga 'affair' then? A hoax circulated by my enemies and reported in the media! Imagine me debating the problems of feminist writing with Lady Gaga! But I'm still getting emails from young men asking for an introduction. I imagine writing back that my friend Lady G has said for them to send a sample of their writing and a photograph of themselves naked. I love the idea of being the mediator of a mess, to introduce disorder and then just disappear.

When not in Ljubljana, you might find me in... Škocjan Caves. I once read that Dante used the place as a model for his description of hell.

FOLK MUSIC

Ljudska glasba (folk music) has developed independently from other forms of Slovenian music over the centuries. Traditional folk instruments include the *frajtonarica* (button accordion), *cimbalom* (a stringed instrument played with sticks), *bisernica* (lute), *zvegla* (wooden cross flute), *okarina* (clay flute), *šurle* (Istrian double flute), *trstenke* (reed pipes), Jew's harp, *lončeni bajs* (earthenware bass), *berdo* (contrabass) and *brač* (eight-string guitar).

Folk-music performances are usually local affairs and are very popular in Dolenjska and Bela Krajina. There's also been a modern folk-music revival in recent years. Listen for the groups Katice and Katalena, who play traditional Slovenian music with a modern twist. Nejc Pačnik is one of the greatest folk accordionists to emerge in the past decades.

Koper date back a century earlier). Renaissance architecture is mostly limited to civil buildings (eg townhouses in Škofja Loka and Kranj, Brdo Castle near Kranj).

Italian-influenced baroque of the 17th and 18th centuries abounds in Slovenia, particularly in Ljubljana; very fine examples there include the Ursuline Church of the Holy Trinity and the Cathedral of St Nicholas. Classicism prevailed in architecture here in the first half of the 19th century; the Kazina building in Ljubljana's Kongresni trg and the Tempel pavilion in Rogaška Slatina are good examples.

The turn of the 20th century was when the Secessionist (or art nouveau) architects Maks Fabiani and Ivan Vurnik began changing the face of Ljubljana after the devastating earthquake of 1895. We can thank them for symmetrical Miklošičev Park, the Prešeren monument and the splendid Cooperative Bank on Miklošičeva cesta. The TIC in Ljubljana distributes the excellent map-guide *Fabiania's Ljubljana*. But its safe to say no architect had a greater impact on his city or nation than Jože Plečnik, a man whose work defies easy definition. You'll find most of his creations in Ljubljana but be on the lookout for things like the Parish Church of the Ascension in far-flung Bogojina.

Postwar architecture is generally forgettable, though Edvard Ravnikar's Trg Republike in Ljubljana has recently been improved with the removal of the car park from its forecourt. For a fascinating look at the ideas behind the planning of some of the capital's districts, get a copy of the free map-guide *Modernist Neighbourhoods of Ljubljana*.

Among the most interesting contemporary architects working today are the award-winning team of Rok Oman and Špela Videčnik, whose OFIS Architechts designed the extraordinary Ljubljana City Museum (2004), the Maribor football stadium (2009) and participated in building the landmark Cultural Centre of European Space Technologies (KSEVT) in Vitanje in 2012. In Ljubljana, Atelier Arhitekti have designed the attractive (and useful) Butchers' Bridge (2010) and Fabiani Bridge (2012) over the Ljublanica, while Vesna and Matej Vozlič have given new life to the riverfront Breg.

Janez Vajkard Valvasor's explanation of how the water system in Lake Cerknica worked earned him membership in London's Royal Society in 1687, the world's foremost scientific institution at the time.

Painting & Sculpture

There are three dozen permanent art museums and galleries in Slovenia and hundreds more temporary exhibition spaces, which will give you a good idea of the role that the visual arts play in the lives of many Slovenes.

Examples of Romanesque fine art are rare in Slovenia, surviving only in illuminated manuscripts. Gothic painting and sculpture is another matter, however, with excellent works at Ptujska Gora (the carved altar in the Church of the Virgin Mary), Bohinj (frescoes in the Church of St

John the Baptist), and Hrastovlje (*Dance of Death* wall painting at the Church of the Holy Trinity).

For baroque sculpture, look at Jožef Straub's epic plague pillar in Maribor and the work of Francesco Robba in Ljubljana (eg the Carniolan Rivers fountain now in the National Gallery). Fortunat Bergant, who painted the *Stations of the Cross* in the church at Stična Abbey, was a master of baroque painting.

The most important painters of the 19th century include the impressionists Rihard Jakopič, whose *Sunny Hillside* (1903) recalls Van Gogh, and Ivan Grohar, whose pointillist *The Sower* (1926) is recalled on the €0.05 coin. In the 20th century, the expressionist school of Božidar Jakac and the brothers France and Tone Kralj put a uniquely Slovenian spin on what had previously been primarily a Germanic school. After the war sculptors Alojzij Gangl, Franc Berneker, Jakob Savinšek and Lojze Dolinar dominated the art scene when art was being used as a great tool of communication and propaganda. The last two in particular would create 'masterpieces' of socialist realism under Tito without losing their credibility or (sometimes) their artistic sensibilities.

From the 1980s and onward, postmodernist painting and sculpture has been dominated by the artists' cooperative Irwin, part of the wider multimedia group Neue Slowenische Kunst (NSK). Among notable names today are the artist Tadej Pogačar, sculptor Marjetica Potrč and video artists Marko Peljhan and Marina Gržinič.

Cinema

Slovenia was never on the cutting edge of filmmaking like some of the former Yugoslav republics (such as Croatia). However, it still managed to produce award-winning films such as Jože Gale's *Kekec* (1951), the story of a young heroic do-gooder in an idyllic Slovenian mountain village, and France Štiglic's *Dolina Miru* (Valley of Peace, 1955), the philosophical tale of two orphans on the lam in war-torn Yugoslavia.

What is now touted as the 'Spring of Slovenian Film' in the late 1990s was heralded by two films: *Ekspres, Ekspres* (Gone with the Train, 1997) by Igor Šterk, an award-winning 'railroad' film and farce, and *Autsajder* (Outsider, 1997), by Andrej Košak, about the love between a Slovenian girl and a Bosnian boy who doesn't fit in.

NEJC GAZVODA: FILMMAKER

Nejc Gazvoda is a scriptwriter (he collaborated on Rok Biček's *Class Enemy*) and director whose most recent work is *Dvojina* (Dual, 2013). This tender film about two female strangers wandering the darkened streets of Ljubljana and falling under one another's spell was well received abroad. We asked him to name his top five Slovenian films of all time.

➡ *Trenutki Odločitve* (Moments of Decision, 1955) by František Čap. Drama about being human in inhuman times.

➡ *Na Papirnatih Avionih* (On Paper Planes, 1967) by Matjaž Klopčič. Wonderful and very quirky romance.

➡ Any of the short films of Karpo Godina. Cinematographer and film director, our master visualist.

➡ *Odgrobadogroba* (Gravehopping, 2006) by Jan Cvitkovič. A very bitter comedy about life and death.

➡ *Kratki Stiki* (Short Circuits, 2006) by Janez Lapajne. Altman-like study of people at the breaking point of their lives.

Subsequent successes included *Kruh in Mleko* (*Bread and Milk*, 2001), the tragic story of a dysfunctional small-town family by Jan Cvitkovič, and Damjan Kozole's *Rezerni Deli* (*Spare Parts*, 2003) about the trafficking of illegal immigrants through Slovenia from Croatia to Italy by a couple of embittered misfits.

Lighter fare is Cvitkovič's *Odgrobadogroba* (*Grave Hopping*, 2006), an Oscar-nominated tragicomedy about a professional funeral speaker, and *Petelinji Zajtrk* (*Rooster's Breakfast*, 2007), a romance by Marko Naberšnik set in Gornja Radgona, on the Austrian border in northeast Slovenia.

More recent productions are *Izlet* (*A Trip*, 2011), Nejc Gazvoda's low-budget road movie about lost friendship and youth, and the award-winning *Razredni Sovražnik* (*Class Enemy*, 2013) by Rok Biček about high-school students rebelling against their teacher.

The website of the Slovenian Film Centre (www.film-center.si) will tell you everything you need to know about films and filming in Slovenia.

THE ARTS CINEMA

Food & Drink

Little Slovenia can boast an incredibly diverse cuisine, with as many as two dozen different regional styles of cooking – from Prekmurje in the northeast to Slovenian Istria in the southwest. Until recently, except for a few national favourites, you were not likely to encounter many regional specialities on restaurant menus. But all that is changing as Slovenia reclaims (and often redefines and updates) its culinary heritage. Whatever you do, don't miss an opportunity to try some of these delights in a Slovenian home, where food is paramount.

When to Eat

Taste Slovenia by ethnographer Janez Bogataj is a richly illustrated and instructive tome that divides Slovenia into two-dozen culinary regions – introducing more than 175 dishes – and takes the reader along for the ride.

On the whole Slovenians are not big eaters of breakfast *(zajtrk)*, preferring a cup of coffee at home or on the way to work. Instead, many people eat a light meal called *malica* (literally, 'snack') at around 10.30 or 11am. Lunch *(kosilo)* is traditionally the main meal in the countryside, and it's eaten at noon if *malica* has been skipped. Sometimes it is eaten much later – sometimes in the middle of the afternoon. Dinner *(večerja)* – supper, really – is less substantial when eaten at home, often just sliced meats and cheese on a platter and salad.

Where to Eat

Restaurants go by many names in Slovenia, and the distinctions are not always very clear. At the top of the heap, a *restavracija* is a restaurant where you sit down and are served by a waiter. A *gostilna* (or *gostišče)* has waiters too, but it's more like an inn, with rustic decor and (usually) traditional Slovenian dishes. A *samopostrežna restavracija* is a self-service place, where you order from a counter and carry your food on a tray. An *okrepčevalnica* and a *bife* serve simple 'fast food' such as grilled meats and sausages. A *krčma* may have snacks, but the emphasis here is on drinking (usually alcohol). A *slaščičarna* sells sweets and ice cream whereas a *kavarna* provides coffee and pastries. A *mlečna restavracija* (milk bar) sells yoghurt and other dairy products as well as *krofi* (jam-filled doughnuts).

Slovenian Cookery: Over 100 Classic Dishes by Slavko Adamlje and *Flavors of Slovenia: Food and Wine from Central Europe's Hidden Gem* by Heike Milhench are practical, highly illustrated guides to making Slovenian dishes.

Almost every sit-down restaurant in Slovenia has a menu with dishes translated into English (and often other languages). It's important to note the difference between *pripravljene jedi* or *gotova jedilna* (ready-made dishes) such as goulash or stew that are just heated up and *jedi po naročilu* (dishes made to order or à la carte). Items under the headings *danes priporočamo* or *nudimo* (daily recommendations or suggestions) are frequently in Slovene only. Many restaurants and inns have an inexpensive *dnevno kosilo* (set-lunch menu).

It's popular among Slovenes at weekends to head 5km or 10km out of town to a *gostilna* or *gostišče* where they know they will find good, home-cooked food and local wine at affordable prices.

What to Eat

There are several truisms concerning Slovenian cuisine. In general, it is plain and simple, pretty heavy and fairly meaty. And it is greatly influenced by its neighbours' cooking styles. From Austria, there's sausage *(klobasa)*, strudel *(zavitek* or *štrudelj)* filled with fruit, nuts and/or curd cheese *(skuta)*, and Wiener schnitzel *(dunajski zrezek)*. The ravioli-like *žlikrofi* (pasta stuffed with potatoes, onion and spiced pork), *njoki* (potato dumplings) and *rižota* (risotto) obviously have Italian origins, and Hungary has contributed *golaž* (goulash), *paprikaš* (piquant chicken or beef 'stew') and *palačinka* ('crèpe' filled with jam or nuts and topped with chocolate). From Croatia and the rest of the Balkans come such popular grills as *čevapčiči* (spicy meatballs of beef or pork) and *pljeskavica* (meat patties).

Bread

Nothing is more Slovenian than bread *(kruh)*, and it is generally excellent, especially wholewheat bread *(kmečki temni kruh)*. Real treats are the braided loaves made for weddings and around Christmas – not dissimilar to Jewish challah – and 'mottled bread' *(pisan kruh)* in which three types of dough (usually buckwheat, wheat and corn) are rolled up together and baked.

Soup

Most Slovenian meals start with *juha* (soup) – of which there are said to be a hundred different varieties – year-round but especially in winter. As a starter, this is usually chicken/beef broth with little egg noodles *(kokošja/goveja juha z rezanci)* or *gobova juha* (mushroom soup). More substantial varieties include *jesprenj* (barley soup); *jota*, a very thick potage of beans, sauerkraut or sour turnip, sometimes potatoes and smoked pork or sausage; and *obara*, a stew-like soup, often made with chicken or veal.

Meat & Fish

For most Slovenes, a meal is incomplete without *meso* (meat). The pig is king of the barnyard in Slovenia and *svinjina* (pork) rules supreme,

Štajerska's distinctive *bučno olje* (pumpkin seed oil) is not just an excellent condiment on salads, but can also be poured over vanilla ice cream and sprinkled with green pumpkin seeds or cracked walnuts.

It's the *burja*, the fiercely cold northeast wind in the Karst region, that gives air-dried *pršut* (ham) its distinctive taste.

FOOD & DRINK WHAT TO EAT

SLOVENIA'S TOP SIX RESTAURANTS

The following half-dozen eateries not only serve local and regional specialities but make a positive obsession – very much to their credit – out of using only locally sourced ingredients. It's all part of the slow-food, local-only trend taking Slovenia by storm. And at times the food can be truly awesome.

Restavracija Mak (p210) Magician/chef David Vračko conjures up some of the most imaginative and artful dishes in the land from his Maribor destination restaurant.

Strelec (p56) Haute cuisine from on high – Ljubljana Castle's Archer's Tower, no less – with a menu that traces the city's history chosen by ethnologist Janez Bogataj and prepared by super-chef Igor Jagodic.

Gostilna Rajh (p221) Probably the best restaurant in Prekmurje, this lovely inn near Murska Sobota serves local specialities with a modern twist – ever hear of *gibanica* ice cream?

Hiša Franko (p116) In Kobarid, a town blessed with great dining, Hiša Franko raises the bar with innovative, ardently locavore tasting menus and perfectly paired Slovenian wines.

Majerija (p120) This village farmhouse in a hamlet beautifully showcases the fine wines and tip-top produce of the fertile Vipava Valley, and wows with inventive accommodation.

Hiša Torkla (p146) Foodies are making the 9km journey from Izola to dine at Hiša Torkla, whose star is rising thanks to warm service, very accomplished cooking and a pretty Istrian village setting.

though *teletina* (veal), *govedina* (beef) and, in season, *divjačina* (game), such as *srna* (deer), *merjasec* (boar) and *fazan* (pheasant), are also eaten. Indeed, even *konj* (horse) finds its way to the Slovenian table. *Piščanec* (chicken) is not as common as *puran* (turkey) on a Slovenian menu; *jagnjetina* (lamb) and *koza* (goat) are rarely seen.

Some excellent prepared meats are *pršut*, air-dried, thinly sliced ham from the Karst region that is related to Italian *prosciutto*, and *divjačinska salama* (salami made from game). Slovenes are big eaters of *riba* (fish) and *morski sadež* (shellfish) even far from the coast. *Postrv* (trout), particularly the variety from the Soča River, can be superb.

Groats

Distinctively Slovenian dishes are often served with *žganci*, groats made from *ječmen* (barley) or *koruza* (corn) but usually *ajda* (buckwheat). A real rib-sticker is *ajdovi žganci z ocvirki*, a kind of dense buckwheat porridge with the savoury addition of *ocvirki* (pork crackling or scratchings). Another is *ajdovi krapi* (buckwheat fritters).

Dessert

Slovenian cuisine boasts several calorific desserts. *Potica*, a national institution, is a kind of nut roll (although it's often made with savoury fillings as well) eaten after a meal or at teatime. *Prekmurska gibanica*, from Slovenia's easternmost province, is a rich concoction of pastry filled with poppy seeds, walnuts, apples and cottage cheese and topped with cream. *Blejska kremna rezina* is a layer of vanilla custard topped with whipped cream and sandwiched between two layers of flaky pastry.

Snacks

The most popular street food in Slovenia is a Balkan import called *burek* – flaky pastry sometimes stuffed with meat but more often cheese or even apple – that is a cousin of Turkish *börek*. It's sold at outdoor stalls or kiosks and is very cheap and filling. Other cheap *malice* (snacks) available on the hoof are *čevapčiči*, *pljeskavica* (spicy meat patties), *ražnjiči* (shish kebab) and pizza (which sometimes appears spelled in Slovene as *pica*).

Vegetarian & Vegan

Slovenia is hardly a paradise for vegetarians, but there are a few of meat-free eateries in Ljubljana and provincial cities, and you're sure to find a few meatless dishes on any menu. *Štruklji*, dumplings made with cheese and often flavoured with chives or tarragon, are widely available, as are dishes like *gobova rižota* (mushroom risotto) and *ocvrti sir* (fried cheese). Slovenes love fresh *solata* (salad) – not a usual Slavic partiality – and you can get one anywhere, even in a countryside *gostilna*. In season (usually late summer and autumn) the whole country indulges in *jurčki* (wild boletus mushrooms or ceps) in soups or salads or grilled.

Wine

Vino (wine) has been made in what is now Slovenia since the arrival of the Celts in the 5th century BC, and many of the country's wines are of a very high quality indeed. Be warned, though, that cheaper 'open wine' *(odprto vino)* sold in bars and restaurants is not always of a high standard.

Slovenes usually drink wine with meals or socially at home. As elsewhere in Central Europe, a bottle or glass of mineral water is ordered along with the wine when eating. It's a different story in summer, when people enjoy a *brizganec* or *špricer* (spritzer or wine cooler) of red or white wine mixed with mineral water. Wine comes in 0.75L bottles or is

Why goose on 11 November? According to legend, Martin, the man who would be proclaimed a saint after his death, hid himself among a flock of geese when the faithful were looking for him to tell him he'd just been made a bishop.

You'll find some excellent recipes from around Slovenia, in English, at www.slovenia.si/en/visit/cuisine/recipes.

WHEN TO GO: A FOOD CALENDAR

Slovenes continue to eat seasonal foods and shop at markets whenever possible. Food festivals, usually timed to welcome the seasonal arrival of a certain fruit, vegetable, nut, wine or even fish, are among the red-letter days of the annual calendar in Slovenia and should not be missed should you be in the area.

Spring

The true harbingers of the spring cycle are *regrat* (dandelion greens added to potato salad) and *motovilec* (valerianella, not unlike lamb's lettuce). Then come asparagus from Istria and *ledenka* (ice lettuce) grown in the Trnovo district of Ljubljana to the first strawberries and cherries from Goriška Brda. At pre-Lenten carnivals *krofi* (jam-filled doughnuts) are enjoyed while Easter is marked by decorated eggs and a ham cooked with herbs or *pršut* from Istria with black olives.

Events to mark in your diary include the **Sevnica Salami Festival** (Sevniška Salam-ijada; www.obcina-sevnica.si; Sevnica; ⊙Mar), the **Salt Festival** (Solinarski Praznik; www. portoroz.si/si/dozivetja/prireditve/dogodki/2015/01/08/841-Solinarski-praznik; Piran; ⊙Apr) and the **Vinska Vigred** (p179) wine event.

Summer

The bounty continues with raspberries and blueberries, then stone fruits like apricots. Next are pears and apples from Kozjansko and the start of the nut harvest, especially almonds and walnuts. Lots of gelato is consumed on city streets, *brizganci* (spritzers or wine coolers) quaffed on cafe terraces, and *golaž* (goulash) stewed outdoors in a *bograč* (cauldron) in the east.

Don't miss the **Cherry Festival** (Praznik Češenj; www.brda.si/events_and_festivals; Dobrovo, Goriška Brda; ⊙Jun), the **Polenta Festival** (Praznik Polente; www.praznik-polente.si; Šempas/Ozeljan, Vipava Valley; ⊙Jul) and the **Fishermen's Festival** (Ribiški Praznik; www. izola.info; Izola; ⊙Aug).

Autumn

Folk engage in the national sport – mushroom-gathering – and chestnut stalls arrive in Ljubljana. St Martin's Day (11 November) is when winemakers' *mošt* (must, or fermenting grape juice) officially becomes wine. In the evening families traditionally dine on *gos* (goose) with *mlinci* (thin dried flatbread) and red cabbage and drink new wine.

Check out the **Pumpkin Festival** (Bučarija; www.td-smartno.si; Šmartno ob Paki, Štajerska; ⊙Sep) and the **Sladka Istra** (Sweet Istria; www.sladka-istra.si/sl; Koper; ⊙Sep) and the **Kozjansko Apple Festival** (Prazni Kozjanskega Jabolka; www.kozjanski-park.si; Podsreada; ⊙Oct) and **Vino Ljubljana** (www.vinoljubljana.si/sejem-vino/mednarodni-vinski-sejem; Ljubljana; ⊙Oct) wine fair.

Winter

Persimmons, olives and lots of root vegetables arrive in the markets. It's time for hearty soups like *jota* and *ričet* and mulled wine (made with white wine here too). A Slovenian Christmas just wouldn't be complete without the national dessert: *potica* (nut roll).

Things quieten down a bit in this season but there's always the **Persimmon Festival** (Pražnik Kakijev; www.portoroz.si/si/dozivetja/prireditve/dogodki/2015/08/13/798-Praznik-kakijev-Strunjan; Strunjan; ⊙Nov) and the delightful Christmas fairs in Ljubljana.

ordered by the deci (decilitre, 0.1L). A normal glass of wine is about *dva* deci (0.2L).

Wine Regions

Slovenia counts three major wine-growing regions. Podravje (literally 'on the Drava'), encompassing the Prekmurje and Štajerska Slovenija (Slovenian Styria) districts, extends from northeast Štajerska into Prekmurje and produces whites almost exclusively, including Laški Rizling (welschriesling) and Renski Rizling (a true German riesling), Beli Pinot (pinot blanc), Traminec (gewürtztraminer) and Šipon (furmint).

Posavje is the region running from eastern Štajerska across the Sava River into Dolenjska and Bela Krajina and includes the Bizeljsko-Sremič, Dolenjska and Bela Krajina districts. This region produces both whites and reds, but its most famous wine is Cviček, a distinctly Slovenian dry light red – almost a rosé – with a low (8.5% to 10%) alcohol content. Reds include ruby-hued Metliška Črnina (Metlika black) and whites such as the sweet Rumeni Muškat (yellow muscatel).

The Primorska wine region, which encompasses the districts of Slovenska Istra (Slovenia Istria), Kras (Karst), Vipavska Dolina (Vipava Valley) and the celebrated Goriška Brda (Gorica Hills), excels at reds, the most famous being Teran, a ruby-red, peppery wine with high acidity made from Slovenian Refošk (Refosco) grapes in the Karst region. Other wines from this region are Malvazija (malvasia), a yellowish white from Slovenian Istria that is light and dry, and red merlots, especially the ones from the Vipava Valley and Goriška Brda. A relatively recent phenomenon from the Vipava Valley is so-called orange wine, a white wine with an orange tinge due to contact with the colouring pigments of red grape skins.

Most of the wine-producing districts have a *vinska cesta* (wine route) or two that you can follow in a car or on a bicycle. Many are outlined on the website of the Slovenian Tourist Board (p257). Along the way, you can stop at the occasional *klet* (cellar) that offers wine tastings or at a *vinoteka* (winery) in wine towns.

Choosing Wine

On a Slovenian wine label, the first word usually identifies where the wine is from and the second specifies the grape variety: Vipavski merlot, Mariborski traminec etc. But this is not always the case, and some wines bear names according to their place of origin, such as Jeruzalemčan, Bizeljčan or Haložan.

Slovenia's version of *Appellation d'Origine Contrôlée* (AOC) is *zaščiteno geografsko poreklo* (ZGP), a trademark protection that guarantees provenance and sets the limits to three quality levels. Some 9% is designated *vrhunsko vino* (premium wine), 54% is *kakovostno vino* (quality wine) and 27% is *deželno vino* (regional wine), not dissimilar to French *vin du pays*. The last 10% are wines classified as *priznano tradicionalno poimenovanje* (recognised traditional designation) such as Cviček, Teran, Metliška Črnina, Belokranjec and Bizeljčan. Wines can be red, white, rosé or orange and dry, semidry, semisweet or sweet. Very roughly, anything costing more than about €6 in the shops is a serious bottle of Slovenian wine; pay more than €10 and you'll be getting something very fine indeed and for €15 to €20, wines are super-premium.

One excellent Slovenian sparkling wine that employs the demanding *méthode classique* is Zlata Radgonska Penina from Gornja Radgona in Slovenian Styria, which is based on chardonnay and Beli Pinot. Kraška

---

Mushroom picking is almost a national pastime in the hills and forests of Slovenia in late summer and autumn.

Wine Cellars in Slovenia (2007) by Vito Hazler, which focuses on the top 75 producers in the country, is one of the few single sources of Slovenian viticulture and wine in English.

A MATCH MADE IN HEAVEN

The pairing of food with wine is as great an obsession in Slovenia as it is in other wine-producing countries. Most people know that *pršut* with black olives and a glass of Teran is a near-perfect match, but what is less appreciated is the wonderful synergy other wines from the Karst, including red Rebula, enjoy with these two foodstuffs. With heavier and/or spicier meat dishes such as goulash and salami, try Cviček. Malvazija, a yellowish white from the coast, is good with fish, as is Laški Rizling. And with sweet food such as strudel and *potica*, it's got to be a glass of late-harvest Rumeni Muškat.

DUŠAN BREJC: WINE-TASTER

Dušan Brejc, who has been studying, making, marketing and, of course, tasting wine for more than three decades and has been referred to as Mr Slovenian Wine, is director of the Ljubljana-based **Wine Association of Slovenia** (Vinska Družba Slovenije; ☎01-244 18 00; www.vinskadruzba.si).

What does a wine taster need beside indulgent taste buds? Laborious years of practice. I take the aesthetic approach when it comes to most things and especially wine – pure intuition tells me what is good and what is not. Of course smells can get in the way. A bad smell for me is really bad. The first thing I realise I've missed about Slovenia when I step off the plane at Brnik is the deep smell of the forest.

So what is your favourite Slovenian wine? I'm an insider, not a consumer. I'm too critical and could never name just one bottle. I like red, I like white; I drink sparkling wine, I drink sweet white. I like beer and water but I never – ever – have soft drinks. If it's a *vin complet* I take the same approach be it a €2 bottle or one costing €200.

Aw, come on, don't let us copycats down. Name some vineyards. In Goriška Brda, Simčič has been around for some time and is one of the best. Also very good and consistent is Ščurek. And let's not forget Movia (p65). Vinakoper has once again been voted tops for offering the best value for money. But it's not just about reds from Primorska. In the last few years there's been much interest in the whites of the northeast: Silvaner from Marof; Riesling from Ducal, Kupljen (p206) and Protner; Furmint from Verus and P&F; and the native Bouvier variety from Radgonske Gorice. In fact, Sauvignon Blanc from the northeast is being compared with New Zealand's very best. And just this year, Pullus (p203) from Ptuj won the coveted Decanter International Trophy for its Welschriesling 2012.

Penina, a sparkling Teran, is unique. Late-harvest dessert wines include Rumeni Muškat from Bela Krajina and Slovenian Istria.

Beer

Pivo (beer) is very popular in Slovenia, especially with younger people. Štajerska *hmelj* (hops) grown in the Savinja Valley are used locally, and are also widely sought by brewers from around the world. They have been described as having the flavour of lemongrass.

Slovenia has two major commercial brewers, both of which are owned by the Laško brewery in the town of that name south of Celje. Laško produces the country's two most popular brands: Laško Zlatorog and Union (which is brewed in Ljubljana). Both brands are standard pilsners, with a light golden colour and a hoppy, almost bitter taste. Of the two, Zlatorog is by far the most popular. Union is generally seen as the working-man's beer – the right choice for a bender, when just about anything will do.

Laško also makes a popular, sweetish dark beer *(temno pivo)* called, appropriately enough, Laško Dark. It's frequently available on tap in bars and pubs. Union makes a very popular, low-alcohol (2.5%) shandy called Radler, flavoured with orange, lemon or grapefruit and available in cans and bottles. Another popular Laško beer blend, Bandidos, throws in other alcohols, including tequila.

In recent years locally made craft beers have become the preferred drink of beer connoisseurs, young professionals and hipsters (not in that order). Human Fish, established by an Australian in 2008 just outside Ljubljana, came first. Others include the superior Pelican, based in the Vipava Valley, and Bevog, brewed just over the border in Austria by a Slovene – reportedly because the bureaucratic paperwork to set up here was just too daunting.

There are an estimated 28,000 producers of wine in Slovenia, many of them just family-size farms.

TASTY TRAVEL

Slovenes eat something nobody else does: *polh* (dormouse or loir), a tree-dwelling nocturnal rodent not unlike a squirrel that grows to about 30cm long and sleeps through several months of the year. But unless you are in Notranjska or Dolenjska, where it was once a staple, during the *polharija* (loir-hunting season) in late September and have friends there, it's unlikely you'll get to taste this incredible edible varmint.

Like the French, Slovenes have a taste for horse flesh – literally – and are especially fond of *žrebe* (colt). They like the taste (it's sweeter than beef or mutton), the low fat and the deep, almost ruby-red colour. You can try it most easily as a burger at a fast-food outlet called Hot Horse (p59) in Ljubljana's Park Tivoli, with a branch at the city's BTC shopping mall.

In a *pivnica* (pub), *točeno pivo* (draught beer) is ordered as a *veliko pivo* ('large beer'; 0.5L) or *malo pivo* ('small beer'; 0.3L). Both locally brewed and imported beers are also available at pubs, shops and supermarkets in 0.5L bottles or 0.3L cans.

Brandy

The oldest vine in the world, planted more than four centuries ago and still producing grapes and wine, is the Stara Trta (Old Vine) in Maribor.

An alcoholic drink as Slovenian as wine is *žganje*, a strong brandy or *eau de vie* distilled from a variety of fruits. Common types are *slivovka* (made with plums), *češnjevec* (with cherries), *sadjevec* (with mixed fruit) and *brinjevec* (with juniper). A favourite type is *medeno žganje* (or *medica*), which is fruit brandy flavoured with honey. One of the most unusual (if not the best) is Pleterska Hruška, a pear brandy (also called *viljamovka*) made by the Carthusian monks at the Pleterje monastery (p171) near Kostanjevica na Krki in Dolenjska. Arguably the best *žganje* in the land, though, is *borovnica*, flavoured with forest blueberries, especially the variety produced by the Kejžar distillery in Zreče in the Central Pohorje region of Štajerska.

Survival Guide

Directory A–Z

Accommodation

Accommodation in Slovenia runs the gamut from riverside camping grounds, hostels, mountain huts, cosy *gostišča* (inns) and farmhouses, to elegant castle hotels in Dolenjska and Štajerska, and five-star hotels in Ljubljana, so you'll usually have little trouble finding accommodation to fit your budget. The only exception may be at the height of the season (July and August) on the coast, at Bled or Bohinj, or in Ljubljana.

Virtually every municipality levies a tourist tax of just over €1 per person per night. For stays of fewer than three nights, many pensions and almost all private rooms charge 30% to 50% more, although the percentage usually drops on the second night.

Camping

There's a *kamp* (camping ground) in virtually every corner of the country; seek out the Slovenian Tourist Board's *Camping in Slovenia* brochure. Some rent inexpensive bungalows. Camping 'rough' is illegal in Slovenia.

Rates Camping grounds generally charge per person. Prices vary according to the site and the season, but expect to pay anywhere from €8 to €20 per person (children are usually charged 20% to 50% of the adult fee). An overnight at one of Slovenia's luxurious 'glamping' spots will cost you considerably more. Many camping grounds offer discounts of 5% to 10% to holders of the **Camping Card International** (CCI; www.campingcardinternational.com).

Opening hours Almost all camping grounds close between mid-October and mid-April.

Farmstays

Hundreds of working farms in Slovenia offer accommodation to paying guests, either in private rooms in the farmhouse itself or in Alpine-style guesthouses. Many farms offer outdoor-sport activities and allow you to help out with the farm chores if you feel so inclined.

Rates Expect to pay from about €18 per person in a room with shared bathroom and breakfast (from €28 for half-board) in the low season (September to mid-December and mid-January to June), rising in the high season (July and August) to a minimum of €20 per person (from €30 for half-board). Apartments for groups of up to eight people are also available. There's no minimum stay, but you usually must pay 30% more if you stay fewer than three nights.

Information Contact the **Association of Tourist Farms of Slovenia** (Združenje Turističnih Kmetij Slovenije; ☎03-491 64 80; www.farmtourism.si; Trnoveljska cesta 1, Celje) or check out the Slovenian Tourist Board's excellent *Farm Stays in Slovenia* brochure, which lists upwards of 185 farms offering accommodation.

BOOKING ROOMS WELL IN ADVANCE

It's always a good idea to book as far in advance as possible. Lodging in the capital, Ljubljana, can be especially tight. During spring and autumn, rooms tend to book up during the week, as this is the prime season for business travel. In summer, weekdays are generally okay, but weekends can get crowded. This is doubly true during festivals.

Outside the capital, the lodging situation eases somewhat, though each region has its peak travel season. Naturally, mountain areas near ski resorts crowd up during the ski season, particularly over the weekend. The week between Christmas and New Year and in mid-February, when school kids have a week-long ski holiday, are especially crowded. Similarly, summer resorts crowd up most weekends in July and August.

BOOK YOUR STAY ONLINE

For more accommodation reviews by Lonely Planet authors, check out http://lonelyplanet.com/hotels/. You'll find independent reviews, as well as recommendations on the best places to stay. Best of all, you can book online.

Hostels & Student Dormitories

Slovenia has a growing stable of excellent hostels including Ljubljana's trendy Celica and Tresor, the MCC in Celje, the Situla in Novo Mesto and the Pekarna in Maribor. Throughout the country there are *dijaški dom* (college dormitories) or *študentski dom* (student residences) moonlighting as hostels for visitors in July and August. Unless stated otherwise hostel rooms share bathrooms.

Rates Hostels usually cost from €15 to €25 for a bed; prices are at their highest in July and August and during the Christmas break.

HI Membership More than 40 hostels nationwide are registered or affiliated with the Maribor-based **Hostelling International Slovenia** (Popotniško Združenje Slovenije; ☑02-234 21 37; www.youth-hostel.si; Gosposvetska cesta 84). You are not required to have a Hostelling International (HI) card to stay at hostels in Slovenia, but it sometimes earns a discount or cancellation of the tourist tax.

Hotels

Rates Slovenia's hotel rates vary seasonally, with July and August the peak season and September/October and May/June the shoulders. Ski resorts such as Kranjska Gora and Maribor Pohorje also have a peak season from December to March. In Ljubljana prices are generally constant throughout the year, though weekends are often cheaper at top-end hotels.

Opening hours Many resort hotels, particularly on the coast, are closed in winter.

Mountain Huts

The **Alpine Association of Slovenia** (PZS; ☑01-434 56 80; www.pzs.si; ⊙Dvoržakova ulica 9, Ljubljana; ⊙9am-3pm Mon & Thu, 9am-5pm Wed, 8am-1pm Fri) maintains some 178 mountain huts throughout the land and these are ranked according to category. A hut is Category I if it is at a height of over 1000m and is more than one hour from motorised transport. A Category II hut is within one hour's walking distance from motorised transport. A Category III hut can be reached by car or cable car directly.

Rates A bed for the night runs from €16 to €22 in a Category I hut, depending on the number of beds in the room, and from €10 to €18 in a Category II. Category III huts are allowed to set their own prices but usually cost less than Category I huts.

Pensions & Guesthouses

Pensions and guesthouses go by several names in Slovenia. A *penzion* is, of course, a pension, but more commonly it's called a *gostišče* – a rustic restaurant with *prenočišče* (accommodation) attached. Generally speaking, a *gostilna* serves food and drink only, but some might have rooms as well. The distinction between a *gostilna* and a *gostišče* isn't very clear – even to most Slovenes.

Rates These options are more expensive than hostels but cheaper than hotels, and might be your only option in small towns and villages.

Private Rooms & Apartments

You'll find private rooms and apartments through tourist offices and travel agencies in most towns. The website of the **Slovenian Tourist Board** (www.slovenia.info) provides photos and the location of the house along with rates.

You don't have to go through agencies or tourist offices; any house with a sign reading 'Sobe' or 'Zimmer frei' means that rooms are available. Depending on the season, you might save yourself a little money by going direct.

In Slovenia, *registered* private rooms and apartments are rated from one to four stars.

Rates Prices vary greatly according to the town and season, but typical rates range from around €18 to €35 for a single and €28 to €45 for a double. The price quoted is usually for a minimum stay of three nights. If you're staying a shorter time, you'll have to pay 30% and sometimes as much as 50% more the first night and 20% to 30% extra the second. The price never includes breakfast (from €5 to €8 when available) or tourist tax.

Holiday apartments Some agencies and tourist offices also have holiday apartments available that can accommodate up to six people. One for two/four people could go for as low as €45/60.

SLEEPING PRICE RANGES

The following price ranges refer to a double room with en suite toilet and bath or shower, and include tax and breakfast.

€ less than €50

€€ €51–100

€€€ more than €100

Customs Regulations

Duty-free shopping within the EU was abolished in 1999; Slovenia, as an EU member, adheres to that rule. You can't buy tax-free goods in, say, Austria, Italy or Hungary and take them to Slovenia. However, you can still enter Slovenia with duty-free items from countries outside the EU. The usual allowances apply:

➡ 200 cigarettes, 50 cigars, 100 cigarillos or 250g of loose tobacco

➡ 4L of wine and 1L of spirits

➡ 50g of perfume and 250cc of eau de toilette.

The total value of the listed items must not exceed €175/90 for those over/ under 15 years of age.

Discount Cards

Camping Card International

➡ The Camping Card International (www. campingcardinternational. com) is available free from local automobile clubs, local camping federations such as the UK's Caravan Club (www. caravanclub.co.uk) and sometimes on the spot at selected campgrounds.

➡ They incorporate third-party insurance for damage you may cause, and many campgrounds in Slovenia offer discounts of 5% or 10% if you sign in with one.

➡ For a list, contact the Caravaning Club Slovenije (CCS; www.ccs-si.com).

Hostel Card

➡ No hostel in Slovenia requires you to be a Hostelling International (HI) card-holder or a member of a related association, but they sometimes offer a discount if you are.

➡ **Hostelling International Slovenia** (Popotniško Združenje Slovenije; ☎02-234 21 37; www. youth-hostel.si; Gosposvetska cesta 84) in Maribor sells hostel cards for those aged up to 15 (€5.50), 16 to 29 (€7.50) and over 30 (€9.20). A family card costs €18.

Student, Youth & Teacher Cards

➡ The **International Student Identity Card** (ISIC; www.isic. org; €12.20) provides students with many discounts on certain forms of transport and cheap admission to museums and other sights.

➡ If you're aged under 26 but not a student, you can apply for ISIC's International Youth Travel Card (IYTC; €112.20) or the Euro<26 card (€19) issued by the European Youth Card Association (EYCA; www.eyca.org), both of which offer the same discounts as the student card.

➡ Teachers can apply for the International Teacher Identity Card (ITIC; €15).

Electricity

Plug your appliances into a standard European adapter with two round pins before connecting to the electricity supply (220V, 50Hz AC).

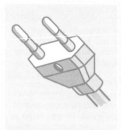

220V/50Hz

Embassies & Consulates

Australian Consulate (☎01-234 86 75; Železna cesta 14, Ljubljana; ⊙9am-noon Mon & Thu, 2-5pm Wed)

Austrian Embassy (☎01-479 07 00; Prešernova cesta 23, Ljubljana; ⊙8.30am-noon Mon-Thu, to 11am Fri) Enter from Veselova ulica.

Canadian Consulate (☎01-252 44 44; Linhartova cesta 49a, Ljubljana; ⊙8am-noon Mon, Wed & Fri)

Croatia Embassy (☎01-425 62 20; Gruberjevo nabrežje 6, Ljubljana; ⊙9am-1pm Mon-Fri)

French Embassy (☎01-479 04 00; Barjanska cesta 1, Ljubljana; ⊙8.30am-12.30pm Mon-Fri)

German Embassy (☎01-479 03 00; Prešernova cesta 27, Ljubljana; ⊙9am-noon Mon-Thu, to 11am Fri)

Hungarian Embassy (☎01-512 18 82; Ulica Konrada Babnika 5, Ljubljana; ⊙8am-5pm Mon-Fri)

Irish Embassy (☎01-300 89 70; 1st fl, Palača Kapitelj, Poljanski nasip 6, Ljubljana; ⊙9.30am-12.30pm & 2.30-4pm Mon-Fri)

Italian Embassy (☎01-426 21 94; Snežniška ulica 8, Ljubljana; ⊙9-11am Mon-Fri)

Netherlands Embassy (☎01-420 14 60; 1st fl, Palača Kapitelj, Poljanski nasip 6, Ljubljana; ⊙9am-noon Mon-Fri)

New Zealand Consulate (☎01-580 30 55; Verovškova ulica 57, Ljubljana; ⊙8am-3pm Mon-Fri) Honorary consulate.

South African Consulate (☎01-241 77 00; Nazorjeva ulica 6, Ljubljana; ⊙9am-noon Mon-Fri) Honorary consulate.

UK Embassy (☎01-200 39 10; 4th fl, Trg Republike 3/4, Ljubljana; ⊙9am-noon Mon-Fri)

US Embassy (☎01-200 55 00; Prešernova cesta 31, Ljubljana; ⊙by appointment)

Food

Slovenia has a highly developed and varied cuisine and a wine-making tradition that goes back to the time of the Romans. For more information, see Food & Drink, p248.

Gay & Lesbian Travellers

Slovenia has a national gay rights law in place that bans discrimination on the basis of sexual preference in employment and other areas, including the military. In recent years a highly visible campaign against homophobia has been put in place across the country; in 2015 it became the first Slavic country to allow same-sex marriage. Outside Ljubljana, however, there is little evidence of a gay presence, much less a community.

➤ **Roza Klub** (Map p46; www.klubk4.org; Kersnikova ulica 4; ⏰10pm-6am Sun Sep-Jun) in Ljubljana is part of the gay and lesbian branches of **ŠKUC** (Študentski Kulturni Center, Student Cultural Centre; www.skuc.org) but is no longer student-orientated as such. It organises the gay and lesbian Ljubljana Pride parade (www.ljubljanapride.

org) in late June and the Gay & Lesbian Film Festival (www.ljudmila.org/siqrd/fglf) in late November/early December. ŠKUC is behind the **Q Cultural Centre** (Kulturni Center Q; Map p46; ☎01-430 35 35; www.kulturnicenterq.org; Metelkova Mesto, Masarykova cesta 24) in Ljubljana's **Metelkova Mesto** (Metelkova Town; Map p46; www.metelkovamesto.org; Masarykova cesta 24), which includes Klub Tiffany for gay men and Klub Monokel for gay women.

➤ Lesbians can contact the Ljubljana-based **Legebitra** (☎01-430 51 44; www.legebitra.si; Truberjeva cesta 76a, Ljubljana; ⏰noon-4pm Mon,Wed & Fri, to 6pm Tue & Thu) and ŠKUC-affiliated LL (www.ljudmila.org/lesbo).

➤ The website of the Slovenian Queer Resources Directory (www.ljudmila.org/siqrd) contains a lot of stuff, both serious and recreational, but is in Slovene only.

➤ Out in Slovenia (www.outinslovenija.com), the first sports and recreational group for gays and lesbians in Slovenia, is where to go for the latest on outdoor activities and events.

➤ The website and blog Narobe (Upside Down; www.narobe.si) is in Slovene only,

though you might be able to glean from the listings.

Health

Medical care in Slovenia corresponds to European standards and is very good. Every large town or city has a *zdravstveni dom* (health centre) or *klinični center* (clinic) that operates from 7am to at least 7pm. Treatment at a public outpatient clinic costs little or nothing; doctors working privately will charge from €40 per consultation.

Pharmacies are usually open from 7.30am to 7.30pm or 8pm, and at least one in each community is open round the clock. A sign on the door of any *lekarna* (pharmacy) will help you find the nearest 24-hour one.

Environmental Hazards

Tick-borne encephalitis (TBE)
Spread by the *klop*, the annoying little insect that burrows under the skin. In recent years, it has become a common problem in parts of Central and Eastern Europe, especially eastern Austria, Germany, Hungary, the Czech Republic and Slovenia. Encephalitis is a serious infection of the brain, and vaccination is advised for campers and hikers who intend on staying in the woods for prolonged periods between May and September. Two doses of vaccine will give a year's protection, three doses up to three years'. For up-to-date information, log on to www.masta-travel-health.com.

Lyme disease Another tick-transmitted infection not unknown in the region. The illness usually begins with a spreading rash at the site of the tick bite and is accompanied by fever, headaches, extreme fatigue, aching joints and muscles and mild neck stiffness. If untreated, these symptoms usually resolve over several weeks, but over subsequent weeks or months disorders of the nervous system, heart and joints might develop.

Mosquitoes These can be a real annoyance, especially around lakes and ponds in the warmer months in Slovenia. The bloodthirsty beasties might not carry malaria, but they can still cause irritation and infection. Just make sure you're armed with a DEET-based insect repellent (*prašek proti mrčesu*) and wear long-sleeved shirts and long trousers around dusk.

Water

Tap water is 100% safe everywhere in Slovenia. If you are hiking or camping in the mountains and are unsure about the water, the simplest way of purifying it is to boil it for 10 minutes. Chlorine tablets will kill many pathogens. Iodine is more effective and is available in tablet form.

Follow the directions carefully, and remember that too much iodine can be harmful.

Insurance

➡ A travel insurance policy to cover theft, loss and medical problems is a good idea. There is a wide variety of policies available, so check the small print. EU citizens on public health insurance schemes should note that they're usually covered by reciprocal arrangements in Slovenia.

➡ Some insurance policies specifically exclude 'dangerous activities', which can include motorcycling and even trekking, so check the small print.

➡ You may prefer a policy that pays doctors or hospitals directly rather than you having to pay on the spot and claim later. If you have to claim later, make sure you keep all documentation. Some policies ask you to call back (reverse charges) to a centre in your home country, where an immediate assessment of your problem can be made. Check that the policy covers ambulances or an emergency flight home.

➡ Paying for your airline ticket with a credit card often provides limited travel accident insurance, and you may be able to reclaim the payment if the operator doesn't deliver. Ask your credit-card company what it will cover.

➡ Worldwide travel insurance is available at www.lonelyplanet.com/travel-insurance. You can buy, extend and claim online anytime – even if you're already on the road.

Internet Access

Virtually every hotel and hostel in the land now has internet access – a computer for guests' use (free or for a small fee), wi-fi – or both.

Most of the country's tourist information centres offer free (or very cheap) access, many libraries in Slovenia have free terminals, and many cities and towns even have free wi-fi in the centre, including Ljubljana.

If you want to get online anywhere, you can get a Visitor SIM for any smart device from €15 for 15 days.

Language Courses

The most famous and prestigious place to learn Slovene is the **Centre for Slovene as a Second/Foreign Language** (Center za Slovenščino kot Drugi/Tuji Jezik; Map p38; ☑01-241 86 47; www.centerslo.net; Kongresni trg 12) at the University of Ljubljana. There are a number of courses available to short-term visitors, students or serious linguists study year-round, including two- and four-week summer courses in July of 40 and 80 hours respectively for €540 and €915, and a two-week (18 hours) elective course for €158. Prices exclude room and board. The centre also sponsors free 1½-hour introductory lessons in Slovene for tourists at 5pm on Wednesday from May to September at the **Slovenian Tourist Information Centre** (STIC; Map p38; ☑01-306 45 76; www.slovenia.info; Krekov trg 10; ☺8am-9pm Jun-Sep, 8am-7pm Mon-Fri, 9am-5pm Sat & Sun Oct-May) in Ljubljana.

A well-received private school offering courses in Slovene in Ljubljana is **Mint International House Ljubljana** (Map p46; ☑01-300 43 00; www.mint.si; Vilharjeva cesta 21), with courses of 51/90 hours costing from €360/565. Individual lessons cost from €33 an hour.

Legal Matters

Persons violating the laws of Slovenia, even unknowingly, may be expelled, arrested or imprisoned. Penalties for possession, use or trafficking of illegal drugs in Slovenia are strict, and convicted offenders can expect heavy fines and even jail terms. The permitted blood-alcohol level for motorists is 0.05%, and it is strictly enforced, especially on motorways. Fines start at €300.

Alcohol may not be purchased from a shop, off-license or bar for consumption off the premises between the hours of 9pm and 7am. You can drink to your heart's content in restaurants and bars, however.

Money

➤ Slovenia uses the euro as its legal tender.

➤ One euro is divided into 100 cents. There are seven euro notes, in denominations of €5, €10, €20, €50, €100, €200 and €500. The designs on the recto (generic windows or portals) and verso (imaginary bridges, a map of the EU) are exactly the same in all 15 countries and symbolise openness and cooperation.

➤ The coins in circulation are in denominations of €1 and €2, then one, two, five, 10, 20 and 50 cents. The 'heads' side of the coin, on which the denomination is shown, is identical throughout the euro zone; the 'tails' side is particular to each member-state, though euro coins can be used anywhere where euros are legal tender, of course.

➤ In Slovenia, the €1 coin (silver centre with brassy outer ring) portrays the Protestant reformer and translator Primož Trubar (1508–86) and the Latin inscription *Stati Inu Obstati* (To Exist and Persevere). The verso of the €2 coin (brassy centre ringed with silver) shows the poet France Prešeren (1800–49) and a line from his poem 'Zdravljica' (A Toast), which forms part of the Slovenian national anthem.

➤ On the three lowest-denomination coins – €0.01, €0.02 and €0.05 (all copper) – are a stork, the Prince's Stone (Knežji Kamen) where the 8th-century Carantanian dukes were installed, and *The Sower* by painter Ivan Grohar (1867–1911). The other

three coins are brass. On the €0.10 coin is a design for a parliament by architect Jože Plečnik (1872–1957) that was never built and the words *Katedrala Svobode* (Cathedral of Freedom). The €0.20 coin features a pair of Lipizzaner horses prancing. The stunning and very symbolic €0.50 coin shows Mt Triglav, the Cancer constellation (under which independent Slovenia was born) and the words *Oj Triglav moj dom* (O Triglav, my home) from the song by Jakob Aljaž (1845–1927).

ATMs
Automated teller machines (ATMs) – called *bančni avtomat* – are ubiquitous throughout Slovenia. If you have a card linked to either the Visa/Electron/Plus or the MasterCard/Maestro/Cirrus network then you can withdraw euros anywhere. Both Abanka and SKB Banka ATMs are linked to both networks.

Credit Cards
Credit cards, especially Visa, MasterCard and American Express, are widely accepted in Slovenia, and you'll be able

---

ADDRESSES & PLACE NAMES

Streets in Slovenian towns and cities are well signposted, although the numbering system can be a bit confusing, with odd and even numbers sometimes running on the same sides of streets and squares.

In small towns and villages, streets are usually not named, with houses simply numbered. Thus Ribčev Laz 13 is house No 13 in the village of Ribčev Laz on Lake Bohinj. As Slovenian villages are frequently made up of one road with houses clustered on or just off it, this is seldom very confusing.

In Slovene, places with double-barrelled names such as Novo Mesto (New Town) and Črna Gora (Black Hill) start the second word in lower case (Novo mesto, Črna gora), almost as if the names were Newtown and Blackhill. This is the correct Slovene orthography, but we've opted to go with the English-language way of doing it to avoid confusion.

Slovene frequently uses the possessive (genitive) case in street names. Thus a road named after the poet Ivan Cankar is Cankarjeva ulica and a square honouring France Prešeren is Prešernov trg. Also, when nouns are turned into adjectives they often become unrecognisable. The town is 'Bled', for example, but 'Bled Lake' is Blejsko Jezero. A street leading to a castle (*grad*) is usually called Grajska ulica. A road going in the direction of Trieste (Trst) is Tržaška cesta, Klagenfurt (Celovec) is Celovska cesta and Vienna (Dunaj) is Dunajska cesta. The words *pri*, *pod* and *na* in place names mean 'at the', 'below the' and 'on the' respectively.

to use them at many restaurants, shops, hotels, car-rental firms, travel agencies and petrol stations. Diner's Club is also accepted but less frequently. Many banks give cash advances on major credit cards but charge both a fee and interest.

A good alternative to credit cards is the Travelex Cash Passport (www.travelex.co.uk/Cash_Passport) – a prepaid travel card that you load up with funds before departure and then withdraw funds in local currency as you go along, throwing it away when you're done.

Moneychangers

It is easy to change cash and travellers cheques at banks, post offices, tourist offices, travel agencies and private exchange offices. Look for the words *menjalnica* or *devizna blagajna* to guide you to the correct place or window. Most banks take a *provizija* (commission) of 1% on travellers cheques but usually nothing at all on cash. Tourist offices, travel agencies and exchange bureaus usually charge around 3%. Hotels can take as much as 5%.

Taxes & Refunds

Value-added tax (known as *davek na dodano vrednost* or DDV in Slovenia) is applied to the purchase of most goods and services at a standard rate of 22% (eg on alcoholic drinks, petrol and so on) and a reduced rate of 9.5% (eg on accommodation, food, books, museum entrance fees etc). It is usually included in the quoted price of goods but not always.

Visitors who are not residents of the European Union can claim refunds on total purchases of €50 (not including tobacco products or spirits) issued on one or more receipts by the same retailer/shop on the same day as long as they take the goods out of the country (and the EU) within three

months. In order to make the claim, you must have a DDV-VP form or Tax Refund Cheque correctly filled out by the salesperson at the time of purchase and have it stamped by a Slovenian customs officer at the border. You can then collect your refund – minus handling fee – from selected offices or have it deposited into your credit-card account. For more information see the Global Blue (www.globalblue.com) website.

Tipping

When a gratuity is not included in your bill, which may or may not be the case, paying an extra 10% is customary. If service is outstanding, you could go as high as 15%. With taxi drivers, however, you usually just round up the sum.

Opening Hours

The *delovni čas* (opening times) are usually posted on the door. *Odprto* is 'open', *zaprto* is 'closed'.

Grocery stores and supermarkets Usually open from 8am to 7pm weekdays and 8am until 1pm on Saturday. Some branches of Mercator supermarket open Sunday mornings.

Restaurants Hours vary tremendously but essentially are from 11am to 10pm daily. Bars are equally variable but are usually open 11am to midnight Sunday to Thursday and to 1am or 2am on Friday and Saturday.

Banks Generally from 8.30 or 9am to 5pm weekdays (often with a lunchtime break from 12.30pm to 2pm) and (rarely) from 8am until noon Saturday.

Main post office Opens from 8am to 6pm or 7pm weekdays and 8am until noon on Saturday.

Museums Usually open from 10am to 6pm Tuesday to Sunday. Winter hours may be shorter (sometimes weekends only) outside the big cities and towns.

Post

The Slovenian postal system (Pošta Slovenije), recognised by its bright yellow logo, offers a wide variety of services – from selling stamps and telephone cards to making photocopies and changing money. Newsstands also sell *znamke* (stamps). Post offices can sell you boxes.

Postal Rates

Domestic Mail costs €0.36 for up to 20g depending on the size, €0.42 for up to 50g and €0.47 for up to 100g. Postcards are €0.42.

International The rate is from €0.60 for 20g or less and €0.97 for up to 100g. A postcard costs €0.56.

Sending & Receiving Mail

➡ Look for the sign 'Pisma – Paketi' if you've got a *pismo* (letter) or *paket* (parcel) to post.

➡ *Poštno ležeče* (poste restante) is kept at the main post office of a city or town. In the capital, address it to Glavni Pošta, Slovenska cesta 32, 1101 Ljubljana, where it will be held for 30 days. Pick it up at window 3.

Public Holidays

Slovenia celebrates 14 *prazniki* (holidays) each year. If any of them fall on a Sunday, then the Monday becomes the holiday.

New Year's holidays 1 and 2 January

Prešeren Day (Slovenian Culture Day) 8 February

Easter & Easter Monday March/April

Insurrection Day 27 April

Labour Day holidays 1 and 2 May

National Day 25 June

Assumption Day 15 August

Reformation Day 31 October

All Saints' Day 1 November

Christmas Day 25 December
Independence Day 26 December

Safe Travel

Slovenia is not a violent or dangerous society. Police say that 90% of all crimes reported in Slovenia involve theft, so take the usual precautions.

➡ Be careful of your purse or wallet in busy areas like bus and train stations, and don't leave it unattended on the beach, or in a hut while hiking.

➡ Lock your car, park in well-lit areas and do not leave valuables visible.

➡ Bicycle theft is also on the increase – one of us had a rental bike stolen in Ljubljana during our last visit. Secure it at all times (or, even better, bring it indoors).

Telephone

➡ Public telephones require a *telefonska kartica* or *telekartica* (telephone card) available at post offices and some newsstands. Phonecards cost €3/4.25/7.25/14.85 for 25/50/100/300 *impulzov* (impulses, or units).

➡ Rates are usually 20% cheaper on calls placed between 7pm and 7am every day.

➡ Slovenian call boxes do not display their telephone numbers, so it's impossible for the other party to phone you back.

➡ To call Slovenia from abroad, dial the international access code, ☎386 (the country code for Slovenia),

the area code (minus the initial zero) and the number. There are six area codes in Slovenia (☎01 to ☎05 and ☎07).

➡ To call abroad from Slovenia, dial ☎00 followed by the country and area codes and then the number. Numbers beginning with ☎80 are toll-free.

Mobile Phones

Network coverage amounts to more than 95% of the country. Mobile numbers carry the prefix ☎030 and ☎040 (SiMobil), ☎031, ☎041, ☎051 and ☎071 (Telekom Slovenija), and ☎070 and ☎080 (Telemach).

Slovenia uses GSM 900, which is compatible with the rest of Europe and Australia but not with the North American GSM 1900 or the Japanese system. SIM cards with €5 credit are available for just €9.50 from providers Si-Mobil, Telekom Slovenija and Telemach (www.telemach.si). Top-up scratch cards are available at post offices, newsstands and petrol stations. Cheap mobile phones with SIM (from €29.50) are available from vending machines at the airport and bus station in Ljubljana.

All three networks have outlets throughout Slovenia, including in Ljubljana.

Simobil (☎040 404 040; www.simobil.si; Prešernov trg 2; ⏰8am-7pm Mon-Fri, 9am-1pm Sat)

Telekom Slovenija (☎01-472 24 60; www.telekom.si/en; Trg Ajdovščina 1; ⏰8am-5pm Mon-Sat)

Tušmobil (☎080 700 700; www.tusmobil.si; Wolfova ulica 4; ⏰9am-8pm Mon-Fri, to 1pm Sat)

Time

➡ Slovenia lies in the Central European time zone. Winter time is GMT plus one hour while in summer it's GMT plus two hours.

➡ Clocks are advanced one hour at 2am on the last Sunday in March and set back at the same time on the last Sunday in October.

➡ Like some other European languages, Slovene tells the time by making reference to the next hour – not the previous one (as in English and other languages). Thus 1.15 is 'one-quarter of two', 1.30 is 'half of two' and 1.45 is 'three-quarters of two'.

Toilets

Finding a public lavatory is not always easy in Slovenia, and when you do, you sometimes have to pay up to €0.50 to use it. They're free in central Ljubljana, however. All train stations have toilets as do most shopping centres and department stores. The standard of hygiene is usually good.

Tourist Information

The **Slovenian Tourist Board** (Slovenska Turistična Organizacija, STO; ☎01-589 18 40; www.slovenia.info; Dunajska cesta 156) based in Ljubljana is the umbrella organisation for tourist promotion, and produces a number of excellent brochures, pamphlets and booklets in English.

Walk-in visitors in Ljubljana can head to the **Slovenian Tourist Information Centre** (STIC; Map p38; ☎01-306 45 76; www.slovenia.info; Krekov trg 10; ⏰8am-9pm Jun-Sep, 8am-7pm Mon-Fri, 9am-5pm Sat & Sun Oct-May). In addition, the STO oversees another five dozen or so local tourist offices and bureaus called 'tourist information centres' (TICs) across the

---

USEFUL TELEPHONE NUMBERS

Domestic Directory Assistance (☎1188)

International Directory Assistance (☎1180)

International Operator/Collect Calls (☎115)

country; there are independent or community-run offices in other smaller cities and towns. In the unlikely event that the place you're visiting doesn't have either, seek assistance at a travel agency or from hotel or museum staff.

The best office in Slovenia for face-to-face information is the **Ljubljana Tourist Information Centre** (TIC; Map p38; ☏01-306 12 15; www.visitljubljana.com; Adamič-Lundrovo nabrežje 2; ◷8am-9pm Jun-Sep, to 7pm Oct-May) run by Ljubljana Tourism (Turizem Ljubljana). The staff know everything about the capital and almost as much about the rest of Slovenia.

Travellers with Disabilities

Facilities found throughout Slovenia include public telephones with amplifiers, pedestrian crossings with beepers, Braille on maps at city bus stops, occasional lifts in pedestrian underpasses, sloped pavements and ramps in government buildings, and reserved spaces in many car parks. A large number of big hotels have at least one room designed for disabled guests (bathrooms big enough for a wheelchair user to turn around in, access door on bath tubs, grip bars alongside toilets etc).

The **Paraplegics Association of Slovenia** (Zveza Paraplegikov Republike Slovenije; ☏01-432 71 38; www.zveza-paraplegikov.si/eng; Štihova ulica 14, Ljubljana) looks after the interests and special needs of paraplegics and tetraplegics, and produces a guide for its members in Slovene only (although their English-language website is fairly complete). Another active group is the **Slovenian Association of Disabled Students** (Društvo Študentov Invalidov Slovenije; ☏01-565 33 51; www.dsis-drustvo.si; Kardeljeva ploščad 5, Ljubljana). Some towns and cities produce useful brochures describing which local sights and attractions are accessible by wheelchair. Ask the Tourist Information Centre.

Visas

➡ Virtually everyone entering Slovenia must have a valid passport, although citizens of the EU as well as Switzerland need only produce their national identity card on arrival for stays of up to 30 days. It's a good idea to carry your passport or other identification at all times.

➡ Citizens of virtually all European countries as well as Australia, Canada, Israel, Japan, New Zealand and the USA do not require visas to visit Slovenia for stays of up to 90 days.

➡ Those who do require visas (including South Africans) can get them at any Slovenian embassy or consulate for up to 90 days – see the website of the Ministry of Foreign Affairs (www.mzz.gov.si) for a full listing. They cost €35 regardless of the type or length of validity. You'll need confirmation of a hotel booking plus one photo and may have to show a return or onward ticket.

Women Travellers

Travelling as a single woman in Slovenia is no different from travelling in most Western European countries. If you can handle yourself in the very occasional less-than-comfortable situation, you'll be fine.

In the event of an emergency call the **police** (☏113) any time or the **SOS Helpline** (☏080 11 55; www.drustvo-sos.si; ◷noon-10pm Mon-Fri, 6-10pm Sat & Sun).

Transport

GETTING THERE & AWAY

Flights, cars and tours can be booked online at lonelyplanet.com/bookings.

Entering the Country

Border formalities with Slovenia's fellow European Union neighbours – Italy, Austria and Hungary are nonexistent. Croatia has been an EU member since 2013 but still does not fall within the Schengen Zone, though it has applied. Until it does join, expect a somewhat closer inspection of your documents – national ID (for EU citizens) or passport and, in some cases, a visa when travelling to/from Croatia.

Passport

Virtually everyone entering Slovenia must have a valid passport, although citizens of the EU as well as Switzerland need only produce their national identity card on arrival for stays of up to 30 days. It's a good idea to carry your passport or other identification at all times.

Air

Airports & Airlines

Slovenia's main international airport receiving regular scheduled flights is Ljubljana's **Jože Pučnik Airport** (Aerodrom Ljubljana; ☑04-206 19 81; www.lju-airport.si/eng; Zgornji Brnik 130a, Brnik), 27km north of Ljubljana. In the arrivals hall there's a **Slovenia Tourist Information Centre desk** (STIC; www.visitljubljana.si; Jože Pučnik Airport, Brnik; ☺8.30am-1.30pm & 4-8pm), five travel agencies and an ATM. Some 10 car-rental agencies, including Avis, Budget, Europcar, Hertz and Sixt, have outlets opposite the terminal.

Adria Airways (☑04-259 45 82, 01-369 10 10; www.adria-airways.com) From its base at Brnik, the Slovenian flag-carrier, Adria Airways, serves more than 20 European destinations on regularly scheduled flights. Adria connects twice or four times daily with Munich, Frankfurt and Zürich; daily with London (Luton) and Paris; and there are useful connections to other former Yugoslav capitals.

Air France (☑01-244 34 47; www.airfrance.com/si) Flights to Paris (CDG).

Air Serbia (☑01-231 43 40; www.airserbia.com) Flights to Belgrade.

EasyJet (☑04-206 16 77; www.easyjet.com) Low-cost flights to London (STN).

Finnair (☑in Helsinki 358-9-818 888; www.finnair.com) Flights to Helsinki.

Lufthansa (☑01-434 72 46; www.lufthansa.com; Gosposvetska cesta 6) Code-shared flights with Adria to Frankfurt and Munich.

CLIMATE CHANGE & TRAVEL

Every form of transport that relies on carbon-based fuel generates CO_2, the main cause of human-induced climate change. Modern travel is dependent on aeroplanes, which might use less fuel per kilometre per person than most cars but travel much greater distances. The altitude at which aircraft emit gases (including CO_2) and particles also contributes to their climate change impact. Many websites offer 'carbon calculators' that allow people to estimate the carbon emissions generated by their journey and, for those who wish to do so, to offset the impact of the greenhouse gases emitted with contributions to portfolios of climate-friendly initiatives throughout the world. Lonely Planet offsets the carbon footprint of all staff and author travel.

Montenegro Airlines
(☑04-259 42 52; www.monte
negroairlines.com) Flights to
Podgorica.

Turkish Airlines (☑04-206
16 80; www.turkishairlines.com)
Flights to Istanbul.

Wizz Air (☑in UK 44-330 977
0444; www.wizzair.com) Flights
to London (LTN).

Land

Slovenia is well connected
by road and rail with its four
neighbours – Italy, Austria,
Hungary and Croatia. Bus
and train timetables sometimes use Slovenian names
for foreign cities (p276).

Bus

Most international buses
arrive and depart from
Ljubljana **bus station** (Avtobusna Postaja Ljubljana; Map
p46; ☑01-234 46 00; www.
ap-ljubljana.si; Trg Osvobodilne
Fronte 4; ⊙5am-10.30pm Mon-
Sat, 5.30am-10.30pm Sun).

CROATIA, BOSNIA &
HERCEGOVINA, & SERBIA

Koper, Piran and Portorož
are the ports of entry from
Croatian Istria and points
farther south by bus. A bus
leaves Koper daily at 9.30am
for Rijeka (€14.50, two hours,
84km), and there are buses
at 9.30am and 6.30pm daily
to Pula (€11.60, 2½ hours,
101km) via Poreč, Umag and
Rovinj.

From Ljubljana, you can
count on at least two daily
departures to Belgrade
(€38.70 to €40.70, eight
hours, 532km) in Serbia.
Buses depart from Ljubljana
daily for the Croatian cities
of Rijeka (€14.20, 2½ hours,
136km), Split (€32.70,
eight hours, 528km), Zadar
(€28.70, 6½ hours, 344km)
and Dubrovnik (€42.70,13
hours, 658km). There are
also daily buses to Sarajevo
in Bosnia & Hercegovina
(€44.70 to €48.70, 9½ to 12
hours, 554km) and Banja
Luka (€27.20, 5½ hours,
336km).

ITALY

Buses from Koper to Trieste
(€3, one hour) run along
the coast via Ankaran and
Muggia Monday to Saturday.
Hourly buses link the train
stations in the Italian city
of Gorizia with Nova Gorica
(€1, 25 minutes) just across
the border. There are multiple daily departures from
Ljubljana to Trieste (€7, 1½
hours, 105km). At least three
daily buses link Ljubljana
with Mestre (€20, four hours,
240km) near Venice, and
there's a daily departure for
Florence (€48, seven hours,
487km).

GERMANY

From Germany, a daily overnight bus links Frankfurt and
Ljubljana (€90, 11½ hours,
777km) via Stuttgart and
Munich. The northbound bus
leaves Ljubljana on Thursday,
Friday and Saturday. There
are at least two daily departures for Munich (€28.70,
five hours, 405km) and
buses three times a week to
Dortmund (€83.70, 17 hours,
1012km) via Cologne.

There's a daily overnight
bus from Maribor across
Austria to Munich, Stutt-
gart and Frankfurt (€95, 14
hours).

HUNGARY

The Hungarian town of
Rédics is only 7km to the
north of Lendava, in northeastern Slovenia, which can
be reached from Murska
Sobota (€3.60, 30 minutes,
29km). Three buses a day
link Murska Sobota and
Ljubljana (€16, three hours,
195km). From Rédics, buses
go to Zalaegerszeg (930Ft,
1¼ hours, 49km) for rail connections to Budapest.

Car & Motorcycle

Slovenia maintains some
150 border crossings with
its neighbours. Motorists will
need the vehicle's registra-
tion papers, liability insurance and a driver's licence.

Train

The **Slovenian Railways**
(Slovenske Železnice, SŽ; ☑01-
291 33 32; www.slo-zeleznice.
si) network links up with the
European railway network
via Austria (Villach, Salzburg, Graz, Vienna), Ger-
many (Munich, Frankfurt),
Czech Republic (Prague),
Croatia (Zagreb, Rijeka),
Hungary (Budapest), Swit-
zerland (Zürich) and Serbia
(Belgrade).

International direct trains
include EuroCity (EC) ones
linking Ljubljana with Vienna as well as Salzburg and
Munich. InterCity (IC) trains
connect Maribor with Vienna and Graz, and Ljubljana
with Villach, Zagreb and
Belgrade. Express trains run
via Ljubljana between Zürich
and Belgrade, Vienna and
Zagreb, Munich and Zagreb,
and Munich and Rijeka. Euro-
Night (EN) trains between
Budapest and Venice go via
Ljubljana and Zagreb.

DISCOUNTS & PASSES

Undiscounted international
tickets on Slovenian Railways trains are valid for two
months. Certain fares bought
at special offer are valid for
just a month, while others
are valid only for the day and
train indicated on the ticket.
Half-price tickets are available for children between the
ages of six and 12 years.

InterRail A Global Pass from
InterRail (www.interrailnet.com)
covers 30 European countries
and can be purchased by
nationals of European countries
(or residents of at least six
months). A pass offers 1st-/2nd-
class travel for five days within
a 10-day period (€267/171),
10 days within a 22-day period
(€380/242), 22 continuous
days (€491/313), or one month
(€636/405). Discounts are
available for those under 26.
Inter Rail now offers a 'One
Country Pass' valid for rail travel
in Slovenia starting at €92/60
for three days' 1st/2nd-class
travel within a month.

Eurail It would be impossible for a standard Eurail pass (www.eurailnet.com) to pay for itself in Slovenia. But if you are a non-European resident, you may consider one of its combination tickets allowing you to travel over a fixed period for a set price. These include the Hungary N' Slovenia/Croatia and Austria N' Slovenia/Croatia passes, offering five/10 days of travel within two months on those countries' rail networks for adults US$271/440 and youths US$218/353; children aged four to 11 travel half-price. Buy the pass before you leave home.

CROATIA, BOSNIA & HERCEGOVINA, & SERBIA

From Croatia, there are five trains a day to Ljubljana from Zagreb via Zidani Most (€16.40, two hours, 141km), two a day from Rijeka (€17, two hours, 135km) via Postojna, and two a day from Split (€58.20, eight to 12 hours, 456km), with a change at Zagreb. There are also two trains a day from Belgrade (€54.80, nine to 10 hours, 569km) in Serbia via Zagreb. One train a day links Sarajevo (€49.20, 12 hours, 670km) in Bosnia & Hercegovina with Ljubljana; change at Zagreb.

ITALY

There is no direct rail link with Italy at this time. One possibility is to go first to Nova Gorica (€10, 3½ hours, 153km), walk across the border to Gorizia then take an Italian train to Venice (about €10).

GERMANY & AUSTRIA

There are three direct trains a day between Ljubljana and Munich (€91.40, six hours, 441km) via Villach and Salzburg; one carries on to Frankfurt (€171.40, 10 hours, 859km). One train links Ljubljana with Villach (€21.40, two hours, 102km).

To get to Vienna (€78.20, six hours, 441km) from Ljubljana there is the direct EC

Emona, or two other trains which require a change at Maribor. Graz (€41.80, three hours, 221km) trains also include a change at Maribor.

While fares to Vienna and Graz from Ljubljana and Maribor are high, so-called SparSchiene fares as low as €29 (valid for travel in one direction in 2nd class) apply on certain trains at certain times. Also, a Praga Spezial fare is available for only €49 to those travelling to Prague via Villach and Vienna, but the number of these discounted tickets per train is limited.

HUNGARY

The *EN Venezia* links Ljubljana directly with Budapest (€49.80, nine hours, 507km) via Zagreb. There are Budapest Spezial fares on this train for as low as €39/29 1st/2nd class.

SWITZERLAND

The overnight MV414/415 links Ljubljana directly with Zürich (€89, 14½ hours, 730km) via Schwarzach-St Veit; the SparSchiene (€29) and SparNight (with couchette; €39) offer enormous savings on the standard fare.

Sea

➡ The travel agency **Kompas** (☑05-617 80 13; www.kompas-online.net; Pristaniška ulica 17, Koper; ☺8am-7.30pm Mon-Fri, 8am-1pm Sat) runs excursions to Venice from Izola on the *Prince of Venice*, a 40m-long, high-speed catamaran. It departs Izola at 8am (Piran at 7.30am) and arrives in Venice at 11am; the return journey departs at 5pm and arrives back at Izola at 8pm. The schedule changes according to the month but essentially there are sailings on Saturday or Sunday from from late April to early October. An adult return ticket costs €60 to €75 (children aged three to 14 pay half-price) depending

on the season and day, including a tour of Venice.

➡ From May to September, **Venezia Lines** (☑in Croatia 385-52 422 896; www.venezialines.com) runs a ferry service service between Piran and Venice, departing at 7.30am and returning at 7.45pm on Wednesday, Friday and Sunday. In July and August the boat sails daily. Same-day return tickets, available at many travel agencies in Piran and Portorož, including Maona Tourist Agency (www.maona.si), are from just €65/35 adult/child aged four to 12. Otherwise it's €67/121 one way/return for adults and €42/76.50 for children.

➡ The Portorož-based agency **Topline** (☑05-674 71 60; www.topline.si; Obala 114, Portorož) runs the 42m-long catamaran *San Frangisk* from Piran to Venice at 8.30am on Saturday from May to September returning at 5.15pm. In July and August the boat sails on Sunday as well at 7.30am, returning at the same time. The adult same-day return fare is from €65, with children aged three to 12 paying €35. If you want to spend the night it's from one-way/return €61/122 for adults and €38/76.50 for children.

➡ A service run by **Trieste Lines** (☑040 200 620; www.triestelines.it) links Piran with Trieste daily except Wednesdays at 7.25pm from May to September, returning the next day at 9am. Buy tickets (one way/return €8/13.50, children six to 14 half-price) from the **Tourist Information Centre** (TIC; Map p148; ☑05-673 44 40; www.portoroz.si; Tartinijev trg 2; ☺9am-10pm Jul & Aug, to 5pm Sep-Jun) in Piran. The same line also sails to/from Rovinj in Croatia at 9.40am, returning at 6.05pm; one way/return is €19.50/33.

GETTING AROUND

Air

Slovenia has no scheduled domestic flights.

Bicycle

Cycling is a popular way of getting around. Bikes can be transported for €3.50 in the baggage compartments of IC and regional trains. Larger buses can also carry bikes as luggage. Cycling is permitted on all roads except motorways. Larger towns and cities have dedicated bicycle lanes and traffic lights.

Bicycle rental places are generally concentrated in the more popular tourist areas such as Ljubljana, Bled, Bovec and Piran, though a fair few cycle shops and repair places hire them out as well. Expect to pay from €2/10 per hour/day; some places may ask for a cash deposit or a piece of ID as security.

Bus

➺ You can buy your ticket at the *avtobusna postaja* (bus station) or simply pay the driver as you board. In Ljubljana you should book your seat (€1.50/3.70 domestic/international) one day in advance if you're travelling on Friday, or to destinations in the mountains or on the coast on a public holiday. Bus services are severely restricted on Sunday and holidays (less so on Saturday).

➺ A range of bus companies serve the country, but prices are uniform: €3.10/5.60/9.20/16.80 for 25/50/100/200km of travel.

➺ Some bus stations have a *garderoba* (left-luggage office) and charge €2 per hour. They often keep banker's hours; if it's an

---

---

option, a better bet is to leave your things at the train station, which is usually nearby and keeps longer hours. If your bag has to go in the luggage compartment below the bus, it will cost from €1.25 extra on domestic routes (more going abroad).

➺ Timetables in the bus station, or posted on a wall or column outside, list all destinations and departure times. If you cannot find your bus listed or don't understand the schedule, get help from the *blagajna vozovnice* (information or ticket window), which are usually one and the same. *Odhodi* means 'departures' while *prihodi* is 'arrivals'.

Car & Motorcycle

Automobile Association

Slovenia's national automobile club is the **AMZS** (Avto-Moto Zveza Slovenije; ☏530 53 00; www.amzs.si; Dunajska cesta 128, Ljubljana). For emergency roadside assistance, call ☏19 87 anywhere in Slovenia. All accidents should

---

be reported to the police immediately on ☏113.

Driving Licence

Foreign driving licences are valid for one year after entering Slovenia. If you don't hold a European driving licence, you might obtain an International Driving Permit (IDP) from your local automobile association before you leave.

Fuel

Petrol stations are usually open from about 7am to 8pm Monday to Saturday, though larger towns have 24-hour services on the outskirts.

The price of *bencin* (petrol) is on par with the rest of Continental Europe: EuroSuper 95 costs €1.25 per litre, with diesel cheaper at €1.15.

Hire

Renting a car in Slovenia allows access to cheaper out-of-centre hotels and farm or village homestays. Rentals from international firms such as Avis, Budget, Europcar and Hertz vary in price; expect to pay from €38/200 per day/week, including unlimited mileage, collision damage waiver (CDW), theft protection (TP), Personal Accident Insurance (PAI) and taxes. Some smaller agencies have somewhat more competitive rates; booking on the internet is always cheaper.

Insurance

Third-party liability insurance is compulsory in Slovenia. If you enter the country in your own car and it is registered in the EU, you're covered. Other motorists must buy a Green Card (www.cobx.org) valid for Slovenia at the border.

Parking

You must pay to park in the centre of most Slovenian towns. 'Pay and display' parking coupons (from €0.50 per hour) are sold at vending machines (no change). In Ljubljana there are underground car parks where fees are charged (€1.20 to €2.40

ROAD DISTANCES (KM)

	Bled	Bovec	Celje	Črnomelj	Koper	Kranj	Kranjska Gora	Ljubljana	Maribor	Murska Sobota	Nova Gorica	Novo Mesto	Postojna	Ptuj
Bovec	83													
Celje	131	207												
Črnomelj	147	223	130											
Koper	156	161	185	193										
Kranj	27	102	105	123	131									
Kranjska Gora	39	45	161	178	186	58								
Ljubljana	59	134	76	93	107	33	89							
Maribor	181	257	54	198	234	156	212	126						
Murska Sobota	245	320	118	266	298	219	275	189	64					
Nova Gorica	156	72	185	193	90	131	168	107	236	299				
Novo Mesto	127	202	95	32	171	101	157	69	151	246	173			
Postojna	102	131	131	139	59	77	133	53	182	245	60	118		
Ptuj	184	260	58	179	237	159	215	129	29	64	238	148	183	
Slovenj Gradec	164	188	50	191	217	138	185	108	71	135	218	146	163	75

for the first hour and €0.60 to €1.80 per hour after that depending on the time of day).

Road Conditions & Tolls

Roads in Slovenia are generally excellent. Driving in the Julian Alps can be hair-raising, with a gradient of up to 18% at the Korensko Sedlo Pass into Austria, and a series of 49 hairpin bends on the road over the Vršič Pass. Many mountain roads are closed in winter and some well into early spring. Motorways and highways are well signposted, but secondary and tertiary roads not always so; take a good map or GPS navigation device (available from car-rental agencies).

There are two main motorway corridors – between the Hungarian border at Lenti and the coast (via the impressive flyover at Črni Kal) and from the Karavanke Tunnel into Austria to Zagreb in Croatia – intersecting at the Ljubljana ring road, with a branch from Postojna to Nova Gorica. Motorways are numbered from A1 to A10 (for *avtocesta*).

Major international roads are preceded by an 'E'. The most important of these are the E70 to Zagreb via Novo Mesto, the E61 to Villach via Jesenice and the Karavanke Tunnel, the E57 from Ljubljana to Graz via Celje and Maribor, and the E59 from Graz to Zagreb via Maribor. National highways contain a single digit and link cities. Secondary and tertiary roads have three digits.

Private-car ownership is high so expect a lot of traffic congestion, especially in summer and on Friday afternoons when entire cities and towns head for the countryside.

Road Rules

➡ Drive on the right.

➡ Speed limits for cars and motorcycles (less for buses) are 50km/h in towns and villages, 90km/h on secondary and tertiary roads, 100km/h on highways and 130km/h on motorways.

➡ Seat belts are compulsory, and motorcyclists must wear helmets.

ROAD TOLLS & THE VINJETA

Tolls are no longer paid separately on the motorways in Slovenia. Instead, all cars must display a *vinjeta* (road-toll sticker) on the windscreen. It costs €15/30/110 for a week/month/year for cars and €7.50/30/55 for motorbikes and is available at petrol stations, post offices and certain newsstands and tourist information centres. A sticker will already be in place on a rental car; armed with a *vinjeta* you just drive straight past the toll booth. Failure to display a sticker risks a fine of up to €300.

National Rail Network

➜ All motorists must illuminate their headlights throughout the day – not just at night.

➜ The permitted blood-alcohol level for drivers is 0.05%.

Hitching

Hitchhiking remains a popular way to get around for young Slovenes, and it's generally easy – except on Friday afternoon, before school holidays and on Sunday, when cars are often full of families. Hitching from bus stops is fairly common, otherwise use motorway access roads or other areas where the traffic will not be disturbed.

Hitching is never entirely safe in any country in the world, and we don't recommend it. Travellers who decide to hitch should understand that they are taking a small but potentially serious risk. People who do choose to hitch will be safer if they travel in pairs and should let someone know where they are planning to go. In particular, it is unwise for females to hitch alone; women are safer hitching with a male companion.

Train

Slovenian Railways (Slovenske Železnice, SŽ; ☎ 01-291 33 32; www.slo-zeleznice.si) runs trains on 1228km of track, about 40% of which is electrified. Very roughly, figure on covering about 60km/h to 65km/h except on the ICS express trains, which hurtle between Ljubljana and Maribor (€16.10, 1¾ hours) at an average speed of 90km/h. In the summer months an ICS train links Koper with Maribor (€28.30, four hours) via Ljubljana (€16.10, two hours).

➜ The provinces are served by *regionalni vlaki* (regional trains) and *primestni vlaki* (city trains), but the fastest are InterCity trains (IC).

➜ An 'R' next to the train number on the timetable means seat reservations

TRAIN TIMETABLE SYMBOLS

⊗ Monday to Friday (except public holidays)

✗ Monday to Saturday (except public holidays)

✖ Monday to Saturday and public holidays

Ⓥ Saturday & Sunday

Ⓥ Saturday, Sunday & public holidays

† Public holidays

7 No Sunday service

Ⓟ Sundays & public holidays

are available. If the 'R' is boxed, seat reservations are obligatory.

→ Purchase your ticket before travelling at the *železniška postaja* (train station) itself; buying it from the conductor on the train costs an additional €3.60. An invalid ticket or fare dodging earns a €40 fine.

→ A *povratna vozovnica* (return ticket) costs double the price of a *enosmerna vozovnica* (a single ticket). A 1st-class ticket costs 50% more than a 2nd-class one.

→ Travelling by train in Slovenia is about 25% cheaper than going by bus. A 100km journey costs €7 in 2nd class.

→ You'll find luggage lockers at train stations in Celje, Divača, Koper, Ljubljana, Maribor, Nova Gorica, Postojna and Sežana. The daily charge is €2 to €3 according to locker size.

Train Timetables

Departures and arrivals are announced by loudspeaker or on an electronic board and are always on a printed timetable somewhere in the station. Those under the heading *Odhod* or *Odhodi Vlakov* are departures; *Prihod* or *Prihodi Vlakov* indicate arrivals. Other useful words are *čas* (time), *peron* (platform), *sedež* (seat), *smer* (direction) and *tir* (rail).

Slovenian Railways (www. slo-zeleznice.si) has a useful online timetable, which includes fares.

Discounts & Passes

There's a 30% discount on return weekend and ICS express train fares.

Slovenian Railways sells the InterRail Country Pass Slovenia from InterRail (www.interrailnet.com), which is valid for rail travel in Slovenia only and available to residents of any European country (excluding Slovenia). The pass, which includes travel on ICS trains, is available for three/four/six/eight days of travel within one month for €78/95/125/148; those under 26 years of age pay €57/69/93/107.

Language

Slovene belongs to the South Slavic language family, along with Croatian and Serbian (although it is much closer to Croatia's northwestern and coastal dialects). It also shares some features with the more distant West Slavic languages through contact with a dialect of Slovak. Most adults speak at least one foreign language, often English, German or Italian.

If you read our coloured pronunciation guides as if they were English, you'll be understood. Note that oh is pronounced as the 'o' in 'note', ow as in 'how', uh as the 'a' in 'ago', zh as the 's' in 'pleasure', r is rolled, and the apostrophe (') indicates a slight y sound. The stressed syllables are indicated with italics.

The markers (m/f) and (pol/inf) indicate masculine and feminine forms, and polite and informal sentence options respectively.

BASICS

Hello.	*Zdravo.*	zdra·vo
Goodbye.	*Na svidenje.*	na svee·den·ye
Excuse me.	*Dovolite.*	do·vo·lee·te
Sorry.	*Oprostite.*	op·ros·tee·te
Please.	*Prosim.*	pro·seem
Thank you.	*Hvala.*	hva·la
You're welcome.	*Ni za kaj.*	nee za kai
Yes.	*Da.*	da
No.	*Ne.*	ne

What's your name?
Kako vam/ti ka·ko vam/tee
je ime? (pol/inf) ye ee·me

My name is ...
Ime mi je ... ee·me mee ye ...

Do you speak English?
Ali govorite a·lee go·vo·ree·te
angleško? ang·lesh·ko

I don't understand.
Ne razumem. ne ra·zoo·mem

ACCOMMODATION

campsite	*kamp*	kamp
guesthouse	*gostišče*	gos·teesh·che
hotel	*hotel*	ho·tel
youth hostel	*mladinski hotel*	mla·deen·skee ho·tel

Do you have a ... room?	*Ali imate ... sobo?*	a·lee ee·ma·te ... so·bo
cheap	*poceni*	po·tse·nee
double	*dvoposteljno*	dvo·pos·tel'·no
single	*enoposteljno*	e·no·pos·tel'·no

How much is it per ...?	*Koliko stane na ...?*	ko·lee·ko sta·ne na ...
night	*noč*	noch
person	*osebo*	o·se·bo

I'd like to share a dorm.
Rad/Rada bi delil/ rad/ra·da bee de·leew/
delila spalnico. (m/f) de·lee·la spal·nee·tso

Is breakfast included?
Ali je zajtrk a·lee ye zai·tuhrk
vključen? vklyoo·chen

Can I see the room?
Lahko vidim sobo? lah·ko vee·deem so·bo

DIRECTIONS

Where's the ...?
Kje je ...? kye ye ...

What's the address?
Na katerem naslovu je? na ka·te·rem nas·lo·voo ye

Question Words

How?	Kako?	ka·ko
How much/ many?	Koliko?	ko·lee·ko
What?	Kaj?	kai
When?	Kdaj?	gdai
Where?	Kje?	kye
Which?	Kateri/ Katera? (m/f)	ka·te·ree/ ka·te·ra
Who?	Kdo?	gdo
Why?	Zakaj?	za·kai

Can you show me (on the map)?
Mi lahko pokažete (na zemljevidu)? — mee lah·ko po·ka·zhe·te (na zem·lye·vee·doo)

How do I get to ...?
Kako pridem do ...? — ka·ko pree·dem do ...

Is it near/far?
Ali je blizu/daleč? — a·lee ye blee·zoo/da·lech

(Go) Straight ahead.
(Pojdite) Naravnost naprej. — (poy·dee·te) na·rav·nost na·prey

Turn left/right at the ...	Obrnite levo/desno pri ...	o·buhr·nee·te le·vo/des·no pree ...
corner	vogalu	vo·ga·loo
traffic lights	semaforju	se·ma·for·yoo

behind	za/zadaj	za/za·dai
far (from)	daleč (od)	da·lech (od)
here	tu	too
in front of	spredaj	spre·dai
near (to)	blizu (do)	blee·zoo (do)
opposite	nasproti	nas·pro·tee
there	tam	tam

EATING & DRINKING

What is the house speciality?
Kaj je domača specialiteta? — kai ye do·ma·cha spe·tsee·a·lee·te·ta

What would you recommend?
Kaj priporočate? — kai pree·po·ro·cha·te

Do you have vegetarian food?
Ali imate vegetarijansko hrano? — a·lee ee·ma·te ve·ge·ta·ree·yan·sko hra·no

I'll have ...	Jaz bom ...	yaz bom ...
Cheers!	Na zdravje!	na zdrav·ye

I'd like the ..., please.	Želim ..., prosim.	zhe·leem ... pro·seem
bill	račun	ra·choon
menu	jedilni list	ye·deel·nee leest

breakfast	zajtrk	zai·tuhrk
lunch	kosilo	ko·see·lo
dinner	večerja	ve·cher·ya

Key Words

bottle	steklenica	stek·le·nee·tsa
breakfast	zajtrk	zai·tuhrk
cold	hladen	hla·den
delicatessen	delikatesa	de·lee·ka·te·sa
dinner	večerja	ve·cher·ya
food	hrana	hra·na
fork	vilica	vee·lee·tsa
glass	kozarec	ko·za·rets
hot	topel	to·pel
knife	nož	nozh
lunch	kosilo	ko·see·lo
market	tržnica	tuhrzh·nee·tsa
menu	jedilni list	ye·deel·nee list
plate	krožnik	krozh·neek
restaurant	restavracija	res·tav·ra·tsee·ya
spoon	žlica	zhlee·tsa
wine list	vinska karta	veen·ska kar·ta
with	z	zuh
without	brez	brez

Meat & Fish

beef	govedina	go·ve·dee·na
chicken	piščanec	peesh·cha·nets
clams	školjke	shkol'·ke
cod	oslič	os·leech
fish	riba	ree·ba
ham	šunka/ pršut	shoon·ka/ puhr·shoot
lamb	jagnjetina	yag·nye·tee·na
pork	svinjina	svee·nyee·na
poultry	perutnina	pe·root·nee·na
prawns	škampi	shkam·pee
squid	lignji	leeg·nyee
trout	postrv	pos·tuhrv
veal	teletina	te·le·tee·na

Fruit & Vegetables

English	Slovene	Pronunciation
apple	jabolko	ya·bol·ko
apricot	marelica	ma·re·lee·tsa
beans	fižol	fee·zhoh
carrots	korenje	ko·re·nye
cauliflower	cvetača/ karfijola	tsve·ta·cha/ kar·fee·yo·la
cherries	češnje/ višnje	chesh·nye/ veesh·nye
grapes	grozdje	groz·dye
hazelnuts	lešniki	lesh·nee·kee
orange	pomaranča	po·ma·ran·cha
peach	breskev	bres·kev
pear	hruška	hroosh·ka
peas	grah	grah
pineapple	ananas	a·na·nas
plum	češplja	chesh·plya
potatoes	krompir	krom·peer
pumpkin	bučke	booch·ke
raspberries	maline	ma·lee·ne
spinach	špinača	shpee·na·cha
strawberries	jagode	ya·go·de
walnuts	orehi	o·re·hee

Other

English	Slovene	Pronunciation
bread	kruh	krooh
butter	maslo	mas·lo
cheese	sir	seer
eggs	jajca	yai·tsa
pasta	testenine	tes·te·nee·ne
pepper	poper	po·per
rice	riž	reezh
salad	solata	so·la·ta
salt	sol	soh
soup	juha	yoo·ha
sugar	sladkor	slad·kor

Drinks

English	Slovene	Pronunciation
beer (lager)	svetlo pivo	svet·lo pee·vo
beer (stout)	temno pivo	tem·no pee·vo
coffee	kava	ka·va
juice	sok	sok
lemonade	limonada	lee·mo·na·da
milk	mleko	mle·ko
plum brandy	slivovka	slee·vov·ka
red wine	črno vino	chuhr·no vee·no

Signs

Slovene	English
Informacije	Information
Izhod	Exit
Moški	Men
Odprto	Open
Prepovedano	Prohibited
Stranišče	Toilets
Vhod	Entrance
Zaprto	Closed
Ženske	Women

English	Slovene	Pronunciation
sparkling wine	peneče vino	pe·ne·che vee·no
tea	čaj	chai
water	voda	vo·da
white wine	belo vino	be·lo vee·no

EMERGENCIES

English	Slovene	Pronunciation
Help!	Na pomoč!	na po·moch
Go away!	Pojdite stran!	poy·dee·te stran
Call ...!	Pokličite ...!	pok·lee·chee·te ...
a doctor	zdravnika	zdrav·nee·ka
the police	policijo	po·lee·tsee·yo

I'm lost.
Izgubil/ Izgubila sem se. (m/f) — eez·goo·beew/ eez·goo·bee·la sem se

I'm ill.
Bolan/Bolna sem. (m/f) — bo·lan/boh·na sem

It hurts here.
Tukaj boli. — too·kai bo·lee

I'm allergic to ...
Alergičen/ Alergična sem na ... (m/f) — a·ler·gee·chen/ a·ler·geech·na sem na ...

Where are the toilets?
Kje je stranišče? — kye ye stra·neesh·che

SHOPPING & SERVICES

Where is a/the ...? — Kje je ...? — kye ye ...

English	Slovene	Pronunciation
bank	banka	ban·ka
market	tržnica	tuhrzh·nee·tsa
post office	pošta	posh·ta
tourist office	turistični urad	too·rees·teech·nee oo·rad

I want to make a telephone call.
Rad/Rada bi telefoniral/ telefonirala. (m/f) — rad/ra·da bee te·le·fon·nee·row/ te·le·fon·nee·ra·la

Where can I get internet access?
Kje lahko dobim — kye lah·ko do·beem
internet povezavo? — een·ter·net po·ve·za·vo

I'd like to buy ...
Rad/Rada bi kupil/ — rad/ra·da bee koo·peew/
kupila ... (m/f) — koo·pee·la ...

I'm just looking.
Samo gledam. — sa·mo gle·dam

Can I look at it?
Ali lahko pogledam? — a·lee lah·ko po·gle·dam

How much is this?
Koliko stane? — ko·lee·ko sta·ne

It's too expensive.
Predrago je. — pre·dra·go ye

TIME & DATES

What time is it?
Koliko je ura? — ko·lee·ko ye oo·ra

It's (one) o'clock.
Ura je (ena). — oo·ra ye (e·na)

half past seven
pol osem — pol o·sem
(literally 'half eight')

in the morning	zjutraj	zyoot·rai
in the evening	zvečer	zve·cher
yesterday	včeraj	vche·rai
today	danes	da·nes
tomorrow	jutri	yoo·tree

Monday	ponedeljek	po·ne·de·lyek
Tuesday	torek	to·rek
Wednesday	sreda	sre·da
Thursday	četrtek	che·tuhrt·tek
Friday	petek	pe·tek
Saturday	sobota	so·bo·ta
Sunday	nedelja	ne·de·lya

January	januar	ya·noo·ar
February	februar	fe·broo·ar
March	marec	ma·rets
April	april	a·preel
May	maj	mai
June	junij	yoo·neey
July	julij	yoo·leey
August	avgust	av·goost
September	september	sep·tem·ber
October	oktober	ok·to·ber
November	november	no·vem·ber
December	december	de·tsem·ber

TRANSPORT

When does	*Kdaj*	gdai
the ... leave?	*odpelje ...?*	od·pe·lye ...
boat	*ladja*	la·dya
bus	*avtobus*	av·to·boos
ferry	*trajekt*	tra·yekt
plane	*avion*	a·vee·on
train	*vlak*	vlak

One ... ticket	*... vozovnico*	... vo·zov·nee·tso
to (Koper),	*do (Kopra),*	do (ko·pra)
please.	*prosim.*	pro·seem
one-way	*Enosmerno*	e·no·smer·no
return	*Povratno*	pov·rat·no

1st/2nd class	*prvi/drugi*	puhr·vee/droo·gee
	razred	raz·red
bus station	*avtobusno*	av·to·boos·no
	postajališče	po·sta·ya·leesh·che
first/last	*prvi/zadnji*	puhr·vee/zad·nyee
ticket office	*prodaja*	pro·da·ya
	vozovnic	vo·zov·neets
train station	*železniška*	zhe·lez·neesh·ka
	postaja	pos·ta·ya

I want to go to ...
Želim iti ... — zhe·leem ee·tee ...

Numbers		
1	*en*	en
2	*dva*	dva
3	*trije*	tree·ye
4	*štirje*	shtee·rye
5	*pet*	pet
6	*šest*	shest
7	*sedem*	se·dem
8	*osem*	o·sem
9	*devet*	de·vet
10	*deset*	de·set
20	*dvajset*	dvai·set
30	*trideset*	tree·de·set
40	*štirideset*	shtee·ree·de·set
50	*petdeset*	pet·de·set
60	*šestdeset*	shest·de·set
70	*sedemdeset*	se·dem·de·set
80	*osemdeset*	o·sem·de·set
90	*devetdeset*	de·vet·de·set
100	*sto*	sto

PLACE NAMES & THEIR ALTERNATIVES

(C) Croatian, (Cz) Czech, (E) English, (G) German, (H) Hungarian, (I) Italian, (P) Polish

Beljak – Villach (G)
Benetke – Venice (E), Venezia (I)
Bizeljsko – Wisell (G)
Bohinj – Wochain (G)
Brežice – Rhain (G)
Budimpešta – Budapest (H)
Čedad – Cividale (I)
Celovec – Klagenfurt (G)
Celje – Cilli (G)
Cerknica – Cirkniz (G)
Črnomelj – Tschernembl (G)
Dolenjska – Lower Carniola (E)
Dunaj – Vienna (E), Wien (G)
Gorenjska – Upper Carniola (E)
Gorica – Gorizia (I)
Gradec – Graz (G)
Gradež – Grado (I)
Idrija – Ydria (G)
Istra – Istria (E)
Izola – Isola (I)
Jadran, Jadransko Morje – Adriatic Sea (E)
Kamnik – Stein (G)
Kobarid – Caporetto (I)
Koper – Capodistria (I)
Koroška – Carinthia (E), Kärnten (G)
Kostanjevica – Landstrass (G)
Kranj – Krainburg (G)
Kranjska – Carniola (E), Krain (G)
Kras – Karst (E)
Krnski Grad – Karnburg (G)
Kropa – Cropp (G)
Lendava – Lendva (H)
Lipnica – Leibnitz (G)
Ljubljana – Laibach (G), Liubliana (I)
Metlika – Möttling (G)
Milje – Muggia (I)

Murska Sobota – Muraszombat (H)
Notranjska – Inner Carniola (E)
Nova Gorica – Gorizia (I), Görz (G)
Oglej – Aquileia (I)
Otočec – Wördl (G)
Piran – Pirano (I)
Pleterje – Pletariach (G)
Pliberk – Bleiburg (G)
Portorož – Portorose (I)
Postojna – Adelsberg (G)
Praga – Prague (E), Praha (Cz)
Ptuj – Pettau (G)
Radgona – Bad Radkersburg (G)
Radovljica – Ratmansdorf (G)
Reka – Rijeka (C), Fiume (I)
Ribnica – Reiffniz (G)
Rim – Rome (E), Roma (I)
Rogaška Slatina – Rohitsch-Sauerbrunn (G)
Rosalnice – Rosendorf (G)
Seča – Sezza (I) Peninsula
Sečovlje – Sicciole (I)
Škocjan – San Canziano (I)
Sredozemsko Morje – Mediterranean Sea (E)
Štajerska – Styria (E), Steiermark (G)
Soča – Isonzo (I)
Stična – Sittich (G)
Strunjan – Strugnano (I)
Trbiž – Tarvisio (I)
Trst – Trieste (I)
Tržaški Zaliv – Gulf of Trieste (E), Golfo di Trieste (I)
Tržič – Monfalcone (I)
Varšava – Warsaw (E), Warszawa (P)
Videm – Udine (I)
Vinica – Weinitz (G)
Železna Kapla – Eisenkappel (G)

How long does the trip take?
Koliko traja | ko·lee·ko tra·ya
potovanje? | po·to·va·nye

Do I need to change?
Ali moram presesti? | a·lee mo·ram pre·ses·tee

Can you tell me when we get to …?
Mi lahko poveste | mee lah·ko po·ves·te
kdaj pridemo …? | gdai pree·de·mo …

Stop here, please.
Ustavite tukaj, | oos·ta·vee·te too·kai
prosim. | pro·seem

I'd like to hire a …	Rad/Rada bi najel/ najela … (m/f)	rad/ra·da bee na·yel/ na·ye·la …
bicycle	kolo	ko·lo
car	avto	av·to
motorcyle	motorno kolo	mo·tor·no ko·lo

GLOSSARY

(m) indicates masculine gender, (f) feminine gender and (n) neutral

AMZS – Avto-Moto Zveza Slovenije (Automobile Association of Slovenia)

bife – snack and/or drinks bar
breg – river bank
burja – bora (cold northeast wind from the Adriatic)

c – abbreviation for cesta
čaj – tea
cerkev – church
cesta – road

DDV – davek na dodano vrednost (value-added tax, or VAT)
delovni čas – opening/ business hours
dijaški dom – student dormitory, hostel
dolina – valley
dom – house; mountain lodge
Domobranci – anti-Partisan Home Guards during WWII
drevored – avenue
dvorana – hall

fijaker – horse-drawn carriage

gaj – grove, park
gledališče – theatre
gora – mountain
gostilna – innlike restaurant
gostišče – inn with restaurant
gozd – forest, grove
grad – castle
greben – ridge, crest
GZS – Geodetski Zavod Slovenije (Geodesic Institute of Slovenia)

Hallstatt – early Iron Age Celtic culture (800–500 BC)
hiša – house
hrib – hill

izvir – source (of a river, stream etc)

jama – cave
jezero – lake

Karst – limestone region of underground rivers and caves in Primorska
kavarna – coffee shop, cafe
klet – cellar
knjigarna – bookshop
knjižnica – library
koča – mountain cottage or hut
kosilo – lunch
kot – glacial valley, corner
kotlina – basin
kozolec – hayrack distinct to Slovenia
kras – karst
krčma – drinks bar (sometimes with food)

lekarna – pharmacy
LPP – Ljubljanski Potniški Promet (Ljubljana city bus network)

mali (m) **mala** (f) **malo** (n) – little
malica – midmorning snack
menjalnica – private currency exchange office
mesto – town
morje – sea
moški – men (toilet)
most – bridge
muzej – museum

na – on
nabrežje – embankment
narod – nation
naselje – colony, development, estate
nasip – dike, embankment
novi (m) **nova** (f) **novo** (n) – new

občina – administrative division; county or commune; city or town hall
odprto – open
okrepčevalnica – snack bar
Osvobodilne Fronte (OF) – Anti-Fascist Liberation Front during WWII
otok – island

pivnica – pub, beer hall
pivo – beer
planina – Alpine pasture
planota – plateau
pletna – gondola
pod – under, below
polje – collapsed limestone area under cultivation
pot – trail
potok – stream
potrditev – enter/confirm (on ATM)
prazniki – holidays
prehod – passage, crossing
prekop – canal
prenočišče – accommodation
pri – at, near, by
PZS – Planinska Zveza Slovenije (Alpine Association of Slovenia)

reka – river
restavracija – restaurant
rob – escarpment, edge

samopostrežna restavracija – self-service restaurant
samostan – monastery
Secessionism – art and architectural style similar to art nouveau
skanzen – open-air museum displaying village architecture
slaščičarna – shop selling ice cream, sweets
smučanje – skiing
sobe – rooms (available)
soteska – ravine, gorge
sprehajališče – walkway, promenade
stari (m) **stara** (f) **staro** (n) – old
stena – wall, cliff
steza – path
STO – Slovenska Turistična Organizacija (Slovenian Tourist Board)
stolp – tower
štruklji – dumplings
Sv – St (abbreviation for saint)
SŽ – Slovenske Železnice (Slovenian Railways)

terme – Italian word for 'spa' used frequently in Slovenia

TIC – Tourist Information Centre

TNP – Triglavski Narodni Park (Triglav National Park)

toplarji – double-linked hayracks, unique to Slovenia

toplice – spa

trg – square

ul – abbreviation for ulica

ulica – street

vas – village

večerja – dinner, supper

veliki (m) **velika** (f) **veliko** (n) – great, big

vila – villa

vinoteka – wine bar

vinska cesta – wine road

vinska klet – wine cellar

vrata – door, gate

vrh – summit, peak

vrt – garden, park

zaprto – closed

zdravilišče – health resort, spa

zdravstveni dom – medical centre, clinic

žegnanje – a patron's festival at a church or chapel

ženske – women (toilet)

žičnica – cable car

zidanica – a cottage in one of the wine-growing regions

Behind the Scenes

SEND US YOUR FEEDBACK

We love to hear from travellers – your comments keep us on our toes and help make our books better. Our well-travelled team reads every word on what you loved or loathed about this book. Although we cannot reply individually to your submissions, we always guarantee that your feedback goes straight to the appropriate authors, in time for the next edition. Each person who sends us information is thanked in the next edition – the most useful submissions are rewarded with a selection of digital PDF chapters.

Visit **lonelyplanet.com/contact** to submit your updates and suggestions or to ask for help. Our award-winning website also features inspirational travel stories, news and discussions.

Note: We may edit, reproduce and incorporate your comments in Lonely Planet products such as guidebooks, websites and digital products, so let us know if you don't want your comments reproduced or your name acknowledged. For a copy of our privacy policy visit lonelyplanet.com/privacy.

OUR READERS

Many thanks to the travellers who used the last edition and wrote to us with helpful hints, useful advice and interesting anecdotes: Ian Andrews, Sarah Anthony, Rinse Balk, Izabela Bogacz, Claire Connorton, Alan Curtis, Nick Gardner, Raquel Gómez, David Hinchliffe, Carlo Iossa, Mark McConnell, John Moratelli, Maciej Nowak, Teresa Oldham

AUTHOR THANKS

Carolyn Bain

Many thanks to Anna Tyler for a great gig, and bouquets to my coauthor Steve Fallon for generously sharing local expertise and contacts. *Hvala lepa* to a fine cast of locals (and fellow travellers) for answering my questions, regaling me with stories and making this job such a rewarding (and scenic) one, including Tine Murn, Zoran Sordjan, Domen & Barbara, Grega, Matic & Katja, Ana & Valter, Matej, Matej, Simon & Marina, Luka, Rok, Mitja, Ivana, Jaka, Bogdan, Mario and Sergeja, and so many more.

Steve Fallon

A warm *najlepša hvala* to Petra Stušek and staff at the Ljubljana Tourist Board as well as Tine Murn at the Slovenian Tourist Board in London. Dušan Brejc of the Wine Association of Slovenia helped with the right vintages (again), Iva Gruden of Ljubljananjam was indispensable with all things culinary, and Dragan Barbutovski of CurioCity told me which way the wind was blowing. I am again eternally grateful to Slovenian Railways' Marino Fakin and both Vojko Anzeljc and Tone Plankar at the Ljubljana bus station for transport information. As always, my efforts here are dedicated to my partner, Michael Rothschild.

ACKNOWLEDGMENTS

Climate map data adapted from Peel MC, Finlayson BL & McMahon TA (2007) 'Updated World Map of the Köppen-Geiger Climate Classification', Hydrology and Earth System Sciences, 11, 163344.

Cover photograph: Tartinijev Trg, Piran; Alan Copson/AWL ©

THIS BOOK

This 8th edition of Lonely Planet's *Slovenia* guidebook was researched and written by Carolyn Bain and Steve Fallon. The previous edition was written by Mark Baker, Paul Clammer and Steve Fallon. This guidebook was produced by the following:

Destination Editor Anna Tyler

Product Editors Grace Dobell, Susan Paterson, Kathryn Rowan

Senior Cartographer Anthony Phelan

Book Designer Mazzy Prinsep

Assisting Editors Jodie Martire, Rosie Nicholson, Monique Perrin, Saralinda Turner

Assisting Cartographers Gabe Lindquist, Diana von Holdt

Cover Researcher Naomi Parker

Thanks to Anita Banh, Kate Chapman, Neill Coen, Ryan Evans, Andi Jones, Karyn Noble, Kirsten Rawlings, Alison Ridgway, Diana Saengkham, Dianne Schallmeiner, Ellie Simpson, Lauren Wellicome, Dora Whitaker

Index

Map Legend

Sights
- Beach
- Bird Sanctuary
- Buddhist
- Castle/Palace
- Christian
- Confucian
- Hindu
- Islamic
- Jain
- Jewish
- Monument
- Museum/Gallery/Historic Building
- Ruin
- Shinto
- Sikh
- Taoist
- Winery/Vineyard
- Zoo/Wildlife Sanctuary
- Other Sight

Activities, Courses & Tours
- Bodysurfing
- Diving
- Canoeing/Kayaking
- Course/Tour
- Sento Hot Baths/Onsen
- Skiing
- Snorkelling
- Surfing
- Swimming/Pool
- Walking
- Windsurfing
- Other Activity

Sleeping
- Sleeping
- Camping

Eating
- Eating

Drinking & Nightlife
- Drinking & Nightlife
- Cafe

Entertainment
- Entertainment

Shopping
- Shopping

Information
- Bank
- Embassy/Consulate
- Hospital/Medical
- Internet
- Police
- Post Office
- Telephone
- Toilet
- Tourist Information
- Other Information

Geographic
- Beach
- Gate
- Hut/Shelter
- Lighthouse
- Lookout
- Mountain/Volcano
- Oasis
- Park
- Pass
- Picnic Area
- Waterfall

Population
- Capital (National)
- Capital (State/Province)
- City/Large Town
- Town/Village

Transport
- Airport
- Border crossing
- Bus
- Cable car/Funicular
- Cycling
- Ferry
- Metro station
- Monorail
- Parking
- Petrol station
- S-Bahn/S-train/Subway station
- Taxi
- T-bane/Tunnelbana station
- Train station/Railway
- Tram
- Tube station
- U-Bahn/Underground station
- Other Transport

Note: Not all symbols displayed above appear on the maps in this book

Routes
- Tollway
- Freeway
- Primary
- Secondary
- Tertiary
- Lane
- Unsealed road
- Road under construction
- Plaza/Mall
- Steps
- Tunnel
- Pedestrian overpass
- Walking Tour
- Walking Tour detour
- Path/Walking Trail

Boundaries
- International
- State/Province
- Disputed
- Regional/Suburb
- Marine Park
- Cliff
- Wall

Hydrography
- River, Creek
- Intermittent River
- Canal
- Water
- Dry/Salt/Intermittent Lake
- Reef

Areas
- Airport/Runway
- Beach/Desert
- Cemetery (Christian)
- Cemetery (Other)
- Glacier
- Mudflat
- Park/F
- Sigh
- S

Published
ABN 36 005
ISBN 978 1 743
8th edition —
© Lonely Planet
10 9 8 7 6 5 4
Printed in China
All rights reserved
chanical, recording
ten permission of
mark Office and
rs, restaurants or

OUR STORY

A beat-up old car, a few dollars in the pocket and a sense of adventure. In 1972 that's all Tony and Maureen Wheeler needed for the trip of a lifetime – across Europe and Asia overland to Australia. It took several months, and at the end – broke but inspired – they sat at their kitchen table writing and stapling together their first travel guide, *Across Asia on the Cheap*. Within a week they'd sold 1500 copies. Lonely Planet was born.

Today, Lonely Planet has offices in Franklin, London, Melbourne, Oakland, Beijing and Delhi, with more than 600 staff and writers. We share Tony's belief that 'a great guidebook should do three things: inform, educate and amuse'.

OUR WRITERS

Carolyn Bain

Lake Bled & the Julian Alps, Western Slovenia & the Soča Valley, The Karst & the Coast, Southern Slovenia & the Krka Valley A sucker for Alpine peaks and fairy-tale lakes, Melbourne-based Carolyn jumped at the chance to add more Central Europe to her guidebook portfolio, which has been heavy on Nordic destinations of late. A travel writer for 15 years, she was delighted to revisit Slovenia on a mission to hike, raft, swim, glamp, explore caves, sample wines, rank waterfalls and castles, and taste-test *kremšnita* in the name of research. Carolyn also wrote Travel with Children. See more at carolynbain.com.au.

Steve Fallon

Ljubljana, Eastern Slovenia Steve has been travelling to Slovenia since the early 1990s, when almost no one but the Slovenes had ever heard of the place. Never mind, it was his own private Idaho for over a decade. Though on *še govori slovensko kot jamski človek* (he still speaks Slovene like a caveman), Steve considers part of his soul to be Slovenian and returns as often as he can for a glimpse of the Julian Alps in the sun, a dribble of *bučno olje* and a dose of the 'dual'. Steve also wrote Plan Your Trip (except Travel with Children), Understand Slovenia and Survival Guide. See more at www.steveslondon.com.

d by Lonely Planet Publications Pty Ltd
507 983
lay 2016
21 572 2
2016   Photographs © as indicated 2016
3 2 1